S0-FCB-440

THE PROPHETIC WRITINGS OF WILLIAM BLAKE

Oxford University Press, Amen House, London E.C.4
GLASGOW NEW YORK TORONTO MELBOURNE WELLINGTON
BOMBAY CALCUTTA MADRAS KARACHI
CAPE TOWN IBADAN NAIROBI ACCRA SINGAPORE

FIRST EDITION 1926
REPRINTED LITHOGRAPHICALLY IN GREAT BRITAIN
AT THE UNIVERSITY PRESS, OXFORD
FROM SHEETS OF THE FIRST EDITION
1957

Milton: the Title-page

THE

PROPHETIC WRITINGS

OF

WILLIAM BLAKE

IN TWO VOLUMES

EDITED WITH A GENERAL INTRODUCTION GLOSSARIAL INDEX OF SYMBOLS COMMENTARY AND APPENDICES

BY

D. J. SLOSS M.A. C.B.E.
PRINCIPAL OF UNIVERSITY COLLEGE, RANGOON

AND

J. P. R. WALLIS M.A.
PROFESSOR OF ENGLISH LANGUAGE AND LITERATURE
TRANSVAAL UNIVERSITY COLLEGE, PRETORIA

VOLUME I

OXFORD: AT THE CLARENDON PRESS

PRINTED IN GREAT BRITAIN

TO

JOHN SAMPSON

AND

OLIVER ELTON

PREFATORY NOTE

THE present edition of Blake's Prophetic writings was undertaken in 1906 at the suggestion of Dr. John Sampson and Professor Oliver Elton. It was intended as supplement to the definitive text of the lyrical poems edited for the Clarendon Press in 1905. A number of causes combined to retard progress and it was not till the close of 1912 that the manuscript was sent to the press. When the first proofs were expected, the war came; and subsequently the prohibitive cost of printing and the remoteness of the editors from the centre of things and from each other in widely sundered parts of the Dominions made it seem as if further progress with the work would be difficult, if not impossible. But means were found within the present year to take up the task again and to revise it throughout, that it might be brought into line with the results of recent researches in the Blakean field. Parts have been remodelled and rewritten, and some additions made both to the text and to the critical apparatus; but on the whole the process of revision has not involved any notable readjustment of the conclusions of the earlier investigation: only here and there a slight modification of emphasis and arrangement has been made.

Our work has stood so long upon the stocks that we cannot now thank some to whom we are deeply indebted for assistance. To members of the Linnell family no longer living we owe it that we had such fullness of opportunity to study the *Four Zoas* manuscript as only the rarest generosity will grant. Through them also we are enabled to reprint the supernumerary Preface to *Europe*. And we have to acknowledge the kindness of the late Mr. B. B. Macgeorge of Glasgow, who allowed us to print from unique copies in his collection the cancelled plates in *America* and *The Book of Urizen*.

In dedicating our work to Dr. John Sampson and Professor Oliver Elton we would express our sense of peculiar indebtedness to them. If our text has merit, the credit lies largely with Dr. Sampson. It was a valuable privilege to be able to enter upon this undertaking under the guidance of him whose Clarendon Press edition of the lyrical poems has set the standard for all similar textual and bibliographical work. Coming to our task with little better than the ordinary notions of editorial responsibility, we were enabled to see what scrupulousness meant in the making-out of a text and the value of carefulness and restraint in the forming and expression of judgements.

We cannot measure what we owe to Professor Elton. Through him in the first place we came to undertake this work, but it is not for that that we would here express our obligation, nor yet for his constant interest in it, nor for our great admiration for the essay on Blake in his *Survey of English Literature*. Rather it is for what we feel has come to us through his teaching and his friendship.

At an early stage in the preparation of our General Introduction we submitted our manuscript of it to the judgement of Professor Alexander Mair, to our great advantage. He has since overlooked the proof-sheets. This does not identify him in any way with its substance or form, but his opinion has been of notable service to us. Mr. Geoffrey L. Keynes has throughout given us most liberal assistance. He has communicated to us without reserve his many valuable Blakean discoveries. Through him we came to the knowledge of and secured permission to include in our text the unique pages in Mr. B. B. Macgeorge's collection. We are obliged to him and to his publishers of the Nonesuch Press for leave to print the newly discovered plate of *Milton*, the extract from the final section of *The Everlasting Gospel* that we quote in our General Introduction, and reliable texts of the Additions to the Catalogue and the Advertizement. Our knowledge of the contents and arrangement of the fourth copy of *Milton* comes through him, and his Bibliography has been as indispensable to us as it must be to all students of Blake. The crowning favour was to allow us to reproduce from originals in his possession facsimiles of *The Ghost of Abel* and the *Laocoön* engraving, the latter the unique copy. We have also to thank Mr. H. M. Lydenberg, Reference Librarian to the New York Public Library, and Mr. V. H. Paltsits of the same institution, for most patient and painstaking replies to a long series of letters of inquiry concerning the Beckford copy of *Milton* and for photographs therefrom. We would also express our indebtedness to Mr. Leslie E. Bliss, Acting Librarian of the Henry E. Huntington Library, California, for information concerning the Butts copy of *Milton*. Mr. S. Foster Damon has unreservedly placed at our service his unmatched knowledge of the recently rediscovered Windus *Milton*, to the owner of which we are also obliged for enlightenment on points of text and arrangement. Mr. Sydney C. Cockerell, the Director, has helped us in matters referred to him in connexion with the copy of *Jerusalem* in the Fitzwilliam Museum, Cambridge.

Finally, we would acknowledge most gratefully the assistance of the Clarendon Press. That the Delegates should accept our work for publication was much, but we would also express our sense of obligation to the staff of the Press whose wisdom and experience in the technical processes of publication have at every stage been set freely and unobtrusively at our service.

D. J. S.

J. P. R. W.

August 1925.

TABLE OF CONTENTS

VOLUME I

Table of Contents

Table of Contents

VOLUME II

LIST OF FACSIMILES

VOLUME I

VOLUME II

TABLE OF ABBREVIATIONS

Advertisement.	'Advertizement' to Blake's Canterbury Pilgrims, written dispersedly in the *Rossetti Manuscript*, pp. 1–67.
Apology.	An Apology for the Bible, in a series of letters addressed to Thomas Paine. By R. Watson, D.D., F.R.S., Bishop of Landaff. 1797. Blake's marginalia are printed for the first time in Keynes's *Bibliography*, pp. 423–438.
B. A.	The Book of Ahania. Lambeth. Printed by W. Blake. 1795.
B. L.	The Book of Los. Lambeth. Printed by W. Blake. 1795.
B. U.	The Book of Urizen. Lambeth. Printed by Will. Blake. 1794.
C. R.	Henry Crabb Robinson: *Diary, Letters and Reminiscences*. The references in the present edition are to A. Symons's collation from the original manuscript in his 'William Blake'. See below under S.
Cat. 1810.	For the year 1810. Additions to Blake's Catalogue of Pictures, &c. Written dispersedly through the latter portion of the *Rossetti Manuscript*, pp. 68–end.
Clar. Press.	The Poetical Works of William Blake . . . by John Sampson. Oxford: at the Clarendon Press. 1905.
D. C.	A Descriptive Catalogue of Pictures, Poetical and Historical Inventions, Painted by William Blake in Water Colours, being the Ancient Method of Fresco Painting Restored: and Drawings, for Public Inspection, and for Sale by Private Contract, London. 1809.
E. G.	The Everlasting Gospel.
E. Y.	The Works of William Blake. Poetic, Symbolic, and Critical. Edited with Lithographs . . . and a Memoir and Interpretation by Edwin John Ellis . . . and William Butler Yeats. 3 volumes. 1893.
F. Z.	The Four Zoa's. The torments of Love and Jealousy in The Death and Judgement of Albion the Ancient Man by William Blake. 1797.
G. A.	The Ghost of Abel. A Revelation In the Visions of Jehovah Seen by William Blake. 1822.
G. L. K.	A Bibliography of William Blake, by Geoffrey Keynes. New York: The Grolier Club of New York. 1921.
J.	Jerusalem. The Emanation of The Giant Albion. 1804. Printed by W. Blake, Sth Molton St.
Lavater.	Aphorisms on Man: Translated from the Original Manuscript of the Rev. John Caspar Lavater. 1788. Blake's marginalia.
M.	Milton, a Poem in 2 Books. The Author & Printer W. Blake. 1804.

Table of Abbreviations

M. H. H.	The Marriage of Heaven and Hell. n. d. about 1790.
N. N. R.	There is No Natural Religion. n. d. about 1790. Two series (a) and (b).
R.	The Letters of William Blake together with a Life by Frederick Tatham, edited . . . by Archibald G. B. Russell. London. 1906.
R. N.	The Works of Sir Joshua Reynolds, Knight. The Second Edition Corrected. London. 1798. 3 volumes. Blake's marginalia.
S.	William Blake, by Arthur Symons. 1907. See above under C. R.
Siris.	Siris : A Chain of Philosophical Reflexions and Inquiries Concerning the Virtues of Tar Water And divers other Subjects connected together and arising one from another. Blake's annotations to Bishop Berkeley's book are printed for the first time in Keynes's *Bibliography*.
S. Los.	The Song of Los. Lambeth. Printed by W. Blake. 1795.
S. Lib.	A Song of Liberty. n. d. about 1790.
Swinburne.	William Blake. A Critical Essay by Algernon Charles Swinburne. A new edition. 1906.
V. D. A.	Visions of the Daughters of Albion. Printed by Willm. Blake. 1793.

THERE IS NO NATURAL RELIGION

and

ALL RELIGIONS ARE ONE

INTRODUCTORY NOTE

BLAKE appears to have engraved three series of plates, containing axioms, or ' principles ', as he calls them, dealing with the nature, the source, and the validity of man's metaphysical and ethical ideas. Mr. Geoffrey L. Keynes in the section of his bibliography of Blake dealing with this work, the proofs of which he permitted the present editors to examine, gives particulars of nine copies, all of which are imperfect and differ both in the number and in the arrangement of the plates. Therefore, in the absence of any authoritative statement of Blake's intention, all attempts to arrange the plates in order must necessarily be conjectural, the clues being found in the numbers engraved above the different axioms, the peculiarities of script or pictorial design, and such traces of logical sequence as can be detected among these scattered affirmations.

All the available material is found in three collections of plates:

A. The copy in the Print-room of the British Museum, consisting of eleven plates, several of which are obviously wrongly placed. This is the set produced, but in a revised order, in the Ellis and Yeats facsimile.

Retaining the order of the Print-room copy, the plates are:

(1) The Argument. Man has no notion of moral fitness but from Education. Naturally he is only a natural organ subject to Sense.

(2) I. Man's perceptions are not bounded by organs of perception: he perceives more than sense (tho' ever so acute) can discover.

(3) II. Man by his reasoning power can only compare and judge of what he has already perceiv'd.

(4) III. From a perception of only 3 senses or 3 elements none could deduce a fourth or fifth.

(5) IV. None could have other than natural or organic thoughts if he had none but organic perceptions.

(6) V. Man's desires are limited by his perceptions: none can desire what he has not perceiv'd.

(7) VI. The desires & perceptions of man untaught by anything but organs of sense must be limited to objects of sense.

(8) I. Man cannot naturally Percieve but through his natural or bodily organs.

(9) II. Reason, or the ratio of all we have known, is not the same that it shall be when we know more.

(10) Therefore God becomes as we are, that we may be as he is.

(11) [Frontispiece; with imprint in reverse, and almost obliterated in the colouring of the design], The Author & Printer W. Blake.

B. Seven loose plates that came into the possession of Mr. William

Muir in 1886. By joining them with the preceding set, and rearranging the whole, he made in his coloured facsimile the first effective attempt towards establishing the plates in their right order. All the plates, except the conclusion (17) which is in a similar hand to numbers (3), (4), (5), (6), (7), and (8), are engraved in the same bold script as numbers (2) and (9) in the Print-room series.

(12) [Title-page, printed in monotone :] ALL RELIGIONS are ONE.

(13) IV. The bounded is loathed by its possessor. The same dull round, even of a univer[s]e would soon become a mill with complicated wheels.

(14) V. If the many became the same as the few when possess'd, More More is the cry of a mistaken soul : less than All cannot satisfy Man.

(15) VI. If any could desire what he is incapable of possessing despair must be his eternal lot.

(16) VII. The desire of Man being Infinite the possession is Infinite & himself Infinite.

(17) Conclusion. If it were not for the Poetic or Prophetic character the Philosophic and Experimental would soon be the ratio of all things & stand still unable to do other than repeat the same dull round over again.

(18) Application. He who sees the Infinite in all things sees God. He who sees the Ratio only sees himself only.

C. Ten plates in monotone, originally in the possession of John Linnell. There is a title-page 'THERE IS NO NATURAL RELIGION', a frontispiece 'The Voice of one crying in the Wilderness', an argument, and seven plates containing seven numbered 'Principles'. With the exception of the title-page none of the plates of this series is found in any other, and with the same exception the series seems to be complete and in order. It is therefore unnecessary to give the contents of the plates at this point.

The question of title-pages to these tractates is a curious one. Only three are known, the two mentioned above, and another, identical with that found in the Linnell series, added to an imperfect series by the owner, Frederick Locker-Lampson in 1878. There can be little doubt that the title-page found in the set B, 'All Religions are One', accurately defines the scope of the argument of the Linnell series and is therefore the correct title-plate of that series. The title-page, 'There is no Natural Religion', found with the Linnell plates can with equal certainty be taken as belonging to the other two collections.

From their substance it might be possible to regard plates (2) and (9) of the British Museum series as intended to supersede (8) and (3), as fuller and less ambiguous statements of the 'principles' they displace. But against this must be put the evidence of the script in (2) and (9) which, differing greatly from that of the other plates of the series, closely resembles that of the Muir group. They are therefore taken in this edition as the first and second 'principles' of the Muir series, the third principle of which has not yet come to light.

The script of plate (10) is similar in character to, though larger and less even than that of (1), but is unlike that of any other plate. It is not obviously related in substance to the 'Argument' or to the ideas on plates (3) to (10). Plate (17) is connected by the nature of its thesis with *All Religions are One*, Principles I—VI, but the character of its script would link it with plates (3) to (8). Plate (10) is indirectly an application of the statement on plate (17) We would therefore conclude that (17) and (9) follow in that order after (7). So to arrange the plates is to ignore what significance may lie in the fact that the phrases 'Ratio of all things' and 'same dull round' occur in (9) and (13), and nowhere else in either of the N. N. R. series. But if, as seems probable, both sets of Principles were composed at about the same time, evidence that rests on similarity of engraved script is of the less validity.

Plate (18) is difficult to place satisfactorily. On grounds of substance we incline to regard it as the conclusion to the series [b].

The present edition differs from the Oxford edition of Blake both in its placing of plate (10) and in dividing the plates (1) to (18) into two distinct tractates. If, however, it be conceded that they are one and not two, plate (10) could well be taken as embodying the conclusion of the whole matter. But in our view, Blake seems rather to offer alternative arguments that reach the same conclusion on similar premisses.

Series [b] lacks Principle III, and it may have had at one time a conclusion of its own, analogous to (10) in series [a].

The title-page to series [a] is regarded as equally suited to series [b].

There is no direct indication of the date of any of these tractates, but there appears to be no doubt of the rightness of the conclusion arrived at independently by Mr. A. G. B. Russell (*The Engravings of William Blake*, p. 205 *note*) and by Dr. Sampson in *Blake's Poetical Works*, Oxford edition (Bibliographical Introduction, p. xxviii), that these tractates are 'Blake's Original Stereotype' assigned to the year 1788 in the colophon to *The Ghost of Abel*.

THERE
is
NO
NATURAL
RELIGION

[a]

The Argument

Man has no notion of moral fitness but from Education. Naturally he is only a natural organ subject to Sense.

I

Man cannot naturally Percieve but through his natural or bodily organs.

II

Man by his reasoning power can only compare & judge of what he has already perciev'd.

III

From a perception of only 3 senses or 3 elements none could deduce a fourth or fifth.

IV

None could have other than natural or organic thoughts if he had none but organic perceptions.

V

Man's desires are limited by his perceptions: none can desire what he has not perciev'd.

VI

The desires & perceptions of man, untaught by any thing but organs of sense, must be limited to objects of sense.

Conclusion

If it were not for the Poetic or Prophetic character, the Philosophic & Experimental would soon be at the ratio of all things, and stand still, unable to do other than repeat the same dull round over again.

Therefore

God becomes as we are, that we may be as he is.

THERE

is

NO

NATURAL

RELIGION

[b]

I

Man's perceptions are not bounded by organs of perception : he percieves more than sense (tho' ever so acute) can discover.

II

Reason, or the ratio of all we have already known, is not the same that it shall be when we know more.

III

[Missing]

IV

The bounded is loathed by its possessor. The same dull round, even of a univer[s]e, would soon become a mill with complicated wheels.

V

If the many become the same as the few, when possess'd, More! More! is the cry of a mistaken soul : less than All cannot satisfy Man.

VI

If any could desire what he is incapable of possessing, despair must be his eternal lot.

VII

The desire of Man being Infinite, the possession is Infinite, & himself Infinite.

Application

He who sees the Infinite in all things sees God. He who sees the Ratio only, sees himself only.

ALL
RELIGIONS
are
ONE

The Voice of one crying in the Wilderness.

The Argument.

As the true method of knowledge is experiment, the true faculty of knowing must be the faculty which experiences. This faculty I treat of.

Principle 1st.

That the Poetic Genius is the true Man, and that the body or outward form of Man is derived from the Poetic Genius. Likewise that the forms of all things are derived from their Genius, which by the Ancients was call'd an Angel & Spirit & Demon.

Principle 2d.

As all men are alike in outward form, So (and with the same infinite variety) all are alike in the Poetic Genius.

Principle 3d.

No man can think, write, or speak from his heart, but he must intend truth. Thus all sects of Philosophy are from the Poetic Genius, adapted to the weaknesses of every individual.

Principle 4th.

As none by traveling over known lands can find out the unknown, So, from already acquired knowledge, Man could not acquire more ; therefore an universal Poetic Genius exists.

Principle 5th.

The Religions of all Nations are derived from each Nation's different reception of the Poetic Genius, which is every where call'd the Spirit of Prophecy.

All Religions are One

Principle 6th.

The Jewish & Christian Testaments are An original derivation from the Poetic Genius: this is necessary from the confined nature of bodily sensation.

Principle 7th.

As all men are alike (tho' infinitely various) So all Religions: & as all similars have one source,
The true Man is the source, he being the Poetic Genius.

THE MARRIAGE OF HEAVEN AND HELL

INTRODUCTORY NOTE

Collation: title-page 1 plate, The Argument 1 plate, text 22 plates, 24 plates relief-engraving, about 6×4 inches. The Grolier Catalogue describes a copy with a slightly different arrangement of the plates, but this is of little importance since there appears to be no strict sequence in the detached notes and ' visions ' that go to make up the book. The small three-page *Song of Liberty* is sometimes bound up with the *Marriage*, but since it also occurs separately, and is in subject-matter more closely related to the later ' prophecy ' *America*, it has here been printed by itself.

The *Argument* stands apart from the rest of the work in that it is written in irregular unrhymed verse. Its crabbed lines state only one of the many themes of the work, namely that in this era the characteristic quality of the expression of virtue is ' rage ', of evil ' mild humility '. A short prose rendering of the allegory might run: ' The just man, once meek, followed the path that leads to death, finding the rose of joy among the thorns of life, and sweetness in wild places, moving among the contraries without which ' there is no progression ' (M. H. H., p. 3). Effort finally made the way of life easy, to be, as it were, a path among trees, beside rivers and springs, till even the horror of death was lost in the wonder of life springing from death (cp. *Thel, passim*, especially ii, ll. 21–27). But the villain, envying his placid career, hypocritically assumed the meekness of the virtuous man, who, driven once more into ' " barren climes " is compelled by his environment to put off meekness and assume rage '. In the terms of the *Marriage* the wicked man becomes an ' Angel ', the just man a ' Devil '.

This paradox, which for Blake is not merely verbal, is much more intelligibly repeated in the *Marriage*, and, in fact, is the substance of Blake's early criticism of conventional moral codes, namely that they engender all forms of deceit and fraud, that they are essentially ' slave-moralities ' rating the compliance of the weak and cunning above the ' honest independence ' of the strong, that their quality is negation, and their effect sterility. Hence the just man is constrained to become a rebel in order to preserve his spiritual integrity. In the splendid vigour of the book the limit suggested in the *Argument* is transcended, and the criticism is carried over, not, however, in any systematic manner, from conventional morality into the region of conventional ideas of reality and knowledge. Incidentally, too, the book gives comparatively straightforward, though incomplete, statements of Blake's own position on these matters. Its directness, and the absence of the perplexing symbolism that darkens the later mystical writings make the *Marriage* of great value as a basis for the exposition of Blake's earlier doctrines and for the definition of his symbols. It has been freely used in the

General Introduction to the present edition, and most of its important points are discussed there.

To the main matters of the book is added a brief satirically barbed criticism of Swedenborg. In adapting Swedenborg's title *De Caelo et Inferno* to his purpose by adding the significant term ' Marriage ' Blake virtually defines one of the chief reasons for his dissent. Swedenborg adopts the normal view that evil is to be eliminated in the interest of good, whereas Blake regards them as the ' Contraries ' that are necessary to ' progression '. The moralist sees Heaven and Hell divided by an impassable gulf; to Blake they are complementary; ' Hell is opened to Heaven ' (J. 77. 34). That the *Marriage* owed its immediate impulse to Blake's antipathy towards the doctrines of Swedenborg is suggested by the satirical reference in the opening lines. In the more explicit indictment on pp. 20–21 Swedenborg is charged with spiritual pride, and his works are set down as mere compilations such as ' any man of mechanical talents ' might produce by thousands from the works of mystics and poets. Again in the most vigorous of the ' Memorable Fancies ', which parody Swedenborg's ' Memorable Relations ', Blake uses that writer's volumes to enable him to sink from ' the glorious clime ' ' above the earth's shadow ' into ' the void between Saturn and the fixed stars ', the place of the moralists, the ' Angels ' who filled ' with a confident insolence sprouting from systematic reasoning ' ' speak of themselves as the only wise '. Swedenborg's conceit made him fit company for ' Angels ', whereas Blake's ' particular friend ' was an Angel converted to Devildom.

Blake's estimate of Swedenborg was not always so contemptuous. Crabb Robinson records one of his utterances: ' Incidentally Swedenborg was mentioned—he [Blake] declared him to be a divine teacher ; he had done and would do much good ; yet he did wrong in trying to explain to Reason what it could not comprehend.' But though the good is admitted, the essential matter of Blake's criticism is maintained, as it is also in *Milton*, p. 20, ll. 46 foll. Such symbols as Blake derived from Swedenborg he modified or transformed with complete freedom.[1]

The *Proverbs of Hell* restate in aphoristic form the cardinal doctrines of the ' Devil's party '. They deny the religious sanction of morality by denying the value of the restraint that is practised in obedience to external authority, including the authority of a transcendent deity ; and condemn as futile prayer and all religious observances. On the positive side they affirm the value of enthusiasm, and of desire and passion carried to the degree conventionally condemned as excess. The *Proverbs* are of very unequal value, but the best are notable exercises in a difficult literary kind.

Next to the lyrical poems the *Marriage* is perhaps the most widely read of Blake's writings. The reasons for this are not difficult to discover: it has won its place, not so much by virtue of its comparative lucidity—it still remains a difficult book in parts—as because

[1] The quality of Blake's criticism of Swedenborg is remarkable, if it be true that at Easter 1789 he and his wife subscribed to a statement affirming a belief that the doctrines taught in the writings of Swedenborg were revealed truths, and proposing the establishment of the New Jerusalem Church as a separate organization (see *The Quest*, vol. xi, No. 1, October 1919, ' Blake and Swedenborg ', by H. N. Morris).

of the freshness and independence of its outlook. Its doctrines would have raised a mighty commotion in sober eighteenth-century households, if by a miracle it had gained access to them; and even now, when heterodoxies have ceased to startle, it can disturb dust in those chambers of the mind where easy generalities lie stored. And again Blake shows himself to be no mean satirist, though he has also to answer for such heinous offences as the *Island in the Moon*. But in the *Marriage* his satire has not vigour merely, but a daring imagination not easily matched. It is difficult to forbear quoting from the *Critical Essay* the whole of Swinburne's tremendous rhapsody. His magnificent praise demands qualification only in respect to the judgment that Blake's book is 'as perfect as his most faultless song'; for unity of final effect is precisely what the book fails to achieve.

Mr. G. L. Keynes notes [Bibliography, p. 151] a single detached copy of plate 11 whereon Blake has written

Death & Hell
Teem with Life.

'Death & Hell' are used in their 'Angelic', 'Life' in its 'Devilish' connotation.

The following catchwords occur in this book:

p. 5. -ah	p. 12. would	p. 21. one
,, 6. ro-	,, 17. root	,, 22. great
,, 8. The	,, 18. us	,, 23. -pulse.
,, 9. The	,, 19. num	

THE

MARRIAGE

of

HEAVEN

and

HELL

[2]

The Argument

RINTRAH roars & shakes his fires in the burden'd air ;
Hungry clouds swag on the deep.

Once meek, and in a perilous path,
The just man kept his course along
The vale of death.
Roses are planted where thorns grow,
And on the barren heath
Sing the honey bees.

Then the perilous path was planted,
And a river and a spring
On every cliff and tomb ;
And on the bleached bones
Red clay brought forth ;

Till the villain left the paths of ease,
To walk in perilous paths and drive
The just man into barren climes.

Now the sneaking serpent walks
In mild humility,
And the just man rages in the wilds
Where lions roam.

Rintrah roars & shakes his fires in the burden'd air ;
Hungry clouds swag on the deep.

The Argument. See Introduction. The verses are suggested by Isa. xxxv, but the theme suffers a characteristic inversion.

1 This is the first mention of Rintrah. He is constantly represented in the Lambeth books as a daemon of wrath and fury, and appears in *Europe* and *Africa* among the sons of Los and Enitharmon ; by their hands Urizen imposes his Laws and Religions on man. The significance of the symbol in the present passage is obscure, though a somewhat similar passage (*Europe*, ll. 127–130) may throw some light on it. There Rintrah helps to frustrate a premature attempt to overthrow the power of Urizen, the symbol of repression. So in the present passage Rintrah may represent the malignity that figures as morality in the scheme of the ' Angel ', the ' villain ' of the Argument.

[3] As a new heaven is begun, and it is now thirty-three [1] years since its advent, the Eternal Hell revives. And lo! Swedenborg is the Angel sitting at the tomb; his writings are the linen clothes folded up. Now is the dominion of Edom, & the return of Adam into Paradise: see Isaiah xxxiv. & xxxv. Chap.[2]

Without Contraries is no progression. Attraction and Repulsion, Reason and Energy, Love and Hate, are necessary to Human existence.

From these contraries spring what the religious call Good & Evil. Good is the passive that obeys Reason. Evil is the active springing from Energy.

Good is Heaven. Evil is Hell.

[4]

The voice of the Devil

ALL Bibles or sacred codes have been the causes of the following Errors: [3]

1. That Man has two real existing principles, Viz. a Body & a Soul.

2. That Energy, call'd Evil, is alone from the Body; & that Reason, call'd Good, is alone from the Soul.

3. That God will torment Man in Eternity for following his Energies.

But the following Contraries to these are True:

1. Man has no Body distinct from his Soul; for that call'd Body is a portion of Soul discern'd by the five Senses, the chief inlets of Soul in this age.

2. Energy is the only life and is from the Body; and Reason is the bound or outward circumference of Energy.

3. Energy is Eternal Delight.

[5] Those who restrain desire, do so because theirs is weak

[1] Swedenborg had foretold the advent in 1757 of a 'New Heaven', the similarity of which to the orthodox hope of 'an Eternal life . . . in an allegorical abode where existence hath never come' (*Europe*, ll. 38, 39) prompts the satirical suggestion that the spirit of revolt that had manifested itself during the thirty-three years following this date must mark the revival of 'the Eternal Hell', its 'Contrary'. The reference to the Swedenborgian prophecy fixes 1790 as the date of the composition of this work.

[2] Read in their 'infernal or diabolical sense' as revolutionary documents these chapters forecast the overthrow of all authority and the attainment of joy and gladness accompanied by the cleansing of the doors of perception (M. H. H., p. 14: cp. Isa. xxxv. 5–7).

[3] For a similar condemnation of 'Bibles or sacred Codes' see *Africa*, ll. 10–35.

enough to be restrained;[1] and the restrainer, or reason, usurps its place & governs the unwilling.

And being restrain'd, it by degrees becomes passive, till it is only the shadow of desire.

The history of this is written in Paradise Lost,[2] & the Governor, or Reason, is call'd Messiah.

And the original Archangel, or possessor of the command of the heavenly host, is call'd the Devil or Satan, and his children are call'd Sin & Death.

But in the Book of Job Milton's Messiah is call'd Satan.

For this history has been adopted by both parties.

It indeed appear'd to Reason as if Desire was cast out, but
[6] the Devil's account is, that the Messi/ah fell, & formed a heaven of what he stole from the Abyss.

This is shewn in the Gospel, where he prays to the Father to send the comforter, or Desire, that Reason may have Ideas to build on; the Jehovah of the Bible being no other than he[3] . . . who dwells in flaming fire.

Know that after Christ's death, he became Jehovah.

But in Milton, the Father is Destiny, the Son a Ratio of the five senses, & the Holy-ghost Vacuum!

Note. The reason Milton wrote in fetters when he wrote of Angels & God, and at liberty when of Devils & Hell, is because he was a true Poet and of the Devil's party without knowing it.

A Memorable Fancy

As I was walking among the fires of hell, delighted with the enjoyments of Genius, which to Angels look like torment and insanity, I collected some of their Proverbs, thinking that, as the sayings used in a nation mark its character, so the Proverbs of Hell shew the nature of Infernal wisdom better than any description of buildings or garments.

When I came home, on the abyss of the five senses, where a flat sided steep frowns over the present world, I saw a mighty Devil, folded in black clouds, hovering on the sides of the

[1] Cp. R. N., p. 180: 'He who Can be bound down is No Genius. Genius cannot be Bound. It may be Rendered Indignant or Outrageous; "Oppression makes the Wise Man Mad"; Solomon' [Eccles. vii. 7].

[2] Blake consistently rejects Milton's theodicy, and here interprets *Paradise Lost* as a perversion of truth to justify the fallacies of 'natural religion', so that the triumph of God over Satan in the Miltonic account is identified with the disastrous ascendancy of restrictive morality over man's fruitful and creative impulses. See *Milton,* Introduction.

[3] he] hiatus in Blake's autotype; apparently an erasure.

[7] rock: with cor/roding fires he wrote the following sentence, now percieved by the minds of men, & read by them on earth:

'How do you know but ev'ry Bird that cuts the airy way,
Is an immense world of delight, clos'd by your senses five?' [1]

Proverbs of Hell

In seed time learn; in harvest teach; in winter enjoy.
Drive your cart and your plow over the bones of the dead.
The road of excess leads to the palace of wisdom.
Prudence is a rich ugly old maid courted by Incapacity.
He who desires but acts not, breeds pestilence.
The cut worm forgives the plow.[2]
Dip him in the river who loves water.
A fool sees not the same tree that a wise man sees.[3]
He whose face gives no light shall never become a star.
Eternity is in love with the productions of time.
The busy bee has no time for sorrow.
The hours of folly are measur'd by the clock; but of wisdom no clock can measure.
All wholsom food is caught without a net or a trap.
Bring out number, weight & measure in a year of dearth.
No bird soars too high, if he soars with his own wings.
A dead body revenges not injuries.
The most sublime act is to set another before you.
If the fool would persist in his folly he would become wise.
Folly is the cloke of knavery.
Shame is Pride's cloke.
[8] Prisons are built with stones of Law, Brothels with bricks of Religion.
The pride of the peacock is the glory of God.
The lust of the goat is the bounty of God.
The wrath of the lion is the wisdom of God.
The nakedness of woman is the work of God.

[1] Cp. V. D. A., ll. 99–104. Cp. Chatterton, *The Dethe of Syr Charles Bawdin*, ll. 133–136: 'How dydd I know that ev'ry darte/That cutte the airie waie/Myghte nott fynde passage toe my harte/And close myne eyes for aie?'

[2] A rejected stanza in 'The Fly' [S. E., Clar. Press, p. 109] has the same phrase: 'The cut worm/Forgives the plow,/And sighs in peace/And so do thou.' In the proverb Blake stigmatizes the weakness that would make its cowardice a virtue. Cp. Proverb 16.

[3] Cp. letter to Dr. Trusler, 23rd August 1799: 'I know that this world is a world of imagination and vision. I see every thing I paint in this world, but every body does not see alike. . . . The tree which moves some to tears of joy is in the eyes of others only a green thing which stands in the way.' Cf. also Proverb 27 below.

Excess of sorrow laughs. Excess of joy weeps.
The roaring of lions, the howling of wolves, the raging of the stormy sea, and the destructive sword are portions of eternity too great for the eye of man.
The fox condemns the trap, not himself.
Joys impregnate: Sorrows bring forth.
Let man wear the fell of the lion, woman the fleece of the sheep.
The bird a nest, the spider a web, man friendship.
The selfish smiling fool & the sullen frowning fool shall be both thought wise, that they may be a rod.
What is now proved was once only imagin'd.
The rat, the mouse, the fox, the rabbet watch the roots; the lion, the tyger, the horse, the elephant watch the fruits.
The cistern contains, the fountain overflows.
One thought fills immensity.
Always be ready to speak your mind, and a base man will avoid you.
Every thing possible to be believ'd is an image of truth.
The eagle never lost so much time as when he submitted to learn of the crow.
[9] The fox provides for himself, but God provides for the lion.
Think in the morning. Act in the noon. Eat in the evening. Sleep in the Night.[1]
He who has suffer'd you to impose on him knows you.
As the plow follows words, so God rewards prayers.[2]
The tygers of wrath are wiser than the horses of instruction.
Expect poison from the standing water.
You never know what is enough, unless you know what is more than enough.
Listen to the fool's reproach: it is a kingly title.
The eyes of fire, the nostrils of air, the mouth of water, the beard of earth.
The weak in courage is strong in cunning.
The apple tree never asks the beech how he shall grow, nor the lion the horse how he shall take his prey.
The thankful reciever bears a plentiful harvest.
If others had not been foolish, we should be so.
The soul of sweet delight can never be defil'd.[3]
When thou seest an Eagle, thou seest a portion of Genius: lift up thy head!

[1] Cp. Proverb 1.
[2] Cp. Proverbs 59 and 60.
[3] Cp. *America*, l. 72.

As the catterpiller chooses the fairest leaves to lay her eggs on, so the priest lays his curse on the fairest joys.[1]

To create a little flower is the labour of ages.

Damn braces. Bless relaxes.

The best wine is the oldest, the best water the newest.

Prayers plow not! Praises reap not!

Joys laugh not! Sorrows weep not!

[10] The head Sublime, the heart Pathos, the genitals Beauty, the hands & feet Proportion.

As the air to a bird or the sea to a fish, so is contempt to the contemptible.

The crow wish'd every thing was black, the owl that every thing was white.

Exuberance is Beauty.

If the lion was advised by the fox, he would be cunning.

Improve[me]nt makes strait roads, but the crooked roads without Improvement are roads of Genius.

Sooner murder an infant in its cradle than nurse unacted desires.

Where man is not, nature is barren.

Truth can never be told so as to be understood, and not be believ'd.

Enough or Too much.

[11] The ancient Poets animated all sensible objects with Gods or Geniuses, calling them by the names and adorning them with the properties of woods, rivers, mountains, lakes, cities, nations, and whatever their enlarged & numerous senses could percieve.

And particularly they studied the genius of each city & country, placing it under its mental deity:

Till a system was formed, which some took advantage of, & enslav'd the vulgar by attempting to realize or abstract the mental deities from their objects: thus began Priesthood,

Choosing forms of worship from poetic tales.

And at length they pronounc'd that the Gods had order'd such things.

Thus men forgot that All deities reside in the human breast.[2]

[1] The priest in the Lambeth books is the agent of moral and mental enslavement. Cp. *Songs of Experience*, 'The Little Vagabond', 'A little Boy Lost': and particularly 'The Garden of Love' (Rossetti MS., Clar. Press, p. 127; quoted, *Europe*, ll. 131–137 *note*). Cp. also M. H. H., p. 11, *passim*.

[2] A later development of this doctrine appears in J. 71. 17–19:

in your own Bosom you bear your Heaven
And Earth; & all you behold, tho' it appears Without, it is Within
In your Imagination, of which this World of Mortality is but a Shadow.

[12] A Memorable Fancy

THE Prophets Isaiah and Ezekiel dined with me, and I asked them how they dared so roundly to assert that God spoke to them; and whether they did not think at the time that they would be misunderstood, & so be the cause of imposition.

Isaiah answer'd: 'I saw no God, nor heard any, in a finite organical perception; but my senses discover'd the infinite in every thing; and as I was then perswaded, & remain confirm'd, that the voice of honest indignation is the voice of God, I cared not for consequences, but wrote.'

Then I asked: 'does a firm perswasion that a thing is so, make it so?'

He replied: 'All poets believe that it does, & in ages of imagination this firm perswasion removed mountains; but many are not capable of a firm perswasion of any thing.'

Then Ezekiel said: 'The philosophy of the east taught the first principles of human perception.[1] Some nations held one principle for the origin, & some another; we of Israel taught that the Poetic Genius[2] (as you now call it) was the first principle, and all the others merely derivative, which was the cause of our despising the Priests & Philosophers of other
[13] countries, and prophecying that all Gods / would at last be proved to originate in ours & to be the tributaries of the Poetic Genius. It was this that our great poet, King David, desired so fervently & invokes so patheticly, saying, by this he conquers enemies & governs kingdoms: and we so loved our God, that we cursed in his name all the deities of surrounding nations, and asserted that they had rebelled. From these opinions the vulgar came to think that all nations would at last be subject to the jews.'

'This,' said he, 'like all firm perswasions, is come to pass; for all nations believe the jews' code and worship the jews' god, and what greater subjection can be?'

I heard this with some wonder, & must confess my own conviction. After dinner, I ask'd Isaiah to favour the world with his lost works; he said none of equal value was lost. Ezekiel said the same of his.[3]

[1] Cp. *Africa*, ll. 10–35.

[2] *All Religions are One*, principle 5: 'The Religions of all Nations are derived from each Nation's different reception of the Poetic Genius, which is everywhere call'd the Spirit of Prophecy.'

[3] Cp. 2 Chron. xxvi. 22 and xxxii. 32. A passage in Josephus, *Antiq*. x. 5, § 1, ascribes to Ezekiel two books dealing with the Babylonian captivity. The source of Blake's knowledge of this is unknown.

I also asked Isaiah what made him go naked and barefoot three years:[1] he answer'd: 'the same that made our friend Diogenes the Grecian.'

I then asked Ezekiel why he eat dung, & lay so long on his right & left side.[2] He answer'd: 'the desire of raising other men into a perception of the infinite. This the North American tribes practise, & is he honest who resists his genius or conscience only for the sake of present ease or gratification?'[3]

14] The ancient tradition that the world will be consumed in fire at the end of six thousand years is true, as I have heard from Hell.

For the cherub with his flaming sword is hereby commanded to leave his guard at [the] tree of life, and when he does, the whole creation will be consumed and appear infinite and holy, whereas it now appears finite & corrupt.[4]

This will come to pass by an improvement of sensual enjoyment.

But first the notion that man has a body distinct from his soul is to be expunged; this I shall do by printing in the infernal method by corrosives, which in Hell are salutary and medicinal, melting apparent surfaces away, and displaying the infinite which was hid.

If the doors of perception were cleansed, every thing would appear to man as it is, infinite.

For man has closed himself up, till he sees all things thro' narrow chinks of his cavern.[5]

[15] A Memorable Fancy[6]

I WAS in a Printing house in Hell & saw the method in which knowledge is transmitted from generation to generation.

In the first chamber was a Dragon-Man, clearing away the rubbish from a cave's mouth; within, a number of Dragons were hollowing the cave.

[1] Cp. Isa. xx. 3.
[2] Cp. Ezek. iv. 12.

[3] The admission of a possible value in asceticism is unusual in Blake's early writings (cf., however, M. H. H., p. 16). But it is to be noted that asceticism here is in obedience to the demand of the individual's 'genius or conscience', not in fulfilment of an external law.

[4] In the later writings the Last Judgement is symbolical of 'an overwhelming of bad art and science. . . . Error or creation will be burn'd up, and then, and not till then, truth or eternity will appear' (Cat. 1810).

[5] Cp. *Europe*, Appendix, 'Five windows light the cavern'd Man'.

[6] Swinburne calls this 'Fancy' a 'vision of knowledge' and adds the following paraphrase: 'First the human nature is cleansed and widened into shape, then decorated, then enlarged and built about with stately buildings for guest-chambers and treasure-houses; then the purged metal of knowledge, melted into form with divine violence, is made fluid and

In the second chamber was a Viper folding round the rock & the cave, and others adorning it with gold, silver and precious stones.

In the third chamber was an Eagle with wings and feathers of air; he caused the inside of the cave to be infinite: around were numbers of Eagle-like men who built palaces in the immense cliffs.

In the fourth chamber were Lions of flaming fire, raging around & melting the metals into living fluids.

In the fifth chamber were Unnam'd forms, which cast the metals into the expanse.

There they were reciev'd by Men who occupied the sixth chamber, and took the forms of books & were arranged in libraries.

[16] The Giants [1] who formed this world into its sensual existence and now seem to live in it in chains, are in truth the causes of its life & the sources of all activity; but the chains are the cunning of weak and tame minds which have power to resist energy: according to the proverb, the weak in courage is strong in cunning.[2]

Thus one portion of being is the Prolific, the other the Devouring. To the devourer it seems as if the producer was in his chains; but it is not so; he only takes portions of existence and fancies that the whole.

But the Prolific would cease to be Prolific unless the Devourer as a sea recieved the excess of his delights.[3]

Some will say: 'Is not God alone the Prolific?' I answer: 'God only Acts & Is, in existing beings or Men.' [4]

These two classes of men are always upon earth, & they
[17] should be enemies: whoever tries / to reconcile them seeks to destroy existence.[5]

vital, that it may percolate and permeate the whole man through every pore of his spirit; then the metal is cast forth and put to use. All forms and forces of the world, viper and lion, half human things and nameless natures, serve to help in this work; all manner of aspiration and inspiration, wrath and faith, love and labour, do good service here' (*Essay*, p. 216).

[1] Giants] 'the Antediluvians who are our Energies' (M. H. H., p. 17). See Index, *Giants*.

[2] Cp. M. H. H., p. 9, Proverb 49.

[3] This curious statement seems to follow from the earlier thesis 'Without Contraries is no progression' (M. H. H., p. 3), but Blake nowhere develops what seems to be a tentative justification of restraint.

[4] 'All deities reside in the human breast' (M. H. H., p. 11): and cp. E. G. γ^2, ll. 31–32:

> Thou art a Man. God is no more.
> Thine own Humanity learn to adore. (Clar. Press, p. 250.)

[5] Later, 'To make One Family of Contraries' (J. 55. 15) is made part of the error of the Spectre. See Index, *Spectre*.

Religion is an endeavour to reconcile the two.

Note. Jesus Christ did not wish to unite, but to seperate them, as in the Parable of sheep and goats : & he says : 'I came not to send Peace, but a Sword.'[1]

Messiah or Satan or Tempter was formerly thought to be one of the Antediluvians who are our Energies.

A Memorable Fancy

An Angel came to me and said : 'O pitiable foolish young man ! O horrible ! O dreadful state ! consider the hot burning dungeon thou art preparing for thyself to all eternity, to which thou art going in such career.'

I said : 'perhaps you will be willing to shew me my eternal lot, & we will contemplate together upon it, and see whether your lot or mine is most desirable.'

So he took me thro' a stable & thro' a church & down into the church vault, at the end of which was a mill. Thro' the mill we went, and came to a cave.[2] Down the winding cavern we groped our tedious way, till a void, boundless as a nether sky, appear'd beneath us, & we held by the roots of trees, and hung over this immensity. But I said : 'if you please, we will commit ourselves to this void, and see whether providence is here also : if you will not, I will.' But he answer'd : 'Do not presume, O young-man : but as we here remain, behold thy lot which will soon appear when the darkness passes away.'

[18] So I remain'd with him, sitting in the twisted / root of an oak :[3] he was suspended in a fungus which hung with the head downward into the deep.

By degrees we beheld the infinite Abyss, fiery as the smoke of a burning city ; beneath us, at an immense distance, was the sun, black but shining :[4] round it were fiery tracks

[1] See below, p. 23, and the whole of *The Everlasting Gospel*, where Jesus is represented as the uncompromising antagonist of all legal and social conventions. The quotation is from Matt. x. 34.

[2] It may possibly be that the stable, the church, and the vault represent the incarnation, the mortal life, and the death and resurrection of Jesus, while the mill and cave, which later become common symbols of religious error, image the repressive influence and the devious ways of the Christian Church, which offers, as reward to its followers, an 'Eternal life' 'in an allegorical abode where existence hath never come' (*Europe*, l. 40), that is, the void immensity of the present parable : see Index, *Ulro, Note II*. See also General Introduction, p. 58.

[3] Blake's seat in the twisted roots of an oak and the Angel's in the fungus overhanging the void continue the allegory.

[4] Cp. *America*, l. 49, where the liberated souls cry, 'The Sun has left his blackness & has found a fresher morning'.

on which revolv'd vast spiders, crawling after their prey, which flew, or rather swum, in the infinite deep, in the most terrific shapes of animals sprung from corruption; & the air was full of them, & seem'd composed of them. These are Devils, and are called Powers of the air. I now asked my companion which was my eternal lot. He said: 'Between the black & white spiders.'

But now, from between the black & white spiders, a cloud and fire burst and rolled thro' the deep, black'ning all beneath, so that the nether deep grew black as a sea, & rolled with a terrible noise. Beneath us was nothing now to be seen but a black tempest, till looking east between the clouds & the waves we saw a cataract of blood mixed with fire, and not many stones' throw from us appear'd and sunk again the scaly fold of a monstrous serpent. At last, to the east, distant about three degrees, appear'd a fiery crest above the waves: slowly it reared like a ridge of golden rocks, till we discover'd two globes of crimson fire, from which the sea fled away in clouds of smoke; and now we saw it was the head of Leviathan. His forehead was divided into streaks of green & purple like those on a tyger's forehead. Soon we saw his mouth & red gills hang just above the raging foam, tinging the black deep
[19] with beams of blood, advancing toward / us with all the fury of a spiritual existence.

My friend the Angel climb'd up from his station into the mill; I remain'd alone, & then this appearance was no more: [1] but I found myself sitting on a pleasant bank beside a river by moon light, hearing a harper, who sung to the harp; & his theme was: 'The man who never alters his opinion is like standing water, & breeds reptiles of the mind.' [2]

But I arose and sought for the mill; & there I found my Angel, who, surprised, asked me how I escaped.

I answer'd: 'All that we saw was owing to your metaphysics; for when you ran away, I found myself on a bank by moonlight hearing a harper. But now we have seen my eternal lot, shall I shew you yours?' He laugh'd at my proposal, but I by force suddenly caught him in my arms, & flew westerly thro' the night, till we were elevated above the earth's shadow; [3] then I flung myself with him directly into the body of the sun. Here I clothed myself in white, & taking in my hand Swedenborg's volumes, sunk from the glorious clime, and passed all the planets till we came to saturn.

[1] See General Introduction, p. 19.

[2] Cp. Proverb 45. See also B. U., chap. iv (a), ll. 11–24, and B. A., chap. iv, ll. 9–13.

[3] See Index, *Cardinal Points* and *Shadow*.

Here I staid to rest, & then leap'd into the void between saturn & the fixed stars.

'Here' said I 'is your lot, in this space, if space it may be call'd.' Soon we saw the stable and the church, & I took him to the altar and open'd the Bible, and lo! it was a deep pit, into which I descended, driving the Angel before me. Soon we saw seven houses of brick:[1] One we enter'd: in it
[20] were a / number of monkeys, baboons, & all of that species, chain'd by the middle, grinning and snatching at one another, but withheld by the shortness of their chains. However I saw that they sometimes grew numerous, and then the weak were caught by the strong, and, with a grinning aspect, first coupled with, & then devour'd by plucking off first one limb and then another, till the body was left a helpless trunk. This, after grinning & kissing it with seeming fondness, they devour'd too; and here & there I saw one savourily picking the flesh off of his own tail. As the stench terribly annoy'd us both, we went into the mill, & I in my hand brought the skeleton of a body, which in the mill was Aristotle's Analytics.[2]

So the Angel said: 'thy phantasy has imposed upon me, & thou oughtest to be ashamed.'

I answer'd: 'we impose on one another, & it is but lost time to converse with you, whose works are only Analytics.'[3]

[21] I have always found that Angels have the vanity to speak of themselves as the only wise: this they do with a confident insolence sprouting from systematic reasoning.

Thus Swedenborg boasts that what he writes is new; tho' it is only the Contents or Index of already publish'd books.

A man carried a monkey about for a shew, & because he was a little wiser than the monkey, grew vain, and conciev'd himself as much wiser than seven men. It is so with Swedenborg: he shews the folly of churches, & exposes hypocrites, till he imagines that all are religious, & himself the single / one
[22] on earth that ever broke a net.

Now hear a plain fact: Swedenborg has not written one new truth. Now hear another: he has written all the old falshoods.

[1] 'The "seven houses of brick" we may take to be a reminiscence of the seven churches of St. John' (Swinburne, *Essay*, p. 220).

[2] Here again, 'A fool sees not the same tree that a wise man sees.' What is to the believer in sense-perception the supreme revelation of reality is to the visionary but the 'skeleton of a body', the antithesis of living truth.

[3] 'It is evident that between pure "phantasy" and mere "analytics" the great gulf must remain fixed, and either party appear to the other deceptive and deceived' (Swinburne, *Essay*, p. 220). Three copies of M. H. H. exhibit at the foot of this plate (20) the words: 'Opposition is true Friendship.'

And now hear the reason. He conversed with Angels, who are all religious, & conversed not with Devils, who all hate religion ; for he was incapable thro' his conceited notions.

Thus Swedenborg's writings are a recapitulation of all superficial opinions and an analysis of the more sublime, but no further.

Have now another plain fact. Any man of mechanical talents may, from the writings of Paracelsus or Jacob Behmen, produce ten thousand volumes of equal value with Swedenborg's, and from those of Dante or Shakespear an infinite number.

But when he has done this, let him not say that he knows better than his master, for he only holds a candle in sunshine.

A Memorable Fancy

Once I saw a Devil in a flame of fire, who arose before an Angel that sat on a cloud, and the Devil utter'd these words :

' The worship of God is : Honouring his gifts in other men,
[23] each according to his genius, and loving the / greatest men best : those who envy or calumniate great men hate God ; for there is no other God.' [1]

The Angel, hearing this, became almost blue ; but mastering himself he grew yellow, & at last white, pink & smiling, and then replied :

' Thou Idolater, is not God One ? & is not he visible in Jesus Christ ? and has not Jesus Christ given his sanction to the law of ten commandments ? and are not all other men fools, sinners & nothings ?'

The Devil answer'd : ' bray a fool in a morter with wheat, yet shall not his folly be beaten out of him. If Jesus Christ is the greatest man, you ought to love him in the greatest degree. Now hear how he has given his sanction to the law of ten commandments. Did he not mock at the sabbath, and so mock the sabbath's God, murder those who were murder'd because of him, turn away the law from the woman taken in adultery, steal the labor of others to support him, bear false witness when he omitted making a defence before Pilate, covet when he pray'd for his disciples and when he bid them shake off the dust of their feet against such as refused to lodge them ? [2] I tell you, no virtue can exist without

[1] Cp. J. 91. 7–12.

[2] Cp. E. G. ε, l. 15 (Clar. Press, p. 256) :

> Yes, but they say he never fell.
> Ask Caiaphas : for he can tell.—

breaking these ten commandments. Jesus was all virtue,
[24] and acted from im/pulse, not from rules.'

When he had so spoken, I beheld the Angel, who stretched out his arms, embracing the flame of fire : & he was consumed, and arose as Elijah.[1]

Note. This Angel, who is now become a Devil, is my particular friend: we often read the Bible together in its infernal or diabolical sense,[2] which the world shall have if they behave well.

I have also The Bible of Hell,[3] which the world shall have whether they will or no.

One Law for the Lion & Ox is Oppression.[4]

He mock'd the Sabbath, and he mock'd
The Sabbath's God, and he unlock'd
The Evil spirits from their Shrines,
And turn'd Fishermen to Divines. . . .
He scorn'd Earth's parents, scorn'd Earth's God,
And mock'd the one, and the other's Rod;
His Seventy Disciples sent
Against Religion and Government . . .
He left his father's trade, to roam,
A wand'ring vagrant without Home;
And thus he others' labour stole,
That he might live above controll.
The Publicans and Harlots he
Selected for his company,
And from the Adulteress turn'd away
God's righteous Law, that lost its Prey.

[1] Elijah in the later writings is the type of the visionary spirit: cp. J. 44. 30, where the Friends of Albion

gave their power to Los,
Naming him the Spirit of Prophecy, calling him Elijah.

[2] Cp. E. G., Prologue (Clar. Press, p. 246):

The Vision of Christ that thou dost see
Is my Vision's Greatest Enemy. . . .
Thine is the Friend of All Mankind;
Mine speaks in Parables to the Blind.
Thine loves the same world that mine hates;
Thy heaven doors are my Hell Gates, . . .
Both read the Bible day & night,
But thou read'st black where I read white.

And cp. J. 91. 36.

[3] Cp. Keynes: *Bibliography*, p. 186: '*Works Lost or Conjectural: THE BIBLE OF HELL*, in Nocturnal Visions collected. Vol. I, Lambeth [?1793]. *Note*: This title is written on the back of a drawing in title-page form. . . . Nothing further is known of any work of this name.'

[4] Cp. *Tiriel*, § 8, ll. 8–9: 'Why is one law given to the lion and the patient ox'; and V. D. A., l. 108: 'And is there not one law for both the lion and the ox.'

VISIONS OF THE DAUGHTERS OF ALBION

INTRODUCTORY NOTE

Collation: 'title-page and "The Argument" 1 plate each, "Visions" 8 plates, full-page design sometimes placed last and sometimes as frontispiece, 1 plate, 11 plates relief engraving, about $6\frac{3}{4} \times 4\frac{5}{8}$ inches' (Clar. Press, p. 334).

The *Visions of the Daughters of Albion* stands with *America*, *Europe*, and *The Song of Los* rather than with *The Book of Urizen* and its complements, the books of *Ahania* and *Los*: that is to say, it is more in the nature of an attack on the generally accepted moral standards, than an attempt to assign a mythical origin to them. It is among the more lucid of Blake's 'prophetic' writings, and what little symbolism it has, is found almost wholly in the first forty lines.

The 'Daughters of Albion' have as yet nothing of their later symbolic significance, and may be best interpreted as 'the female spirits of the dead pining in bonds of religion' (*America*, l. 200), i. e. human souls in the bondage of restrictive morality. They see in vision the vicissitudes of certain supernatural beings, who may be regarded as types of spiritual states in relation to restrictive morality, the source and symbol of which is Urizen. But though vehemently denounced in the course of the book as the prime cause of man's degradation to the mortal state, this tyrant-god of a false religion, 'Creator of Men' and 'mistaken Demon of heaven', does not actually appear in person. Greater prominence is given to other mythical beings, Leutha, Oothoon, Theotormon and Bromion. The first of these is one of the daughters of Los and Enitharmon, who in *Europe* are called to aid their mother in her attempt to subdue mankind to the delusions of morality and religion. Hence she is 'the sweet smiling pestilence' (*Europe*, l. 173), and the mistress of the 'Seven churches' (*ibid.*, l. 181) that 'seek the love' of the masculine spirit, Antamon, to destroy his spiritual life. Similarly her title 'the luring bird of Eden' (*ibid.*, l. 170) may refer to that aspect of the 'feminine delusion' whereby man is led to submit himself to a rule of asceticism in this world in the expectation of Paradise, 'an allegorical abode, where existence hath never come' (*ibid.*, l. 39). She is also called the 'Soft soul of flowers' (*ibid.*, l. 172), an expression akin to the association of the 'soul of sweet delight' with the 'flowers of Leutha' (V. D. A., l. 9). The symbolic plucking of a flower (V. D. A., ll. 7–10), obviously to be interpreted by reference to the lyric cry of pagan love-poetry, would suggest that Leutha is emblematic of bodily delights and sensual impulses which in themselves are wholly pure, and can only become cause of defilement when they are expressed secretly and with shame, or when they are sheltered behind the half-hearted permissives and compromises of current morality. Something of this sense may lie behind the association of Leutha with the 'loose bible' given by Antamon to Mahomet (S. L., ll. 28–29). Other allusions, such as that to 'Leutha's chariot' (B. L., chap. i, l. 2) and the 'dogs of Leutha' (J. 83. 82), with the curious identification of the Isle of Dogs with 'the Isle of Leutha's Dogs' (J. 31. 14–15) cannot be explained. A later modification of the Leutha symbol is considered in M. 9. 28 *note*.

Oothoon, the 'soft soul of America', land of liberty, appears to show the 'pure soul' seeking for delight, and in the pursuit of it transcending the limits of the conventional ethic. Under the lash of the violated moral law, she becomes the mouthpiece of some of Blake's plainest utterances on questions of morality. It may be noticed in passing that an engraved *Book of Outhoon* is among the lost works of Blake.[1]

In *The Song of Los* Theotormon is one of those sons of Los by whom Urizen transmits his restrictive 'Laws and Religions' to mortals; he is the giver of the ascetic Christian gospel to Jesus (*Africa*, ll. 23–24). Later in *Milton* and *Jerusalem* he and Bromion appear among the four sons of Los who assist in their father's labours to regenerate man.[2] In the present book neither of these meanings holds. Concerning Theotormon, it can only be suggested, from the general tenor of the references, that he represents the state of the fearful moralist. When Bromion intercepts and violates Oothoon he binds 'the adulterate pair' back to back in his 'dark religious caves' washed by 'black jealous waves'—clearly a symbolic statement of the common ethical attitude towards unlicensed or abnormal forms of activity. The perplexed inquiries of Theotormon (ll. 83–97) would, on these grounds, seem to be the attempts of the 'religious' man to square the tenets of his creed with the facts of experience.

Bromion is still more obscure. 'A violent Titan', as Swinburne calls him, he sees truths hidden from Theotormon, yet is so far obsessed by the apparent validity of the laws he violates as to appear to be the symbol of mere ravening lust. This view is not free from difficulty, but it is of little importance since no parallel episode occurs elsewhere.

From what has been said, it is clear that the main purpose of the *Visions* is to deny validity to conventional morality; but this, as commonly in Blake, is inextricably bound up with criticism of sense-perception and empiricism. Both forms of error originate in Urizen, against whose 'religion' Blake advances his own doctrine that 'everything that lives is holy' and that the sole criterion of conduct must be its outcome in joy and delight.

The prominence given to the position of women under the moral law is perhaps the most striking feature of the *Visions*, and suggests the question whether the book owes its existence to the publication of *A Vindication of the Rights of Woman* in the previous year (1792). Mary Wollstonecraft and Blake may have met at the house of Johnson the publisher, where many literary men and women of revolutionary sympathies were accustomed to meet. It was at one of these gatherings in this same year (13 September 1792) that Blake is said to have conveyed to Paine the warning whereby he was able to avoid arrest by flight to France.

[1] 'A list drawn up by Mrs. Blake describes it as follows: Outhoon, 12 plates, 6 inches more or less. Price £2 2s. 0.' (Keynes, p. 187.)

[2] See Index, *Los, Note II*, A, i.

VISIONS

of

The Daughters of Albion

The Eye sees more than the Heart knows.

Printed by Willm Blake : 1793.

The Argument

I lovèd Theotormon,
And I was not ashamèd;
I trembled in my virgin fears,
And I hid in Leutha's vale!

I pluckèd Leutha's flower,
And I rose up from the vale;
But the terrible thunders tore
My virgin mantle in twain.

The Argument. These lines are spoken by Oothoon, and present in brief the subject developed in the *Visions.* She, the soul that burns with vigorous youth, plucks the flower of sweet delight that can neither be exhausted nor defiled; but against this native innocence are launched the 'terrible thunders' of the moral law, that declares its purity impure,

> And renders that a Lawless thing
> On which the soul expands its wing.
>
> (E. G., ζ, ll. 67–68, Clar. Press, p. 260.)

Cp. 'Soft Snow' (Ross. MS. xx, Clar. Press, p. 171):

> I walkèd abroad on a snowy day:
> I ask'd the soft snow with me to play:
> She play'd & she melted in all her prime;
> And the winter call'd it a dreadful crime.

Visions

Enslav'd, the Daughters of Albion weep; a trembling lamentation
Upon their mountains; in their valleys, sighs toward America.

For the soft soul of America, Oothoon, wander'd in woe
Along the vales of Leutha, seeking flowers to comfort her;
And thus she spoke to the bright Marygold of Leutha's vale:

'Art thou a flower? art thou a nymph? I see thee now a flower,
Now a nymph! I dare not pluck thee from thy dewy bed!'

The Golden nymph replied: 'pluck thou my flower, Oothoon the mild.
Another flower shall spring, because the soul of sweet delight
Can never pass away.' She ceas'd, & clos'd her golden shrine.

Then Oothoon pluck'd the flower, saying: 'I pluck thee from thy bed,
Sweet flower, and put thee here to glow between my breasts;
And thus I turn my face to where my whole soul seeks.'

Over the waves she went in wing'd exulting swift delight,
And over Theotormon's reign took her impetuous course.

Bromion rent her with his thunders; on his stormy bed
Lay the faint maid, and soon her woes appall'd his thunders hoarse.

1 For the Daughters of Albion, see introductory note to this book.

11–13 Oothoon follows desire, openly and unashamed, and thereby comes into conflict with the central principle of prudential morality, secrecy.

15–25 Bromion breaks the moral law; but he does not deny it. He employs its terrors to maintain his own power (ll. 22–23). Interpretation is almost impossible, but it may perhaps be suggested that in this episode Bromion represents the immoralist, in contrast with the ideal or a-moralist position defined later by Oothoon. Both come under the condemnation of the moralist, Theotormon (ll. 26–28). Yet against this must be set the fact that nowhere else in Blake is there any differentiation of immoralist and a-moralist. An alternative rendering may be made by reference to S. L. *Africa*, ll. 35–37. Bromion's challenge to Theotormon may be

Bromion spoke : ‘ behold this harlot here on Bromion’s bed,
And let the jealous dolphins sport around the lovely maid !
Thy soft American plains are mine, and mine thy north & south :
Stampt with my signet are the swarthy children of the sun.
They are obedient, they resist not, they obey the scourge ;
Their daughters worship terrors and obey the violent.
[2] Now thou maist marry Bromion’s harlot, and protect the child
Of Bromion’s rage, that Oothoon shall put forth in nine moons’ time.’

Then storms rent Theotormon’s limbs : he roll’d his waves around,
And folded his black jealous waters round the adulterate pair ;
Bound back to back in Bromion’s caves, terror & meekness dwell.

At entrance Theotormon sits, wearing the threshold hard
With secret tears ; beneath him sound like waves on a desart shore
The voice of slaves beneath the sun, and children bought with money,
That shiver in religious caves beneath the burning fires
Of lust, that belch incessant from the summits of the earth.

Oothoon weeps not ; she cannot weep ; her tears are lockèd up :
But she can howl incessant, writhing her soft snowy limbs,
And calling Theotormon’s Eagles to prey upon her flesh.

‘ I call with holy voice ! kings of the sounding air,
Rend away this defilèd bosom, that I may reflect
The image of Theotormon on my pure transparent breast ! ’

compared with the state of ‘ War & Lust ’ in Eternity that drove the timorous Har and Heva to create themselves a refuge therefrom in the Vision and Philosophy of the Five Senses.

37–39 For the apparent paradox cp. *America*, ll. 68–72 :

pale religious letchery, seeking Virginity,
May find it in a harlot, and in coarse-clad honesty
The undefil’d, tho’ ravish’d in her cradle night and morn.
For everything that lives is holy : life delights in life ;
Because the soul of sweet delight can never be defil’d.

The reference to ‘ the defiled bosom ’ (l. 38) when related to the substance of Oothoon’s speech, especially ll. 75 foll., perhaps indicates that in some obscure manner moral enlightenment comes to her by the agency of the Eagles (ll. 36 and 40) or of Theotormon’s severe smile (ll. 41–42).

The Eagles at her call descend & rend their bleeding prey.
Theotormon severely smiles ; her soul reflects the smile,
As the clear spring, mudded with feet of beasts, grows pure & smiles.

The Daughters of Albion hear her woes & eccho back her sighs.

'Why does my Theotormon sit weeping upon the threshold,
And Oothoon hovers by his side, perswading him in vain ?
I cry : " arise, O Theotormon, for the village dog
Barks at the breaking day ; the nightingale has done lamenting ;
The lark does rustle in the ripe corn, and the Eagle returns
From nightly prey, and lifts his golden beak to the pure east,
Shaking the dust from his immortal pinions to awake
The sun that sleeps too long. Arise, my Theotormon! I am pure,
Because the night is gone that clos'd me in its deadly black."
They told me that the night & day were all that I could see ;
They told me that I had five senses to inclose me up ;
And they inclos'd my infinite brain into a narrow circle,
And sunk my heart into the Abyss, a red, round globe, hot burning,
Till all from life I was obliterated and erasèd.
Instead of morn arises a bright shadow, like an eye,
In the eastern cloud ; instead of night a sickly charnel house,
That Theotormon hears me not : to him the night and morn
Are both alike, a night of sighs, a morning of fresh tears ;
[3] And none but Bromion can hear my lamentations.

'With what sense is it that the chicken shuns the ravenous hawk ?
With what sense does the tame pigeon measure out the expanse ?
With what sense does the bee form cells ? have not the mouse & frog
Eyes and ears and sense of touch ? yet are their habitations
And their pursuits as different as their forms and as their joys.
Ask the wild ass why he refuses burdens, and the meek camel
Why he loves man : is it because of eye, ear, mouth, or skin,

52 The 'deepest night of Ulro' or error, that obscures all with its delusions of morality and sense-perception. Cp. M. 40. 30 : 'And Ancient Night spread over all the heav'n his Mantle of Laws.'

53–74 This is Blake's first direct statement of the possibility of supersensuous knowledge, a doctrine here based on the analogy of instinct in animals. Cp. N. N. R. [a] and [b], *passim*.

56 This image often recurs in connexion with the later feminine symbols ; cp. B. U., chap. v, 39 *note*.

Or breathing nostrils? No, for these the wolf and tyger have.
Ask the blind worm the secrets of the grave, and why her spires
Love to curl round the bones of death; and ask the rav'nous snake
Where she gets poison, & the wing'd eagle why he loves the sun;
And then tell me the thoughts of man, that have been hid of old:

'Silent I hover all the night, and all day could be silent,
If Theotormon once would turn his lovèd eyes upon me.
How can I be defil'd when I reflect thy image pure?
Sweetest the fruit that the worm feeds on, & the soul prey'd on by woe;
The new wash'd lamb ting'd with the village smoke, & the bright swan
By the red earth of our immortal river. I bathe my wings,
And I am white and pure to hover round Theotormon's breast.'

Then Theotormon broke his silence, and he answerèd:

'Tell me what is the night or day to one o'erflow'd with woe?
Tell me what is a thought, & of what substance is it made?
Tell me what is a joy, & in what gardens do joys grow?
And in what rivers swim the sorrows, and upon what mountains
[4] Wave shadows of discontent? and in what houses dwell the wretched,
Drunken with woe, forgotten, and shut up from cold despair?

'Tell me where dwell the thoughts forgotten till thou call them forth?
Tell me where dwell the joys of old, & where the ancient loves,
And when will they renew again, & the night of oblivion past,

83–97 Theotormon expresses the case of the victim of delusions in thought and morals 'tormented by doubts and fears continually'. This temper is developed in the description of 'the idiot Questioner'

who is always questioning,
But never capable of answering; who sits with a sly grin
Silent plotting when to question, like a thief in a cave;
Who publishes doubt & calls it knowledge, whose Science is Despair,
Whose pretence to knowledge is Envy, whose whole Science is
To destroy the wisdom of ages to gratify ravenous Envy. (M. 43. 12–17.)

That I might traverse times & spaces far remote, and bring
Comforts into a present sorrow and a night of pain ?
Where goest thou, O thought ? to what remote land is thy flight ?
If thou returnest to the present moment of affliction,
Wilt thou bring comforts on thy wings, and dews and honey and balm,
Or poison from the desart wilds, from the eyes of the envier ?'

Then Bromion said, and shook the cavern with his lamentation :

'Thou knowest that the ancient trees seen by thine eyes have fruit ;
But knowest thou that trees and fruits flourish upon the earth
To gratify senses unknown—trees, beasts, and birds unknown,
Unknown, not unperciev'd, spread in the infinite microscope,
In places yet unvisited by the voyager, and in worlds
Over another kind of seas, and in atmospheres unknown ?
Ah ! are there other wars, beside the wars of sword and fire ?
And are there other sorrows beside the sorrows of poverty ?
And are there other joys beside the joys of riches and ease ?
And is there not one law for both the lion and the ox ?
And is there not eternal fire, and eternal chains,
To bind the phantoms of existence from eternal life ?'

Then Oothoon waited silent all the day and all the night ;
[5] But when the morn arose, her lamentation renew'd.
The Daughters of Albion hear her woes, & eccho back her sighs :

'O Urizen ! Creator of men ! mistaken Demon of heaven !
Thy joys are tears, thy labour vain to form men to thine image.
How can one joy absorb another ? are not different joys
Holy, eternal, infinite ? and each joy is a Love.

Does not the great mouth laugh at a gift, & the narrow eyelids mock
At the labour that is above payment ? and wilt thou take the ape

99–110 Bromion realizes the existence of a supersensible world, but fails (ll. 105–110) to see that sorrow and repression are not of the essence of life ; cp. l. 37 *note*.

108 This line occurs in *Tiriel*, § 8, l. 9, and as the last line of M. H. H.

114 See Index, *Urizen*.

For thy councellor, or the dog for a schoolmaster to thy children?
Does he who contemns poverty, and he who turns with abhorrence
From usury, feel the same passion, or are they movèd alike?
How can the giver of gifts experience the delights of the merchant;
How the industrious citizen the pains of the husbandman?
How different far the fat fed hireling with hollow drum,
Who buys whole corn fields into wastes, and sings upon the heath!
How different their eye and ear! how different the world to them!
With what sense does the parson claim the labour of the farmer?
What are his nets & gins & traps, & how does he surround him
With cold floods of abstraction, and with forests of solitude,
To build him castles and high spires, where kings & priests may dwell;
Till she who burns with youth and knows no fixèd lot, is bound
In spells of law to one she loaths? and must she drag the chain
Of life in weary lust? must chilling murderous thoughts obscure
The clear heaven of her eternal spring, to bear the wintry rage
Of a harsh terror driv'n to madness, bound to hold a rod
Over her shrinking shoulders all the day, & all the night
To turn the wheel of false desire and longings that wake her womb
To the abhorrèd birth of cherubs in the human form,
That live a pestilence & die a meteor, & are no more;
Till the child dwell with one he hates, and do the deed he loaths,
And the impure scourge force his seed into its unripe birth,
E'er yet his eyelids can behold the arrows of the day?

121–127 These lines with ll. 144–155 illustrate ll. 116–117.

128–143 For Blake's antagonism to ecclesiastical authority as a blighting influence in mortal life, cp. M. H. H., proverb 55 *and note*.

130 cold floods . . . forests of solitude] These images of spiritual confusion and sterility persist throughout the prophetic books. In the Lambeth prophecies they are almost constantly associated with *Urizen*; cp. B. A., chap. ii, and *Europe*, l. 88.

132–140 This passage on the adversities of the girl in uninspired life is parallel with ll. 141–143, the adversities of the boy.

'Does the whale worship at thy footsteps as the hungry dog ;
Or does he scent the mountain prey because his nostrils wide
Draw in the ocean ? does his eye discern the flying cloud
As the raven's eye, or does he measure the expanse like the vulture ?
Does the still spider view the cliffs where eagles hide their young,
Or does the fly rejoice because the harvest is brought in ?
Does not the eagle scorn the earth & despise the treasures beneath ?
But the mole knoweth what is there, & the worm shall tell it thee.
Does not the worm erect a pillar in the mouldering church yard,
[6] And a palace of eternity in the jaws of the hungry grave ?
Over his porch these words are written : "Take thy bliss, O Man !
And sweet shall be thy taste, & sweet thy infant joys renew !"

'Infancy ! fearless, lustful, happy, nestling for delight
In laps of pleasure ! Innocence, honest, open, seeking
The vigorous joys of morning light, open to virgin bliss !
Who taught thee modesty, subtil modesty, child of night & sleep ?
When thou awakest, wilt thou dissemble all thy secret joys,
Or wert thou not awake when all this mystery was disclos'd ?
Then com'st thou forth, a modest virgin, knowing to dissemble,
With nets found under thy night pillow, to catch virgin joy
And brand it with the name of whore, & sell it in the night,
In silence, ev'n without a whisper, and in seeming sleep.
Religious dreams and holy vespers light thy smoky fires :
Once were thy fires lighted by the eyes of honest morn.
And does my Theotormon seek this hypocrite modesty,

150–151 Cp. *Thel's Motto* :
Does the Eagle know what is in the pit,
Or wilt thou go ask the Mole :
Can Wisdom be put in a silver rod,
Or Love in a golden bowl ?

152–153 Cp. F. Z. viii. 484–485 :
Will you erect a lasting habitation in the mould'ring Church yard,
Or a pillar & palace of Eternity in the jaws of the hungry grave ?

161 Later the whole body of moral and rational error is symbolized by the Tree of Mystery : see Index, *Mundane Shell*, Note I, B.

162–169 Similar criticism of the conventional moral code is to be found in the earlier poems of the Rossetti MS., written about this time, 1793. Cp. *To Nobodaddy*, quoted below, l. 187 *note*, and the poem, Ross. MS. xvii (Clar. Press, p. 169), where Innocence and Modesty are again contrasted. Cp. also F. Z. vii *a*. 20–27.

This knowing, artful, secret, fearful, cautious, trembling hypocrite ?
Then is Oothoon a whore indeed ! and all the virgin joys
Of life are harlots ; and Theotormon is a sick man's dream,
And Oothoon is the crafty slave of selfish holiness.

' But Oothoon is not so, a virgin fill'd with virgin fancies,
Open to joy and to delight where ever beauty appears.
If in the morning sun I find it, there my eyes are fix'd
[7] In happy copulation ; if in evening mild, wearied with work,
Sit on a bank and draw the pleasures of this free born joy.

' The moment of desire ! the moment of desire ! The virgin
That pines for man shall awaken her womb to enormous joys
In the secret shadows of her chamber : the youth shut up from
The lustful joy shall forget to generate & create an amorous image
In the shadows of his curtains and in the folds of his silent pillow.
Are not these the places of religion, the rewards of continence,
The self enjoyings of self denial ? Why dost thou seek religion ?
Is it because acts are not lovely, that thou seekest solitude,
Where the horrible darkness is impressèd with reflections of desire ?

' Father of Jealousy, be thou accursèd from the earth !
Why hast thou taught my Theotormon this accursèd thing,
Till beauty fades from off my shoulders, darken'd and cast out,
A solitary shadow wailing on the margin of non-entity ?

' I cry : Love ! Love ! Love ! happy, happy Love ! free as the mountain wind !
Can that be Love that drinks another as a sponge drinks water,

187 The Father of Jealousy is Urizen. Cp. *To Nobodaddy* (Clar. Press, p. 168) :

Why art thou silent & invisible,
Father of Jealousy ?
Why dost thou hide thyself in clouds
From every searching Eye ?

Why darkness & obscurity
In all thy words & laws,
That none dare eat the fruit but from
The wily serpent's jaws ?
Or is it because Secresy gains females' loud applause ?

' Nobodaddy, obviously " Nobody's Daddy ", antithetical to " Father of All " ' (Clar. Press note on the title of this poem).

190 This phrase often recurs in connexion with Emanations (see Index) divided from their masculine ' counterparts ' ; cp. B. A. v. 9–10, and see Index, *Enion* and *Ahania*.

That clouds with jealousy his nights, with weepings all the day,
To spin a web of age around him, grey and hoary, dark,
Till his eyes sicken at the fruit that hangs before his sight ?
Such is self-love that envies all, a creeping skeleton,
With lamplike eyes watching around the frozen marriage bed.

' But silken nets and traps of adamant will Oothoon spread,
And catch for thee girls of mild silver, or of furious gold.
I'll lie beside thee on a bank, & view their wanton play
In lovely copulation, bliss on bliss, with Theotormon !
Red as the rosy morning, lustful as the first born beam,
Oothoon shall view his dear delight ; nor e'er with jealous cloud
Come in the heaven of generous love, nor selfish blightings bring.

' Does the sun walk in glorious raiment on the secret floor
[8] Where the cold miser spreads his gold ; or does the bright cloud drop
On his stone threshold ? does his eye behold the beam that brings
Expansion to the eye of pity ; or will he bind himself
Beside the ox to thy hard furrow ? does not that mild beam blot
The bat, the owl, the glowing tyger, and the king of night ?
The sea fowl takes the wintry blast for a cov'ring to her limbs,
And the wild snake the pestilence, to adorn him with gems & gold ;
And trees & birds & beasts & men behold their eternal joy.
Arise, you little glancing wings, and sing your infant joy !
Arise, and drink your bliss, for every thing that lives is holy ! '

Thus every morning wails Oothoon ; but Theotormon sits
Upon the margin'd ocean, conversing with shadows dire.

The Daughters of Albion hear her woes, & eccho back her sighs.

The End

195 *To My Mirtle* (Ross. MS., Clar. Press, p. 167).

198–204 So in the symbolism of a later period Blake writes of Beulah, the highest state in mortal existence (see Index, *Beulah*), as a state of being wherein

> every Female delights to give her maiden to her husband.
> The Female searches sea & land for gratifications to the
> Male Genius. (J. 69. 15–17.)

In the passage quoted ' Male Genius ' and ' Female ' have a less directly sexual reference than is implicit in ll. 198–204 above.

214–215 Cp. F. Z. ii. 572–576.

A SONG OF LIBERTY

INTRODUCTORY NOTE

THE *Song of Liberty*, consisting of three plates measuring about 6 × 4 inches, and engraved after Blake's usual manner, occurs both separately and bound up with *The Marriage of Heaven and Hell*. But in subject-matter and phrase it much more closely resembles *America*, as will be seen by reference to the parallel passages quoted in the foot-notes. Its theme is the annihilation of the whole body of restrictive law by the cleansing fires of native passion and desire; in symbol it is the triumph of the 'new born terror' over the 'jealous king', the victory of Orc over Urizen, though neither of these mythical names appears in the work. Here, as in the other Lambeth books, Blake's condemnation extends to all forms of religious, civil, and social law and convention, with the implication, evident enough in his emphatically expressed scorn of priests and priest-craft, that the first is also the direst, and is the source of the others. The purely ethical significance of the conflict is perhaps most clearly stated in the 'Chorus'. On one side is the priestly law, the 'pale religious letchery', the praise of the false virginity 'that wishes but acts not': this receives its fullest and frankest treatment in the *Visions of the Daughters of Albion*, which also uses the same phrase as the present work to suggest the contrary position, Blake's own antinomian or super-moral doctrine, 'everything that lives is Holy'.

In this work occurs the first reference to an obscure feminine symbol which recurs with certain differences in the Preludiums to *America* and *Europe*. Here she is called the 'Eternal Female'; in the other works she is referred to as 'the shadowy daughter of Urthona' and 'the nameless shadowy female' respectively. In each case the symbol is used in association with Orc's coming to destroy the power of Urizen. But in the present 'Song' she is merely mentioned in §§ 1 and 7; so that interpretation on internal evidence is impossible. In the other Prophecies, however, some further information is obtainable, though it is none of the clearest. In the *America* Preludium she feeds Orc from iron vessels, a symbolic act, the significance of which can only be conjectured; and until the day of Orc's embrace she is dumb. He, bound and in chains, projects his spirit in many forms, in the vain hope of seeing her face. The day comes when he bursts his bonds and embraces her. Her timidity is gone, he is revealed as 'the image of God' long obscured, now come to give her life. But life can come to her only through torments and 'eternal death', i. e. by the annihilation of that which she represents.

In the *Europe* Preludium the myth is continued, but with modification arising out of the course of the political events interpreted in *America* and *Europe*. The continuation of the story is even more obscure than its beginning. The 'Shadowy female' is the mother of a 'fiery progeny'. She yearns still (ll. 4–11) for that annihilation promised in the concluding lines of the *America* Preludium, but shown in the prophecy itself to be too high a hope. She remains 'in shady woe and visionary joy' until she realizes the futility of all attempts to set 'bounds to the infinite', i. e. to limit the new spirit that has come into human life. Thus reassured, she is silent.

The symbol can be interpreted as a summary of all the evils, moral, intellectual, and political, that Orc, the spirit of revolt, was born to destroy, or, to use Blake's own phrase, she is the type of 'the female spirits of the dead pining in bonds of religion' (*America*, l. 200), and her flaming passionate antinomianism fits well enough with Orc's mythical relationship to her, either as her son (*Song of Liberty*), or her lover and deliverer (*America* and *Europe*). This interpretation of the 'Shadowy female' is confirmed by her mythical parentage. She is a daughter of Urthona and Enitharmon, the beings in the Lambeth books concerned in promulgating the laws of Urizen that achieve the spiritual enslavement of the human race (*Europe*, ll. 33, 59; *Song of Los*; *Africa*, ll. 44–48), a function widely different from that attributed to them, as Los and Enithermon, in the latest myths. In *Europe* the eighteen centuries of moral slavery, the Christian era, the long sleep of the spirit of man, is Enitharmon's triumph, 'a female dream' (*Europe*, l. 59). In the Preludium to *Europe* the 'shadowy female', partially emancipated by the revolution in America, an overthrow, though not the final overthrow, of the old law, begs Enitharmon not to give 'solid form' to, and so destroy, her 'progeny of fires', the issue of her union with Orc, the revolutionary movements in the countries of Europe that, astonishingly interpreted, are the theme of the prophecy.

There is in the symbol, especially as it is used in the *Song of Liberty*, an undefinable suggestion of the 'earth-mother' which recalls 'The Earth's Answer' (S. E., Clar. Press, p. 107); and it is therefore, of some interest to note a resemblance from this point of view between the relation of Orc and the 'Shadowy Female' and that of Prometheus and the Spirit of Earth in *Prometheus Unbound*, especially in the lines addressed by Earth to Prometheus, beginning:

I am the Earth
Thy mother; she within whose stony veins
To the last fibre of the loftiest tree
Whose thin leaves trembled in the frozen air,
Joy ran, as blood within a living frame,
When thou didst from her bosom, like a cloud
Of glory arise, a spirit of keen joy. (Act I, ll. 152 foll.

[1] # A Song of Liberty

1. The Eternal Female groan'd ! It was heard over all the Earth.

2. Albion's coast is sick, silent ; the American meadows faint !

3. Shadows of Prophecy shiver along by the lakes and the rivers, and mutter across the ocean. ' France, rend down thy dungeon !

4. ' Golden Spain, burst the barriers of old Rome !

5. ' Cast thy keys, O Rome, into the deep, down falling, even to eternity down falling,

6. ' And weep ! '

7. In her trembling hands she took the new born terror howling.

8. On those infinite mountains of light, now barr'd out by the atlantic sea, the new born fire stood before the starry king.

9. Flag'd with grey brow'd snows and thunderous visages, the jealous wings wav'd over the deep.

10. The speary hand burned aloft, unbuckled was the
shield ; forth went the hand of jealousy among the flaming
[2] hair, and / hurl'd the new born wonder thro' the starry night.

11. ' The fire, the fire is falling !

12. ' Look up ! look up ! O citizen of London, enlarge thy countenance ! O Jew, leave counting gold ! return to thy oil and wine. O African ! black African ! (Go, winged thought, widen his forehead !) '

13. The fiery limbs, the flaming hair, shot like the sinking sun into the western sea.

§ 2 Cp. *America*, 21 : ' Albion is sick, America faints.'

§ 3–5 Cp. *America*, 219–220 :

Stiff shudderings shook the heav'nly thrones. France, Spain & Italy
In terror view'd the bands of Albion.

The unrest in these lands was to Blake, as to others of his time, the sign of the coming emancipation of mankind. The term ' Shadows of Prophecy ' cannot be related to the general body of doctrine in the Lambeth books, which contains no specific reference to any source of quickening inspiration external to man such as is implied in this phrase. A similar difficulty arises in connexion with Los as the Eternal Prophet.

§ 8 Cp. *America*, 107–109 ; and see Index, *Atlantic Continent*.

14. Wak'd from his eternal sleep, the hoary element, roaring, fled away.

15. Down rush'd, beating his wings in vain, the jealous king ; his grey brow'd councellors, thunderous warriors, curl'd veterans, among helms, and shields, and chariots, horses, elephants, banners, castles, slings, and rocks,

16. Falling, rushing, ruining, buried in the ruins on Urthona's dens

17. All night beneath the ruins ; then their sullen flames, faded, emerge round the gloomy king

18. With thunder and fire : leading his starry hosts thro'
[3] the waste wilderness, / he promulgates his ten commands,
glancing his beamy eyelids over the deep in dark dismay,

19. Where the son of fire in his eastern cloud, while the morning plumes her golden breast,

20. Spurning the clouds written with curses, stamps the stony law to dust, loosing the eternal horses from the dens of night, crying, 'Empire is no more ! and now the lion & wolf shall cease.'

Chorus

'Let the Priests of the Raven of dawn [1] no longer in deadly black with hoarse note curse the sons of joy ! Nor his accepted brethren, whom, tyrant, he calls free, lay the bound or build the roof ! [2] Nor pale religious letchery call that virginity that wishes but acts not ! [3]

For every thing that lives is Holy ! '

§ 15 Cp. *America*, 142–150. § 19–20 Cp. *America*, 60–63 :

The times are ended : shadows pass : the morning 'gins to break.
The fiery joy that Urizen perverted to ten commands,
What night he led the starry hosts thro' the wide wilderness,
That stony law I stamp to dust.

Cp. *ibid.*, l. 51 :

For Empire is no more, and now the Lion & Wolf shall cease.

§ 16 *Urthona*, see Index, *Los*.

Chorus] Cp. *America*, 68–71.

[1] For the Raven, cp. *The Human Abstract* (S. E., Clar. Press, p. 134) :

And it [the Tree of Mystery] bears the fruit of Deceit,
Ruddy and sweet to eat ;
And the Raven her nest has made
In its thickest shade.

Cp. also M. H. H., proverb 55 : 'As the catterpiller chooses the fairest leaves to lay her eggs on, so the priest lays his curse on the fairest joys.'

[2] Lay . . . roof] the images of the shutting out of eternity are interesting as from them develops the important symbol of the later myths, the 'Mundane Shell' (see Index).

[3] Cp. M. H. H., proverb 5 : 'He who desires but acts not, breeds pestilence.' Cp. V. D. A. 114–218.

AMERICA

INTRODUCTORY NOTE

Collation: 'frontispiece and title-page 1 plate each, 'Preludium' 2 plates, 'A prophecy' 14 plates; 18 plates relief engraving, about $9\frac{1}{4} \times 6\frac{5}{8}$ inches' (Clar. Press, p. 334).

America is a fuller and less rhapsodic treatment of the theme of the *Song of Liberty*. Blake's purpose is to define the forces made manifest in the American Revolution, and to show the significance of that event in the spiritual history of man. He sees in the conflict between the English Government and the Colonies the commencement of the final struggle between the primal 'Contraries', Restraint and Passion or Desire, between 'the passive that obeys Reason' and 'the active springing from Energy' (M. H. H., p. 3). As elsewhere throughout the Lambeth books, these 'Contraries' are symbolized by Urizen and Orc, though in *America* the former does not appear till the close of the story, when his vice-regents have been compelled to give way before the forces of revolt. Up to this point the repressive 'religion' of Urizen operates through 'Albion's Angel', identified with the King of England (l. 29), 'the Guardian Prince of Albion'. It may be mentioned in passing that here, as in the *Marriage*, 'Angel' is used ironically to denote acceptance of the normal moral, civil, and religious codes.

Opposed to these are 'the souls of warlike men', Washington, Franklin, Paine, and others of the revolutionary leaders. They are roused by the quickening fires of Orc, who is for Blake the Liberator of mankind, but to the party of priest and king he is the 'Blasphemous Demon, Antichrist, hater of Dignities, Lover of wild rebellion and transgresser of God's Law' (ll. 56–57). In the conflict that ensues, the 'red flames' of Orc contend with the plagues and blighting winds of Urizen, and triumph over them. Then the spirit of revolt passes eastward over the Atlantic—here, as later, the symbol of the floods of error that 'poured in deluge over the earth-born man'—and reanimates the spiritually enfeebled, till

> They feel the nerves of youth renew, and desires of ancient times
> Over their pale limbs, as a vine when the tender grape appears.

But the time for the emancipation of Europe is not yet. By a supreme effort of the forces of repression, among whom Urizen descends in person, the incipient tendency to rebellion is crushed, and for twelve years 'Angels and weak men' tyrannize over the 'strong'. At the end of this period the unrest in France, Spain, and Italy presages for Blake the final overthrow of all forms of restraint.

From this brief summary it appears that in Blake's view political emancipation was but one, and not the greatest result of the American Revolution. Not the tyranny of the monarchical government alone, but that of all creeds and conventions was to end when men should rise and will their own freedom. Moreover, failure on the part of the colonists would have involved the loss of that undefined portion of truth represented symbolically by America.

> Then had America been lost, o'erwhelm'd by the Atlantic,
> And Earth had lost another portion of the infinite. (ll. 174–175.)

America

Here too, as in the *Visions of the Daughters of Albion*, the perfect existence consists in the complete liberty of man to embody his impulses in act. Every attempt to interfere with this right is a violation of the eternal order, and a root of spiritual corruption. Lines 37–51 and 59–75 state Blake's view of this matter fully and unequivocally.

In an Appendix to the present text of *America* are printed what would seem to be portions of an earlier version of the Prophecy. The new matter consists of three pages, apparently displaced in the complete copies by plates 3, 4, and 12: a fourth, identical with plate 13, is not reprinted: for convenience of reference they are hereafter referred to as pp. 3*, 4*, 12*, 13* respectively. They occupy both sides of two sheets, bound up, along with other plates from the Prophetic Books and elsewhere, with a manuscript copy of Cunningham's *Life of Blake* now in the possession of Mr. B. B. Macgeorge of Glasgow. Printed by the familiar method of relief engraving and uncoloured, they may perhaps be proof sheets which Blake revised and altered, and finally re-engraved. Moreover, p. 12* has been worked over once or twice in pencil, and finally cancelled by a line drawn vertically through the middle of the text.

An examination of the symbolism of these pages seems to show that they are earlier than the corresponding pages in the complete work. One of the most constant features of the symbolism of the Lambeth books from *America* onwards is the association of the imagery of fire and flame with the spirit of ardent passion and desire, which is Orc, while the mythical embodiments of the contrary forces of moral and political tyranny, e. g. Urizen and Albion's Angel, are represented as cold demons of cloud and mist. We find, however, that in the pages under notice this distinction is not observed, but that in plate 3 in the complete work, and still more in the pencilled corrections on p. 12*, Blake sets himself so to alter his text as to bring it into line in this respect with the symbolism that characterizes the Lambeth books as a whole. Thus on p. 3*, l. 14, Albion's Angel, a spirit of error, is described as the 'fiery prince': in the parallel passage on p. 3 Blake alters the phrase to 'wrathful prince'. The significance of the change from 'fierce' (p. 3*, l. 16) to 'red' meteors (p. 3, l. 16) is less certain, but there can be little doubt about the changes made on p. 12*. All the alterations are connected more or less directly with Albion's Angel. In l. 5 'flames' is altered to 'damp mists', 'shining limbs' (l. 6) to 'aged limbs', 'gleam' (l. 7) to 'cold', 'fires' (l. 9) rather awkwardly to 'chill and heavy', 'flames' (l. 13) to 'clouds', 'ardors' (l. 15) to 'clangors', 'glowing' (l. 17) to 'mustering', and 'like a King' (l. 25) to 'like an aged King'. These changes seem clearly to prove that these pages belong to a period when Blake's symbolism was not as definitely established as it was when he made the perfected copies of *America*.

Further, on p. 3*, l. 4, the list of revolutionary leaders is given in this order: 'Washington, Hancock, Paine and Warren, Gates, Franklin and Green.' On p. 3 the names of Franklin and Hancock are transposed. This alteration could not have been made for metrical reasons; the run of the line remains unchanged. The only reason would seem to have been to give the more famous name a more prominent position; and this would be more likely to be done in the later than in the earlier version. Moreover, pp. 4* and 12* describe the session of the King and his Council at such length as to impede the course, and obscure the main theme of the Prophecy, the spiritual significance of the revolt of the colonies; and the description comes nearer than anything else in Blake to passages in *The French Revolution* (1791). But in the corresponding pages 4 and 12 this prolixity is considerably reduced, the main thread of the argument is freed from distracting episodes, and the gist of the matter restated more symbolically. In fact, Blake in these pages seems to be treating the text of a Prophetic Book precisely as, at about the same time, he was treating poems like *To My Mirtle* in the Rossetti MS. (Clar. Press, pp. 166–167).

But the matter of what we may now call the rejected pp. 4* and 12* was afterwards utilized. The similarity of their text with that of *Europe*, ll. 60–126, would seem to suggest that Blake worked their substance into the body of the later Prophecy, inserting it between the first and the second sections of Enitharmon's song, perhaps the most remarkable parallel between the two works being the reference to the collapse of the roof of the Council Chamber upon the heads of those sitting within (p. 4*, ll. 20–24; *Europe*, ll. 63–67). Later still, Blake introduced passages reminiscent of these rejected pages into Nights VI and VII of *The Four Zoas*.

The existence of these two leaves is of interest by reason of the light they throw upon Blake's painstaking methods in producing his Prophetic Books, works which he rarely sold and which very few could have read. That he continually worked over his writings in their manuscript stage has been known ever since the publication of Sampson's edition of the Lyrical Poems; but now it is clear that he also undertook the much more arduous labour of re-engraving plates of text that for any reason did not satisfy him. These leaves also strengthen the theory that what are known as the extra pages in the copy of *Milton* belonging to the New York Public Library are rejected portions of an earlier and perhaps longer version of that poem which Blake, in part at least, re-engraved as he re-engraved plates 3, 4, and 12 of *America*.

The interest of *America* lies not in its range of ideas, as no new idea of value is developed, nor can it compare for vigour and quickness of mind with the *Marriage*. But perhaps better even than *The French Revolution* it shows how the outlines of events and personalities are modified and their aspects transformed as they were merged into the substance of Blake's dreams. As a foot-note to history its value is inconsiderable, but for the light it sheds on the workings of the mind of the mystic it is perhaps first among the non-lyrical works.

The following lines seem to have formed at one time part of *America*. Mr. A. G. B. Russell, who discovered them, gives them on p. 69 of his *Engravings of William Blake*.

> As when a dream of Thiralatha flies the midnight hour,
> In vain the dreamer grasps the joyous images, they fly,
> Seen in obscured traces in the Vale of Leutha; So
> The British Colonies beneath the woful Princes fade.
>
> And so the Princes fade from earth, scarce seen by souls of men,
> But tho' obscur'd, this is the form of the Angelic land.

The fragment cannot be related to *America* as it stands, nor is any symbolic or other value apparent in it.

AMERICA:

a

PROPHECY

LAMBETH:
Printed by WILLIAM BLAKE in the year 1793.

Preludium

The shadowy daughter of Urthona stood before red Orc
When fourteen suns had faintly journey'd o'er his dark abode :
His food she brought in iron baskets, his drink in cups of iron.
Crown'd with a helmet & dark hair the nameless female stood ;
A quiver with its burning stores, a bow like that of night,
When pestilence is shot from heaven : no other arms she need[s],
Invulnerable tho' naked, save where clouds roll round her loins
Their awful folds in the dark air : silent she stood as night ;
For never from her iron tongue could voice or sound arise,
But dumb till that dread day when Orc assay'd his fierce embrace.

'Dark virgin,' said the hairy youth, 'thy father stern, abhorr'd,
Rivets my tenfold chains, while still on high my spirit soars ;
Sometimes an eagle screaming in the sky, sometimes a lion
Stalking upon the mountains, & sometimes a whale I lash
The raging fathomless abyss ; anon a serpent folding
Around the pillars of Urthona, and round thy dark limbs
On the Canadian wilds I fold, feeble my spirit folds ;
For chain'd beneath I rend these caverns ; when thou bringest food
I howl my joy, and my red eyes seek to behold thy face.
In vain ! these clouds roll to & fro, & hide thee from my sight.'

[2] Silent as despairing love, and strong as jealousy,
The hairy shoulders rend the links ; free are the wrists of fire.
Round the terrific loins he siez'd the panting, struggling womb ;

1 The shadowy daughter of Urthona] See S. Lib., Introductory Note.

11–20 Cp. B. U., chap. vii, and F. Z. v. 79–142 for fuller accounts of the binding of Orc by his parents Los (closely identified later with Urthona) and Enitharmon. In these later versions, as here, Orc is still an active influence, though bound in the 'tenfold chain' where the epithet suggests a reference to the Moral Law. The serpent imagery (ll. 15–16) may have relation to Orc and the Tree of Mystery : see Index, *Orc, II*, c.

21–22 These lines recur F. Z. vii *a*. 134 and 138.

It joy'd: she put aside her clouds & smiled her first-born smile,
As when a black cloud shews its lightnings to the silent deep.

Soon as she saw the terrible boy, then burst the virgin cry:

'I know thee! I have found thee & I will not let thee go!
Thou art the image of God who dwells in darkness of Africa,
And thou art fall'n to give me life in regions of dark death.
On my American plains I feel the struggling afflictions
Endur'd by roots that writhe their arms into the nether deep.
I see a serpent in Canada who courts me to his love,
In Mexico an Eagle, and a Lion in Peru;
I see a Whale in the South-sea, drinking my soul away.
O what limb rending pains I feel! thy fire & my frost
Mingle in howling pains, in furrows by thy lightnings rent.
This is eternal death, and this the torment long foretold!'

28 See *The Song of Los*, Introductory Note.

32–34 Cp. ll. 11–20 above, where these creatures are represented as forms assumed by the restricted energy that is enchained Orc. The symbolism of the lines remains unexplained. It is surmised that Blake saw in the revolution in the Colonies merely an instance of a much wider movement covering the whole of the western world. In the symbolism of the later books the West comes to be regarded as the place of truth and liberty.

37 Cp. *Song of Liberty*, §§ 3–6 and *note* to § 3. See also *Song of Los*, Introductory Note.

A
PROPHECY

[3] The Guardian Prince of Albion burns in his nightly tent;
Sullen fires across the Atlantic glow to America's shore,
Piercing the souls of warlike men who rise in silent night.
Washington, Franklin, Paine & Warren, Gates, Hancock & Green
Meet on the coast glowing with blood from Albion's fiery Prince.

Washington spoke: 'Friends of America, look over the Atlantic sea!
A bended bow is lifted in heaven, & a heavy iron chain
Descends link by link from Albion's cliffs across the sea to bind
Brothers & sons of America, till our faces pale and yellow,
Heads deprest, voices weak, eyes downcast, hands work-bruis'd,
Feet bleeding on the sultry sands, and the furrows of the whip
Descend to generations that in future times forget.'

The strong voice ceas'd, for a terrible blast swept over the heaving sea:
The eastern cloud rent: on his cliffs stood Albion's wrathful Prince,

4 Dr. Joseph Warren (1741–1775), of Boston, a leader of the extreme Whig party, and the author of the famous 'Suffolk Resolves', 6th Sept. 1774, was killed in the defence of Bunker Hill. Horatio Gates, 1728–1806, after service with Braddock against Fort Duquesne and active duty in the Seven Years' War, was made adjutant-general by Congress. He was in command of the force that defeated Burgoyne at Saratoga. After his overthrow at Camden an inquiry was held into his conduct, but he was acquitted and retired to his estates. John Hancock, 1737–1793, was president of Congress 1775–1777, and was the first to sign the Declaration of Independence. General Nathaniel Greene, 1742–1786, made for himself a military reputation scarcely, if at all, inferior to that of Washington. Succeeding Gates in the command of the Southern army, he displayed great skill in eluding and dividing the forces of the enemy. Two other names are mentioned (*infra*, l. 159): Ethan Allen, 1739–1789, the eccentric but capable leader of the 'Green Mountain Boys' from Vermont, the captor of Fort Ticonderoga, and author of the once famous deistical work 'Reason, the Only Oracle of Man', and Lee, apparently Richard Henry Lee, 1732–1794, a delegate from Virginia to the first Congress, who introduced the resolutions of 7th June 1776, afterwards known as the Declaration of Independence.

A dragon form, clashing his scales ; at midnight he arose,
And flam'd red meteors round the land of Albion beneath :
His voice, his locks, his awful shoulders and his glowing eyes
[4] Appear to the Americans upon the cloudy night.

Solemn heave the Atlantic waves between the gloomy nations,
Swelling, belching from its deeps red clouds & raging fires.
Albion is sick ! America faints ! enrag'd the Zenith grew.
As human blood shooting its veins all round the orbèd heaven,
Red rose the clouds from the Atlantic in vast wheels of blood,
And in the red clouds rose a Wonder o'er the Atlantic sea,
Intense, naked, a Human fire, fierce glowing as the wedge
Of iron heated in the furnace ; his terrible limbs were fire,
With myriads of cloudy terrors, banners dark & towers
Surrounded ; heat but not light went thro' the murky atmosphere.

The King of England, looking westward, trembles at the vision.

[5] Albion's Angel stood beside the Stone of night, and saw
The terror like a comet, or more like the planet red
That once inclos'd the terrible wandering comets in its sphere.
Then, Mars, thou wast our center, & the planets three flew round
Thy crimson disk ; so, e'er the Sun was rent from thy red sphere,
The Spectre glow'd, his horrid length staining the temple long
With beams of blood ; & thus a voice came forth, and shook the temple :

[6] 'The morning comes, the night decays, the watchmen leave their stations.
The grave is burst, the spices shed, the linen wrappèd up.
The bones of death, the cov'ring clay, the sinews shrunk & dry'd

15 Urizen, at this period the grand symbol of civil and religious tyranny, is commonly represented under serpent or dragon form : see *French Revolution*, ll. 127 and 177, and Index, *Serpent*.

16 Albion is Britain, and not as in F. Z., M., and J., the symbol of the human race (see Index, *Albion*).

24–25 a Wonder . . . fire] Orc. Cp. S. Lib. §§ 11 and 19.

30 Cp. *Europe*, 96 *note*. 'Angel' is here used ironically, as in M. H. H.

35–36 The Spectre's 'horrid length' is apparently equivalent to the dragon- or serpent-form of Urizen or of Albion's Angel ; the voice is Orc's. This is clear from the general tenor of the lines that follow, though later (l. 54) Orc also is described as appearing in the shape of a serpent about

Reviving shake, inspiring move, breathing, awakening,
Spring like redeemèd captives, when their bonds & bars are burst.
Let the slave grinding at the mill run out into the field,
Let him look up into the heavens & laugh in the bright air;
Let the inchainèd soul, shut up in darkness and in sighing,
Whose face has never seen a smile in thirty weary years,
Rise and look out; his chains are loose, his dungeon doors are open;
And let his wife and children return from the o[p]pressor's scourge.
They look behind at every step, & believe it is a dream,
Singing: "The Sun has left his blackness, & has found a fresher morning,
And the fair Moon rejoices in the clear & cloudless night;
For Empire is no more; and now the Lion & Wolf shall cease." '

[7] In thunders ends the voice. Then Albion's Angel wrathful burnt
Beside the Stone of Night; and like the Eternal Lion's howl
In famine & war reply'd: 'Art thou not Orc, who, serpent form'd,
Stands at the gate of Enitharmon to devour her children?
Blasphemous Demon, Antichrist, hater of Dignities,
Lover of wild rebellion, and transgresser of God's Law,
Why dost thou come to Angels' eyes in this terrific form?'

the 'Tree of Moral Virtue': cp. supra, Preludium, ll. 15–16. Cp. Ross. MS. iii (Clar. Press, p. 157):

I saw a chapel all of gold
That none did dare to enter in,
And many weeping stood without,
Weeping, mourning, worshipping.

I saw a serpent rise between
The white pillars of the door,
And he forc'd & forc'd & forc'd;
Down the golden hinges tore,

And along the pavement sweet
Set with pearls & rubies bright,
All his shining length he drew,
Till upon the altar white

He vomited his poison out
On the bread & on the wine.
So I turn'd into a sty,
And laid me down among the swine.

42–48 These lines are repeated, F. Z. ix. 668–674.
54–59 See Index, *Orc*, 1.

[8] The terror answer'd: 'I am Orc, wreath'd round the accursèd tree.
The times are ended; shadows pass; the morning 'gins to break.
The fiery joy that Urizen perverted to ten commands,
What night he led the starry hosts thro' the wide wilderness,
That stony law I stamp to dust, and scatter religion abroad
To the four winds as a torn book, & none shall gather the leaves.
But they shall rot on desart sands, & consume in bottomless deeps,
To make the desarts blossom, & the deeps shrink to their fountains,
And to renew the fiery joy, and burst the stony roof;
That pale religious letchery, seeking Virginity,
May find it in a harlot, and in coarse-clad honesty
The undefil'd, tho' ravished in her cradle night and morn.
For every thing that lives is holy, life delights in life,
Because the soul of sweet delight can never be defil'd.
Fires inwrap the earthly globe, yet man is not consum'd;
Amidst the lustful fires he walks; his feet become like brass,
His knees and thighs like silver, & his breast and head like gold.'

[9] 'Sound! sound! my loud war-trumpets, & alarm my Thirteen Angels!
Loud howls the eternal Wolf; the eternal Lion lashes his tail.
America is dark'ned, and my punishing Demons, terrified,
Crouch howling before their caverns deep like skins dry'd in the wind.
They cannot smite the wheat, nor quench the fatness of the earth;

59 Cp. F. Z. vii. 161–165 and l. 163 *note*: cp. also Index, *Orc, II*. c.

61 Urizen 'the primeval Priest' 'lays his curse on the fairest joys' (M. H. H., proverb 55). The stone with which he overwhelms Fuzon, the fiery spirit that refuses to submit to his laws, becomes 'Mount Sinai in Arabia' (B. A. ii).

63–72 See General Introduction, p. 82, and S. Lib., 'Chorus'.

76–102 These lines are spoken by Albion's Angel (l. 103) whose Thirteen Angels would seem to be the 'mental deities' of the rebellious states: cp. M. H. H., p. 11. Apparently because they 'reflect the genius' of their respective provinces, they afterwards forsake their allegiance to the Urizenic party and appear on the side of the insurgents: cp. *infra*, ll. 115–141.

77 The Wolf and the Lion are symbols of constitutional tyranny of 'Empire': cp. S. Lib., § 20.

78 The 'punishing Demons' are the agents of the Crown, apparently the Governors of the Colonies.

They cannot smite with sorrows, nor subdue the plow and spade ;
They cannot wall the city, nor moat round the castle of princes ;
They cannot bring the stubbèd oak to overgrow the hills :
For terrible men stand on the shores, & in their robes I see
Children take shelter from the lightnings ; there stands Washington,
And Paine and Warren, with their foreheads rear'd toward the east.
But clouds obscure my agèd sight. A vision from afar !
Sound ! sound ! my loud war-trumpets, & alarm my thirteen Angels !
Ah, vision from afar ! Ah, rebel form that rent the ancient
Heavens ! Eternal Viper self-renew'd, rolling in clouds,
I see thee in thick clouds and darkness on America's shore,
Writhing in pangs of abhorrèd birth ; red flames the crest rebellious
And eyes of death ; the harlot womb, oft openèd in vain,
Heaves in enormous circles : now the times are return'd upon thee,
Devourer of thy parent ! now thy unutterable torment renews.
Sound ! sound ! my loud war-trumpets, & alarm my thirteen Angels !
Ah, terrible birth ! a young one bursting ! where is the weeping mouth,
And where the mother's milk ? instead, those ever-hissing jaws
And parchèd lips drop with fresh gore. Now roll thou in the clouds !
Thy mother lays her length outstretch'd upon the shore beneath.
Sound ! sound ! my loud war-trumpets, & alarm my thirteen Angels !
Loud howls the eternal Wolf : the eternal Lion lashes his tail.'

[10] Thus wept the Angel voice ; & as he wept, the terrible blasts
Of trumpets blew a loud alarm across the Atlantic deep.

86 The East is the quarter of error : see Index, *Cardinal Points*.

90 The ' Eternal Viper self-renewed ' is apparently Orc, Albion's Angel giving the ' religious ' view (cp. M. H. H., pp. 5–6, and Gen. iii. 14–15). But the passage remains obscure partly as a result of the contradiction between the epithet ' self-renewed ' and l. 100.

No trumpets answer ; no reply of clarions or of fifes :
Silent the Colonies remain and refuse the loud alarm.

On those vast shady hills between America & Albion's shore,
Now barr'd out by the Atlantic sea, call'd Atlantean hills,
Because from their bright summits you may pass to the Golden world,
An ancient palace, archetype of mighty Emperies,
Rears its immortal pinnacles, built in the forest of God
By Ariston, the king of beauty, for his stolen bride.

Here on their magic seats the thirteen Angels sat perturb'd,
For clouds from the Atlantic hover o'er the solemn roof.
[11] Fiery the Angels rose, & as they rose deep thunder roll'd
Around their shores, indignant burning with the fires of Orc ;
And Boston's Angel cried aloud as they flew thro' the dark night.

He cried : ' Why trembles honesty, and, like a murderer,
Why seeks he refuge from the frowns of his immortal station ?
Must the generous tremble & leave his joy to the idle, to the pestilence
That mock him ? who commanded this ? what God ? what Angel ?
To keep the gen'rous from experience till the ungenerous
Are unrestrain'd performers of the energies of nature,
Till pity is become a trade, and generosity a science
That men get rich by, & the sandy desart is giv'n to the strong ?
What God is he writes laws of peace, & clothes him in a tempest ?
What pitying Angel lusts for tears, and fans himself with sighs ?
What crawling villain preaches abstinence & wraps himself
In fat of lambs ? no more I follow, no more obedience pay.'

107–114 See Index, *Atlantic Continent.*
112 Ariston is only mentioned once elsewhere : cp. *Africa*, l. 4 *note.*
117 The prominence given to Boston's Angel in this episode is apparently reminiscent of the activity of that city's representatives in the Continental Congress, and particularly of John Adams, who took a prominent part in the discussions leading up to the Declaration of Independence.
119 Cp. Letter to Butts, 10th January 1802 (R., p. 100) : ' But if we fear to do the dictates of our angels, and tremble at the tasks set before us ; if we refuse to do spiritual acts because of natural fears or natural desires, who can describe the dismal torments of such a state ! ' The allusion would seem to be to the hesitation on the part of certain delegates in Congress to face the responsibility of declaring for separation from England,
121–123 Cp. S. L., *Africa*, ll. 22–27.

[12] So cried he, rending off his robe & throwing down his scepter
In sight of Albion's Guardian ; and all the thirteen Angels
Rent off their robes to the hungry wind, & threw their golden scepters
Down on the land of America : indignant they descended
Headlong from out their heav'nly heights, descending swift as fires
Over the land ; naked & flaming are their lineaments seen
In the deep gloom ; by Washington & Paine & Warren they stood,
And the flame folded, roaring fierce within the pitchy night
Before the Demon red, who burnt towards America
In black smoke, thunders and loud winds, rejoicing in its terror,
Breaking in smoky wreaths from the wild deep & gath'ring thick
In flames, as of a furnace, on the land from North to South,
[13] What time the thirteen Governors that England sent convene
In Bernard's house ; the flames cover'd the land : they rouze ; they cry.

Shaking their mental chains, they rush in fury to the sea
To quench their anguish : at the feet of Washington down fall'n,
They grovel on the sand and writhing lie, while all
The British soldiers thro' the thirteen states sent up a howl
Of anguish, threw their swords & muskets to the earth & ran
From their encampments and dark castles, seeking where to hide
From the grim flames and from the visions of Orc, in sight
Of Albion's Angel ; who, enrag'd, his secret clouds open'd
From north to south, and burnt outstretch'd on wings of wrath, cov'ring
The eastern sky, spreading his awful wings across the heavens.
Beneath him roll'd his num'rous hosts ; all Albion's Angels, camp'd,
Darken'd the Atlantic mountains, & their trumpets shook the valleys,

142 Bernard's House is Faneuil Hall, Boston, the ' Cradle of Liberty '. Here the delegates from surrounding towns met to protest against certain high-handed actions on the part of the British officials. Francis Bernard, Governor of Massachusetts, was an autocratic person, to whom the leaders of the popular party were ' demagogues '. His misleading reports to the king are held to have been responsible to some extent for the conduct of the home Government towards the Colonies.

Arm'd with diseases of the earth to cast upon the Abyss—
Their numbers forty millions, must'ring in the eastern sky.

[14] In the flames stood & view'd the armies drawn out in the sky,
Washington, Franklin, Paine & Warren, Allen, Gates & Lee,
And heard the voice of Albion's Angel give the thunderous command.
His plagues, obedient to his voice, flew forth out of their clouds,
Falling upon America as a storm, to cut them off
As a blight cuts the tender corn when it begins to appear.
Dark is the heaven above, & cold & hard the earth beneath :
And as a plague wind, fill'd with insects, cuts off man & beast,
And as a sea o'erwhelms a land in the day of an earthquake,
Fury, rage, madness in a wind swept through America,
And the red flames of Orc, that folded, roaring fierce, around
The angry shores, and the fierce rushing of th' inhabitants together.
The citizens of New-York close their books & lock their chests ;
The mariners of Boston drop their anchors and unlade ;
The scribe of Pensylvania casts his pen upon the earth ;
The builder of Virginia throws his hammer down in fear.

Then had America been lost, o'erwhelm'd by the Atlantic,
And Earth had lost another portion of the infinite.
But all rush together in the night in wrath and raging fire.
The red fires rag'd : the plagues recoil'd : then roll'd they back with fury
[15] On Albion's Angels : then the Pestilence began in streaks of red
Across the limbs of Albion's Guardian : the spotted plague smote Bristol's,
And the Leprosy London's Spirit, sickening all their bands.
The millions sent up a howl of anguish and threw off their hammer'd mail,
And cast their swords & spears to earth, & stood a naked multitude.

156. Cp. F. Z. vii *a.* 111–118.

174–177 See Index, *Atlantic Continent.* The act of the colonists, in uniting to oppose and finally to cast off the authority of Britain, is here given a value beyond its political and material consequences. It was an assertion of Liberty against Moral Law, a vindication of the 'wisdom and joy of Eternity'. The revolutionary spirit, the red fires of Orc, repels the 'spiritual diseases' that arise from Urizen's 'Religion'.

Albion's Guardian writhèd in torment on the eastern sky,
Pale, quiv'ring toward the brain his glimmering eyes, teeth chattering,
Howling & shuddering, his legs quivering; convuls'd each muscle & sinew.
Sick'ning lay London's Guardian and the ancient miter'd York,
Their heads on snowy hills, their ensigns sick'ning in the sky.

The plagues creep on the burning winds, driven by flames of Orc,
And by the fierce Americans rushing together in the night,
Driven o'er the Guardians of Ireland and Scotland and Wales.
They, spotted with plagues, forsook the frontiers; and their banners, sear'd
With fires of hell, deform their ancient heavens with shame & woe.
Hid in his caves the Bard of Albion felt the enormous plagues,
And a cowl of flesh grew o'er his head & scales on his back & ribs.
And, rough with black scales, all his Angels fright their ancient heavens.
The doors of marriage are open, and the Priests, in rustling scales,
Rush into reptile coverts, hiding from the fires of Orc
That play around the golden roofs in wreaths of fierce desire,
Leaving the females naked and glowing with the lusts of youth.

For the female spirits of the dead, pining in bonds of religion,
Run from their fetters, reddening; & in long drawn arches sitting,

183–186 Blake seems to antedate George III's mental collapse (1788).

186 London's Guardian is mentioned in l. 4 of the cancelled p. 12* (see Appendix to this Prophecy). The reference may be to Lord Mansfield, the Lord Chief Justice: cp. *Europe*, 120–126. 'Ancient mitred York' is apparently William Markham, Archbishop of York, a friend of Mansfield, through whom he was appointed tutor to the Prince of Wales and Prince Frederick. It was Markham who warned Mansfield of the danger that threatened him in the riots of 2nd June 1780, and helped him to escape. He was in his sixty-first year at the time.

193 William Whitehead was Poet Laureate from 1757 to 1785. But Blake may here be anticipating events, and expressing some of the general derision excited by Pitt's appointment of Henry James Pye—poetical Pye, as Scott calls him—to succeed Thomas Warton in 1790.

196 As in V. D. A. and the earlier Ross. MS. poems—e. g. 'The Fairy', at first called 'The Marriage Ring',—marriage is a type of restrictive morality.

196–197 Cp. F. Z. vii *a*. 111–118.

They feel the nerves of youth renew, and desires of ancient times
Over their pale limbs, as a vine when the tender grape appears.

[16] Over the hills, the vales, the cities, rage the red flames fierce;
The Heavens melted from north to south; and Urizen, who sat
Above all heavens, in thunders wrap'd, emerg'd his leprous head
From out his holy shrine, his tears in deluge piteous
Falling into the deep sublime: flag'd with grey-brow'd snows
And thunderous visages, his jealous wings wav'd over the deep.
Weeping in dismal howling woe, he dark descended, howling
Around the smitten bands, clothèd in tears & trembling, shudd'ring, cold.
His storèd snows he pourèd forth, and his icy magazines
He open'd on the deep, and on the Atlantic sea, white, shiv'ring.
Leprous his limbs, all over white, and hoary was his visage,
Weeping in dismal howlings before the stern Americans,
Hiding the Demon red with clouds & cold mists from the earth,
Till Angels & weak men twelve years should govern o'er the strong;
And then their end should come, when France reciev'd the Demon's light.

Stiff shudderings shook the heav'nly thrones! France, Spain & Italy
In terror view'd the bands of Albion and the ancient Guardians
Fainting upon the elements, smitten with their own plagues.
They slow advance to shut the five gates of their law-built heaven,
Fillèd with blasting fancies and with mildews of despair,
With fierce disease and lust, unable to stem the fires of Orc;
But the five gates were consum'd & their bolts and hinges melted;
And the fierce flames burnt round the heavens & round the abodes of men.

FINIS

212–214 Cp. F. Z. vii. 69–80.

217 Twelve years would seem to be Blake's estimate of the time between the American and the French Revolutions. The emancipation of man, begun in the first of these, is regarded as postponed for a period by a supreme exertion of the powers of Law, till the upheaval in France carried it further.

220–221 Cp. ll. 178–197.

222 The 'five gates of their law-built heaven' are apparently the five senses whose limited powers of perception give rise to the delusions of materialism and morality: cp. General Introduction, pp. 22–25.

APPENDIX

to

AMERICA

The three portions of text here printed have been described in the Introductory Note to *America*. The first, an earlier engraving of the opening passage of the Prophecy, differs very slightly from the later form of the same passage in the published version ; all the changes are indicated in the foot-notes. The other two pages, however, are totally different from the corresponding pp. 4 and 12 in the final form of *America*. The second page, the rejected p. 4, shows no signs of revision, but p. 12 has been worked over once or twice, and finally cancelled, after Blake's usual manner, by a vertical line through the text, from l. 10 to the bottom. Here, as elsewhere, we give Blake's latest reading, all earlier forms being given in foot-notes.

[3*]

A Prophecy

THE Guardian Prince of Albion burns in his nightly tent ;
Sullen fires across the Atlantic glow to America's shore,
Piercing the souls of warlike men, who rise in silent night.
Washington, Hancock, Paine & Warren, Gates, Franklin & Green
Meet on the coast : glowing with blood stood Albion's fiery Prince.
Washington spoke : 'Friends of America, look over the Atlantic sea !
A bended bow in heaven is lifted, & a heavy iron chain
Descends link by link from Albion's cliffs across the sea, to bind
Brothers & sons of America, till our faces pale and yellow,
Heads deprest, voices weak, eyes downcast, hands work-bruis'd,
Feet bleeding on the sultry sands, and the furrows of the whip
Descend to generations that in future times forget '—
The strong voice ceas'd : for a terrible blast swept over the heaving sea.

The quotations given below are from the corresponding page in the final version of *America*, and show all the textual changes. The line-numbers are the same in both cases.

4 Washington, Franklin, Paine & Warren, Gates, Hancock, & Green.
5 stood] from
7 A bended bow in heaven is lifted] A bended bow is lifted in heaven

The eastern cloud rent: on his cliffs stood Albion's fiery Prince,
A dragon form, clashing his scales; at midnight he arose,
And flam'd fierce meteors round the band of Albion beneath.
His voice, his locks, his awful shoulders and his glowing eyes

[4*] Reveal the dragon thro' the human, coursing swift as fire
To the close hall of counsel, where his Angel form renews.
In a sweet vale shelter'd with cedars, that eternal stretch
Their unmov'd branches, stood the hall, built when the moon shot forth,
In that dread night when Urizen call'd the stars round his feet:
Then burnt the center from its orb, and found a place beneath;
And Earth, conglob'd, in narrow room roll'd round its sulphur Sun.
To this deep valley situated by the flowing Thames,
Where George the third holds council & his Lords & Commons meet,
Shut out from mortal sight, the Angel came: the vale was dark
With clouds of smoke from the Atlantic, that in volumes roll'd
Between the mountains; dismal visions mope around the house.
On chairs of iron, canopied with mystic ornaments
Of life by magic power condens'd, infernal forms art-bound,
The council sat; all rose before the agèd apparition.
His snowy beard that streams like lambent flames down his wide breast
Wetting with tears; & his white garments cast a wintry light.
Then, as arm'd clouds arise terrific round the northern drum,
The world is silent at the flapping of the folding banners;
So still terrors rent the house: as when the solemn globe
Launch'd to the unknown shore, while Sotha held the northern helm,
Till to that void it came & fell; so the dark house was rent,
The valley mov'd beneath; its shining pillars split in twain,
And its roofs crack across, down falling on th' Angelic seats.

[12*] [Then Albion's Angel] rose, resolv'd, to the cave of armoury.
His shield, that bound twelve demons & their cities in its orb,
He took down from its trembling pillar; from its cavern deep
His helm was brought by London's Guardian, & his thirsty spear

3*. 14 fiery] wrathful 16 fierce] red
12*. 1 Then Albion's Angel] *del.*: *no 2nd rdg.* cave] ? cove

By the wise spirit of London's river: silent stood the King, breathing damp mists,
And on his agèd limbs they clasp'd the armour of terrible gold.
Infinite London's awful spires cast a dreadful cold
Even on rational things beneath and from the palace walls
Around Saint James's, chill & heavy, even to the city gate.
On the vast stone whose name is Truth he stood, his cloudy shield
Smote with his scepter; the scale bound orb loud howl'd, th[e] pillar
Trembling sunk, an earthquake roll'd along the mossy pile.
In glittering armour, swift as winds, intelligent as clouds,
Four wingèd heralds mount the furious blasts & blow their trumps,
Gold, silver, brass, & iron: clangors clamouring rend the shores.
Like white clouds rising from the deeps, his fifty-two armies
From the four cliffs of Albion rise, mustering around their Prince;
Angels of cities, and of parishes, and villages, and families,
In armour as the nerves of wisdom, each his station holds.
In opposition dire, a warlike cloud, the myriads stood
In the red air before the Demon. But like a constellation ris'n and blazing
Over the rugged ocean, so the Angels of Albion hung
Over the frowning shadow like an agèd King in arms of gold
Who wept over a den in which his only son, outstretch'd,
By rebels' hands was slain; his white beard wav'd in the wild wind;
On mountains & cliffs of snow the awful apparition hover'd;
And like the voices of religious dead heard in the mountains
When holy zeal scents the sweet valleys of the virgin bliss,
Such was the hollow voice that o'er America lamented.

5 London's river :] *a word added after* river *illegible.* damp mists] with flames *1st rdg. del.*; fear forth *2nd rdg. del.*
6 aged limbs] shining limbs *1st rdg. del.*
7 cold] gleam *1st rdg. del.* 8 on rational] to rational *1st rdg.*
9 chill & heavy] glow the fires *1st rdg. del.*; *2nd rdg. del., illegible.*
11 the pillar] th' eternal pillar *1st rdg. del. A word substituted for* eternal *is illegible.*
13 as clouds] as flames *1st rdg. del.* 15 clangors] ardors *1st rdg. del.*
17 mustering] glowing *1st rdg. del.* 19 holds] fixes *1st rdg. del.*
21–23 In . . . blazing] *1st rdg.*:
In the red air before the Demon, seen even by mortal men,
Who call it Fancy, or [& *1st rdg. del.*] shut the gates of sense, or [& *1st. rdg. del.*] in their chambers
Sleep like the dead. But like a constellation, ris'n and blazing
22 Over the] *These are cancelled in the original, apparently through inadvertence.* 23 like an agèd King] like a King *1st rdg.*
29 *America*] the red Demon *1st rdg. del.*

EUROPE

INTRODUCTORY NOTE

Collation (B.M. copy): title 1 plate, Preludium 2 plates, text 11 plates, two full-page designs (pp. 6 and 7) = 16 plates, relief engravings, about $9\frac{1}{4} \times 6\frac{1}{2}$ inches.[1]

The poem that we regard as a rejected Preludium to *Europe* is here printed in an appendix. That by which it was replaced has already been discussed in connexion with the cognate documents, the *America* Preludium and the *Song of Liberty*, in the Introductory Note to the latter work.

The 'Prophecy' itself has affinity with the other writings that bear the names of the continents, *America*, and the two parts of *The Song of Los*, *Africa*, and *Asia*. Its title 'Europe', used almost constantly in the later works to denote the state of subjection to the delusions of the normal metaphysic and ethic, has here in addition a particular reference to the social and political conditions that preceded the French Revolution. The work contains several very difficult passages. One of these is in the first fifty lines. It is possible that a vague suggestion of Milton's *Nativity Ode* in the rhythm and phraseology of the opening stanzas may point to the identity of the 'secret child' (l. 2), and Jesus. If this conjecture holds, the entire passage can be read as a part of Blake's earlier criticism of Christianity, for which the chief documents are other parts of *Europe* and ll. 20–27 of *Africa*. The same purpose would seem to underlie the lines (9–14) that tell how Urthona—an infrequent and obscure symbol in the early books—takes his rest, while Urizen, 'the primeval Priest', freed from his chains, appears in the north, the quarters to which the eternals banished him and his 'religion'. This apparently expresses Blake's opinion that, with the triumph of Christianity, the spiritual energy associated clearly enough in the later books, but not so clearly here, with Urthona becomes dormant, while its contrary, 'the passive that obeys reason', once more asserts itself. These lines are put into the mouth of Los, and it may prevent confusion to notice here that he and Urthona are nowhere related in the Lambeth books as they are in the later writings. Indeed, Blake's conception of Los in the early writings is difficult to determine. This may be due, in great measure, to the absence at this point of any idea of a divine purpose of regeneration, such as makes Los the central figure of the longer 'prophetic' books, from *The Four Zoas* to *Jerusalem*. In the present book it is not even possible to connect with any certainty the activities of Los and the emancipatory influence of Orc, though in the myth they are represented as father and son. An instance of what appears to be the distance between the early and later presentations of Los occurs in the lines following

[1] In this copy quotations from the poets, from Shakespeare and Milton to Mrs. Ann Radcliffe, apposite to Blake's designs, have been written in a hand very like that in the note signed 'F. Tatham' which is to be seen on the drawing in the Print-room, *Blake's Drawings*, vol. i (1874, 12. 12. 148), and in that signed 'Fred. Tatham' on the sheet on which are printed Blake's engravings of Venus, Hermes and the Laocoön group.

those already referred to. Los calls his children and bids them seize 'all the spirits of life' and bind 'their warbling joys' and 'all the nourishing sweets of earth' to the strings of their harps to give bliss to eternals—a presentation of the 'eternal prophet' and of the 'Eternals' that recalls the Epicurean idea of the nature of the gods (cp. ll. 19–23). Finally he commands Orc to rise in his chains, to be crowned, as in mockery, with vine leaves. So commences 'the Night of Enitharmon's joy', the triumph of the moral law. She summons her children by pairs, male and female, to aid her in her work of deluding man, bidding them

Go, tell the human race that Woman's love is Sin ;
That an Eternal life awaits the worms of sixty winters,
In an allegorical abode where existence hath never come. (ll. 37–39.)

Her influence is represented as extending over the eighteen hundred years of the Christian dispensation, the duration of her 'sleep', the 'female dream', during which the life of man is an unreal existence beneath the 'Shadows of a woman', the delusion of sense-perception and repressive morality.

After briefly indicating this valuation of Christianity, the 'Prophecy' turns abruptly to the social and political conditions prevailing over Europe at the close of the eighteenth century. The action becomes centred in Britain, 'o'er-clouded by the terrors of struggling times' (l. 70), the first stirrings of the revolutionary spirit in the Old World. The symbols in this part of *Europe* are almost identical with those of America. On the side of repression is 'Albion's Guardian', with his ministers, called in irony his 'Angels': against these, on the side of revolt, is Orc. The former derive their authority from Urizen, whose 'station', the 'Stone of night', is so described as to identify it with the human skull. The statement that it forms the 'southern porch' to the 'serpent temple' (l. 91)—as it were the citadel or sanctuary of the mundane error arising from reason and sense-perception—recalls the similar image in *The Human Abstract* (S. E., Clar. Press, p. 134), when the 'Tree of Moral Virtue', equivalent in its symbolic content to the 'serpent temple', is said to grow 'in the Human brain'. By reason of his exclusive dependence upon 'the natural organs of sense',

man became an Angel,
Heaven a mighty circle turning, God a tyrant crown'd. (ll. 92–93.)

The Urizenic 'religion' triumphs in 'the night of Enitharmon':

The youth of England, hid in gloom, curse the pain'd heavens, compell'd
Into the deadly night to see the form of Albion's Angel.
Their parents brought them forth, & aged ignorance preaches canting.

Every house is a den, every man bound,

The shadows are fill'd
With spectres, and the windows wove over with curses of iron :
Over the doors 'Thou shalt not' & over the chimneys 'Fear' is written.
With bands of iron round their necks fasten'd into the walls
The citizens ; in leaden gyves the inhabitants of suburbs,
Walk heavy : soft and bent are the bones of villagers. (ll. 132–137.)

But the tyranny that priest and king exercise as Urizen's ministers is threatened by the increasing influence of the rebel Orc. There seems to be an allusion in ll. 120–130 to a popular rising in London, which, though successful at first, was ultimately repressed by the exercise of constitutional authority. It is perhaps worthy of passing notice, in connexion with what has been said above of the nature of Los in these early books, that two of his sons, Rintrah and Palambron, are represented as overwhelming this premature attempt to achieve freedom. Yet in spite of temporary repulse, the revolutionary spirit spreads in the quickening fires of Orc.

The concluding portion of the book is also the most difficult. Alarmed at the growing power of Orc, Albion's Angel

> Siez'd in horror and torment
> The Trump of the last doom : but he could not blow the iron tube.
> Thrice he assay'd presumptuous to awake the dead to Judgment.
> (ll. 143–145.)

Then :

> A mighty Spirit leap'd from the land of Albion,
> Nam'd Newton : he siez'd the Trump & blow'd the enormous blast.
> Yellow as leaves of Autumn the myriads of Angelic hosts
> Fell thro' the wintry skies seeking their graves,
> Rattling their hollow bones in howling and lamentation. (ll. 146–150.)

Nothing can be added to what has already been said of this passage in the General Introduction. What follows is equally obscure, and the utmost that can be attempted is to indicate the main points of the story. The sounding of the trumpet and the falling of the Angelic myriads evidently marks the beginning of the end of the old moral law. Yet this fact seems to be hidden from Enitharmon, who wakes from her sleep, not knowing that she had slept eighteen hundred years (ll. 151–153). She resumes her song as if it had suffered no interruption, and calls the remainder of her sons and daughters to her aid. Last of all she summons Orc, to smile upon her children and give her ' mountains joy of his red light ' (ll. 190–192). This would seem to symbolize Blake's opinion that the ultimate purpose of the forces of empiricism and repressive morality symbolized by Enitharmon is to bring even passion and desire, their contraries, to minister to them. But again difficulty arises because Blake's statement of the matter makes it impossible to discover what response Enitharmon's children make to her call (ll. 193–195). Ultimately, however, the dawn appears ; the morning of universal liberty begins to break. Enitharmon weeps, as Urizen does when, in the close of *Asia*, the Grave quickens beneath the fires of Orc. Apparently the final conflict between the opposed forces of Law and individual freedom is about to begin. Orc descends into France, the terrible agents of revolution begin their work, so that ' Enitharmon groans and cries in anguish and dismay '. The book closes with the descent of Los and his sons to ' the strife of blood '. Unfortunately his part in what is to follow, whether for or against Orc, is not discernible.

EUROPE

a

PROPHECY

LAMBETH
Printed by Willm Blake 1794

[1]

PRELUDIUM

THE nameless shadowy female rose from out the breast of Orc,
Her snaky hair brandishing in the winds of Enitharmon ;
And thus her voice arose :

'O mother, Enitharmon, wilt thou bring forth other sons,
To cause my name to vanish, that my place may not be found ?
For I am faint with travel,
Like the dark cloud disburden'd in the day of dismal thunder.

'My roots are brandish'd in the heavens ; my fruits in earth beneath
Surge, foam and labour into life, first born & first consum'd,
Consumèd and consuming !
Then why shouldst thou, accursèd mother, bring me into life ?

'I wrap my turban of thick clouds around my lab'ring head,
And fold the sheety waters as a mantle round my limbs ;
Yet the red sun and moon
And all the overflowing stars, rain down prolific pains.

[2] 'Unwilling I look up to heaven, unwilling count the stars,
Sitting in fathomless abyss of my immortal shrine ;
I sieze their burning power,
And bring forth howling terrors, all devouring fiery kings,

'Devouring & devourèd, roaming on dark and desolate mountains,
In forests of eternal death, shrieking in hollow trees.
Ah, mother Enitharmon !
Stamp not with solid form this vig'rous progeny of fires.

'I bring forth from my teeming bosom myriads of flames,
And thou dost stamp them with a signet ; then they roam abroad,
And leave me void as death.
Ah ! I am drown'd in shady woe and visionary joy.

1 Cp. S. Lib., Introductory Note.

'And who shall bind the infinite with an eternal band
To compass it with swaddling bands ? and who shall cherish it
With milk and honey ?
I see it smile, & I roll inward, & my voice is past.'

She ceast, & roll'd her shady clouds
Into the secret place.

28–31 The 'infinite' here appears to refer to the 'progeny of fires', the spirits of liberty. The lines express her realization that the restrictive activities identified with Enitharmon cannot permanently triumph.

29–30 In the latest prophetic writings 'to feed with milk' is to establish the feminine delusions of morality and sense experience. Cp. J. 67. 22 : 68. 30 : 82. 40.

[3]

A

PROPHECY

THE deep of winter came,
What time the secret child
Descended thro the orient gates of the eternal day.
War ceas'd, & all the troops like shadows fled to their abodes.

Then Enitharmon saw her sons & daughters rise around ;
Like pearly clouds they meet together in the crystal house ;
And Los, possessor of the moon, joy'd in the peaceful night,
Thus speaking, while his num'rous sons shook their bright fiery wings :

' Again the night is come
That strong Urthona takes his rest,
And Urizen, unloos'd from chains,
Glows like a meteor in the distant north.
Stretch forth your hands and strike the elemental strings !
Awake the thunders of the deep !

[4] ' The shrill winds wake,
Till all the sons of Urizen look out and envy Los.
Sieze all the spirits of life and bind
Their warbling joys to our loud strings !
Bind all the nourishing sweets of earth
To give us bliss, that we may drink the sparkling wine of Los !
And let us laugh at war,
Despising toil and care,
Because the days and nights of joy in lucky hours renew.

1–4 ' Winter ' is constantly associated with the state of error, a condition of spiritual sterility and inanition that harmonizes with Blake's earlier criticism of Christianity already noticed : see *Europe*, Introductory Note. It is difficult to see the connexion of l. 4 with this otherwise than in irony.

6 The image of the ' crystal cabinet ' in the poem bearing that title (Pickering MS., Clar. Press, p. 282) is one of Blake's later symbols of the false world of empiricism and morality, which is controlled by the feminine powers, Vala and the Daughters of Albion, the equivalents of Enitharmon and her children in the present passage. See below, l. 186.

10–12 See Index, *Los*, Note I. Apparently Urthona expresses some form of spiritual energy—later he is represented as labouring at the furnaces and anvil—and is contrasted with Urizen, the negation of all positive creative activity.

'Arise, O Orc, from thy deep den !
First born of Enitharmon, rise,
And we will crown thy head with garlands of the ruddy vine !
For now thou art bound,
And I may see thee in the hour of bliss, my eldest born.'

The horrent Demon rose, surrounded with red stars of fire
Whirling about in furious circles round the immortal fiend.

Then Enitharmon down descended into his red light,
And thus her voice rose to her children : the distant heavens reply :

[5] 'Now comes the night of Enitharmon's joy.
Who shall I call ? Who shall I send,
That Woman, lovely Woman, may have dominion ?
Arise, O Rintrah, thee I call, & Palamabron thee !
Go ! tell the human race that Woman's love is Sin ;
That an Eternal life awaits the worms of sixty winters
In an allegorical abode where existence hath never come.
Forbid all Joy, & from her childhood shall the little female
Spread nets in every secret path.

'My weary eyelids draw towards the evening ; my bliss is yet but new.
[6] Arise, O Rintrah, eldest born, second to none but Orc !
O lion Rintrah, raise thy fury from thy forests black !
Bring Palamabron, hornèd priest, skipping upon the mountains,

27–28 These lines appear to emphasize the point that the restriction of energy is the condition of the continuance of morality.

33–41 Cp. ll. 131–137 and V. D. A. 160–177. In his notes to Lavater's *Aphorisms* Blake writes : ' But the Philosophy of Causes and Consequences mislead Lavater as it has all his contemporaries : . . . the origin of the mistake . . . is, they suppose that Woman's Love is Sin. In consequence, all the loves and graces with them are sins.'

43 The sons and daughters, whom Enitharmon makes the ministers of her purpose of subjugating man, are so described in the course of her song as to suggest that Blake intended in each of them a definite and distinct meaning. Unfortunately, it is not now possible to interpret them with any certainty, since the indications in the present work are insufficient and the symbols are not developed in quite the same way elsewhere. Swinburne's *Essay* (p. 241) contains the following paraphrase of this passage : ' To this end [i. e. the establishment of Woman's dominion] the goddess of Space calls forth her chosen children, the " horned priest " of animal nature, the " silver-bowed queen " of desolate places, the " prince of the sun " with his innumerable race " thick as the summer stars ". . . . Moon and sun, spirit and flesh, all lonely jealous forces and mysteries of the natural world are gathered together under her law, that throughout the eighteen Christian centuries she may have her will of the world.' For Elynittria cp. M. 9. 38 : 11. 36 ; extra p. 8. 14–18 ; and M. 9. 28 *note*.

And silent Elynittria, the silver bowed queen !
Rintrah, where hast thou hid thy bride ?
Weeps she in desart shades ?
Alas, my Rintrah ! bring the lovely jealous Ocalythron.

' Arise, my son ! bring all thy brethren, O thou king of fire !
Prince of the Sun ! I see thee with thy innumerable race
Thick as the summer stars ;
But each, ramping, his golden mane shakes ;
And thine eyes rejoice because of strength, O Rintrah, furious king ! '

[7] Enitharmon slept
Eighteen hundred years. Man was a Dream,
The night of Nature and their harps unstrung !
She slept in middle of her nightly song
Eighteen hundred years, a female dream.

Shadows of men in fleeting bands upon the winds
Divide the heavens of Europe,
Till Albion's Angel, smitten with his own plagues, fled with his bands.
The cloud bears hard on Albion's shore,
Fill'd with immortal demons of futurity.
In council gather the smitten Angels of Albion ;
The cloud bears hard upon the council house, down rushing
On the heads of Albion's Angels.

One hour they lay buried beneath the ruins of that hall ;
But, as the stars rise from the salt lake, they arise in pain,
In troubled mists o'erclouded by the terrors of strug[g]ling times.

[8] In thoughts perturb'd they rose from the bright ruins, silent following
The fiery King, who sought his ancient temple serpent-form'd,
That stretches out its shady length along the Island white.
Round him roll'd his clouds of war ; silent the Angel went
Along the infinite shores of Thames to golden Verulam.

49 For Ocalythron cp. M., extra p. 8. 19–20.

57 The meaning of this line and its relation to the context are equally obscure. But from the general sense of the passage ' Nature ' seems to have a sinister connotation as the world of limited sense-perception and hence of moral law.

60–63 Cp. *America*, 178–181.

64–126 Cp. Appendix to *America*, pp. 4* and 12* *passim*.

72 Cp. F. Z. vii *a*. 1–37 and J. 25. 4 *note*.

There stand the venerable porches that, high-towering, rear
Their oak-surrounded pillars, form'd of massy stones uncut
With tool, stones precious; such eternal in the heavens,
Of colours twelve, few known on earth, give light in the opake,
Plac'd in the order of the stars, when the five senses whelm'd
In deluge o'er the earth-born man: then turn'd the fluxile eyes
Into two stationary orbs, concentrating all things;
The ever-varying spiral ascents to the heavens of heavens
Were bended downward, and the nostrils' golden gates shut,
Turn'd outward, barr'd and petrify'd against the infinite.

Thought chang'd the infinite to a serpent, that which pitieth
To a devouring flame; and man fled from its face and hid
In forests of night: then all the eternal forests were divided
Into earths rolling in circles of space, that like an ocean rush'd
And overwhelmèd all except this finite wall of flesh.
Then was the serpent temple form'd, image of infinite
Shut up in finite revolutions; and man became an Angel,
Heaven a mighty circle turning, God a tyrant crown'd.

Now arriv'd the ancient Guardian at the southern porch,
That, planted thick with trees of blackest leaf & in a vale
Obscure, inclos'd the Stone of Night; oblique it stood, o'er-hung
With purple flowers and berries red, image of that sweet south
Once open to the heavens and elevated on the human neck,
Now overgrown with hair and cover'd with a stony roof.
Downward 'tis sunk beneath th' attractive north, that round the feet,
A raging whirlpool, draws the dizzy enquirer to his grave.

76–85 The punctuation of this passage is conjectural. Blake's autotype gives little assistance.

78–80 Any attempt to identify these stones—as for example with the signs of the Zodiac, or with the gates of the heavenly Jerusalem (Rev. xxi)—must be purely conjectural. They form part of the vision of the infinite and eternal world which was lost to man when he became subject to the limitations of sense-perception.

86 'Thought' is here equivalent to analytic, and therefore destructive reason. In l. 114 it comes near to the later 'Imagination'.

88 A contrast is clearly intended between the 'forests of night' and the 'eternal forests'. The former image the state of mortal error, a dark and endless maze, with tangled roots perplexing the way of the traveller. This use of the expression persists even to *Jerusalem*: cp. J. 14. 8: 80. 43. The 'eternal forests', which clearly relate to the ideal state of existence, are very rarely mentioned.

96–101 The source of this symbol, the Stone of Night, is unknown; but cp. *Paradise Lost*, iv. 543–548. It is mentioned in *America*, 30; B. A., chap. iii, 4–21; F. Z. vii. 18–41, ix. 92; and appears later as the 'Rock of Death' (M. 28. 42), 'a Rock of difficulty and a Cliff of black despair' (J. 44. 11). Its identification in the present passage with the human skull,

[9] Albion's Angel rose upon the Stone of Night.
He saw Urizen on the Atlantic,
And his brazen Book,
That Kings & Priests had copied on Earth,
Expanded from North to South.

[10] And the clouds & fires pale roll'd round in the night of Enitharmon
Round Albion's cliffs & London's walls: still Enitharmon slept.
Rolling volumes of grey mist involve Churches, Palaces, Towers;
For Urizen unclasp'd his Book, feeding his soul with pity.
The youth of England, hid in gloom, curse the pain'd heavens, compell'd
Into the deadly night to see the form of Albion's Angel.
Their parents brought them forth, & agèd ignorance preaches canting,
On a vast rock perciev'd by those senses that are clos'd from thought:
Bleak, dark, abrupt it stands and overshadows London city.
They saw his boney feet on the rock, the flesh consum'd in flames;
They saw the Serpent temple lifted above, shadowing the Island white;

and its association with Urizen, whose place is in the Brain, indicates the origin of mundane error in uninspired reason, whereby truth is perverted into forms destructive to the spiritual life of man. The expression 'attractive north' illustrates the sinister significance in Blake's symbolic use of the North: see Index, *Cardinal Points*.

104 Cp. B. U., chap. ii, l. 33 *note*.

109 Churches, Palaces, and Towers, the symbols of civil and religious tyranny: cp. S.L., *Africa*, ll. 32–35, and S. Lib., § 15.

110 'Pity secret feeding on thoughts of cruelty' (F. Z. iv. 193) is the basis of Urizen's 'religion'. Such is the endeavour to combine in a single concept of God the attributes of mercy and moral justice: cp. B. U., viii. 32–54.

111–119 This apparently is Blake's vision of England at the time, when authority was taking measures to fortify its position by repressing all manifestations of sympathy with the revolutionary spirit in France. It is impossible to say whether the rock whereon the preacher stands is mythically the same as the 'Stone of Night' from which Urizen promulgates the teachings of his Book of Brass; but the essential meaning would seem to be the same in both cases. Cp. 'When I came home, on the abyss of the five senses, where a flat sided steep frowns over the present world . . .' (M. H. H., p. 6).

117 Blake followed certain archaeologists of his time, and chiefly perhaps Jacob Bryant, whose works he knew, in regarding the Druidical remains in Wiltshire and elsewhere as ruins of 'dragon temples', 'Arkite' symbols; and throughout the prophetic writings these are used with constant reference to destructive 'natural religion'. The 'Island white' is of course Albion; cp. M. 4. 20.

They heard the voice of Albion's Angel howling in flames of Orc,
Seeking the trump of the last doom.

Above the rest the howl was heard from Westminster louder and louder.
The Guardian of the secret codes forsook his ancient mansion,
Driven out by the flames of Orc: his furr'd robes & false locks
Adhered and grew one with his flesh, and nerves & veins shot thro' them.
With dismal torment sick, hanging upon the wind, he fled
Groveling along Great George Street, thro' the Park gate; all the soldiers
Fled from his sight: he drag'd his torments to the wilderness.

Thus was the howl thro' Europe.
For Orc rejoic'd to hear the howling shadows;
But Palamabron shot his lightnings, trenching down his wide back,
And Rintrah hung with all his legions in the nether deep.

Enitharmon laugh'd in her sleep to see (O woman's triumph!)
Every house a den, every man bound: the shadows are fill'd
With spectres, and the windows wove over with curses of iron.
Over the doors 'Thou shalt not' & over the chimneys, 'Fear' is written.
With bands of iron round their necks fasten'd into the walls,
The citizens; in leaden gyves the inhabitants of suburbs
Walk heavy: soft and bent are the bones of villagers.

120–126 This passage may be a reference to the London riots of 2nd June 1780, when the mob attacked and burned Lord Mansfield's house: cp. Swinburne, *Essay*, p. 243 *note*, and *America*, 186 *note*.

129–130 The restrictive character of the forces represented by Palamabron and Rintrah, best seen in this passage, is in complete contrast with the conception of the same spiritual beings in the opening myth of *Milton*.

131–137. Cp. 'The Garden of Love' (S. E., Clar. Press, p. 127):

I went to the Garden of Love,
And saw what I never had seen:
A Chapel was built in the midst,
Where I used to play on the green.

And the gates of this Chapel were shut,
And 'Thou shalt not' writ over the door;
So I turn'd to the Garden of Love
That so many sweet flowers bore.

And I saw it was fillèd with graves,
And tombstones where flowers should be:
And Priests in black gouns were walking their rounds
And binding with briars my joys & desires.

Cp. also J. 36. 42–46.

133 The term 'spectre' has here no symbolic significance, but is purely descriptive.

Between the clouds of Urizen the flames of Orc roll heavy
Around the limbs of Albion's Guardian, his flesh consuming:
Howlings & hissings, shrieks & groans & voices of despair
Arise around him in the cloudy
Heavens of Albion. Furious,
[11] The red limb'd Angel siez'd in horror and torment
The Trump of the last doom; but he could not blow the iron tube.
Thrice he assay'd, presumptuous, to awake the dead to Judgment.

A mighty Spirit leap'd from the land of Albion,
Nam'd Newton: he siez'd the Trump & blow'd the enormous blast.
Yellow as leaves of Autumn the myriads of Angelic hosts
Fell thro' the wintry skies, seeking their graves,
Rattling their hollow bones in howling and lamentation.

Then Enitharmon woke, nor knew that she had slept
And eighteen hundred years were fled
As if they had not been.
She call'd her sons & daughters
To the sports of night
Within her crystal house,
And thus her song proceeds:

'Arise, Ethinthus! tho' the earth-worm call,
Let him call in vain,
Till the night of holy shadows
And human solitude is past!

[12] 'Ethinthus, queen of waters, how thou shinest in the sky!
My daughter, how do I rejoice! for thy children flock around,
Like the gay fishes on the wave when the cold moon drinks the dew.
Ethinthus! thou art sweet as comforts to my fainting soul,
For now thy waters warble round the feet of Enitharmon.

'Manatha-Varcyon! I behold thee flaming in my halls!
Light of thy mother's soul, I see thy lovely eagles round!
Thy golden wings are my delight, & thy flames of soft delusion.

142–150 See General Introduction, p. 24.

158 Ethinthus is 'queen of waters' (*infra*, l. 162). The name occurs twice elsewhere, among the daughters of Los, F. Z. viii. 353 and J. 12. 25–27. There is no clue to its meaning.

earth-worm] Cp. J. 34. 57: 'O mortal Man, O worm of sixty winters'.

167 Manatha Varcyon] *not distinctly written*: perhaps Manatha Vorcyon as in F. Z. viii. 353. The source and meaning of this name are obscure.

‘ Where is my lureing bird of Eden ? Leutha, silent love !
Leutha, the many colour’d bow delights upon thy wings !
Soft soul of flowers, Leutha,
Sweet smiling pestilence, I see thy blushing light !
Thy daughters, many changing,
Revolve like sweet perfumes ascending, O Leutha, silken queen !

‘ Where is the youthful Antamon, prince of the pearly dew ?
O Antamon, why wilt thou leave thy mother Enitharmon ?
Alone I see thee, crystal form,
Floting upon the bosom’d air
With lineaments of gratified desire.
My Antamon, the seven churches of Leutha seek thy love.

‘ I hear the soft Oothoon in Enitharmon’s tents.
Why wilt thou give up woman’s secrecy, my melancholy child ?
Between two moments bliss is ripe.
O Theotormon, robb’d of joy, I see thy salt tears flow
Down the steps of my crystal house !

‘ Sotha & Thiralatha ! secret dwellers of dreamful caves,
Arise and please the horrent fiend with your melodious songs.
Still all your thunders golden hoof’d & bind your horses black.
Orc ! smile upon my children,
Smile, son of my afflictions !
Arise, O Orc, and give our mountains joy of thy red light ! ’

She ceas’d ; for All were forth at sport beneath the solemn moon,
Waking the stars of Urizen with their immortal songs,
That nature felt thro’ all her pores the enormous revelry,
Till morning oped the eastern gate :
Then every one fled to his station, & Enitharmon wept.

But terrible Orc, when he beheld the morning in the east,
[13] Shot from the heights of Enitharmon,
And in the vineyards of red France appear’d the light of his fury.

The sun glow’d fiery red ;

176 Cp. *Africa*, l. 11 *note*. The bearing of the present passage upon the meaning of the symbol Antamon has eluded discovery.

181 There may be some connexion between the ‘ seven churches of Leutha ’ and those mentioned in Revelation, but Blake’s meaning has not yet been discovered.

187 Cp. *Africa*, 31. Sotha appears in *America*, p. 4*, l. 21.

196 This apparently is the sign that the darkness of the night of Law draws to an end, and that the morning of freedom is at hand. Here ‘ east ’ is used in its natural sense : later it is the quarter of error, the state of Ulro.

The furious terrors flew around
On golden chariots raging with red wheels dropping with blood.
The Lions lash their wrathful tails;
The Tigers couch upon the prey & suck the ruddy tide;
And Enitharmon groans & cries in anguish and dismay.

Then Los arose: his head he rear'd, in snaky thunders clad;
And with a cry that shook all nature to the utmost pole,
Call'd all his sons to the strife of blood.

FINIS

APPENDIX
to
EUROPE

In the copy of *Europe* that belonged to the Linnell family is a poem of four stanzas in unrhymed lines, normally seven-stressed. But for its explicit last line the poem, marked by a grace beyond all but a few of the best passages of the early 'prophecies', would hardly be taken for what it is, namely, a preface to *Europe*, and hence the reason of its rejection is obvious. It promises the revelation of that joyous spirit life that the senses transform to dead matter, a theme actually dealt with in the Prophecy only incidentally and by implication, for that work is substantially an ethical and political manifesto. The one line of this poem that is germane is:

For stolen joys are sweet, and bread eaten in secret pleasant. (l. 6.)

which defines clearly the 'female dream', the moral atmosphere of the Christian dispensation as Blake conceived it.

'Five windows light the cavern'd Man: thro' one he breathes the air;
Thro' one hears music of the spheres; thro' one the eternal vine
Flourishes, that he may recieve the grapes; thro' one can look
And see small portions of the eternal world that ever groweth;

207–209 No other passage in the Lambeth books brings Los thus close to the actual conflict between the opposing forces of repressive law and liberty. It is therefore quite impossible to assert upon which side his influence was to have been exerted.

1–4 Cp. M. H. H., p. 14: 'If the doors of perception were cleansed, every thing would appear to man as it is, infinite. For man has closed himself up, till he sees all things thro' narrow chinks of his cavern.' Cp. also V. D. A., ll. 99–104.

Thro' one himself pass out what time he please, but he will not;
For stolen joys are sweet, & bread eaten in secret pleasant.'

So sang a Fairy, mocking, as he sat on a streak'd Tulip,
Thinking none saw him: when he ceas'd, I started from the trees,
And caught him in my hat, as boys knock down a butterfly.
'How know you this,' said I, 'small Sir? where did you learn this song?'
Seeing himself in my possession, thus he answer'd me:
'My Master, I am yours! command me, for I must obey.'

'Then tell me, what is the material world, and is it dead?'
He, laughing, answer'd, 'I will write a book on leaves of flowers,
If you will feed me on love-thoughts & give me now and then
A cup of sparkling poetic fancies; so, when I am tipsie,
I'll sing to you to this soft lute, and shew you all alive
This world, where every particle of dust breathes forth its joy.'

I took him home in my warm bosom: as we went along
Wild flowers I gather'd, & he shew'd me each eternal flower.
He laugh'd aloud to see them whimper because they were pluck'd.
They hover'd round me like a cloud of incense: when I came
Into my parlour and sat down, and took my pen to write,
My Fairy sat upon the table and dictated Europe.

13–18 Cp. *Poems from Letters*, ii, ll. 25–32 (Clar. Press, p. 302):

Each grain of Sand,
Each Stone on the Land,
Each rock & each hill,
Each fountain & rill,
Each herb & each tree,
Mountain, hill, earth, & sea,
Cloud, Meteor & Star,
Are Men Seen Afar.

THE BOOK OF URIZEN

INTRODUCTORY NOTE

THE / [FIRST] BOOK / of / URIZEN / Lambeth. Printed by [Will] Wm Blake 1794.

Colophon : ' The End of the / first book of Urizen '.

Collation: title-page 1 plate, Preludium 1 plate. Chaps. i–ix (two chapters being numbered chap. iv) 16 plates, ten full-page plates without illustrations, 10 plates : 28 plates in all, about 6 x 4 inches.

There are two title-pages in existence. One has the word ' FIRST ', and, in the imprint, the abbreviation ' Will ' ; the other has in place of the former word a continuation of the limb of the tree, the trunk of which forms the left side of the design ; and in place of ' Will ' the abbreviation ' W^m '.

Mr. G. L. Keynes in his Bibliography discloses important variations in the constitution and page-order of the six copies collated by him. The page numbered 4 in the present reprint is found only in two copies, both foliated by Blake, though in one most of the numbers have been erased, and the leaves disordered by a later binder. Of the other four copies Blake indubitably paginated three, and probably the fourth. From this it would seem that he could dispense with p. 4, in spite of the fact that by doing so he gave two stanzas 3 to chapter II, one on p. 3, the other on p. 5. Clearly Blake's purpose with regard to this page was not constant. Finally, as is shown below, he seems to have abandoned it.

The second anomaly is the presence of two distinct versions of the first six stanzas of chapter iv, both leading up to stanzas 7–12 on pp. 10 and 11. Of the five copies paginated by Blake, four set p. 9 before p. 8, for reasons that can only be conjectured. The evidence of narrative sequence, stanza structure, style and script indicates that the text on p. 9 was engraved at the same time as the stanzas 7–12 and as the body of the poem. The script on p. 8 is somewhat larger and more open, and may have been engraved at a different time. The difficulty is to find reason (1) for the composition and engraving of p. 8 and (2) for its position after p. 9 in four copies. Finally, why did not Blake reject one or other of these versions of chapter ii, stanzas 1–6 ?

Page 8 looks like an attempt to restate in condensed form the gist of the myth on p. 9, but it is curiously unskilful, as perhaps Blake recognized after engraving it. For one thing, all mention of the passing over of Urizen's ' first Age ' is omitted and to that extent the promised recital of Urizen's ' changes ' (p. 8, l. 12) is maimed. Again, stanzas 1–3 are syntactically incoherent beyond the wont even of this incoherent ' Prophecy '. Perhaps for these reasons, Blake, unable to use this plate as a substitute for p. 9, sought a place for it as a kind of parenthesis inserted after p. 9, between the first and second of Urizen's ' Ages ', where, except for the otiose stanza-numbers, it has, or may be read as having, a relevance of sorts. It is to be noted, by the way, that Blake seems to have added the page-numbers to each copy after it had been made up, so that the foliation alone would not betray incongruities in arrangement.

Yet there were still two sets of stanzas 1–6 in chapter iv. It may be conjectured that Blake retained both through unwillingness to sacrifice the striking design on p. 8. Seemingly he had come to concede so much to his limited public as to defer in some measure to their natural preference for his designs over his verses. Mr. Keynes shows that he made up books of designs from the Lambeth 'prophecies' by binding together prints of plates that bore no text. Three such collections are noted by Mr. Keynes, whose collations show that the *Book of Urizen* was the most frequently drawn upon, in the proportion of thirteen plates out of twenty-three, the balance being divided between *Thel*, the *Visions*, and the *Marriage*. It is likely, then, that in making up copies of this poem Blake was influenced, perhaps unconsciously, by consideration for his patrons' tastes: perhaps also, as his mystical faith developed and he was led further away from the crude thaumaturgies of the Lambeth books, he made such concessions the more easily. Therefore it is at least arguable that p. 8 was retained for its design's sake: the comparatively unimpressive p. 4 could be dropped.

Mr. Keynes helps us to a knowledge of what may be taken as Blake's final mind in the matter of arranging this book. He describes a copy, 'the latest to which a date can be given, and it may be the last that Blake executed'. It cannot be earlier than 1815, the date of the watermark. It is foliated by Blake. The word 'First' disappears from the title-page, the 'Preludium' and the colophon, 'as if by that time he had quite abandoned any intention he may ever have entertained of writing a Second Book of Urizen' (G. L. K., p. 147). Page 4 is omitted and p. 8 precedes p. 9, chapter-headings and stanza-numbers being retained in both. Page 8 thus reads as if its stanzas 1–3 amplified the description of Los in chapter iii, stanza 14, while stanzas 4–6 link up with the myth on p. 9. For convenience of reference the text on p. 9 is in the present edition cited as chapter iv, and that on pp. 9–11 as chapter iv (*a*).

Since the arrangement of the plates in the original copies varies in every instance, the marginal numbering indicating the engraved plates of text has been made consecutive in this edition.

The Book of Urizen is Blake's first detailed attempt at a cosmogonic myth. In the *Marriage* reference is made to the fall of the Messiah who 'formed a heaven of what he stole from the abyss' (M. H. H., p. 6). In another place Blake refers to the 'Giants' who formed this world into its sensual existence and now seem to live in it in chains as 'the causes of its life and the sources of all activity' (M. H. H., p. 16). The 'Giants' are elsewhere identified with the 'Antediluvians who are our Energies' (M. H. H., p. 17). It has not been found possible to relate these statements; indeed they are superficially contradictory. The Messiah fell because he was Acquiescence and not Energy, the positive virtue that Blake's *Marriage* was written to celebrate. The earlier statement appears to us primarily to be an exercise in paradox, aiming at little more than a repudiation of Milton's theology. In the absence of any hint of explanation from Blake and of any like conception elsewhere, the meaning of creation by the Giants 'who are our Energies' remains matter of surmise. Again in *Europe* (ll. 80–93), engraved also in 1794, Blake obscurely states a conception which, if nothing more, is an explicit rejection of the Jewish or Christian tradition. The passage begins:

> The five senses whelm'd
> In deluge o'er the earth-born man. (ll. 80, 81.)

This catastrophic event is not recounted or explained. Apparently the first result (l. 86) is that thought, accepting the witness of the senses, misinterprets 'the Infinite', and consequently

> all the eternal forests were divided
> Into earths rolling in circles of space, that like an ocean rush'd
> And overwhelmed all except this finite wall of flesh.

This appears to mean that man, no longer an 'infinite' being, makes the distinction of the self and the not-self from which proceed the misconceptions of the nature of man and the Divine, the errors in ethic and metaphysic against which Blake wars. But this exposition of the lines leaves unexplained the allusion (l. 81) to the 'Earth-born man' as anterior to the emergence of the 'Earths'. Possibly therefore Blake intends the statement of his doctrine to begin at the mention of the activities of 'Thought', and the 'deluge' of the senses to be the first result. Then would follow the misconception of the 'Infinite', and the notion of earths in Space. But in the one case the 'deluge', in the other 'Thought', is still unaccounted for.

The First Book of Urizen is an attempt to frame a myth to account for the beginnings of things, and also explicitly to reject the notion of providential guidance of human affairs. What we have is only a fragment, but it is enough to show that Blake was influenced by a knowledge, not perhaps very accurate or detailed, of Gnostic thought, and, much more deeply, by the imagery and vast conception of *Paradise Lost*.

The myth assumes the existence of a world of Eternals, of whose nature, however, nothing is said. One of them wilfully isolates himself, Urizen, the Primeval Priest, a title deduced, probably, from his subsequent manifestation in the World of Time, not from his 'Eternal nature'. As a result of his 'self-contemplations', the Void, the 'ideas' of Time and Space, the 'forms' of Elements and Beings arise. He challenges the ordering of the Eternal world: he explains that, 'self-contemplating', he has found only change and pain and death; that in his strivings he has found the elements of fire, air, water, and solid, and finally 'wisdom', by which he knows that all is 'sinful' and that there must be Law. He asserts the necessity that the Eternals, rejecting the unity of their harmonious Being, should separate each for himself a realm in Space, wherein should be

> One command, one joy, one desire,
> One curse, one weight, one measure,
> One King, one God, one Law. (Chap. ii, ll. 47–49.)

The Eternals, rejecting Urizen and his plans, separate him from Eternity by the agency of the 'enormous forms of energy', imaged as fire, whirlwind, and blood. To protect himself against the fires, Urizen, from the products of his 'self-contemplations', frames the spherical roof, 'vast, petrific, around on all sides,' which, seen by the 'sons of eternity' is a black globe 'like a human heart, struggling and beating'. This is the 'vast world of Urizen', afterwards the Universe of man. So far Blake has combined the notions of creation by division and by emanation. The 'forms' out of which the new world is created are the evils emanated from Urizen's self-contemplations, they are Urizen's 'self-begotten armies'; but they have a separate existence because by the power of the Eternals they are 'separated apart'. Separation for the Eternals is the beginning of death, for before, 'Death was not, but Eternal life sprung.'

The process of creation by division continues. From Urizen divides Los, Time, the 'Eternal Prophet', primarily the marking of the beginning of a new mode of existence, the not-Eternal; but while Los is living and active, Urizen lies in hideous formless death. Death, however, is not quiescence, for changes appear in Urizen which Los 'fixes' with his hammer and with the chain of hours, days, and years, and so the human form comes into being. The myth at this point calls for explanation that is not forthcoming. The human form evolves from the 'eternal mind' disorganized, rent from Eternity, figured as 'eddying, sulphureous foam', settling into a lake 'bright and shining clear', a conception probably related to a passage in Godwin's *Political Justice* (see B. U., chap. iv *a*, ll. 19–23 *note*). 'Forgetfulness, Dumbness, Necessity' are 'in chains of the mind locked up'. Whether Los's activity in 'fixing' the changes aimed at limiting the disastrous effects of 'Forgetfulness, Dumbness, Necessity', or whether it was by virtue of these qualities that the human form was evolved, there is nothing definitely to show. But it is to be noted that when the changes are 'fixed' Los pities Urizen, and therefore the three are possibly to be regarded as the marks and governing conditions of life apart from Eternity. At the same time the chain of which the links are 'hours, days and years' apparently is intended to state Blake's conviction that the new form of existence was not indefinitely to endure.

Another matter, on which much in the exposition of the Lambeth books depends, remains obscure. By what power, and to what end does Los labour? There is no clear indication that at this point he was the agent of the Eternals; but, on the other hand, Blake is careful to indicate that he lost his eternal vision only after the changes were completed. The opposed titles used in the book, the 'Eternal Priest' and the 'Eternal Prophet', suggest the severance of a principle of evil in Urizen and of good in Los. But the substance of this and the rest of the Lambeth books forbids a simple Manichaean interpretation, for though Urizen is consistently the evil principle, Los is certainly not consistently the principle of light. The incompleteness of the myth may perhaps be held to be the cause of the obscurities. The changes of Urizen complete, Los deteriorated until his eternal life

Like a dream was obliterated,

or, as in the repetition of the myth (F. Z. iv) Blake phrases it, until 'he became what he beheld', subject to the limitations of the human senses and mind and of the human form. He pities Urizen, and pity 'dividing' the soul, the first female, Enitharmon or Space, comes into being. The eternals call her Pity [1] in horror at the sight, which they close out from Eternity by the tent and curtains called Science. Again difficulties become acute. Herein Blake clearly enough states his convictions that Pity is not an attribute of the Eternals, who therefore do not institute the conception of Pity, and that sex and all that follows from it are no part of a divinely ordered plan. On the other hand, in the Satan-Palamabron myth (M., pp. 5–11) Blake's valuation of Pity is low: there it is the cause of all mundane evils. Hence it may be that the beginning of sex as a result of pity is

[1] 'Pity' is possibly Blake's translation of the πάθος of the Gnostics, the female source of terrestrial life, but the Gnostic Sophia is not Blake's Enitharmon.

condemnatory, so that from Blake's standpoint the Eternals are justified. The use too of the term 'Science' for the curtains that shut out the new phenomenon from the Eternals is not paralleled by any use of the term otherwhere in the prophetic writings. If the meaning is that in the separated world knowledge of a peculiar quality, e. g. the knowledge attained by intuition, is the instrument by which the veil may be pierced, and the secrets hidden from man attained, the image is at least awkward. The only safe deduction that may be made from the episode is that the affairs of the 'world apart' are from that point onward of no concern to the Eternals. Severance is complete.

The myth continues to tell of the establishment of sexual generation in the separated world. Orc the Liberator is born, and afterwards all those children of Los and Enitharmon who in *Europe* and *The Song of Los* are the mythical agents of the moral and intellectual enslavement of men. In relation to the growing to manhood of Orc, Blake's myth attempts to account for the genesis of that most evil result of sex, jealousy, a term used in *The Four Zoas* as a summary title for all forms of evil. Orc, the anarchic Messiah of the Lambeth books, is bound with the chains of jealousy, whereupon Urizen, who so far had lain in a stony stupor, rises to exercise over the creatures of his separated world an authority based upon hypocritical pretences to pity. Religion and moral dominion begin, but not, it is to be noted, until Orc is shackled by the conditions of Time and Space. Henceforth the God of Sinai is enthroned secure in the apathy of his enfeebled subjects, for Blake here regards the acceptance of the witness of the senses and obtuseness to supersensual knowledge as results of the operations of restrictive morality. The infinite senses of the Beings who apparently followed Urizen in his assertion of 'self-hood' are dimmed and diminished to the meagre capacity of physical organs, so that most of them, obsessed by the false appearance of the corporeal; deny the existence of the supersensual. They are 'the weak in courage' who falling readily beneath the sway of the moral law are brought down to the stature of mortals and are confined to the 'pendulous earth', but whether as the parents of men or as the 'sons of God' is not made clear. They proceed to make 'laws of prudence' and call them the 'laws of God'. But a few stronger spirits led by Fuzon, the son of Urizen born of Fire, depart from the earth to prepare for the attempt to overthrow Urizen, which is the theme of *The Book of Ahania*.

The myth is unfinished. When Blake repeated part of it in *The Four Zoas* his mythology had been much elaborated and its foci altered. The two works which at first sight appear to be appendices to the *Book of Urizen*, namely, *Ahania* and the *Book of Los*, are found to add nothing. Therefore the story of the subsequent antagonism of Urizen and Orc can be pieced together only from fragments in *America*, *Europe*, and the *Song of Los*, while the significance and development of Los and Enitharmon, obviously essential to be known, both for a right understanding of that part of the myth that remains and for a hypothetical reconstruction of its conclusion, are left to almost groundless surmise. The loss of the remaining Books, if ever they were written, makes any attempt to state Blake's visions of Eternity and of Time and Space as futile as would be the effort to reconstruct *Paradise Lost* if only the first two Books remained.

THE

BOOK

of

URIZEN

LAMBETH Printed by Will. Blake. 1794.

[2]

PRELUDIUM

TO

THE

BOOK OF

URIZEN.

Of the primeval Priest's assum'd power,
When Eternals spurn'd back his religion
And gave him a place in the north,
Obscure, shadowy, void, solitary. 4

Eternals! I hear your call gladly.
Dictate swift wingèd words, & fear not
To unfold your dark visions of torment. 7

Title: the authority of the copy watermarked 1815 has been accepted for dropping ' First ' from the title, the Preludium and the colophon.

1 The primeval Priest is Urizen. Cp. M. H. H., proverb 55 *note*.

3 The north is the quarter traditionally associated with Satan's revolt. Cp. *Paradise Lost*, v, ll. 754–760, which may have suggested this mythical episode to Blake.

5–7 Similar claims to direct inspiration are made M. 3. 1–10: J. 5. 16–24: 74. 40–41: and perhaps in the rejected Preludium to *Europe*, ll. 22–24. Though the Eternals inspire Blake's Prophecy, it is to be noted that the myth does not represent them as a beneficent providence.

[3]

Chap. I

1. Lo, a shadow of horror is risen
In Eternity, Unknown, unprolific,
Self-clos'd, all-repelling ! What Demon
Hath form'd this abominable void,
This soul-shudd'ring vacuum ? Some said
It is Urizen. But unknown, abstracted,
Brooding secret, the dark power hid.

2. Times on times he divided & measur'd
Space by space in his ninefold darkness,
Unseen, unknown ; changes appear'd
Like desolate mountains, rifted furious
By the black winds of perturbation.

3. For he strove in battles dire,
In unseen conflictions with shapes,
Bred from his forsaken wilderness,
Of beast, bird, fish, serpent & element,
Combustion, blast, vapour and cloud ;

4. Dark revolving in silent activity,
Unseen in tormenting passions,
An activity unknown and horrible,
A self-contemplating shadow,
In enormous labours occupied.

5. But Eternals beheld his vast forests.
Age on ages he lay, clos'd, unknown,
Brooding, shut in the deep ; all avoid
The petrific abominable chaos.

1 Although it does not explain the meaning of the symbol before the separation from Eternity, the description of the ' dark power ' when as yet ' Earth was not ' is suggestive enough in the light of Urizen's subsequent presentation as the source of the errors of reason, sense-perception and morality.

13–17 For the moral content of Urizen's ' self-contemplation ' see B. A., chap. ii, *passim.*

21 Cp. : Reasoning on its own dark Fiction
In doubt which is Self Contradiction
(E. G., γ^2, ll. 95–96, Clar. Press, p. 254.)

23 Cp. V. D. A. 130 *note.*

6. His cold horrors, silent, dark Urizen
Prepar'd ; his ten thousands of thunders,
Rang'd in gloom'd array, stretch out across
The dread world ; & the rolling of wheels,
As of swelling seas, sound in his clouds,
In his hills of stor'd snows, in his mountains
Of hail & ice ; voices of terror
Are heard, like thunders of autumn
When the cloud blazes over the harvests.

Chap. II

1. Earth was not, nor globes of attraction ;
The will of the Immortal expanded
Or contracted his all flexible senses ;
Death was not, but eternal life sprung.

2. The sound of a trumpet the heavens
Awoke, & vast clouds of blood roll'd
Round the dim rocks of Urizen ; so nam'd
That solitary one in Immensity.

3. Shrill the trumpet ; & myriads of Eternity
[4] Muster around the bleak desarts,
Now fill'd with clouds, darkness & waters
That roll'd perplex'd, lab'ring, & utter'd
Words articulate bursting in thunders
That roll'd on the tops of his mountains

4. From the depths of dark solitude : 'From
The eternal abode in my holiness,
Hidden, set apart, in my stern counsels
Reserv'd for the days of futurity,

Chap. II. 1–4. See Index, *Expansion*, &c. The 'globes of attraction' are obscure, unless they are the other heavenly bodies, suns, stars, and planets ; cp. *The French Revolution*, l. 49.

5 Urizen's secret preparations are reminiscent of *Paradise Lost*, vi. 520 seq.

9–42 Urizen's 'self-contemplation', insistence on individuality, or, to use the term so frequently met in the later writings, 'self-hood', breaks the harmony of Eternity. Thus arises a new mode of existence. From the 'self-contemplations' arise the unformed of matter (ll. 11–12) and the notion of Time (l. 18). In ll. 23–32 Urizen tells with more detail of the emergence of the 'ideas' of the four elements. His 'self-contemplation' has results also in the region of conduct. Insistence on 'self-hood' is the beginning of the differentiation of the self and the 'not-self'. Whatever in the 'not-self' is unpleasing to the self is Sin. The recognition of Sin is the wisdom of Urizen (ll. 33–42). The materials of both the physical and moral orders in the world of Time and Space are thus accounted for.

I have sought for a joy without pain,
For a solid without fluctuation.
Why will you die, O Eternals?
Why live in unquenchable burnings?

5. 'First I fought with the fire, consum'd
Inwards into a deep world within,
A void immense, wild, dark & deep,
Where nothing was, Nature's wide womb:
And self balanc'd, stretch'd o'er the void,
I alone, even I, the winds merciless
Bound; but condensing, in torrents
They fall & fall: strong I repell'd
The vast waves; & arose on the waters
A wide world of solid obstruction.

6. 'Here alone I in books form'd of metals
Have written the secrets of wisdom,
The secrets of dark contemplation,
By fightings and conflicts dire
With terrible monsters Sin-bred
Which the bosoms of all inhabit,
Seven deadly Sins of the Soul.

7. 'Lo! I unfold my darkness, and on
This rock place with strong hand the Book
Of eternal brass, written in my solitude,

8. 'Laws of peace, of love, of unity,
Of pity, compassion, forgiveness.
Let each chuse one habitation,
His ancient infinite mansion,
One command, one joy, one desire,
One curse, one weight, one measure,
One King, one God, one Law.'

33 The books of metal, of which the chief are of brass and iron, apparently represent the whole body of false doctrine more commonly referred to as Urizen's 'Web' or 'Veil' of Religion, or more often as Natural Religion. The contents of the Book of Brass are best illustrated by F. Z. vii. 110–129, a keen satire upon the principles of prudential morality. The Book of Iron would seem to have some connexion with Urizen's 'iron laws'. For other passages cp. *Europe*, 104–106, and B. A., chap. iii. 8–28.

35–39 Cp. B. A., chap. ii. 1–19. The Seven deadly Sins are, by inversion, the cardinal virtues.

41 Cp. *Europe*, 96 *note*, 106 and *note*.

43–49 Urizen's error is twofold. First his plan aims at sundering the unity of Eternity into many law-governed universes, the assertion of many 'self-hoods'. Secondly he errs in asserting that peace, love, and unity are to be achieved by law, by the establishment of the principle of dominion.

47–49 Cp. M. H. H., p. 24: 'One Law for the Lion & Ox is Oppression.'

Chap. III

1. The voice ended: they saw his pale visage
Emerge from the darkness, his hand
On the rock of eternity unclasping
The Book of brass. Rage siez'd the strong—

2. Rage, fury, intense indignation
In cataracts of fire, blood & gall,
In whirlwinds of sulphureous smoke;
And enormous forms of energy
[5] In living creations appear'd
In the flames of eternal fury.

3. Sund'ring, dark'ning, thund'ring,
Rent away with a terrible crash,
Eternity roll'd wide apart,
Wide asunder rolling;
Mountainous, all around
Departing, departing, departing,
Leaving ruinous fragments of life
Hanging, frowning cliffs, &, all between,
An ocean of voidness unfathomable.

4. The roaring fires ran o'er the heav'ns
In whirlwinds & cataracts of blood;
And o'er the dark desarts of Urizen
Fires pour thro' the void on all sides
On Urizen's self-begotten armies.

5. But no light from the fires! all was darkness
In the flames of Eternal fury.

6. In fierce anguish & quenchless flames
To the desarts and rocks he ran, raging
To hide, but he could not: combining,
He dug mountains & hills in vast strength.
He piled them in incessant labour,
In howlings & pangs & fierce madness,
Long periods in burning fires labouring,

8 Beneath this line are traces of a deleted line: 'All the seven deadly Sins of the soul'.

10 These eternal flames may be compared with the 'lustful fires' of Orc, the cleansing fires of revolt that in *America* consume error from the earth. Here they represent the 'enormous forms of energy' by means of which the Eternals protect themselves against insurgent evil.

20–21 Cp. B. L., chap. i, ll. 27–30.

Till hoary and age-broke and agèd,
In despair and the shadows of death.

7. And a roof vast, petrific, around
On all sides he fram'd, like a womb,
Where thousands of rivers in veins
Of blood pour down the mountains to cool
The eternal fires beating without
From Eternals; & like a black globe,
View'd by sons of Eternity standing
On the shore of the infinite ocean,
Like a human heart strug[g]ling & beating,
The vast world of Urizen appear'd.

8. And Los round the dark globe of Urizen
Kept watch for Eternals, to confine
The obscure separation alone:
For Eternity stood wide apart,
[6] As the stars are apart from the earth.

9. Los wept, howling around the dark Demon
And cursing his lot; for in anguish
Urizen was rent from his side,
And a fathomless void for his feet
And intense fires for his dwelling.

10. But Urizen, laid in a stony sleep,
Unorganiz'd, rent from Eternity.

. . . .

11. The Eternals said: 'What is this? Death?
Urizen is a clod of clay!'

36 Cp. ll. 41–45. The 'roof' is apparently the separated world of Urizen, man's universe, seen as it were from Eternity. The image is developed later in the symbol Mundane Shell (see Index).

46–50 The sense in which 'for Eternals' is used remains obscure. Neither the present myth nor the use of the symbol Los in the other Lambeth books justifies the deduction that the Eternals plan by Los's activity a final reuniting of the severed 'world of Urizen' with Eternity. Rather it would appear that Time to the Eternals means the confining of the 'obscure separation alone' (cp. chap. iv *a*, ll. 9–10 and ll. 16–18). Time is the prison-house of the fallen Eternal, a doctrine the punitive implication of which Blake was later to modify.

53 This separation of Urizen from Los would seem to indicate that Blake at this period regarded 'the eternal mind' as consisting of two elements, one of Urizen, the other of Los. It is just possible that this view may be connected with the doctrine of 'Contraries' mentioned in M. H. H., p. 3, in which case Urizen might be associated with Reasoner and Devourer (M. H. H., p. 16), and Los with 'Energy' or the 'Prolific'. The treatment of Los in the Lambeth books, however, makes this very uncertain.

[7] 12. Los howl'd in a dismal stupor,
Groaning, gnashing, groaning,
Till the wrenching apart was healèd.

13. But the wrenching of Urizen heal'd not.
Cold, featureless flesh or clay,
Rifted with direful changes,
He lay in a dreamless night,

14. Till Los rouz'd his ⟨his⟩ fires, affrighted
At the formless unmeasurable death—

Chap. IV

[8] 1. Los, smitten with astonishment,
Frighten'd at the hurtling bones

2. And at the surging sulphureous,
Perturbèd, Immortal, mad, raging

3. In whirlwinds & pitch & nitre
Round the furious limbs of Los.

4. And Los formèd nets & gins,
And threw the nets round about.

5. He watch'd in shudd'ring fear
The dark changes, & bound every change
With rivets of iron & brass.

6. And these were the changes of Urizen :—

Chap. IV (a)

[9] 1. Ages on ages roll'd over him ;
In stony sleep ages roll'd over him,

Chap. IV. 7–8 Cp. *Africa*, 10–21, where Urizen gives
his Laws to the Nations
By the hands of the children of Los.

These ' Laws and Religions ' are as ' nets & guns & traps to catch the joys of Eternity ' (*Africa*, l. 33) ; cp. B. U., chap. ii. 19 *note*. Here also, as in *Africa*, the result is to ' obliterate ' and ' erase ' the memory of Eternity : cp. B. U., chap. v. 9–15. The ' Perturbèd Immortal ' (l. 4) is Urizen.

10–12 The changes of Urizen and Los's binding of them are obscure. It is probable that Blake attempts to assign a mythical origin to the human form, making it the symbol of man's fallen state. It is noteworthy that in the Lambeth books there is no mention of the divinity of the human form, such as appears so prominently in the later writings. For the outcome of the changes cp. B. U., chap. v. 9–15.

Chap. IV (a) The question of the two chapters numbered IV is discussed in the Introductory Note. The subject of the present chapter, the changes of Urizen, is found in B. A., chap. iv : B. L., chap. iv : F. Z. iv. 165–245 : and M., extra p. 5.

Like a dark waste stretching, chang'able,
By earthquakes riv'n, belching sullen fires :
On ages roll'd ages in ghastly
Sick torment ; around him in whirlwinds
Of darkness the eternal Prophet howl'd,
Beating still on his rivets of iron,
Pouring sodor of iron, dividing
The horrible night into watches.

2. And Urizen (so his eternal name)
His prolific delight obscur'd more & more
In dark secresy, hiding in surgeing
Sulphureous fluid his phantasies.
The Eternal Prophet heav'd the dark bellows,
And turn'd restless the tongs ; and the hammer
Incessant beat, forging chains new & new,
Numb'ring with links hours, days & years.

3. The eternal mind, bounded, began to roll
Eddies of wrath, ceaseless, round & round ;
And the sulphureous foam, surgeing thick,
Settled, a lake bright & shining clear,
White as the snow on the mountains cold.

4. Forgetfulness, dumbness, necessity !
In chains of the mind lockèd up,
Like fetters of ice shrinking together,
Disorganiz'd, rent from Eternity,
Los beat on his fetters of iron,
And heated his furnaces & pour'd
Iron sodor and sodor of brass.

5. Restless turn'd the immortal, inchain'd,
Heaving dolorous, anguish'd unbearable ;
Till a roof, shaggy, wild, inclos'd
In an orb his fountain of thought.

16–18 The definition of the chain as of 'hours, days, years' is perhaps intended to state Blake's conviction that the new mode of existence is not indefinitely to endure. So with the temporal allusion in ll. 8–10.

19–23 Cp. Godwin's *Political Justice*, ii, p. 24 : 'The Lord, therefore, has no motive to industry and creation, no stimulus to rouse him from the lethargic "oblivious pool" out of which every finite intellect originally rose.'

24–30 An assured interpretation of these lines would dispel most of the difficulties of the book. It is, however, impossible to say whether Los's activity is the limiting of the disastrous results that might proceed from 'Forgetfulness, Dumbness, Necessity', or whether these terms characterize the governing conditions of the fallen mind, and that as a consequence the limitation of the human senses and form follows. But even the punctuation here is dubious.

31–35 Cp. *Europe*, ll. 96–101 and *note*.

6. In a horrible dreamful slumber,
Like the linkèd infernal chain
A vast Spine writh'd in torment
Upon the winds, shooting pain'd
Ribs, like a bending cavern ;
And bones of solidness froze
Over all his nerves of joy :
And a first Age passèd over,
And a state of dismal woe.

[10] 7. From the caverns of his jointed Spine
Down sunk with fright a red
Round globe, hot, burning, deep
Deep down into the Abyss,
Panting, Conglobing, Trembling,
Shooting out ten thousand branches
Around his solid bones :
And a second Age passèd over,
And a state of dismal woe.

8. In harrowing fear rolling round,
His nervous brain shot branches
Round the branches of his heart
On high into two little orbs ;
And fixèd in two little caves,
Hiding carefully from the wind,
His Eyes beheld the deep :
And a third Age passèd over,
And a state of dismal woe.

9. The pangs of hope began.
In heavy pain striving, struggling,
Two Ears in close volutions
From beneath his orbs of vision
Shot spiring out and petrified
As they grew. And a fourth Age passèd,
And a state of dismal woe.

10. In ghastly torment sick,
Hanging upon the wind,
[11] Two Nostrils bent down to the deep.
And a fifth Age passèd over,
And a state of dismal woe.

11. In ghastly torment sick,
Within his ribs bloated round
A craving Hungry Cavern.

Thence arose his channel'd Throat,
And, like a red flame, a Tongue
Of thirst & of hunger appear'd.
And a sixth Age passèd over,
And a state of dismal woe.

12. Enragèd & stifled with torment,
He threw his right Arm to the north,
His left Arm to the south,
Shooting out in anguish deep;
And his Feet stamp'd the nether Abyss
In trembling & howling & dismay.
And a [seventh] Age passèd over,
And a state of dismal woe.

Chap. V

1. In terrors Los shrunk from his task:
His great hammer fell from his hand.
His fires beheld, and sickening
Hid their strong limbs in smoke;
For with noises ruinous, loud,
With hurtlings & clashings & groans
The Immortal endur'd his chains,
Tho' bound in a deadly sleep.

2. All the myriads of Eternity,
All the wisdom & joy of life
Roll like a sea around him,
Except what his little orbs
Of sight by degrees unfold.

3. And now his eternal life
Like a dream was obliterated.

4. Shudd'ring, the Eternal Prophet smote
With a stroke from his north to south region.
The bellows & hammer are silent now;
A nerveless silence his prophetic voice
Siez'd; a cold solitude & dark void
The Eternal Prophet & Urizen clos'd.

83–84 Cp. chap. v, ll. 16–17, and see Index, *Cardinal Points*.

88 seventh] Blake's autograph reads 'second'. This slip is corrected when the same episode is repeated in F. Z. iv. 245 and M., extra page 5, l. 27.

Chap. v. 9–13 For a similar statement of the outcome of limited sense-perception cp. M. H. H., p. 4.

5. Ages on ages roll'd over them,
Cut off from life & light, frozen
Into horrible forms of deformity.
Los suffer'd his fires to decay.
Then he look'd back with anxious desire;
But the space, undivided by existence,
Struck horror into his soul.

6. Los wept, obscur'd with mourning;
His bosom earthquak'd with sighs;
He saw Urizen, deadly, black,
In his chains bound; & Pity began,

7. In anguish dividing & dividing,
For pity divides the soul
In pangs, eternity on eternity.
Life in cataracts pour'd down his cliffs;
The void shrunk the lymph into Nerves
Wand'ring wide on the bosom of night,
And left a round globe of blood
Trembling upon the void.

[12] Thus the Eternal Prophet was divided
Before the death image of Urizen;
For in changeable clouds and darkness,
In a winterly night beneath,
The Abyss of Los stretch'd immense:
And now seen, now obscur'd, to the eyes
Of Eternals the visions remote

27 Of the two powers, Urizen and Los, who divide the new state of existence between them, the former is, by reason of his secession from Eternity, ' unprolific '; the other loses for a time that portion of spiritual energy represented symbolically as his ' fires '. For a later development of this concept of Los cp. M. 16. 31 *note*.

32 Pity becoming apparent as the Female gives rise to the phenomenon of ' Sex ', the basis of much of Blake's later symbolism. Cp. Crabb Robinson (S., p. 269): ' [Blake] replied that the fall produced only generation and death. And then he went off upon a rambling statement of a union of sexes in man, as in Ovid, an androgynous state in which I could not follow him.' For Enitharmon see Introductory Note to this ' prophecy '. The incompleteness of B. U. renders this episode dark, and Blake's casual punctuation augments the obscurity. For ' Pity ' in another sense cp. B. U., chap. viii. 35 *note*.

39 The ' globe of blood ' appears in almost the same connexion as late as J. 86. 50. Its constant association with the ' female ' symbols emphasizes the idea of ' corporeity ' connoted by it. In the latest writings it stands for the distracting influence of mundane environment upon the visionary, the appeal of physical beauty, of social, moral, and artistic conventions.

45 The ' Abyss of Los ' is apparently identical with the world of the fallen Urizen. In such expressions as this the distinction between the two spiritual powers seems to disappear.

Of the dark seperation appear'd.
As glasses discover Worlds
In the endless Abyss of space,
So the expanding eyes of Immortals
Beheld the dark visions of Los
And the globe of life blood trembling.

[13] 8. The globe of life blood trembled,
Branching out into roots,
Fibrous, writhing upon the winds,
Fibres of blood, milk and tears,
In pangs, eternity on eternity.
At length in tears & cries imbodied,
A female form, trembling and pale,
Waves before his deathy face.

9. All Eternity shudder'd at sight
Of the first female now seperate,
Pale as a cloud of snow,
Waving before the face of Los.

10. Wonder, awe, fear, astonishment
Petrify the eternal myriads
At the first female form now separate.
[14] They call'd her Pity, and fled.

11. 'Spread a Tent with strong curtains around them!
Let cords & stakes bind in the Void,
That Eternals may no more behold them!'

12. They began to weave curtains of darkness;
They erected large pillars round the Void,
With golden hooks fasten'd in the pillars:
With infinite labour the Eternals
A woof wove, and callèd it Science.

69–75 The intention of this passage appears to be emphatically to deny the doctrine of an over-ruling Providence in human life.

70–77 The symbols Tent, Tabernacle, Veil, Garment are used freely to summarize the total of human errors in thought and morals. Usually they are attributed to the activities of Vala, or of an equivalent person in Blake's mythology (see Index, *Vala*). Man is imaged as caught in the net of errors, or clad in error; or surrounded and his perception of eternity obstructed by the Tabernacle or Veil. In this instance the Net is woven by the Eternals, powers indifferent, neither friendly to, nor enemies of man. It does not restrain man, but hides him, a hideous sight, from the Eternals. It is called 'Science' (l. 77), a term of equivocal meaning, not here illuminated by the context. Interpretation therefore can only be conjectural.

Chap. VI

1. But Los saw the Female, & pitied ;
He embrac'd her ; she wept, she refus'd ;
In perverse and cruel delight
She fled from his arms, yet he follow'd.

2. Eternity shudder'd when they saw
Man begetting his likeness
On his own divided image.

3. A time passèd over ; the Eternals
Began to erect the tent,
When Enitharmon, sick,
Felt a Worm within her womb.

4. Yet helpless it lay, like a Worm,
In the trembling womb
To be moulded into existence.

5. All day the worm lay on her bosom ;
All night within her womb
The worm lay till it grew to a serpent,
With dolorous hissings & poisons
Round Enitharmon's loins folding.

6. Coil'd within Enitharmon's womb
The serpent grew, casting its scales ;
With sharp pangs the hissings began
To change to a grating cry :
Many sorrows and dismal throes,
Many forms of fish, bird & beast
Brought forth an Infant form
Where was a worm before.

7. The Eternals their tent finishèd,
Alarm'd with these gloomy visions,
When Enitharmon, groaning,
Produc'd a man Child to the light.

8. A shriek ran thro' Eternity,
And a paralytic stroke,
At the birth of the Human shadow.

Chap. VI. 10–27 Creation in the earlier part of the myth is either by emanation, as in the case of the unformed elements from the 'self-contemplations' of Urizen, or by division, as of Los from Urizen and Enitharmon from Los. The mode that distinguishes the life of the world apart, sexual generation, here is mythically accounted for. Blake's embryology (the worm, &c.) probably aims at marking a low valuation of the new mode. Its emergence marks the completion of the severance of Urizen's world from Eternity.

9. Delving earth in his resistless way,
Howling, the Child with fierce flames
Issu'd from Enitharmon.

10. The Eternals closèd the tent;
They beat down the stakes, the cords
[15] Stretch'd for a work of eternity:
No more Los beheld Eternity.

11. In his hands he siez'd the infant;
He bathèd him in springs of sorrow,
He gave him to Enitharmon.

Chap. VII

1. They namèd the child Orc; he grew,
Fed with milk of Enitharmon.

2. Los awoke her. O sorrow & pain!
A tight'ning girdle grew
Around his bosom. In sobbings
He burst the girdle in twain;
But still another girdle
Oppress'd his bosom. In sobbings
Again he burst it. Again
Another girdle succeeds.
The girdle was form'd by day,
By night was burst in twain.

3. These falling down on the rock
Into an iron Chain,
In each other, link by link, lock'd.

4. They took Orc to the top of a mountain.
O how Enitharmon wept!
They chain'd his young limbs to the rock
With the Chain of Jealousy
Beneath Urizen's deathful shadow.

Chap. VII. Cp. F. Z. v. 79–182.

2 This may mean that the quickening spirit of Orc derives nothing of its power from extra-mundane sources. It is nourished and its nature is modified by Enitharmon, who appears here to symbolize the conditions of temporal existence as opposed to those of Eternity. (Cp. *Europe*, Preludium, ll. 28–31 and *note* to ll. 29–30.)

14 The 'Chain of Jealousy' (l. 19) is the symbol of the fettering influence of temporal experience, Los here having the significance of the Time-spirit (B. U., chap. iv *a*. 18 and M. 23. 68). Possibly also Blake wishes to account in his myth for the beginning of Jealousy, the great evil of life.

5. The dead heard the voice of the child
And began to awake from sleep;
All things heard the voice of the child
And began to awake to life.

6. And Urizen, craving with hunger,
Stung with the odours of Nature,
Explor'd his dens around.

7. He form'd a line & a plummet
To divide the Abyss beneath;
He form'd a dividing rule.

8. He formèd scales to weigh,
He formèd massy weights;
He formèd a brazen quadrant;
He formèd golden compasses
And began to explore the Abyss;
And he planted a garden of fruits.

9. But Los encircled Enitharmon
With fires of Prophecy
From the sight of Urizen & Orc.

10. And she bore an enormous race.

Chap. VIII

1. Urizen explor'd his dens,
Mountain, moor & wilderness,
With a globe of fire lighting his journey,
A fearful journey, annoy'd
By cruel enormities, forms
[16] Of life on his forsaken mountains.

2. And his world teem'd vast enormities,
Fright'ning, faithless, fawning;
Portions of life, similitudes
Of a foot, or a hand, or a head,

21–24 The influence of Orc quickens the dead universe of Urizen and Los.

28–36 These lines dimly suggest the Miltonic lines on the creation of the world in the Abyss, *Paradise Lost*, vii. 225–227. Cp. also F. Z. ii. 229–502. The mathematical instruments (ll. 31–34) may have significance as designed to ' set bounds to the infinite ', to fix limits to spiritual aspiration. The ' garden of fruits ', suggesting Eden, is obscure unless it relates to an illusion of a Paradise in the hope of which man is led to subject himself to the moral law on earth; cp. *Europe*, ll. 37–41.

Chap. VIII. Urizen's journey is treated at much greater length in F. Z. vi.

5–12 The lines show curious perversion of the Platonic world of Ideas. They apparently refer back to chap. i, ll. 8–22, and chap. ii, ll. 23–32.

Or a heart, or an eye, they swam misch[i]evous,
Dread terrors, delighting in blood.

3. Most Urizen sicken'd to see
His eternal creations appear,
Sons & daughters of sorrow on mountains,
Weeping, wailing. First Thiriel appear'd,
Astonish'd at his own existence,
Like a man from a cloud born ; & Utha,
From the waters emerging, laments ;
Grodna rent the deep earth, howling,
Amaz'd ; his heavens immense cracks
Like the ground parch'd with heat : then Fuzon
Flam'd out, first begotten, last born of
All his eternal sons ; in like manner
His daughters, from green herbs & cattle,
From monsters & worms of the pit.

4. He, in darkness clos'd, view'd all his race,
And his soul sicken'd ! he curs'd
Both sons & daughters, for he saw
That no flesh nor spirit could keep
His iron laws one moment.

5. For he saw that life liv'd upon death :
[17] The Ox in the slaughter house moans,
The Dog at the wintry door ;
And he wept, & he callèd it Pity,
And his tears flowèd down on the winds.

13–15 Cp. F. Z. vi, ll. 87 seq.

16–22 Of the four sons of Urizen who are associated with the four elements the first, Thiriel, does not appear to be the Tiriel of the book of that name : Fuzon, not essentially different from Orc, comes into the *Book of Ahania*, while Utha and Grodna are not mentioned elsewhere. In a pencil note to a water-colour drawing illustrating *Il Penseroso*, ll. 87–96, the spirits of the four elements are described as surrounding Milton's chair. If Urizen is the creator of the physical universe, then his sons may well be

> those spirits that are found
> In fire, air, flood or underground
> Whose power hath a true consent
> With planet or with element.

But Blake does not develop this nature symbolism.

30–31 Cp. J. 35. 11–12 :

> No individual can keep these Laws, for they are death
> To every energy of man, and forbid the springs of life.

Cp. *Tiriel*, § 8, *passim*.

35 'Pity' here is that false pity 'secret feeding on thoughts of cruelty' (F. Z. iv. 193). It is an attribute of the God of the Moral Law. Cf. the extract from Urizen's 'Book of Brass', F. Z. vii. 110–129.

6. Cold he wander'd on high over their cities
In weeping & pain & woe;
And where-ever he wander'd in sorrows
Upon the agèd heavens,
A cold shadow follow'd behind him,
Like a spider's web, moist, cold & dim,
Drawing out from his sorrowing soul,
The dungeon-like heaven dividing,
Where ever the footsteps of Urizen
Walk'd over the cities in sorrow;

7. Till a Web, dark & cold, throughout all
The tormented element stretch'd
From the sorrows of Urizen's soul.
And the Web is a Female in embrio;
None could break the Web, no wings of fire,

8. So twisted the cords & so knotted
The meshes, twisted like to the human brain.

9. And all call'd it the Net of Religion.

Chap. IX

1. Then the Inhabitants of those Cities
Felt their Nerves change into Marrow;
And hardening Bones began
In swift diseases and torments,
In throbbings & shootings & grindings,
Thro' all the coasts; till, weaken'd,
The Senses inward rush'd, shrinking
Beneath the dark net of infection;

2. Till the shrunken eyes, clouded over,
Discern'd not the woven hipocrisy,
But the streaky slime in their heavens,
Brought together by narrowing perceptions,

37–51 Cp. F. Z. vi. 226–249.

50 The association of the feminine symbols with the ' Veil of Moral Laws ' is constant: see Index, *Vala*.

51–54 Cp. the description in *The Human Abstract* (S. E., Clar. Press, p. 135) of the Tree of Mystery, an equivalent symbol to the Veil or Net of Religion:

The Gods of the earth and sea
Sought thro' Nature to find this Tree;
But their search was all in vain:
There grows one in the Human Brain.

Chap. IX. 1–25 Cp. F. Z. vi. 250–257.

Appear'd transparent air ; for their eyes
Grew small like the eyes of a man ;
And, in reptile forms shrinking together,
Of seven feet stature they remain'd.

3. Six days they shrunk up from existence,
And on the seventh day they rested,
And they bless'd the seventh day in sick hope,
And forgot their eternal life.

4. And their thirty cities divided
In form of a human heart.
No more could they rise at will
In the infinite void ; but bound down
To earth by their narrowing perceptions,
[18] They livèd a period of years,
Then left a noisom body
To the jaws of devouring darkness.

5. And their children wept, & built
Tombs in the desolate places,
And form'd laws of prudence, and call'd them
The eternal laws of God.

6. And the thirty cities remain'd,
Surrounded by salt floods, now call'd
Africa : its name was then Egypt.

17–20 To Blake the Creation, as described in Genesis, was the expression of a decline in spirituality. As man's powers of vision waned, the apprehension of an infinite and eternal world receded, and the illusion of a finite physical universe took its place, till by the end of the 'sixth day' the memory of the transcendent world of Eternity had been obliterated.

21 Cp. *Tiriel*, § 5. 33–34 :

Thirty of Tiriel's sons remained to wither in the palace,
Desolate, loathed, dumb, astonish'd, waiting for black death.

Tiriel closely resembles Urizen : see *Tiriel*, Introductory Note.

22 Cp. ll. 33–35, from which it would seem that this phrase alludes to the general shape of the African continent. Cp. *Africa*, l. 3, 'heart-form'd Africa.'

34–35 The significance of 'Egypt' is not certain. From ll. 36–48 it would appear to indicate the mortal state of subjection to the metaphysical and ethical delusions whereby the perception of the ideal existence is obscured. Hence the origin of the term may be in the bondage of the Israelites. *The Book of Ahania* carries the matter further, for it mentions a period of five hundred years, during which man received a higher vision from Fuzon, who practically repeats the Orc symbol (B. A., chap. i). It is just possible that in this Blake refers to a tradition which he may have met in Jacob Bryant ; that certain 'Shepherd Kings' conquered Egypt and maintained their dominion therein for five hundred years, during which time they destroyed the temples and altars of the older Egyptian religion. This act might be regarded, in terms of Blake's symbolism, as the triumph of Fuzon over Urizen, of light over darkness.

7. The remaining sons of Urizen
Beheld their brethren shrink together
Beneath the Net of Urizen.
Perswasion was in vain;
For the ears of the inhabitants
Were wither'd & deafen'd & cold,
And their eyes could not discern
Their brethren of other cities.

8. So Fuzon call'd all together
The remaining children of Urizen.
And they left the pendulous earth:
They callèd it Egypt, & left it.

9. And the salt ocean rollèd englob'd.

The End of the
book of Urizen.

44–48 The Fuzon myth, here touched upon, is developed in *The Book of Ahania*, which has been regarded by some, though without much probability, as the Second Book of Urizen.

THE BOOK OF LOS

INTRODUCTORY NOTE

Collation: frontispiece and title-page, 1 plate each; 'Los', 3 plates; 5 plates, etched text.

Like *The Book of Ahania*, the present work is more an apparent than a real supplement to the myth of *The Book of Urizen*. Its first five stanzas, etched in a smaller hand than the body of the poem, seem to be in the nature of a Preludium, such as is found in the other books of this period. The theme is a criticism of conventional morality on the familiar lines, setting it over against what Blake exalted as the antinomianism of the 'times remote' before man fell.

The main myth opens at that point in the history of Urizen when the Eternals depute Los to watch over him, lest he should again attempt to establish his own power (B. U., chap. ii). Here Los has something of the attributes of Fuzon or of Orc: he is the spirit whose fiery energy is set against the deadening influence of the 'primeval Priest' and his 'Religion'. This dualism of energy and restraint is maintained throughout *The Book of Los*: the living 'flames of desire', eternal, intelligent, organized, are contrasted with the coldness, darkness and 'obstruction' of Urizen, and the fierce raging rivers of fire of the first are set against the petrific 'solid' of the other (chap. i, l. 54). A similar opposition is seen when in the wild deep into which Los falls there appear two elements: one, the baser, which is called the 'heavy', and sinks; the other, of apparently superior value, the 'thin', which tends towards the fires of the eternals (chap. iii).

At first the forces of restraint are represented as triumphing; for they shut in the 'clear expanding senses' of the Eternal Prophet, Los, obscuring his perceptions of eternity. But when 'impatience could no longer bear the hard bondage' (chap. ii, ll. 5–6), the 'Prophetic wrath, struggling for vent', burst its prison. From this point difficulties increase for the interpreter. In the first place, Los's breaking away from Urizen's restrictions is not, as might have been expected, the definite beginning of a higher condition of being. On the contrary, Los begins to fall into the 'horrid vacuity' of boundless error, and, stranger still, seems to become identified with 'the falling Mind', an aspect of the symbol not paralleled elsewhere, though it may be taken as affording some ground for the interpretation of part of this early myth in terms of psychology.

The 'falling Mind', after breaking from its prison, first manifests itself in wrath, which, subsiding, is succeeded by 'contemplative thought'. 'Contemplative thought' synchronizes with a modification in existence, of which the symbolic statement is that Los's downward fall becomes oblique. The next stage sees the undefined 'Human', apparently synonymous with Los, 'organized' into 'finite flexible organs', the beginnings of physical sensation. Thus the mind undergoes change until it is so far adapted to its new environment as to be able to traverse at will the 'abyss' or horrid vacuity of error. In this there may be implied the principle that objects of sense-perception have no inherent validity, being but illusions created by the physical organs supervening upon and distorting the pure visions of the immortal mind. But it is impossible to feel certainty as to whether Blake also intended that the changes in the falling Los are to be taken as indicating a regenerative purpose. Reading this episode in the light of the books of the post-Lambeth period, one can discern therein something that looks like an intention to attribute a value to the phenomena succeeding Los's fall ; but there is not evidence in the Lambeth books themselves to establish this interpretation.

In the third chapter the processes of change continue. First the lungs appear, and from them is developed a 'fibrous form' wherein Los exists, as it were a 'polypus' in 'a vast world of waters'. All these expressions appear in the post-Lambeth books in association with the symbols of error, though it would be dangerous to say that the later meaning is intended here. What is perhaps the most decisive indication that this continual modification of the state of the fallen Los marks an improvement of spiritual conditions, is that at this point, by a definite act and for the first time since Urizen's succession, Los makes distinction between the two elements in the new world, between the 'heavy' which is of Urizen, and the 'thin' that has affinity with the quickening fires of eternals. Further, the 'thin' becomes the pure medium through which Light first manifests itself. At the same time, there appears in opposition to the Light, the Backbone of Urizen, an obscure expression, except in so far as it may be related to the commoner serpent symbol (see Index, *Serpent*).

The continuation of the conflict between the adverse powers Los and Urizen is full of doubtful points. Los concentrates his energies into 'a form of strength' and enters upon his characteristic labours at the furnaces and anvil. First he forms the light into an Orb, the sun (chap. iv, l. 35), a 'glowing illusion'. To this he binds the 'spine of Urizen', whose 'Brain' and 'Heart' ultimately become the sources of four rivers that obscure the 'Orb of fire' and so give rise to the 'Human Illusion'. There is evidently an intention in the contrasting of Los's 'glowing Illusion' and the 'Human Illusion' that is due to Urizen's influence. Neither represents a perfect vision, but that of Los is nearer to truth than Urizen's, which may perhaps be comparable with the body of error whose root is in the 'Human Brain' (cp. S. E., Clar. Press, p. 134, 'The Human Abstract').

Such is a brief summary of a book which it is difficult to epitomize and impossible to interpret. Its symbolism would seem to be, in its details, purely tentative, for Blake nowhere repeats its most characteristic features in any recognizable form.

THE

BOOK OF LOS

LAMBETH.
Printed by W. Blake, 1795.

[1]

LOS

Chap. I

1. *Eno, agèd Mother,*
Who the chariot of Leutha guides
Since the day of thunders in old time,

2. *Sitting beneath the eternal Oak,*
Trembled and shook the stedfast Earth ;
And thus her speech broke forth :

3. ‘ *O Times remote !*
When Love & Joy were adoration,
And none impure were deem'd,
Not Eyeless Covet,
Nor Thin-lip'd Envy,
Nor Bristled Wrath,
Nor Curlèd Wantonness.

4. ‘ *But Covet was pourèd full,*
Envy fed with fat of lambs,
Wrath with lion's gore,
Wantonness lull'd to sleep
With the virgin's lute
Or sated with her love :

5. ‘ *Till Covet broke his locks & bars,*
And slept with open doors ;
Envy sung at the rich man's feast ;
Wrath was follow'd up and down
By a little ewe lamb ;
And Wantonness on his own true love
Begot a giant race.’

1–26 These lines, etched in a slightly smaller hand than the rest of the book and separated from stanza 6 foll. by a wavy line, correspond to the Preludiums in *America* or *Europe*. Their subject is the pre-mundane state when

The will of the Immortal expanded
Or contracted his all flexible senses.
Death was not, but eternal life sprung. (B. U. ii. 2–4.)

Eno the ‘ aged Mother ’ is referred to, F. Z. i. 1 : ‘ The Song of the Aged Mother which shook the heavens with wrath.’ She is mentioned by name, as a Daughter of Beulah (F. Z. i. 133–143, and see Index, *Erin*). But the significance in this passage does not appear in either of the others.

6. Raging furious, the flames of desire
Ran thro' heaven & earth, living flames,
Intelligent, organiz'd, arm'd
With destruction & plagues. In the midst
The Eternal Prophet, bound in a chain,
Compell'd to watch Urizen's shadow,

7. Rag'd with curses & sparkles of fury.
Round the flames roll, as Los hurls his chains,
Mounting up from his fury, condens'd,
Rolling round & round, mounting on high
Into vacuum, into non-entity,
Where nothing was ; dash'd wide apart,
His feet stamp the eternal fierce-raging
Rivers of wide flame ; they roll round
And round on all sides, making their way
Into darkness and shadowy obscurity.

8. Wide apart stood the fires : Los remain'd
In the void between fire and fire ;
In trembling and horror they beheld him ;
They stood wide apart, driv'n by his hands
And his feet, which the nether abyss
Stamp'd in fury and hot indignation.

9. But no light from the fires : all was
[2] Darkness round Los : heat was not ; for bound up
Into fiery spheres from his fury,
The gigantic flames trembled and hid.

10. Coldness, darkness, obstruction, a Solid
Without fluctuation, hard as adamant,
Black as marble of Egypt, impenetrable,
Bound in the fierce raging Immortal ;
And the seperated fires, froze in
A vast solid without fluctuation,
Bound in his expanding clear senses.

Chap. II

1. The Immortal stood frozen amidst
The vast rock of eternity times
And times, a night of vast durance,
Impatient, stifled, stiffen'd, hard'ned ;

27–59 Cp. B. U., chap. ii. 21–50.

2. Till impatience no longer could bear
The hard bondage: rent, rent the vast solid
With a crash from immense to immense,

3. Crack'd across into numberless fragments.
The Prophetic wrath, strug[g]ling for vent,
Hurls apart, stamping furious to dust,
And crumbling with bursting sobs: heaves
The black marble on high into fragments.

4. Hurl'd apart on all sides as a falling
Rock, the innumerable fragments away
Fell asunder; and horrible vacuum
Beneath him & on all sides round.

5. Falling, falling, Los fell & fell,
Sunk precipitant, heavy, down, down,
Times on times, night on night, day on day—
Truth has bounds, Error none—falling, falling,
Years on years and ages on ages.
Still he fell thro' the void, still a void
Found for falling, day & night without end;
For tho' day or night was not, their spaces
Were measur'd by his incessant whirls
In the horrid vacuity bottomless.

6. The Immortal revolving, indignant,
First in wrath threw his limbs like the babe
New born into our world: wrath subsided,
And contemplative thoughts first arose.
Then aloft his head rear'd in the Abyss,
And his downward borne fall chang'd oblique.

7. Many ages of groans, till there grew
Branchy forms, organizing the Human
Into finite inflexible organs;

8. Till in process from falling he bore
Sidelong on the purple air, wafting
The weak breeze in efforts o'erwearied.

Chap. II. 6 and 11 The punctuation is Blake: his intention eludes us.

20 Later this same statement is expressed symbolically by the attribution of definiteness, in 'form' or 'outline', to truth, either as a whole, or in its parts, the 'minute particulars' (see Index, *Minute Particulars*); whereas the symbols representing the sources or the manifestations of error are 'formless' and 'indefinite'.

24–26 For this reference to the function of Los as Time cp. B. U., chap. iv *a*, ll. 9–10 and 15–18.

9. Incessant the falling Mind labour'd,
Organizing itself till the Vacuum
Became element, pliant to rise,
Or to fall, or to swim, or to fly,
With ease searching the dire vacuity.

Chap. III

1. The Lungs heave incessant, dull and heavy ;
For as yet were all other parts formless,
Shiv'ring, clinging around like a cloud,
Dim & glutinous as the white Polypus
Driv'n by waves & englob'd on the tide.

2. And the unformèd part crav'd repose.
Sleep began ; the Lungs heave on the wave.
Weary, overweigh'd, sinking beneath
In a stifling black fluid, he woke.

3. He arose on the waters ; but soon
Heavy falling, his organs like roots
Shooting out from the seed, shot beneath ;
And a vast world of waters around him
In furious torrents began.

4. Then he sunk, & around his spent Lungs
Began intricate pipes that drew in
The spawn of the waters. Outbranching
[3] An immense Fibrous form stretching out
Thro' the bottoms of immensity, raging,

5. He rose on the floods : then he smote
The wild deep with his terrible wrath,
Seperating the heavy and thin.

Chap. III. 4 The Polypus, here used in simile, becomes in the later book a symbol of the whole body of error : see Index, *Mundane Shell*, Note I, B.
20–26 Cp. *Paradise Lost*, vii. 232–242 :

Thus God the Heaven created, thus the Earth,
Matter unform'd and void. Darkness profound
Covered the Abyss ; but on the watery calm
His brooding wings the Spirit of God outspread,
And vital virtue infused, and vital warmth,
Throughout the fluid mass, but downward purged
The black, tartareous, cold, infernal dregs,
Adverse to life : then founded, then conglobed,
Like things to like, the rest to several place
Disparted, and between spun out the Air,
And Earth, self-balanced, on her centre hung.

'n the heavy sunk, cleaving around
agments of solid ; up rose
., flowing round the fierce fires
ow'd furious in the expanse.

Chap. IV

Then Light first began ; from the fires,
Beams, conducted by fluid so pure,
Flow'd around the Immense. Los beheld
Forthwith, writhing upon the dark void,
The Back bone of Urizen appear
Hurtling upon the wind
Like a serpent, like an iron chain
Whirling about in the Deep.

2. Upfolding his Fibres together
To a Form of impregnable strength,
Los, astonish'd and terrified, built
Furnaces ; he formèd an Anvil,
A Hammer of adamant : then began
The binding of Urizen day and night.

3. Circling round the dark Demon with howlings,
Dismay & sharp blightings, the Prophet
Of Eternity beat on his iron links.

4. And first from those infinite fires
The light that flow'd down on the winds
He siez'd, beating incessant, condensing
The subtil particles in an Orb.

5. Roaring indignant, the bright sparks
Endur'd the vast Hammer ; but unwearied,
Los beat on the Anvil, till glorious
An immense Orb of fire he fram'd.

Chap. IV. 2 The 'fluid' is apparently the obscure 'thin' medium mentioned above, chap. iii. 25–26.

12–13 See Index, *Furnaces*, &c. 14 Cp. B. U. iv, *passim.*

21 The Orb is the Sun (l. 35), frequently associated with Los. The significance of the connexion is not always clear : cp. M. 20. 6–8 : and *Poems from Letters*, iv. 55–58 (Clar. Press, p. 307) :

> Then Los appear'd in all his power :
> In the Sun he appear'd, descending before
> My face in fierce flames ; in my double sight
> 'Twas outward a Sun, inward Los in his might.

It has been suggested that Los is an anagram of the Latin 'sol'.

6. Oft he quench'd it beneath in the Deeps,
Then survey'd the all bright mass. Again
Siezing fires from the terrific Orbs,
He heated the round Globe, then beat;
While, roaring, his Furnaces endur'd
The chain'd Orb in their infinite wombs.

7. Nine ages completed their circles
When Los heated the glowing mass, casting
It down into the Deeps: the Deeps fled
Away in redounding smoke; the Sun
Stood self-balanc'd. And Los smil'd with joy.
He the vast Spine of Urizen siez'd,
And bound down to the glowing illusion.

8. But no light; for the Deep fled away
On all sides, and left an unform'd
Dark vacuity: here Urizen lay
In fierce torments on his glowing bed;

9. Till his Brain in a rock, & his Heart
In a fleshy slough, formèd four rivers,
Obscuring the immense Orb of fire,
Flowing down into night; till a Form
Was completed, a Human Illusion,
In darkness and deep clouds involv'd.

The End of the
Book of Los.

4 Cp. *Europe*, 94–101.

AHANIA

INTRODUCTORY NOTE

Collation: title-page 1 plate, "Ahania" 4 plates; 5 plates, etched text, about $5\frac{3}{8} \times 3\frac{7}{8}$ inches.

In his commentary on *The Book of Ahania* Swinburne writes: 'This we may take—or those may who please—to be the *Second Book of Urizen*' (*Essay*, p. 249). Against this suggestion may be set the fact that it does not take up the main theme of the concluding sections of the earlier work, the myth of Los, Enitharmon, and Orc, but develops what seems to be, in relation to the whole body of Blake's symbolism, an incident of secondary importance mentioned in the last chapter of *The Book of Urizen*, namely, the secession of Fuzon and those of his brethren who were not 'bound down to earth' by 'narrowing perceptions' (B. U. ix. 24–25). These leave the 'pendulous earth', called 'Egypt', to those other sons of Urizen who have become the slaves of their father's repressive 'Religion'.

In the opening chapter of this work Fuzon declares open war against Urizen, whose iron laws none can keep and live. The myth traces the course of the conflict, which, in its various phases, is reflected in mundane history. Fuzon, the fiery spirit of wrath, young and beautiful, whose tresses 'gave light to the mornings of heaven', is hardly distinguishable from Orc, except that he is not born of woman (cp. B. U., chap. viii, ll. 13 foll.); nor is there anything to suggest that his rebellion differs essentially from Orc's. This practical identity may explain the fact that the Fuzon myth does not recur.

To continue the story: the rebel son launches against his adversary his globe of wrath, which, lengthening into a pillar of fire, cleaves the 'disk' Urizen opposes to it, and divides his 'cold loins'. This triumph of the anarchical principle in Fuzon is accompanied by, if it is not the cause of, the separation from Urizen of Ahania, who is called 'Sin' and 'the mother of pestilence'.

For a space of five hundred years Fuzon's pillar of fire gives light to the dwellers in 'Egypt', till it is mysteriously taken up into the body of the Sun. Meanwhile Urizen prepares a poisoned rock that, projected from his 'black bow', overwhelms Fuzon and falls to earth, to be known as Mount Sinai. In this chapter the curious and partially obscure symbolic 'Serpent' appears. It is bred from the 'unnatural productions' of Urizen's 'dire contemplations' and is slain by the power that begot it. From its bones the bow is formed, and its blood, the 'poisonous Source' of the code of penal morality, is smeared upon the rock that overwhelms Fuzon. In the earlier poems of the Rossetti MS. the Serpent symbolizes the defiling influence of priests and priestcraft; and later it images the body of error called 'Natural Religion'. But in the present passage something further, which has so far eluded discovery, would seem to be implied.

The body of the vanquished rebel is nailed to the topmost bough of 'The Tree of Mystery', a symbolic statement of the bondage of energy, the eternal fires of youth, beneath the cold restrictive tyranny of the Urizenic law. The powers of repression triumph in all forms of spiritual, and possibly of bodily, disease, bred from Urizen's atrophied 'nerves of joy' and from the stagnation of 'unacted desires'. For forty years the children of Urizen, in bondage in the 'thirty cities' of 'Egypt' and in the wilderness of moral law endure these torments, with the consequence that they shrink to the mental and corporeal stature of mortal men, and the state of civil and religious tyranny symbolized by 'Asia' commences. The final chapter contains the lamentation of Ahania over Urizen's fall from his primal state. Although Ahania appears frequently in *The Four Zoas*, no adequate interpretation has been found possible. All that can be said will be found in the notes to the present poem and in the Index under *Ahania*.

The following attempt at an interpretation of the central episode of the myth is offered with hesitation. Ahania, severed from Urizen by the flaming hungry beam of Fuzon, i. e. by a single assault of vehement passion, reveals that cessation of harmonious co-operation between intellect and emotion that follows from insistence on 'self-hood' (see B. U., Introductory Note). Urizen, who is Intellect (see Index, *Urizen*), sees his counterpart isolated and revealed as Sin. Without the force that is of the mind the Emotions are shadowy, 'unbodied', 'the mother of pestilence', a phrase that seems to be critical of the unwholesomeness of the purely and exclusively emotional life, such a condition being conceived as possible. Conversely, Intellect unsoftened by Emotion manifests itself in the destructive cruelty of the bow, the nailing on the Tree, in acts rising in climax to the promulgation of the moral law with its plagues and penalties. Spiritual constriction and blindness afflict men until 'they reptilize upon the earth'.

So we see in the myth a restatement in new symbols of Blake's criticism of the God of the Jews and of Christian orthodoxy. What may perhaps be termed the emotional attributes of the anthropomorphically conceived God, Mercy, Pity, Love, are denied in the severance of Ahania from Urizen. The God who conceived the Laws of Sinai and demanded the sacrifice of the Son as the price of atonement is no Being of Mercy and Love, but a monster cruel and destructive.

The catchwords 'Of' and 'But' are found on pp. 3 and 4 respectively.

THE

BOOK of

AHANIA

LAMBETH
Printed by W. Blake 1789

[2]

AHANIA

Chap: Ist

1. FUZON, on a chariot iron-wing'd,
On spikèd flames rose ; his hot visage
Flam'd furious ; sparkles his hair & beard
Shot down his wide bosom and shoulders.
On clouds of smoke rages his chariot ;
And his right hand burns red in its cloud,
Moulding into a vast globe his wrath
As the thunder-stone is moulded,
Son of Urizen's silent burnings.

2. ' Shall we worship this Demon of smoke '
Said Fuzon, ' this abstract non-entity,
This cloudy God seated on waters,
Now seen, now obscur'd, King of sorrow ?'

3. So he spoke in a fiery flame,
On Urizen frowning indignant,
The Globe of wrath shaking on high.
Roaring with fury, he threw
The howling Globe ; burning it flew,
Length'ning into a hungry beam. Swiftly

4. Oppos'd to the exulting flam'd beam,
The broad Disk of Urizen upheav'd
Across the Void many a mile.

5. It was forg'd in mills where the winter
Beats incessant : ten winters the disk
Unremitting endur'd the cold hammer.

6. But the strong arm that sent it remember'd
The sounding beam : laughing it tore through
That beaten mass, keeping its direction,
The cold loins of Urizen dividing.

9 Cp. B. U., chap. viii, l. 22 seq. Fuzon is the son of Urizen, born of Fire.
21 'The broad Disk of Urizen' is not interpreted. It apparently differs from the 'globe of fire' (B. U., chap. viii. 1–3) and from the 'immense Orb of fire' (B. L., chap. iv. 45).
22 Cp. B. U., Preludium, 1–4.
29–37 See Introductory Note and cp. V. D. A. *passim*.

7. Dire shriek'd his invisible Lust.
Deep groan'd Urizen : stretching his awful hand,
Ahania (so name his parted soul)
He siez'd on his mountains of Jealousy.
He groan'd, anguish'd, & callèd her Sin,
Kissing her and weeping over her ;
Then hid her in darkness, in silence,
Jealous tho' she was invisible.

8. She fell down, a faint shadow wand'ring
In chaos, and circling dark Urizen
As the moon, anguish'd, circles the earth,
Hopeless, abhorr'd, a death-shadow,
Unseen, unbodied, unknown,
The mother of Pestilence.

9. But the fiery beam of Fuzon
Was a pillar of fire to Egypt
Five hundred years, wand'ring on earth
Till Los siez'd it and beat in a mass
With the body of the sun.

Chap: II^{d}

[3] 1. But the forehead of Urizen gathering,
And his eyes pale with anguish, his lips
Blue & changing, in tears and bitter
Contrition he prepar'd his Bow

2. Form'd of Ribs that in his dark solitude,
When obscur'd in his forests, fell monsters
Arose. For his dire Contemplations
Rush'd down like floods from his mountains,
In torrents of mud settling thick
With Eggs of unnatural production :
Forthwith hatching, some howl'd on his hills,
Some in vales, some aloft flew in air.

3. Of these, an enormous dread Serpent,
Scalèd and poisonous, hornèd,
Approach'd Urizen even to his knees
As he sat on his dark rooted Oak.

43 See Index, *Ahania.*
44–48 Cp. B. U., chap. ix. 39–43. Los here appears as the Time-spirit the arbiter of mundane existence.
45 See B. U., chap. ix, ll. 34–35 *note.*

4. With his horns he push'd furious :
Great the conflict & great the jealousy
In cold poisons ; but Urizen smote him.

5. First he poison'd the rocks with his blood,
Then polish'd his ribs, and his sinews
Dried, laid them apart till winter ;
Then a Bow black prepar'd ; on this Bow
A poisonèd rock plac'd in silence.
He utter'd these words to the Bow :

6. ' O Bow of the clouds of secresy !
O nerve of that lust form'd monster !
Send this rock swift, invisible, thro'
The black clouds on the bosom of Fuzon.'

7. So saying, In torment of his wounds
He bent the enormous ribs slowly,
A circle of darkness ; then fixèd
The sinew in its rest ; then the Rock,
Poisonous source, plac'd with art, lifting difficult
Its weighty bulk : silent the rock lay,

8. While Fuzon, his tygers unloosing,
Thought Urizen slain by his wrath.
' I am God,' said he, ' eldest of things.'

9. Sudden sings the rock ; swift & invisible
On Fuzon flew, enter'd his bosom ;
His beautiful visage, his tresses
That gave light to the mornings of heaven,
Were smitten with darkness, deform'd
And outstretch'd on the edge of the forest.

10. But the rock fell upon the Earth
Mount Sinai in Arabia.

Chap. II. 26 Secrecy and modesty, or virtue according to common ethical standards, are to Blake inseparable from spiritual corruption. Cp. V. D. A. 156–197 and Ross. MS. xvii (Clar. Press, p. 169) :

Deceit to secresy confin'd,
Lawful, cautious & refin'd, [' modest, prudish & confin'd ' *1st rdg.*]
To any thing but interest blind
And forges fetters for the mind.

36 Cp. M. H. H., proverb 44 : ' The tygers of wrath are wiser than the horses of instruction.'

Chap: III

1. The Globe shook, and Urizen, seated
On black clouds, his sore wound anointed.
The ointment flow'd down on the void
Mix'd with blood: here the snake gets her poison.

2. With difficulty & great pain Urizen
Lifted on high the dead corse:
On his shoulders he bore it to where
A Tree hung over the Immensity.

3. For when Urizen shrunk away
From Eternals, he sat on a rock
Barren, a rock which himself
From redounding fancies had petrified.
Many tears fell on the rock,
Many sparks of vegetation.
Soon shot the painèd root
Of Mystery under his heel:
It grew a thick tree: he wrote
In silence his book of iron,
Till the horrid plant, bending its boughs,
Grew to roots when it felt the earth,
And again sprung to many a tree.

4. Amaz'd started Urizen when
He beheld himself compassèd round
And high roofèd over with trees.
He arose, but the stems stood so thick,
He with difficulty and great pain
Brought his Books, all but the Book
[4] Of iron, from the dismal shade.

5. The Tree still grows over the Void,
Enrooting itself all around,
An endless labyrinth of woe.

6. The corse of his first begotten
On the accursèd Tree of Mystery,
On the topmost stem of this Tree,
Urizen nail'd Fuzon's corse.

Chap. III 2 anointed] anointel in Blake's autotype.
8 See Index, *Mundane Shell, Note II* (1).
9–28 Cp. F. Z. vii. 31–41, and *Europe*, 96 *note*.
15–31 Cp. J. 28. 13–19, where this tree is called ' Moral Virtue, and the Law of God who dwells in Chaos hidden from the human sight '.
27–28 Cp. B. U., chap. ii, l. 33 *note*; and Index, *Mundane Shell, Note I* (*b*).

Chap: IV

1. Forth flew the arrows of pestilence
Round the pale living Corse on the tree.

2. For in Urizen's slumbers of abstraction,
In the infinite ages of Eternity,
When his Nerves of Joy melted & flow'd
A white Lake on the dark blue air,
In perturb'd pain and dismal torment
Now stretching out, now swift conglobing,

3. Effluvia vapor'd above
In noxious clouds; these hover'd thick
Over the disorganiz'd Immortal,
Till petrific pain scurf'd o'er the Lakes
As the bones of man, solid & dark.

4. The clouds of disease hover'd wide
Around the Immortal in torment,
Perching around the hurtling bones,
Disease on disease, shape on shape,
Wingèd, screaming in blood & torment.

5. The Eternal Prophet beat on his anvils,
Enrag'd in the desolate darkness:
He forg'd nets of iron around,
And Los threw them around the bones.

6. The shapes, screaming, flutter'd vain.
Some combin'd into muscles & glands,
Some organs for craving and lust;
Most remain'd on the tormented void,
Urizen's army of horrors.

7. Round the pale living Corse on the Tree
Forty years flew the arrows of pestilence.

8. Wailing and terror and woe
Ran thro' all his dismal world.
Forty years all his sons & daughters

Chap. IV. 2–27 Cp. B. U., chap. iv *a*, *passim*.

3 This apparently refers to the period immediately preceding Urizen's separation from Eternity, when as yet 'Earth was not'.

5–8 Cp. B. U. iv *a*, 19–23 *note*. 19–22 Cp. B. U., chap. iv.

29 The forty years may originate in the wanderings of the Israelites: Blake frequently represents the spiritual desolation that comes of the triumph of moral law as a wilderness.

Felt their skulls harden ; then Asia
Arose in the pendulous deep.

9. They reptilize upon the Earth.

10. Fuzon groan'd on the Tree.

Chap: V

1. The lamenting voice of Ahania,
Weeping upon the void
And round the Tree of Fuzon !
Distant in solitary night
Her voice was heard, but no form
Had she ; but her tears from clouds
Eternal fell round the Tree.

2. And the voice cried : ' Ah, Urizen ! Love !
Flower of morning ! I weep on the verge
Of Non-entity ! how wide the Abyss
Between Ahania and thee !

3. ' I lie on the verge of the deep ;
I see thy dark clouds ascend ;
I see thy black forests and floods,
A horrible waste to my eyes !

4. ' Weeping I walk over rocks,
Over dens, & thro' valleys of death.
Why did'st thou despise Ahania,
To cast me from thy bright presence
Into the World of Loneness ?

5. ' I cannot touch his hand,
Nor weep on his knees, nor hear
His voice & bow, nor see his eyes
And joy ; nor hear his footsteps, and
My heart leap at the lovely sound.
I cannot kiss the place
Whereon his bright feet have trod ;
[5] But I wander on the rocks
With hard necessity.

33 Cp. S. L., Introductory Note.
35 The serpent or worm-form is the common symbol of man in a state of subjection to the delusions of corporeity and morality. Cp. B. U., chap. ix. 1–32.
Chap. V. 10 Non-entity or Non-existence, see Index, *Ulro*. With the whole of this chapter cp. F. Z. iii. 26–37 : v. 190–217 : and viii. 481–520.

6. ‘Where is my golden palace?
Where my ivory bed?
Where the joy of my morning hour?
Where the sons of eternity singing

7. ‘To awake bright Urizen, my king,
To arise to the mountain sport,
To the bliss of eternal valleys;

8. ‘To awake my king in the morn
To embrace Ahania's joy
On the bredth of his open bosom,
From my soft cloud of dew to fall
In showers of life on his harvests?

9. ‘When he gave my happy soul
To the sons of eternal joy;
When he took the daughters of life
Into my chambers of love;

10. ‘When I found babes of bliss on my beds
And bosoms of milk in my chambers
Fill'd with eternal seed,
O! eternal births sung round Ahania,
In interchange sweet of their joys!

11. ‘Swell'd with ripeness & fat with fatness,
Bursting on winds, my odors,
My ripe figs and rich pomegranates
In infant joy at thy feet,
O Urizen, sported and sang.

12. ‘Then thou with thy lap full of seed,
With thy hand full of generous fire,
Walkèd forth from the clouds of morning,
On the virgins of springing joy,
On the human soul to cast
The seed of eternal science.

13. ‘The sweat pourèd down thy temples
To Ahania return'd in evening;
The moisture awoke to birth
My mother's-joys, sleeping in bliss.

55–61 Cp. F. Z. ix 314–341.

14. ' But now alone over rocks, mountains,
Cast out from thy lovely bosom !
Cruel jealousy, selfish fear,
Self-destroying, how can delight
Renew in these chains of darkness,
Where bones of beasts are strown
On the bleak and snowy mountains,
Where bones from the birth are buried
Before they see the light ?'

FINIS

66–70 Cp. ' Earth's Answer ' (S. E., Clar. Press, p. 107) :

Earth rais'd up her head
From the darkness dread & drear.
Her light fled,
Stony dread.
And her locks cover'd with grey despair.

' Prison'd on wat'ry shore,
Starry Jealousy does keep my den :
Cold and hoar,
Weeping o'er,
I hear the father of the ancient men.

' Selfish father of men !
Cruel, jealous, selfish fear !
Can delight,
Chain'd in night,
The virgins of youth and morning bear ?

' Does spring hide its joy,
When buds and blossoms grow ?
Does the sower
Sow by night,
Or the ploughman in darkness plough ?

' Break this heavy chain,
That does freeze my bones around.
Selfish ! vain !
Eternal bane !
That free Love with bondage bound.'

THE SONG OF LOS

INTRODUCTORY NOTE

Collation: title-page 1 plate, *Africa* 2 plates, *Asia* 2 plates, three full-page illustrations variously arranged in different copies; 8 plates, relief engraving, about 9 × 6⅞ inches.

The Song of Los is divided into two parts, *Africa* and *Asia*. The significance of the former title is not clear. 'The deserts of Africa' (*Africa*, l. 51) are the place of the 'Fallen Angels', apparently Los and his fellows (*ibid.*, ll. 1–4). The symbol first occurs in the *Book of Urizen* (chap. ix, l. 35), where it represents the state of those children of Urizen who beneath the 'net of Religion' have diminished in spiritual stature till they have fallen to the low estate of mundane life, shut out from eternity and enslaved to 'laws of prudence' that they call the 'Eternal laws of God'. The cities they inhabit conjoin 'into the form of a heart' (B U. ix, l. 20) now called 'Africa', though formerly known as 'Egypt' (*ibid.*, l. 35), wherein there is probably a reference to the 'house of bondage'. It is impossible to interpret these names with certainty, though it seems that they have reference to different stages of mundane experience. Later in *Jerusalem* (45. 19–23) there is an allusion to a myth, not developed elsewhere, wherein Africa appears to be one of 'the Sons of God in Eternity' into whose company regenerated mankind ultimately returns.

Asia is a common symbol. Throughout the prophetic books it is associated with the state of error, chiefly, though perhaps not exclusively, on its moral side. Its adoption would appear to be due to the fact that most of the great systems of philosophy and religion took their rise within its borders. In *Milton* and *Jerusalem* the 'Twelve Gods of Asia', at once the source and the symbol of all that Blake condemned in life and art as being 'opposed to the Divine Vision' (J. 50. 1–3), are sometimes combined into a single symbol, Satan the Spectre, or the 'Polypus of Death' (see Index, s.v.).

The first section tells how that after the 'golden age' of innocence and liberty, of Adam in Paradise, of Noah before the Flood, and of the African not yet in his nigritude, Urizen imposed his 'Laws and Religion' upon man 'by the hands of the children of Los' or Time; that is to say, temporal existence is definitely connected with the triumph of restrictive morality. But in the present myth Blake again modifies his story of the 'Fall' by the introduction of Har and Heva, personages who appear only in this work and in *Tiriel*. In *Tiriel* is attributed to them the authorship of the code of restrictive morality by means of which Tiriel destroys his children; here they are represented as the first parents of the human race (l. 20), and as fleeing in terror from 'War and Lust' (ll. 36–48), names by which prudential morality condemns the free spirit's exercise of unrestricted energy. Their loss of spiritual stature, the atrophy of vision whereby

all the vast of Nature shrunk
Before their shrunken eyes (ll. 42–43)

is the result of their timid resort to legal codes as a protection against the energy of free souls. It is over this world of 'slave-morality' that Urizen reigns as God, with Time and his children as his ministers.

The Song of Los

Here, as in *The Four Zoas* (Night VI), Urizen is represented as endeavouring to re-establish by laws that state of wisdom and joy of which the condition is pure liberty. This leads up to the main point of the poem, Blake's criticism of the successive philosophic or religious systems by which Urizen sought to accomplish his design. 'Brama', Moses, Trismegistus, Pythagoras, Socrates and Plato are in turn made the prophets of doctrines which fail of their purpose. Then comes Jesus, and it is here that Blake has recorded most clearly his estimate of Christianity at this time. Its ultimate derivation from Urizen plainly implies a general condemnation, while the statement that is transmitted to Jesus through Theotormon, the wretched victim of moral fears (see V. D. A., Introductory Note), emphasizes the more particular criticism of its ascetic teaching. This is still more strongly stressed in the account of its outcome in existence :

> The human race began to wither, for the healthy built
> Secluded places, fearing the joys of love ;
> And the diseased only propagated. (*Africa*, ll. 25–27.)

Therefore, to counteract this destructive tendency, another son of Los, Antamon, 'to Mahomet a loose Bible gave'. Then Blake sees all these systems taken up into a single 'Philosophy of the Five Senses', which Urizen himself gave into the hands of Newton and Locke : these, with Bacon, are constant symbols throughout the prophetic books of the evils in thought and morality that follow from reliance on the witness of the senses. Finally the old Gods die and Deism takes their place, its exponents being Voltaire and Rousseau, who in *Milton* and *Jerusalem* are joined in the same condemnation with the English philosophers just mentioned. But already sounds of the coming revolution are heard, and there may be some significance in the fact that the closing line of *Africa* is identical with the first line of *America*.

In the second section, *Asia*, the powers of civil and religious tyranny, alarmed at the indications of change, seek to strengthen their hold upon power by reasserting the doctrine of divine right. Urizen descends at this critical moment, as in *America* :

> drawing clouds of despair thro' the heavens
> Of Europe as he went.

Orc, bound till now, rises against him, and, as in Ezekiel's vision, the dry bones of man's mortality begin to reassume their former beauty and fullness of life, and the influx of 'wild desire' transforms 'the Grave', the place of man's mundane 'sleep of death' into a universe of joy and gladness.

This is the last book in which Blake makes Orc the symbol of man's ultimate regeneration, of salvation by revolt. From this time a change, equivocal in the earlier written parts of *The Four Zoas*, clear in its later revisions and in *Milton*, takes place in the treatment of the symbol, till in *Milton* (p. 28, l. 34) he is identified with Satan, who is in the later writings what Urizen is in the Lambeth books. It would seem that Blake, like many of his contemporaries, lost his first enthusiasm for the French Revolution : in his case this was due, in part at least, to its association with Rationalism, which was always for him the great evil, but was seen more and more clearly to be so, as his new philosophy of the saving Imagination took shape in a reinterpreted Christianity.

THE

SONG of LOS

Lambeth Printed by W. Blake 1795

[1]

AFRICA

I will sing you a song of Los, the Eternal Prophet.
He sung it to four harps at the tables of Eternity,
In heart-formed Africa.
Urizen faded! Ariston shudder'd!
And thus the Song began:

Adam stood in the garden of Eden,
And Noah on the mountains of Ararat;
They saw Urizen give his Laws to the Nations
By the hands of the children of Los.

Adam shudder'd, Noah faded, black grew the sunny African
When Rintrah gave Abstract Philosophy to Brama in the East.
(Night spoke to the Cloud:
'Lo! these Human form'd spirits, in smiling hipocrisy, War
Against one another; so let them War on, slaves to the eternal Elements')
Noah shrunk beneath the waters;
Abram fled in fires from Chaldea;
Moses beheld upon Mount Sinai forms of dark delusion.

1–5 These introductory lines are engraved in roman characters, the body of the *Song* being in italic.

1 Los in the Lambeth books seems to have little of the 'prophetic' and regenerative significance found in the later use of the symbol. In these earlier works he is of the 'Fallen Angels' (cp. l. 51) or sometimes the Time-Spirit: the fuller sense of the symbol does not clearly appear till the added parts of *The Four Zoas*, Nights VII and VIII. Yet even in the Lambeth books there are vague and intermittent suggestions of this higher significance.

2 Cp. F. Z. ix. 615–644.

4 The 'fading' of Urizen may portend the imminent overthrow of his dominion. The reference to Ariston is obscure. From *America* (ll. 107–112) he would seem to be one of the spirits dwelling in light, but this does not help to explain the present passage.

11 Rintrah, Palamabron (l. 18), Theotormon (l. 24), Antamon (l. 28), and Sotha (l. 30) are 'sons of Los', whose function, as represented in the Lambeth books, is diametrically opposed to that ascribed to them in the later writings. Here and in *Europe* they are the ministers of Urizen or of Enitharmon, and serve them by imposing the bondage of morality and the illusions of sense-perception upon mortals. In *The Four Zoas* and the later books they assist Los in his work of regeneration.

To Trismegistus Palamabron gave an abstract Law;
To Pythagoras, Socrates & Plato.

Times rolled on o'er all the sons of Har: time after time
Orc on Mount Atlas howl'd, chain'd down with the Chain of Jealousy.
Then Oothoon hover'd over Judah & Jerusalem,
And Jesus heard her voice (a man of sorrows); he reciev'd
A Gospel from wretched Theotormon.

The human race began to wither, for the healthy built
Secluded places, fearing the joys of Love;
And the diseasèd only propagated.
So Antamon call'd up Leutha from her valleys of delight,
And to Mahomet a loose Bible gave.

But in the North to Odin Sotha gave a Code of War,
Because of Diralada, thinking to reclaim his joy.

[2] These were the Churches, Hospitals, Castles, Palaces,
Like nets & gins & traps to catch the joys of Eternity;
And all the rest a desart,
Till like a dream Eternity was obliterated & erasèd,
Since that dread day when Har and Heva fled
Because their brethren & sisters liv'd in War and Lust:
And, as they fled, they shrunk
Into two narrow doleful forms
Creeping in reptile flesh upon
The bosom of the ground;
And all the vast of Nature shrunk
Before their shrunken eyes.

18 Trismegistus, cp. J. 91. 32–35, where the 'Smaragdine Table of Hermes' is associated with the anti-visionary activities.

20 Here, as in l. 45, the Sons of Har appear to signify mortal men.

21 The mountain to which Orc is bound is not identified elsewhere.

22 Oothoon] cp. V. D. A., Introductory Note.

23–29 See Introductory Note.

23 In the light of Blake's exaltation of joy as the criterion of conduct the pointed use of the phrase 'man of sorrows' definitely places Jesus and his Gospel among the reprobated repressive influences.

24 Theotormon is the timorous victim of moral scruples in the *Visions*.

28 For Leutha cp. V. D. A., Introductory Note.

29 This seemingly higher valuation of Mohammedanism is based on its less ascetic doctrine on the relation of the sexes.

31 Diralada may be Thiralatha: cp. *Europe*, 187.

32–35 Cp. B. U., chap. iv. 7 *note*.

36 For Har and Heva cp. *Tiriel*, Introductory Note. There appears to be an allusion to a myth not extant.

38 Cp. *Tiriel*, § 8. 9–11:

Why is one law given to the lion and the patient ox?
And why men bound beneath the heavens in a reptile form,
A worm of sixty winters, creeping on the dusty ground?

Thus the terrible race of Los & Enitharmon gave
Laws & Religions to the sons of Har, binding them more
And more to Earth, closing and restraining;
Till a Philosophy of Five Senses was complete.
Urizen wept & gave it into the hands of Newton & Locke.

Clouds roll heavy upon the Alps round Rousseau & Voltaire,
And on the mountains of Lebanon round the deceasèd Gods
Of Asia, & on the desarts of Africa round the Fallen Angels.
The Guardian Prince of Albion burns in his nightly tent.

49 In *The French Revolution*, ll. 274 foll., Rousseau and Voltaire appear as agents of revolution. Here their significance is more doubtful, though their association with the 'deceasèd Gods' tends to show that they are, as in the later books, symbols of 'Abstract Philosophy', the error created by the false reasoning power, or Spectre (J. 54. 16–18). They are often named with Bacon, Newton, and Locke as teachers of 'Atheism', which 'consists in worshipping the natural world, which same natural world, properly speaking, is nothing real but a mere illusion produced by Satan' (Crabb Robinson, Letter to Dorothy Wordsworth, S., p. 274). Identifying 'Atheism' with eighteenth-century Deism, Blake makes his clearest statement against Rousseau and Voltaire in the address 'To the Deists' (J. 52).

52 This repeats *America*, 1.

[4]

ASIA

The Kings of Asia heard
The howl rise up from Europe,
And each ran out from his Web,
From his ancient woven Den ;
For the darkness of Asia was startled
At the thick-flaming thought-creating fires of Orc.

And the Kings of Asia stood
And cried in bitterness of soul :

' Shall not the King call for Famine from the heath,
Nor the Priest for Pestilence from the fen,
To restrain, to dismay, to thin
The inhabitants of mountain and plain
In the day of full-feeding prosperity
And the night of delicious songs ?

' Shall not the Councellor throw his curb
Of Poverty on the laborious,
To fix the price of labour,
To invent allegoric riches ?

' And the privy admonishers of men
Call for Fires in the City,
For heaps of smoking ruins,
In the night of prosperity & wantonness,

' To turn man from his path,
To restrain the child from the womb,
[5] To cut off the bread from the city,
That the remnant may learn to obey,

' That the pride of the heart may fail,
That the lust of the eyes may be quench'd,
That the delicate ear in its infancy
May be dull'd, and the nostrils clos'd up,
To teach mortal worms the path
That leads from the gates of the Grave ?'

Urizen heard them cry ;
And his shudd'ring waving wings

2 The ' howl ' arises from the powers of mental and moral tyranny, whose state is symbolized by ' Europe ' and whose authority is threatened by the revolutionary spirit : cf. *America*, ll. 147–150.

9–32 Cp. F. Z. vii, ll. 111–129.

19 *Read* ' And shall not the privy admonishers of men, &c.'

24 Cp. *Tiriel*, § 8. 12–21.

31–32 The interpretation of these lines is uncertain. They may refer to the illusion of an ' Eternal life ' in an ' allegorical ' or unreal heaven ; cp. *Europe*, 37–41.

33–40 Cp. B. U., chap. viii. 37–54.

Went enormous above the red flames,
Drawing clouds of despair thro' the heavens
Of Europe as he went.
And his Books of brass, iron & gold
Melted over the land as he flew,
Heavy-waving, howling, weeping.

And he stood over Judea,
And stay'd in his ancient place,
And stretch'd his clouds over Jerusalem.

For Adam, a mouldering skeleton,
Lay bleach'd on the garden of Eden ;
And Noah, as white as snow,
On the mountains of Ararat.

Then the thunders of Urizen bellow'd aloud
From his woven darkness above.

Orc, raging in European darkness,
Arose like a pillar of fire above the Alps,
Like a serpent of fiery flame.
The sullen Earth
Shrunk.

Forth from the dead dust, rattling bones to bones
Join ; shaking, convuls'd, the shiv'ring clay breathes,
And all flesh naked stands, Fathers and Friends,
Mothers & Infants, Kings & Warriors.

The Grave shrieks with delight, & shakes
Her hollow womb, & clasps the solid stem :
Her bosom swells with wild desire ;
And milk & blood & glandous wine
In rivers rush & shout & dance
On mountain, dale and plain.

The Song of Los is Ended
Urizen Wept.

38 Cp. B. U., chap. ii. 33–49. The 'book of iron' (cp. B. A., chap. iii. 17–28: F. Z. vii. 39) may have some connexion with Urizen's 'iron laws'. The nature of the Book of Brass is sufficiently indicated in the quotation from it, F. Z. vii. 110–129.

41–43 Urizen is here identified with the God of the Hebrews, the Lawgiver of Sinai, a 'tyrant crowned' (*Europe*, 93). Jerusalem here is his seat, the city of his temple, and has none of its later symbolic meaning.

44–47 The reference would seem to be to the loss of man's 'real and eternal state' and the beginning of a state of subjection to limited sense-perception and moral law, when 'the five senses whelm'd in deluge o'er the earth-born man'. Cp. *Europe*, 80–93.

49 Urizen's 'woven darkness' is his 'Web of Religion'; cp. B. U., chap. viii.

50–64 Cp. the vision of the Last Judgement, F. Z. ix. 1–276.

The Four Zoa's

The torments of Love & Jealousy

in

The Death and Judgement

of Albion the

Ancient Man

by William Blake 1797.

BIBLIOGRAPHICAL PREFACE TO
THE FOUR ZOAS

THE manuscript of *The Four Zoas* consists of seventy loose sheets, varying slightly in size but generally measuring about 16¼ × 12¾ inches.[1] They are made up as follows:

i. Nineteen sheets, drawing paper, with watermark, J Whatman 1794. These contain Nights I (with the exception of the leaves noted below, ii), II, and III, ll. 1–100;

ii. Two sheets, 16½ × 12¼ inches and 10 × 13⅛ inches respectively; originally one sheet bearing a sketch of a male head. They contain Night I, ll. 158–263;

iii. Forty-seven sheets, proofs of Blake's illustrations to Young's *Night Thoughts* (1797). These bear the rest of the text with the exception noted below;

iv. Two sheets, the halves of an historical engraving, *Edward & Elenor* (1793); used for Night VII, ll. 428–494.

In addition there are three small sheets with fragments of text, here printed in Appendix II.

In seven instances one side of the paper contains a full-page drawing, but no text. In all other cases both sides are written upon. In the sheets previously used for proofs of the *Night Thoughts* engravings, the rectangular space, originally intended to receive the text of Young's poem, has been utilized: in every case this side of the leaf is recto.

The title (fo. 1 recto) was twice revised. The first version read:

VALA / or / The Death and / Judgement / of the / Eternal Man / A DREAM / of Nine Nights / by William Blake 1797.

Later, 'Eternal' was deleted and 'Ancient' substituted for it, and 'A Dream of Nine Nights' was scored through with a pen. This version was afterwards modified, the changes being made in pencil. In this, its final form, the title stands:

The Four Zoa's / The torments of Love & Jealousy / in / The Death and / Judgement / of Albion the / Ancient Man / by William Blake 1797.

These changes were not carried through the body of the work, where 'Vala' still stands as the title at the head of each Night; and the poem closes with the phrase 'end of the Dream'. The single fact bearing upon the date of the adoption of *The Four Zoas* as the title is that the word Zoa occurs in no book earlier than *Milton*, which bears the date 1804.

Night I in its earlier form was paginated by Blake, whose figures can still be traced with the exception of that deleted on p. 5.[2] Beyond

[1] All the leaves except those in Nights VII, VIII, and IX have been pierced as if for stitching together after Blake's usual fashion.

[2] In the present text the original manuscript page order is shown throughout so that the earlier forms of Nights I, II, and VII *a* may easily be reconstructed.

this the pages were not numbered ; but at a comparatively early stage the lines were numbered by fifties, and though subsequent changes in the text have falsified these figures, they still afford the surest means of establishing the sequence of the loose leaves. Catchwords, often partially erased, or nullified by alterations in the poem, occur in sixteen instances, all of which are in the first three Nights.[1]

The manuscript has been worked over many times with pen, pencil, and crayon ; all deletions, cancelled passages, transpositions, and additions have been set down in the textual notes. It will be sufficient to notice here the more important changes in the constitution of certain Nights.

Night I, which originally consisted of seven leaves, was subsequently enlarged by the addition of pp. 13 *a* and 13 *b* ; and at a yet later date underwent a further considerable change. A line was drawn across p. 7 beneath l. 157, and above it, in the right margin, was written ' Night the Second '. This would seem to mean that the remaining lines of p. 7, with pp. 8–14, were intended to be taken as the opening passage of Night II. In place of the matter thus transferred, Blake wrote ll. 158–248 on pp. 8*, 9*, 10*, bringing the Night to a close, after his usual manner, with the phrase ' End of the First Night ' ; though this was afterwards deleted when ll. 249–263 on p. 11 were added.

Definite marginal directions, reprinted in the textual notes, indicate the transference or insertion of lengthy passages in Nights IV and VIII. In the latter case the lines so treated are on added pages (VIII, pp. 1*, 2*, 3*). The closing lines of the same Night (ll. 577–591) have been put in their present position for reasons that may be briefly stated here. In the first place, they may reasonably be considered as taking the place of the deleted passage printed in the note to l. 572. Further, the verso of the sheet contains a full-page sketch of Los and Enitharmon. Such designs occur elsewhere only at the end of the Nights, as in Nights V, VI, VII, and IX, and on the last page (p. 12) of the first form of VIII. Again, ll. 585–586 :

> But when she saw the form of Ahania weeping on the Void
> And heard Enion's voice from the caverns of the Grave

refer to the dialogue (ll. 481–571) between ' Ahania weeping in the winds ' (l. 476) and Enion who ' replies from the Caverns of the Grave (l. 521). Finally, Rahab, the subject of the lines in question, is mentioned nowhere but in additions to Nights VIII and IX, and the general tenor of this passage, referring as it does to the momentary triumph of evil before it is finally annihilated, is quite in harmony with its context in the present arrangement, and, as far as we can find, in no other.

The manuscript contains two versions of Night VII, here referred to as VII and VII *a*, and for the following reasons the former has been held to be later than and so to supersede the latter. In the first place, it takes up the story exactly where Night VI leaves it, that is,

[1] The following is a list of the decipherable catchwords : Night I, p. 2, So ; p. 3, Reared ; p. 4, With (*del.*) ; p. 6, They (*del.*). Night II, p. 8, I ; p. 10, They ; p. 11, Stretch ; p. 13, Why ; p. 4, And ; p. 6, That ; p. 7, Spread ; p. 10, The ; p. 13 *a*, Enion. Night III, p. 1, Infolded ; p. 2, Raised ; p. 4, In.

at the point where Urizen, seeking Orc, is opposed by Urthona and Tharmas and sends his comets to open up a way before him. The opening lines of VII describe the rout of his adversaries and the continuation of his journey till Orc is discovered. Moreover, the regenerative activity of Los and Enitharmon, that occupies the closing lines of Night VII, forms the opening theme of Night VIII, while the reference to the binding of Orc (VII, ll. 229–231) rounds off the mention of Orc in Night V, l. 112. The theory of Regeneration through Divine Mercy, previously referred to only in added passages (cp. I. 16–17; II. 82, 105, 208, 475; IV. 246–278), here forms part of the body of the text, in the description of the Tree of Mystery as 'a Shelter from the tempests of Void & Solid' (VII, l. 266; see Index, *Mundane Shell*, IV). Again, Night VII is the keystone of the whole work, in that it tells how Urizen, hoping to subdue Orc, draws him into the Tree of Mystery, with the apparently unpremeditated result that regeneration begins. The comparatively late date of this version is further established by reference to various matters of note treated as in *Milton* and *Jerusalem*, but not elsewhere; e. g. Enitharmon's fear of punishment and utter extinction (F. Z. vii. 368, 420–427; cp. J. 87. 12: 92. 27), and Los's creation of Bodies from the spectres (F. Z. vii. 462 seq.; cp. J. 62. 35–42: 72. 22–50). Then the mention of the appearance of Jesus in 'Luvah's robes of blood' (F. Z. vii. 411), not being, as in Night II, an addition, but in the body of the text, strengthens the contention that this Night was composed at a later date than the preceding Nights.

On the other hand, the symbolism of Night VII *a* is of a distinctly earlier kind. The 'Shadowy Female', one of its main symbols, disappears in *Jerusalem* and occurs in *Milton* only on one of the extra pages (see *Milton*, Introduction). The 'Prester Serpent', emblem of religious tyranny, belongs to the same period as 'The Garden of Love' in *The Songs of Experience* (1794) and to poems of the same date in the Rossetti MS., such as that commencing 'I saw a chapel all of gold' (Clar. Press, p. 157). Further, the original opening to this version closely resembles, and in ll. 136–138 repeats verbatim from, the Preludium to *America* (1793). Then its story has no apparent connexion with either Nights VI or VIII as they now exist. It deals indeed with war, but allegorically, as the general chaotic condition of mundane existence beneath the moral law, and not with the particular conflict of Urizen and Urthona in the close of Night VI. And though Blake tried to adapt it to the first part of Night VIII, the attempt failed; for in the earlier account, 'night or day Los follows war' (VII *a*, l. 73), and continues so throughout as a destructive force. Hence, in passing from Night VII *a* to Night VIII, the reader becomes aware of an abrupt change in the whole symbolic conception of Los, who, from being represented as blindly hostile to vision, suddenly appears as the willing instrument of the providential scheme of regeneration.

Again, though Orc comes under the power of Urizen, there is no indication that this marks, as in VII, the inception of regeneration. Nor are the relations between Urizen and Tharmas at the close of Night VI resumed in VII *a*, while the Tharmas-Vala episode (VII *a*, 220 seq.) can only be compared with the quite early symbolism of the long deleted passages in the first pages of Night I. Moreover, the prominence given to Tharmas is in itself an indication of an early date, since in Blake's later writings, *Milton* and *Jerusalem*, as in

Nights VII and VIII, the symbol is almost entirely ignored, or is practically synonymous with the term Spectre.

If the two versions of Night VII be read consecutively, the myth of Orc and the Tree of Mystery is found to be repeated under quite irreconcilable forms, while the contradictory accounts of Los's activity produce hopeless confusion. The inference would therefore seem to be that VII *a* was the earlier form ; it was afterwards revised and re-arranged, as shown in the textual notes, and finally replaced by a newly written Night VII.

The extensive additions to Night VIII, including those added pages already noticed, mark it as much later than the main body of *The Four Zoas* in respect to symbolism. It was apparently the consciousness of this that led Blake to attempt to bridge a gap by adding ll. 1–89 of Night IX. But this addition causes confusion, for the final annihilation of error, the Last Judgement, is thus twice described, first and more concisely in the added lines, which give prominence to the later doctrines and symbolism of Night VIII, and again in the older portion, which is to be compared with Night II, ll. 214 seq. The early character of this part is clearly seen in the long descriptions of the Eternals, who differ in vital points from the Eternals in *Milton* and *Jerusalem*. The reference to the vision of God appearing in the 'Cloud of the Son of Man' is obviously early, and was written before the great change in Blake's outlook led him to adopt Christian symbolism to express his later doctrines. For in all the many passages relating to Jesus Blake never once uses the title 'Son of Man', the significance of the phrase being completely at variance with his interpretation of the Incarnation. Again, the first part of the 'Vala' interlude (IX. 373–455) is more in the manner of *Thel* (1789) than anything else in Blake. Finally, an examination of the smaller textual emendations indicates an early date of composition. In every case the terms displaced belong to a period much before the adoption of the later doctrines of 'Imagination', and 'Regeneration', and 'Vegetative Nature': e. g. in l. 289, 'Redeem'd Man' replaces 'Fallen Man'; in l. 358, 'Ancient Man' becomes 'Regenerate Man'; in l. 366, 'Imagination' is put for 'Thought', a term that belongs to the period of *The Visions of the Daughters of Albion* and *Europe*; in l. 623 'Generative' is put for 'Vegetative'; and l. 629 reads 'roots of [Eternal] Science' for 'Roots of Nature'.

It may be noticed that there is little similarity between the account of the Last Judgement in Night IX and the prose notes referring to the picture 'The Vision of the Last Judgement'. The chief points of resemblance lie in the references to the Zoas or Living Creatures, the burning of the Tree of Mystery in the flames of Orc, and the description of the women and children ascending to the Judgement seat.

Three small scraps of paper bear fragments of text, all of which, with the exception of the contents of one piece (see 2 below), reappear in modified form in the body of *The Four Zoas*. They are here printed in the Appendix to *The Four Zoas* and consist of:

1. writing-paper, $9 \times 5\frac{1}{2}$ inches; written on one side;
2. writing-paper, $6\frac{1}{8} \times 3\frac{3}{4}$ inches; written on both sides;
3. drawing-paper, $4\frac{1}{2} \times 6\frac{1}{2}$ inches; apparently a leaf from a note-book; the upper portion torn away, rendering illegible the first of three lines on the recto and truncating the second. Beneath the third line is a sketch of a seated figure in the coils of a serpent.

On the verso are seventeen lines, the seventh of which is numbered 140. From this it would appear that the fragment is part of a longer passage, possibly an earlier version of Night I, since these lines are found, in an altered form, in Night I, ll. 110–125.

The Title and Contents of the Book.

Blake's rejection of the title *Vala* may reasonably be attributed to his recognition of its inadequacy. Vala figures prominently in Nights VII–IX, though the conception developed in Nights VII–VIII is in vital particulars out of harmony with that of Night IX. But it is in the rejected Night VII *a* alone that Vala, or the Shadowy Female, occupies indubitably the central position. From the point of view of doctrine also, the title *Vala* was misleading, for the myths of the Nights are concerned far less with Vala, the symbol of the errors that constitute the difference between life in time and the life of eternity, than with the origins and the final annihilation of mortal life. *The Four Zoas* may therefore be regarded as Blake's attempt to find a title more adequately representative of the nature of the myths and of their doctrinal significance. In the revision of the sub-title a phrase was added and words were omitted, but substantially the descriptive part remains; the book purports to give an account of 'The Death and Judgement of the Eternal (ancient) Man', afterwards called 'Albion'.

An exposition of the symbols Zoas and Albion, with a full citation of passages, is given in the Index of Symbols and more briefly in the General Introduction. The conceptions underlying both of them are the basis of the main myth of the book as it was first conceived. Naturally the conceptions grew under Blake's hands; but by reason of many excisions and readjustments of passages the growth cannot be precisely traced. When he wrote *The Marriage* Blake had, at least formally, rejected the conventional differentiation of Being into the finite and the infinite. The incomplete myth of *The Book of Urizen* may express doctrine on this point but equivocally. But the earliest form of *The Four Zoas* develops the doctrine of *The Marriage*. All forms of Being are infinite, the conception of the finite being simply the destruction of the truth consequent upon human reliance on the senses and the logical mind. All forms of Being too are essentially one, a living entity imaged as a sublime human being, the Eternal Man in whom life persists by virtue of the activity of the 'Four Eternal Senses', the Zoas. They are Urizen, the regulative intellect; Luvah, the emotions; Urthona or Los, spiritual energy; and Tharmas, a symbol of obscure and uncertain reference. It is probable that Blake derived a suggestion that led him to use the symbol of the 'Eternal Man' as the summary vision of the Universe from earlier mystics, from the Cabbala, or Böhme or Swedenborg; but his manner of using it is definitely his own. The unity of the All is maintained by the harmonious co-operation of the 'Senses', who in Blake's myths are figured as daemons of immense power. The structure of the myths leads to the conclusion that Blake conceived the four as active, not in the souls of individuals only, but also in 'Man', the aggregate of all souls and of all those spiritual entities which are by the non-mystical mind misinterpreted as material objects. In the individual, loss of harmony by excess or defect of any of the 'Senses' is followed by loss of spiritual vision; in 'Man', or the Universe, it is followed by the infraction of Ideal unity, i. e.

by the ' Fall '. In this book the main myths deal with the wider conception. The ' Fall ' is the consequence of the claim to sovereignty of each of the Zoas in turn. The stories tell of their conflicts and oppositions, which are marked first by the representing of each of these double-sexed beings as dividing, in intense antagonisms of jealousy and destructive selfish love, into male and female ; and secondly, by episodes of cosmic warfare. It is in relation to the ' dividings ' that the added phrase of the sub-title, ' the torments of Love and Jealousy ', is significant.

Passages throughout the book recur to the theme of the Fall, but the conception of the event remains so obscure in detail that the story cannot be restated, even in terms of the myths. A part of the myth of *The Book of Urizen*, with inharmonious elaborations intended to bring the other two Zoas, Luvah and Tharmas, into the story, appears to have been the starting-point of the main myth in the early form of this book, but subsequent omissions and additions, made without regard to the coherence of the whole, produce inextricable confusion.[1] The later alterations were due to changes in Blake's ideas as to the course of human regeneration. He became less interested in the ' Fall ' than in the restoration of ideal unity, or to use the terms of the sub-title, less in the ' Death ' than in the ' Judgement ' of the Ancient Man. The doctrine of the Lambeth books that man may achieve the perfect state by revolt against laws and conventions (in symbol, the establishment of Orc as the anarchic Messiah) was hesitatingly discarded, and a new gospel, a reinterpreted Christianity, which certainly does not grow naturally out of the elaborated myth of the Fall, leaves Orc virtually functionless, notwithstanding the large place he continues to hold in the central myth. In what appears to be an attempt to include him in the more elaborate mythology of *The Four Zoas* he is identified with Luvah, i. e. with Emotion and the emotional life of man. But whereas in *America* Orc, the passionate will to freedom, was of power not merely to destroy legal and social bonds, but also to win and maintain freedom for the spirit of man, in *The Four Zoas* he is represented as powerful only to destroy. Freedom comes only by the saving vision of ' Universal Brotherhood and Love ', the Divine Vision of a Christ differing in almost all respects from the Christ of religious orthodoxy. But though many passages appear to touch on it, the relation of the destroying activity of Orc and the illumination of the Divine Vision is never clearly established. In the earlier written parts of the book, as in Nights V and VII *a*, traces of the anarchic gospel are perceptible in the treatment of the symbol Orc, and these appear to relate to an undefined conception of Necessity as the controlling force in life ; whereas very clearly in Nights VII and VIII and in added passages in other Nights, the doctrine of human regeneration is based on a belief in an immanent Divine Providence, of which the supreme expression is in the Incarnation and Crucifixion (see Index s.v.). When once this providential interpretation of life has been made, the notion of the balance or harmony of the four ' Senses ' in the Eternal Man resolves itself into a simple dualism. Los, the Eternal Prophet of *The Book of Urizen*, becomes the divine instrument of spiritual enlightenment, and opposed to him at different times stand Urizen, Luvah, and Satan. The symbol of the ' Eternal Man ' is retained and interwoven with

[1] For the relation of this ' Fall ' myth with that of *The Book of Urizen* see Index, *Zoas*.

the new doctrine of salvation, for the atonement achieved by the Christ of Blake is not of man with God, but of all forms of life in the Universe into the great Unity, sometimes figured as Man, sometimes as the harmony of the Eternals of whom Man is one. This higher Unity Blake saw also as Man, as the One Man, Jesus; but sometimes, stressing the identity of the One and the Many, he uses the title 'The Council of God'. The 'Fall' myth is almost forgotten, save that there are passing references to that part of it which tells of the infraction of the Ideal Unity by the striving of the Zoas for dominion. In Night IX, however, which, apart from the opening passage of 89 lines and a few short passages elsewhere, is the most considerable relic of the earlier form of the book, is found a vision of the 'Last Judgement' that does attempt to preserve the basic conceptions of the 'Fall' myth. But in the course of many revisions so much in the antecedent circumstances of this new Apocalypse has been eliminated that interpretation becomes in great degree a process of guessing.

Interwoven with the myths are long symbolic episodes in criticism of conventional morality and the 'philosophy of the five senses'. The symbols change from time to time, but the substance and the point of view of the criticism remain almost constant.

In *The Four Zoas* there is no part so crabbed and deformed as the bad pages of *Jerusalem*; indeed, as the selection printed in Dr. Sampson's Oxford edition of Blake shows, there are passages of considerable power or charm. But as a whole the work is among the most obscure. A brief statement of the nature and origins of its peculiar obscurities may serve as warning to the reader who comes to it with expectations based on the mild laudations that have from time to time been written of it:

(1) Despite the appearance of ordered development, *The Four Zoas* tells neither a single myth nor a series of interrelated myths. As this Bibliographical Preface shows, it is a loose congeries of myths showing characteristics that relate them to works so widely separated in time and ideas as *Thel* and *Jerusalem*. Blake indicates a changed belief sometimes by excising, less frequently by modifying a passage, but not uncommonly by loosely interpolating contradictory or unharmonious matters as episodes or parentheses.

(2) The separation of the 'female counterparts' of the Zoas is part of the mechanism of Blake's myths of the 'Fall', as it is told in *The Book of Urizen* and *Ahania*. But as a result of his obsession by the notion of the evil of 'jealousy' in life, the opposition of male and female in his myths is carried far beyond the point necessary for the adequate statement of his doctrine. Consequently, we have many tedious, feebly undramatic scenes of jealousy, long speeches of reproach, faintings, dyings, revivings, and re-dyings. And when all is said, these episodes mean nothing that is not otherwhere and in other symbols expressed more simply, attractively and lucidly.

(3) The width of reference in the symbol Albion has already been indicated. In this book even more than in *Milton* and *Jerusalem* it is often impossible to know in a specific instance whether the symbol stands for the soul of the individual, for mankind generally, for the Universe of Time and Space as it is conceived by the limited mind of the man dependent on sense-experience, or for the Universe as the visionary conceives it to be in its eternal nature. Inevitably a parallel uncertainty arises in respect to the Zoas, whether in

particular cases the reference is to the spiritual life of the individual or to the activities of these beings conceived as daemons of power acting in the Universe. The latter conception strongly possessed Blake when he wrote *Jerusalem*. It is implicit in his treatment of Urizen as the God of Sinai, or as the Creator in *The Four Zoas* and elsewhere. There is ample evidence that Blake believed in the real existence of this malevolent being. It is implicit too, and of practical importance, in the matter of Blake's doctrine in respect of Los and, perhaps, Luvah. But Tharmas, though looming large in the early Nights of the book, apparently means so little that in the later-written portions and in *Milton* and *Jerusalem* he virtually disappears.

It may be that, in spite of many revisions, Blake was so little satisfied with the book that he did not proceed to engrave it, and found use for only the few passages that are embodied in *Jerusalem*. Detailed interpretation is impossible. In the Introductory Notes to the Nights suggestions as to the general sense of the sections of the myths are made, in most cases only when the other books furnish more lucidly expressed matter of a like kind, and always with diffidence. The real interest of *The Four Zoas* appears to us to be in those passages which show the beginnings of doctrines and symbols elaborated in the later books, and in the intermittent faint gleams by which we can trace the poet's progress from the anarchic revolutionary doctrine of the Lambeth books to a not less revolutionary Christianity.

NIGHT I

INTRODUCTORY NOTE

Frequent revision has rendered the First Night incoherent almost beyond the possibility of interpretation. In addition to re-arranging long passages, Blake seems to have taken it up at different times and to have made minor changes without any apparent regard to the consistency of the Night as a whole. The confusion that results is evident even in the opening lines, where a symbol like ' the Aged Mother ' (l. 1) that belongs to the comparatively early period of ' Eno ' in *The Book of Ahania* is almost immediately followed by quite definite references to the doctrines of Brotherhood and the Universal Humanity that constitute the pith and substance of the latest books. Again, in the lament of Tharmas (ll. 19 seq.) the object of Enion's jealousy is sometimes Enitharmon, sometimes Jerusalem. This confusion arises out of Blake's attempt to graft the doctrine of a regenerative purpose in mundane existence, which is implicit in the symbol Jerusalem, upon the pure necessitarianism of his early prophecies. Further, the Tharmas myth, which originally was the main matter of the Night, is almost entirely superseded by the insertion of the later Urizen-Luvah episode. In addition to these difficulties there is the fact that the very decided change in Blake's opinions that dates from a time between the commencement of *The Four Zoas* and the writing of *Milton* led to the practical abandonment of the symbols Tharmas and Enion, and considerably modified the significance of Los and Enitharmon. Hence it has not been found possible to attach any definite meaning to these personages, whose story fills by far the greater part of the Night. For these reasons it is difficult to summarize the contents of the Night. Blake's purpose, according to the statement in ll. 14–18, is to tell first the story of the infraction of the ideal Unity, ' the Fall into the Generation of Decay and Death '. He begins with the story of Tharmas, here called the ' Parent Power ' (l. 18), a title intelligible only when related to references in other books, which show that Tharmas is associated in Blake's mind with the sense of touch, the obstacle popularly proposed to the teacher who begins by denying material reality; therefore he is, as Blake conceived the case, the great original of materialistic philosophies, and of the worthless moralities consequent thereupon. Offering no reason for Tharmas's defection, the myth proceeds to tell of its first result, cessation of unity in the being of Tharmas himself, symbolically expressed by the appearance of the phenomenon of sex; for Enion, his ' counterpart ', divides from him and achieves independent ' will ' or personality. From separated personality grows the notion of the ' self ', and from this, in Blake's view, proceeds moral judgement, moral condemnation and jealousy. Enion is jealous of Enitharmon, for whose name that of Jerusalem was afterwards substituted, but the significance of both names in this relation remains undiscovered. Blake, leaving the main line on which his myth has promised to develop, proceeds to enlarge, in the already familiar manner, on the destructive effects of moral condemnation in life.

Enion in the subsequent passage (ll. 60–66) is said to weave for Jerusalem or, in the earlier reading, for Enitharmon a ' tabernacle ' which, in some manner not defined, is connected with the ' circle of destiny ' that Tharmas rotates. The ' circle ', mentioned again in Night I, ll. 81 and 93, and in Night III, ll. 129 and 171, cannot be interpreted, as it then disappears from among the symbols. Vaguely the story suggests that the ' tabernacle ' is the physical universe, an interpretation supported by the next episode of the myth (ll. 101–111) where Enion combines with the Spectre of Tharmas, another undefinable symbol, into the monstrous form of Nature. Of Nature are born Los and Enitharmon, here clearly identified as Time and Space. It is to be noted that in this episode and in that which tells of the preparing of a ' tabernacle ', two added passages, not brought into harmony with the staple of the narrative, superimpose the conception that these events are controlled by a Divine Providence. Hence the new creation of Time and Space is not to be regarded as completely severed from Eternity, as it was in the earlier myth of *The Book of Urizen*. At what date these additions were made it is impossible to surmise, but they clearly belong to the range of ideas out of which the new Nights VII and VIII grew.

The remainder of the Night (ll. 158–263) is added to replace the manuscript pages transferred to the beginning of Night II. It opens with the lament of the ' Council of God ', Blake's vision of the ultimate Unity (see Index, *Jesus*), over the fallen Albion, that is to say, over the ' fall ' of one element of the Eternal and the beginning of a new mode of existence, the ' Generation of Decay and Death '. A new story is told to account for the Fall. To it references are made both in the succeeding Nights and in later works, while to the Tharmas myth references are few and unimportant. Whether the new myth is substituted for, or is complementary to that of Tharmas, it is impossible to discover. The first consequence of the emergence of the ideas of Nature and Time and Space is that Urizen desires to ' lay (his) sceptre upon Jerusalem ', the image of the state of spiritual harmony, to destroy her. The opposition, frequently to reappear, of Reason in Urizen and Emotion in Luvah is indicated by the latter's refusal to share in the design, and by his counterclaim to sole dominion in the world of the fallen Eternal.

The flight of Urthona's ' feminine counterpart ' or Emanation, Enitharmon, to Tharmas for protection, an episode to which attention is called specifically in the added lines 27–28, serves mechanically to unite the earlier and later myths of the Night. Not only is the meaning of the episode entirely hidden by the confusion of the mythical personages Jerusalem and Enitharmon in the earlier part of the Night, but it raises the question, never satisfactorily solved, as to Blake's intention in duplicating, as it were, the one personality, sometimes calling him Los, sometimes Urthona (see Index, *Los*). After again affirming the existence of an active Divine Providence, and after still another completely obscure episode in which Jerusalem and Enitharmon figure, the Night closes with a reference to the opposing forces in the cosmic strife : on the one side, the creative ' wheels of intellect ' or of the spirit ; on the other, the destructive wheels of morality and critical reason.

[1] Οτι οὐκ ἔστιν ἡμῖν ἡ πάλη πρὸς αἷμα καὶ σάρκα, ἀλλὰ πρὸς τὰς ἀρχάς,
πρὸς τὰς ἐξουσίας, πρὸς τοὺς κοσμοκράτορας τοῦ σκότους τοῦ αἰῶνος
τούτου, πρὸς
τὰ πνευματικὰ τῆς πονηρίας ἐν τοῖς ἐπουρανίοις.

Εφες 5 κεφ. 12.

VALA.

Night the First.

The Song of the Agèd Mother, which shook the heavens with wrath,
Hearing the march of long resounding, strong, heroic Verse,
Marshall'd in order for the day of Intellectual Battle.

The verse from the Epistle to the Ephesians would seem to have been transcribed at some later date. It is written without breathings or accents; the final form of sigma is used throughout; and the symbol ȣ is used for the diphthong *ου*. The reference to the chapter has been corrected, possibly by another hand than Blake's, the correct number, VI, being written in roman numerals above the figure 5; at the same time 'ver' was written after 12.

1–5 Traces of two deleted versions remain. Of the earlier of these, only part of the first line is decipherable:

This is the Song of Eno . . . of Vala.

The following is the second version, with Blake's numbering of the lines:

1 The Song of the Agèd Mother, which shook the heavens with wrath,
2 And thus beginneth the Book of Vala, which whosoever reads
3 If with his Intellect he comprehend . . .
6 The heavens quake [shall quake *1st rdg.*]; the Earth was moved [shall move *1st rdg.*] & shudder'd [shudder *1st rdg.*], & the mountains
7 With all their woods: the streams & valleys wail'd in dismal fear.
4 To hear the Sound of long resounding strong heroic verse
5 Marshall'd in order for the day of Intellectual Battle.

Apparently the lines numbered 1, 2, 3, 6, and 7 were first written. Then ll. 4 and 5 were added in a smaller hand in the space below l. 7, and the whole passage was re-arranged by means of the figures to the left. Later these numbers were cancelled by a vertical line drawn through them; ll. 2–3 were erased, and the first part of l. 4 altered from 'To hear the Sound' to 'Hearing the March'. The passage was then renumbered and stood as follows:

1 The Song of the Aged Mother which shook the heavens with wrath
2 Hearing the March of long resounding strong heroic verse
3 Marshall'd in order for the day of Intellectual Battle.

At the same time Blake joined up this passage with the succeeding paragraph by marking the first line of the latter, 'Four Mighty Ones are in every Man: a Perfect Unity', as the fourth of his new version. Finally, ll. 2–3, 'Hearing . . . Battle', were cancelled and re-written over the erasure below l. 1.

The second numbering of the lines clearly eliminated ll. 6–7, but it is possible that Blake silently reinstated them, with the alterations noted in l. 6.

Οτι ουκ εστιν ημιν η παλη προς αιμα και σαρκα, αλλα προς τας αρχας, προς τας εξουσιας, προς τους κοσμοκρατορας του σκοτους του αιωνος τουτου, προς τα πνευματικα της πονηριας εν τοις επουρανιοις.

Εφεσ: VI Κεφ 12 ver

2

1

VALA

Night the First

The Song of the Aged Mother which shook the heavens with wrath
Hearing the march of long resounding strong heroic Verse
Marshalld in order for the day of Intellectual Battle
The heavens quake: the earth moved & shudderd & the mountains
With all their woods, the streams & valleys: wail in dismal fear

Four Mighty Ones are in every Man; a Perfect Unity
Cannot Exist. but from the Universal Brotherhood of Eden
The Universal Man. To Whom be Glory Evermore Amen

John XVII c. 21 & 22 & 23 v

John I c. 14 v
και εσκηνωσεν εν ημιν

Los was the fourth immortal starry one, & in the Earth
Of a bright Universe, Empery attended day & night
Days & nights of revolving joy, Urthona was his name

In

The Four Zoas: Night I, page 1

Night I

Four Mighty Ones are in every Man: a Perfect Unity
Cannot exist but from the Universal Brotherhood of Eden,
The Universal Man, To Whom be Glory Evermore, Amen.
What are the Natures of those Living Creatures the Heavenly Father only
Knoweth: No Individual Knoweth, nor Can Know in all Eternity.
Los was the fourth immortal starry one, & in the Earth
Of a bright Universe, Empery attended day & night,
Days & nights of revolving joy. Urthona was his name
[2] In Eden: in the Auricular Nerves of Human Life,
Which is the Earth of Eden, he his Emanations propagated,

4 See Index, *Zoas*. They are the Living Creatures: see below, l. 7. In the margin, opposite to this line, is the reference ' John **xvii**. c, 21 & 22 & 23 v '. The passage is part of Christ's prayer for those who believe: ' That they all may be one; as thou, Father, art in me, and I in thee, that they also may be one in us: that the world may believe that thou hast sent me. And the glory which thou gavest me I have given them; that they may be one, even as we are one: I in them, and thou in me, that they may be made perfect in one; and that the world may know that thou hast sent me, and hast loved them, as thou hast loved me.'

5 Opposite to this line is the reference: John I c. iv v / *καὶ ἐσκήνωσεν* / *ἐν ἡμῖν*: i. e. ' and [the Word] dwelt among us '. As before, Blake marks neither breathings nor accents.

6 The . . . Man] Not in this case Albion, but the ' One Man, Jesus ', the symbol of the ultimate unity in which Albion is comprehended (see Index, *Jesus* and *Albion*).

8 Knoweth . . . Eternity] Knoweth: Individual Man Knoweth not, nor Can Know in all Eternity: *1st rdg.*

9 Los is the fourth Zoa (M. 23. 8) and the ' Vehicular Form of strong Urthona ' (J. 53. 1). Cp. J. 82. 79–80:

> I [Los] know I am Urthona, keeper of the Gates of Heaven,
> And that I can at will expatiate in the Gardens of bliss.

For the somewhat confused relations between Los and Urthona see Index, *Los, Note I*.

Page 2 has been worked over several times both with pencil and pen.

12 In the series of fourfold correspondences connected with the Zoas Los is associated with the Ear: cp. M. 28. 40–41:

> And in the Nerves of the Ear (for the Nerves of the Tongue are closed),
> On Albion's Rock Los stands.

And in F. Z. vi. 247–248 the Ear is ' as a golden ascent winding round to the heavens of heavens '. Further, the Ear is the medium of inspiration in mortal life: cp. J. 3, ll. 7–8, where Blake declares:

> Even from the depths of Hell his [Jesus'] voice I hear
> Within the unfathom'd caverns of my Ear.

From these references there would appear to be a definite connexion between the Ear and Prophecy or Inspiration in Los.

13–14 Cp. M. 31. 20–26:

> The Fairies, Nymphs, Gnomes & Genii of the Four Elements . . .
> These are the Gods of the Kingdoms of the Earth, in contrarious
> And cruel opposition, Element against Element opposed in War,

Fairies of Albion, afterwards Gods of the Heathen. Daughter of Beulah, Sing
His fall into Division & his Resurrection to Unity,
His fall into the Generation of Decay & Death & his
Regeneration by the Resurrection from the dead !
Begin with Tharmas, Parent power, dark'ning in the West !

' Lost ! Lost ! Lost ! are my Emanations ! Enion ! O Enion !
We are become a Victim to the Living. We hide in Secret.
I have hidden Jerusalem in silent contrition. O, Pity Me !
I will build thee a Labyrinth also. O pity me, O Enion !
Why hast thou taken sweet Jerusalem from my inmost Soul ?
Let her Lay secret in the soft recess of darkness & silence.
It is not Love I bear to Enitharmon : It is Pity.
She hath taken refuge in my bosom, & I cannot cast her out.
The Men have reciev'd their Death wounds, & their Emanations are fled
To me for refuge, & I cannot turn them out, for Pity's Sake.'

Enion said : ' Thy fear has made me tremble, thy terrors have surrounded me.

Not Mental, as in the Wars of Eternity, but a Corporeal Strife,
In Los's Halls, continual labouring in the Furnaces of Golgonooza.

These spiritual agents are more directly related to Los in M. 23. 74–75 :

All the Gods of the Kingdoms of Earth labour in Los's Halls ;
Every one is a fallen Son of the Spirit of Prophecy [i. e. of Los].

14 Fairies . . . Heathen] Like Sons & Daughters *1st rdg. del.*
16–17 His . . . Dead] *an addition.* See Index, *Albion*, II. 6.
18 Tharmas as the Parent power may refer to the fact that he is here the father of Los, or more probably that he represents the Tongue, the sense of touch (M. 24. 44–46). In the latter case there is possibly a vague reminiscence of Blake's reading of Berkeley's *Essay Towards a new Theory of Vision*, where the visual perception of solid things, the empirical warrant of material reality, is in the sense of touch (see Night I, Introductory Note).
19 Enion ! O Enion !] Enion ! come forth. *1st rdg. del.* Emanations here seem to be equivalent to Sons and Daughters : see above, ll. 13–14 and the textual note to the latter line.
20 Tharmas's exclamation that he and Enion have become Victims to the Living may indicate the beginnings in him of the error of morality. So Los's Spectre (J. 10. 38–59) speaks of his subjection to the illusion of a transcendent deity, a God of Moral Law :

Life lives on my
Consuming ; & the Almighty hath made me his Contrary,
To be all evil, all reversed & for ever dead, knowing
And seeing life, yet living not. (J. 10. 55–58.)

21 Jerusalem . . . contrition] thee, Enion, in Jealous Despair *1st rdg. del.*
22 also . . . Enion] where we may remain for ever alone *1st rdg. del.*
23–24 why . . . silence] *an addition.*
27–28 The Men . . . Sake] *marginal addition.* Cp. F. Z. i. 213–214.
29 Cp. J. 22. 1.

All Love is lost. Terror succeeds & Hatred instead of Love,
And stern demands of Right & Duty instead of Liberty.
Once thou wast to Me the loveliest son of heaven. But now,
Why art thou Terrible? and yet I love thee in thy terror, till
I am almost Extinct, & soon shall be a Shadow in Oblivion,
Unless some way can be found that I may look upon thee & live.
Hide me, some shadowy semblance, secret whisp'ring in my Ear,
In Secret of Soft Wings, in mazes of delusive beauty!
I have look'd into the secret soul of him I lov'd,
And in the Dark recesses found Sin & cannot return.'

Trembling & pale sat Tharmas weeping in his clouds:

'Why wilt thou Examine every little fibre of my soul,
Spreading them out before the Sun like stalks of flax to dry?
The infant Joy is beautiful, but its anatomy
Horrible, Ghast & Deadly: nought shalt thou find in it
But Death, Despair & Everlasting brooding Melancholy.

'Thou wilt go mad with horror if thou dost Examine thus
Every moment of my secret hours. Yea, I know
That I have sinn'd, & that my Emanations are become harlots.
I am already distracted at their deeds, & if I look
Upon them more, Despair will bring self-murder on my soul.
O Enion! thou art thyself a root growing in hell,
Tho' thus heavenly beautiful to draw me to Destruction.

'Sometimes I think thou art a flower expanding;
Sometimes I think thou art fruit breaking from its bud
In dreadful dolor & pain; & I am like an atom,

30–32 Cp. J. 22. 10–12.

38–40 I . . . clouds] *an addition*. Cp. J. 22. 14–15. These lines give the general significance of the contention between Male and Female that is one of the characteristic features of the earlier version of *The Four Zoas*, viz. it implies a state of existence where the ideal values are perverted, where a censorious morality replaces the law of liberty.

41–52 Why . . . Destruction] *marginal addition*, position not indicated, but in a similar hand to the added lines 38–40.

41–45 Cp. J. 22. 20–24.

47–48 The Emanations here are 'the Loves and Graces', the 'infant thoughts and desires' (J. 8. 44–9. 2), the beauty and the increase of the spiritual life, that the moral law would condemn as impure. This phrase is expanded later (J., p. 21, *passim*) in connexion with Albion. As it stands inserted here, it is difficult to relate to the general trend of the Tharmas myth.

51–52 The allusion to the beauty of Enion, the destructive appeal of objects of sense is paralleled in passages referring to Vala and her equivalents, the Daughters of Albion (see Index, *Vala*).

53–57 Sometimes . . . terrible] *marginal addition*; position not indicated.

A Nothing left in darkness ; yet I am an identity.
I wish, & feel, & weep, & groan. Ah terrible ! terrible !

[3] In Eden Females sleep the winter in soft silken veils
Woven by their own hands, to hide them in the darksom grave :
But Males immortal live, renew'd by female deaths in soft
Delight ; they die, & they revive in spring with music & songs.'
Enion said : ' Farewell ! I die. I hide from thy searching eyes.'

So saying, From her bosom weaving soft in sinewy threads
A tabernacle for Jerusalem, She sat among the Rocks,
Singing her lamentation. Tharmas groan'd among his Clouds,
Weeping ; then bending from his Clouds, he stoop'd his innocent head,
And, stretching out his holy hand on the vast deep sublime,
Turn'd round the circle of Destiny with tears & bitter sighs,
And said : ' Return, O wanderer, when the day of Clouds is o'er.'

So saying, he sunk down into the sea, a pale white corse.
In torment he sunk down & flow'd among her filmy Woof,
His spectre issuing from his feet in flames of fire,
In gnawing pain drawn out by her lov'd fingers : every nerve
She counted, every vein & lacteal, threading them among
Her woof of terror. Terrified & drinking tears of woe,
Shudd'ring she wove nine days & nights, sleepless ; her food was tears.
Wond'ring she saw her woof begin to animate, & not
As Garments woven subservient to her hands, but having a will
Of its own, perverse & wayward. Enion lov'd & wept.

Nine days she labour'd at her work & nine dark sleepless nights.

58–62 In Eden . . . Eyes] *an addition.*
58 Eden] Beulah *1st rdg. del.* 63 So saying] *an addition.*
64 for Jerusalem] of delight *1st rdg. del.* ; for Enitharmon *2nd rdg. del.*
66 innocent] holy. then] and *1st rdg. del.*
68 The ' circle of Destiny ', an obscure expression. Cp. F. Z. iii. 129 and 171. Cp. also F. Z. vii. 206, ' the troops of Destiny '.
70 So . . . corse] *an addition.* 71 In torment] So saying *1st rdg. del.*
72 His . . . fire] *an addition.* 73 gnawing] dismal *1st rdg. del.*
77–79 Wond'ring . . . wept] *marginal addition.*
77 The ' woof ', like the Veil, Tent, and Tabernacle, represents the fallacies associated with ' feminine ' or non-visionary activities of the mind. The error implied in the symbol is indicated by its attribute of a perverse and wayward ' will ', an instance of the insistence on ' individuality ' or ' selfhood ' that conflicts with Blake's ideal of selflessness.

But on the tenth trembling morn, the Circle of Destiny complete,
Round roll'd the Sea, Englobing in a wat'ry Globe, self-balanc'd.
A Frowning Continent appear'd, where Enion in the Desart,
Terrified in her own Creation, viewing her woven Shadow,
Sat in a dread intoxication of Repentance & Contrition.

There is from Great Eternity a mild & pleasant rest
Nam'd Beulah, a Soft Moony Universe, feminine, lovely,
Pure, mild & Gentle, given in Mercy to those who sleep,
Eternally Created by the Lamb of God, around,
On all sides, within & without the Universal Man.
The Daughters of Beulah follow sleepers in all their Dreams,
Creating Spaces lest they fall into Eternal Death.
The Circle of Destiny complete, they gave to it a Space,
And nam'd the Space Ulro, & brooded over it in care & love.
They said: 'The Spectre is in every man insane & most
Deform'd. Thro' the three heavens descending in fury & fire,
We meet it with our songs & loving blandishments & give
To it a form of vegetation. But this Spectre of Tharmas
Is Eternal Death. What shall we do? O God, pity & help!'
So spoke they, & clos'd the Gate of the tongue in trembling fear.

85 dread] sweet *1st rdg. del.*
Repentance & Contrition] falsewoven bliss *1st rdg. del.*; self woven sorrow *2nd rdg. del.*
86–100 There . . . fear] *marginal addition* marked for insertion here.
87 See Index, *Beulah.* 91 Dreams] wanderings *1st rdg.*
91–92 A specific instance is that of Eno in F. Z. i. 133–139. Cp. J. 48. 46–52. Cp. also F. Z. viii. 359: M. 6. 42–44: 11. 12–44.
94 See Index, *Ulro.* 96 'Thro' . . . fire,' relates to the Spectre.
99 God pity] God help pity *1st rdg.* See Index, *Spectre* and *Vegetation.*
100 tongue] Auricular power *1st rdg.*; Auricular nerves *2nd rdg. del.* The tongue is generally associated with Tharmas whose quarter is the West; cp. J. 13. 6 *note.* After l. 100 a passage of fourteen lines has been deleted:

He spurn'd Enion with his foot: he sprang aloft in Clouds
[Alighting down from, *del.*] Alighting in his drunken joy in a far distant Grove.

'What have I done?' said Enion, 'accursed wretch! What deed?
Is this a deed of Love? I know what I have done. I know
Too late now to repent. Love is chang'd to deadly Hate.
A life is blotted out, & I alone remain, possess'd with Fears.
I see the Shadow [remembrance *del.*] of the dead within my Soul [eyes *del.*], wandering
In darkness & solitude, forming Seas of Doubt & rocks of Repentance [Sorrow *del.*].
Already are my Eyes reverted; all that I behold
Within my Soul has lost its splendor, & a brooding Fear
Shadows me o'er & drives me outward to a world of woe.'

[4] She drew the Spectre forth from Tharmas in her shining loom
Of Vegetation, weeping in wayward infancy & sullen youth.
List'ning to her soft lamentations, soon his tongue began
To lisp out words ; & soon in masculine strength augmenting, He
Rear'd up a form of gold, & stood upon the glittering rock,
A shadowy human form, wingèd ; & in his depths
The dazzlings as of gems shone clear : rapturous in fury,
Glorying in his own eyes, Exalted in terrific Pride,

So wail'd She, trembling before her own Created Phantasm,
Who animating times on times by the force of her sweet song.

But standing on the Rocks her woven shadow Glowing bright,

101–102 She . . . youth] *an addition.* 102 shining] silken *1st rdg. del.*
103–104 List'ning . . . He] *an addition.*
After l. 108 a passage of 31 lines *del.* :

Searching for glory, wishing that the heavens had eyes to see,
And courting that the Earth would ope her Eyelids & behold
Such wondrous beauty, repining in the midst of all his glory
That nought but Enion could be found to praise, adore & love ;
Three days in self admiring raptures on the rocks he flam'd,
And three dark nights repin'd the solitude ; but the third morn,
Astonish'd, he found Enion hidden in the darksom Cave.

She spoke : ' What am I ? wherefore was I put forth on these rocks,
Among the Clouds to tremble in the wind in solitude ?
Where is the voice that lately woke the desart ? Where the Face
That wept among the clouds, & where the voice that shall reply ?
No other living thing is here. The Sea, the Earth, the Heaven,
And Enion, desolate ! Where art thou, Tharmas ? O return ! '

Three days she wail'd & three dark nights, sitting among the Rocks,
While the bright spectre hid himself among the dark'ning clouds.
Then sleep fell on her eyelids in a Chasm of the Valley.
The Sixteenth morn the Spectre stood before her, manifest.

The Spectre thus spoke : ' Who art thou, Diminutive husk & shell [Art thou not my slave & shalt thou dare *1st rdg. del.*]
Broke from my bonds ? I scorn my prison, I scorn & yet I love.
Art thou not my slave, & shalt thou dare
To smite me with thy tongue ? beware lest I sting also thee.
If thou hast sinn'd & art polluted, know that I am pure
And unpolluted, & will bring to rigid strict account
All thy past deeds : hear what I tell thee ! mark it well ! remember !
This world is Thine [Mine *1st rdg. del.*] in which thou dwellest ; that within thy soul,
That dark & dismal infinite where Thought roams up & down,
Is Mine, & there thou goest when with one Sting of my tongue
Envenom'd, thou roll'st inwards to the place whence I emerg'd [of death & hell *1st rdg. del.*]

She trembling answer'd : ' Wherefore was I born & what am I ?
A sorrow & a fear, a living torment, & naked Victim !
I thought to weave a Covering for [from *1st rdg. del.*] my Sins from wrath of Tharmas ;

[5] Mingling his brightness with her tender limbs; then high she soar'd
Above the ocean, a bright wonder, Nature,
Half Woman & half Spectre; all his lovely changing colours mix
With her fair crystal clearness; in her lips & cheeks his poisons rose
In blushes like the morning and his scaly armour softening,
A monster lovely in the heavens, or wandering on the earth;
[6] Till with fierce pain she brought forth on the rocks her sorrow & woe.
Behold! two little Infants wept upon the desolate wind:

p. 5 The following passage continuing the cancelled passage on manuscript p. 4 is written above l. 109 and cancelled:

Examining the sins of Tharmas I soon [have *del.*] found my own,
O slay me not! thou art his Wrath embodied in Deceit.
I thought Tharmas a Sinner, & I murder'd his Emanations,
His secret loves & Graces. Ah me wretched! what have I done?
For [But *del.*] now I find that all those Emanations were my Children's Souls,
And I have murder'd them with Cruelty above atonement.
Those that remain have fled from my cruelty into the desarts.

' [Among wild beasts to roam. *del.*] And thou the delusive tempter [sit'st before me. *1st rdg.*] to these deeds. [*2nd rdg.*]
And art thou [But where is *1st rdg. del.*; Thou art not *2nd rdg. del.*] Tharmas: all thy soft delusive beauty cannot
Tempt me to murder my own soul, [honest love *del.*] & wipe my tears & smile
In this thy world, not mine, [for ah! *del.*] tho' [how *del.*] dark I feel my world within.' [This line to come in, *marginal addition partially del.*]

The Spectre said: ' Thou sinful Woman, was it thy desire
That I should hide thee with my power & delight thee with my beauty?
And now thou dark'nest in my presence: never from my sight
Shalt thou depart to weep in secret. In my jealous wings
I evermore will hold thee, when thou goest out or comest in.
'Tis thou hast darken'd all My World, O Woman, lovely bane!

Thus they contended all the day among the Caves of Tharmas,
Twisting in fearful forms & howling, howling harsh, shrieking.
Howling harsh, shrieking, mingling, their bodies join in burning anguish.'

ll. 13–14 of this passage appear in Fragment I: see below, Appendix II, p. 338.

109 his brightness] his horrible brightness *1st rdg.*

110 Above] Shrieking *2nd rdg. del.*
Nature] that Beulah shudder'd at *1st rdg. del.*

111 Spectre] (? Serpent) *1st rdg. del.* Later in *Jerusalem* mundane error is symbolized by Vala ' the Goddess Nature, Mystery, Babylon the Great, the Druid Dragon ' (J. 93. 24–25). Again in J. 96. 12 the whole extent of mundane existence appears as ' a Serpent of precious stones & gold '. The symbol of the Woman-Spectre is not used hereafter. It is replaced by the symbols ' Vala ' and ' Serpent '.

Below 113 Three lines *del.*:

With Spectre [Serpent *del.*] voice incessant wailing in incessant thirst
Beauty all blushing with desire, mocking her fell despair.

Wandering desolate, a wonder abhorr'd by Gods & Men.

The first state weeping they began, & helpless as a wave
Beaten along its sightless way, growing enormous in
Its motion to its utmost goal; till strength from Enion
Rais'd the fierce boy & girl, with glories from their heads out beaming,
Drawing forth drooping mother's pity, drooping mother's sorrow.

They sulk upon her breast: her hair became like snow on mountains:
Weaker & weaker, weeping woful, wearier and wearier,
Faded; & her bright Eyes decay'd, melted with pity & love.
[7] And then they wander'd far away: she sought for them in vain.
In weeping blindness stumbling, she follow'd them o'er rocks & mountains,
Rehumanizing from the Spectre in pangs of maternal love.
Ingrate they wander'd, scorning her, drawing her Spectrous Life,
Repelling her away & away, by a dread repulsive power,
Into Non Entity, revolving round in dark despair,
And drawing in the Spectrous Life in pride & haughty joy.
Thus Enion gave him all her Spectrous life.

118–119 Beaten . . . Enion]

Beaten along its sightless way, growing enormous in its motion to
Its utmost goal, till strength from Enion like summer shining

1st rdg. After ' like ' ' richest ' *added*: Then ' like richest summer shining ' *deleted* and the lines redivided. 120 fierce] bright *1st rdg. del.*

After 121 a passage of 13 lines of which the first four are an addition, *del.*:

But those in Great Eternity Met in the Council of God
As One Man, hovering over Gilead & Hermon;
He is the Good Shepherd, He is the Lord & Master,
To Create Man Morning by Morning, to Give gifts at Noon day.

Enion brooded o'er the rocks: the rough rocks, groaning, vegetate:
Such power was given to the Solitary wanderer.
The barkèd Oak, the long-limb'd Beech, the Chestnut tree, the Pine,
The Pear-tree mild, the frowning Walnut, the sharp Crab & Apple sweet;
The rough bark opens; twittering peep forth little beaks & wings,
The Nightingale, the Goldfinch, Robin, Lark, Linnet, & Thrush.
The Goat leap'd from the craggy cliff, the Sheep awoke from the mould;
Upon its green stalk rose the Corn, waving innumerable,
Infolding the bright Infants from the desolating winds.

127 Rehumanizing . . . love] *an addition.* ' Maternal love ' is here a ' rehumanizing influence ' from the state of the Spectre-woman. For the later use of ' Maternal Love ', cp. J. 5. 47 *note.*

128 Spectrous Life] life; ingrate *1st rdg. del.*

131 And . . . joy] *an addition.*

132–135 Thus . . . Eden and ll. 138–142 Astonish'd . . . repose] a single *marginal addition* marked for insertion here.

132 life] life in deep despair *1st rdg.*

Then Eno, a daughter of Beulah, took a Moment of Time,
And drew it out to seven thousand years with much care & affliction
And many tears; & in ⟨the⟩ every year⟨s⟩ made windows into Eden.
She also took an atom of space, & open'd its center
Into Infinitude, & ornamented it with wond'rous art.
Astonish'd sat her Sisters of Beulah to see her soft affections
To Enion & her children; & they ponder'd these things wond'ring.
And they Alternate kept watch over the Youthful terrors.
They saw not yet the Hand Divine, for it was not yet reveal'd.
But they went on in Silent Hope & Feminine repose.

But Los and Enitharmon Delighted in the Moony spaces of Eno.
Nine Times they liv'd among the forests feeding on sweet fruits;
And nine bright Spaces wander'd, weaving mazes of delight,
Snaring the wild Goats for their milk; they eat the flesh of Lambs,
A male & female, naked & ruddy as the pride of summer.

Alternate Love & Hate his breast, hers Scorn & Jealousy,
In embryon passions: they kiss'd not, nor embrac'd, for shame & fear.
His head beam'd light, & in his vigorous voice was prophecy.
He could controll the times & seasons & the days & years:
She could controll the spaces, regions, desart, flood & forest,
But had no power to weave a Veil of covering for her Sins.
She drave the Females all away from Los,
And Los drave all the Males from her away.

133 Eno] Ona *1st rdg.* Nothing can be discovered concerning Ona, except that she is a daughter of Urizen (F. Z. vii. 95). The name is found in the lyrical poem 'A Little Girl Lost' (S. E., Clar. Press, p. 132), without any elucidation of meaning. For 'Eno', cp. B. L., chap. i. 1 *note*, and see Index, *Daughters of Beulah, Note I.*

134 seven thousand] twenty *1st rdg. del.*

135 every] twenty *1st rdg. del.*

made windows into Eden] gave visions to sweet heaven, *1st rdg. del.* With the whole of this passage, cp. J. 48. 26–52; cp. also F. Z. i. 91–92.

136–137 She . . . art] *an addition*: position not indicated.

141 The explicit references to Divine Providence are all, save two, in added passages. The two exceptions (F. Z. vi. 154–163 and ix. 624–640) are casual rather than doctrinal, having no discernible relation with the doctrine of such early parts of *The Four Zoas* as are interpretable, and where the doctrine, as in the Lambeth books generally, is necessitarian.

143 But . . . Eno] *an addition.* Eno] Ona *1st rdg. del.*

151–152 Cp. M. 23. 68, 'Los is by mortals nam'd Time; Enitharmon is nam'd Space.' 153 But . . . sins] *an addition.*

154–155 She . . . away] *marginal addition.*

They wander'd long, till they sat down upon the margin'd sea
Conversing with the visions of Beulah in dark slumberous bliss.

[8*] Then those in Great Eternity met in the Council of God
As one Man: for Contracting their Exalted Senses,
They behold Multitude; or Expanding, they behold as one,
As One Man all the Universal family, & that One Man
They Call Jesus the Christ: & they in him & he in them
Live in Perfect harmony in Eden, the land of life,
Consulting as One Man above the Mountain of Snowdon Sublime.

For messengers from Beulah come in tears & dark'ning clouds,
Saying: 'Shiloh is in ruins; our brother is sick. Albion, He
Whom thou lovest, is sick: he wanders from his house of Eternity.
The Daughters of Beulah, terrified, have clos'd the Gate of the Tongue.
Luvah & Urizen contend in war around the holy tent.'

So spoke the Ambassadors from Beulah: & with solemn mourning
They were introduc'd to the Divine presence: & they kneelèd down
In Conway's Vale, thus recounting the Wars of Death Eternal:

'The Eternal Man wept in the holy tent. Our Brother in Eternity,
Even Albion, whom thou lovest, wept in pain: his family
Slept round on hills & valleys, in the regions of his love.
But Urizen awoke, & Luvah woke, & thus conferr'd:

Beneath l. 157, 'Conversing . . . bliss', Blake has drawn a line across the page through a verse added in pencil, 'Nine years they view the glowing spheres, leading [? feeding] the Visions of Beulah', as though cancelling it. Above the line, in the right margin, he has written 'Night the Second'. Thus the passages of text on four sheets and more than half of a fifth are transferred from the First Night to the beginning of the Second. The ll. 158–263 are written on two added leaves. They are clearly substituted for that portion of the original First Night which now stands at the commencement of the Second, for beneath l. 248 Blake wrote 'End of the First Night', though when ll. 249–263 were added, this phrase was *deleted*.

158–164 See General Introduction, p. 48.

164 the Mountains of Snowden] Mount Gilead *1st rdg. del.*

166 Shiloh] Cp. J. 49. 9 *note*.

Albion] Shiloh *1st rdg.*, see Index, *Albion*. The lines which follow purpose to show the effects in mortal life, here first symbolized by Albion, of the matter dealt with in the story of Tharmas in the earlier part of the Night; l. 168 (cp. l. 100) marks this intention.

172 Conway's Vale] Beth Peor *1st rdg. del.* Wars of Death Eternal] Cp. M., Preface, *note* 2. 174 Albion] Shiloh *1st rdg. del.*

'"Thou, Luvah!" said the Prince of Light, "behold our sons & daughters
Repos'd on beds! Let them sleep on; do thou alone depart
Into thy wishèd Kingdom, where in Majesty & Power
We may erect a throne. Deep in the North I place my lot,
Thou in the South. Listen attentive! In silent of this night
I will infold the Eternal tent in clouds opake; while thou,
Siezing the chariots of the morning, Go, outfleeting, ride
Afar into the Zenith high, bending thy furious course
Southward, with half the tents of men inclos'd in clouds
Of Tharmas & Urthona. I, remaining in porches of the brain,
Will lay my scepter on Jerusalem the Emanation,
On all her sons, & on thy sons, O Luvah, & on mine,
Till dawn was wont to wake them; then, my trumpet sounding loud,
Ravish'd away in night: my strong command shall be obey'd,
For I have plac'd my centinels in stations: each tenth man
Is bought & sold, & in dim night my Word shall be their law."

[9*] 'Luvah replied: "Dictate to thy Equals! am not I
The Prince of all the hosts of Men, nor Equal know in Heaven?
If I arise into the Zenith, leaving thee to watch
The Emanation & her Sons, the Satan & the Anak,
Sihon & Og, wilt thou not, rebel to my laws, remain
In darkness, building thy strong throne; & in my ancient night,
Daring my power, wilt arm my sons against me in the Atlantic,
My deep, My night, which thou assuming, hast assum'd my Crown?
I will remain as well as thou, & here with hands of blood
Smite this dark sleeper in his tent; then try my strength with thee."

'While thus he spoke, his fires redden'd o'er the holy tent.
Urizen cast deep darkness round him, silent brooding death,
Eternal death to Luvah. Raging, Luvah pour'd
The Lances of Urizen from chariots round the holy tent.
Discord began: & yells & cries shook the wide firmament.

177 The Prince of Light is Urizen, who is associated with the north in the Lambeth books: cp. B. U., Preludium, l. 3 *note*, and see Index, *Cardinal Points*.

186 Cp. F. Z. ii. 45–46:

the Human Brain
Where Urizen & all his Hosts hang their immortal lamps.

Cp. also F. Z. ii. 223.

196–197 Cp. M. 18. 29 *note*.

199 Atlantic] deep *1st rdg. del.* See Index, *Atlantic*.

203 o'er] round *1st rdg. del.*

'Beside his anvil stood Urthona dark: a mass of iron
Glow'd furious on the anvil, prepar'd for spades & coulters. All
His sons fled from his side to join the conflict. Pale, he heard
The Eternal voice: he stood: the sweat chill'd on his mighty limbs.
He drop'd his hammer: dividing from his aking bosom fled
A portion of his life; shrieking upon the wind she fled,
And Tharmas took her in, pitying. Then Enion in jealous fear
Murder'd her, & hid her in her bosom, embalming her for fear
She should arise again to life. Embalm'd in Enion's bosom,
Enitharmon remains a corse. Such thing was never known
In Eden, that one died a death never to be reviv'd.

'Urthona stood in terror, but not long. His spectre fled
To Enion, & his body fell. Tharmas beheld him fall
Endlong, a raging Serpent, rolling round the holy tent.
The sons of war, astonish'd at the Glitt'ring monster, drove
Him far into the world of Tharmas, into a cavern'd rock.

'But Urizen, with darkness overspreading all the armies,
Sent round his heralds, secretly commanding to depart
Into the north. Sudden, with thunder's sound, his multitudes
Retreat from the fierce conflict, all the sons of Urizen at once,
Mustering together in thick clouds, leaving the rage of Luvah
To pour its fury on himself & on the Eternal Man.

Sudden down fell they all together into an unknown Space,
Deep, horrible, without End, Separated from Beulah, far beneath.
The Man's exteriors are become indefinite, open'd to pain,
In a fierce hungering void; & none can visit his regions.

208 See Index, *Los, Note I.*

209 Blake commonly represents the state of man before the Fall by images of patriarchal and pastoral life. Thus, when the general upheaval comes, Urthona is preparing 'spades and coulters'; cp. vii. 280 *seq.*

216 Cp. F. Z. i. 27–28, part of added passage inserted to bring the earlier Tharmas myth into connexion with this later Urizen-Luvah episode.

218 In Eden . . . reviv'd] *marginal addition.* See above, ll. 58–62, for a similar statement that in the ideal existence 'death', or lapse into error is not made permanent by any unforgiving spirit of moral law. This notion is developed in the symbol Beulah as described in *Milton*, 30. 8–31. 7, and belongs to a later period than the main portion of the present work.

226–229 The Urizen-Luvah myth is only found in *The Four Zoas*, so that points like this, which do not explain themselves, can receive no light from without.

Night I

[10] ' Jerusalem his Emanation is become a ruin,
Her little ones are slain on the top of every street,
And she herself led captive, & scatter'd into the indefinite.
Gird on thy sword, O thou most mighty in glory & majesty!
Destroy these op[p]ressors of Jerusalem, & those who ruin Shiloh.'

So spoke the Messengers of Beulah. Silently removing,
The Family Divine drew up the Universal tent
Above High Snowdon, & clos'd the Messengers in clouds around
Till the time of the End. Then they Elected Seven, callèd the Seven
Eyes of God & the Seven lamps of the Almighty.
The Seven are one within the other; the Seventh is namèd Jesus,
The Lamb of God, blessèd for ever: & he follow'd the Man,
Who wander'd in mount Ephraim, seeking a Sepulcher,
His inward eyes closing from the Divine vision, & all
His children wandering outside from his bosom, fleeing away.

234 is] will soon *1st rdg. del.*
235 are] will be *1st rdg. del.*
236 the indefinite] all nations *1st rdg. del.* 'Indefiniteness' is always connoted of sense-percepts and hence appears in association with symbols of moral and intellectual error as the Spectre, Void, Chaos, and Ulro. The 'definite', or truth apprehended in vision, is associated with the symbols Minute Particulars, and Human Form (see Index, *Minute Particulars*, and General Introduction, p. 38) led] *dubious rdg.: perhaps* let.
241 High Snowdon] Mount Gilead *1st rdg. del.*
242–243 'The Seven Eyes of God', originating in the 'seven Spirits of God' described in Rev. v. 6, are here represented as beneficent powers, made apparent in Jesus. So in *Milton* (12. 25: 14. 3: 22. 50: 28. 52: 35. 64: 36. 4) they instruct and comfort fallen man, sustaining him 'with food of Eden'. But in another part of the same book (M. 11. 14–27), as in F. Z. viii. 388–396, seven spirits are named, Lucifer, Molech, Elohim, Shaddai, Pahad, Jehovah, Jesus: they are identified with the 'Seven Eyes of God' (J. 55. 31). These are represented as chosen to watch over Man, but all except the last, Jesus, fail to fulfil the charge. The significance of this mythical episode is not apparent: cp. F. Z. viii. 388 *note*.
247 The vision of the 'inward eyes' is truth: cp. Blake's account of his own spiritual labours:

I rest not from my great task,
To open the Eternal Worlds, to open the immortal Eyes
Of Man inwards into the Worlds of Thought, into Eternity.
(J. 5. 17–19.)

248 Beneath this line Blake has written 'End of The First Night'. But at a later date he added, on the other side of the leaf, fifteen lines (249–263) which carry on the previous episode. The passage is followed by no formal indication of the end of the Night.

[11] The Daughters of Beulah beheld the Emanation : they pitied,
They wept before the Inner gates of Enitharmon's bosom
And of her fine wrought brain & of her bowels within her loins.
Three gates within, Glorious & bright, open into Beulah
From Enitharmon's inward parts ; but the bright female terror
Refus'd to open the bright gates ; she clos'd & barr'd them fast,
Lest Los should enter into Beulah thro' her beautiful gates.

The Emanation stood before the Gates of Enitharmon
Weeping : the Daughters of Beulah silent in the Porches
Spread her a Couch, unknown to Enitharmon ; here repos'd
Jerusalem in slumbers soft, lull'd into silent rest.

Terrific rag'd the Eternal Wheels of intellect : terrific rag'd
The living creatures of the wheels in the Wars of Eternal life ;
But perverse roll'd the wheels of Urizen & Luvah, back revers'd
Downwards & outwards, consuming in the Wars of Eternal Death.

[End of the First Night]

249 The Emanation is Jerusalem.

249–263 The Daughters . . . Death] *pencilled addition*.

250 Blake uses the expressions, Inner and Outer, Interior and Exterior, Within and Without, with definite symbolic meaning. What is Within is of Eternity or Truth (J. 71. 6) ; what is Without is of Error, ' the Void Outside of Existence ' (M. 43. 37), Existence here referring to the Ideal state, and not to mundane life. The Gates, according as they are represented as open or closed, indicate the acceptance or the rejection of the mystical communion with the Divine Humanity. See Index, *Head, Heart, Loins, Stomach.*

252 Three] *dubious rdg.* Beulah] Eternity *1st rdg. del.*

260–263 For the moral implication of the passage cp. J. 22. 34–35 :

Why should Punishment Weave the Veil with Iron Wheels of War
When Forgiveness might it Weave with Wings of Cherubim.

For the ' Wars of Eternal life ' and ' Wars of Eternal Death ' see M., Preface, *note* 2.

261 Cp. Ezekiel i. 263 consuming] bending *1st rdg. del.*

NIGHT II

INTRODUCTORY NOTE

Night II is not less confused and obscure than Night I. It continues the myth of Tharmas from Night I, l. 157, and refers only in passing and towards the end to that of Urizen and Luvah.

There are discernible two main themes: first, the mutual 'jealousy' of Los and Enitharmon, by which is figured the strife that must arise when an ethic based on vision is practised in a world given over to repressive morality; and secondly, Urizen's labours in building in the Abyss the 'golden world' for fallen man.

Detailed interpretation of the myth which develops the first theme is impossible because of our uncertainty as to Blake's meaning in Los at this point. References to Los in the Lambeth books are equivocal, while in the later-written parts of the book and in *Milton* and *Jerusalem* the symbol is first in importance of those used to state the doctrines of regeneration. Certainly the Enitharmon of this Night is the personage of *Europe*, not of *Jerusalem*. She represents error in the regions both of thought and morality. In so far as she also symbolizes Space, emphasis falls upon her beauty, that is, she appears to represent the beauty of man's world as it appears in sense-presentation, dangerously attractive to the visionary. Los is called the 'fierce prophetic boy' (l. 2), a 'visionary' (l. 51), and in an added line 'the visionary of Jesus' (l 80). In spite of these names no definite notion of regenerative activity attaches to the symbol; yet, on the other hand, his opposition to Urizen, the 'god of this world', is more marked than in the Lambeth books. Whatever of spiritual quality is implied in the titles is soon subdued by Enitharmon's power, and, together, they appear as powers 'of this world', sustained by the sufferings of their mythical parents, Tharmas and Enion, and by the 'fleshly bread' and 'nervous wine' of mortal and perishing delights. Men come to debase their immortal powers to do them worship. Time and Space, no longer made intelligible by the light of vision, become deities, sharing with Urizen, the deified rational power of man, 'Doubt' and no longer 'Faith and Certainty', a tyranny over mankind.

A brief survey of the myth will show how Blake treats the theme. Enitharmon mocks Los because he pities Enion and Tharmas, their parents (l. 4), and exults in a 'Song of Death' over fallen man (ll. 14–31). When the visionary spirit in him asserts itself and he smites her to the earth she calls on Urizen for aid (l. 50). He descends and the spiritual subjection of Los is completed in an alliance with Urizen and a reconciliation with Enitharmon (ll. 93–96). Los's decline is emphasized in the long description of the marriage feast, when he and Enitharmon are served by the 'Elemental Gods' of Vegetative existence, i.e. of the apparently real material (ll. 97–126). The song of the 'Demons of the Deep' (ll. 127–175) proclaims the triumph of the forces of intellectual and moral tyranny and shows how beneath the power of the two, aided by the might of Urizen, the life of the spirit is perverted into confusion and sterility, till the ' real and immortal self ' of man is no more (l. 149). A like condemnation of the influence of a non-visionary conception of Time and Space is expressed in changed symbols in Enion's lament (ll. 187–202).

The second theme, which has no apparent relation with the above matters, nor directly with anything in Night I, Urizen's building of a new world, is one of Blake's many myths in criticism of the creation story in Genesis. Since the material Universe is known intuitively by the mystic to be mere illusion, it is the work, not of God, but of the unenlightened mind, of which Urizen is the symbol.[1] Blake's myth tells how Albion on his ' couch of Death ', ' losing the Divine vision ', calls to Urizen, saying, ' Take thou possession.' An obscure line that follows (l. 217) assigns responsibility for the Fall to Luvah and so mechanically connects this myth with that of the second part of Night I (cp. I, ll. 224–229) ; but it explains nothing. From his place 'in the Human Brain' (l. 222 Urizen sees in dismay the ' body ' or state of Man, whose ' golden porches ', the avenues of perception, grow pale in his sickening light (l. 223). Horror impels him to build in ' the deeps of Non Entity ' (l. 347) a ' golden world ' within which 'spirits mourn'd their bondage night and day ' (l. 454). His sons assist him ; ' spirits of strongest wing ' create ' the vehicles of light ', spiders and worms weave the atmospheres, and then the ' weak begin their work ' (ll. 366–368), forming nets, gins and traps, ' condensing the strong energies into little compass ' (l. 373). Thus the elements are divided in ' finite bonds ' (l. 379), the eternal forms of wisdom and joy are perverted to narrowed perceptions of physical reality and moral law. In the west of this newly created world is built a shrine for Ahania, the mother of moral pestilence, Urizen's ' Shadow of Despair ' (l. 397), the soul-destroying feminine principle that lives on sacrifice. All of this seems to be an expansion of chapters viii–ix of the *Book of Urizen*, and Urizen's association with the brain may be intended to indicate that the metaphysical and moral errors of mundane life are in their nature and origin primarily intellectual, though, as will be seen in other places, in attributing the Fall to the maleficent activity of Luvah, Blake appears sometimes to think the errors are of the emotions. Further, a long added passage (ll. 248–275), full of Blake's later symbolism, identifies this Urizenic world with the body of error which, in *Milton* and *Jerusalem*, is attributed to the operation of the spectrous Reason. Both the original and the added passages recount the overthrow of Jerusalem, the image of the ideal existence ; i.e. the disintegration of the perfect unity in Man.

But difficulties arise when, by the insertion of ll. 235 and 456, Blake seeks to relate the creation of Urizen's world with a divine plan for human regeneration ; that is, to identify the new created Universe with the Mundane Shell (see Index, *Mundane Shell*, IV) or the ' Bower for heaven's darling in the grizly deep ' (l. 234). A similar purpose seems implied in ll. 474–476, with their equivocal hint of a providence in the creation of the stars, vehicles of light, to ' bind the body of Man to heaven from falling into the Abyss ' (l. 473). Like most of Blake's attempts to adapt the earlier myths

[1] In conversation with Crabb Robinson Blake said : ' Nature is the work of the Devil . . . God [the Creator] was not Jehovah but the Elohim ' (S., p. 297).

of *The Four Zoas* to those of the later books, these added passages result only in confusion. In the indisputably early part of this episode there is no indication of a regenerative purpose in the labours of Urizen and his sons, for the reference to the former as the 'Architect divine' (l. 376), like the common title of 'prince of light', is merely reminiscent of Urizen's function in the ideal Unity. The Golden World here described does not reappear elsewhere in the present work, unless it be identified with the desolate universe explored by Urizen in the first part of Night VI.

The long sections in this Night that deal with Luvah and Vala are completely obscure. Both these mythical beings appear to suffer beneath Urizen's tyranny (ll. 425–443); while Luvah, like Tharmas and Los, is also the victim of the 'feminine' delusions in Vala (ll. 291–326).

Towards the end of the Night Los and Enitharmon are depicted rejoicing over the labour and sorrow of Urizen and his sons, seeking to plant division in the newly created world, and mocking the bondage of Luvah and Vala (ll. 421–423, 444–447). In ll. 510–590, where Enitharmon triumphs over Los because of his love of her, Blake apparently describes the fate of the soul dominated by falsehood. For though Los, who appears in this instance to be the type of the creative masculine spirit, is strong and Enitharmon weak (l. 540), yet she subdues him, singing:

> The joy of woman is the Death of her most best beloved
> Who dies for Love of her. (ll. 557–558.)

The apparent realities of non-visionary thought and morality destroy the souls that surrender to their specious appeal. Certain additional lines (567–576) appear seriously to conflict with the sentiment of Enitharmon's song of triumph. In ll. 572–574 she speaks lines repeated from V. D. A. (ll. 214–215) proclaiming the holiness of life and liberty. How these lines are to be harmonized, not only with the rest of the song, but with the conception of Enitharmon throughout this Night, we are unable to discover.

VALA.

Night the [Second]

[7] But the two Youthful wonders wander'd in the world of Tharmas.
'Thy name is Enitharmon,' said the fierce prophetic boy.
'While thy mild voice fills all these Caverns with sweet harmony,
O! how our Parents sit & mourn in their silent secret bowers!'

[8] But Enitharmon answer'd with a dropping tear, & frowning
Dark as a dewy morning when the crimson light appears:
'To make us happy, let them weary their immortal powers,
While we draw in their sweet delights, while we return them scorn
On scorn to feed our discontent: for if we grateful prove,
They will withhold sweet love, whose food is thorns & bitter roots.
We hear the warlike clarions, we view the turning spheres;
Yet Thou in indolence reposest, holding me in bonds.
Hear! I will sing a Song of Death: it is a song of Vala:

'The Fallen Man takes his repose: Urizen sleeps in the porch.
Luvah and Vala wake, & fly up from the Human Heart
Into the Brain: from thence upon the pillow Vala slumber'd,
And Luvah siez'd the Horses of Light & rose into the Chariot of Day.
Sweet laughter siez'd me in my sleep, silent & close I laugh'd;
For in the visions of Vala I walk'd with the mighty Fallen One.
I heard his voice among the branches & among sweet flowers:

1 But . . . Tharmas] *marginal addition.*

2 Thy . . . boy] Above this, and apparently cancelled by the line drawn across the page to mark the commencement of the Night, is the line:

Nine years they view'd the living spheres leading [? feeding] the visions of Beulah.

4 our] thy *1st rdg. del.* mourn] weep *1st rdg. del.*

7 let them] how they *1st rdg. del.* Cp. with this speech of Enitharmon, *Europe*, ll. 9–26, and references to Los and Enitharmon in the Introduction to that book.

11–12 We hear . . . bonds] *an addition* inserted between ll. 6 and 7 and marked to come in here.

14 Fallen] Eternal *1st rdg. del.*

15 wake] woke *1st rdg. del.* fly] flew *1st rdg. del.*

17 Cp. *Thel*, § ii, l. 8 *note.*

" Why is the light of Enitharmon darken'd in dewy morn ?
Why is the silence of Enitharmon a terror, & her smile a whirlwind,
Uttering this darkness in my halls, in the pillars of my Holy-ones ?
Why dost thou weep as Vala, & wet thy veil with dewy tears,
In slumbers of my night-repose infusing a false morning,
Driving the Female Emanations all away from Los ?
I have refus'd to look upon the Universal Vision ;
And wilt thou slay with death him who devotes himself to thee,
Once born for the sport & amusement of Man, now born to drink up all his Powers ? "

[9] ' I heard the sounding sea. I heard the voice weaker and weaker.
The voice came & went like a dream. I awoke in my sweet bliss.'

Then Los smote her upon the Earth : 'twas long e'er she reviv'd.
He answer'd, dark'ning more, with indignation hid in smiles :

' I die not, Enitharmon, tho' thou sing'st thy song of death :
Nor shalt thou me torment. For I behold the Fallen Man
Seeking to comfort Vala : she will not be comforted.
She rises from his throne and seeks the shadows of her garden,
Weeping for Luvah lost in the bloody beams of your false morning.
Sick'ning lies the Fallen Man ; his head sick, his heart faint—
Mighty atchievement of your power. Beware the punishment !

21 in dewy] in her dewy *1st rdg.* 22 terror] *1st rdg. illeg.*; Cloud *2nd rdg. del.* 26 Driving . . . Los] *an addition.*
After l. 28, a line divided by Blake, *del.* :

If thou drivest all the Females away from Luvah I will drive all / The Males away from thee.

28–29 And . . . Powers] *an addition.* The perversive effects of morality and reliance on sense-perception are in the later writings frequently imaged as a female dominion over the male ; cp. J. 68. 65–68 :

Once Man was occupied in intellectual pleasures & energies,
But now my soul is harrow'd with grief & fear & love & desire ;
And now I hate & now I love, & Intellect is no more ;
There is no time for any thing but the torments of love & desire.

32 Then . . . reviv'd] *pencilled addition.*
33 He] Los *1st rdg. del.* with indignation] with foul indignation *1st rdg.*
40 Mighty . . . punishment] *an addition.*

‘ I see invisible descend into the Gardens of Vala
Luvah, walking on the winds. I see the invisible knife ;
I see the shower of blood ; I see the swords & spears of futurity.
Tho’ in the Brain of Man we live & in his circling Nerves,
Tho’ this bright world of all our joy is in the Human Brain
Where Urizen & all his Hosts hang their immortal lamps,
Thou ne’er shalt leave this cold expanse where wat’ry Tharmas mourns.’

So spoke Los. Scorn & Indignation rose upon Enitharmon.

Then Enitharmon, redd’ning fierce, stretch’d her immortal hands :
‘ Descend, O Urizen ! descend with horse & chariot !
Threaten not me, O Visionary : thine the punishment.
The Human Nature shall no more remain, nor Human acts
Form the rebellious Spirits of Heaven ; but War & Princedom & Victory & Blood.’

[10] Night darken’d as she spoke ; a shudd’ring ran from East to West ;
A Groan was heard on high. The warlike clarions ceas’t ; the Spirits
Of Luvah & Vala shudder’d in their Orb, an orb of blood.

Eternity groan’d & was troubled at the Image of Eternal Death.
The Wandering Man bow’d his faint head and Urizen descended :
And the one must have murdered the Man if he had not descended.

After 40 *a deleted marginal passage* :

Refusing to behold the Divine image which all behold
And live thereby, he is sunk down into a deadly sleep.
But we, immortal in our own strength, survive by stern debate,
Till we have drawn the Lamb of God into a mortal form.
And that he must be born is certain ; for One must be All,
And comprehend within himself all things both small & great.
We therefore for whose sake all things aspire to be & live,
Will so receive the Divine Image that among the Reprobate
He may be devoted to destruction from his mother’s womb.

41–43 Los’s visions apparently have relation to the punishment of which he warns Enitharmon (l. 40). Their exact significance is obscure.

After l. 49 an added line, identical with l. 51, *del.*

52–53 The . . . Blood] *an addition.* 53 rebellious] free *1st rdg. del.*

57 Eternity . . . Death] *an addition* ; cp. l. 204 *infra.* The line is also found in *Jerusalem*, 48. 12.

59–60 And . . . descended] *an addition.* The identity of ‘ the one ’ is obscure, and the interpolation of these lines, with their suggestion of an

Indignant, muttering low thunders, Urizen descended,
Gloomy sounding: 'Now I am God from Eternity to Eternity!'

Sullen sat Los, plotting Revenge. Silent he eyed the Prince
Of Light. Silent the prince of Light view'd Los. At length a brooded
Smile broke from Urizen; for Enitharmon brighten'd more & more.
Sullen he lower'd on Enitharmon, but he smil'd on Los,

Saying: 'Thou art the Lord of Luvah: into thine hands I give
The prince of Love, the murderer: his soul is in thine hands.
Pity not Vala, for she pitied not the Eternal Man;
Nor pity thou the cries of Luvah. Lo, these starry hosts!
They are thy Servants, if thou wilt obey my awful Law.'

So spoke the Prince of Light & sat beside the Seat of Los:
Upon the sandy shore rested his chariot of fire.

Los answer'd furious: 'Art thou one of those who when most complacent
Mean mischief most? If you are such, Lo! I am also such.
One must be master. Try thy Arts; I also will try mine:
For I percieve Thou hast Abundance which I claim as mine.'
Urizen startled stood, but not Long. Soon he cried:

'Obey my voice, young Demon. I am God from Eternity to Eternity.'

Thus Urizen spoke, collected in himself in awful pride:
'Art thou a visionary of Jesus, the soft delusion of Eternity?
Lo! I am God, the terrible destroyer, & not the Saviour.

ulterior purpose in the descent of Urizen, increases the difficulty of this part of the story. It is just possible that the reference is to Luvah who is called 'the murderer' (l. 67): cp. the Urizen-Luvah myth, F. Z. i, ll. 177 seq.; but the context, especially ll. 52–53, seems rather to identify the 'one' with Enitharmon, here, as in the Lambeth books, the 'Female', the symbol of the life of the senses. 62 he] Urizen *1st rdg. del.*

63–72 Of . . . fire] *marginal addition*, marked to come in here.

68 Urizen's concern for the Eternal Man in this passage inexplicably replaces his usual antagonism. The nearest parallel is in the added lines at the commencement of the earlier form of Night II (ll. 211 seq.).

73–83 Los . . . spectre] *an addition*.

73–77 With this account of Urizen, cp. the description of Satan in the Satan-Palamabron myth, M. 5. 5–41.

80–81 Cp. M. 7. 19–29: 9. 10–14. According to the standards of the Spectrous metaphysic and ethic, the visionary ideas of reality and of right conduct are delusions: cp. J. 82. 42, and J. 28. 6 *note*.

Why should the Divine Vision compell the Sons of Eden
To forego each his own delight to war against his spectre ?
The Spectre is the Man : the rest is only delusion & fancy.'

Ten thousand thousand were his hosts of spirits on the wind,
Ten thousand thousand glittering Chariots shining in the sky.
They pour upon the golden shore beside the silent ocean,
Rejoicing in the Victory : & the heavens were fill'd with blood.

The Earth spread forth her table wide ; the Night, a silver cup
Fill'd with the wine of anguish, waited at the golden feast.
But the bright Sun was not as yet : he, filling all the expanse,
Slept as a bird in the blue shell that soon shall burst away.

Los saw the wound of his blow : he saw, he pitied, he wept.
Los now repented that he had smitten Enitharmon : he felt love
Arise in all his Veins : he threw his arms around her loins
To heal the wound of his smiting.

They eat the fleshly bread, they drank the nervous wine,
[11] They listen'd to the Elemental Harps & Sphery Song.
They view'd the dancing Hours, quick sporting thro' the sky,
With wingèd radiance scattering joys thro' the everchanging light.
But Luvah & Vala, standing in the bloody sky,
On high remain'd alone, forsaken, in fierce jealousy.
They stood above the heavens, forsaken, desolate, suspended in blood.
Descend they could not, nor from Each other avert their eyes.
Eternity appear'd above them as One Man infolded
In Luvah's robes of blood & bearing all his afflictions.
As the sun shines down on the misty earth, such was the Vision.

82–83 These lines contain the first reference to the opposition between the Divine Vision and the Spectre. The Spectre here is symbolic (see Index, *Spectre*) ; elsewhere in *The Four Zoas*, except in similar added passages, it is used descriptively.

84 The Spectre . . . fancy] *marginal addition* ; position not indicated.

85–126 Cp. *Europe*, 1–32 and 154–195.

93 Los . . . wept] *an addition*. 94–95 Los . . . loins] *an addition*.

96 To . . . smiting] *marginal addition* ; in red crayon like l. 93.

97 ' fleshly ' and ' nervous ' are written over erasures.

101–102 But . . . jealousy] *an addition*. The significance of this added passage is quite obscure, as is the entire myth of Luvah and Vala in this book. Vala has here very little of her later significance.

103–107 They . . . Vision] *marginal addition*, marked for insertion here. Like the additions in Night I that have a similar reference to the later doctrine of Providence, these lines stand quite apart from the main body of the story. For the manifestation of the providential purpose of regeneration

But purple night and crimson morning & golden day, descending
Thro' the clear changing atmosphere, display'd green fields among
The varying clouds, like paradises stretch'd in the expanse,
With towns & villages and temples, tents, sheep-folds and pastures,
Where dwell the children of the elemental worlds in harmony.
Not long in harmony they dwell; their life is drawn away,
And wintry woes succeed, successive driven into the Void
Where Enion craves, successive drawn into the golden feast.

And Los & Enitharmon sat in discontent & scorn.
The Nuptial Song arose from all the thousand thousand spirits
Over the joyful Earth & Sea, and ascended into the Heavens;
For Elemental Gods their thunderous Organs blew, creating
Delicious Viands. Demons of Waves their wat'ry Eccho's woke.
Bright Souls of vegetative life, budding and blossoming,
[12] Stretch their immortal hands to smite the gold & silver Wires
And with immortal Voice soft warbling fill all Earth & Heaven;
With doubling Voices & loud Horns wound round sounding,
Cavernous dwellers fill'd the enormous Revelry Responsing,
And Spirits of Flaming fire on high govern'd the mighty Song.

And This the Song sung at The Feast of Los & Enitharmon:

'Ephraim call'd out to Zion: "Awake, O Brother Mountain!
Let us refuse the Plow & Spade, the heavy Roller & spikèd
Harrow: burn all these Corn fields: throw down all these fences!
Fatten'd on Human blood & drunk with wine of life is better far

'"Than all these labours of the harvest & the vintage. See the river,
Red with the blood of Men, swells lustful round my rocky knees!

becoming apparent in Eternity as 'One Man', Jesus, in Luvah's robes of blood, see Index, *Luvah*, and cp. M. 19. 37–42: J. 29. 4–27.

108 golden] the golden *1st rdg.* 117–126 Cp. M. 31. 17–27.

128–143 Ephraim . . . blood] written over a deletion. The Song of the elemental spirits is continued on the added pp. 13 *a*, 13 *b*.

128 Ephraim] The Mountain *1st rdg. del.* Zion] the Mountain *1st rdg. del.*

My clouds are not the clouds of verdant fields & groves of fruit,
But Clouds of Human Souls : my nostrils drink the lives of Men."

'The Villages Lament! they faint outstretch'd upon the plain:
Wailing runs round the Valleys from the Mill & from the Barn.
But most the polish'd Palaces dark, silent, bow with dread,
Hiding their books & pictures underneath the dens of Earth.

'The Cities send to one another saying : "My sons are Mad
With wine of cruelty. Let us plat a Scourge, O Sister City !"
Children are nourish'd for the Slaughter. Once the Child was fed
With Milk ; but wherefore now are Children fed with blood ?

[13*a*] 'The horse is of more value than the Man ; The Tyger fierce
Laughs at the Human form ; the Lion mocks, & thirsts for blood.
They cry : "O Spider, spread thy web ! Enlarge thy bones, & fill'd
With marrow, sinews & flesh, Exalt thyself ! attain a voice !"

'Call to thy dark arm'd hosts, for all the Sons of Men muster together
To desolate their cities. Man shall be no more. Awake, O Hosts !
The bow string sang upon the hills. Luvah & Vala ride
Triumphant in the bloody sky, & the Human form is no more."

'The list'ning Stars heard, & the first beam of the morning started back.
He cried out to his Father : "Depart ! depart !" but sudden Siez'd
And clad in steel & his Horse proudly neigh'd : he smelt the battle
Afar off. Rushing back, redd'ning with rage, the Mighty Father

'Siez'd his bright Sheephook studded with gems & gold : he Swung it round
His head, shrill sounding in the Sky. Down rush'd the Sun with noise

153–154 but . . . neigh'd] so in MS. 'Siez'd' is written over an erasure.
155 Mighty] Eternal *1st rdg. del.*

Of war. The Mountains fled away: they sought a place beneath.
Vala remain'd in desarts of dark solitude, nor Sun nor Moon

'By night nor day to comfort her. She labour'd in thick smoke.
Tharmas endur'd not: he fled howling; then a barren waste sunk down,
Conglobing in the dark confusion. Mean time Los was born,
And Thou, O Enitharmon. Hark, I hear the hammers of Los!

[13 b] 'They melt the bones of Vala & the bones of Luvah into wedges.
The innumerable sons & daughters of Luvah, clos'd in furnaces,
Melt into furrows. Winter blows his bellows: Ice & Snow
Tend the dire anvils. Mountains mourn, & Rivers faint & fail.

'There is no City, nor Cornfield, nor Orchard: all is Rock & Sand.
There is no Sun nor Moon nor Star, but rugged wintry rocks
Justling together in the void, suspended by inward fires.
Impatience now no longer can endure. Distracted Luvah

'Bursting forth from the Loins of Enitharmon! Thou fierce Terror!
Go, howl in vain! Smite, Smite his fetters! Smite, O wintry hammers!
Smite, Spectre of Urthona! mock the fiend who drew us down
From heavens of joy into this Deep! Now rage, but rage in vain!'

Thus sang the Demons of the Deep: the Clarions of war blew loud.
The Feast redounds, & Crown'd with roses & the circling vine,
The Enormous Bride & Bridegroom sat: beside them Urizen
With faded radiance sigh'd, forgetful of the flowing wine
And of Ahania his Pure Bride: but she was distant far.

But Los & Enitharmon sat in discontent & scorn,
Craving the more, the more enjoying; drawing out sweet bliss
From all the turning wheels of heaven & the chariots of the Slain.

171–175 The bursting forth of Luvah from Enitharmon's Loins, and his binding at the hands of Urthona's Spectre, suggest that here, as later, Luvah is identified with Orc. See Index, *Orc*.

176 War here is the Corporeal strife, the state of error; see M., Preface, *note* 2.

At distance, Far in Night repell'd, in direful hunger craving,
Summers & Winters round revolving in the frightful deep,
[13] Enion, blind & age-bent, wept upon the desolate wind:

'Why does the Raven cry aloud and no eye pities her?
Why fall the Sparrow & the Robin in the foodless winter?
Faint, shivering, they sit on leafless bush or frozen stone,

'Wearied with seeking food across the snowy waste, the little
Heart cold, and the little tongue consum'd that once in thoughtless joy
Gave songs of gratitude to waving corn fields round their nest.

'Why howl the Lion & the Wolf? why do they roam abroad?
Deluded by summer's heat they sport in enormous love,
And cast their young out to the hungry wilds & sandy desarts.

[14] 'Why is the Sheep given to the knife? The Lamb plays in the Sun.
He starts; he hears the foot of Man; he says: "Take thou my wool
But spare my life": but he knows not that winter cometh fast.

'The Spider sits in his labour'd Web, eager watching for the Fly:
Presently comes a famish'd Bird, & takes away the Spider.
His Web is left all desolate that his little anxious heart
So careful wove & spread it out with sighs and weariness.'

This was the Lamentation of Enion round the golden Feast.
Eternity groan'd & was troubled at the image of Eternal Death
Without the body of Man, an Exudation from his sick'ning limbs.

Now Man was come to the Palm tree & to the Oak of Weeping,
Which stand upon the Edge of Beulah; & he sunk down

189 Faint . . . stone] *written over erasure.*
192 to waving] to the waving *1st rdg.*
194 summer's] the summer's *1st rdg.*
198 but] *an addition.* that winter] that the winter *1st rdg.*
204–210 Eternity . . . Care] *an addition*; written over 'End of the [? First] Night' *del.*: cp. F. Z. i, l. 157 *note.*
204–205 The 'Body of Death' is a comparatively frequent symbol in the later writings, imaging the state of mundane error. 'Without' (205) has here a definite symbolic reference to the unreal forms of physical life: cp. F. Z. i. 250 *note.*
206–207 Cp. J. 23. 24–25. The Palm Tree and the Oak have so far eluded interpretation. Elsewhere (J. 59. 6) the 'Oak of Weeping & the Palm of Suffering' are mentioned, without throwing light on the symbols. In Gen. xxxv. 8, where Allon Bachuth signifies 'Oak of Weeping'.

From the supporting arms of the Eternal Saviour, who dispos'd
The pale limbs of his Eternal Individuality
Upon The Rock of Ages, Watching over him with Love & Care.

[1] Rising upon his Couch of Death, Albion beheld his Sons.
Turning his Eyes outward to Self, losing the Divine Vision,
Albion call'd Urizen & said : ' Behold these sick'ning Spheres !
Whence is this voice of Enion that soundeth in my Porches ?
Take thou possession ! take this Scepter ! go forth in my might !
For I am weary & must sleep in the dark sleep of Death.
Thy brother Luvah hath smitten me; but pity thou his youth,
Tho' thou hast not pitied my Age, O Urizen, Prince of Light ! '

Urizen rose from the bright Feast like a star thro' the evening sky,
Exulting at the voice that call'd him from the Feast of envy.
First he beheld the body of Man, pale, cold. The horrors of death
Beneath his feet shot thro' him as he stood in the Human Brain ;
And all its golden porches grew pale with his sickening light,
No more Exulting, for he saw Eternal Death beneath.
Pale he beheld futurity, pale he beheld the Abyss

208–212 Cp. J. 48. 1–4, and M. 14. 10–16 :

for when he enter'd into his Shadow, Himself,
His real and immortal Self, was, as appear'd to those
Who dwell in immortality, as One sleeping on a couch
Of gold : and those in immortality gave forth their Emanations
Like Females of sweet beauty, to guard round him & to feed
His lips with food of Eden in his cold and dim repose.
But to himself he seem'd a wanderer lost in dreary night.

211–212 Rising . . . Vision] *an addition.* At this point the earlier form of Night II began. Above l. 211 is written ' Vala / Night the [First *1st rdg. del.* ; First *2nd rdg. del.*

211 See Index, *Spectre.*

212 Cp. F. Z. i. 250 *note.* ' Self ' here is ' the Self-hood ' or Spectre, the Individual, in opposition to the Universal spirit : see Index, *Spectre.*

213 Albion] The Man *1st rdg. del.*

214 Whence . . . Porches] *an addition.* Porches] Ears *1st rdg. del.* This line recurs with a slight change in J. 29. 59.

218 Tho' . . . Light] *an addition.*

219–220 The Feast is apparently that of Los and Enitharmon : cp. ll. 177–180.

220 Exulting] Indignant *2nd rdg. del.* : *1st rdg. restored.*

222 This would seem to imply a definitely mental or intellectual significance in this part of the myth ; but the details are too vague for interpretation.

Where Enion, blind & age bent, wept, in direful hunger craving,
All rav'ning like the hungry worm & like the silent grave.
[2] Mighty was the draught of Voidness to draw Existence in.

Terrific Urizen strode above in fear & pale dismay.
He saw the indefinite space beneath, & his soul shrunk with horror,
His feet upon the verge of Non Existence. His voice went forth.

Luvah & Vala, trembling & shrinking, beheld the great Work master,
And heard his Word: 'Divide, ye bands, influence by influence!
Build we a Bower for heaven's darling in the grizly deep;
Build we the Mundane Shell around the Rock of Albion!'

The Bands of Heaven flew thro' the air, singing & shouting to Urizen.
Some fix'd the anvil, some the loom erected, some the plow
And harrow form'd, & fram'd the harness of silver & ivory,
The golden compasses, the quadrant & the rule & balance.
They erected the furnaces; they form'd the anvils of gold, beaten in mills
Where winter beats incessant, fixing them firm on their base.
The bellows began to blow: & the Lions of Urizen stood round the anvil,
[3] And the leopards, cover'd with skins of beasts, tended the roaring fires;
Sublime, distinct their lineaments divine of human beauty.
The tygers of wrath callèd the horses of instruction from their mangers.
They unloos'd them & put on the harness of gold & silver & ivory.

232–235 Cp. J. 58. 16–51. The association of Urizen with this task, which apparently implies a regenerative purpose, is not easily reconciled with the commoner use of the symbol. The statement that the world he is about to create is for 'heaven's darling' (l. 234) and its identification with the Mundane Shell (see Index) sufficiently indicate a providential purpose. The ll. 235 and 456 wherein Urizen's world is identified with the Mundane Shell are, it is to be noted, added lines.

235 Build . . . Albion] *an addition.*

244 Sublime . . . beauty] *an addition.*

245 Cp. M. H. H., proverb 44: 'The tygers of wrath are wiser than the horses of instruction.'

In human forms distinct, they stood round Urizen, prince of Light,
Petrifying all the Human Imaginations into rock & sand.
Groans ran along Tyburn's brook and along the River of Oxford,
Among the Druid Temples. Albion groan'd on Tyburn's brook.
Albion gave his loud death groan: the Atlantic Mountains trembled.
Aloft the Moon fled with a Cry, the Sun with streams of blood;
From Albion's Loins fled all Peoples, And Nations of the Earth
Fled with the noise of Slaughter, & the Stars of heaven fled.
Jerusalem came down in a dire ruin over all the Earth:
She fell cold from Lambeth's Vales in groans & dewy death,
The dew of anxious Souls, the death-sweat of the dying,
In every pillar'd hall & archèd roof of Albion's Skies.
The brother & the brother bathe in blood upon the Severn,
The Maiden weeping by; The father & the mother, with
The Maiden's father & her mother, fainting over the body;
And the Young Man, the Murderer, fleeing over the mountains.

Reuben slept on Penmaenmawr, & Levi slept on Snowdon.
Their eyes, their ears, nostrils & tongues roll outward; they behold
What is within, now seen without: they are raw to the hungry wind;

248–275 Petrifying . . . Stones] *an addition.*

249–251 Cp. J. 27. poem. Tyburn with its 'fatal Tree' (J. 12. 26) has constant reference to the repressive and punitive operation of the Moral Law. It is the place of the 'Victims' of Natural Religion (J. 62. 34), the 'Nations and Families of the Dead' (J. 63. 33), who are dominated by the Daughters of Albion. It is also associated with 'Druidism', and its 'Offerings of Human [i. e. Spiritual or Visionary] Life', the sacrifice of the 'real and eternal' in man before the unreal forms of Law. The 'Tree of Moral Virtue' 'the Law of God who dwells in Chaos', i. e. of Satan, has root here, and is watered by Tyburn's brook (J. 28. 14). Blake couples this place of execution, standing outside London, with Golgotha (J. 63. 33).

250 The 'Druid Temples' are associated with the idea of Sacrifice, the repression or destruction of the spiritual life of Imagination: for an earlier use of the symbol, cp. *Europe*, 117 *note*. See Index, *Druid*.

252–254 Cp. J. 27: 'You have a tradition that Man anciently contain'd in his mighty limbs all things in Heaven & Earth . . . But now the Starry Heavens are fled from the mighty limbs of Albion.' The illusion of discrete physical entities obscures the perception of the essential unity of all things which Blake expresses in his symbolic treatment of the Eternal Man or Albion. See General Introduction, p. 46.

256 Cp. M. 4. 14 *note*.

263–265 See Index, *Reuben*, and cp. J. 34. 43–58 and 36. 1–24. The significance of Levi is not discerned. 265 Cp. F. Z. i. 250 *note*.

They become Nations far remote in a little & dark Land.
The Daughters of Albion girded around their garments of Needlework,
Stripping Jerusalem's Curtains from mild demons of the hills.
Across Europe & Asia to China & Japan, like lightnings
They go forth & return to Albion on his rocky couch,
Gwendolen, Ragan, Sabrina, Gonorill, Mehetabel, Cordella,
Boadicea, Conwenna, Estrild, Gwinefrid, Ignoge, Cambel,
Binding Jerusalem's Children in the dungeons of Babylon.
They play before the Armies, before the hounds of Nimrod,
While The Prince of Light on Salisbury plain among the Druid Stones . . .

Rattling the adamantine chains & hooks heave up the ore,
In mountainous masses plung'd in furnaces : & they shut & seal'd
The furnaces a time & times. All the while blew the North
His cloudy bellows, & the South & East & dismal West :
And all the while the plow of iron cut the dreadful furrows
In Ulro, beneath Beulah, where the Dead wail Night & Day.

Luvah was cast into the Furnaces of affliction & sealèd,
And Vala fed in cruel delight the furnaces with fire.
Stern Urizen beheld, urg'd by necessity to keep
The evil day afar, & if perchance with iron power

267 The garments of Needlework seem equivalent to the commoner symbol, the 'Net' or 'Veil' of Religion, a perversion of the visionary faith symbolized by Jerusalem.

269 So the 'Wheel of Religion' against which Jesus strove, goes from west to east, that is, from the quarter of Eden or Imagination to Ulro or Error. For 'Europe' and 'Asia' as symbols, cp. Introductions to the prophecies bearing these names. Japan is frequently mentioned in *Jerusalem* as the eastern, and Ireland as the western limit of the earth : cp. J. 34. 42 : 63. 34 ; 67. 7.

271–272 See Index, *Vala, Note I*, A. 273 See Index, *Jerusalem, Note I.*

274 Nimrod appears to represent the spirit of hostility to Imagination, the repressive activity of the Spectre, Corporeal War :

> Great is the cry of the Hounds of Nimrod along the valley
> Of Vision ; they scent the odor of War in the Valley of Vision.
> All Love is lost ; terror succeeds, & Hatred instead of Love,
> And stern demands of Right & Duty instead of Liberty.
>
> (J. 22. 8–11.)

275 Cp. *supra*, 250 *note*. This line concludes the marginal addition, but its incompleteness would suggest that it was intended to be followed by a passage now lost. It has no connexion, syntactical or other, with l. 276, where a return is made to the main body of the text, following upon l. 247.

280 See Index, *Plow*, ii. 281 In . . . Day] *an addition*.

282–289 These lines are repeated, J. 7. 30–37. Their meaning is quite obscure.

285–286 The ordinary rules of syntax are somewhat strained in these lines, but Blake's intention is clear enough.

He might avert his own despair. In woe & fear he saw
[4] Vala incircle round the furnaces where Luvah was clos'd.
In joy she heard his howlings, & forgot he was her Luvah
With whom she walk'd in bliss in times of innocence & youth.

Hear ye the voice of Luvah from the furnaces of Urizen :

' If I indeed am Vala's King, & ye, O sons of Men,
The workmanship of Luvah's hands—in times of Everlasting,
When I call'd forth the Earth-worm from the cold & dark obscure,
I nurtur'd her, I fed her with my rains & dews. She grew
A scalèd Serpent ; yet I fed her, tho' she hated me.
Day after day she fed upon the mountains in Luvah's sight.
I brought her thro' the Wilderness, a dry & thirsty land,
And I commanded springs to rise for her in the black desart,
Till she became a Dragon, wingèd, bright & poisonous.
I open'd all the floodgates of the heavens to quench her thirst,
[5] And I commanded the Great deep to hide her in his hand,
Till she became a little weeping Infant a span long.
I carried her in my bosom as a man carries a lamb.
I lovèd her : I gave her all my soul & my delight.
I hid her in soft gardens & in secret bowers of Summer,
Weaving mazes of delight along the sunny Paradise,
Inextricable labyrinths. She bore me sons & daughters
And they have taken her away & hid her from my sight.
They have surrounded me with walls of iron & brass. O Lamb
Of God, clothèd in Luvah's garments, little knowest thou
Of death Eternal, that we all go to Eternal Death,
To our Primeval Chaos, in fortuitous concourse of incoherent
Discordant principles of Love & Hate. I suffer affliction
Because I love ; for I was love : but hatred awakes in me :
And Urizen, who was Faith & Certainty, is chang'd to Doubt.

291 Vala's King] *written over erasure.*

292 Blake has a semicolon after ' hands ', but the incoherence of the passage makes punctuation uncertain.

302 To become ' a weeping Infant ', an expression fairly frequent in *Jerusalem* (63. 17 : 82. 8 : 83. 5), indicates a decline into the errors of ' Natural Religion '. It apparently indicates entry into the state of the ' Spectre ' or ' Shadow ' (see Index, *Spectre*) : cp. Poems from Letters, ii, ll. 42–44 (Clar. Press, p. 303) :

We like Infants descend
In our Shadows on Earth
Like a weak mortal birth.

309–313 O . . . affliction] *an addition,* over erased passage. For ' Luvah's garments ' see Index, *Incarnation.*

314 was] am *1st rdg. del.* but] & *1st rdg. del.*

315 And . . . doubt] *an addition.*

The hand of Urizen is upon me because I blotted out
That Human delusion, to deliver all the sons of God
From bondage of the Human form. O first born Son of Light!
O Urizen, my enemy! I weep for thy stern ambition,
But weep in vain. O when will you return, Vala the wanderer?'
[6] These were the words of Luvah, patient in afflictions,
Reasoning from the loins in the unreal forms of Ulro's night.

And when Luvah, age after age, was quite melted with woe,
The fires of Vala faded like a shadow, cold & pale,
An evanescent shadow: last she fell, a heap of Ashes
Beneath the furnaces, a woful heap in living death.

Then were the furnaces unseal'd with spades, & pickaxes
Roaring let out the fluid: the molten metal ran in channels
Cut by the plow of ages held in Urizen's strong hand
In many a valley; for the Bulls of Luvah drag'd the Plow.

With trembling horror, pale, aghast, the Children of Man
Stood on the infinite Earth, & saw these visions in the air,
In waters & in Earth beneath. They cried to one another:
'What! are we terrors to one another? Come, O brethren! wherefore
Was this wide Earth spread all abroad?—not for wild beasts to roam.'
But many stood silent, & busied in their families.
And many said: 'We see no Visions in the darksom air.
Measure the course of that sulphur orb that lights the darksom day,

317 delusion] terror. *1st rdg. del.* Cp. F. Z. ii. 80 *note.* The difficulty of this passage consists in the quite unusual function attributed to Urizen, of vindicating 'the Human form', that is, Vision or Imagination, against those who call it a delusion and seek to overthrow it. See above, ll. 213–218.

319 Cp. F. Z. v. 189 seq.

322 Reasoning . . . night] *an addition.* Cp. J. 33. 4: 'the back & loins, where dwell the spectrous Dead': and see Index, *Head, Heart, and Loins.*

330 Cp. *Thel,* § ii, 8 *note.*

331–344 With . . . severity] *an addition* which comes awkwardly here as it interrupts the narrative of the creation of the world which the 'Children of Men' appear in these lines already to inhabit. But the phrase, 'the infinite Earth' (l. 332), otherwise unintelligible, suggests that this is a prevision in the Divine mind showing not what is, but what is to become.

337–341 Blake here represents the materialists' attitude towards the realities of vision, which are obscured for them by the illusory interests, scientific and other, of mundane life. For Blake's symbolic use of the sun cp. *Thel,* § ii, l. 8. The orb of the sun, regarded as a material object, is quoted as a case of the illusion following upon the loss or denial of vision (J. 77, *poem,* l. 7). On the other hand, what Blake calls 'the spiritual sun' is closely associated with Jesus and the equivalent symbols, 'the Divine Family' (M. 19. 37–42), and Los (M. 20. 6).

338 darksom] dismal *1st rdg. del.*

Set stations on this breeding Earth, & let us buy & sell.'
Others arose, & schools Erected, forming Instruments
To measure out the course of heaven. Stern Urizen beheld
In woe his brethren & his Sons, in dark'ning woe lamenting
Upon the winds, in clouds involv'd, Uttering his voice in thunders,
Commanding all the work with care & power & severity.

Then siez'd the Lions of Urizen their work; & heated in the forge
Roar the bright masses. Thund'ring beat the hammers. Many a pyramid
Is form'd, & thrown down thund'ring into the deeps of Non Entity.
Heated red hot, they hizzing rend their way down many a league,
Till resting, each his [basement] finds: suspended there they stand,
Casting their sparkles dire abroad into the dismal deep.
For measur'd out in order'd spaces, the Sons of Urizen
With compasses divide the deep: they the strong scales erect
[7] That Luvah rent from the faint Heart of the Fallen Man,
And weigh the massy Cubes, then fix them in their awful stations.

And all the time in Caverns shut, the golden Looms, erected,
First spun, then wove the Atmospheres: there the Spider & Worm
Plied the wing'd shuttle, piping shrill thro' all the list'ning threads.
Beneath the Caverns roll the weights of lead & spindles of iron;
The enormous warp & woof rage direful in the affrighted deep:

While far into the vast unknown the strong wing'd Eagles bend
Their venturous flight in Human forms distinct; thro' darkness deep

346 pyramid] Globe *1st rdg. del.*
349 basement] *2nd rdg. del.*; center *1st rdg. del.*
353 Fallen] Eternal *1st rdg. del.*; Ancient *2nd rdg. del.* Luvah is frequently mentioned in association with the Heart: see above, l. 15. This agrees with the interpretation of the symbol as connected with the Affections or Love, which in the fallen state becomes Hate (l. 314). The significance of the 'strong scales' is uncertain.
354 Cubes] Globes *1st rdg. del.*

They bear the woven draperies ; on golden hooks they hang abroad
The universal curtains, & spread out from Sun to Sun
The vehicles of light : they separate the furious particles
Into mild currents, as the water mingles with the wine.

While thus the Spirits of strongest wing enlighten the dark deep,
The threads are spun, & the cords twisted & drawn out. Then the weak
Begin their work : & many a net is netted, many a net
[8] Spread, & many a Spirit caught : innumerable the nets,
Innumerable the gins & traps : & many a soothing flute
Is form'd, & many a corded lyre. Outspread over the immense
In cruel delight they trap the listeners & in cruel delight
Bind them, condensing the strong energies into little compass.
Some became seed of every plant that shall be planted ; some
The bulbous roots thrown up together into barns & garners.

Then rose the Builders. First the Architect divine his plan
Unfolds. The wondrous scaffold rear'd all round the infinite,
Quadrangular the building rose : the heavens squared by a line.
Trigons & cubes divide the elements in finite bonds.
Multitudes without number work incessant. The hewn stone
Is plac'd in beds of mortar mingled with the ashes of Vala :
Severe the labour : female slaves the mortar trod, oppressèd.

Twelve halls, after the names of his twelve sons, compos'd
The wondrous building ; & three Central Domes, after the Names

362–366 This passage presents some difficulty, if, as elsewhere (see above, l. 222 *note*), a definitely mental significance is to be read into this myth. For it is impossible to reconcile the intellectual light proceeding from the labours of certain of Urizen's sons with the obscurantism denoted by Urizen himself, and manifested in the creation of his new world. It may be therefore that the reference is to the light of the sun, not to mental light.

367–375 Cp. *Africa*, 32–35, where Blake writes of Urizen's 'Laws & Religions':

These were the Churches, Hospitals, Castles, Palaces,
Like nets & gins & traps to catch the joys of Eternity ;
And all the rest a desart :
Till like a dream Eternity was obliterated & erased.

See also B. U., chaps. viii–ix.

376 'The Architect divine' is apparently Urizen : cp. J. 58. 21 seq. In both passages the connexion between Urizen and the Divine Power is quite obscure.

378–379 Quadrangular . . . bonds] *an addition.*

383–418 Twelve . . . Repentance] *an addition.*

384 wondrous] golden *1st rdg. del.*

Of his three daughters, were encompass'd by the twelve bright halls,
Every hall surrounded by bright Paradises of Delight,
In which were towns & Cities, Nations, Seas, Mountains & Rivers.
Each Dome open'd toward four halls; & the Three Domes Encompass'd
The Golden Hall of Urizen, whose western side glow'd bright
With ever streaming fires beaming from his lawful limbs.
His Shadowy Feminine Semblance here repos'd on a White Couch,
Or hover'd o'er his Starry head; & when he smil'd, she brighten'd
Like a bright Cloud in harvest; but when Urizen frown'd, she wept
In mists over his carvèd throne; & when he turn'd his back
Upon his Golden hall, & sought the Labyrinthine porches
Of his wide heaven, Trembling, cold, in jealous fears she sat,
A Shadow of Despair. Therefore toward the West Urizen form'd
A recess in the wall for fires to glow upon the pale
Female's limbs in his absence; & her Daughters oft upon
A Golden Altar burnt perfumes, with Art Celestial form'd,
Foursquare, sculptur'd & sweetly Engrav'd, to please their shadowy mother:
As[c]ending into her misty garments, the blue smoke roll'd, to revive
Her cold limbs in the absence of her Lord. Also her sons,
With lives of Victims sacrificed upon an altar of brass
On the East side, Reviv'd her Soul with lives of beasts & birds
Slain on the Altar, up ascending into her cloudy bosom.
Of terrible workmanship the Altar, labour of ten thousand Slaves:
One thousand Men of wondrous power spent their lives in its formation.
It stood on twelve steps, nam'd after the names of her twelve sons,
And was Erected at the chief entrance of Urizen's hall.

391 Urizen's 'Shadowy Feminine Semblance' a 'Shadow of Despair' (l. 397) would seem to be Ahania: cp. B. A. i. 30–43. Here apparently she is identical with the generic symbol 'Female' (see Index, *Sex*), the repressive spirit of the Moral Law that demands obedience involving the sacrifice of 'all the energies of Man', the 'lives of Victims sacrificed upon an altar of brass' (l. 404). 402 misty] cloudy *1st rdg. del.*

405 Later the quarter of the East is always associated with the errors of morality and empiricism: see Index, *Cardinal Points*.

When Urizen return'd from his immense labours & travels,
Descending, she repos'd beside him, folding him around
In her bright skirts. Astonish'd & Confounded, he beheld
Her shadowy form now separate : he shudder'd & was silent,
Till her caresses & her tears reviv'd him to life & joy.
Two wills they had, two intellects, & not as in times of old.
This Urizen perciev'd, & silent brooded in dark'ning Clouds.
To him his Labour was but Sorrow, & his Kingdom was Repentance.
He drave the Male Spirits all away from Ahania,
And she drave all the Females from him away.

Los joy'd & Enitharmon laugh'd, saying : ' Let us go down,
And see this labour & sorrow.' They went down to see the woes
Of Vala & the woes of Luvah, to draw in their delights.

And Vala, like a shadow, oft appear'd to Urizen.
[9] The King of Light beheld her mourning among the Brick kilns, compell'd
To labour night & day among the fires : her lamenting voice
Is heard when silent night returns & the labourers take their rest :

' O Lord, wilt thou not look upon our sore afflictions,
Among these flames incessant labouring ? our hard masters laugh
At all our sorrow. We are made to turn the wheel for water,
To carry the heavy basket on our scorchèd shoulders, to sift
The sand & ashes, & to mix the clay with tears & repentance.
The times are now return'd upon us : we have given ourselves
To scorn, and now are scornèd by the slaves of our enemies.

411 return'd] descended *1st rdg. del.*

416 This line is repeated J. 86. 61. It relates to the spiritual division symbolized by Sex.

419–420 He . . . away] *an addition.* These lines are found, with slight change, in F. Z. i, ll. 154–155.

425 In this reference to Vala's labours among the ' Brick Kilns ', and in the lines that follow (ll. 426–436) there is a clear allusion to the slavery in Egypt, which is often used by Blake to denote subjection to a repressive morality. Cp. the use of the symbol ' Egypt ' to represent ' Urizen's world ', B. U. ix. 1–45.

432–434 Opposite these lines in the right margin the following lines are written in pencil :

I see not Luvah as of old.
I only see his feet / Like pillars
of fire travelling thro' darkness
& non entity.

They apparently belong to Vala's lament, though no position is indicated for them.

Our beauty is cover'd over with clay & ashes, & our backs
Furrow'd with whips, & our flesh bruisèd with the heavy basket.
Forgive us, O thou piteous one, whom we have offended: forgive
The weak remaining shadow of Vala, that returns in sorrow to thee.'

Thus she lamented day & night, compell'd to labour & sorrow.
Luvah in vain her lamentations heard; in vain his love
Brought him in various forms before her. Still she knew him not:
[10] Still she despis'd him, calling on his name & knowing him not;
Still hating, still professing love, still labouring in the smoke.

And Los & Enitharmon joy'd: they drank in tenfold joy
From all the sorrow of Luvah & the labour of Urizen.
And Enitharmon joy'd, Plotting to rend the secret cloud,
To plant divisions in the Soul of Urizen & Ahania.

But infinitely beautiful, the wondrous work arose
In sorrow & care, a Golden World, whose porches round the heavens,
And pillar'd halls & rooms, reciev'd the eternal wandering stars,
A wondrous golden Building. Many a window, many a door,
And many a division let in & out into the vast unknown.
[Circled] in [infinite orb] immoveable, within its walls & cielings
The heavens were clos'd, and spirits mourn'd their bondage night & day.
And the Divine Vision appear'd in Luvah's robes of blood.

Thus was the Mundane Shell builded by Urizen's strong Power.

Sorrowing went the Planters forth to plant, the Sowers to sow.
They dug the channels for the rivers, & they pour'd abroad
[11] The seas & lakes: they rear'd the mountains & the rocks & hills

444–445 And . . . Urizen] *deleted*; then marked in the right margin: 'To come in'.
446–447 And . . . Ahania] *an addition.* 448 But] For *1st rdg.*
453 Circled] *deleted*: no other word substituted. infinite orb] *deleted*: two words deleted above, illegible. walls & cielings] arches all *1st rdg. del.*
454 spirits . . . day] *written over deletion.*
455–456 And . . . Power] *an addition.* See above, l. 235 *and note.*
457 Sorrowing] Then *1st rdg. del.* Sowers] Sowers forth *1st rdg.*

On broad pavilions, on pillar'd roofs & porches & high towers,
In beauteous order : thence arose soft clouds & exhalations,
Wandering even to the sunny Cubes of light & heat ;
For many a window, ornamented with sweet ornaments,
Look'd out into the World of Tharmas, where in ceaseless torrents
His billows roll, where monsters wander in the foamy paths.

On clouds the Sons of Urizen beheld Heaven wallèd round.
They weigh'd & order'd all ; & Urizen, comforted, saw
The wondrous work flow forth like visible out of the invisible.
For the Divine Lamb, Even Jesus, who is the Divine Vision,
Permitted all lest Man should fall into Eternal Death.
For when Luvah sunk down, himself put on the robes of blood,
Lest the state call'd Luvah should cease : & the Divine Vision
Walkèd in robes of blood, till he who slept should awake.

Thus were the stars of heaven created like a golden chain,
To bind the Body of Man to heaven from falling into the Abyss.
Each took his station, & his course began with sorrow & care ;

. . . .

In sevens & tens & fifties, hundreds, thousands, number'd all
According to their various powers, subordinate to Urizen
And to his sons in their degrees & to his beauteous daughters ;
Travelling in silent majesty along their order'd ways
In right lined paths outmeasur'd by proportions of number, weight
And measure, mathematic motion wondrous along the deep,
In fiery pyramid, or Cube, or unornamented pillar square
Of fire, far shining, travelling along even to its destin'd end ;
Then falling down, a terrible space : recovering in winter dire
Its wasted strength, it back returns upon a nether course,
Till, fired with ardour fresh recruited in its humble season,

462 Cubes] orbs *1st rdg. del.*

464 The World of Tharmas cannot be explained : its origin is described, F. Z. i. 70 seq.

460–473 For . . . awake] *written over deletion,* illegible except the last words, 'the Mundane Egg', an image probably derived from Jacob Bryant, *Ancient Mythology,* vol. ii, plate iv.

471 See Index, *Incarnation.*

476 sorrow & care] '[*word illegible*] & fear' written beneath, underlined and partly erased : to the right, the sign '+ 1' refers to a missing passage, which according to Blake's numbering must have been of some seven lines.

477–479 In . . . daughters] *an addition* at foot of page, numbered '2'.

480–494 Travelling . . . deep] *an addition* ; numbered '3'.

481 number, weight] weight & measure *1st rdg.*

487 season] spring *1st rdg. del.*

It rises up on high all summer ; till its wearied course
Turns into autumn : such the periods of many worlds.
Others triangular right angled course maintain, others obtuse,
Acute, Scalene, in simple paths : but others move
In intricate ways, biquadrate, Trapeziums, Rhombs, Rhomboids,
Paralellograms triple & quadruple, polygonic,
In their amazing hard subdued course in the vast deep.

[12] And Los & Enitharmon were drawn down by their desires,
Descending sweet upon the wind among soft harps & voices
To plant divisions in the Soul of Urizen & Ahania,
To conduct the Voice of Enion to Ahania's midnight pillow.

Urizen saw & envied, & his imagination was fillèd.
Repining he contemplated the past in his bright sphere,
Terrified with his heart & spirit at the visions of futurity
That his dread fancy form'd before him in the unform'd void.

For Los & Enitharmon walk'd forth on the dewy Earth,
Contracting or expanding their all flexible senses ;
At will to murmur in the flowers, small as the honey bee ;
At will to stretch across the heavens & step from star to star,
Or standing on the Earth erect, or on the stormy waves
Driving the storms before them, or delighting in sunny beams,
While round their heads the Elemental Gods kept harmony.

And Los said : 'Lo ! the Lilly pale & the rose redd'ning fierce
Reproach thee, & the beamy gardens sicken at thy beauty.
I grasp thy vest in my strong hand : in vain, like water springs
In the bright sands of Los evading my embrace : then I alone
Wander among the virgins of the summer. "Look ! " they cry,
"The poor forsaken Los, mock'd by the worm, the shelly snail,
The Emmet & the beetle : hark ! they laugh & mock at Los." '

490 right angled] their *1st rdg. del.*
491 Scalene] & Oblong *1st rdg. del.*
494 hard subdued] fructifying *1st rdg. del.*
497–498 To . . . pillow] *an addition.*
501 Urizen's 'horrible fear of the future' (F. Z. vii. 86), that seems 'teeming with Endless destruction' (F. Z. viii. 93), indicates the limitation of perception that accompanies the Fall of Man, when 'Urizen who was Faith & Certainty, is chang'd to Doubt' (F. Z. ii. 315).
503 For] Now *1st rdg. del.* 510–556 And . . . king] *an addition.*

Enitharmon answer'd : ' Secure now from the smitings of thy Power, demon of fury,
If the God Enraptur'd me infolds,
In clouds of sweet obscurity my beauteous form dissolving,
Howl thou over the body of death ; 'tis thine. But if among the Virgins
Of summer I have seen thee sleep & turn thy cheek delighted
Upon the rose or lilly pale, or on a bank where sleep
The beaming daughters of the light, starting they rise, they flee
From thy fierce love. For tho' I am dissolv'd in the bright God,
My spirit still pursues thy false love over rocks & valleys.'

Los answer'd : ' Therefore fade I, thus dissolv'd in raptur'd trance.
Thou canst repose on clouds of secrecy, while o'er my limbs
Cold dews & hoary frost creeps, tho' I lie on banks of summer
Among the beauties of the World. Cold & repining, Los
Still dies for Enitharmon, nor a spirit springs from my dead corse.
Then I am dead till thou revivest me with thy sweet song,
Now taking on Ahania's form, & now the form of Enion.
I know thee not as once I knew thee in those blessèd fields,
Where memory wishes to repose among the flocks of Tharmas.'

Enitharmon answer'd : ' Wherefore didst thou throw thine arms around
Ahania's Image ? I deciev'd thee, & will still decieve.
Urizen saw thy sin, & hid his beams in dark'ning Clouds.
I still keep watch, altho' I tremble & wither across the heavens
In strong vibrations of fierce jealousy ; for thou art mine,
Created for my will, my slave, tho' strong, tho' I am weak.
Farewell ! the God calls me away. I depart in my sweet bliss.'

She fled vanishing on the wind, And left a dead cold corse
In Los's arms. Howlings began over the body of death.
Los spoke : ' Thy God in vain shall call thee, if by my strong power
I can infuse my dear revenge into his glowing breast.

517 Enitharmon . . . fury] Enitharmon answer'd : ' If the God Enraptur'd me infolds ' *1st rdg.*

520 Howl . . . thine] *written over erasure.* 523 beaming] ? beamy.

534 Tharmas is often represented as a shepherd : cp. F. Z. ix. 836–838. The significance of the imagery has not been discovered.

540 Created . . . weak] *an addition.*

543 In . . . death] *written over erasure.*

Then jealousy shall shadow all his mountains, & Ahania
Curse thee, thou plague of woful Los, & seek revenge on thee.'

So saying, in deep sobs he languish'd, till dead he also fell.
Night pass'd & Enitharmon, e'er the dawn, return'd in bliss.
She sang O'er Los, reviving him to Life: his groans were terrible.
But thus she sang: 'I sieze the sphery harp; I strike the Strings!

'At the first Sound the Golden sun arises from the deep,
And shakes his awful hair;
The Eccho wakes the moon to unbind her silver locks.
The golden sun bears on my song,
And nine bright spheres of harmony rise round the fiery king.

'The joy of woman is the Death of her most best belovèd
Who dies for Love of her
In torments of fierce jealousy & pangs of adoration:
The Lovers' night bears on my song,
And the nine Spheres rejoice beneath my powerful controll.

'They sing unceasing to the notes of my immortal hand.
The solemn silent moon
Reverberates the living harmony upon my limbs;
The birds & beasts rejoice & play,
And every one seeks for his mate to prove his inmost joy.

'Furious & terrible they sport & rend the nether deep;
The deep lifts up his rugged head,
And, lost in infinite hum[m]ing wings, vanishes with a cry.
The fading cry is ever dying;
The living voice is ever living in its inmost joy.

'Arise, you little glancing wings & sing your infant joy!
Arise & drink your bliss!
For every thing that lives is holy; for the source of life
Descends to be a weeping babe;
For the Earthworm renews the moisture of the sandy plain.

548 So . . . fell] *an addition.*
550–551 She . . . Strings] 'She sang O'er Los "I sieze the sphery harps: strike the Strings"' *1st rdg.*
557–561 The . . . controll] *marginal addition*: position not indicated. These lines illustrate the repressive character of Natural Religion as symbolized by the Female. Cp. J. 68. 62–70, and see Index, *Sex.*
562–590 They . . . fading] *marginal addition*, marked for insertion here. See Introductory Note to the present Night.
569 huming] indistinctly written in MS.: perhaps 'hov'ring'.
572–574 Cp. V. D. A. 214–215.
574–576 To the passage (572–574) stressing the inherent holiness of life, Blake adds what would seem to be a statement of the significance of birth

'Now my left hand I stretch to earth beneath,
And strike the terrible string.
I wake sweet joy in dens of sorrow, & I plant a smile
In forests of affliction,
And wake the bubbling springs of life in regions of dark death.

'O, I am weary! lay thine hand upon me or I faint.
I faint beneath these beams of thine;
For thou hast touchèd my five Senses, & they answer'd thee.
Now I am nothing, & I sink,
And on the bed of silence sleep till thou awakest me!'

Thus sang the Lovely one, in Rapturous delusive trance.
Los heard, reviving: he siez'd her in his arms; delusive hopes
Kindling, she led him into Shadows & thence fled, outstretch'd
Upon the immense like a bright rainbow, weeping & smiling & fading.

Thus liv'd Los, driving Enion far into the deathful infinite,
That he may also draw Ahania's spirit into her Vortex.
Ah, happy blindness! Enion sees not the terrors of the uncertain.
Thus Enion wails from the dark deep: the golden heavens tremble:

[13] 'I am made to sow the thistle for wheat, the nettle for a nourishing dainty:
I have planted a false oath in the earth; it has brought forth a poison tree:
I have chosen the serpent for a councellor, & the dog
For a schoolmaster to my children:

in the regeneration of man, though it does not appear whether the allusion is to the universal phenomenon or to the particular instances of Orc, and, in the later writings, of Jesus. See Index, *Incarnation*. The great difficulty lies in the fact that these lines, enunciating apparently approved Blakean doctrine, are put into the mouth of Enitharmon.

584 This line would seem to indicate that Los's error, as a visionary, lay in admitting the appeal of physical beauty. It may also be that the rest of the stanza stresses the fact that this power in Nature is dormant till the creative or poetic spirit in Los calls it forth. It must, however, be admitted that the earliest clear expression of this idea is in *Jerusalem*.

594 Thus Enion] And oft she *1st rdg.*: And thus she *2nd rdg.*

595–626 The connexion between this song and the rest of the Night is not clear, its interpretation apparently depending upon a fuller understanding of the symbol Enion than has yet been attained.

596 The 'false oath' is developed later, in the 'oath of blood' (J. 65. 7), and the 'Spectrous Oath' (J. 98. 53), into the symbol of the Moral Law, with its 'Vengeance for Sin' (G. A., ll. 46–50). In the present passage it may have a more general reference to the errors of morality and sense-perception with which Enion is associated in the first part of Night I. Cp. F. Z. vii *a*. 163.

I have blotted out from light & living the dove & nightingale,
And I have causèd the earth worm to beg from door to door:
I have taught the thief a secret path into the house of the just:
I have taught pale artifice to spread his nets upon the morning.
My heavens are brass, my earth is iron, my moon a clod of clay,
My sun a pestilence burning at noon & a vapour of death in night.

'What is the price of Experience? do men buy it for a song,
Or wisdom for a dance in the street? No! it is bought with the price
Of all that a man hath—his house, his wife, his children.
Wisdom is sold in the desolate market where none come to buy,
And in the wither'd field where the farmer plows for bread in vain.

'It is an easy thing to triumph in the summer's sun
And in the vintage, & to sing on the waggon loaded with corn.
It is an easy thing to talk of patience to the afflicted,
To speak the laws of prudence to the houseless wanderer,
[14] To listen to the hungry raven's cry in wintry season,
When the red blood is fill'd with wine & with the marrow of lambs.

'It is an easy thing to laugh at wrathful elements;
To hear the dog howl at the wintry door, the ox in the slaughter house moan;
To see a god on every wind & a blessing on every blast;
To hear sounds of love in the thunder storm that destroys our enemies' house,
To rejoice in the blight that covers his field, & the sickness that cuts off his children,
While our olive & vine sing & laugh round our door, & our children bring fruits & flowers.

'Then the groan & the dolor are quite forgotten, & the slave grinding at the mill,
And the captive in chains, & the poor in the prison, & the soldier in the field,
When the shatter'd bone hath laid him groaning among the happier dead.

'It is an easy thing to rejoice in the tents of prosperity—
Thus could I sing, & thus rejoice; but it is not so with me.'

Ahania heard the Lamentation, & a Swift Vibration 627
Spread thro' her Golden frame. She rose up e'er the dawn of day,
When Urizen slept on his couch. Drawn thro' unbounded space,
On to the margin of Non Entity the bright Female came.
There she beheld the Spectrous form of Enion in the Void;
And never from that moment could she rest upon her pillow.

End of the Second Night

627–632 Ahania heard . . . pillow] written over 'The End of the Second Night' *del.*
631 Spectrous] terrible *1st rdg. del.*

NIGHT III

INTRODUCTORY NOTE

THE Night is mainly concerned with a myth of Urizen and Ahania which is entirely different in conception from that of Night II, ll. 383–420, where Ahania, as in *The Book of Ahania*, chap. i, ll. 30–43, is the symbol of that ' pestilence ' of the soul, called morality. Here, on the contrary, the symbol has the significance that sometimes appertains confusingly to certain of the female symbols, namely, capacity for vision, or the content of a vision apprehended. The divergent use of the symbols is sometimes marked by epithets, in the former case implying disobedience or self-will, in the latter subservience; but frequently the significance of the symbol is to be gathered from the context. In the present instance Ahania's devotion to Urizen is the basis of interpretation. She is the image, or form, of right reason, persisting after his apostasy as a faint perception, or a remote memory, of his perfect being (cp. B. A., chap. v, *passim*, and Index, *Ahania*, I, *a*).

Ahania pleads with Urizen, begging him no longer to set himself against the Eternal Man. Urizen, apparently recognizing the limitation of his sovereignty, tells of his ultimate fate, that he is to become subject to Orc, a conception of the triumph of the antinomian principle that links this myth much more intimately with the Lambeth books, especially *America* and *Europe*, than with the later-written Nights of the present work and the books that follow. He prophesies also that Vala shall be born of Enitharmon, an obscure matter.

Ahania continues to plead, telling him, as it were in warning, of the attempt of Luvah and Vala to impose upon man the illusion of a transcendent deity, which is, indeed, nothing more than a shadow from his wearied intellect (l. 45). The general sense of the episode is clear: it is offered in criticism of non-visionary conceptions of the deity. But when ' the shadow ' is called ' that son of Man ' and identified with Luvah, and when sentence is pronounced by man against Luvah, his deceiver (ll. 63–64), condemning him to die vicariously for Vala (l. 80), the suggestion arises, in view of the visionary relation of Luvah and Christ in Nights II, IV, and VIII (see Index, *Incarnation*), that the particular implication of this passage is in some manner bound up with that conventional interpretation of the being and message of Christ that Blake rejects in *The Everlasting Gospel*. The myth goes on to relate how, for their deception, Luvah and Vala are cast out into ' the world of death ', where they are divided by the ' serpent form ' of Nature, the emblem of that ' Natural Religion ' of which the illusion imposed on man is an example (ll. 41–98; cp. J. 29. 33–82).

The completeness of Urizen's apostasy is emphasized in what follows (ll. 100–128). He ignores Ahania's warning vision and casts her into the world of ' non-entity ' where among ' the caverns of the Grave ' she persists among the impressions of ' Despair and Hope ' that there enroot eternally. This act of Urizen is catastrophic, as the confusion that follows indicates. The bounds of destiny are broken (l. 129) and out of the confusion Tharmas appears, a spirit of despair, seeking Enion, the faint shadow of Hope (VIII. 475), who remain a ' voice eternal wailing in the elements ' (l. 200). This episode, treated with great appearance of consideration and with great labour, is one of the many unexplained matters.

VALA

Night the Third

[1] Now sat the King of Light on high upon his starry throne,
And bright Ahania bow'd herself before his splendid feet:

'O Urizen! look upon Me: like a mournful stream
I embrace round thy knees & wet My bright hair with my tears.
Why sighs my Lord? Are not the morning stars thy obedient Sons?
Do they not bow their bright heads at thy voice? At thy command
Do they not fly into their stations & return their light to thee?
The immortal Atmospheres are thine; there thou art seen in glory
Surrounded by the ever changing Daughters of the Light.
Why wilt thou look upon futurity, dark'ning present joy?'

She ceas'd: the Prince his light obscur'd, & the splendors of his crown
[2] Infolded in thick clouds, from whence his mighty voice burst forth:

'O bright Ahania! a Boy is born of the dark Ocean
Whom Urizen doth serve, with Light replenishing his darkness.
I am set here, a King of trouble, commanded here to serve
And do my ministry to those who eat of my wide table.
All this is mine, yet I must serve, & that Prophetic boy
Must grow up to command his Prince: but hear my determin'd decree.

Night the Third] 'Third' written over an erasure: very indistinctly, in pencil to the right, 'Second'.

3 Me] thy Wife that *1st rdg. del.*

4 I embrace] Embraces *1st rdg. del.* wet . . . tears] wets her bright hair with her tears *1st rdg.*

After l. 9, line del.:

Thou sit'st in harmony, for God hath set thee over all

10 Why . . . joy] *an addition.* Cp. F. Z. ii. 501 *note* and ix. 179–182.

13 Ahania] Ahania *1st rdg. del.*; Shadow *2nd rdg. del.* The 'Boy' is Orc: see Index, *Orc.*

17–18 Cp. F. Z. vi, ll. 152–155 and F. Z. viii, ll. 450–455.

18 but . . . decree] & all my Kingly power *1st rdg. del.*

Vala shall become a Worm in Enitharmon's Womb,
Laying her seed upon the fibres, soon to issue forth :
And Luvah in the loins of Los a dark & furious death.
Alas for me ! what will become of me at that dread time ! '

Ahania bow'd her head & wept seven days before the King.
And on the eighth day, when his clouds unfolded from his throne,
She rais'd her bright head, sweet perfum'd, & thus with heavenly voice :

' O Prince ! the Eternal One hath set thee leader of his hosts.
[3] Leave all futurity to him ; resume thy fields of Light.
Why didst thou listen to the voice of Luvah that dread morn,
To give the immortal steeds of light to his deceitful hands,
No longer now obedient to thy will ? thou art compell'd
To forge the curbs of iron & brass, to build the iron mangers,
To feed them with intoxication from the wine presses of Luvah,
Till the Divine Vision & Fruition is quite obliterated.
They call thy lions to the fields of blood ; they rouze thy tygers
Out of the halls of justice, till these dens thy wisdom fram'd,
Golden & beautiful, but O how unlike those sweet fields of bliss
Where liberty was justice, & eternal science was mercy !
Then, O my dear lord, listen to Ahania, listen to the vision,
The vision of Ahania in the slumbers of Urizen,
When Urizen slept in the porch, & the Ancient Man was smitten :

' The Dark'ning Man walk'd on the steps of fire before his halls,

19 Vala] But Vala *1st rdg.* For the fulfilment of this prophecy cp. F. Z. vii *a*, ll. 312–331.

21 This line cannot be explained by reference to anything in the subsequent course of the myth.

26 The ' Eternal One ' is apparently the Eternal Man (cp. F. Z. ii. 213–216), not Divine Providence.

27 Two lines *del.* above l. 27 :

Raise then thy radiant eyes to him ; raise thy obedient hands ;
And comforts shall descend from heaven into thy dark'ning clouds.

27 Leave . . . Light] *an addition.* 28–29 See Index, *Luvah*, II.

32 See Index, *Wine-press.*

33 Till . . . obliterated] *written over erasure.* The ' Divine Vision and Fruition ' is Imagination, ' the Human Existence itself ' (M. *extra page* 32, 32) : see Index, *Imagination.* Its obliteration is in the later books the beginning of error. 40 Ancient] Eternal *1st rdg. del.*

41–98 These lines, with the exception of 67–71, 79, 86–87, are repeated with slight changes in J. 29. 33–82.

And Vala walk'd with him in dreams of soft deluding slumber.
He lookèd up & saw thee, Prince of Light, thy splendor faded.

[4] 'Then Man ascended mourning into the splendors of his palace.
Above him rose a Shadow from his wearied intellect,
Of living gold, pure, perfect, holy; in white linen pure he hover'd,
A sweet entrancing self delusion, a wat'ry vision of Man,
Soft exulting in existence, all the Man absorbing.

'Man fell upon his face prostrate before the wat'ry shadow,
Saying: "O Lord, whence is this change? thou knowest I am nothing."
And Vala trembled & cover'd her face, & her locks were spread on the pavement.
We heard, astonish'd at the Vision, & our hearts trembled within us;
We heard the voice of the Slumberous Man, & thus he spoke,
Idolatrous to his own Shadow, words of Eternity uttering:

'"O I am nothing when I enter into judgment with thee!
If thou withdraw thy breath, I die & vanish into Hades.

42 Vala is here connected, perhaps as cause, with the illusion of a transcendent deity, 'the vision of God . . . clos'd in clouds of Albion's Spectre' or Reasoning Power. See Index, *Vala*.

43 thee . . . thy] the Prince of Light with *1st rdg*. After l. 43 two lines, the last on MS. p. 3 and the first on MS. p. 4, have been deleted:

But saw not Los nor Enitharmon; for Luvah hid them in shadow
In [Of *1st rdg. del.*] a soft cloud outstretch'd across; & Luvah dwelt in the cloud.

45 Intellect is here used in a sinister sense, as equivalent to the Spectre, or 'Reasoning power in Man' (see Index, *Spectre*), always closely associated with the feminine activities as the source of Natural Religion, with its doctrine of a transcendent deity opposed to the Divine Humanity.

52 We . . . our hearts . . . us] I . . . my heart . . . me *1st rdg. del.*

52–54 We . . . uttering] These lines are bracketed, and marked with a cross. Similar crosses stand before l. 48 and the second deleted line (see *supra*, l. 43 *note*). The meaning of these signs is not apparent.

53 We] I *1st rdg. del.* Slumberous] *written over erasure*.

55–60 Albion's prayer with its echoes of scriptural phrases is a sufficient clue to the interpretation of the 'wat'ry shadow' as the orthodox conception of the deity. Usually Blake's criticism of conventional theology leads him to offer the figure of Urizen as the God of religious orthodoxy, thereby emphasizing his belief that the false conception grows primarily out of undue reliance on the rational mind. Here, however, the false god arising from the mind is related to the unillumined emotions and, therefore, takes the form of Luvah. Cp. D. C. iii, p. 31, quoted F. Z. ix. 361–372 *note*. Cp. also (allowing for difference of point of view) Thomas Hardy, 'Satires of Circumstance', *God's Funeral*, ll. 21–32:

O man-projected Figure, of late
Imaged as we, thy knell who shall survive?

If thou dost lay thine hand upon me, behold! I am silent.
If thou withhold thine hand, I perish like a fallen leaf.
O! I am nothing, & to nothing must return again:
If thou withdraw thy breath, behold! I am oblivion."

'He ceas'd; the shadowy voice was silent: but the cloud hover'd over their heads
[5] In golden wreathes, the sorrow of Man; & the balmy drops fell down.
And Lo! that Son of Man, that shadowy Spirit of Albion,
Luvah, descended from the cloud. In terror Albion rose;
Indignant rose the Awful Man, & turn'd his back on Vala.

'We heard the Voice of ⟨the⟩ Albion starting from his sleep:

"Why roll thy clouds in sick'ning mists? I can no longer hide
The dismal vision of mine eyes. O love & life & light!
Prophetic dreads urge me to speak: futurity is before me
Like a dark lamp. Eternal death haunts all my expectation.
Rent from Eternal Brotherhood we die, & are no more.

'"Whence is this voice crying, Enion! that soundeth in my ears?
O cruel pity! O dark deceit! can Love seek for dominion?"

'And Luvah strove to gain dominion over mighty Albion:
They strove together above the Body where Vala was inclos'd,

Whence comes it we were tempted to create
One whom we can no longer keep alive.

Framing him jealous, fierce, at first,
We gave him justice as the ages rolled,
Will to bless those by circumstance accurst,
And long-suffering, and mercies manifold.

And tricked by our own early dream
And need of solace, we grew self deceived,
Our making soon our maker did we deem
And what we had imagined we believed.

63 Albion] Eternal *1st rdg. del.*: the Fallen One *2nd rdg.*
64 In terror Albion rose] The Eternal Man arose *1st rdg.*
66 We] I *1st rdg.* This line follows l. 73: the changed position is clearly indicated. Albion] fallen One *1st rdg. del.*
71 Rent . . . more] *an addition.* For Blake's doctrine of Brotherhood cp. General Introduction, p. 62.
73 Love seeks for dominion when the 'Slaves and Captives' of Natural Religion are compelled to worship a 'God of cruelty and Laws', 'the God of this World, Satan' as a 'God of Mercy' (J. 90. 56–57). In the present passage Luvah invests himself with the attributes of a transcendent deity (ll. 74 seq.).
74 mighty Albion] the Ancient Man *1st rdg.*
75 The 'dark Body of Albion' is an example of the use of the symbol Albion (see Index, *Albion*) as the victim of Law, the civil and religious ministers of which are the 'smiters with disease' (E. G. β. 22–29, Clar.

And the dark Body of Albion, left prostrate upon the crystal pavement,
Cover'd with boils from head to foot, the terrible smitings of Luvah.

'Then frown'd Albion & put forth Luvah from his presence,
(I heard him : frown not, Urizen, but listen to my Vision !)
[6] Saying : " Go & die the Death of Man for Vala, the sweet wanderer.
I will turn the volutions of your Ears outward, & bend your Nostrils
Downward ; & your fluxile Eyes, englob'd, roll round in fear ;
Your with'ring Lips & Tongue shrink up into a narrow circle,
Till into narrow forms you creep. Go take your fiery way,
And learn what 'tis to absorb the Man, you Spirits of Pity & Love ! "

'O Urizen, why art thou pale at the visions of Ahania ?
Listen to her who loves thee, lest we also are driven away.

'They heard the Voice & fled swift as the winter's setting sun.
And now the Human Blood foam'd high. I saw that Luvah & Vala
Went down the Human Heart, where Paradise & its joys abounded,
In jealous fears, in fury & rage ; & flames roll'd round their fervid feet,
And the vast form of Nature like a Serpent play'd before them.
And as they went in folding fires & thunders of the deep,
Vala shrunk in like the dark sea that leaves its slimy banks,
And from her bosom Luvah fell, far as the east & west ;

Press, p. 248). But l. 78 shows another use of the symbol arising out of Blake's doctrine of the Divine Humanity (see Index, *Jesus*). Man appears in his perfect state as God, having authority over the Zoas (cp. ll. 80–85 and 87). This dual aspect of Albion is developed in the subsequent books : cp. M. 14. 1–16.

76 Albion] Man *1st rdg. del.*

78 Albion] the Eternal Man *1st rdg.* ; the Fallen Man *2nd rdg.*

80–85 Some light is thrown upon this passage by its sequel, F. Z. ix. 356–372, where the cause and purpose of this decree of banishment are explained. Pity and Love are the emotions perverted to morally destructive ends as noted above, l. 71 *note.*

86–87 O Urizen . . . away] *an addition.*

90–91 Opposite these lines in the left margin is written : 'Albion clos'd the Western Gate &/shut America out by the Atlantic/for a Curse and hidden horror/and an altar of victims, to Sin/& Repentance.' No line-divisions are inserted, and no place indicated for it in the text.

92 Later Vala is called 'Nature, Mother of all' (J. 34. 9), 'the Goddess Nature' (J. 93. 24).

And the vast form of Nature like a Serpent roll'd between.
Whether this is Jerusalem or Babylon, we know not.
All is Confusion! All is tumult! & we alone are escaped.'

She ended, for his wrathful throne burst forth the black hail storm.

'Am I not God?' said Urizen, 'Who is Equal to me?
Do I not stretch the heavens abroad, or fold them up like a garment?'
He spoke, mustering his heavy clouds around him, black, opake.
[7] Then thunders roll'd around, & lightnings darted to & fro.
His visage chang'd to darkness, & his strong right hand came forth
To cast Ahania to the Earth. He siez'd her by the hair
And threw her from the steps of ice that froze around his throne,
Saying: 'Art thou also become like Vala? Thus I cast thee out!
Shall the feminine indolent bliss, the indulgent self of weariness,
The passive idle sleep, the enormous night & darkness of Death,
Set herself up to give her laws to the active masculine virtue?
Thou little diminutive portion that dar'st be a counterpart!
Thy passivity, thy laws of obedience & insincerity,
Are my abhorrence. Wherefore hast thou taken that fair form?
Whence is this power given to thee? Once thou wast in my breast
A sluggish current of dim waters, on whose verdant margin
A cavern shagg'd with horrid shades, dark, cool & deadly, where
I laid my head in the hot noon after the broken clods
Had wearied me: there I laid my plow, & there my horses fed.
And thou hast risen with thy moist locks into a wat'ry image
Reflecting all my indolence, my weakness & my death,

97–98 Whether . . . escaped] *an addition.* Jerusalem is the vision of Eternity as Vala is the sum of false physical percepts.

100–102 Am I . . . opake] *an addition.* Urizen repeats the error of Luvah: cp. F. Z. ix. 364–372.

To weigh me down beneath the grave into non Entity,
Where Luvah strives scornèd by Vala, age after age wandering,
Shrinking & shrinking from her Lord & calling him the Tempter.
And art thou also become like Vala? Thus I cast thee out.'

So loud in thunders spoke the King, folded in dark despair,
And threw Ahania from his bosom obdurate. She fell like lightning.
Then fled the Sons of Urizen from his thunderous throne petrific:
They fled to East & West, & left the North & South of Heaven.

A crash ran thro' the immense. The bounds of Destiny were broken.
The bounds of Destiny Crash'd direful, & the swelling sea
Burst from its bonds in whirlpools fierce, roaring with Human voice
Triumphing even to the Stars at bright Ahania's fall.

Down from the dismal North, the Prince, in thunders & thick clouds,
[8] As when the thunderbolt down falleth on the appointed place,
Fell down, down, rushing, ruining, thundering, shuddering,
Into the Caverns of the Grave & places of Human Seed,
Where the impressions of Despair & Hope enroot for ever,
A world of Darkness. Ahania fell far into Non Entity.

She Continued falling. Loud the Crash continu'd, loud & Hoarse.
From the Crash roar'd a flame of blue sulphureous fire; from the flame
A dolorous groan that struck with dumbness all confusion,
Swallowing up the horrible din in agony on agony:
Thro' the Confusion, like a crack across from immense to immense,

125–126 So . . . lightning] *an addition.*

128 The significance of the cardinal points in this line is not identical with their meaning in other passages, and eludes interpretation.

129 Blake does not afford any clear indication of the meaning attached to Destiny in this and other passages: cp. F. Z. i. 68 and 81. In *Jerusalem* it is associated with the extreme form of error 'the Hermaphroditic Satan World of Rocky destiny' (J. 58. 51: cp. J. 66. 6).

130–132 See Index, *Atlantic Continent.*

135 shuddering] darkening *1st rdg. del.* 137 & Hope] *an addition.*

139–146 The punctuation of this passage is tentative. The MS. gives no help.

Loud, strong, a universal groan of death, louder
Than all the wracking elements, deafen'd & rended worse
Than Urizen & all his hosts in curst despair down rushing.
But from the Dolorous Groan one like a shadow of smoke appear'd,
And human bones rattling together in the smoke & stamping
The nether Abyss, & gnasshing in fierce despair, panting in sobs,
Thick, short, incessant, bursting, sobbing, deep despairing, stamping, struggling,
Struggling to utter the voice of Man, struggling to take the features of Man, Struggling
To take the limbs of Man. At length, emerging from the Smoke
Of Urizen, dashèd in pieces from his precipitant fall,
Tharmas rear'd up his hands, & stood on the affrighted Ocean.
The dead rear'd up his Voice & stood on the resounding Shore,

Crying: 'Fury in my limbs! destruction in my bones & marrow!
My skull riven into filaments, my eyes into sea jellies
Floating upon the tide, wander bubbling & bubbling;
Uttering my lamentations & begetting little monsters
Who sit mocking upon the little pebbles of the tide
In all my rivers, & on dried shells that the fish
[9] Have quite forsaken! O fool! fool! to lose my sweetest bliss!
Where art thou, Enion? ah! too near to (? cunning), too far off,
And yet too near! Dash'd down, I send thee into distant darkness,
Far as my strength can hurl thee: wander there, & laugh & play
Among the frozen arrows; they will tear thy tender flesh.
Fall off afar from Tharmas! come not too near my strong fury!
Scream, & fall off, & laugh at Tharmas, lovely summer beauty,
Till winter rends thee into Shivers, as thou hast rended me!'

So Tharmas bellow'd o'er the ocean, thund'ring, sobbing, bursting.
The bounds of Destiny were broken, & hatred now began

151 Struggling to utter the voice of Man] *written over deletion.*
163 (? cunning)] *not legibly written.*

Instead of love to Enion. Enion, blind & age bent,
Plung'd into the cold billows, living a life in midst of waters.
In terrors she wither'd away to Entuthon Benithon,
A world of deep darkness where all things in horrors are rooted.

These are the words of Enion, heard from the cold waves of despair:
'O Tharmas! I had lost thee: & when I hopèd I had found thee,
O Tharmas, do not thou destroy me quite; but let
A little shadow, but a little showery form of Enion
Be near thee, lovèd Terror! Let me still remain, & then do thou
Thy righteous doom upon me: only let me hear thy voice!
Driven by thy rage, I wander like a cloud into the deep
Where never yet Existence came; there losing all my life,
I back return, weaker & weaker. Consume me not away
In thy great wrath, tho' I have sinnèd, tho' I have rebell'd.
Make me not like the things forgotten, as they had not been:
Make not the thing that loveth thee a tear wipèd away.'

Tharmas replied, riding on storms; his voice of Thunder roll'd:

'Image of grief, thy fading lineaments make my eyelids fail.
What have I done? Both rage & mercy are alike to me.
Looking upon thee, Image of faint waters, I recoil
From my fierce rage into thy semblance. Enion, return!
Why does thy piteous face Evanish like a rainy cloud
[10] Melting, a shower of falling tears, nothing but tears? Enion,
Substanceless, voiceless, weeping, vanish'd, nothing but tears! Enion,
Art thou for ever vanish'd from the wat'ry eyes of Tharmas?
Rage, Rage shall never from my bosom; winds & waters of woe,
Consuming, all to the end consuming! Love & Hope are ended!'

For now no more remain'd of Enion in the dismal air,
Only a voice eternal wailing in the Elements.

174 See Index, *Ulro, Note III*. 177 O Tharmas . . . thee] *an addition.*
188 his] the *1st rdg. del.* Thunder] Tharmas *1st rdg. del.*
198 Hope] Joy *1st rdg. del.*

Where Enion, blind & age bent, wander'd, Ahania wanders now.
She wanders in Eternal fear of falling into the indefinite ;
For her bright eyes behold the Abyss. Sometimes a little Sleep
Weighs down her eyelids : then she falls : then, starting, wakes in fears,
Sleepless, to wander round, repell'd on the margin of Non Entity.

The End of the Third Night

NIGHT IV

INTRODUCTORY NOTE

This Night continues the myth of Tharmas, the victim of despair, from Night III, ll. 139 seq. Pursuing Enion, ' the vain shadow of hope ', he bids his children, Los and Enitharmon, create beneath his power a world wherein the ' lineaments of ungratified desire ' may take on the soft delusive forms of the moralistic life (ll. 24–33). Los refuses to obey, claiming to be supreme god now that Urizen is fallen (ll. 34–43).

What follows is quite obscure and can only be stated as briefly as possible in Blake's own terms. Tharmas carries off Enitharmon from Los, who falls, becoming a dark Spectre, an expression in this place descriptive rather than symbolic. Tharmas repeats his proposal, offering to restore Enitharmon if it is accepted. The Spectre of Los is then revealed as the Spectre of Urthona, and these symbols, together with Los, are, for a time, inextricably confused. But as Blake states the matter, fallen Urthona declares himself to be the victim of Urizen's attempt on Man, as described in Night I, ll. 210–225. Tharmas recognizes him as his former fellow in Eternity, and gives back Enitharmon, proposing that the Spectre shall assist Los to bind Urizen, lest he rise again to destroy (ll. 111–128). Tharmas now proclaims himself god over all, but still laments the loss of the age of innocence and bliss in the world of Eternity. He then departs to his proper place in the west, leaving Los to the binding of Urizen (ll. 165–245), the description of which is transferred almost verbatim from B. U., chap. iv *a*. One important change is made. Los ' fixes ' the changes of Urizen in obedience to Tharmas's command. The explanation of this is possibly to be sought in the emphatic repetition (ll. 39 and 41) of the title given to Tharmas, ' father of worms and clay ', the most elementary forms of existence in Blake's view (cp. *Thel*, iii). The limiting of Urizen into the human form would seem, therefore, to stress Blake's low valuation, at this stage in his writings, of the ' worm of sixty winters ' (J. 34. 57), its brain and senses.

The succeeding passage (ll. 246–278) is an interpolation in the manner of the later writings, dealing with the promise of regeneration through the Divine Vision. It is not, however, interwoven with the substance of the Night. The concluding passage (ll. 279–294) describes the infection of Los by the evil of his environment.

VALA

Night the Fourth

[1] But Tharmas rode on the dark Abyss; the voice of Tharmas roll'd
Over the heaving deluge; he saw Los & Enitharmon emerge
In strength & brightness from the Abyss; his bowels yearn'd over them.
They rose in strength above the heaving deluge in mighty scorn,
Red as the Sun in the hot morning of the bloody day.
Tharmas beheld them; his bowels yearn'd over them.

And he said: 'Wherefore do I feel such love & pity?
Ah Enion! Ah Enion! Ah, lovely lovely Enion!
How is this? All my hope is gone, for ever fled!
Like a famish'd Eagle, Eyeless, raging in the vast expanse,
Incessant tears are now my food, incessant rage & tears;
Deathless for ever now I wander, seeking oblivion
In torrents of despair in vain; for if I plunge beneath,
Stifling I live. If dash'd in pieces from a rocky height,
I reunite in endless torment: would I had never risen
From death's cold sleep beneath the bottom of the raging Ocean!
And cannot those who once have lov'd, ever forget their Love?
Are love & rage the same passion? they are the same in me.
Are those who love like those who died, risen again from death,
Immortal in immortal torment, never to be deliver'd?
Is it not possible that one risen again from Death
Can die? When dark despair comes over, can I not
Flow down into the sea & slumber in oblivion? Ah Enion!
[2] Deform'd I see these lineaments of ungratified Desire.

7–10 fled] *an addition over erasure.*
9 for ever fled] Enion for ever fled *1st rdg.*
16 beneath] upon *1st rdg. del.*
24 Cp. Ross. MS. xxv (Clar. Press, p. 173):

Abstinence sows sand all over
The ruddy limbs & flaming hair,
But Desire Gratified
Plants fruits of life & beauty there

and 'Several Questions Answered', 4:

What is it men in women do desire?
The lineaments of Gratified Desire.
What is it women do in men require?
The lineaments of Gratified Desire.

The all powerful curse of an honest man be upon Urizen & Luvah!
But thou, My Son, Glorious in brightness, comforter of Tharmas,
Go forth! Rebuild this Universe beneath my indignant power,
A Universe of Death & Decay. Let Enitharmon's hands
Weave soft delusive forms of Man above my wat'ry world.
Renew these ruin'd souls of Men thro' Earth, Sea, Air, & Fire,
To waste in endless corruption: renew those I will destroy.
Perhaps Enion may resume some little semblance,
To ease my pangs of heart & to restore some peace to Tharmas.'

Los answer'd in his furious pride, sparks issuing from his hair:
'Hitherto shalt thou come; no further: here thy proud waves cease.
We have drunk up the Eternal Man by our unbounded power;
Beware lest we also drink up thee, rough demon of the waters.
Our God is Urizen the King, King of the Heavenly hosts.
We have no other God but he, thou father of worms & clay;
And he is fall'n into the Deep, rough Demon of the waters;
And Los remains God over all, weak father of worms & clay!
I know I was Urthona, keeper of the gates of heaven;
But now I am all powerful Los, & Urthona is but my shadow.'

Doubting stood Tharmas in the solemn darkness; his dim Eyes
Swam in red tears: he rear'd his waves above the head of Los
In wrath; but pitying, back withdrew with many a sigh.
Now he resolv'd to destroy Los; & now his tears flow'd down.

In scorn stood Los: red sparks of blighting from his furious head
Flew over the waves of Tharmas: pitying, Tharmas stay'd his Waves.

28–29 The obscurity of Tharmas as a symbol makes it difficult to assign any clear meaning to Enitharmon's weaving at this point. Since it is desired that she should produce 'soft delusive forms', it would seem that the weaving has reference to the creation of forms of mundane illusion: see Index, *Weaving*, § I.

30 Cp. B. U. viii, l. 16 *note*.

42 This line is repeated, J. 82. 79. See Index, *Los, Note I*. Apparently in l. 43 Los speaks as one in error, Urthona being the true and Los the perverted form of spiritual activity. This is clearly stated in the closing lines of F. Z. ix. 847–853: cp. F. Z. vii. 353–356.

44 solemn] dismal *1st rdg. del.*

For Enitharmon shriek'd amain, crying: 'O! my sweet world,
Built by the Architect divine whose love to Los & Enitharmon,
Thou, rash abhorrèd Demon, in thy fury hast o'erthrown!

[3] 'What Sovereign Architect', said Tharmas, 'dare my will controll?
For if I will, I urge these waters. If I will, they sleep
In peace beneath my awful frown: my will shall be my Law.

So saying, in a Wave he rap'd bright Enitharmon far
Apart from Los, but cover'd her with softest brooding care
On a broad wave in the warm west, balming her bleeding wound.

O! how Los howl'd at the rending asunder! all the fibres rent,
Where Enitharmon join'd to his left side, in griding pain!
He, falling on the rocks, bellow'd his Dolor, till the blood
Stanch'd; then in ululation wail'd his woes upon the wind.

And Tharmas call'd to the Dark Spectre who upon the shores
With dislocated Limbs had fall'n. The Spectre rose in pain,
A Shadow blue, obscure & dismal; like a statue of lead
Bent by its fall from a high tower, the dolorous shadow rose.

'Go forth!' said Tharmas, 'works of joy are thine: obey & live!
So shall the spungy marrow issuing from thy splinter'd bones
Bonify; & thou shalt have rest when this thy labour is done.
Go forth! bear Enitharmon back to the Eternal Prophet.
Build her a bower in the midst of all my dashing waves.
Make first a resting place for Los & Enitharmon; then
Thou shalt have rest. If thou refusest, dash'd abroad on all
My waves, thy limbs shall separate in stench & rotting, & thou
Become a prey to all my Demons of despair & hope.'

50–51 Cp. F. Z. ii. 232–494. Enitharmon appears here to speak as Space and of Los as Time in the Urizenic world.

60 griding] dismal *1st rdg. del.*

63 The Spectre is Los divided from Enitharmon (ll. 60–61), or the Spectre of Urthona (l. 76), the symbols being inextricably confused. The significance of the change in Los is, however, indicated in ll. 80–82, which seem to show that the spiritual energy of the Eternal Prophet, which properly is creative, becomes merely destructive when divorced from vision, that is, in the fallen state. See below, ll. 201–207.

71 Inability to interpret adequately the Tharmas myth make it impossible to suggest an explanation of the interest of Tharmas in Enitharmon. His command for the building of a 'bower' or world for Los and Enitharmon may be compared with Urizen's charge 'to the Bands of Heaven': cp. F. Z. ii. 232 *note.* Tharmas's purpose is apparently opposed to the re-establishment of the former state of Man: see below, ll. 129–136.

The Spectre of Urthona, seeing Enitharmon, writh'd
His cloudy form in jealous fear ; & muttering thunders hoarse
And casting round thick glooms, thus utter'd his fierce pangs of heart :

' Tharmas, I know thee : how are we alter'd, our beauty decay'd !
But still I know thee, tho' in this horrible ruin whelm'd.
Thou, once the mildest son of heaven, art now become a Rage,
A terror to all living things. Think not that I am ignorant
That thou art risen from the dead ; or that, my power forgot,
[4] I slumber here in weak repose. I well remember the Day,
The day of terror & abhorrence,
When fleeing from the battle, thou, fleeting like the raven
Of dawn, outstretching an expanse where ne'er expanse had been,
Drew'st all the Sons of Beulah into thy dread vortex, following
Thy Eddying spirit down the hills of Beulah. All my sons
Stood round me at the anvil, where new heated, the wedge
Of iron glow'd furious, prepar'd for spades & mattocks.
Hearing the symphonies of war loud sounding, All my sons
Fled from my side : then pangs smote me unknown before. I saw
My loins begin to break forth into veiny pipes & writhe
Before me in the wind : englobing, trembling with strong vibrations,
The bloody mass began to animate. I, bending over,
Wept bitter tears incessant, still beholding how the piteous form
Dividing & dividing from my loins, a weak & piteous
Soft cloud of snow, a female pale & weak. I soft embrac'd
My counter part, & call'd it Love. I nam'd her Enitharmon
But found myself & her together issuing down the tide
Which now our rivers were become, delving thro' caverns huge
Of goary blood, strugg[l]ing to be deliver'd from our bonds.
She strove in vain : not so Urthona strove, for breaking forth,
A Shadow blue, obscure & dismal, from the breathing Nostrils

76 seeing] answer'd *1st rdg. del.*
85 abhorrence] abhorrence eternal *1st rdg.* Cp. F. Z. i. 165–238.
87 dread] great *1st rdg. del.* The ' sons of Beulah ' appear to be equivalent to Eternals, the symbolic use of the term Beulah being apparently of later date than this ' Night '. Similarly Vortex would seem to be merely a descriptive term and not symbolic as in F. Z. vi. 184.
93–100 Cp. B. U., chap. v. 33–69, for a similar account of the separation of the female from the male. See Index, *Sex*.
94 My . . . writhe] *written over erasure.*

Of Enion, I issued into the air, divided from Enitharmon.
I howl'd in sorrow. I beheld thee rotting upon the Rocks;
I pitying hover'd over thee, I protected thy ghastly corse
From Vultures of the deep; then wherefore should'st thou rage
Against me who thee guarded in the night of death from harm?'

Tharmas replied: 'Art thou Urthona, My friend, my old companion,
With whom I liv'd in happiness before that deadly night
When Urizen gave the horses of Light into the hands of Luvah?
Thou knowest not what Tharmas knows. O! I could tell thee tales
That would enrage thee as it has Enragèd me, even
From Death, in wrath & fury. But now come! bear back
Thy lovèd Enitharmon, For thou hast her here before thine Eyes.
[5] But my sweet Enion is vanish'd, & I never more
Shall see her, unless thou, O Shadow, wilt protect this Son
Of Enion, & him assist to bind the fallen King,
Lest he should rise again from death in all his dreary furor.
Bind him! take Enitharmon for thy sweet reward; while I
In vain am driven on false hope—hope, sister of Despair!'

Groaning the terror rose, & drave his solid rocks before
Upon the tide; till underneath the feet of Los a World
Dark, dreadful, rose; & Enitharmon lay at Los's feet.
The dolorous shadow joy'd: weak hope appear'd around his head.

Tharmas before Los stood; & thus the Voice of Tharmas roll'd:

'Now all comes into the power of Tharmas. Urizen is fall'n
And Luvah hidden in the Elemental forms of Life & Death.
Urthona is My Son. O Los, thou art Urthona, & Tharmas
Is God. The Eternal Man is seal'd, never to be deliver'd.
I roll my floods over his body, my billows & waves pass over him;
The sea encompasses him, & monsters of the deep are his companions;

119 The 'Son of Enion' is Los. The relationship between Urthona, his Spectre, and Los at this point is still obscure. The terror (l. 124) is apparently this same Spectre of Urthona. The 'fallen King' (l. 120) is Urizen.
121 dreary] dismal *1st rdg. del.* furor] *dubious rdg.*: ? power.

Dreamer of furious oceans, cold sleeper of weeds & shells !
Thy Eternal form shall never renew ; my uncertain prevails against thee.
Yet tho' I rage, God over all, A portion of my Life,
That in Eternal fields in comfort wander'd with my flocks
At noon, & laid her head upon my wearied bosom at night,
She is divided. She is vanish'd, even like Luvah & Vala.
O ! why did foul ambition sieze thee, Urizen, Prince of Light ;
And thee, O Luvah, prince of Love, till Tharmas was divided ?
And I, what can I now behold but an Eternal Death
Before my Eyes, & an Eternal weary work, to strive
Against the monstrous forms that breed among my silent waves ?
Is this to be A God ? Far rather would I be a Man,
To know sweet Science & to do with simple companions,
Sitting beneath a tent, & viewing Sheepfolds & soft pastures.
Take thou the hammer of Urthona : rebuild these furnaces.
Dost thou refuse ? mind I the sparks that issue from thy hair ?
[6] I will compell thee to rebuild by these my furious waves.
Death choose or life ! thou strugglest in my waters ; now choose life,
And all the Elements shall serve thee to their soothing flutes ;
Their sweet inspiriting lyres thy labours shall administer,
And they to thee ; only remit not, faint not thou, my Son !
Now thou dost know what 'tis to strive against the God of waters.'

So saying, Tharmas, on his furious chariots of the Deep
Departed far into the Unknown, & left a wondrous void
Round Los. Afar his waters bore on all sides round with noise
Of wheels & horses' hoofs & Trumpets, Horns & Clarions.

135 The Dreamer is the Eternal Man, the ideal form of being, whom Tharmas purposes to destroy.

137 The portion of Tharmas's Life is Enion.

147 The content of Science in this passage cannot be defined. Elsewhere (cp. F. Z. vii *a.* 162 seq.) the shepherd and the husbandman stand for the visionary life, with its 'simple rules' as contrasted with the complex and destructive machinery of Natural Religion, that brings 'sorrowful drudging', 'ignorance', and 'a scanty pittance of bread' to its victims. In writing this passage Blake may have remembered the King's speech in *3 Henry VI*, II. v. 19–54.

153–156 In the later books 'the Fairy hands of the Four Elements', though of themselves incapable of right action, labour beneath Los's control in the work of regeneration (M. 27. 60 *and passim*). Here their purpose is entirely to delude man.

158–245 These lines repeat the account of Los's labours in the Void and

Terrified, Los beheld the ruins of Urizen beneath,
A horrible Chaos to his eyes, a formless unmeasurable Death,
Whirling up broken rocks on high into the dismal air,
And fluctuating all beneath in Eddies of molten fluid.

Then Los with terrible hands siez'd on the Ruin'd Furnaces
Of Urizen, Enormous work ; he builded them anew,
Labour of Ages in the Darkness & the war of Tharmas.
And Los form'd Anvils of Iron petrific ; for his blows
Petrify with incessant beating many a rock, many a planet.

But Urizen slept in a ston[i]ed stupor in the nether Abyss ;
A dreamful horrible state, in tossings on his icy bed.
Freezing to Solid all beneath, his grey oblivious form,
Stretch'd over the immense, heaves in strong shudders—silent his voice—
In brooding contemplation stretching out from North to South
In mighty power. Round him Los roll'd furious
His thunderous wheels from furnace to furnace, tending diligent
The contemplative terror, frighten'd in his scornful sphere,
Frighten'd with cold infectious madness ; in his hand the thundering
Hammer of Urthona, forming under his heavy hand the hours,
[7] The days & years in chains of iron round the limbs of Urizen,
Link'd hour to hour & day to night & night to day & year to year,
In periods of pulsative furor : mills he form'd, & works
Of many wheels resistless in the power of dark Urthona.

But Enitharmon, wrap'd in clouds, wail'd loud : for as Los beat
The anvils of Urthona, link by link the chains of sorrow,
Warping upon the winds & whirling round in the dark deep,
Lash'd on the limbs of Enitharmon ; & the sulphur fires,
Belch'd from the furnaces, wreath'd round her. Chain'd in ceaseless fire

of Urizen's 'stony stupor' and subsequent 'binding', first told in the Books of *Urizen* and *Los*. According to the present myth, Los works in obedience to the command of Tharmas, the 'father of worms and clay' (ll. 39 and 41 above). The 'fixing' of Urizen's changes would therefore seem here to be allegorically a low valuing of the human form, senses and intellect. What more is implied is matter of conjecture merely.

175–183 Cp. B. U., chap. iv (*a*), ll. 15–18.

185 The 'chains of sorrow' have clear reference to the enslavement of man by the illusions of his mundane environment. See below, l. 203.

The lovely female howl'd, & Urizen beneath deep groan'd
Deadly between the hammer's beating, grateful to the Ears
Of Los. Absorb'd in dire revenge, he drank with joy the cries
Of Enitharmon & the groans of Urizen—fuel for his wrath
And for his pity, secret feeding on thoughts of cruelty.

The Spectre wept at his dire labours, when from Ladles huge
He pour'd the molten iron round the limbs of Enitharmon :
But when he pour'd it round the bones of Urizen, he laugh'd
Hollow upon the hollow wind, his Shadowy form obeying
The voice of Los ; compell'd, he labour'd round the Furnaces.

And thus began the binding of Urizen day & night in fear.
Circling round the dark Demon with howlings, dismay & sharp blightings,
The Prophet of Eternity beat on his iron links & links of brass ;
And as he beat round the hurtling Demon, terrified at the Shapes
Enslav'd humanity put on, he became what he beheld.
Raging against Tharmas his God, & uttering
Ambiguous words blasphemous, fill'd with envy, firm resolv'd
On hate Eternal, in his vast disdain he labour'd, beating
The Links of fate, link after link, an endless chain of sorrows.

[8] The Eternal Mind, bounded, began to roll eddies of wrath, ceaseless,
Round & round, & the sulphureous foam, surgeing thick,
Settled, a Lake bright & shining clear, White as the snow.

Forgetfulness, dumbness, necessity ! in chains of the mind lock'd up,
In fetters of ice shrinking, disorganiz'd, rent from Eternity,
Los beat on his fetters, & heated his furnaces,
And pour'd iron sodor & sodor of brass.

Restless the immortal, inchain'd, heaving dolorous,
Anguish'd, unbearable ; till a roof, shaggy, wild, inclos'd
In an orb his fountain of thought.

195 As the pouring of molten iron round the bones of Urizen is the process of limiting him to the condition of mortal life, so the like activity in the case of Enitharmon may be intended to refer to the limited human conception of Space, the emergence of which is the first consequence, according to this myth, of the constriction of the 'eternal mind'.

203–207 See above, l. 63 *note*. 208–245 Cp. B. U. iv (*a*). 19–89.

213 heated] pour'd *1st rdg. del.*

In a horrible dreamful slumber, like the linkèd chain
A vast spine writh'd in torment upon the wind,
Shooting pain'd ribbs, like a bending Cavern ;
And bones of solidness froze over all his nerves of joy.
A first age passèd, a State of dismal woe.

From the Caverns of his jointed spine down sunk with fright
A red round globe, hot, burning, deep deep down into the Abyss ;
Panting, Conglobing, trembling, shooting out ten thousand branches
Around his solid bones ; & a second age passèd over.

In harrowing fear rolling, his nervous brain shot branches
On high into two little orbs, hiding in two little caves :
Hiding carefully from the wind, his eyes beheld the deep ;
And a third age passèd : a State of dismal woe.

The pangs of hope began : in heavy pain, striving, struggling,
Two Ears in close volutions from beneath his orbs of vision
Shot spiring out, & petrified as they grew. And a Fourth
Age passèd over, & a State of dismal woe.

In ghastly torment sick, hanging upon the wind,
Two nostrils bent down to the deeps.
[9] And a fifth age passèd, & a state of dismal woe.

In ghastly torment sick, within his ribs bloated round
A craving hungry cavern. Thence arose his channel'd
Throat ; then, like a red flame, a tongue of hunger
And thirst appear'd : and a sixth age passèd of dismal woe.

Enragèd & stifled with torment, he threw his right arm to the north,
His left arm to the south, shooting out in anguish deep ;
And his feet stamp'd the nether abyss in trembling, howling & dismay.
And a seventh age passèd over, & a state of dismal woe.

The Council of God, on high watching over the Body
Of Man, cloth'd in Luvah's robes of blood, saw & wept,

After l. 227 : 'Round the branches of his heart' *del.*
233 they grew] as they grew *1st rdg.*
246–278 After l. 245 Blake has the note 'The Council of God &c as below to Immensity, 31 lines'. This direction transfers to this place an added passage, ll. 246–278, written beneath l. 294, which originally concluded this Night, the partially deleted phrase 'The End of the Fourth Night' being visible beneath the first two lines of the added passage.
246–249 The phrase 'cloth'd in Luvah's robes of blood' relates to the Council of God, the 'Universal Family' who live as 'One Man, Jesus the Christ' (J. 38. 16–22). See F. Z. ii. 105–106 and Index, *Jesus* and *Incarnation*, II. β. i.

De[s]cending over Beulah's mild moon cover'd regions.
The daughters of Beulah saw the Divine Vision ; they were comforted ;
And as a Double female form, loveliness & perfection of beauty,
They bow'd the head & worshipp'd, & with mild voice spoke these words :

[10] ' Lord Saviour, if thou had'st been here, our brother had not died.
And now we know that whatsoever thou wilt ask of God
He will give it thee : for we are weak women, & dare not lift
Our eyes to the Divine pavilions : therefore in mercy thou
Appearest cloth'd in Luvah's garments, that we may behold thee
And live. Behold ! Eternal Death is in Beulah. Behold !
We perish & shall not be found, unless thou grant a place
In which we may be hidden under the Shadow of wings.
For if we, who are but for a time & who pass away in winter,
Behold these wonders of Eternity, we shall consume.'

Such were the words of Beulah, of the Feminine Emanation.
The Empyrean groan'd throughout. All Eden was darken'd.
The Corse of Albion lay on the Rock ; the Sea of Time & Space
Beat round the Rock in mighty waves ; & as a Polypus
That vegetates beneath the Sea, the limbs of Man vegetated
In monstrous forms of Death, a Human polypus of Death.

The Saviour mild & gentle bent over the corse of Death,
Saying : ' If Ye will Believe, Your brother shall rise again.'
And first he found the Limit of Opacity, & nam'd it Satan,
In Albion's bosom : for in every human bosom these limits stand.
And next he found the Limit of Contraction, & nam'd it Adam ;
While yet those beings were not born, nor knew of good or Evil.

250 In the later books the general significance of symbols compounded with ' double '—e. g. the ' Double Female ' who is Vala or Rahab—is evil. Here its association with the Daughters of Beulah would seem to indicate that it is used in the contrary and spiritual sense.

254–261 See Index, *Beulah*. The vision of Eternity is so tempered in ' Jesus in Luvah's robes of blood ', as to adapt it to the weakness of the Daughters of Beulah, who are of those who could not endure the full revelation : cp. M. 30, ll. 8–31.

259–261 These lines are repeated in M. 30. 25–27.

262–267 Such . . . Death] *written over erasure*.

264 Albion] Man *1st rdg. del*. The ' Sea of Time & Space ' is symbolically equivalent to the ' Atlantic Deep ' : see Index, *Atlantic*.

269 Saying . . . again] *an addition*.

270–272 See Index, *Expansion*, &c.

271 In . . . stand] *marginal addition in pencil*.

Then wondrously the Starry Wheels felt the Divine hand. Limit
Was put to Eternal Death. Los felt the Limit & saw
The Finger of God touch the Seventh furnace, in terror;
And Los beheld the hand of God over his furnaces
Beneath the Deeps, in dismal Darkness beneath immensity.

[9] In terrors Los shrunk from his task; his great hammer
Fell from his hand; his fires hid their strong limbs in smoke.
For with noises ruinous, hurtlings & clashings & groans,
The immortal endur'd, tho' bound in a deadly sleep.
Pale terror siez'd the Eyes of Los as he beat round
The hurtling Demon. Terrified at the shapes
Enslav'd humanity put on, he became what he beheld;
He became what he was doing; he was himself transform'd.
Spasms siez'd his muscular fibres writhing to & fro; his pallid lips
Unwilling mov'd as Urizen howl'd: his loins wav'd like the sea.
At Enitharmon's shrieks his knees each other smote, & then he look'd
With stony Eyes on Urizen, & then swift writh'd his neck
Involuntary to the Couch where Enitharmon lay.
The bones of Urizen hurtle on the wind, the bones of Los
Twinge, & his iron sinews bend like lead & fold
Into unusual forms, dancing & howling, stamping the Abyss.

End of the Fourth Night [Book *del.*]

274 Starry Wheels] Deep beneath *1st rdg. del.* The 'Starry Wheels' are generally assigned to the 'Spectre Sons of Albion'. The symbol stresses the oppressive force of the empiricist and moralistic errors. 'Natural Religion', the total of mundane delusions, is represented as such a wheel, and

Jesus died because he strove
Against the current of this Wheel: its Name
Is Caiaphas, the dark Preacher of Death,
Of Sin, of sorrow & of punishment. (J. 77, *poem*, 16–19.)

278 Beneath . . . immensity] written over 'The End of the Fourth Night', *del.* After this line Blake notes 'In terrors &c to Abyss, as 31 lines above', referring to the change in the order of the passages noted above: see l. 246 *note.* After l. 286 is an obscure pencil note: 'Bring in here the Globe of Blood as in the B. of Urizen.' Since ll. 279–282 practically repeat the opening stanza of B. U., chap. v, it may have been Blake's intention, which he never carried out, to introduce at this point the episodes of the Globe of Blood and the subsequent separation of Enitharmon, which occupy stanzas 7–12 of that chapter. Above the pencilled drawing that occupies the bottom of this page is written 'Christ's Crucifix shall be made an excuse for Executing Criminal'. It has no apparent place in the text.

281 with] in *1st rdg. del.*

NIGHT V

INTRODUCTORY NOTE

The infection of error in Los and Enitharmon is described in its consequences; the Prophet and his Emanation shrink into fixed space; though still majestic and beautiful, they remain ' unexpansive '; the furnaces and bellows, symbols of creative activity, stand idle. The daylight wanes, the wheels of turning darkness arise, and winter holds the earth (ll. 1–35). At this point, Orc is born. In a line that is almost certainly an addition, he is identified with Luvah, the King of Love, who, as Orc, is become the King of rage and death (l. 42). This change in the concept of Orc presents some considerable difficulty (see Index, *Orc*); but the main point that comes out clearly is that the birth of the ' man-child ' synchronizes with the nadir of suspended spirituality,[1] and with the awakening of the ' Demons of the deep ', the ministers of empirical and moral law, who summon Vala, the latest manifestation of the ' feminine ' illusion, from the womb of Enitharmon, or Space (ll. 62–64: cp. F. Z. iii, ll. 19–21). But though no longer the triumphant liberator of *America* and *Europe*, Orc is not wholly in bondage to error: later (ll. 114–142) he enjoys communion with the ideal world, and ultimately becomes the instrument of the overthrow of Urizen's ' religion ' (cp. F. Z. vii. and ix.).

The account of the binding of Orc (ll. 79–112) is repeated from *The Book of Urizen*, chap. vii, with significant additions. Among these is Blake's ascription of Los's act to jealousy of the new force that threatens to supersede his power in the world of Enitharmon. Jealousy grows, obstructing the ' prophetic ' activity of Los, and ultimately imposing a partial restraint upon Orc. But the limitations of temporal existence, the Chain of Jealousy, apparently affect only physical acts, for the spirit of Orc is still free. Flames of fire bring to it the virtues of the eternal world, spirits of life minister sustenance from the heavens of heavens, the thrilling joys of sense quell his rage, while his eyes, ' the lights of his large soul ', behold the secrets of infinite being (ll. 114–142).

The binding of Orc, the jealous inhibition of energy, definitely reveals the extent of Los's defaillance (cp. ll. 110–113); and later the inextricable intertwining of the Chain with the limbs of Orc symbolizes the power of mundane environment to pervert spiritual energy, so that not even Los's repentance can undo the work of his mistaken act (ll. 143–172). The final triumph of error in mundane existence would seem to be the quickening of Vala within the heart of Enitharmon (ll. 176–182).

Closed up in dens of death by Los (cp. F. Z. iv, ll. 165–245), Urizen feels the influence of Orc and Vala. In a passage (ll. 189–241) hardly in keeping with the general character of the symbol, he repents his schism and declares his purpose of exploring his dens, to discover the power that quickens them. The final words of the Night (ll. 239–241) mark the synchronism of the appearance of Orc and Vala with the beginnings of regeneration.

[1] So in J. 93. 21–26, the denial of ' a conscience in Man, and the communion of Saints and Angels ', and the rejection of Vision for what Blake calls ' Deism ', is said to be ' that Signal of the Morning which was told us in the Beginning '.

VALA

Night the Fifth

INFECTED, Mad, he danc'd on his mountains high & dark as heaven.
Now fix'd into one stedfast bulk, his features Stonify:
From his mouth curses, & from his eyes sparks of blighting.
Beside the anvil cold he danc'd with the hammer of Urthona
Terrific. Pale, Enitharmon, stretch'd on the dreary earth,
Felt her immortal limbs freeze, stiffening, pale, inflexible.
His feet shrink with'ring from the deep, shrinking & withering;
And Enitharmon shrunk up, all their fibres with'ring beneath;
As plants, wither'd by winter, leaves & stems & roots decaying,
Melt into thin air, while the seed, driv'n by the furious wind,
Rests on the distant Mountain's top. So Los & Enitharmon,
Shrunk into fixèd space, stood trembling on a Rocky cliff;
Yet mighty bulk & majesty & beauty remain'd, but unexpansive.
As far as highest Zenith from the lowest Nadir, so far shrunk
Los from the furnaces, a Space immense; & left the cold
Prince of Light bound in chains of intellect among the furnaces.
But all the furnaces were out, & the bellows had ceast to blow.

He stood trembling, & Enitharmon clung around his knees:
Their senses unexpansive in one stedfast bulk remain.
The night blew cold, & Enitharmon shriek'd on the dismal wind:
[2] Her pale hands cling around her husband, & over her weak head
Shadows of Eternal Death sit in the leaden air.

Night] Book *1st rdg. del.* 5 dreary] dismal *1st rdg. del.*
13 See Index, *Expansion*, and see below, l. 19.
15 Here the Furnaces represent the visionary activities proper to Los in the supreme state of existence: his shrinking from them expresses the change to the state of error. In ll. 16–17 Blake varies the image. The cold furnaces and idle bellows image the fallen state, the cessation of all spiritual vitality, the world where Urizen lies bound. The bonds are of 'intellect', i.e. they are the outcome of the limitation of Urizen to the life of the senses and the rational mind. 'Intellect' is more commonly used in antithesis with 'Reason' and refers to the higher life of vision or 'Imagination'.

But the soft pipe, the flute, the viol, organ, harp & cymbal,
And the sweet sound of silver voices calm the weary couch
Of Enitharmon : but her groans drown the immortal harps.
Loud & more loud the living music floats upon the air ;
Faint & more faint the daylight wanes, the wheels of turning darkness
Began in solemn revolutions. Earth, convuls'd with rending pangs,
Rock'd to & fro, & ⟨&⟩ cried sore at the groans of Enitharmon.
Still the faint harps & silver voices calm the weary couch ;
But from the caves of deepest night ascending in clouds of mist,
The winter spread his wide black wings across from pole to pole ;
Grim frost beneath & terrible snow, link'd in a marriage chain,
Began a dismal dance. The winds around on pointed rocks
Settled like bats innumerable, ready to fly abroad.
The groans of Enitharmon shake the skies, the lab'ring Earth ;
Till from her heart rending his way, a terrible Child sprang forth
In thunder, smoke & sullen flames & howlings & fury & blood.

Soon as his burning Eyes were open'd on the Abyss,
The horrid trumpets of the deep bellow'd with bitter blasts.
The Enormous Demons woke & howl'd around the new born king,
Crying : ' Luvah, King of Love, thou art the King of rage & death.'
Urizen cast deep darkness round him. Raging, Luvah pour'd
The spears of Urizen from Chariots round the Eternal tent.
Discord began ; then yells & cries shook the wide firmament.

23–30 Cp. F. Z. ii, ll. 117 foll., for a similar description of elemental music in connexion with Enitharmon and Los. See also *Europe*, 13–23. Such music would properly pertain to them, since as Time and Space they are vaguely, in *The Four Zoas*, the regents of ' vegetative ' or physical existence.

37 The child is Orc. It is only in added passages (e. g. ll. 43–45) that Blake identifies him with Luvah, a modification that apparently reflects the change in Blake's attitude towards mere passion as a regenerative influence ; see Index, *Luvah*.

41 new born] youthful *1st rdg. del.*

42 Crying . . . death] *an addition.*

43–45 Urizen . . . firmament] *written over erased passage.* The precise significance of the spears of Urizen in the hands of Luvah (cp. F. Z. i. 205–207) cannot be discerned. It is clearly an instance of confusion of functions to which the ' fall ' is sometimes attributed (see F. Z. iii. 27–33 : cp. v. 234–237 and the Satan-Palamabron myth, M., pp. 5–11, and M., Introduction).

45 then] & *1st rdg. del.*

[3] 'Where is Sweet Vala, gloomy prophet? where the lovely form
That drew the body of Man from heaven into this dark Abyss?
Soft tears & sighs, where are you? come forth! shout on bloody fields!
Shew thy soul, Vala! shew thy bow & quiver of secret fires!

'Draw thy bow, Valan! from the depths of hell thy black bow draw,
And twang the bow string to our howlings! let thine arrows black
Sing in the Sky, as once they sang upon the hills of Light
When dark Urthona wept in torment of the secret pain!

'He wept & he divided, & he laid his gloomy head
Down on the Rock of Eternity, on darkness of the deep,
Torn by black storms & ceaseless torrents of consuming fire;
Within his breast his fiery sons chain'd down & fill'd with cursings;

'And breathing terrible blood & vengeance, gnashing his teeth with pain,
Let loose the Enormous Spirit on the darkness of the deep:
And his dark wife, that once fair crystal form, divinely clear,
Within his ribs producing serpents, whose souls are flames of fire.

'But now the times return upon thee. Enitharmon's womb
Now holds thee, soon to issue forth. Sound, Clarions of war!
Call Vala from her close recess in all her dark deceit,
Then rage on rage shall fierce redound out of her crystal quiver.'

So sung the Demons round red Orc & round faint Enitharmon.
Sweat & blood stood on the limbs of Los in globes; his fiery Eyelids
Faded. He rouz'd; he siez'd the wonder in his hands, & went
Shudd'ring & weeping thro' the Gloom & down into the deeps.

Enitharmon nurs'd her fiery child in the dark deeps,
Sitting in darkness: over her Los mourn'd in anguish fierce,
Cover'd with gloom. The fiery boy grew, fed by the milk
Of Enitharmon. Los around her builded pillars of iron

50 Valan] This form of 'Vala' is found in *The Four Zoas* below, l. 179 and ix. 373. A dubious instance occurs in F. Z. iv. 140.

56–57: 60–61 These lines are repeated in J. 40. 39–42, 'his own' being added before 'consuming' and 'Eon', i.e. 'Emanations' substituted for 'wife'

62–63 Cp. F. Z. iii, ll. 19–21, where Urizen foretells the birth of Vala.

[4] And brass & silver & gold, fourfold, in dark prophetic fear;
For now he fear'd Eternal Death & uttermost Extinction.
He builded Golgonooza on the Lake of Udan Adan,
Upon the Limit of Translucence; then he builded Luban;
Tharmas laid the Foundations, & Los finish'd it in howling woe.

But when fourteen summers & winters had revolvèd over
Their solemn habitation, Los beheld the ruddy boy
Embracing his bright mother, & beheld malignant fires
In his young eyes, discerning plain that Orc plotted his death.
Grief rose upon his ruddy brows: a tight'ning girdle grew
Around his bosom like a bloody cord. In secret sobs
He burst it: but next morn another girdle succeeds
Around his bosom. Every day he view'd the fiery youth
With silent fear, & his immortal cheeks grew deadly pale;
Till many a morn & many a night pass'd over in dire woe,
Forming a girdle in the day & bursting it at night.
The girdle was form'd by day, by night was burst in twain,
Falling down on the rock, an iron chain, link by link lock'd.

Enitharmon beheld the bloody chain of nights & days
Depending from the bosom of Los, & how with griding pain
He went each morning to his labours with the spectre dark;
Call'd it the chain of Jealousy. Now Los began to speak
His woes aloud to Enitharmon, since he could not hide
His uncouth plague. He siez'd the boy in his immortal hands,
While Enitharmon follow'd him, weeping in dismal woe,
Up to the iron mountain's top; & there the Jealous chain
Fell from his bosom on the mountain. The Spectre dark
Held the fierce boy: Los nail'd him down, binding around his limbs
The accursed chain. O how bright Enitharmon howl'd & cried
Over her Son! Obdurate, Los bound down her lovèd Joy.
[5] The hammer of Urthona smote the rivets, in terror, of brass.
Tenfold. The Demon's rage flam'd tenfold forth, rending,
Roaring, redounding, Loud, Loud, Louder & Louder, & fir'd

76–78 He . . . woe] *an addition.* For these symbols, that belong to the period of *Milton* and *Jerusalem*, see Index, *Los, Note III*, A., *Expansion*, and *Ulro, Note III*. For Luban cp. F. Z. vii, l. 429 *note*.

83–91 Cp. B. U., chap. vii, ll. 3–15.

93 griding] dismal *1st rdg. del.*

93–95 The Spectre is the Spectre of Urthona: cp. F. Z. vii, ll. 215–230 and ll. 265–306.

95 Cp. B. U., chap. vii, l. 14, and Index, *Orc*, II, *b*.

102 accursed] dismal *1st rdg. del.*

103 lovèd] *perhaps* love's.

The darkness, warring with the waves of Tharmas & Snows of Urizen.
Crackling the flames went up with fury from the immortal Demon.
Surrounded with flame the Demon grew, loud howling in his fires.
Los folded Enitharmon in a cold white cloud in fear;
Then led her down into the deeps & into his labyrinth,
Giving the Spectre sternest charge over the howling fiend,
Concenter'd into Love of Parent, Storgous Appetite, Craving.
His limbs, bound down, mock at his chains; for over them a flame
Of circling fire unceasing plays, to feed them with life & bring
The virtues of the Eternal worlds. Ten thousand thousand spirits
Of life lament around the Demon, going forth & returning.
At his enormous call they flee into the heavens of heavens,
And back return with wine & food, or dive into the deeps
To bring the thrilling joys of sense to quell his ceaseless rage.
His eyes, the lights of his large soul, contract or else expand.
Contracted they behold the secrets of the infinite mountains,
The veins of gold & silver & the hidden things of Vala,
Whatever grows from its pure bud or breathes a fragrant soul.
Expanded they behold the terrors of the Sun & Moon,
The Elemental Planets, & the orbs of eccentric fire.
His nostrils breathe a fiery flame, his locks are like the forests
Of wild beasts; there the lion glares, the tyger & wolf howl there,
And there the Eagle hides her young in cliffs & precipices.
His bosom is like starry heaven expanded; all the stars

113 Concenter'd . . . Craving] *an addition.* The meaning of this line is obscure. It may apply to Los or to his Spectre, since the two are practically identical in meaning at this point. In that case it would seem that Blake is speaking in condemnation of the allegation of parental affection as a reason for restraint. Compare the lines in the final section of *Tiriel* and *The Little Boy Lost* in the *Songs of Experience*, which in some respects presents a curiously close parallel to the present passage. There may be in it something of the notion of 'Love seeking for Dominion': cp. F. Z. iii. 71 *note*. The original of the word, στοργή (love of parents and children), appears in M. 34. 30 as the 'River Storge (which is Arnon)'. Here again the exact meaning is obscure, though its association with error is plain enough.

114–142 This passage recalls the earlier concept of Orc in *America*. The superiority of energy over the external restraints of law is expressed in the continual intercourse of the former with the visionary world of eternal wisdom and delight in spite of the restrictions of moral and other codes.

117 lament] *2nd rdg.*; *1st rdg. illegible.*

127 a] with *1st rdg. del.*

Sing round ; there waves the harvest, & the vintage rejoices ; the Springs
Flow into rivers of delight ; there the spontaneous flowers
Drink, laugh & sing ; the grasshopper, the Emmet & the Fly ;
The golden Moth builds there a house & spreads her silken bed.
[6] His loins, inwove with silken fires, are like a furnace, fierce
As the strong Bull in summer time, when bees sing round the heath,
Where the herds low after the shadow & after the water spring ;
The num'rous flocks cover the mountain & shine along the valley.
His knees are rocks of adamant & rubie & emerald.
Spirits of strength in Palaces rejoice in golden armour ;
Armèd with spear & shield they drink & rejoice over the slain.
Such is the Demon, such his terror on the nether deep.

But when return'd to Golgonooza, Los & Enitharmon
Felt all the sorrow Parents feel. They wept toward one another,
And Los repented that he had chain'd Orc upon the mountain ;
And Enitharmon's tears prevail'd : parental love return'd,
Tho' terrible his dread of that infernal chain. They rose
At midnight, hasting to their much belovèd care.
Nine days they travel'd thro' the Gloom of Entuthon Benithon :
Los, taking Enitharmon by the hand, led her along
The dismal vales & up to the iron mountain's top, where Orc
Howl'd in the furious wind. He thought to give to Enitharmon
Her son in tenfold joy, & to compensate for her tears
Even if his own death resulted : so much pity him pain'd.

But when they came to the dark rock & to the spectrous cave,
Lo ! the young limbs had strucken root into the rock, & strong

140 strength in] strength rejoice *1st rdg. del.*

156–170 This is a symbolical expression of the growth and ramification of the power of error, when once it is established : a somewhat similar conception underlies the symbolic ' Tree of Moral Virtue ', ' Albion's Tree ', or the ' Polypus ' in the later writings. It is noteworthy that the limbs of Orc grow into its fibres—as if even the spirit of energy were at length drawn into the service of its contrary, Law, by the influence of its mundane environment.

Fibres had from the Chain of Jealousy inwove themselves
In a swift vegetation round the rock & round the Cave,
And over the immortal limbs of the terrible fiery boy.
In vain they strove now to unchain, In vain, with bitter tears
To melt the chain of Jealousy: not Enitharmon's death,
Nor the Consummation of Los could ever melt the chain,
Nor unroot the infernal fibres from their rocky bed.
Nor all Urthona's strength, nor all the power of Luvah's Bulls,
Tho' they each morning drag the unwilling Sun out of the deep,
Could uproot the infernal chain; for it had taken root
[7] Into the iron rock, & grew a chain beneath the Earth
Even to the Center, wrapping round the Center; & the limbs
Of Orc entering with fibres, became one with him, a living Chain,
Sustainèd by the Demon's life. Despair & Terror & Woe & Rage
Inwrap the Parents in cold clouds, as they bend howling over
The terrible boy; till fainting by his side the Parents fell.

Not long they lay. Urthona's spectre found herbs of the pit:
Rubbing their temples, he reviv'd them. All their lamentations
I write not here, but all their after life was lamentation.

When satiated with grief they return'd back to Golgonooza,
Enitharmon, on the road of Dranthon, felt the inmost gate
Of her bright heart burst open, & again close with a deadly pain.
Within her heart Valan began to reanimate in bursting sobs;
And when the Gate was open she beheld that dreary Deep
Where bright Ahania wept. She also saw the infernal roots
Of the chain of Jealousy, & felt the rendings of fierce howling Orc,

Rending the Caverns like a mighty wind pent in the Earth.
Tho' wide apart as furthest north is from the furthest south,
Urizen trembled where he lay, to hear the howling terror.
The rocks shook; the Eternal bars, tugg'd to & fro, were rifted.

164–165 Cp. *Thel*, § ii, l. 8.

177 Dranthon, mentioned elsewhere only in a deleted line (F. Z. vii. 452 *note*), cannot be explained.

178 deadly] dismal *1st rdg. del.* 180 dreary] dismal *1st rdg. del.*

Outstretch'd upon the stones of ice, the ruins of his throne,
Urizen shudd'ring heard: his trembling limbs shook the strong caves.

The Woes of Urizen, shut up in the deep dens of Urthona:

'Ah! how shall Urizen the King submit to this dark mansion?
Ah! how is this? Once on the heights I stretch'd my throne sublime.
The mountains of Urizen, once of silver, where the sons of wisdom dwelt
And on whose tops the Virgins sang, are rocks of Desolation.

'My fountains, once the haunt of Swans, now breed the scaly tortoise,
The houses of my harpers are become a haunt of crows,
The gardens of wisdom are become a field of horrid graves,
And on the bones I drop my tears, & water them in vain.

[8] 'Once how I walkèd from my palace in gardens of delight!
The sons of wisdom stood around, the harpers follow'd with harps.
Nine virgins cloth'd in light compos'd the song to their immortal voices,
And at my banquets of new wine my head was crown'd with joy.

'Then in my ivory pavilions I slumber'd in the noon,
And walkèd in the silent night among sweet smelling flowers,
Till on my silver bed I slept, & sweet dreams round me hover'd:
But now my land is darken'd & my wise men are departed.

'My songs are turnèd to cries of Lamentation
Heard on my Mountains, & deep sighs under my palace roofs;
Because the Steeds of Urizen, once swifter than the light,
Were kept back from my Lord & from his chariot of mercies.

'O did I keep the horses of the day in silver pastures?
O I refus'd the lord of day the horses of his prince!
O did I close my treasuries with roofs of solid stone,
And darken all my Palace walls with envyings & hate!

189 See above, ll. 15–17, and cp. S. Lib. § 16. Urizen's speech (ll. 190–241) does not appear to be in harmony with the normal significance of the symbol.

202 slumber'd in] slumber'd with *1st rdg.* 206 to] into *1st rdg. del.*

'O Fool, to think that I could hide from his all piercing eyes
The gold & silver & costly stones, his holy workmanship !
O Fool, could I forget the light that fillèd my bright spheres
Was a reflection of his face who call'd me from the deep !

'I well remember, for I heard the mild & holy voice
Saying: "O light ! spring up & shine !" & I sprang up from the Deep.
He gave to me a silver scepter & crown'd me with a golden crown,
& said "Go forth & guide my Son who wanders on the ocean !"

'I went not forth: I hid myself in black clouds of my wrath.
I call'd the stars around my feet in the night of councils dark;
The stars threw down their spears & fled naked away.
We fell: I siez'd thee, dark Urthona. In my left hand, falling,

'I siez'd thee, beauteous Luvah; thou art faded like a flower,
And like a lilly thy wife Vala wither'd by winds.
When thou didst bear the golden cup at the immortal tables,
Thy children smote their fiery wings, crown'd with the gold of heaven.

[9] 'Thy pure feet step'd on the steps divine, too pure for other feet,
And thy fair locks shadow'd thine eyes from the divine effulgence.
Then thou didst keep with Strong Urthona the living gates of heaven;
But now thou art bow'd down with him, even to the gates of hell,

'Because thou gavest Urizen the wine of the Almighty
For Steeds of Light, that they might run in thy golden chariot of pride.
I gave to thee the Steeds. I pour'd the stolen wine,
And drunken with the immortal draught fell from my throne sublime.

218 The 'mild and holy voice' would seem to be the voice of 'the Eternal One', the Eternal Man, but the 'Son' (l. 221) cannot be identified.
221 & said] Saying *1st rdg. del.*
227 thy] is thy *1st rdg.* 234–237 See Index, *Luvah*, II.

' I will arise, Explore these dens, & find that deep pulsation
That shakes my caverns with strong shudders: perhaps this is the night
Of Prophecy, & Luvah hath burst his way from Enitharmon.
When Thought is clos'd in Caves, Then love shall shew its root in deepest Hell.' 241

End of the Fifth Night [Book *del.*]

239–240 The 'night of Prophecy' would seem to be 'the night foretold', the time immediately preceding the dawn of regeneration: cp. F. Z. iii, ll. 13–22.

241 This idea that at a certain point in man's spiritual decline a providential purpose manifests itself, is common in Blake's later writings. Cp. F. Z. viii, ll. 1–4: J. 73, ll. 22–27: and see Index, *Expansion*, &c. 'Thought clos'd in Caves' apparently interprets the fallen Urizen.

NIGHT VI

INTRODUCTORY NOTE

Night VI elaborates the eighth chapter of *The Book of Urizen* without adding anything of interest. Blake depicts, in the allegory of Urizen's journey to the northern world of Urthona, the efforts of the unillumined mind to attain truth. The long accounts of horrors he encounters represent, in general, Blake's vision of the misery and cruelty inseparable from the 'philosophy of five senses', and from the moralities that are its results. It is impossible, perhaps unnecessary to try to assign a definite meaning to each occasion of horror. The repetitions and restatements probably aim at achieving an effect by the accumulation of impressions. The only effect achieved, however, is one of monotony, for the details are very little varied and emphasis is ignored. The opening passage (ll. 1–46), strongly reminiscent of *Tiriel*, deals with Urizen's encounter with the obscure personages, his daughters, who appear elsewhere only in F. Z. VII. and IX. Then he meets Tharmas, who in despair proposes that Urizen shall withhold light from him, while he withholds food from Urizen, that by extinction both may obtain release from their sufferings (l. 71). Urizen, unheeding, pursues his way through the forms of enormity that crowd the world of death, bearing with him his books of iron and brass, the repositories of his perverted wisdom (l. 85). Himself the cause of the universal desolation, he cannot release his children from it, for he is subject to some undefined power (cp. l. 142 and *note*). So he passes through his own world, through the southern world of Los and Orc, into the eastern Void. Here he experiences cycles of death and resurrection (ll. 143–225), described symbolically in a passage which is noted here because it is connected with the only certain references in this book to an ulterior providential purpose that are not in added passages (ll. 154–163, and 279–281). He traverses the void by creating a bridge of 'Vortices' or 'Sciences' (l. 184), apparently systems of error. At length, wearied by the confusion, he builds another world 'better suited to obey his will' (ll. 228–229). So he gains a new dominion over his creatures, weaving round them his 'Web of Religion', till their senses grow weaker and narrower; a form of statement apparently intended to stress the view that a false philosophy most effectually entangles the souls of mortals when it is woven with terms of religion. Ultimately 'by Providence Divine conducted' (l. 280) he arrives at the northern world where the Spectre of Urthona, Orc, and Tharmas bar his way.

VALA

Night the Sixth

So Urizen arose, & leaning on his Spear explor'd his dens.
He threw his flight thro' the dark air to where a river flow'd,
And taking off his silver helmet, fillèd it & drank.
But when unsatiated his thirst he assay'd to gather more,
Lo ! three terrific women at the verge of the bright flood,
Who would not suffer him to approach, but drove him back with storms.

Urizen knew them not, & thus address'd the spirits of darkness :

' Who art thou, Eldest Woman, sitting in thy clouds ?
What is that name written on thy forehead ? what art thou,
And wherefore dost thou pour this water forth in sighs & care ? '

She answer'd not, but fill'd her Urn & pour'd it forth abroad.

' Answerest thou not ? ' said Urizen. ' Then thou maist answer me,
Thou terrible woman clad in blue, whose strong attractive power
Draws all into a fountain at the rock of thy attraction.
With frowning brow thou sittest, mistress of these mighty waters.'

She answer'd not, but stretch'd her arms & threw her limbs abroad.

' Or wilt thou answer, youngest Woman, clad in shining green ?
With labour & care thou dost divide the current into four.
Queen of these dreadful rivers, speak & let me hear thy voice ! '

They rear'd up a wall of rocks, and Urizen rais'd his spear.
[2] They gave a scream ; they knew their father ; Urizen knew his daughters.

5 These three daughters of Urizen reappear, F. Z. vii, ll. 92–110 ; viii. 70–76 ; and ix. 200–202 and 331–332. Their symbolic significance is obscure.

18 current] river *1st rdg. del.*

20 They . . . spear] ' And [Then *del.*] Urizen rais'd his spear [but *del.*] they rear'd up a wall of rocks.' *1st rdg.* The numerals ' 2 ' and ' 1 ' over ' Then ' and ' they ' respectively indicate the transposition.

They shrunk into their channels—dry the rocky strand beneath his feet—
Hiding themselves in rocky forms from the Eyes of Urizen.

Then Urizen wept, & thus his lamentation pourèd forth:

'O horrible, O dreadful state! those whom I lovèd best,
On whom I pour'd the beauties of my light, adorning them
With jewels & precious ornament labour'd with art divine,
Vests of the radiant colours of heaven & crowns of golden fire!
I gave sweet lillies to their breasts & roses to their hair;
I taught them songs of sweet delight; I gave their tender voices
Into the blue expanse, & I invented with laborious art
Sweet instruments of sound. In pride encompassing my knees,
They pour'd their radiance above all. The daughters of Luvah Envied
At their exceeding brightness, & the sons of eternity sent them gifts.
Now will I pour my fury on them & I will reverse
The precious benediction: for their colours of loveliness
I will give blackness; for jewels, hoary frost; for ornament, deformity;
For crowns, wreath'd Serpents; for sweet odors, stinking corruptibility;
For voices of delight, hoarse croakings inarticulate thro' frost.
For labour'd fatherly care & sweet instruction I will give
Chains of dark ignorance & cords of twisted self conceit,
And whips of stern repentance & food of stubborn obstinacy;
That they may curse Tharmas their God & Los his adopted son;
That they may curse & worship the obscure demon of destruction;
That they may worship terrors & obey the violent.
Go forth, sons of my curse! Go forth, daughters of my abhorrence!'

Tharmas heard the deadly scream across his wat'ry world,
And Urizen's loud sounding voice lamenting on the wind.
And he came riding in his fury: froze to solid were his waves.
[3] Silent, in ridges he beheld them stand round Urizen,
A dreary waste of solid waters, for the King of Light

35–46 Cp. *Tiriel*, § 5, *passim*. Urizen's cursing of his sons and daughters (cp. B. U., chap. viii, ll. 27–54) is Blake's criticism of the conception of a God who sets up an impossibly high standard and punishes failure to attain to it (cp. F. Z. ii. 81). 45 Cp. V. D. A. l. 23.

Darken'd his brows with his cold helmet, & his gloomy spear
Darken'd before him. Silent on the ridgy waves he took
His gloomy way; before him Tharmas fled, & flying fought,

Crying: 'What & who art thou, Cold Demon? art thou Urizen?
Art thou, like me, risen again from death, or art thou deathless?
If thou art he, my desperate purpose hear & give me death;
For death to me is better far than life—death, my desire,
That I in vain in various paths have sought; but still I live.
The Body of Man is given to me; I seek in vain to destroy,
For still it surges forth in fish & monsters of the deeps,
And in these monstrous forms I Live in an Eternal woe.
And thou, O Urizen, art fall'n, never to be deliver'd!
Withhold thy light from me for ever & I will withhold
From thee thy food; so shall we cease to be & all our sorrows
End, & the Eternal Man no more renew beneath our power.
If thou refusest, in eternal flight thy beams in vain
Shall pursue Tharmas, & in vain shalt crave for food. I will
Pour down my flight, thro' dark immensity Eternal falling.
Thou shalt pursue me but in vain; till starv'd upon the void
Thou hang'st, a dried skin, shrunk up, weak, wailing in the wind.'

So Tharmas spoke, but Urizen replied not. On his way
He took, high bending over hills & desarts, floods & horrible chasms.
Infinite was his labour, without end his travel: he strove
In vain, for hideous monsters of the deeps annoy'd him sore:
Scalèd & finn'd with iron & brass, they devour'd the path before him.
Incessant was the conflict. On he bent his weary steps
Making a path toward the dark world of Urthona: he rose
With pain upon the dreary mountains, & with pain descended,
And saw their grizly fears; & his eyes sicken'd at the sight.
The howlings, gnashings, groanings, shriekings, shudderings, sobbings, burstings
Mingle together to create a world for Los. In cruel delight
[4] Los brooded on the darkness, nor saw Urizen with a Globe of fire
Lighting his dismal journey thro' the pathless world of death,

62 Live] lie *1st rdg. del.* 66 End] Cease *1st rdg. del.*
73 bending] ? bounding. 79 dreary] dismal *1st rdg. del.*
82 The 'world' here mentioned may be that referred to in F. Z. iv. ll. 70–72 and ll. 124–136. But the point is quite uncertain.
83–86 Los . . . joy] *an addition.*

Writing in bitter tears & groans in books of iron & brass
The enormous wonders of the Abysses, once his brightest joy.
For Urizen beheld the terrors of the Abyss, wandering among
The ruin'd spirits, once his children & the children of Luvah,
Scar'd at the sound of their own sigh that seems to shake the immense.
They wander Moping; in their heart a Sun, a dreary moon;
A Universe of fiery constellations in their brain;
An earth of wintry woe beneath their feet, & round their loins
Waters or winds or clouds or brooding lightnings & pestilential plagues.
Beyond the bounds of their own self their senses cannot penetrate.
As the tree knows not what is outside of its leaves & bark,
And yet it drinks the summer joy & fears the winter sorrow;
So in the regions of the grave none knows his dark compeer,
Tho' he partakes of his dire woes & mutual returns the pang,
The throb, the dolor, the convulsion, in soul sickening woes.
The horrid shapes and sights of torment in burning dungeons & in
Fetters of red hot iron, some with crowns of serpents, & some
With monsters girding round their bosoms, some lying on beds of sulphur
On racks & wheels, he beheld: women marching o'er burning wastes

85 Cp. B. U. ii. 33 *note*.

87–88 For Urizen . . . Luvah] *marginal addition*.

89–99 Scar'd . . . woes] written over an erasure of thirteen lines. In the right margin is the following couplet, written in crayon:

Till thou dost [*word illegible*] the distrest
Thou shalt never have peace within thy breast

For the fourth word of the first line Dr. Sampson reads 'conquer'. Messrs. Ellis and Yeats print 'injure', adding the note: 'After fruitless efforts, we reluctantly leave the deciphering of the word that cannot be *injure* to future editors.' The present editors can only follow the example of Messrs. Ellis and Yeats.

After l. 99 three lines, of which the first and third are later than the second, have been cancelled. 'For' in l. 2 is a later addition:

Not so clos'd up the Prince of Light, now darken'd, wand'ring among
For Urizen beheld the terrors of the Abyss wand'ring among
The Ruin'd Spirits, once his Children & the Children of Luvah.

100–127 The horrid . . . world.] *bracketed in the left margin*. Below the bracket there remain two lines on the page. On MS. p. 5 ll. 128–137 are lined round, the upper line being curved upward into the margins. The bracketed passages (ll. 100–127 and 128–137) are read consecutively, followed by the two lines below the bracketed passage on p. 4 and by the four lines above the bracket on p. 5.

Of Sand, in bands of hundreds & of fifties & of thousands, strucken with
Lightnings which blazèd after them upon their shoulders in their march,
In successive volleys with loud thunders. Swift flew the King of Light
Over the burning desarts. Then, the desarts pass'd, involv'd in clouds
Of smoke, with myriads moping in the stifling vapours, Swift
Flew the King, tho' flag'd his powers; labouring, till over rocks
And Mountains, faint, weary, he wander'd where multitudes were shut
Up in the solid mountains & in rocks which heavèd with their torments.
Then came he among fiery cities, & castles built of burning steel.
Then he beheld the forms of tygers & of Lions, dishumaniz'd men.
Many in serpents & in worms stretch'd out, enormous length,
Over the sullen mould: & slimy tracks obstruct his way,
Drawn out from deep to deep, woven by ribb'd
And scalèd monsters, or arm'd in iron shell or shell of brass
Or gold, a glittering torment shining & hissing in eternal pain:
Some, columns of fire or of water, sometimes stretch'd out in heighth
Sometimes in length, sometimes englobing, wandering in vain seeking for ease.
His voice to them was but an inarticulate thunder, for their Ears
Were heavy & dull, & their eyes & nostrils closèd up.
Oft he stood by a howling victim, Questioning in words
Soothing or Furious: no one answer'd; every one wrap'd up
In his own sorrow howl'd regardless of his words; nor voice

113 The phrase 'dishumaniz'd men' may perhaps be explained by reference to a subsequent passage where Blake describes the regeneration of the world:

> All spirits deceas'd, let loose from reptile prisons, come in shoals:
> Wild furies from the tyger's brain & from the lion's eyes;
> And from the ox & ass come moping terrors. (F. Z. ix. 234–236.)

So apparently does Blake turn the opinion of Pythagoras to his own purposes. Those who are dead to the visionary life appear in mundane existence under every variety of physical form. But 'all are Men in Eternity', and so the visionary sees them.

119 heighth] length *1st rdg. del.* 120 length] breadth *1st rdg. del.*

Of sweet response could he obtain, tho' oft assay'd with tears.
He knew they were his Children, ruin'd in his ruin'd world.
[5] Oft would he stand & question a fierce scorpion glowing with gold.
In vain; the terror heard not: then a lion he would Sieze
By the fierce mane, staying his howling course: in vain the voice
Of Urizen, in vain the Eloquent tongue. A Rock, a Cloud, a Mountain
Were not now Vocal as in Climes of happy Eternity,
Where the lamb replies to the infant voice, & the lion to the man of years,
Giving them sweet instructions; Where the Cloud, the River & the Field
Talk with the husbandman & shepherd. But these attack'd him sore,
Siezing upon his feet, & rending the Sinews, that in Caves
He hid to recure his obstructed powers with rest & oblivion.
[4] Here he had time enough to repent of his rashly threatenèd curse.
He saw them curs'd beyond his Curse: his soul melted with fear.
[5] He could not take their fetters off, for they grew from the soul;
Nor could he quench the fires, for they flam'd out from the heart;
Nor could he calm the Elements, because himself was subject:
So he threw his flight in terror & pain & in repentant tears.
When he had pass'd these southern terrors, he approach'd the East,
Void, pathless, beaten with iron sleet & eternal hail & rain.
No form was there, no living thing; & yet his way lay thro'
This dismal world. He stood awhile & look'd back o'er his former
Terrific voyage, Hills & Vales of torment & despair,

127 He . . . world] *an addition.*
130 his] their *1st rdg. del.*
139 He . . . fear] *an addition in pencil.*
142 Scattered passages up and down *The Four Zoas* contain vague references to Urizen's subjection to some undefined power which may be Providence, Destiny, or possibly Orc (cp. F. Z. iii, ll. 14–19). Three passages, F. Z. vi. 154–155, vi. 173, and vi. 279–280, distinctly point to the existence of an external, benevolent power, 'The ever pitying one who seeth all things' (cp. *Tiriel*, § 2. 4); but the general tone of *The Four Zoas*, apart from added passages and the later-written portions, is distinctly necessitarian or deterministic.
144–145 See Index, *Cardinal Points.*
145 iron] eternal *1st rdg. del.* rain] snow *1st rdg. del.*

Sighing & wiping a fresh tear: then turning round, he threw
Himself into the dismal void, falling: he fell & fell,
Whirling in unresistible revolutions, down & down
In the horrid bottomless vacuity, falling, falling, falling
Into the Eastern vacuity, the empty world of Luvah.
The ever pitying one, who seeth all things, saw his fall,
And in the dark vacuity created a bosom of clay.
When wearied, dead he fell, his limbs repos'd in the bosom of slime.
As the seed falls from the sower's hand, so Urizen fell, & death
Shut up his powers in oblivion: then as the seed shoots forth
In pain & sorrow, So the slimy bed his limbs renew'd.
At first an infant weakness: periods pass'd; he gather'd strength,
But still in solitude he sat; then rising, threw his flight
Onward, tho' falling thro' the waste of night & ending in death
And in another resurrection to sorrow & weary travel.
But still his books he bore in his strong hands, & his iron pen:
For when he died they lay beside his grave, & when he rose
He siez'd them with a gloomy smile; for wrap'd in his death clothes
He hid them when he slept in death. When he reviv'd, the clothes
Were rotted by the winds; the books remain'd still unconsum'd,
Still to be written & interleav'd with brass & iron & gold
Time after time: for such a journey none but iron pens
Can write, And adamantine leaves recieve; nor can the man who goes
[6] The journey obstinate refuse to write time after time.
Endless had been his travel, but the Divine hand him led.
For infinite the distance & obscur'd by Combustions dire,
By rocky masses frowning in the abysses, revolving erratic
Round Lakes of fire in the dark deep, the ruins of Urizen's world.
Oft would he sit in a dark rift & regulate his books,

153 Into . . . Luvah] *an addition.* 155 clay] slime *1st rdg. del.*
155–163 Cp. F. Z. ix, ll. 629–636, and vi. ll. 219–225.
164 Cp. B. U. ii. 33 *note.* The death clothes (l. 166), in which Urizen wraps his books and which are rotted away when he sleeps in death, would seem to represent the forms under which, at different periods, the Moral Law is presented to man. Cp. also M. 44. 11–15 and see Index, *Weaving*, § iii.
166 gloomy] dismal *1st rdg. del.*
173–180 Endless . . . remote] *written over erasure.*

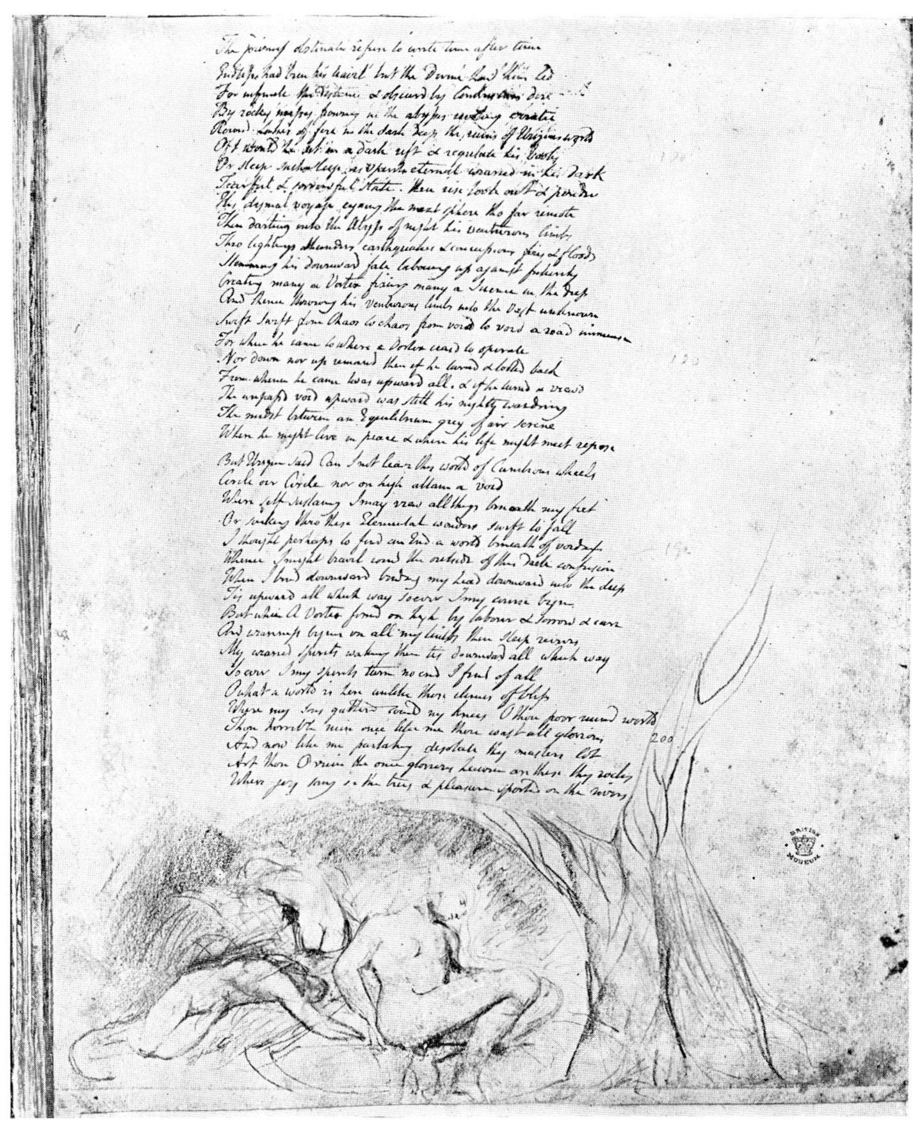

The Four Zoas: Night VI, page 6

Or sleep such sleep as spirits eternal, wearied in his dark
Tearful & sorrowful state ; then rise, look out, & ponder
His dismal voyage, eyeing the next sphere tho' far remote;
Then darting into the Abyss of night his venturous limbs
Thro' lightnings, thunders, earthquakes & concussions, fires & floods,
Stemming his downward fall, labouring up against futurity,
Creating many a Vortex, fixing many a Science in the deep ;
And thence throwing his venturous limbs into the Vast unknown,
Swift, swift, from Chaos to chaos, from void to void, a road immense.

For when he came to where a Vortex ceas'd to operate,
Nor down nor up remain'd ; then if he turn'd & look'd back
From whence he came, 'twas upward all ; & if he turn'd & view'd
The unpass'd void, upward was still his nightly wand'ring :
The midst between, an Equilibrium grey of air serene,
Where he might live in peace & where his life might meet repose.

But Urizen said : ' Can I not leave this world of Cumbrous wheels
Circle o'er Circle, nor on high attain a void
Where, self sustaining, I may view all things beneath my feet ?
Or sinking thro' these Elemental wonders, swift to fall,
I thought perhaps to find an End, a world beneath of voidness,
Whence I might travel round the outside of this dark confusion.
When I bend downward, bending my head downward into the deep,
'Tis upward all, which way soever I my course begin :
But when A Vortex form'd on high by labour & sorrow & care,
And weariness begins on all my limbs, then sleep revives
My wearied spirits : waking then, 'tis downward all, which way

183 fall] *not legibly written* : ? fate.

184 Vortex appears to signify a milieu of error, such as is usually associated with Urizen and the fallen man. It seems to correspond to the later symbol ' state ' (see Index, *State*) except that it is no way connected with a regenerative purpose. In F. Z. vii *a*, l. 123, it is identified with the Female, Vala, the symbol of ' Natural Religion '. In the present passage the ' Vortexes ' represent the forms under which the false ' Science ' of Urizen manifests itself at different times or to different individuals (cp. F. Z. viii. 170–172).

So ever I my spirits turn ; no end I find of all.
O what a world is here, unlike those climes of bliss
Where my sons gather'd round my knees ! O thou poor ruin'd world !
Thou horrible ruin ! once like me thou wast all glorious ;
And now like me, partaking desolate thy master's lot !
Art thou, O ruin, the once glorious heaven ? are these thy rocks
Where joy sang on the trees, & pleasure sported on the rivers,
[7] And laughter sat beneath the Oaks, & innocence sported round
Upon the green plains, & sweet friendship met in palaces ?
And books & instruments of song & pictures of delight,
Where are they ?—whelm'd beneath these ruins in horrible destruction.
And if, Eternal falling, I repose on the dark bosom
Of winds & waters, or thence fall into a Void where air
Is not, down falling thro' immensity, ever & ever,
I lose my powers, weaken'd every revolution, till a death
Shuts up my powers. Then a seed in the vast womb of darkness,
I dwell in dim oblivion: brooding over me the Enormous worlds
Reorganize me : shooting forth in bones & flesh & blood,
I am regenerated to fall or rise at will, or to remain
A labourer of ages, a dire discontent, a living woe,
Wandering in vain. Here will I fix my foot & here rebuild :
Here Mountains of Brass promise much riches in their dreadful bosoms.'

So he began to form of gold, silver & iron
And brass, vast instruments to measure out the immense & fix
The whole into another world better suited to obey

214 destruction] confusion *1st rdg. del.*

222–224 It is not clear what Urizen's choice is, or precisely what is intended in his liberty to rise or fall or to remain a 'labourer of ages', a title which later is applied to Los as the agent of man's regeneration. In l. 222 'regenerated' has nothing of its later meaning.

225 Here . . . bosoms] *an addition.* bosoms] bowels *1st rdg. del.* The Mountains of Brass have apparently some connexion with Urizen's Book of Brass, the body of Moral Law. Cp. J. 4. 26 *note.*

226 So] So saying *1st rdg.* iron] brass *1st rdg. del.*

This and the following lines are clearly reminiscent of *Paradise Lost*, vii, ll. 225 foll. It is impossible with certainty to relate this new world with the Mundane Shell created by Urizen (F. Z. ii, ll. 235–494). The latter seems to be a world guided by providence, the former a world of moral law represented after the manner of the Miltonic Hell. In ll. 250 foll. there is the suggestion that the new created world is entirely subjective.

His will, where none should dare oppose his will, himself being King
Of All; & all futurity be bound in his vast chain.
And the Sciences were fix'd & the Vortexes began to operate
On all the sons of men; & every human soul, terrified
At the turning wheels of heaven, shrunk away inward, with'ring away;
Gaining a New Dominion over all his Sons & Daughters,
& over the Sons & Daughters of Luvah in the horrible Abyss.
For Urizen lamented over them in a selfish lamentation,
Till a white woof cover'd his cold limbs from head to feet.
Hair white as snow cover'd him in flaky locks terrific,
Overspreading his limbs. In pride he wander'd weeping,
Clothèd in agèd venerableness, obstinately resolv'd,
Travelling thro' darkness; & wherever he travel'd a dire Web
Follow'd behind him, as the Web of a Spider, dusky & cold,
Shiv'ring across from Vortex to Vortex, drawn out from his mantle of years,
A living Mantle adjoin'd to his life & growing from his Soul.
And the Web of Urizen stre[t]ch'd direful, shiv'ring in clouds
And uttering such woes, such Cries, such thunderings;
The eyelids expansive as morning & the Ears
As a golden ascent winding round to the heavens of heavens,
Within the dark horrors of the Abysses, lion, or tyger, or scorpion.

[8] For every one open'd within into Eternity at will;
But they refus'd because their outward forms were in the Abyss.
And the wing-like tent of the Universe, beautiful, surrounding all
Or drawn up or let down at the will of the immortal man,
Vibrated in such anguish, the eyelids quiver'd;

234–235 Gaining . . . Abyss] *an addition.*

236–244 Compare with these lines the corresponding description of the 'Net of Religion' and its association with false 'Pity', 'a selfish lamentation', B. U., chap. viii, ll. 32–54.

244 A living . . . Soul] *an addition.* 246 Cries] burstings *1st rdg.*

247–249 These lines have been found unintelligible in this context.

250–251 This is perhaps the plainest statement of Blake's belief, expressed in symbols in the added passage F. Z. i. 133–137, that man may enter at will into visionary communion with the world of Eternity. That this power is not exercised is due to the predominance of the 'outward form', later called the 'Spectre' (see Index, *Spectre,* and cp. F. Z. i. 250 *note*). The passage to l. 257 is a short summary of the allegory of Urizen's journey, marking the contrast between the perceptualist and visionary notions of the Universe.

254–257 Cp. B. U., chap. ix, ll. 1–23.

Weak & Weaker their expansive orbs began shrinking:
Pangs smote thro' the brain, & a universal shriek
Ran thro the Abysses, rending the web, torment on torment.

Thus Urizen in sorrows wandered many a dreary way,
Warring with monsters of the Deeps in his most miserable pilgrimage,
Till his bright hair scatter'd in snows, his skin bark'd o'er with wrinkles.
Four Caverns rooting downwards their foundations, thrusting forth
The metal, rock & stone in ever painful throes of vegetation.
The Cave of Orc stood to the South, a furnace of dire flames
Quenchless unceasing. In the west the Cave of Urizen,
For Urizen fell as the Midday Sun falls down into the West.
North stood Urthona's stedfast throne, a World of Solid darkness,
Shut up in stifling obstruction, rooted in dumb despair.
The East was Void. But Tharmas roll'd his billows in ceaseless eddies,
Void, pathless, beat with Snows eternal & iron hail & rain
All thro' the caverns of fire & air & Earth, Seeking
For Enion's limbs, nought finding but the black sea weed & sick'ning slime,
Flying away from Urizen that he might not give him food,
Above, beneath, on all sides round in the vast deep of immensity;
That he might starve the sons & daughters of Urizen on the winds,
Making between horrible chasms into the vast unknown.
All these around the world of Los cast forth their monstrous births.
But in Eternal times the Seat of Urizen is in the South,
Urthona in the North, Luvah in East, Tharmas in West.

And now he came into the Abhorrèd world of Dark Urthona,
By Providence Divine conducted—not bent from his own will,
Lest Death Eternal should be the result; for the Will cannot be violated—
Into the doleful vales where no tree grew, nor river flow'd,
Nor man nor beast nor creeping thing, nor sun nor cloud nor star.
Still he with his globe of fire immense in his venturous hand
Bore on thro' the Affrighted vales, ascending & descending,

263–278 See Index, *Cardinal Points*. 280–281 Cp. J. 44. 18–19.

O'erwearied; or in cumberous flight he ventur'd o'er dark rifts,
Or down dark precipices, or climb'd with pain & labour high,
Till he beheld the world of Los from the Peakèd rock of Urthona,
And heard the howling of red Orc distincter & distincter.
[9] Redoubling his immortal efforts, thro' the narrow vales
With difficulty down descending, guided by his Ear
And by his globe of fire, he went down the Vale of Urthona
Between the enormous iron walls built by the Spectre dark.
Dark grew his globe, reddening with mists; & full before his path,
Striding across the narrow vale, the Shadow of Urthona,
A Spectre Vast, appear'd, whose feet & legs, with iron scalèd,
Stamp'd the hard rocks, expectant of the unknown wanderer
Whom he had seen wand'ring his nether world when distant far,
And watch'd his swift approach. Collected, dark, the Spectre stood.
Beside him Tharmas stay'd his flight & stood in stern defiance,
Communing with the Spectre who rejoic'd along the Vale.
Round his loins a girdle glow'd with many colour'd fires;
In his hand a knotted Club whose knots like mountains frown'd,
Desart among the Stars, them withering with its ridges cold.
Black scales of iron arm the dread visage; iron spikes instead
Of hair shoot from his orbèd scull; his glowing eyes
Burn like two furnaces. He call'd with Voice of Thunder:
Four wingèd heralds mount the furious blasts & blow their trumps;
Gold, Silver, Brass, & iron clangors clamoring rend the shores.
Like white clouds rising from the Vales, his fifty two armies
From the four Cliffs of Urthona rise, glowing around the Spectre.

291 by] with *1st rdg. del.* 300 Beside him] Beside his *in MS.*
309 shores] deeps *1st rdg. del.*
310 The four cliffs and the fifty-two armies would seem to signify the seasons and weeks of the year. Los, hardly distinguishable from Urthona in many parts of *The Four Zoas,* is definitely identified with Time (see Index, *Los*): cp. B. U., chap. iv *a,* ll. 17–18, where Los forges the links of hours, days, and years. The curious point is that sons of Urizen lead Urthona's squadrons against their father. In *The Book of Urizen* four of these sons are identified with the physical elements (cp. B. U., chap. viii, l. 16 *note*); and Los's connexion with the world of time and space would suggest that the explanation of the unusual alliance in the present passage is to be found in the earlier hint of a nature-myth.

Four sons of Urizen the Squadrons of Urthona led in arms
Of gold & silver, brass & iron : he knew his mighty sons.

Then Urizen arose upon the wind, back many a mile
Retiring into his dire Web, scattering fleecy snows
As he ascended howling : loud the Web vibrated strong
From heaven to heaven, from globe to globe. In vast excentric paths
Compulsive roll'd the Comets at his dread command the dreary way,
Falling with wheel impetuous down among Urthona's vales,
And round red Orc, returning back to Urizen gorg'd with blood.
Slow roll the massy Globes at his command, & slow o'erwheel
The dismal squadrons of Urthona, weaving the dire Web
In their progressions & preparing Urizen's path before him.

End of the Sixth Night

NIGHT VII

INTRODUCTORY NOTE

EVIDENCE has already been given in the Bibliographical Preface to *The Four Zoas* in support of the view that this Night was written to replace that printed in the Appendix as Night VII *a*. The account of Urizen's journey is here continued from Night VI. The Spectre of Urthona and Tharmas give way before the powers that weave the Web of Religion, and Urizen descends into the caves where Orc lies bound. Surrounded by forms of restricted or perverted activity, Urizen takes his seat upon a rock whence springs the Tree of Moral Virtue (ll. 18–41). In the important section that follows, Blake develops his concept of the antagonism between the rebellious spirit of ' wrath ' and ' fiery indignation ' in Orc, and Urizen's forces of physical and moral restraint. For the latter, being the negation of all energy, would subdue to his own passivity the vehement spirit of revolt in Orc, the sources of which lie outside his comprehension, though at the same time he recognizes therein the sole living force in an otherwise dead world (ll. 45–47). Though the unceasing fires of his own passion prey upon him, though bitter anguish and stifling despair assail him, Orc in bondage is triumphant. The strength to endure torments comes from ' visions of delight so lovely that they urge (his) wrath tenfold with fierce desire to rend his chain ' (ll. 65–66). Hence, when Urizen pretends pity, Orc replies with curses and accusations of hypocrisy (ll. 69–89). Then the other, to achieve his purpose, summons his daughters, who prepare for Orc ' the bread of sorrow ', while Urizen reads from his ' book of brass words of wisdom ', the selfish counsels of prudential morality (ll. 110–134). The outcome of this is the degradation of Orc's energy : the spirit of wrath is compelled into the ineffectual limits of a worm, and his strength is made subservient to the deceits of ' Natural Religion ' (ll. 137–150). At this point Orc is definitely identified with Luvah, both being symbols of a perverted emotionalism. This significance appears again in the case of Orc when he is described as organizing a serpent body (l. 152), a destructive power, ' turning affection into fury and thought into abstraction ' (l. 155). The same association with the subversive forces of Urizen's religion is symbolized in Orc's ascent into the Tree of Mystery or Moral Virtue : for at this point, apparently, Blake can conceive energy to be capable of corruption, and so of becoming an agent in spiritual defection : by it men are drawn into bondage to Urizen (ll. 164–165). Herein Blake appears to take account of the fact of his own experience, that passionate devotion was not infrequently the mark of the teachers of ' Urizen's religion ', among orthodox Christians and otherwhere. But this triumph of Urizen over Orc, like the appearance of Deism in *Jerusalem* (p. 93. 21–26) is ' the Signal of the Morning ', the prelude to the final consuming of the Tree of Mystery in the fires of Orc.

The remainder of the Night deals with Los, Enitharmon, the Spectre of Urthona, and Enitharmon's Shadow. This last symbol, not found elsewhere, may represent that definitely sinister aspect of

Enitharmon outlined in the earlier Nights and in the Lambeth books, where she is the emblem of the non-mystical conception of Space that results in ' the philosophy of five senses ' (cp. ll. 215–216) ; for in the later-written parts of *The Four Zoas* Enitharmon herself appears co-operating in Los's regenerative labours. Further, it is to be noted that the term Spectre has here nothing of its later meaning of antagonism to visionary truth ; it appears to connote a degree of difference from the ideal relation that is yet compatible with conscious efforts to attain truth. This is made abundantly clear in the closing section of the present Night.

Los laments the desolation of his state ; since ' all things beside the woful Los enjoy the delights of beauty ' (l. 196) apparently spiritual energy is not yet triumphant over the evil of its environment. The story proceeds to tell of Urthona's Spectre set to guard Orc, of Enitharmon's Shadow beneath the poisonous Tree of Mystery. The latter episode adds something to the second ' Fall ' myth of Night I by telling of Urizen's birth as the child of man and Vala. Luvah's conspiracy with Urizen (cp. F. Z. i, ll. 175 foll.) is also referred to. Enitharmon finally begs the Spectre's aid that Vala may be brought into subjection to Orc (l. 264). All this matter is obscure because it has no apparent relation with the present *dénouement* of *The Four Zoas*, which belongs to a date earlier than that of the present Night. The first clear idea emerges when the Spectre interprets mundane existence as the divinely appointed means towards the re-establishment of the unity of the Ideal World (ll. 265–273). He promises to aid Enitharmon against Vala, and from this alliance is to follow, first the destruction of all delusions, and then the return to Unity. Vala, now appearing with the later meaning of the symbol, as the summary of influences and activities antagonistic to vision or Jerusalem, is represented as born of Enitharmon, i. e. as becoming manifest in the world of Space (ll. 312–327), a restatement, in symbols changed in order to bring the theme more intimately into relation with human life, of the matter with which Blake had dealt in his account of Urizen's wanderings in Night VI (see particularly VI, ll. 250–257). But there is a significant difference ; for here references to Blake's new interpretation of mundane existence frequently occur. Now also the ' Tree of Mystery ' appears in the world. This is the manifestation of the establishment of the Urizenic law in life. But simultaneously the new gospel which is to destroy the ' Tree ' is manifested also. Los embraces the Spectre, ' first as a brother, then as another Self ' ; in ' Self-abasement ' he abandons his ' domineering lust ' (ll. 337, 365), and becomes the servant and not the master of man. So is established the new law of ' Self-sacrifice and Brotherhood ', the foundation principle of the moral teaching of *Milton* and *Jerusalem* (ll. 338–356). Resurrection into Unity would have been consummated immediately but that, as in *Jerusalem*, pp. 87–88, Enitharmon relapses into error (l. 368). So when the Spectre, divinely inspired, bids him destroy the body of error which is the created world, and ' rebuild Jerusalem ', Los appears as if assailed by doubts and the temptations of weakness, symbolized by the ' female ' (ll. 381–392). Only the intervention of Urthona's Spectre, here the symbol of divine inspiration, saves him (ll. 394–406). Explanation comes in the following passage. Los's spiritual dejection is the mechanism by which Blake aims at grafting on to the symbols of his own invention his reinterpreted Christianity. Los failing, there comes the promise of the Lamb of God 'descending to redeem' (ll. 407–427).

The close of the Night deals with the regenerative labours of Urthona's Spectre, Los, and Enitharmon. To save the 'Spectres of the Dead' from 'Eternal death' beneath Urizen's tyranny, they create for them 'bodies', 'embodied semblances in which the dead may live' (l. 436: cp. ll. 443–451, 462–470). These 'forms' are apparently revelations of truth in which the soul may live in communion with the world of vision and secure against the assaults of mundane error. They may be related to the regenerative aspects of the Mundane Shell (see Index). Blake also emphasizes the necessity for continual sacrifice of self for others (ll. 439, 477–480), while in an otherwise obscure passage (ll. 489–494), Los's pity for Urizen can only be read as stressing the importance of forgiveness, a precept that is more distinctly mentioned in l. 417. The distance between the ethical doctrine of the earlier Lambeth books and these revised portions of *The Four Zoas* is again made clear in the statement that return to the ideal Unity can only be accomplished through

> Cares & Sorrows & Troubles
> . . . self denial & . . . bitter Contrition. (ll. 395–396.)

VALA

Night the Seventh

[1] Then Urizen arose. The Spectre fled & Tharmas fled.
The dark'ning Spectre of Urthona hid beneath a rock.
Tharmas threw his impetuous flight thro' the deeps of immensity,
Revolving round in whirlpools fierce all round the cavern'd worlds.

But Urizen silent descended to the Caves of Orc & saw
A Cavern'd Universe of flaming fire. The horses of Urizen,
Here bound to fiery mangers, furious dash their golden hoofs,
Striking fierce sparkles from their brazen fetters. Fierce his lions
Howl in the burning dens; his tygers roam in the redounding smoke
In forests of affliction; the adamantine scales of justice
Consuming in the raging lamps of mercy; pour'd in rivers,
The holy oil rages thro' all the cavern'd rocks. Fierce flames
Dance on the rivers & the rocks, howling & drunk with fury.
The plow of ages & the golden harrow wade thro' fields
Of goary blood; the immortal seed is nourish'd for the Slaughter.
The bulls of Luvah, breathing fire, bellow on burning pastures
Round howling Orc, whose awful limbs cast forth red smoke & fire,
That Urizen approach'd not near but took his seat on a rock,
And rang'd his books around him, brooding Envious over Orc.
Howling & rending his dark caves the awful Demon lay.
Pulse after pulse beat on his fetters; pulse after pulse his spirit
Darted & darted higher & higher to the shrine of Enitharmon;
As when the thunder folds himself in thickest clouds
The wat'ry nations couch & hide in the profoundest deeps,
Then bursting from his troubled head with terrible visages & flaming hair,
His swift wing'd daughters sweep across the vast black ocean.

10–12 The incoherence of these lines renders all attempts at punctuation purely conjectural.

16 Cp. *Thel*, § ii. 8 *note*.

19 Cp. B. U., chap. ii. 33 *note*.

Los felt the Envy in his limbs like to a blighted tree.
[2] For Urizen, fix'd in Envy, sat brooding & cover'd with snow,
His book of iron on his knees ; he trac'd the dreadful letters,
While his snows fell & his storms beat to cool the flames of Orc,
Age after Age, till underneath his heel a deadly root
Struck thro' the rock, the root of Mystery, accursèd. Shooting up
Branches into the heaven of Los they, pipe form'd, bending down,
Take root again whereever they touch, again branching forth
In intricate labyrinths o'erspreading many a grizly deep.

Amaz'd started Urizen when he found himself compass'd round
And high roofèd over with trees : he arose, but the stems
Stood so thick he with difficulty & great pain brought
His books out of the dismal shade—all but the book of iron.
Again he took his seat, & rang'd his Books around
On a rock of iron frowning over the foaming fires of Orc.

And Urizen hung over Orc & view'd his terrible wrath,
Sitting upon an iron Crag : at length his words broke forth :

'Image of dread, whence art thou ? whence is this most woful place,
Whence these fierce fires but from thyself ? No other living thing
In all this Chasm I behold. No other living thing
Dare thy most terrible wrath abide. Bound here to waste in pain

27 It is difficult to understand the reference to Los in this place, unless it be that as Time he represents mundane existence dominated by the influence of Urizen's religion with its jealousy of passion and desire in Orc. See below, ll. 32–33.

31–35 See Index, *Mundane Shell, Note I*, B. Cp. J. 28. 13–19.

36–39 Repeated, with slight change, from B. A., chap. iii, ll. 22–28.

43 an] his *1st rdg. del.*

44–68 This speech and the reply (ll. 69–89) illustrate the essential opposition between Urizen and Orc. Blake emphasizes the inability of 'the philosophy of the five senses' to comprehend the strength of native passion and desire that, though bound down by the restrictions of mundane existence, can transcend the limitations of physical being and despise the fears that obsess the 'weak and tame minds' who accept the delusions of 'Natural Religion'. Yet the conception of Orc in this Night is widely different from that in *America*. Passion is no longer sufficient in itself to compass man's regeneration, for Blake now sees that the powers of tyranny may subvert revolutionary enthusiasm to their own extension. The history of the years following the first successes of the Revolution in France is the likeliest cause of his modified view.

Thy vital substance in these fires that issue new & new
Around thee: sometimes like a flood, & sometimes like a rock
Of living pangs thy horrible bed, glowing with ceaseless fires
Beneath thee & around. Above a Shower of fire now beats,
Moulded to globes & arrowy wedges, rending thy bleeding limbs;
And now a whirling pillar of burning sands to overwhelm thee,
Steeping thy wounds in salts infernal & in bitter anguish;
And now a rock moves on the surface of this lake of fire,
To bear thee down beneath the waves in stifling despair.
Pity for thee mov'd me to break my dark & long repose,
And to reveal myself before thee in a form of wisdom.
Yet thou dost laugh at all these tortures & this horrible place:
Yet throw thy limbs these fires abroad that back return upon thee,
While thou reposest, throwing rage on rage, feeding thyself
With visions of sweet bliss far other than this burning clime.
Sure thou art bath'd in rivers of delight, on verdant fields
Walking in joy, in bright Expanses sleeping on bright clouds,
With visions of delight so lovely that they urge thy rage
Tenfold with fierce desire to rend thy chain & howl in fury
And dim oblivion of all woe & desperate repose.
Or is thy joy founded on torment which others bear for thee?'

Orc answered: 'Curse thy hoary brows! What dost thou in this deep?
Thy Pity I contemn: scatter thy snows elsewhere.
[3] I rage in the deep, for Lo! my feet & hands are nail'd to the burning rock.
Yet my fierce fires are better than thy snows. Shudd'ring thou sittest.
Thou art not chain'd. Why shouldst thou sit, cold grovelling demon of woe,
In tortures of dire coldness? Now a Lake of waters deep
Sweeps over thee, freezing to solid: still thou sit'st clos'd up
In that transparent rock, as if in joy of thy bright prison,
Till overburden'd with its own weight, drawn out thro' immensity,
With a crash breaking across, the horrible mass comes down
Thund'ring; & hail & frozen iron, hail'd from the Element,
Rends thy white hair: yet thou dost fix'd, obdurate, brooding sit,
Writing thy books. Anon a cloud fill'd with a waste of snows

57 This is Urizen's false pity: cp. B. U., chap. viii, l. 35 *note*.
74–80 Cp. B. L., chap. i, l. 53–chap. ii, l. 16.

Covers thee, still obdurate, still resolved, & writing still.
Tho' rocks roll o'er thee, tho' floods pour, tho' winds black as the Sea
Cut thee in gashes, tho' the blood pours down around thy ankles,
Freezing thy feet to the hard rock, still thy pen obdurate
Traces the wonders of Futurity in horrible fear of the future.
I rage furious in the deep, for lo ! my feet & hands are nail'd
To the hard rock ; or thou shouldst feel my enmity & hate
In all the diseases of man falling upon thy grey accursèd front.'

Urizen answer'd : 'Read my books : explore my Constellations.
Enquire of my Sons & they shall teach thee how to War.
Enquire of my Daughters who, accurs'd in the dark depths,
Knead bread of Sorrow by my stern command : for I am God
Of all this dreadful ruin. Rise, O daughters, at my stern command !'

Rending the Rocks, Eleth & Uveth rose, & Ona rose,
Terrific with their iron vessels, driving them across
In the dim air : they took the book of iron, & plac'd above
On clouds of death, & sang their songs, Kneading the bread of Orc.
Orc listen'd to the song, compell'd, hungering on the cold wind
That swagg'd heavy with the accursed dough. The hoar frost rag'd
Thro' Ona's sieve : the torrent rain pour'd from the iron pail
Of Eleth, & the icy hands of Uveth kneaded the bread.
The heavens bow with terror underneath their iron hands,
Singing at their dire work the words of Urizen's book of iron,
While the enormous scrolls roll'd dreadful in the heavens above.
And still the burden of their song in tears was pourèd forth :
'The bread is Kneaded : let us rest, O cruel father of children !'

But Urizen remitted not their labours upon his rock.

91 Cp. F. Z. vi, l. 5 *note*.
93 Cp. F. Z. ix, ll. 815–818 :

Men are bound to sullen contemplations. In the night
Restless they turn on beds of sorrow, in their inmost brain
Feeling the crushing Wheels. They rise : they write the bitter words
Of stern Philosophy & knead the bread of knowledge with tears & groans.

[4] And Urizen Read in his book of brass in sounding tones :
'Listen, O Daughters, to my voice ! Listen to the Words of Wisdom !
Compell the poor to live upon a Crust of bread by soft mild arts :
So shall [ye] govern over all ; let Moral Duty tune your tongue,
But be your hearts harder than the nether millstone.
To bring the Shadow of Enitharmon beneath our wondrous tree,
That Los may Evaporate like smoke & be no more,
Draw down Enitharmon to the Spectre of Urthona,
And let him have dominion over Los the terrible shade !
Smile when they frown, frown when they smile ; & when a man looks pale
With labour & abstinence, say he looks healthy & happy ;
And when his children sicken, let them die : there are enough
Born, even too many, & our Earth will be overrun
Without these arts. If you would make the poor live with temper,
With pomp give every crust of bread you give ; with gracious cunning
Magnify small gifts ; reduce the man to want a gift, & then give with pomp.
Say he smiles if you hear him sigh. If pale, say he is ruddy.
Preach temperance : say he is overgorg'd & drowns his wit
In strong drink, tho' you know that bread & water are all
He can afford. Flatter his wife, pity his children, till we can
Reduce all to our will, as spaniels are taught with art.
Lo, how the heart & brain are formèd in the breeding womb
Of Enitharmon ! how it buds with life & forms the bones,
The little heart, the liver, & the red blood in its labyrinths !

109 Read . . . tones] *written over erasure.* Cp. *Europe,* ll. 102–106.

110 Listen . . . wisdom] *an addition.*

112–113 So . . . millstone] *an addition* ; written in one line. ye] be *MS. rdg.*

114–117 *marginal addition* ; *written below l. 113.* See below, ll. 208–327. In these added lines the Daughters of Urizen are made practically equivalent to the female symbols of *Milton* and *Jerusalem*, the Daughters of Albion (see Index, *Vala*), who control man's perceptions through the physical senses (cp. J. 68. 5–9), bringing him beneath the power of the moral law and perverting the spiritual influences symbolized by Los and Enitharmon (cp. M. 28. 51–54). There is also a reference to the enfeeblement of the masculine creative powers through the weakened 'feminine' perceptions expressed as Enitharmon's 'Shadow'. This highly symbolic parenthesis merely repeats what Blake writes elsewhere of the spiritual effects of the hypocritical morality of Urizen's 'book of brass'.

130–132 Enitharmon figures here and in *Europe* as *Genetrix Mundi* and hence as the symbolic source of worldly morals. The conception is entirely out of keeping with the use of the symbol in *Milton* and *Jerusalem*. The Enitharmon of these times is the Vala of the later books (see Index, *Vala*).

By gratified desire, by strong devouring appetite she fills
Los with ambitious fury, that his race shall all devour.'

Then Orc cried: 'Curse thy Cold hypocrisy! already round thy Tree,
In scales that shine with gold & rubies, thou beginnest to weaken
My divided Spirit. Like a worm I rise in peace, unbound
From wrath. Now When I rage, my fetters bind me more.
O torment! O torment! A Worm compell'd! Am I a worm?
Is it in strong deceit that man is born? In strong deceit
Thou dost restrain my fury, that the worm may fold the tree.
Avaunt, Cold hypocrite! I am chain'd or thou couldst not use me thus.
The Man shall rage, bound with this chain; the worm in silence creep.
Thou wilt not cease from rage. Grey Demon, silence all thy storms.
Give me example of thy mildness, King of furious hail storms!
Art thou the cold attractive power that holds me in this chain?
I well remember how I stole thy light, & it became fire
Consuming. Thou Know'st me now, O Urizen, Prince of Light,
And I know thee: is this the triumph, this the Godlike State
That lies beyond the bounds of Science in the Grey obscure?'

Terrified, Urizen heard Orc, now certain that he was Luvah.
And Orc ⟨he⟩ begins to Organize a Serpent body,
Despising Urizen's light & turning it into flaming fire,
Recieving as a poison'd Cup Recieves the heavenly wine,
And turning affection into fury & thought into abstraction,
A Self consuming dark devourer issuing into the heavens.

135 Then] *an addition.* cried] answer'd *1st rdg. del.*
135–165 See Index, *Orc*, II. *c*.
147–156 Orc's identification with Luvah is apparently an attempt to relate the simple dualism of the Lambeth books, the contraries Urizen and Orc, with the more elaborate scheme of *The Four Zoas*. The antagonism of the two is maintained, but it is complicated by the forces which Blake symbolized in Urthona and Tharmas, and by the growth into greater and greater prominence of the notion of a Divine Providence acting continuously in human life.
151 Terrified . . . Luvah] *an addition.*
152 And Orc] So saying *1st rdg. del.*
152–155 In these lines there appears to be an assigning of value to Urizen's light: cp. F. Z. v. 190–241.
155 affection] wisdom *1st rdg. del.*

Urizen envious brooding sat & saw the secret terror
Flame high in pride, & laugh to scorn the source of his deceit;
Nor knew the source of his own, but thought himself the sole author
[5] Of all his wandering Experiments in the horrible Abyss.
He knew that weakness stretches out in breadth & length; he knew
That wisdom reaches high & deep; & therefore he made Orc,
In serpent form compell'd, stretch out & up the mysterious tree.
He suffer'd him to Climb that he might draw all human forms
Into submission to his will, nor knew the dread result.

Los sat in showers of Urizen, watching cold Enitharmon.
His broodings rush down to his feet, producing Eggs that, hatching,
Burst forth upon the winds above the tree of Mystery.
Enitharmon lay on his knees. Urizen trac'd his Verses.
In the dark deep the dark tree grew: her shadow was drawn down,
Down to the roots: it wept over Orc, the Shadow of Enitharmon.

Los saw her stretch'd, the image of death, upon his wither'd valleys.
Her Shadow went forth & return'd. Now she was pale as snow
When the mountains & hills are cover'd over & the paths of Men shut up;
But when her spirit return'd, as ruddy as a morning when
The ripe fruit blushes into joy in heaven's eternal halls.

Sorrow shot thro' him from his feet; it shot up to his head,
Like a cold night that nips the roots & shatters off the leaves.
Silent he stood o'er Enitharmon, watching her pale face.

159–160 Cp. F. Z. vi. 142 *note*.

163 In view of the definite statement in ll. 160–161, Blake's use of 'out' and 'up' in this line would seem to suggest both weakness and strength in the serpent-form of Orc. The weakness, of course, has reference to the enfeebling of Orc's spirit beneath Urizen's power: the strength would appear to relate to the fact that the Tree is finally destroyed by the passionate fires of Orc (F. Z. ix. 69–70; cp. ix. 356–357), a result unforeseen by Urizen (cp. l. 165).

166 Urizen . . . Enitharmon] Urizen, cold, watching Enitharmon *1st rdg.*

167–168 Cp. B. A. ii, ll. 5–12.

After 176 two lines *del.*:

She secret joy'd to see, She fed herself on his Despair;
She said: 'I am aveng'd for all my sufferings of old.'

He spoke not; he was silent till he felt the cold disease.
Then Los mourn'd on the dismal wind in his jealous lamentation:

'Why can I not Enjoy thy beauty, Lovely Enitharmon?
When I return from clouds of Grief in the wandering Elements,
Where thou in thrilling joy, in beaming summer loveliness,
Delectable reposest, ruddy in my absence, flaming with beauty,
Cold, pale in sorrow at my approach; trembling at my terrific
Forehead & eyes, thy lips decay like roses in the spring.
How art thou shrunk! Thy grapes that burst in summer's vast Excess,
Shut up in little purple covering faintly bud & die:
Thy olive trees that pour'd down oil upon a thousand hills,
Sickly look forth & scarcely stretch their branches to the plain:
Thy roses that expanded in the face of glowing morn,
[6] Hid in a little silken veil, scarce breathe, & faintly shine:
Thy lillies that gave light, what time the morning lookèd forth,
Hid in the Vales faintly lament, & no one hears their voice.
All things beside the woful Los enjoy the delights of beauty.
Once how I sang & call'd the beasts & birds to their delights
Nor knew that I, alone exempted from the joys of love,
Must war with secret monsters of the animating worlds!
O that I had not seen the day! then should I be at rest,
Nor felt the stingings of desire, nor longings after life;
For life is sweet to Los the wretchèd; to his wingèd woes
Is given a craving cry, that they may sit at night on barren rocks,
And whet their beaks, & snuff the air, & watch the opening dawn,
And shriek till at the smells of blood they stretch their boney wings,
And cut the winds like arrows shot by troops of Destiny.'

Thus Los lamented in the night, unheard by Enitharmon;
For the Shadow of Enitharmon descended down the tree of Mystery.
The Spectre saw the Shade Shiv'ring over his gloomy rocks
Beneath the tree of Mystery, which in the dismal Abyss

182–206 Los, now infected with 'the error and delusion' of mundane environment, falls beneath the power of 'Female Jealousy' and thereby experiences the futility and barrenness of all uninspired endeavour. This notion is carried much further in *Jerusalem*, particularly on p. 68. 62–68.
187 the] early *1st rdg. del.*

Began to blossom in fierce pain, shooting its writhing buds
In throes of birth ; & now, the blossoms falling, shining fruit
Appear'd of many colours & of various poisonous qualities
Of Plagues hidden in shining globes that grew on the living tree.

The Spectre of Urthona saw the Shadow of Enitharmon
Beneath the Tree of Mystery, among the leaves & fruit.
Redd'ning the Demon strong prepar'd the poison of sweet Love;
He turn'd from side to side in tears ; he wept & he embrac'd
The fleeting image, & in whispers mild woo'd the faint shade :

' Loveliest delight of Men, Enitharmon, shady hiding
In secret places where no eye can trace thy watery way,
Have I found thee ? have I found thee ? tremblest thou in fear
Because of Orc, because he rent his discordant way
From thy sweet loins of bliss ? Red flow'd thy blood ;
Pale grew thy face ; lightnings play'd around thee ; thunders hover'd
Over thee, & the terrible Orc rent his discordant way.
But the next joy of thine shall be in sweet delusion,
And its birth in fainting & sleep & sweet delusions of Vala.'

The Shadow of Enitharmon answer'd : 'Art thou, terrible Shade,
Set over this sweet boy of mine to guard him, lest he rend
[7] His mother to the winds of heaven ? Intoxicated with
The fruit of this delightful tree, I cannot flee away
From thy embrace ; else be assur'd so horrible a form
Should never in my arms repose. Now listen ! I will tell
The Secrets of Eternity which ne'er before Unlock'd
My golden lips, nor took the bar from Enitharmon's breast.
Among the Flowers of Beulah walk'd the Eternal Man & saw
Vala the lilly of the Desart. Melting in high noon
Upon her bosom in sweet bliss he fainted. Wonder siez'd
All heaven : they saw him dark : they built a golden wall

218 tears] veins *1st rdg.* 228 Sweet] woe *1st rdg. del.*

229–264 Enitharmon's narration carries the account of the Fall still farther back, but without throwing any light upon the matter. The birth of Urizen from Vala marks the growing importance of the ' Female ' symbols in Blake's system (see Index, *Sex*). It also implies the criticism that the conventional conception of God is the outcome of man's subjection to the delusion of a physical world, Nature, of which Vala is the symbol.

230 Cp. F. Z. v. 112.

237 Beulah is here the symbol of the state of innocence, the ' lower Paradise ' of F. Z. ix. 458, which is also associated with Vala : and see below, ll. 268–275.

Round Beulah. There he revel'd in delight among the Flowers.
Vala was pregnant & brought forth Urizen, Prince of Light,
First born of Generation. Then behold ! a wonder to the Eyes
Of the now fallen Man, a double form Vala appear'd, a Male
And female. Shudd'ring, pale, the Fallen Man recoil'd
From the Enormity, & call'd them Luvah & Vala, turning down
The vales to find his way back into Heaven, but found none ;
For his frail eyes were faded & his ears heavy & dull.

' Urizen grew up in the plains of Beulah. Many sons
And many daughters flourish'd round the holy Tent of Man,
Till he forgot Eternity, delighted in his sweet joy
Among his family, his flocks & herds & tents & pastures.

' But Luvah close conferr'd with Urizen in darksom night
To bind the father & enslave the brethren. Nought he knew
Of sweet Eternity. The blood flow'd round the holy tent & riv'n
From its hinges, uttering its final groan, all Beulah fell
In dark confusion. Mean time Los was born & Enitharmon,
But how I know not : then forgetfulness quite wrap'd me up
A period, nor do I more remember till I stood
Beside Los in the Cavern dark, enslav'd to vegetative forms,
According to the Will of Luvah, who assum'd the Place
Of the Eternal Man & smote him. But thou, Spectre dark,
Maist find a way to punish Vala in thy fiery South,
To bring her down, subjected to the rage of my fierce boy.'

[8] The Spectre said : ' Thou lovely Vision, this delightful Tree
Is given us for a Shelter from the tempests of Void & Solid,
Till once again the morn of ages shall renew upon us,
To reunite in those mild fields of happy Eternity
Where thou & I in undivided Essence walk'd about
Imbodied, thou my garden of Delight & I the spirit in the garden.
Mutual there we dwelt, in one another's joy revolving

242 Vala] Valan *1st rdg.* 245–246 Cp. F. Z. iii. 41–96.
261–262 Cp. F. Z. ix. 364–372. 265 Vision this] *an addition.*
265–270 There appears here to be an indication of a regenerative purpose in mundane existence as symbolized by the Tree of Mystery. Such a valuation of life is more commonly expressed in the *Mundane Shell*, a symbol inclusive of the Tree and other matters. It is ' the Habitation of the Spectres of the Dead ' that becomes through mercy ' the Place of Redemption & of awaking again into Eternity ' (J. 59. 8–9 and see Index, *Mundane Shell*).

Days of Eternity with Tharmas mild & Luvah sweet, melodious,
Upon our waters. This thou well rememberest: listen, I will tell
What thou forgettest. They in us & we in them alternate Liv'd,
Drinking the joys of Universal Manhood. One dread morn—
Listen, O vision of delight!—One dread morn of goary blood,
The manhood was divided; for the gentle passions, making way
Thro' the infinite labyrinths of the heart & thro' the nostrils issuing
In odorous stupefaction, stood before the Eyes of Man,
A female bright. I stood beside my anvil dark: a mass
Of iron glow'd bright, prepar'd for spades & plowshares: sudden down
I sunk with cries of blood, issuing downward in the veins
Which now my rivers were become, rolling in tubelike forms,
Shut up within themselves. Descending, down I sunk along
The goary tide even to the place of seed, & there dividing,
I was divided in darkness & oblivion, thou an infant woe,
And I an infant terror in the womb of Enion.
My masculine spirit, scorning the frail body, issu'd forth
From Enion's brain In this deformèd form, leaving thee there
Till times pass'd over thee; but still my spirit, returning, hover'd,
And form'd a Male to be a counterpart to thee, O Love
Darken'd & Lost. In due time issuing forth from Enion's womb,
Thou & that demon Los wert born. Ah, jealousy & woe!
Ah, poor divided dark Urthona! now a Spectre, wandering
The deeps of Los, the slave of that Creation I created!
I labour night & day for Los, but listen thou my vision.
I view futurity in thee. I will bring down soft Vala
To the embraces of this terror, & I will destroy
That body I created: then shall we unite again in bliss.
Thou knowest that the Spectre is in Every Man insane, brutish,

277 manhood . . . for] *written over erasure*. See Index, *Sex*, and cp. M. 10. 3–8.

280–290 Cp. F. Z. i. 208 seq.

289 From Enion's brain] *marginal addition*.

293 It has not been found possible to arrive at any understanding of the changes of Urthona and Enitharmon, and particularly of their relationship to Los and Enitharmon, the children of Enion.

300–304 Thou . . . Living] *marginal addition* marked for insertion here. After l. 303 *two lines del.*:

I have thee in my arms & am again united to Los,
To be one body & One Spirit with him.

Deform'd; that I am thus a ravening devouring lust, continually
Craving & devouring: but my Eyes are always upon thee, O lovely
Delusion, & I cannot crave for any thing but thee. Not so
The spectres of the Dead, for I am as the Spectre of the Living.
For till these terrors, planted round the Gates of Eternal life,
Are driven away & annihilated, we can never repass the Gates.'

. . . .

[9] Astonish'd, fill'd with tears, the spirit of Enitharmon beheld
And heard the Spectre: bitterly she wept, Embracing fervent
Her once lov'd Lord, now but a Shade, herself also a shade,
Conferring times on times among the branches of that Tree.

Thus they conferr'd among the intoxicating fumes of Mystery,
Till Enitharmon's shadow, pregnant, in the deeps beneath
Brought forth a wonder horrible. While Enitharmon shriek'd
And trembled thro' the Worlds above, Los wept; his fierce soul was terrified
At the shrieks of Enitharmon, at her tossings; nor could his eyes percieve
The cause of her dire anguish; for she lay the image of Death,
Mov'd by strong shudders, till her shadow was deliver'd: then she ran
Raving about the upper Elements in maddening fury.

She burst the Gates of Enitharmon's heart with direful Crash,
Nor could they ever be Clos'd again: the golden hinges were broken,

303 Not so] & till *1st rdg. del.* From Blake's numbering of the lines it would seem that something is missing at this point. The course of the myth shows no clear sign of a lacuna.

307–310 Astonish'd . . . Tree] *an addition.*

317 Enitharmon's 'shadow' would seem to be Vala. It is not easy to discover between Enitharmon and Vala a connexion such as Blake expresses by representing one as the daughter of the other. For Enitharmon is 'Space' controlling 'spaces, regions, desart, flood & forest' (F. Z. i. 152), while Vala is Nature, the whole body of error that Blake associated with a belief in physical reality. Apart from this, it is noteworthy that when Enitharmon, who up to this point has been the type of the perversive 'feminine' influences of empiricism and morality, joins with Los in his regenerative labours, a new symbol, the Shadow of Enitharmon (see Index, *Shadow*), takes her former place in Blake's scheme. Indeed, both in *The Four Zoas* and the later books, it is often difficult to discover any difference between Enitharmon when opposed to the visionary labours of Los, and Vala. This episode also fulfils Urizen's prophecy, F. Z. iii. 19–20.

319 'She' is Vala. Enitharmon's broken Heart Gate, the Gate of Pity, cannot be interpreted with certainty. In Night VIII it seems to be connected with Blake's theory of regeneration through mortal life; while

And the gates broke in sunder, & their ornaments defac'd
Beneath the tree of Mystery: for the immortal shadow, shuddering,
Brought forth this wonder horrible. A cloud she grew & grew,
Till many of the dead burst forth from the bottoms of their tombs
In male forms without female counterparts or Emanations,
Cruel & ravening with Enmity & Hatred & War
In dreams of Ulro, dark, delusive, drawn by the lovely shadow.

The Spectre, terrified, ⟨&⟩ gave her Charge over the howling Orc.
Then took the tree of Mystery root in the World of Los,
Its topmost boughs shooting a fibre beneath Enitharmon's couch.
The double rooted Labyrinth soon wav'd around their heads.

But then the Spectre enter'd Los's bosom. Every sigh & groan
Of Enitharmon bore Urthona's Spectre on its wings.
Obdurate Los felt Pity. Enitharmon told the tale
Of Urthona. Los Embrac'd the Spectre, first as a brother,
Then as another Self, astonish'd, humanizing & in tears,
In Self abasement Giving up his Domineering lust.

'Thou never canst embrace sweet Enitharmon, terrible Demon, Till

in the account of the appearance of the Divine Vision in this Gate, there appears to be an allusion to the Incarnation. If this last suggestion holds, Enitharmon's Heart Gate may be compared with the Gate of Birth (J. 27, stanza 16).

321 broke] burst *1st rdg.*

325–327 In . . . war] *marginal addition*, marked for insertion here. See Index, *Emanation*.

327 dark] sweet *1st rdg. del.* See Index, *Ulro*.

328 terrified] smiled *1st rdg. del.*

330 boughs] branches *1st rdg. del.* fibre] stem *1st rdg. del.*

332–333 But . . . wings] *written over* 'End of the S[even]th Night' *del.*

337 Los's 'Domineering lust' cannot be defined, since no complete interpretation has been discovered for Los in the earlier Nights. That he is a 'visionary of Jesus' (F. Z. ii. 80) and controls 'the times and seasons and the days and years' (F. Z. i. 151) only partially explains his part in the myth, and it is not evident in what manner either of these activities could develop into 'domineering lust'. On present knowledge, the phrase can only be interpreted as emphasizing the necessity for harmony among the powers of man (see Index, *Zoas*): this is also the condition of the perfect form of being, the Eternal Man. The destruction of this harmony by the predominance of one form of activity over the other is the cause of error: cp. F. Z. ix. 364–372.

338–367 Thou . . . uniting] *an addition*.

Thou art united with thy Spectre, Consummating by pains & labours
That mortal body, & by Self annihilation back returning
To Life Eternal. Be assur'd I am thy real self,
Tho' thus divided from thee & the Slave of Every passion
Of thy fierce Soul. Unbar the Gates of Memory: look upon me,
Not as another, but as thy real Self. I am thy Spectre,
Tho' horrible & Ghastly to thine Eyes, tho' buried beneath
The ruins of the Universe: hear what inspir'd I speak & be silent!
Thou didst subdue me in old times by thy Immortal Strength,
When I was a ravening, hungering & thirsting cruel lust & murder.
If we unite in one, another better world will be
Open'd within your heart & loins & wondrous brain,
Threefold, as it was in Eternity; & this the fourth Universe
Will be Renew'd by the three, & consummated in Mental fires.
But if thou dost refuse, Another body will be preparèd
[10] For me; & thou, annihilate, evaporate & be no more.
For thou art but a form & organ of life, & of thyself
Art nothing, being Created Continually by Mercy & Love divine.'

Los furious answer'd: 'Spectre horrible, thy words astound my Ear
With irresistible conviction. I feel I am not one of those
Who, when convinc'd, can still persist: tho' furious, controllable
By Reason's power. Even I already feel a World within
Opening its gates, & in it all the real substances

339–346 The Spectre at this point is quite other than the 'Spectre' of the later books (see Index, *Spectre*). Here he is inspired (l. 346), and is the 'real Self' though fallen, while Los in himself is nothing, being but a 'form and organ of life', an instrument of 'Mercy & Love divine', existing only for the sake of the Spectre (ll. 353–356). Such a concept does not occur elsewhere.

340 That] Thy *1st rdg. del.* See Index, *Self-annihilation.*

343–344 Of . . . Spectre] *written over* 'The End of the S[eventh] Night' *del.*

347–348 Thou . . . murder] *marginal addition*: position not indicated, but probably intended for insertion here. These lines appear to be an attempt to bring the view of the Spectre in ll. 339–346 (see note *ad loc.*) into harmony with the later use of the symbol.

349 we] once we *1st rdg.*

349–352 First Los is to be regenerated; then he is to proceed with the work of the regeneration of this world. For 'Consummation' cp. F. Z. ix. 32 *note.*

360–362 See General Introduction, p. 22. For the 'World within' and 'the outward World' see F. Z. i. 250 *note.* 'Reason' here has, of course, nothing of the sinister significance that it has when associated with fallen Urizen or the Spectre.

Of which these in the outward World are shadows which pass away.
Come then into my Bosom, & in thy shadowy arms bring with thee
My lovely Enitharmon. I will quell my fury & teach
Peace to the soul of dark revenge, & repentance to Cruelty.'

So spoke Los: & Embracing Enitharmon & the Spectre,
Clouds would have folded round in Extacy & Love uniting:
[11] But Enitharmon trembling fled & hid beneath Urizen's tree.
But mingling together with his Spectre, the Spectre of Urthona
Wondering beheld the Center open'd. By Divine Mercy inspir'd,
He in his turn Gave Tasks to Los, Enormous, to destroy
That body he created, but in vain: for Los perform'd
Wonders of Labour.
They builded Golgonooza. Los, labouring, builded pillars high,
And Domes terrific in the nether heavens; for beneath
Was open'd new heavens & a new Earth, beneath & within,
Threefold, within the brain, within the heart, within the loins,
A Threefold Atmosphere Sublime, continuous from Urthona's world,
But yet having a Limit Twofold namèd Satan & Adam.

But Los Stood on the Limit of Translucence, weeping & trembling;
Fillèd with doubts, in self accusation, beheld the fruit
Of Urizen's Mysterious tree. For Enitharmon thus spake:

367 Clouds . . . round] *written over erasure.*
368–427 But Enitharmon . . . destroy] written on back of half of 'Edward and Elenor' proof. In the space above the print, and having no apparent place in the text, are the lines:

The Christian Religion teaches that No Man is Indifferent to you but that every one is/
Either Your friend or your enemy: he must necessarily be either the one [of *del.*] or the other;
And that he will be equally profitable both ways if you treat him as he deserves.

Line 3 is a later addition.
369 But] Then *1st rdg. del.* 370 Wondering...open'd] *written over erasure.*
371–373 He . . . Labour] *an addition.*
374 labouring] labouring inspir'd *1st rdg.* See Index, *Golgonooza.*
377 See Index, *Head, Heart, and Loins.*
378 Urthona's] *written over erasure*: ? Urizen's.
380 See Index, *Expansion*, &c. This is not in accord with J. 42. 35–36:

But there is no Limit of Expansion, there is no Limit of Translucence
In the bosom of Man for ever from Eternity to Eternity.

381 beheld] *written over erasure*: ? gather'd.

'When In the Deeps beneath I gather'd of this ruddy fruit,
It was by that I knew that I had Sinn'd; & then I knew
That, without a ransom, I could not be sav'd from Eternal death;
That Life lives upon Death; & by devouring appetite
All things subsist on one another. Thenceforth in despair
I spend my glowing time, but thou art strong & mighty
To bear this Self conviction. Take then. Eat thou also of
The fruit, & give me proof of life Eternal, or I die.'

Then Los pluckèd the fruit, & Eat, & sat down in Despair,
And must have given himself to death Eternal, But
Urthona's Spectre, in part mingling with him, comforted him,
Being a medium between him & Enitharmon. But This Union
Was not to be Effected without Cares & Sorrows & Troubles
Of Six thousand Years of self denial & of bitter Contrition.

Urthona's Spectre, terrified, beheld the Spectres of the Dead,
Each male form'd without a counter part, without a concentering vision.
The Spectre of Urthona wept before Los, saying: 'I am the cause
That this dire state commences. I began the dreadful state
Of Separation, & on my dark head the curse & punishment
Must fall, unless a way be found to Ransom & Redeem.
But I have thee, my [Counterpart] miraculous.
These Spectres have no Counter[parts]; therefore they ravin
Without the food of life. Let us Create them Coun[terparts];
For without a Created body the Spectre is Eternal Death.'

Los trembling answer'd: 'Now I feel the weight of stern repentance.
Tremble not so, my Enitharmon, at the awful gates
Of thy poor broken Heart. I see thee like a shadow withering

386–396 Cp. B. U., chap. viii, l. 32.

394–396 This is the clearest statement of Blake's new point of view that mundane existence is valid as the divinely appointed means for the achieving of reunion in the Eternal.

396 of bitter Contrition] many Tears *1st rdg. del.*

398–406 The Counterpart is identified with the Emanation: cp. F. Z. vii. 325–327, and Index, *Emanation.*

402 found] found the *1st rdg.*

403–406 But . . . Death] *marginal addition,* marked to come in here.

403 Counterpart] *1st rdg. del.*; Vegetation *2nd rdg. del.* Counterpart evidently failed to convey Blake's meaning and was deleted, but for want of a better word, truncated forms of the term were used in ll. 404–405 till such time as he might discover an adequate expression. For the creation of bodies for the Spectres, cp. M. 26. 13–28. 53, and see Index, *Enitharmon,* III.

As on the outside of Existence : but look ! behold ! take comfort !
Turn inwardly thine Eyes, & there behold the Lamb of God,
Clothèd in Luvah's robes of blood, descending to redeem.
O Spectre of Urthona, take comfort ! O Enitharmon,
Couldst thou but cease from terror & trembling & affright,
When I appear before thee in forgiveness of ancient injuries !
Why shouldst thou remember, & be afraid ? I surely have died in pain
Often enough to convince thy jealousy & fear & terror.
Come hither ; be patient ; let us converse together, because
I also tremble at myself & at all my former life.'

Enitharmon answer'd : ' I behold the Lamb of God descending
To Meet these Spectres of the Dead. I therefore fear that he
Will give us to Eternal Death, fit punishment for such
Hideous offenders—Uttermost extinction in eternal pain,
An ever dying life of stifling & obstruction, shut out
Of existence to be a sign & terror to all who behold,
Lest any should in futurity do as we have done in heaven.
Such is our state, nor will the Son of God redeem us, but destroy.'

[12] So Enitharmon spoke, trembling & in torrents of tears.

Los sat in Golgonooza, in the Gate of Luban, where
He had erected many porches, where branch'd the Mysterious tree,
Where the Spectrous dead wail ; & sighing, thus he spoke to Enitharmon :

410 Cp. M. 43. 38 : ' The Void Outside of Existence ' ; see Index, *Ulro.*
413 O Spectre . . . comfort] written first in pencil, then with a pen.
415 ancient injuries] former injuries *1st rdg. del.*
425–426 Something of this idea of the persistence of the phenomena of error after the regeneration is repeated in J. 92. 13–22, where the same motive of warning is expressed :

that we may Foresee & Avoid
The terrors of Creation & Redemption & Judgment,

these three ' states ' combining to form Ulro or Error.
427 Such . . . destroy] *a pencilled addition.*
428–494 So . . . himself] written on the back of the remaining half of the ' Edward and Elenor ' print.
429 See Index, *Golgonooza.* The name ' Luban ' is apparently derived from the following passage in Jacob Bryant's *Ancient Mythology,* vol. iii, p. 21 : ' The place where mankind first resided was undoubtedly the region of the Minyae at the bottom of Mount Baris or Luban, which was the Ararat of Moses : here I imagine that the Patriarch resided, and Berosius mentions that in this place he gave instructions to his children and vanished from the sight of men.'
430 where] which *1st rdg. del.* where . . . tree] *written over erasure.*

'Lovely delight of Men, Enitharmon, shady refuge from furious war,
Thy bosom translucent is a soft repose for the weeping souls
Of those piteous victims of battle: there they sleep in happy obscurity.
They feed upon our life: we are their victims. Stern desire
I feel to fabricate embodied semblances in which the dead
May live before us in our palaces & in our gardens of labour,
Which, now open'd within the Center, we behold spread abroad,
To form a world of sacrifice of brothers & sons & daughters
To comfort Orc in his dire sufferings. Look, my fires enlume afresh,
Before my face ascending with delight as in ancient times.'

Enitharmon spread her beaming locks upon the wind & said:
'O Lovely terrible Los, wonder of Eternity, O Los, my defence & guide,
Thy works are all my joy, & in thy fires my soul delights.
If mild they burn in just proportion, & in secret night
And silence build their day in Shadow of soft clouds & dews,
Then I can sigh forth on the winds of Golgonooza piteous forms
That vanish again into my bosom: but if thou, my Los,
Wilt in sweet moderated fury fabricate forms sublime,
Such as the piteous spectres may assimilate themselves into,
They shall be ransoms for our Souls that we may live.'

So Enitharmon spoke; & Los, his hands divine inspirèd, began
To modulate his fires: studious the loud roaring flames
He vanquish'd with the strength of Art, bending their iron points
And drawing them forth, delighted, upon the winds of Golgonooza,

432 shady refuge] shady sweet refuge *1st rdg.* See Index, *Enitharmon*.
435 They . . . desire] *an addition*. 437 labour] pleasure *1st rdg. del.*
438 Which . . . abroad] *an addition*.
439 This marks the introduction of the new ethic of self-sacrifice and brotherhood into mortal life. sacrifice] life & love *1st rdg. del.*
440 The reviving of Los's fires indicate the beginning of regenerative activities in the 'separated' world.
443 Lovely terrible Los] Lovely *1st rdg. del.*
449 forms sublime] sweet forms *1st rdg.* 451 They . . . live] *an addition*.
After l. 452 *line del.*:

To hew the cavern'd rocks of Dranthon into forms of beauty

455 forth, delighted, upon] forth upon *1st rdg.*

From out the ranks of Urizen's war & from the fiery lake
Of Orc, bending down as the binder of the sheaves follows
The reaper, in both arms embracing the furious raging flames.
Los drew them forth out of the deeps, planting his right foot firm
Upon the Iron crag of Urizen, thence springing up aloft
Into the heavens of Enitharmon in a mighty circle.

And first he drew a line upon the walls of shining heaven,
And Enitharmon tinctur'd it with beams of blushing love.
It remain'd permanent, a lovely form inspir'd, divinely human,
Dividing into just proportions. Los unwearied labour'd
The immortal lines upon the heavens, till with sighs of love
Sweet Enitharmon, mild, Entranc'd, breath'd forth upon the wind
The Spectrous dead. Weeping the Spectres view'd the immortal works
Of Los, Assimilating to those forms, Embodied & Lovely
In youth & beauty, in the arms of Enitharmon mild reposing.

First Rintrah, & then Palamabron, drawn from out the ranks of war,
In infant innocence repos'd on Enitharmon's bosom.
Orc was comforted in the deeps; his soul reviv'd in them.
As the Eldest brother is the father's image, So Orc became,
As Los, a father to his brethren, & he joy'd in the dark lake,
Tho' bound with chains of Jealousy & in scales of iron & brass.

But Los lovèd them, & refus'd to Sacrifice their infant limbs,
And Enitharmon's smiles & tears prevail'd over self protection.
They rather chose to meet Eternal Death than to destroy
The offspring of their Care & Pity. Urthona's Spectre was comforted;
But Tharmas most rejoic'd in hope of Enion's return;
For he beheld new Female forms born forth upon the air,

460 Cp. above, ll. 40–43, and B. A., chap. iii, ll. 9–21.

462 Cp. M. 27. 16 *note*.

471 In the earlier works Rintrah and Palamabron, with the other children of Los, transmit Urizen's Laws and Religions to mortals (*Africa*, ll. 8–9). But at this point, apparently, they are regenerated, and henceforth appear as assistant to Los and Enitharmon in the work of regeneration, except only in the Satan-Palamabron myth, M., pp. 5–11.

474 father's image] second father *1st rdg.* In the later books Orc is never associated with Rintrah, Palamabron and the rest of the brethren who assist Los in his labours.

482–484 For . . . veil] *an addition.* The Females would seem to be either the Daughters of Los or the Daughters of Beulah, though nowhere else is the distinction made between either of these and Enitharmon, that is

Who wove soft silken veils of covering in sweet raptur'd trance,
Mortal & not as Enitharmon, without a covering veil.
First his immortal spirit drew Urizen's Spectre away
From out the ranks of war, separating him in sunder,
Leaving his Spectrous form, which could not be drawn away.
Then he divided Thiriel, the Eldest of Urizen'[s] sons;
Urizen became Rintrah; Thiriel became Palamabron;
Thus dividing the power of Every Warrior.
Startled was Los: he found his Enemy Urizen now
In his hands: he wonder'd that he felt love, & not hate.
His whole soul lovèd him: he beheld him an infant
Lovely breath'd from Enitharmon: he trembled within himself.

made in l. 484, where 'without a covering veil' appears to be antithetical to 'mortal'. See above, ll. 403–406 and note *ad loc.*

485–494 First . . . himself] *marginal addition*, position not indicated.

485 Spectre] Shadow *1st rdg.* This alteration makes l. 487 meaningless, since it is not possible to discover any difference between 'Urizen's Spectre' and 'his Spectrous form'. It is true that 'Urizen's Shadow', the first reading, is not satisfactorily explained by Blake, though some light may be thrown upon it by reference to an apparently similar use of the symbols 'shadow' and 'spectre' in connexion with Milton, where the former represents the victim of error, the latter the principle of error.

488 Cp. B. U., chap. viii, l. 16.

489–494 This form of the myth of Los and Urizen is not developed elsewhere.

NIGHT VIII

INTRODUCTORY NOTE

WHEN in his spiritual decline man reaches a point predetermined by Providence and called the Limit of Contraction, or Adam, the 'Council of God', seen as One Man, Jesus, intervenes to create or recreate the fallen man. The revelation of the divine purpose in the Incarnation (ll. 15–16) sustains Los and Enitharmon in their task of creating bodies for the Spectres of the Dead (F. Z. vii. 398 seq.). To Urizen the Divine Vision appears as 'a new Luvah, or One who assum'd Luvah's form and stood before him opposite' (ll. 56–57); that is, Jesus appears as Love in the form of Luvah, the Prince of Love who, as Orc, has been drawn into the Tree of Mystery, becoming destructive Hate, the King of rage and death (ll. 58–82). From this follows the conflict of the forces that contend about or within Man (ll. 83–133): on one side Jesus, with Los and Enitharmon; on the other, Satan, the serpent Orc and the Synagogue of Satan (l. 90). For Urizen's 'battle' becomes apparent as Satan (ll. 104–108, 238–249), and in the Tree of Mystery appears the Shadowy Female, the sum of the 'feminine' delusions of religion (ll. 133–174).

Meanwhile, the 'forms' created by Los and Enitharmon combine into Jerusalem, 'a vast family' seen as

> a Universal female form, created
> From those who were dead in Ulro, from the spectres of the dead;
>
> (ll. 181–182.)

and in the midst appears the Lamb of God. In this instance, therefore, Jerusalem appears to represent all revelations of truth and morality, and these are, as it were, consummated in Christ, the final revelation of the regenerative function of mundane life. The Sons of Eden, the Eternals, whose relation with the 'Council of God' (ll. 1–2) is not defined, proclaim the imminence of man's redemption (ll. 190, 230–236), for the 'holy Lamb of God . . . beginneth to put off the dark Satanic body' (ll. 188–189). They tell also (ll. 193–236) of the labours of Los and Enitharmon, and of the 'Satanic Mills' that destroy their work to set up in its place the delusive 'forms' of the 'false females' Rahab and Tirzah (ll. 208–213).

Then follows the account of the Incarnation and Crucifixion (ll. 250–326), the latter being represented at first as the triumph of the forces of mundane error, the synagogue of Satan and its 'female counterpart', Rahab (ll. 267–311). Even to Los and Jerusalem the Crucifixion appears at first to be the victory of these forces (ll. 319–329); but shortly the true significance of the event is revealed as the final unmasking of the errors in religion and thought represented in Satan and Rahab (ll. 330–333).

The succeeding passage, on the added pp. 1*–3*, stands quite apart from all else in *The Four Zoas*, consideration of it belonging more properly to *Milton* (see *Milton*, Introduction). Los gives

Rahab still another account of the Fall, in the Satan-Palamabron myth, declaring also the doctrine of ' States ' (see Index), and the value of Jesus' act of sacrifice (ll. 340–398). When the Night wanders back to its former channel it describes a further change in Urizen (ll. 404–454), ascribed to the supremacy of the ' Female ', whom he embraces, thereby being changed into a serpent, his ' human form '—an unintelligible expression in its present connexion—remaining as ' a form of senseless stone '.

> Incessant stern disdain his scaly form gnaws inwardly,
> With deep repentance for the loss of that fair form of Man.
> (ll. 423–424.)

The episode has no parallel in any other treatment of the myth of Urizen, and can only be related to that of the present work mechanically, for its closing lines indicate that the event is the fulfilment of the prophecy (F. Z. iii. 17–19) foretelling that Urizen should become subservient to Orc, for ' Orc reign'd over all, and Urizen's wisdom serv'd but to augment the indefinite lust ' (ll. 453–454). Tharmas, Urthona, Los, and Enitharmon are affected by the resultant suspension of all activity in a ' universal stupor '. The first two daemons, Tharmas and Urthona, surrender their power to Los ' for love of Enitharmon ' ; that is, apparently, to further the work of regeneration in mortal life. Thus all things are bound in a living death in the nameless Shadow, the body of error, which Jesus ' puts off ', that is, discovers and annihilates, in his Crucifixion (ll. 459–471).

In its earlier form Night VIII closed with two songs. The first (ll. 481–520), sung by Ahania, whose memory beholds man's ancient days and whose eyes behold his existence in the dark body of corruptible death (ll. 492–493), describes the desolation of man's fallen state : her visions reveal nothing of ultimate regeneration. But Enion, the shadow of Hope, tells how Jesus has rent the Veil of Mystery (l. 544) ; and though it has been reconstituted, its final annihilation is predicted ; for the promise of a final spiritual awakening is inherent in all the forms of life (ll. 569–571).

The Night in its present form ends with an added passage of a later date (ll. 577–600). Here Blake tries to relate eighteenth-century deism to the errors of earlier dogmatic theologies by representing the latter, symbolized by Rahab, as effete. Hence they are burnt by the synagogue of Satan, as ineffectual weapons, but from their ashes arise Deism and Natural Religion :

> so now anew began
> Babylon again in Infancy call'd Natural Religion. (ll. 599–600.)

VALA

Night the Eighth

THEN All in Great Eternity Met in the Council of God
As One Man, Even Jesus, upon Gilead & Hermon,
Upon the Limit of Contraction, to create the fallen Man.
The fallen Man, stretch'd like a Corse upon the oozy Rock,
Wash'd with the tides, Pale, overgrown with weeds,
Yet mov'd with horrible dreams : hovering high over his head
Two wingèd immortal shapes, one standing at his feet
Toward the East, one standing at his head toward the west :
Their wings join'd in the Zenith over head.

Such is a Vision of All Beulah hov'ring over the Sleeper.

The limit of Contraction now was fix'd & Man began
To wake upon the Couch of Death : he sneezèd Seven times ;
A tear of blood droppèd from either eye : again he repos'd
In the Saviour's arms, in the arms of tender mercy & loving
kindness.

Then Los said : ' I behold the Divine Vision thro' the broken
Gates

1–44 Cp. F. Z. iv. 246–278. 1 Met in] which is call'd *1st rdg. del.*
2 As] Met as *1st rdg.* Gilead and Hermon, lying to the east of the Jordan, are constantly used in association with the state of mundane error : see Index, *Cardinal Points*. Cp. also Hos. vi. 8 : ' Gilead is the city of them that work iniquity.'
3 Fallen] Eternal *1st rdg. del.* For ' Limit of Contraction ' see Index, *Expansion*, &c.
4–9 The fallen . . . head] *written over deleted passage.*
4–5 Cp. F. Z. viii. 497–515 and J. 94. 1–12. In this latter passage Blake appears to interpret the geographical situation of Britain, or Albion, as symbolic of the fallen state of Man, see Index, *Atlantic*. It seems likely that a similar meaning is implied in the present passage.
6 The six thousand years of mundane existence is a ' dreamful slumber ' in the ' Dreams of Chastity & Moral Law ' (J. 94. 23).
7–10 Cp. J. 94. 12–14.
9 Their . . . head] Their wings join'd in the Zenith over head, but other wings *1st rdg.* A marginal addition, continuing this line, is also deleted :

They had which cloth'd their bodies like a garment of soft down,
Silvery white, shining upon the dark blue sky in silence [? silver].
Their wings touch'd the heavens, their fair feet hover'd above
The swelling tides : they bent over the dead corse like an arch
Pointed at top in highest heavens of precious stones & pearl.

10 Such . . . sleeper] the undeleted last line of the marginal addition given above.
15 Cp. F. Z. vii. 319 *note.* Then . . . behold] Then Los beheld *1st rdg.* ; First Los beheld *2nd rdg. del.*

Of thy poor broken heart, astonish'd, melted into Compassion & Love.'
And Enitharmon said : ' I see the Lamb of God upon Mount Zion.'
Wondering, with love & Awe, they felt the divine hand upon them.

For nothing could restrain the dead in Beulah from descending
Into Ulro's night : tempted by the Shadowy female's sweet
Delusive cruelty, they descend away from the Daughters of Beulah,
And Enter Urizen's temple, Enitharmon pitying & her heart
Gates broken down : they descend thro' the Gate of Pity,
The broken heart Gate of Enitharmon. She sighs them forth upon the wind
Of Golgonooza,
[2] From out the War of Urizen & Tharmas recieving them.
[1] Into his hands Los stood recieving them ;
For Los could enter into Enitharmon's bosom & explore
Its intricate Labyrinths, now the Obdurate heart was broken.
[2] Then Enitharmon erected Looms in Luban's Gate,
And call'd the Looms Cathedron ; in these Looms she wove the Spectres
Bodies of Vegetation, Singing lulling Cadences to drive away
Despair from the poor wondering spectres : and Los lovèd them
With a parental love, for the Divine hand was upon him
And upon Enitharmon, & the Divine Countenance shone
In Golgonooza. Looking down, the Daughters of Beulah saw
With joy the bright Light, & in it a Human form,
And knew he was The Saviour, Even Jesus, & they worshippèd.

16 thy poor broken] Enitharmon's *1st rdg. del.*
24 The broken . . . wind]

The broken heart Gate of Enitharmon which joins to Urizen's temple
Which is the Synagogue of Satan. She sighs them forth upon the wind

1st rdg.

25–30 Of . . . Gate] These lines originally stood in the following order :

Of Golgonooza. Los stood recieving them ;
For Los could enter into Enitharmon's bosom & explore
Its intricate Labyrinths, now the Obdurate heart was broken ;
[2] From out the War of Urizen & Tharmas recieving them.
Then Enitharmon erected Looms in Luban's Gate.

The re-arrangement of this passage is in accordance with the note 'Los stood &c.' written below l. 4*.

30–31 See Index, *Enitharmon* and *Weaving*. For 'Luban' cp. F. Z. vii. 429 *note*.

Astonish'd, Comforted, Delighted, in notes of Rapturous Extacy,
All Beulah stood astonish'd, looking down to Eternal Death
They saw the Saviour beyond the Pit of death & destruction :
For whether they look'd upward, they saw the Divine Vision ;
Or whether they look'd downward, still they saw the Divine Vision
Surrounding them on all sides, beyond sin & death & hell.

Enitharmon wove in tears, singing Songs of Lamentation
And pitying comfort, as she sigh'd forth on the wind the Spectres.
Also the Vegetated bodies, which Enitharmon wove,
Open'd within their hearts & in their loins & in their brain
To Beulah ; & the dead in Ulro descended from the War
Of Urizen & Tharmas, & from the Shadowy female's clouds.
And some were woven single, & some two fold, & some three fold
In Head, or Heart, or Reins, according to the fittest order
Of most merciful pity & compassion to the Spectrous dead.

[3] When Urizen saw the Lamb of God clothèd in Luvah's robes,
Perplex'd & terrified he stood, tho' well he knew that Orc
Was Luvah. But he now beheld a new Luvah, Or One
Who assum'd Luvah's form & stood before him opposite.

But he saw Orc, a Serpent form, augmenting times on times
In the fierce battle ; & he saw the Lamb of God & the World of Los
Surrounded by his dark machines ; for Orc augmented swift
In fury, a Serpent wondrous, among the Constellations of Urizen.
A crest of fire rose on his forehead, red as the carbuncle ;
Beneath, down to his eyelids, scales of pearl ; then gold & silver,
Immingled with the ruby, overspread his Visage ; down
His furious neck, writ[h]ing contortive in dire budding pains,

After l. 38, 'Astonish'd Comforted Delighted the Daughters of Beulah saw' *del.*

47–53 See Index, *Head, Heart, and Loins*. The 'single', 'two-fold', and 'three-fold' Vegetated bodies apparently referred to the varieties of visionary endowment in mundane existence. See General Introduction, pp. 21–43, and cp. the 'three classes' in *Milton* (M. 3. 26 *note*).

51 single] One fold *1st rdg.* 54 See Index, *Incarnation*, II, *b*, i.

58–73 Cp. F. Z. vii. 151–165 ; and see Index, *Orc*, II, *c*.

60–61 Urizen's 'dark machines', his 'Constellations', appear to be the 'starry wheels' : cp. F. Z. iv. 274 *note*.

The scaly armour shot out. Stubborn down his back & bosom,
The Emerald, Onyx, Sapphire, jasper, beryl, amethyst
Strove in terrific emulation which should gain a place
Upon the mighty Fiend—the fruit of the mysterious tree
Kneaded in Uveth's kneading trough. Still Orc devour'd the food
In raging hunger. Still the pestilential food in gems & gold
Exuded round his awful limbs, Stretching to serpent length
His human bulk, While the dark shadowy female, brooding over,
Measur'd his food, morning & evening in cups & baskets of iron.
With tears of sorrow, incessant she labour'd the food of Orc,
Compell'd by the iron hearted sisters, Daughters of Urizen.
Gath'ring the fruit of that mysterious tree, circling its root,
She spread herself thro' all the branches in the power of Orc.
Thus Urizen in self deceit his warlike preparations fabricated ;
And when all things were finish'd, sudden wav'd among the Stars,
His hurtling hand gave the dire Signal ; thunderous Clarions blow,
And all the hollow deep rebellow'd with the wonderous war.

[2] But Urizen his mighty rage let loose in the mid deep.
Sparkles of dire affliction issu'd round his frozen limbs.
Horrible hooks & nets he form'd, twisting the cords of iron
And brass, & molten metals cast in hollow globes, & bor'd
Tubes in petrific steel, & ramm'd combustibles, & wheels
And chains & pullies fabricated all round the heavens of Los,
Communing with the Serpent of Orc in dark dissimulation,

69 Upon the mighty] On the immortal *1st rdg. del.*
70 Uveth, a daughter of Urizen: cp. F. Z. vi. 5 *note*, and F. Z. vii. 90–107.
71 The gems and gold are the allegoric fruits of Urizen's ' mysterious tree ' (see below, ll. 161–162), the outcome of the moral law imposed upon man's passions and desires. Cp. M., extra p. 17. 22–24 :

the gold of broken hearts
And the precious stones of anxiety & care & desperation & death,
And repentance for sin & sorrow & punishment & fear.

73 The ' shadowy female ' in the present passage would seem to be Vala. For the earlier use of the symbol, cp. *Song of Liberty*, Introductory Note.
76 Compell'd . . . Urizen] *an addition.*
80 among the Stars] his hurtling hand *1st rdg. del.*
81 His hurtling hand] Among the Stars *1st rdg. del.*
After l. 82 Blake notes ' " But Urizen his mighty rage " comes in here to " quenchless rage " '. The passage referred to consists of the last nine lines of MS. p. 2 and the first three on MS. p. 3.
84 round] from *1st rdg. del.*

And with the Synagogue of Satan in dark Sanhedrim,
To undermine the World of Los & tear bright Enitharmon
[3] To the four winds, hopeless of future. All futurity
Seems teeming with Endless destruction, never to be expell'd.
Desperate remorse swallows the present in a quenchless rage.

The battle howls : the terrors, fir'd, rage in the work of death.
Enormous Works Los Contemplated, inspir'd by the Holy Spirit.
Los builds the Walls of Golgonooza against the stirring battle,
That only thro' the Gates of Death they can enter to Enitharmon.
Raging they take the human visage & the human form,
Feeling the hand of Los in Golgonooza & the force
Attractive of his hammer's beating, & the Silver looms
Of Enitharmon singing lulling cadences on the wind.
They humanize in the fierce battle, where, in direful pain,
Terrified & astonish'd, Urizen beheld the battle take a form
Which he intended not, a Shadowy hermaphrodite, black & opake.
The Soldiers nam'd it Satan ; but he was yet unform'd & vast.
Hermaphroditic it at length became, hiding the Male
Within as in a Tabernacle, Abominable, Deadly.
Troop by troop the beastial droves rend one another, sounding loud
The instruments of sound ; & troop by troop in human forms they urge
[4] The dire confusion, till the battle faints ; those that remain
Return in pangs & horrible convulsions to their beastial state.
For the monsters of the Elements, Lions or Tygers or Wolves,
Sound loud the howling music. Inspir'd by Los & Enitharmon, sounding loud, terrific men

90 The Synagogue of Satan, practically equivalent to 'Satan' (see Index, *Satan*), is set over against the Council of God, which appears as Jesus.
92 Cp. F. Z. ii. 501 *note*. 96 Enormous . . . Spirit] *an addition*.
97 See Index, *Golgonooza*.
98 This line is not clear. It may have the same meaning as J. 86. 42, that none can 'consummate bliss without being Generated on Earth', that is to say, regeneration can only come through mundane life. Death here may emphasize the fallen state of the Spectres ; or since the new sphere of existence is higher than the state of war, it may be used in the sense that birth into the new existence demands rejection of the old errors.
100–103 Feeling . . . pain] *marginal addition*, marked to come in here. The first word is written 'Feelling'.
104–108 Terrified . . . Deadly] *marginal addition* : position not indicated.
105 hermaphrodite] male *1st rdg. del.* See Index, *Hermaphrodite*.
113–123 Cp. F. Z. vi. 113 *note*.
114 Inspir'd . . . Enitharmon] *an addition*. See Index, *Human Form*.

They seem to one another, laughing terrible among the banners ;
And when, the revolution of their day of battles over,
Relapsing in dire torment, they return to forms of woe,
To moping visages returning, inanimate tho' furious,
No more erect tho' strong, drawn out in length they ravin
For senseless gratification ; & their visages, thrust forth,
Flatten above & beneath, & stretch out into beastial length.
Weaken'd, they stretch beyond their power in dire droves, till war begins,
Or secret religion in their temples before secret shrines.

And Urizen gave life & sense by his immortal power
To all his Engines of deceit, that linkèd chains might run
Thro' ranks of war spontaneous, & that hooks & boring screws
Might act according to their forms by innate cruelty.
He formèd also harsh instruments of sound
To grate the soul into destruction, or to inflame with fury
The spirits of life, to pervert all the faculties of sense
Into their own destruction ; if perhaps he might avert
His own despair, even at the cost of every thing that breathes.

Thus in the temple of the Sun his books of iron & brass
And silver & gold he consecrated, reading incessantly
To myriads of perturbèd spirits. Thro' the universe
They propagated the deadly words, the Shadowy Female absorbing
The enormous Sciences of Urizen, ages after ages exploring
The fell destruction. And she said : 'O Urizen, Prince of Light,
What words of Dread pierce my faint Ear, what falling snows around
My feeble limbs infold my destin'd misery !
I alone dare the lash abide, to sit beneath the blast
Unhurt, & dare the inclement forehead of the King of light
From dark abysses of the times remote fated to be
[5] The Sorrower of Eternity, in love with tears. Submiss I rear
My Eyes to thy Pavilions : hear my prayer for Luvah's sake !
I see the murderer of my Luvah clothèd in robes of blood,
He who assum'd my Luvah's throne in times of Everlasting.

131–132 Cp. F. Z. iii. 1–22 for a statement of Urizen's cause of despair.
132 avert] invert *1st rdg.* 133 Cp. B. U., chap. ii, l. 33 *note.*
137 Urizen's 'enormous Sciences' are his Laws and Religions.
139 falling] *a dubious reading : indistinctly written.*
146–147 Cp. *supra*, ll. 56–57. There is no other passage where Jesus is called the murderer of Luvah : possibly the words are put into Vala's

Where hast thou hid him whom I love? in what remote Abyss
Resides that God of my delight? O, might my eyes behold
My Luvah! then could I deliver all the sons of God
From Bondage of these terrors, & with influences sweet,
As once in those eternal fields, in brotherhood & Love
United, we should live in bliss as those who sinnèd not.
The Eternal Man is seal'd by thee, never to be deliver'd.
We are all servants to thy will. O King of Light! relent
Thy furious power: be our father & our lovèd King!
But if my Luvah is no more, If thou hast smitten him
And laid him in the Sepulcher, Or if thou wilt revenge
His murder on another, Silent I bow with dread.
But happiness can never [come] to thee, O King, nor me;
For he was source of every joy that this mysterious tree
Unfolds in Allegoric fruit. When shall the dead revive?
Can that which has existed cease; or can love & life Expire? '

Urizen heard the Voice & saw the Shadow underneath
His woven darkness; & in laws & deceitful religions,
Beginning at the tree of Mystery, circling its root,
She spread herself thro' all the branches in the power of Orc,
A shapeless & indefinite cloud, in tears of sorrow incessant
Steeping the Direful Web of Religion. Swagging heavy it fell
From heaven to heaven, thro' all its meshes altering the Vortexes,
Misplacing every Center. Hungry desire & lust began
Gathering the fruit of that Mysterious tree, till Urizen
Sitting within his temple, furious felt the numming Stupor,
Himself tangled in his own net in sorrow, lust, repentance.

Enitharmon wove in tears, Singing Songs of Lamentations

mouth as part of the dramatic treatment of the symbol in its antagonism to vision.

150–153 That 'these terrors' are the 'simple rules of life' associated with the 'Human Nature', the 'Divine Vision', is clear from the earlier reading of l. 151. Cp. J. 28. 6 *note*.

151 these terrors] the human form *1st rdg. del.*

157 If thou] if that thou [*word illeg.*] *1st rdg. del.*

158 if thou] if that *1st rdg.*

160 A word appears to have been omitted in MS., probably 'come'.

162 Cp. J. 30. 18 *note*.

164 Vala is the 'Shadow' of Enitharmon: cp. F. Z. vii. 317 *note*.

167 See above, l. 78. This line may be connected with the fragment of an Orc myth on extra p. 17 of *Milton*. It apparently restates the notion that the errors of the rational mind summarized in the Tree and the Web are effective in enslaving mankind only when they can be made to appeal under a form that moves the emotions (cp. F. Z. vii. 164–165 and Introductory Note to that Night). 173 'numming' a dubious reading.

And pitying comfort as she sigh'd forth on the wind the spectres,
And wove them bodies, calling them her belovèd sons & daughters,
Employing the daughters in her looms ; & Los employ'd the Sons
In Golgonooza's Furnaces, among the Anvils of time & space ;
Thus forming a Vast family, wondrous in beauty & love.
And they appear'd a Universal female form, created
From those who were dead in Ulro, from the spectres of the dead :
[6] And Enitharmon nam'd the Female Jerusalem the holy.
Wond'ring she saw the Lamb of God within Jerusalem's Veil,
The Divine Vision seen within the inmost deep recess
Of fair Jerusalem's bosom in a gently beaming fire.

Then sang the Sons of Eden round the Lamb of God, & said :
'Glory ! Glory ! Glory ! to the holy Lamb of God,
Who now beginneth to put off the dark Satanic body !
Now we behold redemption. Now we know that life Eternal
Depends alone upon the Universal hand, & not in us
Is aught but death, In individual weakness, sorrow & pain.
[1*] We behold with wonder Enitharmon's Looms & Los's Forges,
And the Spindles of Tirzah & Rahab and the Mills of Satan & Beelzeboul.
In Golgonooza Los's Anvils stand & his Furnaces rage.
Ten thousand Demons labour at the forges, Creating Continually
The times & spaces of Mortal Life, the Sun, the Moon, the Stars ;
In periods of Pulsative furor beating into wedges & bars,

178 See Index, *Los, Note II.* ii.

183 The identification of the redeemed sons and daughters of Los and Enitharmon with Jerusalem is peculiar to this Night.

189 For the content of the symbol 'Satanic body', cp. M. 42. 34–43. 28, and see Index, *Incarnation*, II, *b*.

190–192 Cp. J. 45. 3–16.

After l. 192 Blake has written 'We behold with wonder &c'. This refers to a passage on the first added page, 1*.

193 We . . . wonder] 'Daughter of Beulah, describe' *1st rdg. del.*

194 For Rahab and Tirzah see Index, *Vala*. Beelzeboul] Baal *1st rdg.* Beelzeboul (Βεελζεβούλ, Matt. xii. 24) does not add anything to what is already implied in the symbol 'Satan': see Index, *Spectre, Note II, b.*

After l. 195 *two lines del.* :

The hard dentant hammers are lull'd by the flute, lula, lula ;
The bellowing furnaces blown by the long-sounding Clarion.

196–208 Cp. M. 27 *passim.* The Demons are children of Los ; cp. M. 23. 74–75 : 31. 17–23. 197 wedges] bars *1st rdg. del.*

Then drawing into wires, the terrific Passions & Affections
Of Spectrous dead. Thence to the Looms of Cathedron convey'd,
The Daughters of Enitharmon weave the ovarium & the integument
In soft silk drawn from their own bowels in lascivious delight
With songs of sweetest cadence to the turning spindle & reel
Lulling the weeping spectres of the dead, Clothing their limbs
With gifts & gold of Eden. Astonish'd, stupified with Delight,
The terrors put on their sweet clothing on the banks of Arnon,
Whence they plunge into the river of space for a period, till
The dread Sleep of Ulro is past. But Satan, Og, & Sihon
Build Mills of resistless wheels to unwind the soft threads & reveal,
Naked of their clothing, the poor spectres before the accusing heavens;
While Rahab & Tirzah far different mantles prepare, webs of torture,
Mantles of despair, girdles of bitter compunction, shoes of indolence,
Veils of ignorance, covering from head to feet with a cold web.
We look down into Ulro; we behold the Wonders of the Grave.
Eastward of Golgonooza stands the Lake of Udan Adan In
Entuthon Benithon, a Lake not of Waters, but of Spaces,
Perturb'd, black & deadly: on its Islands & its Margins
The Mills of Satan & Beelzeboul stand round the roots of Urizen's tree;

201 Integument] See Index, *Weaving*, III. No interpretation has been found for 'ovarium'.

206 Arnon] the Moon *1st rdg. del.* According to J. 89. 25, the river Arnon, constantly associated with error by reason, apparently, of its geographical position in relation to the heathen peoples of Bashan and Moab, was once called Pison, and was therefore one of the four rivers of Paradise. Hence its change of name is symbolic of the Fall. In the present passage, however, Blake uses the name in a somewhat different way, by making the fact that when the Israelites crossed it after their wanderings in the wilderness, they entered into their inheritance of the Promised Land, the symbol of the beginning of regeneration.

207 The 'river of space' is mortal life, 'the sea of time and space' (R., p. 100). 208 *After* Satan *a word del. illegible.*

208–213 Cp. M. 28. 51–63.

213 The Web is the Web of Religion: see Index, *Weaving*, I.

214 We . . . Grave] *an addition.* The Grave is the state of error; Ulro, Void, Chaos, Udan Adan and Enthuthon Benython are equivalent symbols: see Index, *Ulro.*

216 a Lake] it is *1st rdg. del.*

217 its] the *1st rdg. del.* its Margins] the Margins of this Lake *1st rdg.*

For this Lake is form'd from the tears & sighs & death sweat of the Victims
Of Urizen's laws, to irrigate the roots of the tree of Mystery.
They unweave the soft threads; then they weave them anew in the forms
Of dark death & despair, & none from Eternity to Eternity could Escape.
But thou, O Universal Humanity, who is One Man, blessèd for Ever,
Receivest the Integuments woven. Rahab beholds the Lamb of God;
She smites with her knife of flint; she destroys her own work
Times upon times, thinking to destroy the Lamb blessèd for Ever.
He puts off the Clothing of blood; he redeems the spectres from their bonds;
He awakes the sleepers in Ulro; the Daughters of Beulah praise him;
They anoint his feet with ointment; they wipe them with the hair of their head.

[6] 'We now behold the Ends of Beulah, & we now behold
Where Death Eternal is put off Eternally.
Assume the dark Satanic body in the Virgin's womb,
O Lamb divine! it cannot thee annoy. O pitying one!
Thy pity is from the foundation of the World, & thy Redemption
Begun Already in Eternity. Come then, O Lamb of God!
Come, Lord Jesus! come quickly!'

So sang they in Eternity, looking down into Beulah.
The war roar'd round Jerusalem's Gates; it took a hideous form;
Seen in the aggregate, a Vast Hermaphroditic form
Heav'd like an Earthquake, lab'ring with convulsive groans
Intolerable. At length an awful wonder burst
From the Hermaphroditic bosom; Satan he was nam'd,
Son of Perdition; terrible his form, dishumaniz'd, monstrous,
A male without a female counterpart, a howling fiend

223 thou, O] All *1st rdg. del.*
223–236 See Index, *Incarnation* and *Crucifixion.*
235 Begun Already] Already *1st rdg.*
238–249 See Index, *Spectre, Note II, b.*
239 See Index, *Hermaphrodite.*
240 Heav'd like] Heaving [*word illegible*], *1st rdg. del.*
244 The 'female counterpart' or emanation is the capacity for vision or sometimes the vision itself: see Index, *Emanation,* I. So in l. 268 Vala

Fo[r]lorn of Eden, & repugnant to the forms of life ;
Yet hiding the shadowy female Vala as in an ark & Curtains ;
Abhorr'd, accursèd, ever dying an Eternal Death,
Being multitudes of tyrant Men in union blasphemous
Against the Divine image, Congregated Assemblies of wicked men.

Los said to Enitharmon : ' Pitying I saw,
Pitying the Lamb of God Descended thro' Jerusalem's gates,
To put off Mystery time after time ; & as a Man
Is born on Earth, so was he born of Fair Jerusalem,
In mystery's woven mantle & in the Robes of Luvah.

' He stood in fair Jerusalem to awake up into Eden
The fallen Man ; but first to Give his vegetated body
To be cut off & separated, that the Spiritual body may be Reveal'd.'

[7] The Lamb of God stood before Satan opposite
In Entuthon Benithon, in the shadows of torments & woe,
Upon the heights of Amalek : taking refuge in his arms,
The Victims fled from punishment; for all his words were peace.

Urizen call'd together the Synagogue of Satan in dire Sanhedrim
To judge the Lamb of God to Death as a murderer & robber :
As it is written, he was number'd among the transgressors.

Cold, dark, opake, the Assembly met twelvefold in Amalek,
Twelve rocky unshap'd forms, terrific forms of torture & woe.

is a ' False Feminine Counterpart ' ; that is, in this instance, the body of falsified perceptions, the sum of moral and perceptual error.

245 Cp. J. 50. 4–5 :

a Providence oppos'd to the Divine Lord Jesus,
A murderous Providence, A Creation that groans, living on Death.

246 Yet . . . curtains] *an addition.*

250 Los . . . saw] *an addition.* The interpolation disturbs the whole passage. The words between ' said ' and ' Pitying ' are indistinctly written.

251–257 See Index, *Incarnation* and *Crucifixion.* ' Mystery ', ' mystery's woven mantle ', the ' Robes of Luvah ', and the ' Vegetated Body ' all symbolize the moral and metaphysical errors of mundane life, in contrast to the truth of Eternity, the ' Spiritual Body '. Jesus, by ' annihilating ' them, putting them off from his ' real and immortal self ', reveals their falsity.

256 Give his vegetated body] rend the Veil of Mystery *1st rdg. del.* After l. 256 a line deleted :

And then Call Urizen & Luvah & Tharmas & Urthona.

260 Amalek, and the other races who opposed the Israelites either before or after their entry into Canaan, are constantly used to symbolize the state of moral error.

261 The Victims are those subject to the repressive operation of Natural Religion.

Such seem'd the Synagogue to distant view: amidst them beam'd
A False Feminine Counterpart of Lovely Delusive Beauty,
Dividing & Uniting at will in the Cruelties of Holiness,
Vala, drawn down into a Vegetated body, now triumphant.
The Synagogue of Satan Clothèd her with Scarlet robes & Gems,
And on her forehead was her name written in blood, ' Mystery.'
When view'd remote, She is One; when view'd near, she divides
To multitude: as it is in Eden, so permitted because
It was the best possible, in the State call'd Satan, to Save
From Death Eternal & to put off Satan Eternally.
The Synagogue Created her from Fruit of Urizen's tree
By Devilish arts abominable, unlawful, unutterable;
Perpetually vegetating in detestable births
Of female forms, beautiful thro' poisons hidden in secret
Which give a tincture to false beauty. There was hidden within
The bosom of Satan The false Female, as in an ark & veil,
Which Christ must rend & her reveal. Her daughters are Call'd
Tirzah; She is nam'd Rahab; their various divisions are call'd
The daughters of Amalek, Canaan & Moab, binding on the Stones
Their victims, & with knives tormenting them, singing with tears
Over their victims. Hear ye the song of the Females of Amalek:

267 amidst] around *1st rdg. del.* beam'd] stood *1st rdg. del.*
268–284 A False . . . call'd] *marginal addition*, marked for insertion here.
269 The ' Cruelties of Holiness ' refer to the tyranny of the Moral Law.
270 Vala . . . triumphant] *an addition*: cp. Rev. xvii. 5.
273–274 Cp. *Cat.*: 1810. 'These various states I have seen in my imagination: when distant they appear as one man, but as you approach they appear as multitudes of nations.'
274–276 The relation of these lines to their context is not clear: they seem to state the doctrine that Providence permits all things, even the temporary triumph of anti-spiritual powers, ' lest man should fall into Eternal Death.'
281 There was hidden within] therefore they were call'd *1st rdg. del.*
282 ' The daughters, &c.' deleted at the beginning of the line.
284 The names Tirzah, Rahab, and Vala are practically interchangeable among these persons of the myth, though Blake sometimes attempts to differentiate them. nam'd] call'd *1st rdg. del.*
285 Amalek] *an addition.* Stones] Stems *1st rdg. del.*

'O thou poor human form ! O thou poor child of woe !
Why dost thou wander away from Tirzah ? why me compell to bind thee ?
If thou dost go away from me, I shall consume upon the rocks.
These fibres of thine eyes, that used to wander in distant heavens
Away from me, I have bound down with a hot iron.
These nostrils, that Expanded with delight in morning skies,
I have bent downward with lead molten in my roaring furnaces.
My soul is seven furnaces ; incessant roars the bellows
Upon my terribly flaming heart ; the molten metal runs
In channels thro' my fiery limbs. O love ! O pity ! O pains !
O the pangs, the bitter pangs, of love forsaken !
Ephraim was a wilderness of joy where all my wild beasts ran.
The river Kanah wander'd by my sweet Manasseh's side.
Go, Noah ! fetch the girdle of strong brass ; heat it red hot ;
Press it around the loins of this expanding cruelty.
Shriek not so, my only love.
Bind him down, Sisters, bind him down on Ebal, mount of Cursing !
Malah, come forth from Lebanon, & Hoglah from Mount Sinai !
Come ! circumscribe this tongue of sweets, & with a Screw of iron
Fasten this Ear into the Rock. Milcah, the task is thine.
Weep not so, sisters, weep not so ! our life depends on this ;
Or mercy & truth are fled away from Shechem & Mount Gilead,
Unless my belovèd is bound upon the Stems of Vegetation.'

288–310 Cp. J. 67. 44–68. 9, where these lines are repeated with a few slight verbal changes.

290 Error ceases to exist as soon as Man refuses to accept it as true. The following passages, where the symbol 'Woman' stands for the errors of mundane life, support this :

If once a Delusion be found
Woman must perish & the Heavens of Heavens [i. e. Natural Religion] remain no more. (J. 80. 14–15.)

291–294 The alteration of the organs of perceptions, whereby the illusion of physical reality with its ethical corollary is set up, is the peculiar function of the Female in Blake's symbolism. Cp. J. 66. 35–56 and 83. 33–48.

After l. 300 *line deleted* :

To see the boy spring into heavens sounding from my sight.

301–311 Noah, Malah, Hoglah, Milcah and Tirzah, the daughters of Zelophehad of the tribe of Manasseh (M. 28. 58, and Num. xxviii. 1), all appear as feminine symbols, particularly in *Milton*. Their significance is that of the last-named sister, Tirzah : see Index, *Vala, Note I*, C.

304–307 This again refers to the alteration of the organs of perception by the 'Female' powers : see above, ll. 291–294.

309 The 'mercy & truth' here referred to are the delusions of Natural

Such are the songs of Tirzah, such the loves of Amalek.
The Lamb of God descended thro' the twelve portions of Luvah,
Bearing his sorrows, & [? recieving] all his cruel wounds.
[8] Thus was the Lamb of God condemn'd to Death:
They nail'd him upon the tree of Mystery, weeping over him,
And then mocking & then worshipping, calling him Lord & King.
Sometimes as twelve daughters lovely, & sometimes as five,
They stood in beaming beauty; & sometimes as one, even Rahab,
Who is Mystery, Babylon the Great, the Mother of Harlots.

Jerusalem saw the Body dead upon the Cross. She fled away
Saying: 'Is this Eternal Death? Where shall I hide from Death?
Pity me, Los! pity me, Urizen! & let us build
A Sepulcher & worship Death in fear, while yet we live—
Death, God of All, from whom we rise, to whom we all return.
And Let all Nations of the Earth worship at the Sepulcher
With Gifts & Spices, with lamps rich emboss'd, jewels & gold.'

Religion, with which also Shechem is associated, on the analogy of its relation to Jerusalem in Jewish history, as the capital of Rehoboam's kingdom. For Gilead cp. F. Z. viii. 2 *note*.

312 The significance of the 'twelve portions' is not apparent. Another use of 'twelve', probably symbolic, is in ll. 265–266 above.

314–316 See Index, *Crucifixion*.

315 The Stems of Vegetation are equivalent to the Tree of Mystery: see Index, *Mundane Shell, Note I*, B. As in the case of Fuzon and Orc, the binding of the beloved symbolizes the imposition of the restraints of moral law.

317 The 'twelve' are the 'Daughters of Albion' (see Index, *Vala*): the 'five' may be the five Daughters of Zelophehad: see above, l. 302 *note*

318–319 See Index, *Vala*.

320 Jerusalem] She *1st rdg. del.*

321–329 Saying . . . Eternal] *marginal addition* marked for addition here. Cp. J. 61. 49–51. The assigning of these lines to Jerusalem brings out very clearly what is noticeable elsewhere, that Blake regarded the highest visionary endowment in mortality as intermittent: here Jerusalem and Los mistakenly regard the death of the Body as the final triumph of moral law: see Index, *Crucifixion*. The Sepulchre represents the state wherein the spiritual energies are atrophied by the repressive law. Cp. J. 80. 27–29:

But I, Vala, Luvah's daughter, keep his [Man's] body embalm'd in moral laws,
With spices of sweet odours of lovely jealous stupefaction
Within my bosom, lest he arise to life & slay my Luvah.

The 'Body' is the body of error or 'Death' which was 'put off', that is rejected as false, upon the Cross: it is equivalent to the 'Mantle of Luvah' (l. 330), the 'Mantle of Laws' (M. 40. 30). Cp. F. Z. ix. 4–5. At the end of this marginal passage, Blake notes '"But when Rahab, &c.": turn back 3 leaves'. The passage indicated is found on two added sheets (pp. 1*, 2*, and 3*). 322 *After* '&' *a word del., perhaps* Luvah.

Los took the Body from the Cross, Jerusalem weeping over.
They bore it to the Sepulcher which Los had hewn in the rock
Of Eternity: for himself he hew'd it, despairing of Life
    Eternal.

1* But when Rahab had cut off the Mantle of Luvah from
The Lamb of God, it roll'd apart, revealing to all in heaven
And all on Earth the Temple & the Synagogue of Satan, &
    Mystery,
Even Rahab in all her turpitude. Rahab divided herself.
She stood before Los in her Pride among the Furnaces,
Dividing & uniting in Delusive feminine pomp, questioning
    him.
He answer'd her with tenderness & love, not uninspir'd.
Los sat upon his anvil stock; they sat beside the forge.
Los wip'd the sweat from his red brow & thus began
To the delusive female forms shining among his furnaces:

'I am that shadowy Prophet who, Six thousand years ago,
Fell from my station in the Eternal bosom. I divided
To multitude, & my multitudes are children of Care & Labour.
O Rahab! I behold thee. I was once like thee, a Son
Of Pride, and I also have pierc'd the Lamb of God in pride
    & wrath.
Hear me repeat my Generations, that thou maist also repent.
[2*] And these are the Sons of Los & Enitharmon: Rintrah,
    Palamabron,
Theotormon, Bromion, Antamon, Ananton, Ozoth, Ohana,
Sotha, Mydon, Ellayol, Natho, Gon, Harhath, Satan,
Har, Ochim, Ijim, Adam, Reuben, Simeon, Levi, Judah, Dan,
    Naphtali,
Gad, Asher, Issachar, Zebulun, Joseph, Benjamin, David,
    Solomon,
Paul, Constantine, Charlemaine, Luther, Milton.

330 But] And *1st rdg. del.*
330–336 But . . . uninspir'd] *written over erasure.*
334 among the Furnaces] above the Furnaces *1st rdg.*
339 To the . . . furnaces] *an addition.*
340–341 I . . . bosom] This sentence is repeated M. 20. 15–16. The fall can only be related to that of Urthona. Cp. F. Z. i. 210–223: vii. 276–295.
346 are] were *1st rdg. del.* Of the names in ll. 347–348 Ananton, Ohana, Mydon, Ellayol, Natho, Gon, Harhath and Ochim (l. 349) occur nowhere else, nor can any source be discovered for them.
349 Ochim, Ijim] *an addition.* For Ijim see *Tiriel*, § 4. The twelve sons of Israel appear as the sons of Los in *Milton* and *Jerusalem*: cp. J. 16. 35 *note*, and see Index, *Los.*
351 Paul . . . Milton] *an addition.* Paul, Constantine, Charlemaine, and Luther, reappear in *Milton* and *Jerusalem*, not as sons of Los, but as

These are our daughters: Ocalythron, Elynittria, Oothoon, Leutha,
Elythiria, Enanto, Manathu-Vorcyon, Ethinthus, Moab, Midian,
Adah, Zillah, Caina, Naamah, Tamar, Rahab, Tirzah, Mary,
And myriads more of Sons & Daughters to whom our love increas'd,
To each according to the multiplication of their multitudes.
But Satan accus'd Palamabron before his brethren; also he madden'd
The horses of Palamabron's harrow: wherefore Rintrah & Palamabron
Cut him off from Golgonooza. But Enitharmon in tears
Wept over him, Created him a Space clos'd with a tender moon;
And he roll'd down beneath the fires of Orc, a Globe immense,
Crusted with snow, in a dim void. Here by the Arts of Urizen
He tempted many of the Sons & Daughters of Los to flee
Away from Me. First Reuben fled, then Simeon, then Levi, then Judah,
Then Dan, then Naphtali, then Gad, then Asher, then Issachar,
Then Zebulun, then Joseph, then Benjamin, twelve sons of Los.
And this is the manner in which Satan became the Tempter.

'There is a State nam'd Satan—learn distinct to know, O Rahab,

Churches, that is, aspects of the general error of formal Religion. The names of the warlike champions of Christianity, Constantine and Charlemaine, are used to establish Blake's criticism that religion, when it denies Imagination and the mystical doctrine of Brotherhood, is in its essence War (see M. Preface, *note* 2). The significance of Luther in this connexion is best shown in the passage M. 22. 47–50:

Remember how Calvin and Luther in fury premature
Sow'd War and stern division between Papists & Protestants.
Let it not be so now. O go not forth in Martyrdoms & Wars!
We [Los and his sons] were plac'd here by the Universal Brotherhood & Mercy.

Milton is the theologian of *Paradise Lost*, Paul of the Epistles which Blake omits from his Canon of the Scriptures (J. 48. 4–11).

352 are our] were their *1st rdg. del.* 355 our] their *1st rdg. del.*

357 his brethren] Los *1st rdg. del.*

357–385 Cp. M. pp. 5–11, where this myth of Satan and Palamabron is expanded. See also Introduction to *Milton*.

363–367 Cp. M. 22. 62–23. 4. It has not been found possible to suggest an interpretation of this passage.

364 Me] Los *1st rdg. del.* 367 twelve sons of Los] *an addition.*

368 Rahab] Mortals *1st rdg.* See Index, *States*.

The difference between States & Individuals of those States.
The State nam'd Satan never can be redeem'd in all Eternity :
But when Luvah in Orc became a Serpent, he descended into
That State call'd Satan. Enitharmon breath'd forth on the Winds
Of Golgonooza her well belovèd, knowing he was Orc's human remains.
She tenderly lov'd him above all his brethren ; he grew up
In mother's tenderness. The Enormous worlds rolling in Urizen's power
Must have given Satan by these mild arts Dominion over all ;
Wherefore Palamabron, being accus'd by Satan to Los,
Call'd down a Great Solemn assembly. Rintrah in fury & fire
Defended Palamabron, & rage fill'd the Universal Tent.
Because Palamabron was good natur'd, Satan suppos'd he fear'd him.
And Satan, not having the Science of Wrath, but only of Pity,
Was soon condemn'd, & wrath was left to wrath, & Pity to Pity.
Rintrah & Palamabron Cut sheer off from Golgonooza
Enitharmon's Moony Space & in it Satan & his companions.
They roll'd down, a dim world, Crusted with Snow, deadly & dark.
Jerusalem, pitying them, wove them mantles of life & death
Times after times. And those in Eden sent Lucifer for their Guard.
Lucifer refus'd to die for Satan, & in pride he forsook his charge.
Then they sent Molech. Molech was impatient. They Sent—
Molech impatient—They Sent Elohim, who created Adam
To die for Satan. Adam refus'd, but was compell'd to die
By Satan's arts. Then the Eternals Sent Shaddai.
Shaddai was angry. Pachad descended. Pachad was terrified,
And then they Sent Jehovah who, leprous, stretch'd his hand to Eternity.

377 Wherefore Palamabron] Wherefore Rintrah & Palamabron *1st rdg.*
380 Because . . . him] *an addition.* 381–385 Cp. M. 7. 46 *note.*
387–395 Cp. F. Z. i. 244–246 and M. 11. 12–29. These are the 'Seven Eyes of God', commanded to labour for Man's regeneration : cp. Rev. v. 6 : 'And I beheld, and, lo, in the midst of the throne and of the four beasts, and in the midst of the elders, stood a Lamb as it had been slain, having seven horns and seven eyes, which are the seven Spirits of God sent forth into all the earth.' In the present passage, as in M. 11. 12–29, all save the seventh, Jesus, fail; but in M. 14. 3–7: 35. 64–65: 36. 4–5 and extra p. 32*. 9, the 'seven Eyes of God' are represented as channels of inspiration to mortal man, supporting, comforting, and instructing him. Moreover, Jesus is normally the Divine Humanity and not merely one of its agents.
394 In the prophetic books preceding *Jerusalem*, the Jehovah of the

Then Jesus Came, & Died willing beneath Tirzah & Rahab.
Thou art that Rahab. Lo, the Tomb ! what can we purpose more ?
[3*] Lo, Enitharmon, terrible & beautiful in Eternal youth !
Bow down before her, you her children, & set Jerusalem free ! '

Rahab, burning with pride & revenge, departed from Los.
Los drop'd a tear at her departure, but he wip'd it away in hope.
She went to Urizen in pride : the Prince of Light beheld,
Reveal'd before the face of heaven, his secret holiness.

[8] Darkness & sorrow cover'd all flesh. Eternity was darken'd.

Urizen sitting in his web of deceitful Religion
Felt the female death, a dull & numming stupor, such as ne'er
Before assaulted the bright human form : he felt his pores
Drink in the deadly dull delusion : horrors of Eternal Death
Shot thro' him. Urizen sat stonied upon his rock.
Forgetful of his own Laws, pitying he began to Embrace
The shadowy Female. Since life cannot be quench'd, Life exuded.
His eyes shot outwards : then his breathing nostrils drawn forth,
Scales cover'd over a cold forehead & a neck outstretch'd
Into the deep to sieze the shadow. Scales his neck & bosom
Cover'd, & scales his hands & feet. Upon his belly falling
Outstretch'd thro' the immense, his mouth wide opening, tongueless,
His teeth a triple row, he strove to sieze the shadow in vain,
And his immense tail lash'd the Abyss : his human form a Stone,

Pentateuch is commonly identified with Satan : see Index, *Jesus*, &c., III. He is represented, somewhat after the Gnostic doctrine, as a recusant spirit, creating this world and the mortal body, with the moral law, against Imagination and Divine Brotherhood and Love. Cp. Crabb Robinson, *Letter to Dorothy Wordsworth*, ' " For whoever believes in Nature," said Mr B[lake] " disbelieves in God, for Nature is the work of the Devil ". On my obtaining from him the declaration that the Bible was the Word of God, I referred him to Genesis " In the beginning God created the heavens and the earth ". But I gained nothing by this, for I was triumphantly told that this God was not Jehovah, but the Elohim ; and the doctrine of the Gnostics was repeated with sufficient consistency to silence one so unlearned as myself.' Cp. E. G., ζ, ll. 29–42.

396 Thou art . . . more] *an addition.* 400 Los . . . hope] *an addition.*

After l. 402 Blake notes ' " Darkness & sorrow &c ", turn over leaf '. This refers back to MS. p. 8.

404 Religion] Religion, was darken'd *1st rdg.*

405 Felt] He felt *1st rdg.* 410–442 See Index, *Serpent.*

415 thro'] *2nd rdg.* : *1st rdg. illegible, del.*

A form of Senseless Stone, remain'd in terrors on the rock,
Abominable to the eyes of mortals who explore his books.
His wisdom still remain'd, & all his memory stor'd with woe.

And still his stony form remain'd in the Abyss, immense,
Like the pale visage in its sheet of lead, that cannot follow.
Incessant stern disdain his scaly form gnaws inwardly,
With deep repentance for the loss of that fair form of Man.
With Envy he saw Los, with Envy Tharmas & the Spectre.
With envy & in vain he swam around his stony form.

No longer now Erect, the King of Light, outstretch'd in fury,
Lashes his tail in the wild deep : his Eyelids, like the Sun
Arising in his pride, enlighten all the Grizly deeps ;
His scales transparent give forth light like windows of the morning ;
His neck flames with wrath & majesty ; he lashes the Abyss,
Beating the desarts & the rocks : the desarts feel his power ;
They shake their slumbers off. They wave in awful fear,
Calling the Lion & the Tyger, the horse & the wild Stag,
[9] The Elephant, the wolf, the Bear, the Lamia, the Satyr.
His Eyelids give their light around ; his folding tail aspires
Among the stars ; the Earth & all the Abysses feel hot fury
When, as the snow covers the mountains, oft petrific hardness
Covers the deeps : at his vast fury mo[a]ning in his rock,
Hardens the Lion, & the Bear trembling in the Solid mountain :
They view the light, & wonder, crying out, in terrible existence
Up bound : the wild stag & the horse behold the King of Pride.

Oft doth his Eyes emerge from the Abyss into the realms
Of his Eternal day, & memory strives to augment his ruthfulness.
Then weeping he descends in wrath, drawing all things in his fury
Into obedience to his will : & now he finds in vain

425 the Spectre] Urthona *1st rdg. del.* 428 wild] wide *1st rdg. del.* 438 hardness] hardness covers *1st rdg.* 442 behold] beholds *1st rdg.*

446–454 Here as elsewhere in the preceding Nights, Urizen is represented as subject to some undefined form of control : see F. Z. vi. 142 *note.* In the present instance there is good ground for identifying it with a beneficent providence, 'permitting all things lest man should fall into Eternal Death.' In *Night III*, ll. 13–22, where Urizen foretells that Orc shall dominate him in the manner here described in ll. 449–450, mention is made of 'the Eternal One' as the supreme power, without any explanation of the term. The matter is still further confused by the apparently

That not of his own power he bore the human form erect,
Nor of his own will gave his Laws in times of Everlasting.
For now fierce Orc in wrath & fury rises into the heavens,
A King of wrath & fury, a dark enragèd horror.
And Urizen, repentant, forgets his wisdom in the abyss
In forms of priesthood, in the dark delusions of repentance,
Repining in his heart & spirit that Orc reign'd over all,
And that his wisdom serv'd but to augment the indefinite lust.

Then Tharmas & Urthona felt the stony stupor rise
Into their limbs. Urthona shot forth a Vast Fibrous form:
Tharmas like a pillar of sand roll'd round by the whirlwind,
An animated Pillar rolling round & round in incessant rage.

Los felt the stony stupor, & his head roll'd down beneath
Into the Abysses of his bosom: the vessels of his blood
Dart forth upon the wind in pipes writhing about in the Abyss.
And Enitharmon, pale & cold, in milky juices flow'd
Into a form of Vegetation, living, having a voice,
Moving in rootlike fibres, trembling in fear upon the Earth.

And Tharmas gave his Power to Los. Urthona gave his Strength
Into the youthful Prophet, for the Love of Enitharmon
And of the nameless Shadowy female in the nether deep,
And for the dread of the dark terrors of Orc & Urizen.

Thus in a living death the nameless shadow all things bound,
All mortal things made permanent, that they may be put off
Time after time by the Divine Lamb who died for all:
And all in him died, & he put off all mortality.

necessitarian basis of the greater part of the earlier written parts of *The Four Zoas*.

After l. 449 a line identical with l. 452 is deleted.

451 repentant, forgets] forgets repentant *1st rdg.*: the transposition is indicated by numerals over the words affected.

452 Blake regarded repentance as part of the delusion of morality; he speaks later (J. 43. 75) of 'the infection of Sin & stern Repentance'; and describes the state figuratively as 'the struggles of intanglements with incoherent roots'. Cp. also the language of Albion in prayer to the deluding image of a transcendent deity: F. Z. iii. 55–60.

459–464 For a similar change in Enitharmon cp. J. 86. 50–61. In both instances there appears to be a wholly inexplicable disturbance in the spiritual nature of Los immediately preceding the consummation of his regenerative labours.

465–468 Cp. J. 44. 28–31.

470–472 All . . . mortality] *an addition* Cp. J. 12. 10–15.

[10] Tharmas on high rode furious thro' the afflicted worlds,
Pursuing the Vain Shadow of Hope, fleeing from identity
In abstract false Expanses, that he may not hear the Voice
Of Ahania wailing on the winds: in vain he flies, for still
The voice incessant calls on all the children of Men;
For she spoke of all in heaven & all upon the Earth.
[She] Saw not as yet the Divine vision: her Eyes are toward Urizen,
And thus Ahania cries aloud to the Caverns of the Grave:

'Will you keep a flock of wolves & lead them? will you take the wintry blast
For a covering to your limbs, or the summer pestilence for a tent to abide in?
Will you erect a lasting habitation in the mouldering Church yard,
Or a pillar & palace of Eternity in the jaws of the hungry grave?
Will you seek pleasure from the festering wound, or marry for a Wife
The ancient Leprosy, that the King & Priest may still feast on your decay,
And the grave mock & laugh at the plow'd field, saying:
"I am the nourisher, thou the destroyer: in my bosom is milk & wine,
And a fountain from my breasts: to me come all multitudes;
To my breath they obey, they worship me. I am a goddess & queen?"
But listen to Ahania, O ye sons of the Murder'd one,
Listen to her whose memory beholds your ancient days:
Listen to her whose eyes behold the dark body of corruptible death,
Looking for Urizen in vain. In vain I seek for morning.
The Eternal Man sleeps in the Earth, nor feels the vig'rous sun,
Nor silent moon, nor all the hosts of heaven move in his body.
His fiery halls are dark, & round his limbs the Serpent Orc,
Fold without fold, incompasses him, And his corrup[?ting] members
Vomit out the scaly monsters of the restless deep.

473 on high] above *1st rdg. del.*

474 The 'Vain Shadow of Hope' would seem to be Enion.

478–479 For . . . Urizen] *an addition*. 'She' seems to have been omitted at the beginning of l. 479.

483–484 Cp. V. D. A. 152–153.

495 This would appear to be a reference to the 'tradition' of Albion: see Index, *Albion* I. Cp. also l. 549 below.

They come up in the rivers, & annoy the nether parts
Of Man who lays upon the Shores, leaning his faded head
Upon the Oozy rock, inwrappèd with the weeds of death.
His eyes sink hollow in his head, his flesh cover'd with slime
And shrunk up to the bones: alas, that Man should come to this,
His strong bones beat with snows & hid within the caves of night,
Marrowless, bloodless, falling into dust, driven by the winds!
O, how the horrors of Eternal Death take hold on Man!
His faint groans shake the caves, & issue thro' the desolate rocks.
[11] And the Strong Eagle, now with num[b]ing cold blighted of feathers,
Once like the pride of the sun, now flagging on cold night,
Hovers with blasted wings aloft, watching with Eager Eye
Till Man shall leave a corruptible body: he, famish'd, hears him groan;
And now he fixes his strong talons in the pointed rock,
And now he beats the heavy air with his enormous wings.
Beside him lies the Lion dead, & in his belly worms
Feast on his death, till universal death devours all.
And the pale horse seeks for the pool to lie him down & die,
But finds the pools fillèd with serpents devouring one another:
He droops his head & trembling stands, & his bright eyes decay.
These are the Visions of My Eyes, the Visions of Ahania.'

Thus cries Ahania. Enion replies from the Caverns of the Grave:

' Fear not, O poor forsaken one! O land of briars & thorns,
Where once the Olive flourish'd & the Cedar spread his wings!
Once I wail'd desolate like thee: my fallow fields in fear
Cried to the Churchyards, & the Earthworm came in dismal state.
I found him in my bosom & I said: " The time of Love
Appears upon the rocks & hills in silent shades." But soon
A voice came in the night, a midnight cry upon the mountains:
" Awake! the bridegroom cometh!" I awoke to sleep no more.
But an Eternal Consummation is dark Enion,
The wat'ry Grave. O thou Corn field! O thou Vegetater happy!

501–506 Cp. F. Z. viii. 2 *note*. 530 Cp. F. Z. ix. 32 *note*.

More happy is the dark consumer. Hope drowns all my torment,
For I am now surrounded by a shadowy vortex drawing
The Spectre quite away from Enion, that I die a death
Of better hope, altho' I consume in these raging waters.
The furrow'd field replies to the grave, I hear her reply to me :
" Behold the time approaches fast, that thou shalt be as a thing
Forgotten : when one speaks of thee, he will not be believ'd.
When the man gently fades away in his immortality,
When the mortal disappears in improvèd knowledge, cast away
The former things. So shall the Mortal gently fade away,
And so become invisible to those who still remain."
Listen ! I will tell thee what is done in the caverns of the grave.
12] The Lamb of God has rent the Veil of Mystery, soon to return
In Clouds & Fires around the rock & the Mysterious tree.
As the seed waits, Eagerly watching for its flower & fruit,
Anxious its little soul looks out into the clear expanse,
To see if hungry winds are abroad with their invisible array :
So Man looks out in tree & herb & fish & bird & beast,
Collecting up the scatter'd portions of his immortal body
Into the Elemental forms of every thing that grows.
He tries the sullen north wind, riding on its angry furrows,
The sultry south when the sun rises, & the angry east
When the sun sets, when the clods harden, & the cattle stand
Drooping, & the birds hide in their silent nests. He stores his thoughts,
As in a store house, in his memory ; he regulates the forms
Of all beneath & all above, & in the gentle West
Reposes, where the Sun's heat dwells. He rises to the Sun,
And to the Planets of the Night, & to the stars that gild
The Zodiac, & the stars that sullen stand to north & south.
He touches the remotest pole ; & in the Center weeps,
That Man should labour, & sorrow, & learn, & forget, & return
To the dark valley whence he came, to begin his labour anew.
In pain he sighs, in pain he labours in his universe,
Sorrowing in birds over the deep, & howling in the wolf
Over the slain, & moaning in the cattle & in the winds,

540–541 It is difficult to discover the syntactical connexion between the words ' cast away The former things ' and their context.

541 Mortal] Man *1st rdg. del.* 544 See above, ll. 330–333.

549–570 See General Introduction, pp. 46–47.

And weeping over Orc & Urizen in clouds & flaming fires:
And in the cries of birth & in the groans of death his voice
Is heard throughout the Universe. Wherever a grass grows,
Or a leaf buds, The Eternal Man is seen, is heard, is felt,
And all his sorrows, till he reassumes his ancient bliss.'

Such are the words of Ahania & Enion. Los hears & weeps.

And Los & Enitharmon took the Body of the Lamb
Down from the Cross, & plac'd it in a Sepulcher which Los had hewn
For himself in the Rock of Eternity: trembling & in despair
Jerusalem wept over the Sepulcher two thousand Years.
[13] Rahab triumphs over all. She took Jerusalem
Captive, A Willing Captive, by delusive arts impell'd
To worship Urizen's Dragon form, to offer her own Children
Upon the bloody Altar. John saw these things Reveal'd in Heaven
On Patmos Isle, & heard the souls cry out to be deliver'd.
He saw the Harlot of the Kings of Earth, & saw her Cup
Of fornication, food of Orc & Satan, press'd from the fruit of Mystery.
But when she saw the form of Ahania weeping on the Void,
And heard Enion's voice sound from the caverns of the Grave,
No more spirit remain'd in her. She secretly left the Synagogue of Satan:

567 flaming] dismal *1st rdg. del.*

572 Such . . . weeps] *an addition.* Beneath is a carefully deleted passage of nine lines:

But Rahab (? hew'd) a Sepucher in the Rock of Eternity,
And placing in the Sepulcher the body which she had taken
The End of the Eighth Night.
From the divine Lamb, wept over the Sepulcher, weaving
Her web of Religion around the Sepulcher times after times beside Jerusalem's Gate.
But as she wove, behold! the bottom of the Sepulcher
Rent & a door (? was) open'd thro' the bottom of the Sepulcher
Into Eternity. And as she wove, she heard a Voice behind her calling her.
She (? turn'd) & (? saw) the Divine Vision & her . . .

573–576 Cp. F. Z. viii. 327–329. 574 Cp. F. Z. viii 321 *note.*

575 despair] fear *1st rdg. del.*

576 The 'two thousand Years' may indicate the duration of Christianity. This religion rationalized has been concerned only with the 'body', which the 'visionary of Jesus' has cast away as valueless, a dead thing. Cp. Enitharmon's dream of eighteen hundred years: *Europe*, ll. 151–153. Beneath l. 576, End of [the] Eighth Night. *del.*

577–597 Rahab . . . will] *an addition.* The lines are not numbered, and the usual indication of the end of the Night is wanting. The subject-matter, however, establishes the position of the passage.

584–597 Nothing corresponding to this mythical treatment of Rahab occurs elsewhere, nor can any satisfactory interpretation be derived from the passage itself: but see below, l. 598 *note.*

She commun'd with Orc in secret. She hid him with the flax
That Enitharmon had number'd away from the Heavens.
She gather'd it together to consume her Harlot Robes
In bitterest Contrition, sometimes Self condemning, repentant,
And sometimes kissing her Robes of Jewels & weeping over
them ;
Sometimes returning to the Synagogue of Satan in Pride,
And sometimes weeping before Orc in humility & trembling.
The Synagogue of Satan therefore, uniting against Mystery,
Satan divided against Satan, resolv'd in open Sanhedrim
To burn Mystery with fire, & form another from her ashes ;
For God put it into their heart to fulfill all his will.

The Ashes of Mystery began to animate ; they call'd it Deism
And Natural Religion ; as of old, so now anew began
Babylon again in Infancy, Call'd Natural Religion.

598–600 The ashes . . . Religion] *an addition*. These lines contain the first statement of Blake's later attitude towards Deism (cp. J. 52, *To the Deists*). His position is that in process of time the religions of the churches were become effete, so that ' a new Religion ' was created to perpetuate the old errors (M. 20. 40–42). Its apostles were Voltaire and Rousseau, with whom Hume, Gibbon, and Bolingbroke were joined later (M. 42. 12). This curious theory of a lapse of the dogmatic theologies through exhaustion may explain ll. 586–597, where Rahab is represented as hesitating between the retention and the abandonment of the body of falsehood, her ' Harlot Robes ' (see Index, *Weaving*, III).

NIGHT IX

THE LAST JUDGMENT

Two accounts of the beginnings of the Last Judgment are included in this Night. The earlier version (ll. 90 seq.) completes the original form of *The Four Zoas* myth : the second and later account (ll. 1–89) presents the conclusion of the regenerative process described in added passages in the earlier Nights, but most completely in Nights VII and VIII. Blake does not attempt to relate the two accounts ; and the description of the Harvest and Vintage of the Nations (ll. 290 seq.), which is reminiscent of the Apocalypse, would seem to follow equally well upon either. It may be noticed in passing that the closing lines of *Milton* seems to refer back to the vision of the Harvest and Vintage in this Night.

In the first account, the immediate cause of the influx into mundane life of the cleansing fires of Eternity is obscurely described as Los's fear lest the annihilation of temporal error by the inspiration of the Divine Vision in Jesus should involve his own extinction or Non-Existence. Therefore in terror he pulls the sun and moon from the firmament with his ' vegetable hands ', a reference to the imperfection of Los's spiritual powers that cannot be explained. But by this act the heavens and the earth are removed, and the foundations of the Eternal hills discovered (ll. 16–17). Kings, priests, and warriors, the agents of moral and civil tyranny, are overthrown before the multitudes of their slaves now set at liberty : Rahab and Tirzah, symbols of the ' feminine ' delusions of Natural Religion, are consumed in the Eternal fires with the Dragon form of Urizen, his books of brass and iron, the Tree of Mystery and the Serpent body of Orc (ll. 32–41). And when all tyranny is cut off from the face of the earth, the liberated souls begin to enter the Holy City (ll. 80–89).

The earlier myth which follows, represents the awaking of fallen man as a spontaneous act. Rising upon his Rock of Death, he laments the confusion of his universe, and calls upon Urizen to cast aside his ' slumbers of cold abstraction ', the sleep of error (l. 128). Urizen obeys, repentant, and throws from him the ' excrementitious husk and covering ' of his moral codes (ll. 179–183, 224–228). He no longer restrains the activities of Orc, Tharmas and Los. Urizen reassumes his real and immortal form, and Ahania rises to reunite with him. But in an extremely difficult passage she is described as falling dead from excess of joy, and the three daughters of Urizen (cp. F. Z. vi. 5 : vii. 95) are said to guard her body in the grave, till error shall be entirely consumed from the earth (ll. 194–202).

Then as in the preceding account the temporal universe is rent asunder (l. 229), King and Priest are overthrown ; their victims are set free ; and Jesus descends, surrounded, as in Revelation, by the twenty-four venerable patriarchs and the four ' Wonders of the Almighty ', the ' Lifes in Eternity '. These last, it may be noticed as an additional indication of the early date of this part of Night IX, are not specifically identified with the four Zoas.

Fallen Man sees the revelation of Jesus, and rises with Urizen, desiring unity with the Divine. But the flames repel him, for the process of spiritual regeneration is not yet complete. Therefore Urizen takes the Plow of Ages, drawn by his eternal horses, and drives it over the cities and villages, the mountains and valleys, the graves and caverns of the world of death. The Souls of all the Dead are cast into the furrows (ll. 314–315) and harrowed in; while the quickening flames of Orc 'heat the black mould and cause the human harvest to begin' (ll. 335–336). Then 'like the harvest moon' Ahania rises, and is finally reunited with Urizen. And Orc, having 'quite consumed himself in mental flames', is revealed as Luvah, and ascends with Vala. They are put into Urizen's charge and commanded to serve man. In obedience to the command they descend into mundane life to labour for its regeneration (ll. 373–377). This, of course, marks the change from the state of error wherein Urizen and Luvah conspire against Man, and at the same time are antagonistic to each other (F. Z. i. 173 seq.). For Urizen now appears as a controlling intellectual force, the power of right reason (cp. F. Z. vii. 359–360): he is pre-eminently the director of the regenerative labours in this Night. The significance of the ascended Luvah is less clear; it can only be suggested that he represents purified passion 'controllable by Reason's power' and directed to spiritual ends.

Then follows (ll. 383–556) a long quasi-pastoral interlude which is written in the imagery and diction of *Thel*. It describes the state of Luvah and Vala in the renewal of their 'ancient golden age'. It has no apparent connexion with any other part of *The Four Zoas*, and its independent value seems to be negligible. Like *Thel* again, what meaning it has it carries on the surface.

After this digression the story reverts to the progress of the Human Harvest. 'Times are ended' (l. 566) and Luvah reascends into the heavens. Urizen and his sons reap and bind the sheaves (ll. 577–584); then Enion and Tharmas reunite and rise to the feast of the Eternals, who mourn over the Generative World (ll. 620–644). Urizen threshes and Tharmas winnows the human grain, and the chaff, Mystery, with its Kings, Councillors, and Warriors, is driven into the caves. The emancipated souls 'from every Earth in the wide Universe' rejoice in their liberty (ll. 666–689).

The Harvest completed, Luvah is sent to the Vintage of the Nations (ll. 691–792). The purpose of this is not clear, unless it refer to the cleansing of human passions and desires, and the restoration of the primal state of innocence and love (cp. ll. 699–706). Finally, when the wine has been separated from the lees, the corn is taken from the Stores of Urizen, and converted into the Bread of Ages by Los, who now appears in his regenerate power as Urthona (ll. 799–822). Then,

Man walks forth from the midst of the fires: the evil is all consum'd.

The perverted or partial visions of the Spectre of Prophecy, the delusive Phantom Los disappear before the fuller revelation, when Urthona rises

to form the golden armour of science
For intellectual War. The war of swords departed now;
The dark Religions are departed; & sweet Science reigns.

VALA

Night the Ninth

Being

The Last Judgment

AND Los & Enitharmon builded Jerusalem, weeping
Over the Sepulcher, & over the Crucified body,
Which to their Phantom Eyes appear'd still in the Sepulcher.
But Jesus stood beside them in the Spirit, Separating
Their Spirit from their body. Terrified at Non Existence—
For such they deem'd the death of the body—Los his vegetable hands
Outstretch'd; his right hand, branching out in fibrous strength,
Siez'd the Sun; His left hand like dark roots cover'd the Moon,
And tore them down, cracking the heavens across from immense to immense.
Then fell the fires of Eternity, with loud & shrill
Sound of Loud Trumpet thundering along from heaven to heaven,
A mighty sound articulate: 'Awake, ye dead, & come
To Judgment, from the four winds! Awake, & Come away!'
Folding like scrolls of the Enormous volume of Heaven & Earth,
With thunderous noise & dreadful shakings, rocking to & fro,
The heavens are shaken, & the Earth removèd from its place,
The foundations of the Eternal hills discover'd.
The thrones of Kings are shaken, they have lost their robes & crowns;
The poor smite their oppressors, they awake up to the harvest.
The naked warriors rush together down to the sea shore,
Trembling before the multitudes of slaves now set at liberty:

1–13 And . . . away] *written over deleted passage.*
1 Cp. F. Z. viii. 175–186 and 183 *note.*
2–3 Cp. F. Z. viii. 321–329 *note.*
10 The 'fires of Eternity' represent the spiritual influx in which the whole creation which now is 'finite and corrupt' 'will be consumed and appear infinite and holy' (M. H. H., p. 14).
16–31 Cp. *America*, ll. 37–51 and ll. 144–150.
19 The poor . . . harvest] *an addition.*
21 Trembling . . . liberty] *an addition.*

They are become like wintry flocks, like forests strip'd of leaves.
The oppressèd pursue like the wind ; there is no room for escape.
The Spectre of Enitharmon, let loose on the troubled deep,
Wail'd shrill in the confusion ; & the Spectre of Urthona
[2] Reciev'd her in the darkening south. Their bodies lost, they stood
Trembling & weak, a faint embrace, a fierce desire, as when
Two shadows mingle on a wall : they wail, & shadowy tears
Fell down, & shadowy forms of joy mix'd with despair & grief.
Their bodies, buried in the ruins of the Universe,
Mingled with the confusion. Who shall call them from the Grave ?

Rahab & Tirzah wail aloud in the wild flames : they give up themselves to Consummation.
The books of Urizen unroll with dreadful noise : the folding Serpent
Of Orc began to Consume in fierce raving fire ; his fierce flames
Issu'd on all sides, gathering strength in animating Volumes,
Roaming abroad on all the winds, raging intense, reddening
Into resistless pillars of fire, rolling round & round, gathering
Strength from the Earths consum'd & heavens & all hidden abysses,
Wheree'er the Eagle has Explor'd, or Lion or Tyger trod,

23 The . . . escape] *an addition.*

24 The Spectre of Enitharmon is not mentioned elsewhere.

32 Rahab . . . Consummation] *an addition.* The use of ' Consummation ' suggests that Blake derives it from ' consume ', making it equivalent to the ' consuming ' or the annihilation of error. Cp. *Cat. 1810*, the description of Blake's picture ' The Last Judgment ' : ' Between the figures of Adam & Eve appears a fiery Gulph descending from the sea of fire before the throne. In this Cataract Four Angels descend . . . to awake the dead : beneath these is the Seat of the Harlot nam'd Mystery in the Revelations. She is siezed by Two Beings, each with three heads : they Represent Vegetative Existence : as it is written in Revelations, they strip her naked & burn her with fire : it represents the Eternal Consummation of Vegetable Life & Death with its Lusts. The wreathed Torches in their hands represent Eternal Fire, which is the fire of Generation or Vegetation : it is an Eternal Consummation. Those who are blessed with Imaginative Vision see This Eternal Female & tremble at what others fear not, while they despise & laugh at what others fear. Her Kings & Councelors & Warriors descend in Flames Lamenting & looking on her in astonishment & Terror.'

35 Cp. F. Z. vi. 164 *note*, and see Index, *Orc.*

36 Roaming] Not clearly written—perhaps ' Roaring '.

Or where the Comets of the night or stars of day
Have shot their arrows or long beamèd spears in wrath & fury.

And all the while the trumpet sounds.
From the clotted gore & from the hollow den
Start forth the trembling millions into flames of mental fire,
Bathing their limbs in the bright visions of Eternity.

Then, like the doves, from pillars of Smoke the trembling families
Of women & children throughout every nation under heaven
Cling round the men in bands of twenties & of fifties, pale
As snow that falls around a leafless tree upon the green.
Their oppressors are fall'n ; they have stricken them ; they awake to life.
Yet pale the just man stands, erect & looking up to heav'n.
Trembling & strucken by the Universal stroke, the trees unroot ;
The rocks groan horrible & run about ; the mountains &
Their rivers cry with a dismal cry ; the cattle gather together ;
Lowing they kneel before the heavens ; the wild beasts of the forests
Tremble; the Lion shuddering asks the Leopard : 'Feelest thou
The dread I feel, unknown before ? My voice refuses to roar,
And in weak moans I speak to thee. This night,
Before the morning's dawn, the Eagle call'd the Vulture,
The Raven call'd the hawk. I heard them from my forests,
Saying : "Let us go up far, for soon I smell upon the wind
A terror coming from the south." The Eagle & Hawk fled away
At dawn, & E'er the sun arose, the raven & Vulture follow'd.
Let us flee also to the north.' They fled. The Sons of Men
Saw them depart in dismal droves. The trumpet sounded loud
And all the Sons of Eternity Descended into Beulah.
[3] In the fierce flames the limbs of Mystery lay consuming with howling
And deep despair. Rattling go up the flames around the Synagogue

40 day] eternal day *1st rdg.* ; asterial day *2nd rdg.*
42–3 And . . . den]

And all the while the trumpet sounds 'Awake ye dead & come
To Judgment' : from the clotted gore & from the hollow den *1st rdg.*

43–45 Cp. *infra*, ll. 87–89.
50 Their . . . life] *an addition.*
51 Yet] Then *1st rdg. del.*
60 forests] forests black *1st rdg.*
65–66 The trumpets . . . Beulah] *written over three and a half lines erased.*
66–80 And . . . Earth] written over deleted title 'Vala / Night the Ninth / Being / The Last Judgment'.

Of Satan. Loud the Serpent Orc rag'd thro' his twenty seven
Folds. The tree of Mystery went up in folding flames.
Blood issu'd out in mighty volumes, pouring in whirlpools fierce
From out the flood gates of the Sky. The Gates are burst; down pour
The torrents black upon the Earth; the blood pours down incessant.
Kings in their palaces lie drown'd; shepherds, their flocks, their tents,
Roll down the mountains in black torrents. Cities, Villages,
High spires & Castles, drown'd in the black deluge; shoal on shoal
Float the dead carcases of Men & Beasts driven to & fro on waves
Of foaming blood beneath the black incessant Sky, till all
Mystery's tyrants are cut off & not one left on Earth.
And when all Tyranny was cut off from the face of Earth,
Around the Dragon form of Urizen, & round his strong form,
The flames, rolling intense thro' the wide Universe,
Began to Enter the Holy City. Entering the dismal clouds,
In furrowèd lightnings break their way the wild flames, whirring up
The Bloody Deluge, living flames wingèd with intellect
And Reason; round the Earth they march in order, flame by flame.
From the clotted gore & from the hollow den
Start forth the trembling millions into flames of mental fire,
Bathing their limbs in the bright visions of Eternity.
Beyond this Universal Confusion, beyond the remotest Pole,
Where their vortexes begin to operate, there stands
A Horrible rock far in the South: it was forsaken when
Urizen gave the horses of Light into the hands of Luvah.

69 The twenty-seven folds of the Serpent Orc may well have some affinity with the Twenty-seven Heavens of the Mundane Shell: see Index, *Mundane Shell, Note II.*

81–89 Around . . . Eternity] *marginal addition,* marked for insertion here.

83–86 Entering . . . flame] Punctuation doubtful; 'flames' is taken as subject of the sentence.

83 Began to Enter the Holy City] Began to draw near to the Earth *1st rdg. del.*

84 whirring] *not legibly written*: a dubious reading.

86 Reason here is used in its higher sense: cp. F. Z. vii. 360 *note.*

88 See above, l. 10 *note.*

90 Beyond] Without *1st rdg. del.*

91 Cp. F. Z. vi. 184 *note.*

92 Cp. *Europe,* l. 96 *note.*

On this rock lay the faded head of the Eternal Man,
Enwrappèd round with weeds of death, pale, cold, in sorrow & woe.
He lifts the blue lamps of his Eyes, & cries with heavenly voice.
Bowing his head over the consuming Universe, he cried :
' O weakness & O weariness ! O war within my members !
My sons, exilèd from my breast, pass to & fro before me.
My birds are silent on my hills ; flocks die beneath my branches ;
My tents are fallen ; my trumpets & the sweet sounds of my harp
Is silent on my clouded hills that belch forth storms & fires.
My milk of cows & honey of bees & fruit of golden harvest
Are gather'd in the scorching heat & in the driving rain.
My robe is turnèd to confusion, & my bright gold to stone.
Where once I sat, I weary walk in misery & pain ;
For from within my wither'd breast, grown narrow with my woes,
The Corn is turn'd to thistles, & the apples into poison ;
The birds of song to murderous crows, My joys to bitter groans ;
[4] The voices of children in my tents to cries of helpless infants ;
And all exilèd from the face of light & shine of morning,
In this dark world, a narrow house, I wander up & down.
I hear Mystery howling in these flames of Consummation.
When shall the Man of future times become as in days of old ?
O weary life ! why sit I here, & give up all my powers
To indolence, to the night of death, when indolence & mourning
Sit hovering over my dark threshold ? Tho' I arise, look out
And scorn the war within my members, yet my heart is weak
And my head faint. Yet will I look again into the morning.
Whence is this sound of rage of Men drinking each other's blood,
Drunk with the smoking gore, & red, but not with nourishing wine ? '

The Eternal Man sat on the Rocks & cried with awful voice :

' O Prince of Light, where art thou ? I behold thee not, as once
In those Eternal fields, in clouds of morning stepping forth
With harps & songs, where bright Ahania sang before thy face,

94 Cp. F. Z. viii. 4 *note*. 97 Bowing . . . cried] *an addition*.
107 wither'd] narrow *1st rdg. del.* 113 Cp. F. Z. ix. 32 *note*.
123–126 Cp. F. Z. v. 189 seq.

And all thy sons & daughters gather'd round my ample table.
See you not all this wracking furious confusion ?
Come forth from slumbers of thy cold abstraction! come forth!
Arise to Eternal births ! shake off thy cold repose !
Schoolmaster of souls, great opposer of change, arise !
That the Eternal worlds may see thy face in peace & joy ;
That thou, dread form of Certainty, maist sit in town & village
While little children play around thy feet in gentle awe,
Fearing thy frown, loving thy smile, O Urizen Prince of Light ! '

He call'd : the Deep buried his voice ; & answer none return'd.
Then wrath burst round ; the Eternal Man was wrath : again he cried :

' Arise, O strong form of Death ! O dragon of the Deeps !
Lie down before my feet, O Dragon ! let Urizen arise !
O ! how could'st thou deform those beautiful proportions
Of life & person ? for as the Person, so is his life proportion'd.
Let Luvah rage in the dark deep, even to Consummation :
For if thou feedest not his rage it will subside in peace.
But if thou darest, obstinate, refuse my stern behest,
Thy crown & scepter I will sieze, & regulate all my members
In stern severity, & cast thee out into the indefinite
Where nothing lives, there to wander : & if thou returnest weary,
Weeping at the threshold of Existence, I will steel my heart
Against thee to Eternity, & never recieve thee more.
Thy self destroying, beast form'd Science shall be thy eternal lot.
My anger against thee is greater than against this Luvah ;
For war is energy Enslav'd : but thy religion,
The first author of this war, & the distracting of honest minds

127 See . . . confusion] *an addition.* 128 Cp. B. A. iv. 3–18.
132 Cp. F. Z. ii. 315 : ' Urizen who was Faith & Certainty.'
139–140 O . . . proportion'd] *an addition.* The Human Form is the symbol of the ideal state of existence, the rightly proportioned life. In Blake's later writings this connexion between Form and Life is among the most striking features of his aesthetic.
140 Person] Person is *1st rdg.* 141 See above, l. 32 *note.*
149 ' Science ' here is apparently Urizen's ' Philosophy of the Five Senses ' (*Africa,* l. 47), which has an ethical as well as a metaphysical content. ' Beast-form'd ' here would seem to mean ' in the form of a beast ': not spiritual or ' human-formed ' (see B. A., chap. ii, and Index, *Human Form*). The phrase ' eternal lot ' is explained in l. 157 : ' Error can never be redeem'd in all Eternity.'
151 energy Enslav'd] honest energy *1st rdg.*
152 distracting] *dubious reading : perhaps* destruction *or* distrusting.

Into confused perturbation & strife & honour & pride,
Is a deceit so detestable, that I will cast thee out
If thou repentest not ; & leave thee, as a rotten branch, to be burnèd
With Mystery the Harlot & with Satan for Ever & Ever.
Error can never be redeem'd in all Eternity ;
But Sin, Even Rahab, is redeem'd in blood & fury & jealousy,
That line of blood that stretch'd across the windows of the morning
Redeem'd from Error's power. Wake, thou dragon of the deeps ! '

[5] Urizen wept in the dark deep, anxious his scaly form
To reassume the human ; & he wept in the dark deep,
Saying : ' O that I had never drank the wine nor eat the bread
Of dark mortality ; nor cast my view into futurity, nor turn'd
My back, dark'ning the present, clouding with a cloud ;
And building arches high, & cities, turrets & towers & domes,
Whose smoke destroy'd the pleasant gardens & whose running kennels
Chok'd the bright rivers ; burdening with my Ships the angry deep,
Thro' Chaos seeking for delight, & in spaces remote
Seeking the Eternal, which is always present to the wise ;
Seeking for pleasure which unsought falls round the infant's path
And on the fleeces of mild flocks who neither care nor labour.
But I, the labourer of ages, whose unwearied hands
Are thus deform'd with hardness, with the sword & with the spear
And with the chisel & the mallet, I, whose labours vast
Order the nations, separating family by family,
Alone enjoy not : I alone in misery supreme,
Ungratified, give all my joy unto this Luvah & Vala.
Then Go, O dark futurity ! I will cast thee forth from these
Heavens of my brain, nor will I look upon futurity more.
I cast futurity away, & turn my back upon that void
Which I have made : for lo, futurity is in this moment.

153 honour] *perhaps* horrour.
156–160 With . . . deeps] *an addition*, l. 159 being later than the rest. Nothing can be discovered to throw light upon the ' line of blood '.
164 futurity] the past *1st rdg. del.* Cp. F. Z. iii. 10.
166 towers] high towers *1st rdg.* 168 Cp. F. Z. vii *a*, 11 *note*.
173–176 See Index, *Urizen*.
179 futurity] remembrance *1st rdg. del.*: cp. ll. 180 and 181.
182 futurity] Remembrance *1st rdg. del.*

Let Orc consume; let Tharmas rage; let dark Urthona give
All strength to Los & Enitharmon, & let Los, self-curs'd,
Rend down this fabric as a wall ruin'd & family extinct!
Rage, Orc! Rage, Tharmas! Urizen no longer curbs your rage.'

So Urizen spoke. He shook his snows from off his shoulders & arose
As on a Pyramid of mist, his white robes scattering
The fleecy white. Renew'd, he shook his agèd mantles off
Into the fires. Then glorious, bright, Exulting in his joy,
He sounding rose into the heavens in naked majesty,
In radiant Youth: when Lo! like garlands in the Eastern sky
When vocal May comes dancing from the East, Ahania came
Exulting in her flight. As when a bubble rises up
On to the surface of a lake, Ahania rose in joy.
Excess of Joy is worse than grief; her heart beat high, her blood
Burst its bright vessels: she fell down dead at the feet of Urizen
Outstretch'd, a Smiling corse. They buried her in a silent cave.
Urizen dropt a tear: the Eternal Mind Darken'd with sorrow.

The three daughters of Urizen Guard Ahania's death couch;
Rising from the confusion in tears & howlings & despair;
Calling upon their father's Name upon their Rivers dark.

And the Eternal Man Said: 'Hear my words, O Prince of Light!
[6] Behold Jerusalem, in whose bosom the Lamb of God
Is seen, tho' slain before her Gates! he, self renew'd, remains
Eternal, & I thro' him awake to life from death's dark vale.
The times revolve; the time is coming when all these delights
Shall be renew'd, & all these Elements that now consume
Shall reflourish. Then bright Ahania shall awake from death,

186 Urizen's abandonment of his former restrictive power is immediately followed by the disappearance of those attributes that characterized him as the God of Moral Law.

193 May] Blake has 'may'.

195–199 Like much else connected with Ahania, this episode is obscure.

199 Mind] Man *1st rdg.*

200–202 The . . . dark] *marginal addition*; position not indicated. Cp. F. Z. vi. 5 *note*.

203 words] voice *1st rdg. del.* 204–206 Behold . . . vale] *an addition.*

204 God] God is seen *1st rdg.* 204–205 Cp. F. Z. viii. 184–187.

209–212 Cp. F. Z. i. 58–62. The significance of these lines is obscure. It may be, though the suggestion is made with all diffidence, that the

A glorious Vision to thine Eyes, a Self renewing Vision,
The spring, the summer to be thine; then sleep the wintry days
In silken garments spun by her own hands against her funeral.
The winter thou shalt plow & lay thy stores into thy barns,
Expecting to recieve Ahania in the spring with joy,
Immortal thou, Regenerate She; & all the lovely Sex
From her shall learn obedience, & prepare for a wintry grave,
That spring may see them rise in tenfold joy & sweet delight.
Thus shall the male & female live the life of Eternity,
Because the Lamb of God Creates himself a bride & wife
That we, his Children, evermore may live in Jerusalem,
Which now descendeth out of heaven, a City, Yet a Woman,
Mother of myriads redeem'd & born in her Spiritual palaces,
By a New Spiritual birth Regenerated from Death.'

Urizen said: 'I have Errèd & my Error remains with me.
What Chain encompasses? in what Lock is the river of light confin'd,
That issues forth in the morniñg by measure, & the evening by carefulness?
Where shall we take our stand, to view the infinite & unbounded?
Or where are human feet? for Lo! our eyes are in the heavens.'

He ceas'd: for, riv'n link from link, the bursting Universe explodes.
All things revers'd flew from their centers: rattling bones
To bones Join: shaking, convuls'd, the shivering clay breathes;
Each speck of dust to the Earth's center nestles round & round
In pangs of an Eternal Birth, in torment & awe & fear.

'glorious Vision' represented by Ahania is intermittent, the period of its immediate apprehension being symbolized by spring and summer. Between these moments of direct spiritual influx, i. e. in 'winter', man is sustained by a mediate form of vision, Ahania sleeping in silken garments (see Index, *Weaving* III), as it were the form under which the ecstatic vision is recollected in tranquillity. Unfortunately there is no other passage by which this explanation can be tested.

210 to] of *1st rdg. del.*

216 Cp. *Cat. 1810*: 'In Eternity Woman is the Emanation of Man; she has No Will of her own. There is no such thing in Eternity as a Female Will.'

219–223 This conception of Jerusalem comes nearer to that in the Apocalypse than to Blake's later treatment of the symbol.

226 Cp. M. H. H., Proverb 14: 'Bring out number, weight & measure in a year of dearth.' The allusion is to the restrictive operation of morality.

231 To bones] These words originally stood at the end of l. 230: then they were deleted and inserted in their present position.

All spirits deceas'd, let loose from reptile prisons, come in shoals:
Wild furies from the tyger's brain & from the lion's Eyes,
And from the ox & ass come moping terrors, from the Eagle
And raven; numerous as the leaves of Autumn every species
Flock to the trumpet, mutt'ring over the sides of the grave, & crying
In the fierce wind round heaving rocks & mountains fill'd with groans.
On rifted rocks suspended in the air by inward fires
Many a woful company, & many on clouds & waters,
Fathers & friends, Mothers & Infants, Kings & Warriors,
Priests & chain'd Captives, met together in a horrible fear.
And every one of the dead appears as he had liv'd before,
[7] And all the marks remain of the Slave's scourge & tyrant's Crown,
And of the Priest's o'ergorgèd Abdomen, & of the merchant's thin
Sinewy deception, & of the warrior's outraving & thoughtlessness,
In lineaments too extended & in bones too strait & long.

They shew their wounds: they accuse, they sieze the oppressor: howlings began
On the golden palace, songs & joy on the Desart. The Cold babe
Stands in the furious air; he cries; the children of six thousand years
Who died in infancy rage furious; a mighty multitude rage furious,
Naked & pale, standing on the expecting air to be deliver'd,
Rend limb from limb the warrior & the tyrant, reuniting in pain.
The furious wind still rends around: they flee in sluggish effort.
They beg, they intreat in vain now; they listen'd not to intreaty.
They view the flames, red rolling on thro' the wide universe,

234 Cp. B. U. ix. 1–16, and F. Z. vi. 113 *note.*
245–248 Cp. F. Z. ix. 18–50 and 139 *note.*
247 outraving] *doubtful word, indistinctly written.*
248 Cp. F. Z. ix. 139–140 and *note.*
249 Howlings began] *indistinctly written in ink: repeated more clearly above in pencil.*
253 on the] *perhaps* in the.
254 The relation of this line to its context is not evident.
255 'they' are 'the warrior & the tyrant' of l. 254.
256 They . . . intreaty] *an addition.*

From the dark jaws of death beneath & desolate shores remote,
These covering vaults of heaven, & these trembling globes of earth.
One Planet calls to another, & one star enquires of another :
' What flames are these coming from the South ? what noise, what dreadful rout
As of a battle in the heavens ? Hark ! heard you not the trumpet
As of fierce battle ? ' While they spoke the flames come on, intense, roaring.

They see him whom they have pierc'd ; they wail because of him.
They magnify themselves no more against Jerusalem, Nor
Against her little ones. The innocent, accusèd before the Judges,
Shines with immortal Glory : trembling, the Judge springs from his throne,
Hiding his face in the dust beneath the prisoner's feet, & saying :
' Brother of Jesus, what have I done ? intreat thy lord for me !
Perhaps I may be forgiven !' While he speaks, the flames roll on ;
And after the flames appears the Cloud of the Son of Man
Descending from Jerusalem with power & great Glory.
All nations look up to the Cloud, & behold him who was Crucified.
The Prisoner answers : ' You scourg'd my father to death before my face
While I stood bound with cords & heavy chains. Your hipocrisy
Shall now avail you nought ! ' So speaking, he dash'd him with his foot.

The Cloud is Blood, daz[z]ling upon the heavens ; & in the cloud
Above, upon its volumes, is beheld a throne & a pavement
Of precious stones, surrounded by twenty four venerable patriarchs ;

258 dark] black *1st rdg. del.* 260 calls] cries *1st rdg. del.*

271 Blake uses the title ' Son of Man ' only in one other place (F. Z. iii. 63), but there it is used of Luvah, not directly of Christ.

274–276 The Prisoner . . . foot] *marginal addition*, marked for insertion here. For the ethical basis of these lines, see E. G. γ^2 , l. 25 (Clar. Press, p. 251) : ' He who loves his Enemies betrays his Friends.'

277–283 Cp. Rev. iv. and *Cat. 1810*.

278 a throne & a] as a throne & as a *1st rdg. del.*

And these again surrounded by four Wonders of the Almighty,
Incomprehensible, pervading all, amidst & round about,
Fourfold each in the other reflected : they are namèd Life's in Eternity,
Four Starry Universes, going forward from Eternity to Eternity.
And the Fall'n Man, who was arisen upon the Rock of Ages,
[8] Beheld the Vision of God ; & he arose up from the Rock.
And Urizen arose up with him, walking thro' the flames
To meet the Lord coming to Judgment ; but the flames repell'd them
Still to the Rock : in vain they strove to Enter the Consummation
Together ; for the Redeem'd Man could not enter the Consummation.

Then siez'd the sons of Urizen the Plow : they polish'd it
From rust of ages : all its ornament of gold & silver & ivory
Reshone across the field immense, where all the nations
Darken'd like Mould in the divided fallows, where the weed
Triumphs in its own destruction. They took down the harness
From the blue walls of heaven, starry, jingling, ornamented
With beautiful art, the study of angels, the workmanship of Demons
When Heaven & Hell in Emulation strove in sports of Glory.

The noise of rural work resounded thro' the heavens of heavens :
The horse[s] neigh from the battle, the wild bulls from the sultry waste,
The tygers from the forests, & the lions from the sandy desarts.
They sing ; they sieze the instruments of harmony ; they throw away
The spear, the bow, the gun, the mortar ; they level the fortifications ;

280–283 See Index, *Zoas*, and *Cat. 1810*.

284 The ' Rock of Ages ' seems to be equivalent to temporal existence, as the fallen state of Man. It is represented as surrounded by the ' Sea of Time and Space ' (M. 14. 36–38), and is one of the symbols arising out of Blake's mythical interpretation of the Deluge. See Index, *Atlantic Continent*, and cp. F. Z. viii. 4 *note*.

289 Redeem'd] Fallen *1st rdg. del.* Man] man *1st rdg.* The flames were to destroy, not the spirit, the Redeemed Man, but the error of his *milieu*.

290 See Index, *Plow*.

They beat the iron engines of destruction into wedges;
They give them to Urthona's sons: ringing the hammers sound
In dens of death, to forge the spade, the mattock & the ax,
The heavy roller to break the clods, to pass over the nations.

The Sons of Urizen shout. Their father rose. The Eternal horses
Harness'd, They call'd to Urizen: the heavens movèd at their call.
The limbs of Urizen shone with ardor. He laid his hand on the Plow,
Thro' dismal darkness drave the Plow of ages over Cities
And all their Villages, over Mountains & all their Vallies,
Over the graves & caverns of the Dead, Over the Planets
And over the void Spaces, over sun & moon & star & constellation.

Then Urizen commanded, & they brought the Seed of Men.
The trembling souls of All the Dead stood before Urizen,
Weak, wailing in the troubled air, East, west & north & south.
[9] He turn'd the horses loose, & laid his Plow in the northern corner
Of the wide Universal field, then step'd forth into the immense.

Then he began to sow the seed. He girded round his loins
With a bright girdle, & his skirt fill'd with immortal souls.
Howling & Wailing fly the souls from Urizen's strong hand.

For from the hand of Urizen the myriads fall like stars
Into their own appointed places: driven back by the winds,
The naked warriors rush together down to the sea shores.
They are become like wintry flocks, like forests strip'd of leaves.
The Kings & Princes of the Earth cry with a feeble cry,
Driven on the unproducing sands & on the harden'd rocks.
And all the while the flames of Orc follow the vent'rous feet
Of Urizen; & all the while the Trump of Tharmas sounds.

309 The limbs of Urizen shone with ardor: he rose up from the Rock: The Fallen Man wond'ring beheld. He laid his hand on the plow. *1st rdg.*
314 Cp. B. A. v. 56–65, where Urizen sows the 'seed of eternal science'.
318 forth] out *1st rdg. del.* 324–325 Cp. F. Z. ix. 20 and 22.
328 The quickening fires of Orc, 'thick flaming, thought creating' (*Asia*, l. 6).

Weeping & wailing fly the souls from Urizen's strong hands.
The daughters of Urizen stand with Cups & measures of foaming wine
Immense upon the heavens, with bread & delicate repasts.
Then follows the golden harrow in the midst of Mental fires.
To ravishing melody of flutes & harps & softest voice
The seed is harrow'd in, while flames heat the black mould & cause
The human harvest to begin. Towards the south first sprang
The myriads, & in silent fear they look out from their graves.

Then Urizen sits down to rest ; & all his wearied Sons
Take their repose on beds ; they drink, they sing, they view the flames
Of Orc ; in joy they view the human harvest springing up.
A time they give to sweet repose till all the harvest is ripe.

And Lo ! like the harvest Moon, Ahania cast off her death clothes.
She folded them up in care, in silence, & her bright'ning limbs
Bath'd in the clear spring of the rock ; then from her darksom cave
Issu'd in majesty divine. Urizen rose up from his couch
On wings of tenfold joy, clapping his hands, his feet, his radiant wings
In the immense, as when the Sun dances upon the mountains ;
A shout of jubilee in lovely notes responding from daughter to daughter,
From son to son, as if the stars beaming innumerable
Thro' night should sing, soft warbling, filling Earth & heaven.
And bright Ahania took her seat by Urizen in songs & joy.

The Eternal Man also sat down upon the Couches of Beulah,
Sorrowful that he could not put off his new risen body
In mental flames : the flames refus'd ; they drave him back to Beulah.
His body was redeem'd to be permanent thro' Mercy Divine.

[10] And now fierce Orc had quite consum'd himself in Mental flames,
Expending all his energies against the fuel of fire.
The Regenerate Man stoop'd his head over the Universe, & in

331–332 The daughters . . . repasts] *an addition.*
333 See Index, *Plow etc.* 336 See Index, *Cardinal Points.*
350 Earth] earth *1st rdg.*
352–355 The Eternal . . . Divine] *an addition.*
357 energies] *perhaps* energy. 358 Regenerate] Ancient *1st rdg.*

His holy hands reciev'd the flaming Demon & Demoness of smoke,
And gave them to Urizen's hands. The Immortal frown'd saying :

'Luvah & Vala, henceforth you are Servants : obey & live !
You shall forget your former state. Return, O Love, in peace
Into your place, the place of seed, not in the brain or heart.
If Gods combine against Man, Setting their dominion above
The Human form Divine, Thrown down from their high Station
In the Eternal heavens of Human Imagination, buried beneath
In dark Oblivion with incessant pangs ages on ages
In enmity & war first weaken'd ; then in stern repentance
They must renew their brightness, & their disorganiz'd functions
Again reorganize, till they resume the image of the human,
Co-operating in the bliss of Man, obeying his Will,
Servants to the infinite & Eternal of the Human form.'

Luvah & Valan descended & enter'd the Gates of Dark Urthona,
And walk'd from the hands of Urizen in the shadows of Vala's Garden,
Where the impressions of Despair & Hope for ever vegetate
In flowers, in fruits, in fishes, birds & beasts & clouds & waters,

359 The Demon and Demoness of Smoke are Luvah or Orc and Vala.

361–372 Cp. D. C. iii, p. 21 : 'Visions of these eternal principles or characters of human life appear to poets, in all ages : the Grecian gods were the ancient Cherubim of Phoenicia ; but the Greeks, and since them, the Moderns, have neglected to subdue the gods of Priam. These gods are visions of the eternal attributes or divine names, which, when erected into gods, become destructive to humanity. They ought to be the servants and not the masters of man, or of society. They ought to be made to sacrifice to man, and not man compelled to sacrifice to them ; for when separated from man, or humanity, who is Jesus the Saviour, the vine of eternity, they are thieves and rebels, they are destroyers.'

363 See Index, *Head, Heart, and Loins.*

364 The Gods are the 'eternal attributes' of man. The passages in the earlier *Nights* where the Zoas in turn assume the place of Gods over man are apparently related to the present lines ; though inability to identify with certainty the particular attributes represented by the Zoas still makes interpretation difficult.

366 Imagination] Thought *1st rdg. del.*

373 Cp. J. 39. 7–10 :

In the Fourth region of Humanity, Urthona nam'd,
Mortality begins to roll the billows of Eternal Death
Before the Gate of Los. Urthona here is named Los,
And here begins the System of Moral Virtue named Rahab.

The Land of doubts & shadows, sweet delusions, unform'd hopes.
They saw no more the terrible confusion of the wracking universe ;
They heard not, saw not, felt not all the terrible confusion ;
For in their orbèd senses, within clos'd up, they wander'd at will.
And those upon the Couches view'd them in the Dreams of Beulah
As they repos'd from the terrible wide universal harvest.
Invisible, Luvah in bright clouds hover'd over Vala's head,
And thus their ancient golden age renew'd ; for Luvah spoke
With voice mild from his golden Cloud upon the breath of morning :

' Come forth, O Vala, from the grass & from the silent dew ;
Rise from the dews of death, for the Eternal Man is Risen ! '

She rises among flowers & looks toward the Eastern clearness ;
She walks, yea runs—her feet are wing'd—on the tops of the bending grass.
Her garments rejoice in the vocal wind & her hair glistens with dew.

She answer'd thus : ' Whose voice is this in the voice of the nourishing air,
In the spirit of the morning, awaking the Soul from its grassy bed ?
[11] Where dost thou dwell ? for it is thee I seek, & but for thee
I must have slept Eternally, nor have felt the dew of thy morning.
Look how the opening dawn advances with vocal harmony !
Look how the beams foreshew the rising of some glorious power !
The sun is thine ; he goeth forth in his majestic brightness.
O thou creating voice that callest, & who shall answer thee ?'

377 Land] *not legibly written* ; perhaps ' Sand '.
381–382 And . . . harvest] *an addition*. Cp. F. Z. ix. 338–341.
385 With . . . morning] *an addition*.
386–554 This long interlude, wherein Blake almost reverts to the facile prettiness of imagery and diction, not always free from feebleness, that characterizes *Thel*, does not clearly join itself to any other myth in *The Four Zoas*. Like *Thel*, again, what meaning it has, is, in the main, visible upon the surface. For the association of Luvah with the Sun in the opening lines, cp. *Thel*, § ii, l. 8 *note*.
397 he] when he *1st rdg*.

'Where dost thou flee, O fair one! where dost thou seek thy happy place?'

'To yonder brightness: there I haste, for sure I came from thence;
Or I must have slept eternally, nor have felt the dew of morning.'

'Eternally thou must have slept, nor have felt the morning dew,
But for yon nourishing sun: 'tis that by which thou art arisen.
The birds adore the sun; the beasts rise up & play in his beams;
And every flower & every leaf rejoices in his light.
Then, O thou fair one, sit thee down, for thou art as the grass;
Thou risest in the dew of morning, & at night art folded up.'

'Alas! am I but as a flower? then will I sit me down;
Then will I weep, then I'll complain & sigh for immortality,
And chide my maker, thee, O Sun, that raisèdst me to fall.'

So saying she sat down & wept beneath the apple trees:

'O! be thou blotted out, thou Sun, that raisedst me to trouble,
That gavest me a heart to crave & raisedst me, thy phantom,
To feel thy heat & see thy light & wander here alone,
Hopeless, if I am like the grass, & so shall pass away.'

'Rise sluggish Soul! why sit'st thou here? why dost thou sit & weep?
Yon Sun shall wax old & decay, but thou shalt ever flourish.
The fruit shall ripen & fall down & the flowers consume away,
But thou shalt still survive: arise! O dry thy dewy tears!'

'Hah! shall I still survive? whence came that sweet & comforting voice,
And whence that voice of sorrow? O sun! thou art nothing now to me:
Go on thy course rejoicing, & let us both rejoice together!
I walk among his flocks & hear the bleating of his lambs.
O! that I could behold his face & follow his pure feet!
I walk by the footsteps of his flocks: come hither, tender flocks!
Can you converse with a pure soul that seeketh for her maker?
You answer not: then am I set your mistress in this garden.

I'll watch you & attend your footsteps : you are not like the birds
[12] That sing & fly in the bright air ; but you do lick my feet,
And let me touch your wooly backs : follow me as I sing ;
For in my bosom a new song arises to my Lord :

" Rise up, O Sun ! most glorious minister & light of day !
Flow on, ye gentle airs, & bear the voice of my rejoicing !
Wave freshly, clear waters, flowing around the tender grass ;
And thou, sweet smelling ground, put forth thy life in fruit & flowers ! "
Follow me, O my flocks, & hear me sing my rapturous song !
I will cause my voice to be heard on the clouds that glitter in the sun.
I will call, & who shall answer me ? I will sing ; who shall reply ?
For from my pleasant hills, behold the living living springs
Running among my green pastures, delighting among my trees !
I am not here alone : my flocks, you are my brethren ;
And you birds, that sing & adorn the sky, you are my sisters.
I sing, & you reply to my song ; I rejoice, & you are glad.
Follow me, O my flocks ! we will now descend into the valley.
O, how delicious are the grapes flourishing in the sun !
How clear the spring of the rock, running among the golden sand !
How cool the breezes of the valley ! & the arms of the branching trees
Cover us from the sun ; come & let us sit in the Shade.
My Luvah here hath plac'd me in a sweet & pleasant land,
And given me fruits & pleasant waters & warm hills & cool valleys.
Here will I build myself a house, & here I'll call on his name ;
Here I'll return when I am weary, & take my pleasant rest.'

So spoke the sinless soul, & laid her head on the downy fleece
Of a curl'd Ram who stretch'd himself in sleep beside his mistress,
And soft sleep fell upon her eyelids in the silent noon of day.

Then Luvah pass'd by & saw the sinless Soul
And said : ' Let a pleasant house arise, to be the dwelling place

453–455 These lines almost perfectly describe one of the most attractive of the engraved designs in *America*, where two children, naked, nestle against the fleece of a sleeping ram, while overhead birds perch among the drooping branches of a tree.

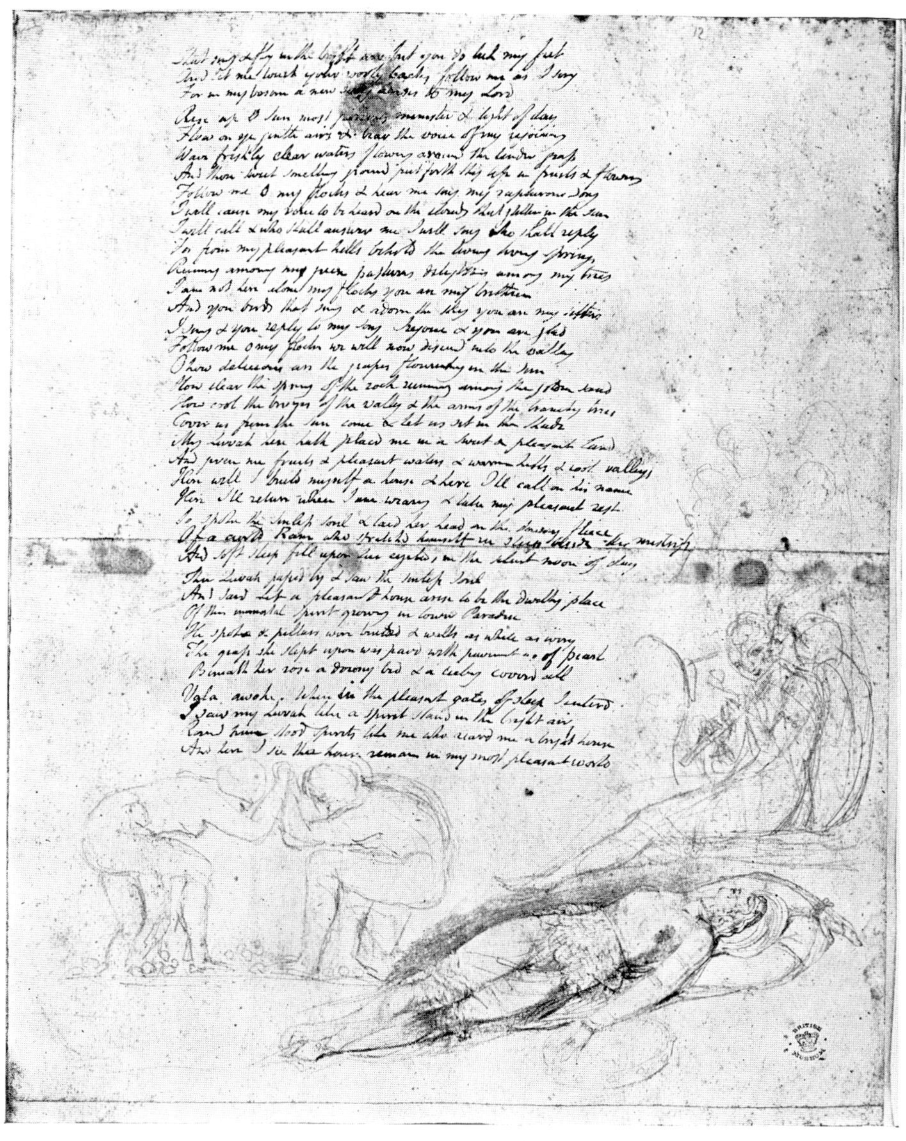

12

That sing & joy in the bright air. But you do lick my feet
And let me touch your wooly backs; follow me as I sing
For in my bosom a new song arises to my Lord

Rise up O Sun most glorious minister & light of day
Flow on ye gentle airs & bear the voice of my rejoicing
Wave freshly clear waters flowing around the tender grass
And thou sweet smelling ground put forth thy life in fruits & flowers
Follow me O my flocks & hear me sing my rapturous Song
I will cause my voice to be heard on the clouds that glitter in the sun
I will call & who shall answer me I will sing who shall reply
For from my pleasant hills behold the living living springs
Running among my green pastures delighting among my trees
I am not here alone my flocks you are my brethren
And you birds that sing & adorn the sky you are my sisters
I sing & you reply to my Song I rejoice & you are glad
Follow me O my flocks we will now descend into the valley
O how delicious are the grapes flourishing in the Sun
How clear the spring of the rock running among the golden sand
How cool the breezes of the valley & the arms of the branching trees
Cover us from the Sun come & let us sit in the Shade
My Luvah here hath placed me in a sweet & pleasant Land
And given me fruits & pleasant waters & warm hills & cool valleys
Here will I build myself a house & here I'll call on his name
Here I'll return when I am weary & take my pleasant rest
So spoke the sinless soul & laid her head on the downy fleece
Of a curld Ram who stretchd himself in sleep beside his mistress
And soft sleep fell upon her eyelids in the silent noon of day
Then Luvah passed by & saw the sinless Soul
And said Let a pleasant house arise to be the dwelling place
Of this immortal Spirit growing in lower Paradise
He spoke & pillars were builded & walls as white as ivory
The grass she slept upon was pavd with pavement as of pearl
Beneath her rose a downy bed & a ceiling covered all
Vala awoke. When in the pleasant gates of sleep I entered
I saw my Luvah like a spirit stand in the bright air
Round him stood spirits like me who reard me a bright house
And here I see thee house remain in my most pleasant world

The Four Zoas: Night IX, page 12

Of this immortal spirit growing in lower Paradise ! '
He spoke, & pillars were builded & walls as white as ivory.
The grass she slept upon was pav'd with pavement as of pearl.
Beneath her rose a downy bed ; & a cieling cover'd all.

Vala awoke : 'When in the pleasant gates of sleep I enter'd,
I saw my Luvah, like a spirit, stand in the bright air.
Round him stood spirits like me, who rear'd me a bright house
And here I see thee, house, remain in my most pleasant world.
[13] My Luvah smil'd. I kneelèd down. He laid his hand on my head ;
And when he laid his hand upon me, from the gates of sleep I came
Into this bodily house, to tend my flocks in my pleasant garden.'

So saying, she arose & walkèd round her beautiful house ;
And then from her white door she look'd to see her bleating lambs ;
But her flocks were gone up from beneath the trees into the hills.

' I see the hand that leadeth me doth also lead my flocks.'
She went up to her flocks & turnèd oft to see her shining house.
She stop'd to drink of the clear spring & eat the grapes & apples ;
She bore the fruits in her lap ; she gather'd flowers for her bosom.
She callèd to her flocks, saying : ' Follow me, O my flocks ! '

They follow'd her to the silent valley beneath the spreading trees,
And on the river's margin she ungirded her golden girdle ;
She stood in the river & view'd herself within the wat'ry glass,
And her bright hair was wet with the waters. She rose up from the river,
And as she rose, her Eyes were open'd to the world of waters :
She saw Tharmas sitting upon the rocks beside the wavy Sea.
He strok'd the water from his beard & mour[n]'d faint thro' the summer vales.

And Vala stood on the rocks of Tharmas & heard his mournful voice :

' O Enion ! my weary head is on the bed of death ;
For weeds of death have wrap'd around my limbs in the hoary deeps.

I sit in the place of shells & mourn, & thou art clos'd in clouds.
When will the time of Clouds be past, & the dismal night of Tharmas ?
Arise, O Enion ! Arise & Smile upon my head,
As thou dost smile upon the barren mountains & they rejoice.
When wilt thou smile on Tharmas, O thou bringer of golden day ?
Arise, O Enion, arise ! for Lo ! I have calm'd my seas.'

So saying, his faint head he laid upon the Oozy rock
And darkness cover'd all the deep : the light of Enion faded
Like a faint flame quivering upon the surface of the darkness.

Then Vala lifted up her hands to heaven to call on Enion.
She call'd, but none could answer her ; & the Eccho of her voice return'd :

' Where is the voice of God that call'd me from the silent dew ?
Where is the Lord of Vala ? dost thou hide in clefts of the rock ?
Why shouldst thou hide thyself from Vala, from the soul that wanders desolate ? '

She ceas'd, & light beamèd round her like the glory of the morning ;
[14] And She arose out of the river & girded her golden girdle.
And now her feet step on the grassy bosom of the ground
Among her flocks, & she turn'd her eyes toward her pleasant house,
And saw in the door way, beneath the trees, two little children playing.
She drew near to her house, & her flocks follow'd her footsteps.
The Children clung around her knees : she embrac'd them & wept over them.

'Thou, little Boy, art Tharmas ; & thou, bright Girl, Enion !
How are ye thus renew'd, & brought into the Gardens of Vala ? '

She embrac'd them in tears till the sun descended the western hills,
And then she enter'd her bright house, leading her mighty children.
And when night came, the flocks laid round the house beneath the trees.

489–492 Arise . . . seas] *an addition.*

She laid the Children on the beds which she saw prepar'd in the house ;
Then last herself laid down & clos'd her Eyelids in soft slumbers.

And in the morning, when the Sun arose in the crystal sky,
Vala awoke & call'd the children from their gentle slumbers :

'Awake, O Enion, awake ! & let thine innocent Eyes
Enlighten all the Crystal house of Vala. Awake, awake !
Awake, Tharmas ! Awake, awake, thou child of dewy tears !
Open the orbs of thy blue eyes & smile upon my gardens.'

The Children woke & smil'd on Vala ; she kneel'd by the golden couch ;
She pres'd them to her bosom, & her pearly tears drop'd down.
'O my sweet Children ! Enion, let Tharmas kiss thy Cheek.
Why dost thou turn thyself away from his sweet wat'ry eyes ?
Tharmas, henceforth in Vala's bosom thou shalt find sweet peace.
O bless the lovely eyes of Tharmas & the Eyes of Enion !'

They rose ; they went out, wand'ring sometimes together, sometimes alone.

'Why weep'st thou, Tharmas, Child of tears, in this bright house of joy ?
Doth Enion avoid the sight of thy blue heavenly Eyes,
And dost thou wander with my lambs, & wet their innocent faces
With thy bright tears because the steps of Enion are in the gardens ?
Arise, sweet boy, & let us follow the path of Enion.'

So saying, they went down into the garden among the fruits,
And Enion sang among the flowers that grew among the trees.
And Vala said: 'Go, Tharmas, weep not. Go to Enion.'

[15] He said : 'O Vala, I am sick, & all this garden of Pleasure
Swims like a dream before my eyes ; but the sweet smelling fruit
Revives me to new deaths. I fade even like a water lilly
In the sun's heat, till in the night, on the couch of Enion,
I drink new life, & feel the breath of sleeping Enion.
But in the morning, she arises to avoid my Eyes.
Then my loins fade, & in the house I sit me down & weep.'

530 wet] with *1st rdg. del.*

‘ Chear up thy Countenance, bright boy, & go to Enion.
Tell her that Vala waits her in the shadows of her garden.’

He went with timid steps ; & Enion, like the ruddy morn
When infant spring appears in swelling buds & opening flowers,
Behind her Veil withdraws : so Enion turn’d her modest head.

But Tharmas spoke : ‘ Vala seeks thee, sweet Enion, in the shades.
Follow the steps of Tharmas, O thou brightness of the gardens ! ’
He took her hand : reluctant she follow’d in infant doubts.

Thus, in Eternal Childhood straying among Vala’s flocks,
In infant sorrow & joy alternate, Enion & Tharmas play’d
Round Vala in the Gardens of Vala & by her river’s margin :
They are the shadows of Tharmas & of Enion in Vala’s world.

And the Sleepers who rested from their harvest work, beheld these visions :
Thus were the Sleepers entertain’d upon the Couches of Beulah.

When Luvah & Vala were clos’d up in their world of shadowy forms,
Darkness was all beneath the heavens ; only a little light,
Such as glows out from sleeping spirits, appear’d in the deeps beneath.
As when the wind sweeps over a Corn field, the noise of souls
Thro’ all the immense : borne down by Clouds swagging in autumnal heat,
Mutt’ring along from heaven to heaven, hoarse roll the human forms.
Beneath thick clouds dreadful lightnings burst & thunders roll ;
Down pour the torrent floods of heaven on all the human harvest.
Then Urizen, sitting at his repose on beds in the bright South,
Cried : ‘ Times are Ended ! ’ He exulted ; he arose in joy ; he exulted.

549 brightness] bright’ning *1st rdg. del.*
555–556 And . . . Beulah] *an addition* : cp. ll. 381–382.
558–559 In the illustration to Blair’s *Grave*, entitled ‘ The Soul exploring the Recesses of the Grave ’, light flames are seen to come from the body of the dead man, or, as Blake here calls him, the ‘ sleeping spirit ’.
565 See Index, *Cardinal Points*.

He pour'd his light, & all his sons & daughters pour'd their light
To exhale the spirits of Luvah & Vala thro' the atmosphere.
And Luvah & Vala saw the Light: their spirits were exhal'd
In all their ancient innocence. The floods depart; the clouds
Dissipate or sink into the Seas of Tharmas. Luvah sat
Above on the bright heavens in peace. The Spirits of Men beneath
Cried out to be deliver'd, & the Spirit of Luvah wept
Over the human harvest & over Vala the sweet wanderer.
In pain the human harvest wav'd in horrible groans of woe.
[16] The Universal Groan went up: the Eternal Man was Darken'd.

Then Urizen arose & took his Sickle in his hand.
There is a brazen Sickle & a Scythe of iron hid
Deep in the South, guarded by a few solitary stars.
This Sickle Urizen took; the scythe his sons embrac'd,
And went forth & began to reap; & all his joyful sons
Reap'd the wide Universe, & bound in Sheaves a wondrous harvest.
They took them into the wide barns with loud rejoicings & triumph
Of flute & harp & drum & trumpet, horn & clarion.

The feast was spread in the bright South, & the Regenerate Man
Sat at the feast rejoicing, & the wine of Eternity
Was serv'd round by the flames of Luvah all Day & all the Night.

And when Morning began to dawn upon the distant hills,
A whirlwind rose up in the Center; & in the Whirlwind a Shriek,
And in the Shriek a rattling of bones, & in the rattling of bones
A dolorous groan, & from the dolorous groan in tears
Rose Enion, like a gentle light; & Enion spoke, saying:

'O Dreams of Death, the human form dissolving, companied
By beasts & worms & creeping things & darkness & despair!
The clouds fall off from my wet brow, the dust from my cold limbs

577–584 Cp. Rev. xiv. 15–20.
588 And . . . hills] *an addition.*
588–592 Cp. F. Z. iii. 139–155 for a parallel account of the appearance of Tharmas.
589 A whirlwind] Then a whirlwind *1st rdg.*
594 By] With *1st rdg. del.*

Into the Sea of Tharmas. Soon renew'd, a Golden Moth,
I shall cast off my death clothes & Embrace Tharmas again.
For Lo, the winter melted away upon the distant hills,
And all the black mould sings! She speaks to her infant race; her milk
Descends down on the sand; the thirsty sand drinks & rejoices,
Wondering to behold the Emmet, the Grasshopper, the jointed worm.
The roots shoot thick, thro' the solid rocks bursting their way;
They cry out in joys of existence; the broad stems
Rear on the mountains, stem after stem; the scaly newt creeps
From the stone, & the armèd fly springs from the rocky crevice;
The spider, The bat burst from the harden'd slime, crying
To one another: "What are we, & whence is our joy & delight?
Lo! the little moss begins to spring, & the tender weed
Creeps round our secret nest." Flocks brighten the Mountains:
Herds throng up the Valley; wild beasts fill the forests.'

Joy thrill'd thro' all the Furious form of Tharmas: humanizing
Mild he Embrac'd her whom he sought; he rais'd her thro' the heavens.
Sounding his trumpet to awake the Dead, on high he soar'd
Over the ruin'd worlds, the smoking tomb of the Eternal Prophet.

[17] The Eternal Man arose; he welcom'd them to the Feast.
The feast was spread in the bright South, & the Eternal Man
Sat at the feast rejoicing, & the wine of Eternity
Was serv'd round by the flames of Luvah all day & all the night.
And Many Eternal Men sat at the golden feast, to see
The female form now separate. They shudder'd at the horrible thing,
Not born for the sport & amusement of Man, but born to drink up all his powers.

600 down] of *1st rdg. del.*

614 See F. Z. viii. 321 *note*. In the present passage the physical universe is regarded as the 'tomb' or place of regeneration of Los rather than of Albion. In this Blake comes nearer to the *Book of Urizen* and the *Book of Los* than to *Milton* and *Jerusalem*. 620–621. See Index, *Sex*.

621 Not . . . powers] an addition repeating in slightly different form F. Z. ii. 29: see *note ad loc.* Cp. B. U. v. 62–68.

They wept to see their shadows: they said to one another: ' This is sin ;
This is the Generative world.' They remember'd the days of old.

And One of the Eternals spoke. All was silent at the feast.

' Man is a Worm. Wearied with joy, he seeks the caves of sleep
Among the Flowers of Beulah, in his Selfish cold repose
Forsaking Brotherhood & Universal love, in Selfish clay
Folding the pure wings of his mind, seeking the places dark,
Abstracted from the roots of Science ; then inclos'd around
In walls of Gold we cast him like a Seed into the Earth
Till times & spaces have pass'd over him. Duly every morn
We visit him, covering with a Veil the immortal Seed:
With windows from the inclement sky we cover him, & with walls
And hearths protect the Selfish terror ; till, divided all
In families, we see our shadows born, & thence we know
That Man subsists by Brotherhood & Universal Love.
We fall on one another's necks, more closely we embrace.
Not for ourselves, but for the Eternal family we live.
Man liveth not by Self alone ; but in his brother's face
Each shall behold the Eternal Father, & love & joy abound.'

So spoke the Eternal at the Feast: they embrac'd the New born Man,

622 See Index, *Shadow*. They] And *1st rdg. del.*

623 Generative] Vegetative *1st rdg. del.* Generative and Vegetative, in the later books, are often indistinguishable, though it is possible that the former term may have a more definitely moral connotation. Its content is best seen in M. 42. 35–43. 28.

625–640 The attitude of carefulness distinguishes the Eternals here from Blake's representation of them in the *Book of Urizen*. But the conception developed here has no definable place in relation to the ideas expressed in such parts of the early form of this book as remain. The definitely providential ideas belong to the time at which *Night VIII* and additions to the earlier Nights were written.

626 Here and in the following line ' selfish ' has a definite symbolic meaning, relating to the ' Self-hood ' or ' Spectre '. See Index, *Spectre*.

629 Science] Nature *1st rdg. del.* Science appears to be ' Eternal Science ', ' the wisdom & joy of life '. B. U. v. 10.

630–636 These lines would seem to indicate a regenerative purpose in mortal life : see Index, *Mundane Shell*.

635–637 In . . . embrace] To these lines, bracketed in the right margin, Blake gives the reference ' Ephesians iii c, 10 v '. The verse reads : ' To the intent that now unto the principalities and powers in heavenly places might be known by the church the manifold wisdom of God.' The scriptural parallel emphasizes the exemplary function in mundane existence.

Calling him Brother, image of the Eternal Father: they sat down
At the immortal tables, sounding loud their instruments of joy,
Calling the Morning into Beulah. The Eternal Man rejoic'd.

When Morning dawn'd, The Eternals rose to labour at the Vintage.
Beneath they saw their Sons & daughters, wondering inconcievable
At the dark myriads in Shadows in the worlds beneath.

The morning dawn'd. Urizen rose, & in his hand the Flail
Sounds on the Floor, heard terrible by all beneath the heavens.
Dismal, loud resounding, the nether floor shakes with the sound;
[18] And all Nations were threshèd out & the stars thresh'd from their husks.

Then Tharmas took the Winnowing fan. The winnowing wind, furious
Above, veer'd round by the violent whirlwind, driven west & south,
Tossèd the Nations like Chaff into the seas of Tharmas.

'O Mystery!' Fierce Tharmas cries: 'Behold, thy end is come!
Art thou she that made the nations drunk with the cup of Religion?
Go down, ye Kings & Councillors & Giant Warriors,
Go down into the depths; go down & hide yourselves beneath;
Go down with horse & Chariots & Trumpets of hoarse war!'

Lo! how the Pomp of Mystery goes down into the Caves.
Her great men howl & throw the dust & rend their hoary hair.
Her delicate women & children shriek upon the bitter wind,
Spoil'd of their beauty, their hair rent & their skin shrivel'd up.
Lo! darkness covers the long pomp of banners on the wind,
And black horses & armèd men & miserable bound captives!
Where shall the graves recieve them all, & where shall be their place,
And who shall mourn for Mystery, who never loos'd her Captives?
Let the slave, grinding at the mill, run out into the field;

655–667 Cp. F. Z. ix. 32 *note*.
668–674 These lines occur in *America*, ll. 42–48.

Let him look up into the heavens & laugh in the bright air.
Let the inchain'd soul, shut up in darkness & in sighing,
Whose face has never seen a smile in thirty weary years,
Rise & look out; his chains are loose, his dungeon doors are open;
And let his wife & children return from the op[p]ressor's scourge!
They look behind at every step & believe it is a Dream.
Are these the slaves that groan'd along the streets of Mystery?
Where are your bonds & task masters? Are these the prisoners?
Where are your chains? where are your tears? why do you look around?
If you are thirsty, there is the river; go, bathe your parchèd limbs!
The good of all the Land is before you, for Mystery is no more.'

Then All the Slaves from every Earth in the wide Universe
Sing a New Song, drowning confusion in its happy notes;
While the flail of Urizen sounded loud, & the winnowing wind of Tharmas,
So loud, so clear in the wide heavens; & the song that they sung was this,
Composèd by an African Black from the little Earth of Sotha:

'Aha! Aha! how came I here so soon in my sweet native land?
How came I here? Methinks I am as I was in my youth,
[19] When in my father's house I sat & heard his chearing voice.
Methinks I see his flocks & herds & feel my limbs renew'd.
And Lo, my Brethren in their tents, & their little ones around them!'

The song arose to the Golden feast: the Eternal Man rejoic'd.
Then the Eternal Man said: 'Luvah, the Vintage is ripe; arise!
The sons of Urizen shall gather the vintage with sharp hooks.
And all thy sons, O Luvah, bear away the families of Earth.
I hear the flail of Urizen; his barns are full, no room
Remains; & in the Vineyards stand the abounding sheaves beneath
The falling Grapes that odorous burst upon the winds. Arise!
My flocks & herds trample the Corn, my cattle browze upon

684 Sotha is the Son of Los by whom Urizen's 'Code of War' was transmitted to Odin (*Africa*, ll. 30–31). The 'little Earth of Sotha' is not mentioned elsewhere.

The ripe Clusters. The shepherds shout for Luvah, prince of Love.
Let the Bulls of Luvah tread the Corn, & draw the loaded waggon
Into the Barn, while children glean the Ears around the door.
Then shall they lift their innocent hands & stroke his furious nose,
And he shall lick the little girl's white neck & on her head
Scatter the perfume of his breath; while from his mountains high
The lion of terror shall come down, & bending his bright mane
And couching at their side shall eat from the curl'd boy's white lap
His golden food, and in the Evening sleep before the door.'

'Attempting to be more than Man, We become less,' said Luvah
As he arose from the bright feast, drunk with the wine of ages.
His crown of thorns fell from his head; he hung his living Lyre
Behind the seat of the Eternal Man, & took his way,
Sounding the Song of Los, descending to the Vineyards bright.
His sons arising from the feast, with golden baskets follow,
A fiery train, as when the Sun sings in the ripe vineyards.
Then Luvah stood before the Wine press; all his fiery sons
Brought up the loaded Waggons with shoutings. Ramping tygers play
In the jingling traces; furious lions sound the song of joy
To the golden wheels circling upon the pavement of heaven, & all
The Villages of Luvah ring. The golden tiles of the villages
Reply to violins & tabors, to the pipe, flute, lyre & cymbal.
Then fell the Legions of Mystery in madd'ning confusion,
Down, down, thro' the immense, with outcry, fury & despair,
Into the wine presses of Luvah. Howling fell the Clusters
Of human families thro' the deep: the wine presses were fill'd:
The blood of life flow'd plentiful. Odors of life arose

699 Cp. *Thel*, § ii, l. 8 *note*. Cp. S. E., 'The Little Girl Lost' (Clar. Press, pp. 116–117).

707 Cp. F. Z. ix. 364–368. 709 Cp. F. Z. vii *a*. 164–166.

711 It is remotely possible that the 'Song of Los' here mentioned may be the Lambeth book bearing that title, for its subject is the imminent overthrow of the power of Priest and King by the rebel Orc.

722 See Index, *Wine press*.

724 The 'Odors of life' would appear to be 'those risen again from Death' (l. 727), those whose error has been put off in the wine press. The further account of the operations at the wine press (ll. 730–771) is, however,

All round the heavenly arches ; & the Odors rose, singing this song :

[20] ' O terrible wine presses of Luvah ! O caverns of the Grave !
How lovely the delights of those risen again from Death !
O trembling joy ! excess of joy is like Excess of grief.'

So sang the Human Odors round the wine presses of Luvah.

But in the Wine presses is wailing, terror & despair.
Forsaken of their Elements, they vanish & are no more—
No more but a desire of Being, a distracted ravening desire,
Desiring like the hungry worm & like the gaping grave.
They plunge into the Elements : the Elements cast them forth,
Or else consume their shadowy semblance. Yet they, obstinate
Tho' painèd to distraction, Cry : ' O ! let us Exist, for
This dreadful Non Existence is worse than pains of Eternal Birth.
Eternal Death who can Endure ! let us consume in fires,
In waters stifling, or in air corroding, or in earth shut up !
The Pangs of Eternal birth are better than the Pangs of Eternal Death ! '

How red the Sons & Daughters of Luvah ! how they tread the Grapes !
Laughing & shouting, drunk with odors, many fall o'erwearied.
Drown'd in the wine is many a youth & maiden : those around
Lay them on skins of tygers or the spotted Leopard or wild Ass
Till they revive ; or bury them in cool Grots, making lamentation.

But in the Wine Presses the Human Grapes Sing not nor dance.
They howl & writhe in shouts of torment, in fierce flames consuming,
In chains of iron & in dungeons circled with ceaseless fires,

more difficult to understand, unless, following the Apocalyptic narrative, Blake intends to represent the destruction of error as at first partial, and afterwards universal.

731 ' they ' apparently refers to the non-essentials, the errors which it is the function of the wine press to separate from the ' Elements '.

733 gaping] silent *1st rdg. del.* 737 Birth] death *1st rdg. del.*

741–769 These lines recur, slightly rearranged and with the addition of certain lines, in M. 24. 3–41.

In pits & dens & shades of death, in shapes of torment & woe ;
The Plates, the Screws and Racks & Saws & cords & fires & floods,
The cruel joy of Luvah's daughters lacerating with knives
And whips their Victims, & the deadly sport of Luvah's Sons.
Timbrels & Violins sport round the Wine Presses. The little Seed,
The sportive root, the Earthworm, the small beetle, the wise Emmet,
Dance round the Wine Presses of Luvah : the Centipede is there,
The ground Spider with many Eyes, the Mole clothèd in Velvet,
The Earwig arm'd, the tender maggot, emblem of Immortality,
The Slow Slug, the grasshopper that sings & laughs & drinks :
The winter comes ; he folds his slender bones without a murmur.
There is the Nettle that stings with soft down, & there
The indignant Thistle, whose bitterness is bred in his milk
And who lives on the contempt of his neighbour : there all the idle weeds
That creep about the obscure places shew their various limbs,
Naked in all their beauty, dancing round the Wine Presses.

They Dance around the Dying, & they drink the howl & groan ;
[21] They catch the shrieks in cups of gold ; they hand them to one another.
These are the sports of love, & these the sweet delights of amorous play,
Tears of the grape, the death sweat of the Cluster, the last sigh
Of the mild youth who listens to the luring songs of Luvah.
The Eternal Man darken'd with Sorrow, & a wintry mantle
Cover'd the Hills. He said : ' O Tharmas, rise ! & O Urthona ! '

Then Tharmas & Urthona rose from the Golden feast, satiated
With Mirth & Joy. Urthona, limping from his fall, on Tharmas lean'd ;
In his right hand his hammer. Tharmas held his Shepherd's crook

750 Screws] Screws, the nets *1st rdg.* Saws] *2nd rdg.* : *1st rdg. illegible.*
769 This reference to Luvah is confusing in view of his regeneration already described. Here, however, the allusion is clearly to the unregenerate Luvah, the King of Rage and Death : see Index, *Luvah.*

Beset with gold; gold were the ornaments, form'd by the sons of Urizen.

Then Enion & Ahania & Vala & the wife of Dark Urthona
Rose from the feast, in joy ascending to their Golden Looms.
There the wing'd shuttle Sung; the spindle & the distaff & the Reel
Rang sweet the praise of industry. Thro' all the golden rooms
Heaven rang with wingèd Exultation. All beneath howl'd loud.
With tenfold rout & desolation roar'd the Chasms beneath,
Where the wide woof flow'd down, & where the Nations are gather'd together.

Tharmas went down to the Wine presses, & beheld the sons & daughters
Of Luvah quite exhausted with the labour, & quite fill'd
With new wine, that they began to torment one another & to tread
The weak. Luvah & Vala slept on the floor o'erwearied.

Urthona call'd his sons around him, Tharmas call'd his sons
Num'rous: they took the wine; they separated the Lees,
And Luvah was put for dung on the ground by the Sons of Tharmas & Urthona.
They formèd heavens of sweetest wood, of gold & silver & ivory,
Of glass & precious stones. They loaded all the waggons of heaven,
And took away the wine of ages with solemn songs & joy.

Luvah & Vala woke, & all the sons & daughters of Luvah
Awoke: they wept to one another, & they reascended
To the Eternal Man in woe: he cast them wailing into
The world of shadows thro' the air till winter is over & gone.

But the Human Wine stood wondering in all their delightful Expanses.
The Elements subside, the heavens roll'd on with vocal harmony.

Then Los, who is Urthona, rose in all his regenerate power.
The Sea, that roll'd & foam'd with darkness & the shadows of death,
Vomited out & gave up all: the floods lift up their hands,

785 tread] tread the weak *1st rdg.*

Singing & shouting to the Man ; they bow their hoary heads,
And murmuring in their channels, flow & circle round his feet.

22] Then Dark Urthona took the Corn out of the Stores of Urizen :
He ground it in his rumbling Mills. Terrible the distress
Of all the Nations of Earth ground in the Mills of Urthona.
In his hand Tharmas takes the Storms ; he turns the whirlwind loose
Upon the wheels ; the stormy seas howl at his dread command,
And Eddying fierce, rejoice in the fierce agitation of the wheels
Of Dark Urthona. Thunders, Earthquakes, Fires, Water-floods
Rejoice to one another : loud their voices shake the Abyss,
Their dread forms tending the dire mills. The grey hoar frost was there,
And his pale wife the agèd snow : they watch over the fires,
They build the Ovens of Urthona. Nature in darkness groans,
And Men are bound to sullen contemplations. In the night
Restless they turn on beds of sorrow, in their inmost brain
Feeling the crushing Wheels. They rise ; they write the bitter words
Of stern Philosophy & knead the bread of knowledge with tears & groans.

Such are the works of Dark Urthona. Tharmas sifted the corn.
Urthona made the Bread of Ages, & he placèd it
In golden & in silver baskets in heavens of precious stone,
And then took his repose in Winter, in the night of Time.

The Sun has left his blackness & has found a fresher morning ;
And the mild moon rejoices in the clear & cloudless night.
And Man walks forth from the midst of the fires : the evil is all consum'd.
His eyes behold the Angelic spheres arising night & day ;
The stars consum'd like a lamp blown out, & in their stead, behold !
The Expanding Eyes of Man beholds the depths of wondrous worlds,
One Earth, one sea beneath ; nor Erring Globes wander, but Stars
Of fire rise up nightly from the Ocean, & one Sun
Each morning, like a New born Man, issues with songs & joy,

817 Cp. F. Z. iv. 274 *note.* 818 Cp. F. Z. vii. 90–107.
823–824 Cp. *America,* ll. 49–50. 826–832 Cp. M. H. H , p. 14.
803 And murmuring] *indistinctly written : a dubious reading.*
830–838 Of . . . Sounds] *an addition over deleted passage.*

Calling the Plowman to his Labour, & the Shepherd to his rest.
He walks upon the Eternal Mountains, raising his heavenly voice,
Conversing with the Animal forms of wisdom night & day,
That, risen from the Sea of fire, renew'd walk o'er the Earth.
For Tharmas brought his flocks upon the hills, & in the Vales
Around the Eternal Man's bright tent the little Children play
Among the wooly flocks. The hammer of Urthona Sounds
In the deep caves beneath: his limbs renew'd, his Lions roar
Around the Furnaces, & in Evening sport upon the plains.
They raise their faces from the Earth, conversing with the Man:

'How is it we have walk'd thro' fires, & yet are not consum'd?
How is it that all things are chang'd, even as in ancient time?
[23] The Sun arises from his dewy bed, & the fresh airs
Play in his smiling beams, giving the seeds of life to grow;
And the fresh Earth beams forth ten thousand thousand springs of life.

'Urthona is arisen in his strength, no longer now
Divided from Enitharmon, no longer the Spectre Los.
Where is the Spectre of Prophecy, where the delusive Phantom?

'Departed: & Urthona rises from the ruinous Walls
In all his ancient strength, to form the golden armour of science
For intellectual War. The war of swords departed now;
The dark Religions are departed; & sweet Science reigns.'

End of The Dream

843–844 Cp. *America*, ll. 73–75.

847–850 Cp. F. Z. viii. 540–541, and see Index, *Los*, IV. The term 'Spectre' is here descriptive rather than symbolic: it is equivalent to 'Phantom' in the latter half of the line. Cp. also l. 12 of the deleted passage given in the note to F. Z. i. 100.

The Four Zoas

Appendix I

Night VII *a*

THE present order of the lines of this rejected Night (see Bibliographical Preface to the book) is in accordance with Blake's directions, here printed in foot-notes. The earlier form of the Night can be reconstructed by the aid of the manuscript page-numbers, which indicate the original order of the sheets. The only passage that does not appear to have found part of the original text is on manuscript p. 5, where an earlier version has been carefully washed out and the present lines (ll. 1–19, 286–299) substituted. Thus the lateness in character of the symbolism of these passages can be accounted for.

The subject matter of the Night is more than usually difficult. Its main theme is the triumph of the forces of repression and its most prominent symbol is the 'nameless shadowy Female' (l. 143), who is also referred to as the 'Shadow' brooding beneath Urizen's tree of Mystery (ll. 1–2), as the 'nameless shadowy Vortex' (l. 123) and as Vala (l. 135). The first of these titles has already been noticed (cp. *S. Lib.*, Introductory Note); but here for the first time it is clearly identified with the notable symbol in the later books, Vala, the 'Feminine delusions', the false visions of morality and corporeity. Urizen, to whom the 'shadowy Female' is subject, proclaims himself God, reducing men to obedience by the establishment of trades and commerce, materializing influences that militate against the true spiritual life (ll. 11–15); and in his temple the order of delight is reversed (l. 21), just as in *America* the fiery joy is perverted to ten commands (*America*, l. 61). Further, Los is represented as following War, the 'strife of swords', night and day (l. 72); that is, he represents the negation of all visionary activity. Then Tharmas, under whom, as in F. Z. iv, Los seems to hold his power, is described as a God who loves those who hate, and rewards with his hate the loving soul (l. 89). Mundane existence is also described as entirely a state of conflict against the ideal mode of being: it is controlled by the 'Prester Serpent', the Priest of that God who blotted man from life and light, who was the author of the 'Seven Diseases of the Soul' (ll. 111–112, 115–116).

Considerable space is also given to the myth of Orc, who appears as the symbol of perverted passion and desire. The moral temptations to which this aspect of man's being is subjected would seem to be expressed in the Song of the Demons, the Spirits of vegetative, that is, uninspired, life. These tell of Urizen's sons who have changed the arts of life into the arts of death, and of Vala's delight in War. Apparently under such influences as these, passion in Orc becomes merely destructive, 'rending the form of life into a formless indefinite' (l. 214) till it passes entirely under the domination of error. For the form of Orc, the saviour in *America*, *Europe*, and *The Song of Los*, vanishes, and his energy is made to serve the powers of civil and moral tyranny ; or symbolically stated, nothing remains of Orc but the 'serpent round the tree of Mystery', rearing his bulk among the stars of Urizen (ll. 212–214). It is quite possible that his view of Orc may reflect the change which seems to have taken place in Blake's attitude towards the French Revolution (cp. *Song of Los*, Introductory Note).

But perhaps the obscurest part of the Night is the episode of Tharmas (ll. 221–287), whom Vala seeks to deceive in order that his despair may not lead to the overthrow of Urizen's hold over man. Tharmas curses the voice of the delusive female that mocks him with false hope (ll. 257–258), yet it would seem that he also is ultimately subdued (ll. 284–285). Thus all the powers concerned with the life of man appear in this Night as more or less completely subjected to Urizen and Vala.

The closing lines, an added passage (ll. 288–299), introduce the later doctrine of a providential purpose of regeneration : the eternal promise is repeated that man shall rise again. The Night ends with the identification of all the forms of mundane error with Satan.

Such is a brief summary of the contents of this Night. As has already been pointed out in the Bibliographical Introduction, it cannot easily be related to Nights VI and VIII, and the opinion of the present editors is that, having failed to adapt it to his liking, Blake rejected it altogether, substituting for it the section printed in the body of the poem as Night VII.

VALA

Night the Seventh

Beginning of the [Seventh Night Book *1st rdg.*]

[5] But in the Deeps beneath the Roots of Mystery, in darkest night,
Where Urizen sat on his rock, the Shadow brooded.
Urizen saw & triumph'd, & he cried to his warriors :

' The time of Prophecy is now revolv'd, & all
This Universal ornament is mine, & in my hands
The ends of heaven : like a Garment will I fold them round me,
Consuming what must be consum'd. Then in power & majesty
I will walk forth thro' those wide fields of endless Eternity,
A God & not a Man, a Conqueror in triumphant glory ;
And all the Sons of Everlasting shall bow down at my feet.'

First Trades & Commerce, Ships & armèd vessels he builded laborious,
To swim the deep ; & on the land children are sold to trades
Of dire necessity, still laboring night & day till, all
Their life extinct, they took the spectre form in dark despair.
And slaves in myriads, in ship loads, burden the hoarse sounding deep :
Rattling with clanking chains the Universal Empire groans.

1–19 But . . . heart] These lines form the latter portion of MS. p. 5, according to the earlier arrangement of this Night, which originally began at l. 122 of the present text : cp. l. 121 *note* and l. 286 *note*. The numbers indicating the MS. pages are those of the earlier version, which can thereby easily be reconstructed.

1 Roots] trees *1st rdg. del.* 2 brooded] brooded dismal *1st rdg.*

3 his warriors] the Shadowy female *1st rdg. del.*

10 After this line a line deleted :

The shadowy voice answer'd : ' O Urizen, Prince of Light '

11 Cp. *Epigrams*, v (Clar. Press, p. 321) :

When Nations grow Old, the Arts grow Cold,
And Commerce settles on every Tree.

Cp. also Ross. MS., cxxvii, ll. 13–14, *1st rdg.* (Clar. Press, p. 237) :

Spirit who lovest Brittannia's shore,
Round which the Fiends of Commerce roar.

15 Cp. J. 65. 33–36.

And he commanded ; his sons found a Center in the Deep,
And [Urizen] laid the first Stone, & all his myriads
Builded a temple in the image of the human heart.
[6] And in the inner part of the Temple, wondrous workmanship,
They form'd the Secret place, reversing all the order of delight,
That whosoever enter'd into the temple might not behold
The hidden wonders allegoric of the Generations
Of secret lust, when, hid in chambers dark, the nightly harlot
Plays in Disguise, in whisper'd hymn & mumbling prayer. The priests
He ordain'd, & Priestesses cloth'd in disguises beastial,
Inspiring secrecy ; & lamps they bore. Intoxicating fumes
Roll round the Temple ; & they took the Sun that glow'd o'er Los,
And with immense machines down rolling the terrific orb
Compell'd. The sun, redd'ning like a fierce lion in his chains,
Descended to the sound of instruments that drown'd the noise
Of the hoarse wheels & the terrific howlings of wild beasts
That drag'd the wheels of the Sun's chariot ; & they put the Sun
Into the temple of Urizen to give light to the Abyss,
To light the War by day, to hide his secret beams by night.
For he divided day & night in different order'd portions,
The day for war, the night for secret religion in his temple.

Los rear'd his mighty stature : on Earth stood his feet, Above
The moon his furious forehead, circled with black bursting thunders ;
His naked limbs glitt'ring upon the dark blue sky, his knees
Bathèd in bloody clouds, his loins in fires of war where spears
And swords rage, where the Eagles cry & Vultures laugh, saying :
' Now comes the night of Carnage, now the flesh of Kings & Princes
Pamper'd in palaces for our food, the blood of Captains nurtur'd
With lust & murder for our drink. The drunken Raven Shall wander

17–19 Cp. J. 33. 17–24, and F. Z. ii. 235–494.
18 Urizen] *del.* : *no alternative rdg. given.*
21 Cp. *America*, l. 61 :

The fiery joy that Urizen perverted to ten commands.

23 Cp. J. 30. 18 *note.* 28–37 Cp. F. Z. ii. 337 *note.*
35 ' beams ' is the present editors' reading of a word very indistinctly written. Ellis and Yeats read ' braves '. Neither guess is satisfactory.
After l. 37 ' Urizen nam'd it [*word illegible*] . . . ' *del.*
38 stature] forehead *1st rdg. del.* Los here is the ' unregenerate ' Los of *Nights I–VI.*

All night among the slain, & mock the wounded that groan in the field.'

Tharmas laugh'd furious among the Banners, cloth'd in blood,

Crying: 'As I will I rend the Nations, all asunder rending
The People: vain their combinations; I will scatter them.
But thou, O Son, whom I have crownèd & inthron'd, thee Strong
I will preserve, tho' Enemies arise around thee numberless.
I will command my winds, & they shall scatter them; or call
[7] My Waters like a flood around thee. Fear not: trust in me;
And I will give thee all the ends of heaven for thy possession.
In war shalt thou bear rule; in blood shalt thou triumph for me;
Because in times of Everlasting I was rent in sunder,
And what I lovèd best was divided among my Enemies:
My little daughters were made captives, & I saw them beaten
With whips among the sultry sands. I heard those whom I lov'd
Crying in secret tents at night, & in the morn compell'd
To labour: & behold! my heart sunk down beneath
In sighs & sobbings, all dividing till I was divided
In twain: & lo! my Crystal form, that livèd in my bosom,
Follow'd her daughters to the fields of blood. They left me naked,
Alone, & they refus'd to return from the fields of the mighty.
Therefore I will reward them as they have rewarded me.
I will divide them in my anger, & thou, O my King,
Shalt gather them from out their graves, & put thy fetter on them,
And bind them to thee, that my crystal form may come to me.'

So cried the Demon of the Waters in the Clouds of Los.
Outstretch'd upon the hills lay Enitharmon: clouds & tempests
Beat round her head all night: all day she riots in Excess.
But night or day Los follows War: & the dismal moon rolls over her,
That, when Los warr'd upon the South, reflected the fierce fires
Of his immortal head into the North upon faint Enitharmon.
Red rage the furies of fierce Orc: black thunders roll round Los;

50–55 Cp. F. Z. iv. 149 seq.
59 sands] roads *1st rdg. del.* 62 all] till all *1st rdg.*
63 The 'Crystal form' is Enion: see Index, *Enion*.
73 night or] day by *1st rdg. del.*

Flaming his head, like the bright sun seen thro' a mist that magnifies
His disk into a terrible vision to the Eyes of trembling mortals.

And Enitharmon, trembling & in fear, utter'd these words :

' I put not any trust in thee, nor in thy glittering scales.
Thy eyelids are a terror to me, & the flaming of thy crest ;
The rushing of thy scales confound me, thy hoarse rushing scales.
And if that Los had not built me a tower upon a rock
I must have died in the dark desart among noxious worms.
How shall I flee ! how shall I flee into the tower of Los !
My feet are turnèd backward, & my footsteps slide in clay,
And clouds are clos'd around my tower : my arms labour in vain.
Does not the God of waters in the wracking Elements
Love those who hate, rewarding with his hate the Loving Soul ?
[8] And must not I obey the God, thou Shadow of Jealousy ?
I cry : the watchman heareth not. I pour my voice in roarings.
Watchman ! the night is thick, & darkness cheats my rayie sight.
Lift up ! Lift up ! O Los ! awake my watchman, for he sleepeth !
Lift up ! Lift up ! Shine forth, O Light ! watchman, thy light is out !
O Los ! unless thou keep my tower, the Watchman will be slain ! '

So Enitharmon cried upon her terrible Earthy bed,
While the broad Oak wreath'd his roots round her, forcing his dark way
Thro' caves of death into Existence. The Beech, long limb'd, advanc'd
Terrific into the pain'd heavens. The fruit trees, humanizing,
Shew'd their immortal energies in warlike desperation,
Rending the heavens & earths, & drinking blood in the hot battle
To feed their fruit, to gratify their hidden sons & daughters
That, far within the close recesses of their secret palaces,
View'd the vast war & joy'd, wishing to vegetate
Into the Worlds of Enitharmon. Loud the roaring winds,

91 The watchman may be Los (cp. M. 23. 8), but the purpose of Enitharmon's speech is too uncertain to justify any attempt to identify either the Shadow in l. 90 or the watchman. 92 choaks] *perhaps* cheats.

Burden'd with clouds, howl round the Couch. Sullen the wooly sheep
Walks thro' the battle. Dark & fierce the Bull his rage
Propagates thro' the warring Earth. The Lion raging in flames,
The Tyger in redounding smoke, The Serpent of the woods
And of the waters, & the scorpion of the desart, irritate
With harsh songs every living soul. The Prester Serpent runs
Along the ranks, crying: 'Listen to the Priest of God, ye warriors!
This Cowl upon my head he plac'd in times of Everlasting,
And said: "Go forth, & guide my battles: like the jointed spine
Of Man I made thee, when I blotted Man from life & light.
Take thou the Seven Diseases of Man: store them for times to come
In store houses, in secret places that I will tell the[e] of,
To be my great & awful curses at the time appointed."'

The Prester Serpent ceas'd: the War song sounded loud & strong
Thro' all the heavens. Urizen's web vibrated, torment on torment.

Then I heard the Earthquake &c.

Now in the Caverns of the Grave & Places of human seed,

108 raging] *not legibly written: perhaps* 'rages'. Lion] Lions *1st rdg.*
109 Tyger] Tygers *1st rdg.*
111 The Serpent is constantly associated with priests and priestcraft in Blake's earlier work; cp. poems in the Ross. MS., written *circa* 1793: e. g. nos. iii commencing 'I saw a chapel all of gold' and x, 'Infant Sorrow.'
114 Cp. Ross. MS. xvi (Clar. Press, p. 169):

> They said this mystery never shall cease:
> The priest promotes war, & the soldier peace.

114–115 Cp. B. U. iv. 35–43: and B. L. iv. 37–38.
116 The 'Seven diseases of the Soul' (J. 19. 26), the 'hypocritic virtues', the seven cardinal virtues of the moral law.
120 Cp. B. U. viii. 37–54.
121 Then . . . Earthquake &c.] This refers to a passage, now lost, which was intended to follow here. Beneath l. 121 is written the further direction 'Then follows "Thus in the Caverns of the Grave &c." as it stands now in the beginning of Night the Seventh'. Below this again is written 'End of the Seventh Night', since the last line of the transferred passage would conclude the Night in its revised form. Above l. 122, which was the first line of the earlier arrangement of Night VII, is written: 'VALA/Night the Seventh/This Night begins at l. 153: the following comes in at the end.'

The nameless shadowy Vortex stood before the face of Orc.
The shadow rear'd her dismal head over the flaming youth:
With sighs & howlings & deep sobs, that he might lose his rage,
And with it lose himself in meekness, she embrac'd his fire.
As when the Earthquake rouzes from his den, his shoulders huge
Appear above the crum[b]ling Mountains; Silence waits around him
A moment; then astounding horror belches from the Centers;
The fiery dogs arise; the shoulders huge appear:
So Orc roll'd round his clouds upon the deeps of dark Urthona.
Knowing the arts of Urizen were Pity & Meek affection,
And that by these arts the Serpent form exuded from his limbs,
Silent as despairing love & strong as Jealousy,
Jealous that she was Vala, now become Urizen's harlot
And the Harlot of Los & the Deluded harlot of the Kings of Earth,
His soul was gnawn in sunder.
The hairy shoulders rend the links; free are the wrists of fire;
Red rage redounds. He rouz'd his lions from his forests black.
They howl around the flaming youth, rending the nameless shadow,
And running their immortal course, thro' solid darkness borne.

Loud sounds the war song round red Orc in his fury,
And round the nameless shadowy Female in her howling terror,
When all the Elemental Gods join'd in the wondrous Song:

'Sound the War trumpet, terrific Souls clad in attractive steel!
Sound the shrill fife, serpents of war! I hear the northern drum!
Awake! I hear the flappings of the folding banners!
The dragons of the North put on their armour;
Upon the Eastern sea direct they take their course;

123 Cp. F. Z. vi. 184 *note*.
132–133 Knowing . . . limbs] *an addition*. Orc's 'Serpent form' symbolizes the temporary triumph of the repressive forces over Energy: cp. F. Z. vii. 152–156, and see Index, *Orc*.
132 affection] love *1st rdg. del.* 134 Cp. *America*, Preludium, l. 21.
135–137 Jealous . . . sunder] *an addition*, written originally to follow l. 141. The changed position is clearly indicated.
138 Cp. *America*, Preludium, l. 22.
142 fury] *2nd rdg.*: *1st rdg. del, illegible*.
146 The north is the quarter of Urthona: cp. F. Z. vi. 266–267. Here Orc is bound: cp. F. Z. vi. 288–289. The east is the quarter of Error, the World of Voidness, Ulro.

The Glitt'ring of their horses' trappings stains the vault of night.

'Stop we the rising of the glorious king! spur, spur your clouds
[2] Of death! O northern drum, awake! O hand of iron, sound
The northern drum! Now give the charge! bravely obscur'd
With darts of wintry hail! Again the black bow draw!
Again the elemental strings to your right breasts draw,
And let the thund'ring drum speed on the arrows black!

'The arrows flew from cloudy bow all day, till blood
From east to west flow'd like the human veins in rivers
Of life upon the plains of death & valleys of despair.

'Now sound the Clarions of Victory! now strip the slain!
Clothe yourselves in golden arms, brothers of war!

'They sound the clarions strong; they chain the howling captives;
They give the Oath of blood. They cast the lots into the helmet,
They vote the death of Luvah & they nail'd him to the tree;
They pierc'd him with a spear & laid him in a Sepulcher,
To die a death of Six thousand years bound round with desolation.

151 clouds] steeds *1st rdg. del.*
154 Cp. J. 52, stanza 5:

> When Satan first the black bow bent,
> And the Moral Law from the Gospel rent,
> He forg'd the Law into a Sword
> And spill'd the blood of mercy's Lord.

161 Clothe] Now clothe *1st rdg.*
162–207 This portion of the Song of the 'demons of the deep' is repeated with slight changes in J. 65. 6–55, as the Song of 'the Spectre Sons of Albion round Luvah's Stone of Trial' (J. 65. 56).
163 They . . . helmet] 'They cast the lots into the helmet, they give the Oath of blood' *1st rdg.* The changed order of the clauses is indicated by the figure '1' above 'they' and '2' above 'They'. Cp. F. Z. ii. 596 *note.*
164–165 Considerable obscurity surrounds the relations between the symbols Luvah and Jesus in this book. Later Jesus is the 'new Luvah Or One who assum'd Luvah's form' (F. Z. viii. 56–57), i. e. Luvah's 'robes of blood' (see Index, *Luvah*). But in the present passage, Luvah appears to be equivalent to Orc, and the symbolic treatment of the Crucifixion to have the same meaning as the binding of Orc. Cp. the myth of Fuzon, B. A., chap. iii, ll. 5–35. It is noteworthy that in the corresponding passage, J. 65. 8–9, the alterations made are such as destroy the close similarity between this episode and the crucifixion of Jesus, which in the later books has another and quite definite symbolic significance (see Index, *Crucifixion*). 166 Cp. J. 96. 11.

'The sun was black & the moon roll'd a useless globe thro' heaven.

'Then left the Sons of Urizen the plow & harrow, the loom,
The hammer & the chisel, & the rule & compasses.
They forg'd the sword, the chariot of war, the battle ax,
The trumpet fitted to the battle, & the flute of summer,
And all the arts of life they chang'd into the arts of death:
The hour glass contemn'd because its simple workmanship
Was as the workmanship of the plowman, & the water wheel
That raises water into Cisterns broken & burn'd in fire
Because its workmanship was like the workmanship of the Shepherd:
And in their stead, intricate wheels invented, Wheel without wheel,
To perplex youth in their outgoings, & to bind to labours
Of day & night the myriads of Eternity, that they might file
And polish brass & iron hour after hour, laborious workmanship,
Kept ignorant of the use; that they might spend the days of wisdom
In sorrowful drudgery, to obtain a scanty pittance of bread,
In ignorance to view a small portion & think that All,
And call it Demonstration, blind to all the simple rules of life.

'Now, now the Battle rages round thy tender limbs, O Vala!
Now smile among thy bitter tears, now put on all thy beauty!
Is not the wound of the sword sweet, & the broken bone delightful?
'Wilt thou now smile among the slain, when the wounded groan in the field?
[3] Lift up thy blue eyes, Vala, & put on thy sapphire shoes.
O Melancholy Magdalen! behold, the morning breaks.
Gird on thy flaming Zone, descend into the Sepulcher.
Scatter the blood from thy golden brow, the tears from thy silver locks.
Shake off the waters from thy wings, & the dust from thy white garments.

183 Cp. M. H. H., p. 14: 'If the doors of perception were cleansed, every thing would appear to man as it is, infinite. For man has closed himself up, till he sees all things thro' narrow chinks of his caverns,' i. e. through the natural organs of sense, the 'five windows' which light 'the cavern'd man'. In l. 184 Blake implies the futility of all argument based on sense-perceptions. 188 Cp. J. 43. 31–45.

190 O . . . breaks] *an addition*. The significance of 'Melancholy Magdalen' applied to Vala by the 'demons of the deep' is not apparent.

'Remember all thy feignèd terrors on the secret Couch,
When the sun rose in glowing morn, with arms of mighty hosts
Marching to battle, who was wont to rise with Urizen's harps,
Girt as a sower with his seed, to scatter life abroad.

'Arise, O Vala! bring the bow of Urizen, bring the swift arrows of light.
How rag'd the golden horses of Urizen bound to the chariot of Love,
Compell'd to leave the plow to the Ox, to snuff up the winds of desolation,
To trample the corn fields in boastful neighings! This is no gentle harp,
This is no warbling brook, nor Shadow of a Myrtle tree;
But blood & wounds & dismal cries & clarions of war,
And hearts laid open to the light by the broad grizly sword,
And bowels hidden in hammer'd steel ripp'd forth upon the Ground.
Call forth thy smiles of soft deceit, call forth thy cloudy tears!
We hear thy sighs in trumpets shrill when Morn shall blood renew.'

So sung the demons of the deep: the Clarions of war blew loud.
Orc rent her; & his human form, consum'd in his own fires,
Mingled with her dolorous members strewn thro' the Abyss.
She joy'd in all the Conflict, Gratified & dropping tears of woe.
No more remain'd of Orc but the Serpent round the tree of Mystery.
The form of Orc was gone: he rear'd his Serpent bulk among
The stars of Urizen in Power, rending the form of life
Into a formless indefinite & strewing her on the Abyss,
Like clouds upon the winter sky broken with winds & thunders.
This was to her supreme delight. The Warriors mourn'd disappointed.

205 And . . . Ground] *an addition.* in hammer'd steel] in darkness are *1st rdg. del.*

After l. 207 a pencil line runs to a marginal note:

Unorganis'd Innocence An Impossibility.
Innocence dwells with Wisdom but never with Ignorance.

The second line was apparently written at a later date than the first. Cp. line written in reverse at the top of p. 30 of *Milton*:

How wide the Gulf & Unpassable between Simplicity & Insipidity!

211 She . . . woe] *an addition.*

214 Power] furor *1st rdg.* Cp. F. Z. ix. 139 *note.*

217–219 This . . . weeping] *an addition*, the last two lines being written as one, and the division indicated after 'Pity'.

They go out to war with strong shouts & loud Clarions. O Pity !
They return with lamentations, mourning & weeping.
Invisible or visible, drawn out in length or stretch'd in breadth,
The Shadowy Female varied in the War in her delight,
Howling in discontent, black & heavy, uttering brute sounds,
Wading thro' fens, among the slimy weeds making Lamentations
To decieve Tharmas in his rage, to sooth his furious soul,
To stay him in his flight, that Urizen might live, tho' in pain.
He said : 'Art thou bright Enion ? is the Shadow of hope return'd ? '

And She said : 'Tharmas, I am Vala, bless thy innocent face !
Doth Enion avoid the sight of thy blue wat'ry eyes ?
Be not perswaded that the air knows this, or the falling dew.'

Tharmas repli'd : 'O Vala! once I liv'd in a garden of delight.
[4] I waken'd Enion in the morning, & she turn'd away
Among the apple-trees, & all the garden of delight
Swam like a dream before my eyes. I went to seek the steps
Of Enion in the gardens, & the shadows compass'd me
And clos'd me in a wat'ry world of woe, where Enion stood
Trembling before me, like a shadow, like a mist, like air.
And she is gone, & here alone I war with darkness & death.
I hear thy voice, but not thy form see : thou & all delight
And life appear & vanish, mocking me with shadows of false hope.
Hast thou forgot that the air listens thro' all its districts, telling
The subtlest thoughts shut up from light in chambers of the Moon ?'

'Tharmas, The Moon has chambers where the babes of love lie hid,
And whence they never can be brought in all Eternity,
Unless expos'd by their vain parents. Lo ! him whom I love
Is hidden from me, & I never in all Eternity
Shall see him. Enitharmon & Ahania, combin'd with Enion,
Hid him in that Outrageous form of Orc, which torments me for Sin,

221 The Shadowy . . . delight] *an addition.*
225 stay] not legibly written : perhaps 'slay'. Cp. F. Z. vi. 64–68.
231–237 Cp. F. Z. ix. 528–550.
242–256 Tharmas . . . wrath] *an addition.* 247 of Orc] *an addition.*

For all my Secret faults which he brings forth upon the light
Of day in jealousy & blood. My Children are led to Urizen's war
Before my eyes, & for every one of these I am condemn'd
To Eternal torment in these flames. For tho' I have the power
To rise on high, Yet love here binds me down, & never, never
Will I arise till him I love is loos'd from this dark chain.'

Tharmas replied: ' Vala, thy sins have lost us heaven & bliss.
Thou art our Curse, and till I can bring love into the light,
I never will depart from my great wrath.'

So Tharmas wail'd wrathful, then rode upon the Stormy Deep,
Cursing the Voice that mock'd him with false hope in furious mood.
Then She returns, swift as a blight upon the infant bud,
Howling in all the notes of woe to stay his furious rage,
Stamping the hills, wading or swimming, flying furious or falling,
Or like an Earthquake rumbling in the bowels of the earth,
Or like a cloud beneath, & like a fire flaming on high;
Walking in pleasure of the hills or murmuring in the dales,
Like to a rushing torrent beneath & a falling rock above,
A thunder cloud in the south & a lulling voice heard in the north.

And she went forth & saw the forms of life & of delight
Walking on Mountains, or flying in the open expanse of heaven.
She heard sweet voices in the winds, & in the voices of birds
That rose from waters; for the waters were as the voice of Luvah,
Not seen to her like waters, or like this dark world of death;
Tho' all those fair perfections, which men know only by name,
In beautiful substantial forms appear'd, & servèd her
As food or drink or ornament, or in delightful works
To build her bowers. For the Elements brought forth abundantly
The living soul in glorious forms; & every one came forth,
Walking before her Shadowy face & bowing at her feet.
But in vain delights were pourèd forth on the howling melancholy.
For her delight the horse his proud neck bow'd, & his white mane;
And the Strong Lion deign'd in his mouth to wear the golden bit;

257 wrathful, then] then furious *1st rdg. del.*

While the far beaming Peacock waited on the fragrant wind
To bring her fruits of sweet delight from trees of richest wonders ;
And the strong pinion'd Eagle bore the fire of heaven in the night season.
Woo'd & subdu'd into Eternal Death the Demon lay
In rage against the dark despair, the howling Melancholy.
[5] For far & wide she stretch'd thro' all the worlds of Urizen's journey,
And was Adjoin'd to Beulah as the Polypus to the Rock.
Mourning the daughters of Beulah saw, nor could they have sustain'd
The horrid sight of death & torment. But the Eternal Promise
They wrote on all their tombs & pillars, & on every Urn
These words : ' If ye will believe, your Brother shall rise again ',
In golden letters ornamented with sweet labours of love,
Waiting with Patience for the fulfilment of the Promise Divine.

And all the Songs of Beulah sounded comfortable notes,
Not suffering doubt to rise up from the Clouds of the Shadowy Female.
Then myriads of the Dead burst thro' the bottoms of their tombs,
Descending on the shadowy female's clouds in Spectrous terror,
Beyond the Limit of Translucence on the Lake of Udan Adan.
These they nam'd Satans, & in the Aggregate they nam'd them Satan.

End of The Seventh Night

284 lay] not legibly written : perhaps ' Sang '.
285 rage against] anguish for *1st rdg. del.*
286–299 These lines, that show a much later symbolism than the rest of this Night, appear to have been written over a previous draft, deleted. An examination of the surface of the paper suggests that Blake removed the earlier text by washing.
293 for] of *1st rdg. del.* 298 See Index, *Limit* and *Udan Adan.*
299 See Index, *Satan.*

APPENDIX II

FRAGMENTS

The following passages are written upon three small pieces of paper found among the manuscript sheets of *The Four Zoas*: see Bibliographical Introduction.

I. Drawing-paper, about $4\frac{1}{2} \times 6\frac{1}{2}$ inches. The upper portion has been torn away and traces of stitching indicate that this sheet once formed part of a note-book. Further, the number 140, written over against l. 7 of the passage on verso, 'A wonder . . . earth', shows that it was originally part of a considerable piece of manuscript, which, judging from the contents of this fragment, may have been an earlier draft of Night I.

i. On the recto, three lines, the first torn through and illegible, and the latter part of the second line also torn away. Both lines printed below appear as ll. 13–14 of the deleted passage in F. Z. i. 109 *note*. Beneath them is a pencil sketch of a seated figure with a serpent coiled about him.

THAT I should hide thee with my power & delig[ht thee with my beauty ;]
And now thou dark'nest in my presence : never from my sight

ii. On the verso, seventeen lines. The changes in ll. 1–9 are made in pencil.

Opening his rifted rocks; mingling together, they join in burning anguish,
Mingling his horrible darkness with her tender limbs; then high she soar'd,
Shrieking above the ocean, a bright wonder that nature shudder'd at,
Half Woman & half desart: all his darkly waving colours mix
With her fair crystal clearness; in her lips & cheeks his metals rose
In blushes like the morning & his rocky features soft'ning;
A wonder lovely in the heavens, or wand'ring on the earth,
With female voice warbling upon the hills & hollow vales,
Beauty all blushing with desire, a Self enjoying wonder.

1 Opening his rifted rocks] *an addition.* together, they] their bodies *1st rdg. del.* 2–7 Cp. F. Z. i. 111–116.
2 darkness] brightness 4 desart] Serpent *1st rdg.* darkly waving] lovely changing *1st rdg. del.*
5 metals] poisons *1st rdg. del.*
6 rocky features] scaly armour *1st rdg. del.*
7 wonder] monster *1st rdg. del.*
8–9 Cp. F. Z. i. 115 *note, deleted passage*, ll. 1–2.

For Enion brooded, groaning loud: the rough seas vegetate.
Golden rocks rise from the vast,
And thus her voice: 'Glory, delight & sweet enjoyment, born
To mild Eternity, shut in a threefold shape delightful,
To wander in sweet solitude enraptur'd at every wind!'

Shining across the ocean
Enion brooded, groaning: the golden rocks vegetate. The...
Infolding the bright woman from the desolating winds
& thus her voice & . . .

II. Writing-paper, about $6\frac{1}{8} \times 3\frac{3}{4}$ inches. All the passages have references to the myth of Tharmas and Enion, remains of which appear in Night I, particularly in deleted passages. The sign '&c.', as elsewhere in Blake, shows that the continuation of the lines is to be sought elsewhere. It is not unlikely that these fragments were intended as additions to an earlier form of Night I. None of the lines appear in *The Four Zoas* in its present form.

i. On the recto, sixteen lines, four of which are deleted, followed by a second passage of four lines.

[*a*] Beneath the veil of Vala rose Tharmas from dewy tears.
The eternal man bow'd his bright head, & Urizen, prince of light,
Astonish'd look'd from his bright portals. Luvah, king of Love,
Awaken'd Vala. Ariston ran forth with bright Anana;
And dark Urthona rouz'd his shady bride from her deep den.
Pitying they view'd the new born demon, for they could not love.
Male form'd the demon mild, athletic force his shoulders spread,
And his bright feet firm as a brazen altar; but the parts
To love devoted, female: all astonish'd stood the hosts
Of heaven, while Tharmas with wing'd speed flew to the sandy shore.
He rested on the desart wild & on the raging sea
He stood, & stretch'd his wings &c.

[*β*] With printless feet scorning the concave of the joyful sky.
Female her form, bright as the summer; but the parts of love

10 For . . . vast] *an addition.* Cp. F. Z. i. 123 *note*, l. 5. vast] vortex *1st rdg. del.*

14–17 Shining . . . voice] *an addition: all but the first part of l. 16* 'Infolding . . . woman' *del.*

16 Cp. F. Z. i. 123 *note*, l. 13. 16 Infolding] To Infolding, *1st rdg.*

1 Vala] Mystery *1st rdg. del.* 2 eternal] ancient *1st rdg. del.*

After l. 2 two lines *del.*:

Astonish'[d] look'd from his bright portals, calling thus to Luvah
O Luvah [*word illeg.*] the

After l. 5 'Awaking from his stony slumber' *an addition del.*

After l. 6 *an addition* Of [*word illegible*] sea *del.*

Male ; & her brow, radiant as day, darted a lovely scorn.
Tharmas beheld from his rock &c.

ii. On the verso, ten lines divided into three sections by lines drawn below the fifth and seventh lines. They are written in pencil.

[α] The ocean calm the clouds fold round, & fiery flames of love
Inwrap the immortal limbs struggling in terrific joy.
Not long : thunders, lightnings, swift rendings & blasting winds
Sweep o'er the struggling copulation ; in fell writhing pangs
They lie, in twisting agonies beneath the covering heavens.

[β] The womb impress'd, Enion fled & hid in verdant mountains.
Yet here his heavenly orbs &c.

[γ] From Enion pours the seed of life, & death in all her limbs
Froze : in the womb of Tharmas rush the rivers of Enion's pain.
Trembling he lay, swell'd with the deluge, stifling in the anguish.

III. Writing-paper, 9 × 5½ inches. This fragment is written on one side, the verso being blank. Its symbolism is that of Blake's later period, and it would appear to have been written after the greater part of *The Four Zoas*, but before the present form of Night VIII, with which its matter has been incorporated at different points and with minor verbal changes.

The Lamb of God stood before Urizen opposite
In Entuthon Benithon, in the shadows of torment & woe,
Upon the heights of Amalek : taking refuge in his arms
The victims fled from punishment, for all his words were peace.
Urizen call'd together all the synagogue of Satan in dark Sanhedrim
To judge the lamb of God to death as a murderer & robber ;
As it is written : ' He was number'd among the transgressors.'

Cold, dark, opake, the Assembly met twelvefold in Amalek,
Twelve rocky unshap'd forms terrific, forms of torture & woe.
Such seem'd the Synagogue to distant view ; around them stood
The daughters of Canaan & Moab, binding on the Stones
Their victims, & with knives tormenting them, singing with tears

1–10 Cp. F. Z. viii. 259–268. 1 The . . . opposite] *an addition*.
3 Amalek] Entuthon that *1st rdg. del.* 4 for] that *1st rdg. del.*
5 Urizen] He *1st rdg. del.*
11–13 The . . . victims] Cp. F. Z. viii. 286–288.
12 knives] songs *1st rdg. del.*

Over their victims. Thus was the Lamb of God condemn'd to death. 13
They nail'd him upon the tree of Mystery, & weeping over him,
And mocking & then worship[p]ing, calling him Lord & King.
Sometimes as twelve daughters lovely, & sometimes as five,
They stood in beaming beauty, & sometimes as One, even Rahab,
Who is Mystery, Babylon the Great, Mother of Harlots.

And Rahab strip'd off Luvah's robes from off the lamb of God.
Then first she saw his glory, & her harlot form appear'd 20
In all its turpitude beneath the divine light; & of Luvah's robes
She made herself a Mantle.

Also the Vegetated bodies which Enitharmon wove in her looms
Open'd within the heart & in the loins & in the brain,
To Beulah, & the dead in Beulah descended thro' their gates.
And some were woven one fold, some two fold, & some three fold, 26
In head or heart or reins, according to the fittest order
Of most merciful pity & compassion to the spectrous dead.
Darkness & sorrow coverèd all flesh; eternity was darken'd.
Urizen sitting in his web of deceitful religion was tormented.
He felt the female &c.

13–18 Cp. F. Z. viii. 315–320. After l. 17 is a deleted line, only partly decipherable:

In which is Tirzah [*word illegible*] translucent as [*word illegible*] opake covering.

19–22 Three oblique lines cancel this passage, which appears, much altered, in F. Z. viii. 331–334.

23–28 This passage is cancelled: it occurs, with changes, in F. Z. viii. 47–49 and 51–53.

29–31 Cp. F. Z. viii. 404–405.

MILTON

Milton is the first of the Prophetic Books belonging entirely to the later period of Blake's life. Yet though it was written under the inspiration of his maturer faith, when, out of great spiritual perturbation he had ' emerged into the light of the day ', certain elements of his earlier symbolism occasionally appear in modified forms. There is, however, somewhat less of the confusion of styles that constitutes the peculiar difficulty of *The Four Zoas*, and in spite of considerable incoherences, chiefly in the first pages, the poem comes nearer to achieving unity than any other of Blake's longer writings. It contains many passages that read like transcripts from actual visionary experience, and shows how confidently Blake believed that he was the divinely appointed agent to expose and annihilate the fallacies of materialism in life and art. Further, the style is comparatively simple and direct; the incidents are varied and move rapidly, and there is something also of the re-awakened sense of wonder and delight in nature that marks his first letters from Felpham. For all these reasons, as well as on account of its more manageable bulk, *Milton* is more easily readable than *Jerusalem*.

Though the title-pages of both *Milton* and *Jerusalem* are dated 1804, an examination of the symbolism proves conclusively that the former is, as a whole, the earlier work. In the first place, the personages Orc and Urizen, the great protagonists of the Lambeth books, are of more importance in the development of the myths of *Milton* than of *Jerusalem*. Again in *Milton* and *The Four Zoas*, Nights VII and VIII, the chief ' feminine ' symbols are Rahab and Tirzah. Vala is rarely mentioned, while the Daughters of Albion, who appear so constantly with her in *Jerusalem*, have no place at all.[1] So again Los is represented in *Milton* rather after the manner of the earlier works than of *Jerusalem*: his mythical functions are more developed and much more clearly defined in the last-named work. Finally, in the use of the curious topographical symbolism that is the mark of Blake's latest manner, *Milton*, except in p. 4, a later addition, and in p. 25 (also a late page, see p. 25, ll. 48–50 *note*), is clearly intermediate between *The Four Zoas* and *Jerusalem*.

It is not unlikely that an earlier and more extended form of *Milton* than the present is the poem referred to in Blake's letters of the years 1803–1805. He speaks of ' an immense number of verses on one grand theme, similar to Homer's *Iliad* or Milton's *Paradise Lost*: the persons and machinery entirely new to the inhabitants of earth (some of the persons excepted) '. The phrase in parenthesis may refer to the presence of such names as Satan, Milton, Wesley, and Whitefield; or more probably the whole passage may merely state the fact that the myth of *Milton* is constructed on a different basis from that of the Lambeth books, and that in the main the personages are new. Again he says that this long poem is descriptive of the ' spiritual acts of [his] three years' slumber on the banks of ocean ',

[1] The fact that the Daughters of Albion are named in F. Z. ii. 268 shows that Blake still turned to that work even after he had written *Milton*. Cp. F. Z. ii. 263, the symbolism of which can be matched only in *Jerusalem*.

and that he will soon publish it. *Milton* alone of Blake's works deals directly with his life at Felpham. Moreover, in the early part of these years he was engaged in engraving plates, after designs by Romney, Flaxman and himself, for Hayley's edition of Milton's poems (R., p. 120), and it may well be that this circumstance caused him to formulate the characteristic criticism of the theodicy of *Paradise Lost* that is the distinguishing feature of the present poem. But it is very unlikely that Blake would have spoken of the work as it now stands as containing an immense number of verses. There is, however, reason to think that a longer work was contemplated when the title-page was engraved in 1804. The title-page of the New York Public Library copy, reproduced as frontispiece to volume I of the present edition, reads : ' a Poem in 12 Books '. Indeed Blake seems to have been at pains to give special distinctness to the ' 1 ', though there are but two Books in all known copies of the poem. Doubtless the twelve was suggested by the number of the Books in *Paradise Lost*, just as the nine Nights of *The Four Zoas* (1797) are reminiscent of the Nine Nights of Young's *Night Thoughts*, for which Blake was making drawings in 1796 and 1797. But other evidence of a discarded purpose to compose a longer poem seems to be implicit in the supernumerary pages and in the Satan-Palamabron myth.

The extra pages, here printed as an appendix to *Milton*, are numbered 2, 3, 5, 8*, 17, and 32*. Of these, pages 2, 3 and 32* would seem on internal evidence to be later than the main body of the poem, and demand separate treatment. But the remainder show a comparatively early type of symbolism; p. 2 is in part an almost verbatim repetition of the binding of Urizen (cp. B. U., chap. iv and F. Z. iv), and pp. 8* and 17 treat mainly of Orc and the Shadowy Female. In the body of the poem, however, the Shadowy Female has no place, and the other personage appears only in passages that cannot easily be reconciled with their contexts. The most striking of these is the 'old Prophecy in Eden ', to the effect that

> Milton of the Land of Albion should up ascend
> Forwards from Ulro, from the Vale of Felpham, and set free
> Orc from the Chain of Jealousy. (M. 18. 59–61.)

These lines define the task which, according to the first intention, the reincarnate Milton was to perform ; but in the work as it stands no such purpose is pursued. He comes, in fact, to annihilate his own ' self-hood ' that is, to give example of the Divine law of brotherhood and self-sacrifice, and, in the person of Blake, to wipe out the evil effects of the erroneous doctrine of *Paradise Lost* by a new gospel and a new art based on vision and the life of the spirit. In the ending of the extant poem Orc is not mentioned. Again, the episode of Milton's wrestling with Urizen (M. 16. 36–17. 14), though referred to later (M. 41. 53–45 and 42. 4–5), is not specifically concluded: Urizen disappears from the myth. It would seem as if these passages and others having a similar reference were either overlooked in revision or were allowed to remain because to remove them would have involved the removal of passages which for some special significance, rather than for their contribution to the story, Blake wished to retain.

The conclusion that suggests itself after an examination of the symbolism of the supernumerary pages is that *Milton* was originally based upon a myth closely resembling that of the later written parts of *The Four Zoas*, i.e. Nights VII and VIII, wherein Urizen or Satan, with Rahab and Tirzah, who combine into the Shadowy Female, appeared as the sources and symbols of all forms of mundane error. To Blake's mind, *Paradise Lost* had been singularly persuasive in advocacy of these errors; wherefore Milton descended from the region of Truth and united with Blake to release the enslaved spirit of man, Orc in the 'Chains of Jealousy'. The poem would have contained, probably in modified forms, much of the myths of Urizen and of the Los of the later-written parts of *The Four Zoas*, with a developed myth of Orc (cp. extra p. 17 *passim*). Such a story, treated after the manner of *The Four Zoas* or of the existing *Milton*, could have been wrought by Blake into 'a long poem'.

The occasion of the revision of *Milton* is obscure. In part it may be hidden in the dim symbolism of the Satan-Palamabron myth, in part it may be connected with the development of the doctrine of Self-annihilation, which supersedes the cruder theory of regeneration embodied in the combat between Milton and Urizen over the enchained Orc. A curious record of this change exists in the inscription beneath the design on p. 15. The drawing would seem to have been intended to illustrate Milton's struggle with Urizen (p. 17. 4–14), but, in revising the poem, Blake gave a new interpretation to the group. The figure of the aged man, forced to his knees and seeking to sustain himself by his tables of the law, is no longer Urizen but Milton's Spectre, as is shown by the words engraved beneath it, 'To Annihilate the Self-hood of Deceit and False Forgiveness'. The fact that this is the only clear instance in the engraved books where a design is interpreted by Blake is in itself significant. Another indication is the manner in which the poem is hurried to a close. Its last five lines are a most summary *précis* of *The Four Zoas*, ix. Probably they are all that Blake retained of an earlier account of the Last Judgment on the lines and scale of Night IX, like it wholly catastrophic and a sequel to the Urizen-Orc myth. But in the recension of *Milton* the doctrine of regeneration through the individual discipline of 'Self-annihilation' displaces most of the elaborate processes of a universal 'Harvest and Vintage of the Nations'. This may explain the exceedingly brief reference to this theme in the present text of *Milton*. At the same time it illustrates Blake's reluctance lightly to cast aside his outworn symbols.

It is practically certain that the Satan-Palamabron myth did not form part of the original poem.[1] In the first place it is complete in itself and has no organic connexion with the rest of the work. Secondly, it is this episode, here embodied in the 'Bard's prophetic song', that is said to have impelled Milton to descend a second time to earth; but this explanation is not sustained, and confusion arises later when Milton's act is attributed to a different cause, the conduct of the dwellers of Ololon, 'those who Milton drove down into Ulro' (19. 16–17). Finally, its doctrine, inculcating the iniquity of moral judgement, and its mythical representation of Satan, are not easily reconciled with the fragments of the Orc myth that remain, or with the identification of Urizen and Satan.[2]

[1] Though the Satan-Palamabron myth in F. Z. viii. 357 *seq.* is later than the body of that Night, being written on an added page, it is earlier than the *Milton* version. It is rudimentary; its later reference to Blake's Felpham experiences is only faintly adumbrated in an added line (l. 380), and it has not yet developed the elaborate system of complementary episodes that emphasize the obligation to continual sacrifice of self for others: see General Introduction, pp. 67–69.

[2] Extra p. 8*. 1–2.

Attention may be called at this point to extra page 3, which, unlike the three noticed above, belongs to the comparatively late period of Blake's return from Felpham : it mentions South Molton Street, where he went to live on 6th October 1803 (cp. l. 21). Yet the presence of the refrain (ll. 20. 26 : cp. M. 3–25 : 5. 17 and 49, &c.) would seem to show that it was intended to form a part of the Bard's song, although it is now impossible to place it satisfactorily. The matter is still further complicated by the presence of p. 4, which, on the evidence of symbolism and decoration, clearly belongs to the same period as *Jerusalem*.[1] It is evident that pp. 3 and 5 were originally consecutive and that Blake adapted the end of the added p. 4 to the opening lines of p. 5. But there is an awkward hiatus between pp. 3 and 4. In the Beckford copy extra p. 3 does in some sort bridge the gap, but in the Windus copy the sequence is again deranged by the intrusion of extra p. 5.

The last of the extra pages, 32*, is also later in its symbolism than the main body of the poem, and once more it is difficult to discover to what end Blake composed it. The page is of the first importance, however, as a document dealing with the theory of States and the symbolic significance of Milton.

To sum up : the discrepancies in symbolism show that in its present form *Milton* is the outcome of vital if unharmonized modifications. Primarily Blake meant to express, in extended form, the concepts he had been and was still striving to engraft upon the original stock of *The Four Zoas*, particularly in Nights VII and VIII. But as he worked, his position was changing. The older mythopoeic machinery was disintegrating ; and the newly revealed importance of the principles of individual responsibility was extending its hold upon his mind and imagination. The mechanical complexities of the myths of Urizen, Luvah, Orc and the Shadowy Female fell away, and their places were taken by a succession of exemplary episodes emphasizing the fundamental obligations to unconditional and unremitted abstinence from judgement, and especially from moral censure, and to perpetual self-discipline and spiritual purgation. The details, or much even of the main history of this reconstitution must remain obscure and debatable. It may or may not have involved a contraction from twelve books to two. But unless the remarkably consistent development traceable in Blake's symbolic writings, from *Thel* to *The Ghost of Abel*, is to be gainsaid or ignored, it is impossible to deny that *Milton* bears the signs of being the product of a period of transition only less critical and significant than that which disorganized *The Four Zoas*.

The two main episodes in *Milton* are the Satan-Palamabron myth and the descent of Milton the Awakener. The first is more than usually difficult and calls for treatment in detail. In the first place, it speaks of the three classes into which mankind is divided. The first division is the Dead, the Elect, or the ' Spectrous ' class, identified with Satan, who joins to his commoner Blakean attributes the spirit of ' officious brotherhood ', uninspired benevolence that imagines itself competent to control the spiritual labours of the visionary. The second class, the Redeemed, ' live in doubts and fears, perpetually tormented by the Elect ' (M. 25–26) until they are redeemed by Mercy from Satan's Law (M. 9. 23). Finally, the

[1] M. 4. 26 repeats, with slight alteration, J. 70. 32, and also bears a similar drawing of a Druid monument, a very late symbol.

Reprobate are they who 'never cease to Believe' (M. 25–35). Rintrah, the typical Reprobate, a demon of wrath, may stand for the convinced and uncompromising mystic, but the evidence is too scanty and equivocal to admit of certain interpretation of either this or the preceding class.

The opening part of the myth defines Satan's prime offence. He seeks to usurp Palamabron's function, to guide the 'Harrow of the Almighty'. Los, arbiter of this sphere of existence, inadvertently permits him to do so, while Palamabron takes charge of the Mills of Satan. As in the earlier Urizen-Luvah myth, confusion follows the interchange of tasks, and the matter is referred to the Eternals for judgement. From this point difficulties increase rapidly.

> . . . Palamabron appeal'd to all Eden and reciev'd
> Judgment ; and Lo ! it fell on Rintrah and his rage,
> Which now flam'd high & furious in Satan against Palamabron,
> Till it became a proverb in Eden : 'Satan is among the Reprobate.'
> (M. 7. 9.)

Satan accuses Palamabron of ingratitude and malice, and, shutting himself off from the Divine Vision, declares himself sole God, whose power is founded upon Moral Law in 'a world of deeper Ulro' or error. Providence intervenes on behalf of Palamabron, 'the wrath falling on Rintrah' (M. 7. 8–42) : for

> If the guilty should be condemn'd, he must be an Eternal Death :
> And one must die for another throughout all Eternity. (M. 9. 17.)

The incident would seem to be an illustration, exaggerated for the sake of emphasis, of the iniquity of the exercise of moral judgement, and of the cruelty of the law of punishment for sin. The true ethic demands that the innocent suffer for the guilty, in order that the law of brotherhood and mutual forgiveness may be fulfilled. The point of view is interesting and characteristic, even in its neglect of logic.

Rintrah's conduct, here and later, is perplexing. A curious point is his apparent unwillingness, the absence of spontaneity in his act of self-sacrifice. He

> rear'd up walls of rocks, and pour'd rivers & moats
> Of fire round the walls ; columns of fire guard around
> Between Satan and Palamabron in the terrible darkness
>
> And Satan, not having the Science of wrath, but only of pity,
> Rent them asunder ; and wrath was left to wrath & pity to pity.
> He sunk down, a dreadful Death, unlike the slumbers of Beulah.
> (M. 7. 43.)

In passages like this, Pity has a sinister connotation. It involves an assumption of superiority and a passing of judgement ; it is a spiritual trespass, infringing the sanctity of the individuality. The will must not be bended : each must keep his proper function.

Up to this point, Blake's purpose would seem to be to correct what he considered the errors of *Paradise Lost*, and, by means of the Bard's divinely inspired song, 'to Justify the Ways of God to Men'. For in the first place, Satan did not fall through ambition, nor was the first sin that of rebellion against the Creator of Man and this world, whom Blake always regarded, after the Gnostic fashion, as a disobedient 'Angel of the Divine Presence'. Satan fell because of 'officious brotherhood' or unenlightened benevolence. It has been suggested that the allusions to Satan's 'soft dissimulation of friendship',

> Seeming a brother, being a tyrant, even thinking himself a brother
> While he is murdering the just (M. 5. 23),

and the frequent denunciation of 'corporeal friends' glance at Hayley, whose 'genteel ignorance and polite disapprobation' of visionary enthusiasm appear to have disturbed Blake's peace of mind at Felpham. It is possible to support this identification by reference to passages in the letters, and particularly in those to Thomas Butts. But complete certainty on this point can only come with a much fuller knowledge of the relations existing between Blake and Hayley than is at present attainable. Indeed it would seem that the false friendship complained of in the Satan-Palamabron myth has reference to something of much longer standing than his acquaintance with Hayley. For in the *Advertizement* (Ross. MS., p. 52) Blake writes: 'The manner in which my Character has been blasted these forty years, both as an Artist and a Man, may be seen particularly in a Sunday Paper called the *Examiner*, Publish'd in Beaufort Buildings; . . . & the manner in which I have routed out the nest of villains will be seen in a Poem concerning my Three years' Herculean Labours at Felpham, which I will soon Publish. Secret Calumny & open Professions of Friendship are common enough all the world over, but have never been so good an occasion of Poetic Imagery. When a Base Man means to be your Enemy, he always begins with being your Friend.' From this passage it is arguable that Blake intended to pillory not Hayley, but certain unknown persons who, like the critics in the *Examiner*, sought to pervert his spiritual labours, and that too, apparently, under the guise of friendship. But whatever the origin of the myth, Blake's meaning in this part of it would seem to be that Satan's error was not that he rebelled against the God of this world, but that he obstructed the Holy Ghost, the Poetic Genius, in others.

The remainder of the myth is chiefly concerned with the Miltonic fallacy of supposing Satan to have been punished by Providence for his fault. Blake deliberately sets himself to controvert this view by representing Divine Mercy as active from the first, and by means of several agents, to protect Satan from punishment. One instance of this, the suffering of Rintrah for the sin of Satan, has already been noticed. Another is the devotion of Enitharmon, who creates a 'Space' to shield the erring spirit; and the Eternals 'ratify the kind decision', giving 'a Time to the Space, even six thousand years' (M. 11. 16).[1] This divinely appointed purpose of regeneration in temporal existence is itself a manifestation of Mercy and Forgiveness.

The contrast between the Miltonic and Blakean points of view is still greater in the lines that follow (ll. 17–27). Not only is the notion of punishment entirely absent, but the 'solemn Assembly' of Eternals elects seven spirits, Lucifer, Molech, Elohim, Shaddai, Pahad, Jehovah and Jesus, to guard the newly created Space and to give themselves to 'Eternal Death' for Satan's sake. In spite of the obscure statement, found also in the corresponding passage in *The Four Zoas* viii, that all save Jesus fail, Blake's intention is clearly enough to emphasize the doctrine that the ideal ethic consists

[1] Cp. M. 23. 72:

> Time is the mercy of Eternity: without Time's swiftness
> Which is the swiftest of all things, all were eternal torment.

in mercy and forgiveness, and abhors moral condemnation and punishment. The same idea is restated in the subsidiary myth of Leutha, the Blakean parallel to the figure of Sin in *Paradise Lost*. She offers herself as a 'ransom' for Satan, assuming the guilt of his fall. She tells how, by stultifying the 'masculine perceptions' and keeping only the 'feminine' active (M. 10. 5), she originated the illusions through which Satan fell. Finally, Elynittria, an indefinable female figure, who, as the counterpart to Palamabron, is opposed to Leutha, is represented as laying aside all enmity and jealousy to aid her rival. 'She soothed her with soft words and brought her to Palamabron's bed.'

Thus though many details of symbolism remain dark, two at least of the main principles embodied in the myth are evident enough, the perversive influence of 'corporeal' or uninspired 'friendship' and the necessity of continual forgiveness and mercy.

The second theme of the poem, Milton's purpose of self-annihilation, can best be illustrated by reference to Blake's own experiences at Felpham during the years 1800–1803, his 'three years' slumber on the banks of ocean', a period of 'sore travail', when he 'passed through perils and darkness not unlike a champion' (*Letter to Butts*, 22 November 1802). His difficulties were concerned with religion and art, which from that time forward are often inseparably denoted under the same symbols, till they are ultimately identified in the declaration that 'Christianity is Art' (*Laocoön*, 32). But on reflection this period of mental and spiritual tribulation appeared to him to be a divinely appointed means to the attainment of truth (cp. M. 36. 21–25). In the letter already quoted he writes: 'I am again emerged into the light of day: I still and shall to eternity embrace Christianity, and adore him who is the express image of God. My enthusiasm is still what it was, only enlarged and confirmed.' So in the matter of his art, he came to a clearer understanding of his own position. The revelation came to him after visiting the Truchsessian Gallery exhibition of old masters. Writing on the subject to Hayley immediately afterwards (22 June 1804), he says: 'I was again enlightened with the light I enjoyed in my youth, and which has for exactly twenty years been closed to me as by a door and by window-shutters.' At the time he was engraving after Romney, whose 'spiritual aid' contributed not a little to his 'restoration to the light of art'. But the most interesting point is that he describes his experience in symbols that resemble those in *Milton*. 'For now! O Glory! and O Delight! I have entirely reduced that spectrous fiend to his station, whose annoyance has been the ruin of my labours for the last passed twenty years of my life . . . I was a slave bound in a mill among beasts and devils. These beasts and these devils are now, together with myself, become children of life and liberty, and my feet and my wife's feet are free from fetters.'

In the present work, the impulse to achieve freedom in art and religion by the annihilation of the 'spectrous fiend' or 'Selfhood' is symbolized by Milton, who, as has already been noticed, becomes one with Blake himself. The content of this symbolic act, in so far as it relates to the destruction of error, is fully set forth in the vigorous passage 42. 34–43. 28. The Self or Selfhood is identified with the common 'spectrous' symbols, the Polypus, the Covering Cherub, the Shadow, and Satan. But there is also another sense, in which self-annihilation expresses the willing sacrifice of self for others, the principle of continual and unconditional forgiveness.

And just as in *Jerusalem* Blake associates such ' feminine ' powers as Vala and the Daughters of Albion with the ' spectrous ' activities, so here, using the tradition that Milton's daughters acted as their father's amanuenses, he creates a sixfold Emanation suggested by the number of the poet's wives and daughters, and relates it to the Miltonic Spectre or Shadow. It does not seem different from the common female symbols, except that it is given a particular significance to represent the opinions embodied in *Paradise Lost*, the errors that Milton left the world of Eternity to redeem. The greatest of these was that he had identified the supreme deity with the creator of this world, the author of the Moral Law, and so traversed the almost unvarying doctrine of Blake's later works that the physical universe was created by the Elohim or Satan. Crabb Robinson, writing to Dorothy Wordsworth on Blake's opinion of her brother's poetry, gives what is perhaps the best statement of the matter: ' Now, according to Blake, atheism consists in worshipping the natural world, which same natural world, properly speaking, is nothing real but a mere illusion produced by Satan. Milton was for a great part of his life an atheist, and therefore his fatal errors in *Paradise Lost*, which he often begged Blake to refute.' [1]

So it is that, a hundred years after his death, Milton leaves his place in eternity, and laying aside his spiritual being, his ' real and immortal self ', becomes subject to the conditions of mortality in order to redeem his former errors. The immediate impulse to this act, as has already been pointed out, is not quite unequivocally stated. In the opening pages Milton is impelled by ' a Bard's prophetic song ' (M. 3. 16–24), that is, the myth of Satan and Palamabron; but later (M. 19. 52–53) he is described as obeying a ' Universal Dictate ', a decree of Providence.

Descending, Milton joins with Blake, from whom a cloud separates itself and spreads over Europe. This is Milton's ' Shadow ', and in its division would seem to express the fact that an influx of spirituality reveals the body of error which is now seen, as if from without, in the form of a cloud. Then Los unites with Blake, setting him down in Felpham, that ' in three years ' he ' might write all these Visions To display Nature's cruel holiness, the deceits of Natural Religion ' (M. 36. 23–25). That Blake looked upon himself as destined to consummate the regeneration of the world is clear from this statement as well as from passages in other works.[2]

The latter part of *Milton* is confused by the introduction of Ololon, a symbol not found elsewhere. The entire episode is exceedingly obscure, and there are indications that it is, in part at least, reminiscent of visions that appeared to Blake at Felpham.[3] Primarily Ololon is the name of a river in Eden, one of the ' rivers of the waters of life ', but it is used to represent the Eternals who dwell on its banks. These appear to be set in opposition to the seven Angels of the Divine Presence who sustain with ' food of Eden ' the immortal Form that Milton put off when he descended into the mundane state. A similar division among Eternals is found in *Jerusalem* (55. 1–22), though it is not developed to the same extent. In the present myth

[1] Symons, p. 274. Crabb Robinson also records that ' Blake declared him (Dante) a mere politician and atheist, busied in this world's affairs: as Milton was, till in his old age he returned back to the God he had abandoned in childhood ' (ibid., p. 294).

[2] Cp. Ross. MS. (Clar. Press, p. 236).

[3] Cp. M. 36. 13–20: 44. 7–28.

the dwellers in or by Ololon refuse to acquiesce in the act of the seven, who, combining with the form of Milton into a 'Starry Eight', are driven by Ololon into the Ulro. The subsequent relation of the 'Seven' to the descended Milton is quite obscure, unless they can be regarded as affording him spiritual guidance.

Ololon is almost immediately enlightened as to the error of its action, which involves an exercise of moral judgement. This appears from the repentant cry: 'Is Virtue a Punisher? O No!' Uniting with the Divine family in Jesus, they descend through the chaos or Ulro that lies about Los's world of time and space. But they are compelled to combine into a female form, lest they destroy that 'Vegetative world' they come to save. The significance of this change is difficult to discover; it may, however, represent the substitution of a mediate for an immediate presentation of truth, lest the latter should prove too great and terrible for man's comprehension. Some such idea, in a different connexion though still associated with the symbolic use of the 'Female', occurs in the description of Beulah (M. 30. 21 *seq.*) and in the important passage on the 'Female' and 'Human' forms on the extra p. 17. But whatever the explanation, Ololon is seen by Blake, as he walks before his cottage in Felpham, as 'a Virgin of twelve years'. She questions him concerning Milton, who straightway appears before her and commands her to aid him in his struggle against his Selfhood, the Spectre Satan. At this point the opposites are definitely revealed, ranged one against another. The Miltonic Shadow, Satan, the symbol of the entire body of mundane error, faces Milton the Awakener, who is associated with Los, now unequivocally the symbol of Divine inspiration. Following an elaborate symbolic description of the first of these comes a wholly obscure association of Ololon with Milton's 'Sixfold Emanation', which is identified with the source of Deism (M. 42. 4–16: 43. 30–36). In the succeeding lines confusion is worse confounded:

The Virgin (Ololon) divided Six-fold & with a shriek
Dolorous that ran thro' all Creation, a Double Six-fold Wonder,
Away from Ololon she divided, & fled into the depths
Of Milton's Shadow as a Dove upon the stormy Sea.
Then as a Moony Ark Ololon descended to Felpham's Vale
In clouds of blood, in streams of gore, with dreadful thunderings,
Into the Fires of Intellect that rejoic'd in Felpham's Vale
Around the Starry Eight: with one accord the Starry Eight became
One Man, Jesus the Saviour, wonderful; round his limbs
The Clouds of Ololon folded as a Garment dippèd in blood,
Written within & without in woven letters; & the Writing
Is the Divine Revelation in the Litteral expression,
A Garment of War: I (Blake) heard it nam'd the Woof of Six Thousand
Years. (M. 44. 3–15.)

Then the trumpet sounded for the Last Judgement, and Blake came out from his trance; his soul

return'd into its mortal state
To Resurrection & Judgment in the Vegetable Body.

The poem closes with the preparations for 'the Great Harvest & Vintage of the Nations'.

The general significance of Ololon remains dark, and perhaps necessarily so, since so much of it appears to be a record of Blake's own mystical experience. All that can be attempted in the way of exposition is to notice the points of contact with the body of Blake's more familiar symbolism, and to suggest with all diffidence a possible line of interpretation. The initial conflict of Ololon with the Starry Eight repeats the main doctrine of this poem, the iniquity of any attempt at moral judgement such as is implied in the expulsion of the Eight. Incidentally it illustrates the curious conception of the possibility of error even among Eternals, and this again is brought into relation to the notion that the principles of continual forgiveness and self-sacrifice are fundamental in the supreme state of existence. It is also noteworthy that, as in the earlier *Book of Urizen*, some at least among the Eternals act without fore-knowledge : the dwellers in Ololon do not know that in banishing the Eight they are fulfilling part of the divine purpose of regeneration (M. 19. 31–57). All this is very confusing and not easily to be reconciled with the commoner statement of ideal unity in the supreme state of existence, expressed symbolically as the appearance of the 'Eternals' or of 'all Eternity' as 'One Man, Jesus', the 'Divine Humanity' or as a 'Divine Family'.

What is perhaps the surest clue to the interpretation of Ololon is to be found in the last lines of the passage quoted above, wherein the Clouds of Ololon that, like Luvah's 'robes of blood', enfold Jesus are compared to a 'Garment' whereon is woven 'the Divine Revelation in the Litteral expression'. This expression, taken in association with the further identification of Ololon with the 'Woof of Six Thousand Years', suggests that the symbol represents dramatically the revelation within temporal existence of the divine scheme of regeneration : its error is made the means to ultimate salvation for man. She is the 'Moony Ark' of the promise, the vehicle of the providential purpose. Evidently there is significance in the statement that she enfolds the Starry Eight whom before she had driven forth : it is a symbolic act of self-abasement to serve others. Yet so complete an identification of Eternals with the errors of mortality is singular.

In conclusion, one further matter of some interest may be noticed here. Though Blake's doctrinal antagonism to 'Nature' continues throughout *Milton* and the later writings, there are passages (M. 25. 26–M. 26. 12) where a definite modification of his attitude is faintly discernible. Though the 'created' universe is the world of Satan, Blake is conscious that aspects of it are beautiful. He remembers too that it is the world of Los and Enitharmon, of divinely given Time and Space, the place of human salvation. Hence the beauty of the Universe may have its place in the scheme of human regeneration. The 'constellations in the deep and wondrous Night', the 'gorgeous clothed flies that dance and sport in summer', the trees that 'thunder thro' the darksom Sky'

> Uttering prophesies & speaking instructive words to the sons
> Of men ; These are the sons of Los, These the Visions of Eternity.
> But we see only as it were the hem of their garments
> When with our vegetable eyes we behold these wondrous Vistas.

This passage and others on p. 31 not only are evidence of the renewed sense of the beauty in Nature which quickens the book of *Milton*, but suggest a basis for a mediate vision of truth that associates Blake with others of the Romantic poets. But when the vehemence of prophecy returns upon him, he finds no place for it, and denounces the 'imitation of Nature's Images' as destructive of Imagination and an obstacle to truth.

Catchwords, answering in every instance to the initial word of the following page, are found on pp. 9, 10, 14, 16, 18, 20, 24, 25, 27, 30, and 31.

Milton

Four copies of *Milton* have been described by Mr. Keynes. For reasons given below the present edition follows the British Museum copy, and in the following bibliographical notes its arrangement of the plates has been taken as the norm. The copies are :

(*a*) The British Museum copy : title-page and ' Preface ' 1 plate each ; ' Book the First ' 26 plates ; ' Book the Second ' 17 plates : 45 plates. Watermark, Whatman 1808.

(*b*) ? The Butts copy : in the Henry E. Huntington Library. Forty-five plates : arrangement of plates and the watermark as in (*a*).

(*c*) The Beckford copy : in the New York Public Library : lacks ' Preface ' but has 5 extra pages, 2, 3, 8*, 17, 32* : total 49 plates, arranged 1, 3, 5, extra p. 2, 4, extra p. 3, 6–8, extra p. 8*, 9–16, extra p. 17, 17–20, 22, 23, 25, 26, 24, 27–32, extra p. 32*, 32–42, 21, 43–45.

The following erasures have been made upon the paper (i.e. not on the engraved plate) :

p. 4, l. 35. and woven.

p. 5, l. 1. By Enitharmon's Looms & Spun beneath the Spindle of Tirzah.

p. 24. *Catchword* : Loud. p. 25. *Catchword* : These.

(*d*) The Windus copy : lacks ' Preface ' but has 6 extra pages : total 50 plates, arranged : 1, 3, extra pages 2, 3, and 5 ; 4, 5, 6–8, extra p. 8*, 9–16, 17, 17–20, 22–23, 25, 26, 24, 27–31, extra p. 32*, 32–42, 21, 43–45. Watermark, Ruse and Turner 1815.

These details are taken from the Nonesuch Blake and from Mr. Keynes' letter to the *Times Literary Supplement*, 13 December 1923.

Though (*d*) was latest compiled, (*a*) and (*b*) are more homogeneous and consistent. The disruptive effect of the intruded pages in (*c*) has been noted, but extra p. 5 is even more inconsequent and pointless. It has no clear relevance to its context and is compact of additions and interpolations more discordant than the worst of *The Four Zoas* pages, though the engraved plate does not show as plainly as does the manuscript page how they were put together. The latter part of l. 2 may be a survival from an earlier version, modelled more closely than the present poem upon *Paradise Lost*. The symbolic cast of the first reference to the Daughters of Albion is comparatively primitive, while the appearance of Charles (apparently the First), Cromwell, and James is unlike anything later than *America*. The fact that ll. 19–26 appear in *Jerusalem* seems to indicate that at one time Blake had abandoned this page, though later he bound it up with the 1815 copy, perhaps for no deeper reason than to bring up the tale of plates to fifty.

The variations in the four copies of *Milton* suggest the following conclusions : (*a*) and (*b*) represent Blake's endeavour to state his mystical faith with precision ; (*c*) appears to be a characteristically unhappy second thought, marring the earlier version by thrusting in plates previously rejected and by altering the order of pp. 24–26. The fourth copy we are inclined to regard as primarily a work of art. By 1815 Blake had outgrown the position defined in *Milton*, and was content that the text in this fourth copy should be subordinated to the splendours of its coloured and gilded page. Therefore the (*a*) text has been adopted here, the six extra pages being printed in an Appendix, so that, by the aid of the bibliographical data given above, any of the longer texts may be reconstructed.

MILTON a Poem

in 2 Books

'To Justify the Ways of God to Men'

The Author & Printer, W. Blake,
1804

[2]

PREFACE

THE Stolen and Perverted Writings of Homer & Ovid, of Plato & Cicero, which all Men ought to contemn, are set up by artifice against the Sublime of the Bible;[1] but when the New Age is at leisure to Pronounce, all will be set right, & those Grand Works of the more ancient & consciously & professedly Inspired Men will hold their proper rank, & the Daughters of Memory shall become the Daughters of Inspiration. Shakspeare & Milton were both curb'd by the general malady & infection from the silly Greek & Latin slaves of the Sword.

Rouze up, O Young Men of the New Age! set your foreheads against the ignorant Hirelings! For we have Hirelings in the Camp, the Court, & the University, who would, if they could, for ever depress Mental & prolong Corporeal War.[2] Painters! on you I call. Sculptors! Architects! Suffer not

[1] The Stolen . . . Inspiration] Cp. *On Homer's Poetry* and *On Virgil*, *passim*, and D. C. ii, pp. 4–5. 'No man can believe that either Homer's Mythology or Ovid's were the production of Greece or of Latium; neither will any one believe that the Greek statues, as they are called, were the invention of Greek Artists: perhaps the Torso is the only original work remaining; all the rest are evidently copies, though fine ones, from the greater works of the Asiatic Patriarchs. The Greek Muses are daughters of Mnesmosyne, or Memory, and not of Inspiration or Imagination, therefore not authors of such sublime conceptions.'

[2] Mental or Spiritual War expresses the activities of the perfect visionary state: cp. J. 27: 'The Return of Israel is a return to Mental Sacrifice & War,' and J. 38. 14, where the Eternals say:

> Our wars are wars of life & wounds of love,
> With intellectual spears & long wingèd arrows of thought.

Brotherhood and perfect forgiveness find their expression therein:

> For the Soldier who fights for Truth, calls his enemy his brother.
> They fight & contend for life & not for eternal death. (J. 43. 41–42.)

A sentence from the *Laocoön* plate expounds the symbol on the aesthetic side: 'Spiritual War: Israel deliver'd from Egypt is Art deliver'd from Nature & Imitation.' It is also used for the visionary's part in the struggle against error:

> He [Jesus] bound old Satan in His Chain,
> And, bursting forth, his furious ire
> Became a Chariot of fire.
> Throughout the land he took his course
> And trac'd diseases to their source.
> He curs'd the Scribe & Pharisee,
> Trampling down Hipocrisy.

the fashionable Fools to depress your powers by the prices they pretend to give for contemptible works, or the expensive advertizing boasts that they make of such works : [1] believe Christ & his Apostles that there is a Class of Men whose whole delight is in Destroying. We do not want either Greek or Roman Models if we are but just & true to our own Imaginations, those Worlds of Eternity in which we shall live for ever in Jesus our Lord.

And did those feet in ancient time
Walk upon England's mountains green ?
And was the holy Lamb of God
On England's pleasant pastures seen ?

And did the Countenance Divine
Shine forth upon our clouded hills ?
And was Jerusalem builded here
Among these dark Satanic Mills ? [2]

Bring me my Bow of burning gold !
Bring me my Arrows of desire !
Bring me my Spear ! O clouds, unfold !
Bring me my Chariot of fire !

Where'er His Chariot took its way,
There Gates of death let in the Day,
Broke down from every Chain & Bar,
And Satan in his [Jesus'] Spiritual War
Drag'd at his Chariot Wheels.

(E. G. *β*, 32–43, Clar. Press, p. 248.)

Corporeal War, on the contrary, expresses the destructive operation of Morality and Empiricism, and, with reference to art, it is used in connexion with what Blake held to be the pernicious influence of classical tradition, and particularly of the tradition of the Venetian and Flemish painters (but not of the Florentines and Dürer). 'Art Degraded, Imagination Denied, War Govern'd the Nations' [*Laocoön*]. But the aspect of Corporeal War most commonly stressed is the moral. Blake declares 'The Moral Virtues are continual Accusers of Sin & promote Eternal Wars & Domineering over others.' Hence it is commonly associated with the feminine and spectrous symbols, especially 'Vala' and 'Satan', as well as with symbols of unregenerate mundane existence, e.g. Wine Press, the Veil or Garment : see Index under these terms.

[1] In the *Advertizement* Blake vehemently attacks the fashionable vogue of certain artists whose practice he held to be antagonistic to the principles of imaginative art. The Rossetti MS. also contains epigrams ridiculing the ignorance of English connoisseurs. It will suffice to quote the titles to two of these :

'A Pretty Epigram for the encouragement of those Who have paid great sums in the Venetian and Flemish ooze' (Clar. Press, p. 220).

'On the great encouragement given by English Nobility & Gentry to Corregio, Rubens, Reynolds, Gainsborough, Catalani, Du Crow and Dilbury Doodle' (ibid., p. 223).

[2] Cp. stanzas in J. p. 77. England here is identified with Albion or Man : see Index, *Albion*.

I will not cease from Mental Fight,
Nor shall my Sword sleep in my hand,
Till we have built Jerusalem
In England's green & pleasant Land.

Would to God that all the Lord's people were Prophets.[1]
Numbers XI. Ch. 29 v.

[1] Cp. Letter to Hayley, 11 Dec. 1805 (R., p. 188): 'Oh! what wonders are the children of men! Would to God that they would consider it—that they would consider their spiritual life, regardless of that faint shadow called natural life, and that they would promote each other's spiritual labours, each according to its rank, and that they would know that receiving a prophet as a prophet is a duty which, if omitted, is more severely punished than every sin or wickedness beside.'

[3]

MILTON

Book the First

DAUGHTERS of Beulah ! Muses who inspire the Poet's Song!
Record the journey of immortal Milton thro' your Realms
Of terror & mild moony lustre, in soft sexual delusions
Of varied beauty to delight the wanderer and repose
His burning thirst & freezing hunger ! Come into my hand,
By your mild power descending down the Nerves of my right arm
From out the Portals of my Brain, where by your ministry
The Eternal Great Humanity Divine planted his Paradise,
And in it caus'd the Spectres of the Dead to take sweet forms
In likeness of himself. Tell also of the False Tongue vegetated
Beneath your land of shadows, of its sacrifices and
Its offerings ; even till Jesus, the image of the Invisible God,
Became its prey, a curse, an offering and an atonement
For Death Eternal in the heavens of Albion & before the Gates
Of Jerusalem his Emanation in the heavens beneath Beulah !

Say first, what mov'd Milton, who walk'd about in Eternity
One hundred years, pond'ring the intricate mazes of Providence?

Page 3. 1–5 See Index, *Beulah*. Lines 3–5 have no reference to Milton, but allude to the general character of the State as a ' pleasant retreat ', a mode of existence undisturbed by doubts.

7–9 This Paradise, planted within the Brain by the Daughters of Beulah, the true Muses, appears to symbolize the vision of truth granted to such as Blake, wherein those ideas that to uninspired mortal man are ' forms of death ' are seen in their ' real and eternal form ', which is human. Further, these visions of truths, retaining their identity, are seen by the visionary merged in the Vision of Truth, also human-formed, the ' One Man, Jesus '. Cp. J. 98. 28–99. 5.

10 The Tongue is the ' seat of Satan ' (M. 24. 45). Vala is also described as ' vegetated into a hungry Stomach & a devouring Tongue '. The symbol would seem, therefore, to represent the destructive operation of error, but particularly to refer to the inter-relation of materialism and restrictive morality, the latter proceeding out of the former. The association of the Tongue with Tharmas carries also the same significance : cp. F. Z. i. 18 and *note* : J. 14. 4–9 : 63. 5–6.

12–14 See Index, *Incarnation* and *Crucifixion*.

17 Blake, who elsewhere identifies his own mission as prophet with that here ascribed to Milton (cp. M. 14. 47–50), gives one hundred years as

Unhappy tho' in heav'n, he obey'd; he murmur'd not; he was silent,
Viewing his Sixfold Emanation scatter'd thro' the deep
In torment. To go into the deep, her to redeem & himself perish,
That cause at length mov'd Milton to this unexampled deed,
A Bard's prophetic Song: for sitting at eternal tables,
Terrific among the Sons of Albion, in chorus solemn & loud
A Bard broke forth: all sat attentive to the awful man.

'Mark well my words! they are of your eternal salvation.

'Three Classes are Created by the Hammer of Los, & Woven
[4] From Golgonooza, the spiritual Four-fold London eternal,
In immense labours & sorrows ever building, ever falling,
Thro' Albion's four Forests, which overspread all the Earth
From London Stone to Blackheath east, to Hounslow west,
To Finchley north, to Norwood south; and the weights

approximately the period between John Milton's death and the commencement of his own career as visionary.

19 See *Milton*, Introduction.

21 That] What *in New York Public Library and Butt's copies.* The British Museum copy shows traces of the 'W' beneath the 'T'.

23 The 'Sons of Albion' here appear to be the 'Eternals'. For the later meaning of the symbol, see Index, *Spectre, Note II* (*a*).

26 This division of men into the Elect, the Redeemed, and the Reprobate is confined to *Milton*. The first and third, for which Blake adopts in irony the names assigned to them according to the fallacy of the moral law, seem the clearest, and appear to represent the contrary modes of existence in mundane life. The former, 'who cannot Believe in Eternal Life Except by Miracle and a New Birth' (M. 25. 33–34) include Satan (M. 5. 5) and are associated with the 'Virtues and Cruel Goodnesses' (M. 11. 34) of the Moral Law of Horeb. The Reprobate are they 'who never cease to Believe' (M. 25. 35); of these is Rintrah, an Orc-like daemon, the vehement assailant of Satan's dissimulations (M. 6. 34). Difficulty arises in the statement that they are 'form'd to destruction from the mother's womb' (M. 5. 4: 6. 34). This may be explained by reference to Blake's doctrine of Self-annihilation: see General Introduction, p. 88. Between the Elect and the Reprobate 'stand the Redeemed', the least distinct of the Classes. They 'live in doubts & fears, perpetually tormented by the Elect. Palamabron, the type of the Elect, is here quite obscure: he is 'redeemd from Satan's Law, the wrath falling on Rintrah' (M. 9. 22).

Page 4 appears to be an interpolation. It interrupts the sequence of pp. 3 and 5; its use of geographical symbols relating to Britain is common to *Jerusalem*, rare in *Milton*.

3–5 It would seem, from J. 42. 73–81, that Albion's Four Forests are symbolically identical with the Veil of Vala: see Index, *Weaving*. The dark labyrinth of mundane error is frequently described under the image of a forest: cp. S. E., *The Voice of the Ancient Bard.*

4–5 It is difficult to discover the archaeological theory that Blake adopted with regard to London Stone. As a symbol it is always associated with repressive morality, being sometimes mentioned in connexion with

From Golgonooza the spiritual Four-fold London eternal
In immense labours & sorrows, ever building, ever falling,
Thro Albions four Forests which overspread all the Earth,
From London Stone to Blackheath east: to Hounslow west:
To Finchley north: to Norwood south: and the weights
Of Enitharmons Loom play lulling cadences on the
winds of Albion
From Caithness in the north, to Lizard-point & Dover in the south

Loud sounds the Hammer of Los, & loud his Bellows is heard
Before London to Hampsteads breadths & Highgates heights To
Stratford & old Bow: & across to the Gardens of Kensington
On Tyburns Brook: loud groans Thames beneath the iron Forge
Of Rintrah & Palamabron of Theotorm & Bromion, to
forge the instruments
Of Harvest: the Plow & Harrow to pass over the Nations

The Surrey hills glow like the clinkers of the furnace: Lambeths Vale
Where Jerusalems foundations began; where they were laid in ruins
Where they were laid in ruins from every Nation & Oak Groves rooted
Dark gleams before the Furnace-mouth a heap of burning ashes
When shall Jerusalem return & overspread all the Nations
Return: return to Lambeths Vale O building of human souls
Thence stony Druid Temples overspread the Island white
And thence from Jerusalems ruins.. from her walls of salvation
And praise: thro the whole Earth were reard from Ireland
To Mexico & Peru west, & east to China & Japan: till Babel
The Spectre of Albion frownd over the Nations in glory & war
All things begin & end in Albions ancient Druid rocky shore
But now the Starry Heavens are fled
from the mighty limbs of
Albion

Loud sounds the Hammer of Los, loud turn the Wheels of Enitharmon
Her Looms vibrate with soft affections, weaving the Web of Life
Out from the ashes of the Dead; Los lifts his iron Ladles
With molten ore: he heaves the iron cliffs in his rattling chains
From Hyde Park to the Alms-houses of Mile-end & old Bow
Here the Three Classes of Mortal Men take their fixd destinations
And hence they overspread the Nations of the whole Earth & hence
The Web of Life is woven: & the tender sinews of life created
And the Three Classes of Men regulated by Los's Hammer, and
woven

Milton : page 4

Of Enitharmon's Loom play lulling cadences on the winds of Albion
From Caithness in the north to Lizard-point & Dover in the south.

' Loud sounds the Hammer of Los & loud his Bellows is heard
Before London to Hampstead's breadths & Highgate's heights, To
Stratford & old Bow, & across to the Gardens of Kensington
On Tyburn's Brook: loud groans Thames beneath the iron Forge
Of Rintrah & Palamabron, of Theotorm & Bromion, to forge the instruments
Of Harvest, the Plow & Harrow, to pass over the Nations.

' The Surrey hills glow like the clinkers of the furnace; Lambeth's Vale,
Where Jerusalem's foundations began, where they were laid in ruins,
Where they were laid in ruins from every Nation, & Oak Groves rooted,

Druidical monuments, e.g. Stonehenge, as a place of sacrifice. Norwood, Finchley, Blackheath, and Hounslow, lying to the south, north, east, and west respectively of London, are identified with the Four Forests noted above, and represent the antagonism of Natural Religion which in mortal life besets on all sides the imaginative activity, symbolized by London or Golgonooza. Cp. J. 13. 30 seq.

7 Similarly the Furnaces of Los (see Index, *Los, Note III*, A) are ranged from ' South to North ' (J. 53. 14). The Spectres of the Dead ' revolve into the Furnaces Southward & are driven forth Northward '. See also Index, *Weaving*, II–IV.

9 These districts lying to the north of London are identified with the error against which the inspired Prophet, Los, labours. A curious passage in one of Blake's letters may have some bearing on the adoption of these names as symbols: 'When I was young, Hampstead, Highgate, Hornsey, Muswell Hill, and even Islington, and all places north of London, always laid me up the day after, and sometimes two or three days, with precisely the same complaint, and the same torment of the stomach; easily removed, but excruciating while it lasts, and enfeebling for some time after' (Letter to John Linnell, 1 February 1826, R., p. 211). For Tyburn see F. Z. ii. 249 *note*.

12 See Index, *Los, Note II* (*a*). 13 See Index, *Plow and Harrow*.

14 It was in Lambeth that Blake engraved his early books, and where he heard spiritual voices: cp. J. 38. 40. Hence, apparently, it is always spoken of in connexion with the highest forms of visionary aspiration and achievement in mundane life, ' Jerusalem's Inner Court.' It is the place of refuge for ' Jerusalem ' (see Index, *Jerusalem*) from the assaults of ' Satan's watch fiends ', the powers of moral law and destructive reason. From another point of view, it is the starting-point of human regeneration, where ' Jerusalem's Foundation began '.

16 Following upon Blake's identification of mundane error with Druidism (see Index, *Druid*), all the forms and appurtenances of Druidical worship—

Dark gleams before the Furnace-mouth a heap of burning ashes.
When shall Jerusalem return & overspread all the Nations ?
Return, return to Lambeth's Vale, O building of human souls!
Thence stony Druid Temples overspread the Island white ;
And thence from Jerusalem's ruins, from her walls of salvation
And praise, thro' the whole Earth were rear'd, from Ireland
To Mexico & Peru west, & east to China & Japan, till Babel,
The Spectre of Albion, frown'd over the Nations in glory & war.
All things begin & end in Albion's ancient Druid rocky shore ;
But now the Starry Heavens are fled from the mighty limbs of Albion.

'Loud sounds the Hammer of Los, loud turn the Wheels of Enitharmon.
Her Looms vibrate with soft affections, weaving the Web of Life
Out from the ashes of the Dead. Los lifts his iron Ladles
With molten ore ; he heaves the iron cliffs in his rattling chains
From Hyde Park to the Alms-houses of Mile-end & old Bow.
Here the Three Classes of Mortal Men take their fix'd destinations ;
And hence they overspread the Nations of the whole Earth ; & hence
The Web of Life is woven, & the tender sinews of life created,
And the Three Classes of Men regulated by Los's Hammer, and woven
[5] 'By Enitharmon's Looms, & Spun beneath the Spindle of Tirzah.

oak groves, temples, stones of trial and sacrifice, wicker cage and sacrificial knife—are used in elaboration of the main idea of moral and intellectual tyranny and destructiveness. 19 Cp. F. Z. viii. 176–184.

20 Cp. *Europe*, 117 *note*, and F. Z. viii. 4 *note*.

23 Babel, Babylon, or Shinar are used to express the contrary of the visionary state, Jerusalem : see Index, *Vala*. This is the only place where Babel or Babylon is identified with a masculine symbol such as Albion's Spectre.

25–26 Cp. J. 27 and 75. 27.

28–29 Cp. M. 28. 47–54, and see Index, *Weaving*.

31 The direction from west to east symbolizes the purpose of Los's labours, which are bent against Ulro or Error, located in the east. The west is associated with Eden, the high spiritual state that Man forsook at the Fall.

35–p. 5. 1 and woven . . . Tirzah] These words are deleted in the copy of *Milton* in the New York Public Library and in the Windus copy.

Page 5. 1 The mention of Tirzah as spinning in the company of Los and Enitharmon is a difficulty, unless, as in M. 28. 53, she perverts the 'mild

The first, The Elect from before the foundation of the World;
The second, The Redeem'd; The Third, The Reprobate, & form'd
To destruction from the mother's womb: follow with me my plow!

'Of the first class was Satan: with incomparable mildness
His primitive tyrannical attempts on Los: with most endearing love
He soft intreated Los to give to him Palamabron's station;
For Palamabron return'd with labour wearied every evening.
Palamabron oft refus'd; and as often Satan offer'd
His service, till, by repeated offers and repeated intreaties,
Los gave to him the Harrow of the Almighty; alas, blamable!
Palamabron fear'd to be angry lest Satan should accuse him of
Ingratitude, & Los believe the accusation thro' Satan's extreme
Mildness. Satan labour'd all day—it was a thousand years:
In the evening, returning terrified, overlabour'd & astonish'd,
Embrac'd soft with a brother's tears Palamabron, who also wept.

'Mark well my words! they are of your eternal salvation.

'Next morning Palamabron rose: the horses of the Harrow
Were madden'd with tormenting fury, & the servants of the Harrow,
The Gnomes, accus'd Satan with indignation, fury and fire.
Then Palamabron, reddening like the Moon in an eclipse,
Spoke, saying: "You know Satan's mildness and his self-imposition;

influences' of the Eternal Prophet and his Emanation, or unless the distinction is made as in J. 18. 7 'Vala [=Tirzah] produc'd the Bodies, Jerusalem gave the Souls'.

4 To . . . plow] engraved as two lines, but the last part of one and the first part of the other were deleted between the words 'womb' and 'follow'.

7–11 Los, 'whose Will both Time and Space obey' (M. 20. 17), permits the Redeemed, those who 'live in doubts and fears', to be tormented by Satan, who is of the Elect; those who 'cannot Believe in Eternal Life without Miracle and a New Birth'. This may be reminiscent of Blake's relations with Hayley: see *Milton*, Introduction.

18–20 The exact significance of the Horses and Gnomes of the Harrow has not been discovered. All that seems certain is that, from M. 10. 14–17, the former would seem to represent a higher degree of spiritual perception than the latter. Blake shows this by contrasting their conduct when they are confronted with Leutha's usurpation of Elynittria's control of the Harrow. While the Horses instantly discern the presence of the false Leutha and refuse to submit to her power, the Gnomes are unable to discover the illusion, and are compelled to become the servants of Satan. For a different use of the symbol Gnomes see M. 31. 17–27.

Seeming a brother, being a tyrant, even thinking himself a brother
While he is murdering the just: prophetic I behold
His future course thro' darkness and despair to eternal death.
But we must not be tyrants also! He hath assum'd my place
For one whole day under pretence of pity and love to me.
My horses hath he madden'd, and my fellow servants injur'd.
How should he ⟨he⟩ know the duties of another? O foolish forbearance!
Would I had told Los all my heart! but patience, O my friends!
All may be well: silent remain, while I call Los and Satan."

'Loud as the wind of Beulah that unroots the rocks & hills
Palamabron call'd, and Los & Satan came before him;
And Palamabron shew'd the horses & the servants. Satan wept;
And mildly cursing Palamabron, him accus'd of crimes
Himself had wrought. Los trembled. Satan's blandishments almost
Perswaded the Prophet of Eternity that Palamabron
Was Satan's enemy, & that the Gnomes, being Palamabron's friends,
Were leagued together against Satan thro' ancient enmity.
What could Los do? how could he judge, when Satan's self believ'd
That he had not oppres'd the horses of the Harrow nor the servants?

'So Los said: "Henceforth, Palamabron, let each his own station
Keep; nor in pity false, nor in officious brotherhood, where
None needs, be active." Mean time Palamabron's horses
Rag'd with thick flames redundant, & the Harrow madden'd with fury.
Trembling Palamabron stood; the strongest of Demons trembled,
Curbing his living creatures: many of the strongest Gnomes
They bit in their wild fury, who also madden'd like wildest beasts.

26 Cp. J. 31. 29–35.

32 The 'wind of Beulah' is not mentioned elsewhere, and is not clearly related to the common use of the symbol 'Beulah'.

42–44 Cp. F. Z. ix. 361–372 and the myth of Luvah and Urizen: see Index, *Luvah, II*.

'Mark well my words! they are of your eternal salvation.

[6] 'Mean while wept Satan before Los, accusing Palamabron,
Himself exculpating with mildest speech, for himself believ'd
That he had not op[p]ress'd nor injur'd the refractory servants.

'But Satan, returning to his Mills (for Palamabron had serv'd
The Mills of Satan as the easier task), found all confusion,
And back return'd to Los, not fill'd with vengeance but with tears.
Himself convinc'd of Palamabron's turpitude, Los beheld
The servants of the Mills drunken with wine and dancing wild
With shouts and Palamabron's songs rending the forests green
With ecchoing confusion, tho' the Sun was risen on high.

'Then Los took off his left sandal, placing it on his head,
Signal of solemn mourning. When the servants of the Mills
Beheld the signal, they in silence stood, tho' drunk with wine.
Los wept. But Rintrah also came; and Enitharmon on
His arm lean'd tremblingly, observing all these things.

'And Los said: "Ye Genii of the Mills, the Sun is on high:
Your labours call you. Palamabron is also in sad dilemma.
His horses are mad, his Harrow confounded, his companions enrag'd.
Mine is the fault! I should have remember'd that pity divides the soul,
And man unmans. Follow with me my Plow! this mournful day
Must be a blank in Nature; follow with me, and tomorrow again
Resume your labours, & this day shall be a mournful day."

'Wildly they follow'd Los and Rintrah, & the Mills were silent.
They mourn'd all day this mournful day of Satan & Palamabron;
And all the Elect & all the Redeem'd mourn'd one toward another
Upon the mountains of Albion, among the cliffs of the Dead.

Page 6. 4 The Mills of Satan, like the Starry Wheels of Albion's Sons (cp. F. Z. iv. 274 *note*) symbolize the destructive operation of moral law and empiricism. Nothing has been discovered that throws light upon the significance of Palamabron's service in the Mills.

19–20 Cp. B. U. v. 34, where the phrase 'pity divides the soul' is used in connexion with the first manifestation of sex. Here apparently the sense is best given by a phrase of Blake's found elsewhere 'He who keeps not right onwards is lost' (Letter to Butts, 10 January 1802, R., p. 100).

21 'Nature' occurs in Blake in so many different senses that it is impossible to discover its meaning here.

'They Plow'd in tears! incessant pour'd Jehovah's rain; & Molech's
Thick fires, contending with the rain, thunder'd above, rolling
Terrible over their heads. Satan wept over Palamabron;
Theotormon & Bromion contended on the side of Satan,
Pitying his youth and beauty, trembling at eternal death.
Michael contended against Satan in the rolling thunder;
Thulloh, the friend of Satan, also reprov'd him; faint their reproof.

'But Rintrah, who is of the reprobate, of those form'd to destruction,
In indignation for Satan's soft dissimulation of friendship,
Flam'd above all the plowèd furrows, angry, red and furious,
Till Michael sat down in the furrow, weary, dissolv'd in tears.
Satan, who drave the team beside him, stood angry & red.
He smote Thulloh & slew him; & he stood terrible over Michael,
Urging him to arise: he wept. Enitharmon saw his tears,
But Los hid Thulloh from her sight, lest she should die of grief.
She wept: she trembled: she kissèd Satan: she wept over Michael.
She form'd a Space for Satan & Michael & for the poor infected;
Trembling she wept over the Space & clos'd it with a tender Moon.

'Los secret buried Thulloh, weeping disconsolate over the moony Space.

'But Palamabron callèd down a Great Solemn Assembly,
That he who will not defend Truth may be compellèd to
Defend a Lie, that he may be snared & caught & taken.

27 Jehovah and Molech are among the Seven Angels of the Divine Presence, set to guard the 'space' of mundane existence providentially created to receive the fallen spirits (cp. F. Z. viii. 388 *note*). Both fail to perform the charge, and appear as sources of repressive morality. Molech 'rejoices In moral law and its severe penalties' (J. 68. 38–39), and Jehovah, or Jehovah Elohim, is represented, somewhat after the manner of the Gnostics, as a rebellious spirit whose Law and Temple, the body of error apparent to physical perception as the physical body, Jesus descends to put off and annihilate. Jehovah in this connexion is the God of this World, Satan (cp. F. Z. viii. 395 *note*). On the other hand, such explicit statements of the doctrine of unconditional forgiveness as appear in J. 61 and *The Ghost of Abel*, are described as Visions of Jehovah or Jehovah Elohim. Elsewhere, too, Jehovah is apparently identical with God, the Divine Humanity: cp. J. 98. 40.

32–33 Michael and Thulloh are obscure symbols not found elsewhere.

43–44 See Index, *Space*.

47–48 These lines recur J. 9. 29–30 with the addition 'That Enthusiasm and Life may not cease'.

[7] ‘ And all Eden descended into Palamabron's tent
Among Albion's Druids & Bards, in the caves beneath Albion's
Death Couch, in the caverns of death, in the corner of the Atlantic.
And in the midst of the Great Assembly Palamabron pray'd :
“ O God, protect me from my friends, that they have not power over me.
Thou hast giv'n me power to protect myself from my bitterest enemies.”

‘ Mark well my words ! they are of your eternal salvation.

‘ Then rose the Two Witnesses, Rintrah & Palamabron.
And Palamabron appeal'd to all Eden, and reciev'd
Judgment : and Lo ! it fell on Rintrah and his rage,
Which now flam'd high & furious in Satan against Palamabron,
Till it became a proverb in Eden : “ Satan is among the Reprobate.”

‘ Los in his wrath curs'd heaven & earth ; he rent up Nations,
Standing on Albion's rocks among high-rear'd Druid temples
Which reach the stars of heaven & stretch from pole to pole.
He displac'd continents ; the oceans fled before his face :
He alter'd the poles of the world, east, west & north & south ;
But he clos'd up Enitharmon from the sight of all these things.

‘ For Satan, flaming with Rintrah's fury hidden beneath his own mildness,

Page 7. 2 See Index, *Druids*. On ‘ Albion's Death Couch ’ the ‘ real and immortal Self ’ is reposed (M. 14. 9–16), guarded round by the Angels of the Divine Presence, and fed with ‘ food of Eden ’ till the fallen Man shall have consummated his ‘ passage through Eternal Death ’ in ‘ the awaking to Eternal Life ’. The Death Couch may therefore be taken as significant of man's ultimate regeneration. See Index, *Mundane Shell*, IV.

3 See Index, *Atlantic Continent*.

5–6 Cp. Letter to Butts, 25th April 1803 (R., p. 114) : ‘ If a man is the enemy of my spiritual life while he pretends to be the friend of my corporeal, he is a real enemy ; but the man may be the friend of my spiritual life while he seems the enemy of my corporeal, though not *vice versa*.’ Cp. M., extra p. 3. 26 : ‘ Corporeal Friends are Spiritual Enemies.’

8–12 This passage, with its reference to the ‘ Witnesses ’ and the ‘ Judgment ’, remains obscure. For the Witnesses cp. Rev. xi. 3.

13–18 These difficult lines may have something of the same meaning as J. 91. 50–52 :

> Thus Los alter'd his Spectre, & every Ratio of his Reason
> He alter'd, time after time, with dire pain & many tears,
> Till he had completely divided him into a separate space.

Cp. also J. 11. 5 where Los labours ‘ Striving with Systems to deliver Individuals from those Systems ’.

18 Cp. B. U., chap. vii, ll. 37–39 and M. 9. 2–4.

Accus'd Palamabron before the Assembly of ingratitude, of malice.
He created Seven deadly Sins, drawing out his infernal scroll
Of Moral laws and cruel punishments upon the clouds of Jehovah,
To pervert the Divine voice in its entrance to the earth
With thunder of war & trumpets' sound, with armies of disease,
Punishments & deaths muster'd & number'd ; Saying : "I am God alone ;
There is no other : let all obey my principles of moral individuality.
I have brought them from the uppermost innermost recesses
Of my Eternal Mind : transgressors I will rend off for ever,
As now I rend this accursèd Family from my covering."

'Thus Satan rag'd amidst the Assembly, and his bosom grew
Opake against the Divine Vision ; the pavèd terraces of
His bosom inwards shone with fires ; but the stones becoming opake,
Hid him from sight in an extreme blackness and darkness :
And there a World of deeper Ulro was open'd in the midst
Of the Assembly In Satan's bosom, a vast unfathomable Abyss.

'Astonishment held the Assembly in an awful silence, and tears
Fell down as dews of night ; & a loud solemn universal groan
Was utter'd from the east & from the west & from the south
And from the north : and Satan stood opake, immeasurable,
Covering the east with solid blackness round his hidden heart,
With thunders utter'd from his hidden wheels accusing loud
The Divine Mercy for protecting Palamabron in his tent.

'Rintrah rear'd up walls of rock and pour'd rivers & moats
Of fire round the walls : columns of fire guard around
Between Satan and Palamabron in the terrible darkness.

22 Cp. M. 6. 17 *note*.
26–28 Cp. B. U., chap. ii, ll. 9–42 *note*, and Introduction to that book.
29 'This accurs'd Family' is the Divine Family united in Jesus. Satan's 'covering' is the 'Satanic body of Holiness', the 'sexual garments' described at length, M. 42. 35–43. 27.
31 See Index, *Expansion*, &c. 34 See Index, *Ulro*.
40 The east is the quarter of Ulro or Error : see Index, *Cardinal Points*.
41 Satan's hidden wheels do not seem to differ from those of Albion's Sons : cp. F. Z. iv. 274 *note*.

'And Satan, not having the Science of Wrath but only of Pity,
Rent them asunder, and wrath was left to wrath, & pity to pity.
He sunk down a dreadful Death, unlike the slumbers of Beulah.

'The Separation was terrible: the Dead was repos'd on his Couch
Beneath the Couch of Albion, on the seven mou[n]tains of Rome,
In the whole place of the Covering Cherub, Rome, Babylon & Tyre.
His Spectre, raging furious, descended into its Space.

[9] 'He set his face against Jerusalem to destroy the Eon of Albion.

'But Los hid Enitharmon from the sight of all these things
Upon the Thames, whose lulling harmony repos'd her soul,
Where Beulah lovely terminates in rocky Albion,
Terminating in Hyde Park, on Tyburn's awful brook.

'And the Mills of Satan were separated into a moony Space
Among the rocks of Albion's Temples; and Satan's Druid sons
Offer the Human Victims throughout all the Earth: and Albion's
Dread Tomb, immortal on his Rock, overshadow'd the whole Earth,

46–48 The corresponding passage (F. Z. viii. 382–386) differs from these lines in certain details, the significance of which is not apparent. In the earlier account Satan is condemned, and Rintrah and Palamabron are cut off from Golgonooza, the space created by Enitharmon for Satan and his companions. Swinburne has the following note to l. 46: 'That is, being unable to reconcile qualities, to pass beyond the legal and logical grounds of good and evil into the secret places where they are not. The whole argument hinges on this difference between Pantheism, which can, and Theism, which cannot, and is therefore no surer or saner than a mere religion based on Church or Bible, nor less incompetent to include, to expound, to redeem the world' (*Essay*, p. 263).

51 See Index, *Mundane Shell, Note I*, A.

Page 8. Full-page engraving, without text. It may represent Satan 'flaming' before Los and Enitharmon.

Page 9. 1 The Eon is the Emanation: see Index, *Emanation*.

5 Hyde Park, from its situation in relation to London, has the usual symbolic significance of the western quarter, the place of vision. For Tyburn cp. F. Z. ii. 249 *note*.

6 Cp. M. 6. 4 *note*. 9–10 'Albion's dread Tomb', cp. M. 7. 2 and *note*.

Where Satan, making to himself Laws from his own identity,
Compell'd others to serve him in moral gratitude & submission,
Being call'd God, setting himself above all that is callèd God.
And all the Spectres of the Dead, calling themselves Sons of God,
In his Synagogues worship Satan under the Unutterable Name.

'And it was enquir'd: Why in a Great Solemn Assembly
The Innocent should be condemn'd for the Guilty? Then an Eternal rose,

'Saying: "If the Guilty should be condemn'd, he must be an Eternal Death;
And one must die for another throughout all Eternity.
Satan is fall'n from his station, & never can be redeem'd,
But must be new Created continually, moment by moment.
And therefore the Class of Satan shall be call'd the Elect, & those
Of Rintrah the Reprobate, & those of Palamabron the Redeem'd;
For he is redeem'd from Satan's Law, the wrath falling on Rintrah.
And therefore Palamabron dared not to call a solemn Assembly
Till Satan had assum'd Rintrah's wrath in the day of mourning,
In a feminine delusion of false pride self-deciev'd."

'So spoke the Eternal, and confirm'd it with a thunderous oath.

But when Leutha (a Daughter of Beulah) beheld Satan's condemnation,

10–14 Cp. J. 90. 52–56, and M. 7. 26.

15–26 See General Introduction, p. 96. The 'Innocent' may be Rintrah: cp. M. 7. 10.

28 For the earlier use of Leutha cp. V. D. A., Introduction. The present myth, with its vague suggestion of the Miltonic description of Sin (*Paradise Lost*, ii. 747–814), is not repeated elsewhere. Though called a Daughter of Beulah, Leutha appears to belong rather to the same class of symbols as Vala and the Daughters of Albion. She is contrasted with Elynittria as Vala with Jerusalem (J., pp. 20–24), and ultimately gives birth to 'the Spectre of Sleep, nam'd Death' and to 'Rahab' (M. 11. 41). The only point in which she differs from the general nature of the 'disobedient Female' is in her act of self-sacrifice, in offering herself a ransom for Satan, and taking on herself his sin. Possibly here, as elsewhere (see *Milton*, Introduction), Blake's chief purpose is to correct the Miltonic history of

She down descended into the midst of the Great Solemn Assembly,
Offering herself a Ransom for Satan, taking on her his Sin.

'Mark well my words! they are of your eternal salvatiòn.

'And Leutha stood glowing with varying colours, immortal, heart-piercing
And lovely; & her moth-like elegance shone over the Assembly.

'At length, standing upon the golden floor of Palamabron,
She spake: "I am the Author of this Sin: by my suggestion
My Parent power Satan has committed this transgression.
I lovèd Palamabron, & I sought to approach his Tent,
But beautiful Elynittria with her silver arrows repell'd me,
[10] For her light is terrible to me. I fade before her immortal beauty.
O wherefore doth a Dragon-form forth issue from my limbs
To sieze her new born son? Ah me! the wretched Leutha!
This to prevent, entering the doors of Satan's brain night after night,
Like sweet perfumes I stupified the masculine perceptions,
And kept only the feminine awake; hence rose his soft
Delusory love to Palamabron, admiration join'd with envy,
Cupidity unconquerable. My fault, when at noon of day
The Horses of Palamabron call'd for rest and pleasant death,
I sprang out of the breast of Satan, over the Harrow beaming
In all my beauty, that I might unloose the flaming steeds
As Elynittria used to do: but too well those living creatures
Knew that I was not Elynittria, and they brake the traces.
But me the servants of the Harrow saw not but as a bow
Of varying colours on the hills: terribly rag'd the horses.
Satan, astonish'd, and with power above his own controll
Compell'd the Gnomes to curb the horses, & to throw banks of sand

Satan, by carefully avoiding any suggestion of vengeance against Satan, and emphasizing the contrary doctrine of forgiveness and self-sacrifice by exhibiting it even in Leutha.

36 For the term 'Parent power' cp. F. Z. i. 18 *note*.
38 See *Europe*, 43 *note*.
5 Cp. *Europe*, 174–175. 5–6 See Index, *Sex*.
12–19 Cp. M. 5. 18 *note*.

Around the fiery flaming Harrow in labyrinthine forms,
And brooks between to intersect the meadows in their course.
The Harrow cast thick flames: Jehovah thunder'd above.
Chaos & ancient night fled from beneath the fiery Harrow.
The Harrow cast thick flames, & orb'd us round in concave fires, 22
A Hell of our own making: see, its flames still gird me round.
Jehovah thunder'd above. Satan, in pride of heart,
Drove the fierce Harrow among the constellations of Jehovah,
Drawing a third part in the fires as stubble north & south,
To devour Albion and Jerusalem the Emanation of Albion,
Driving the Harrow in Pity's paths. 'Twas then, with our dark fires,
Which now gird round us (O eternal torment!), I form'd the Serpent
Of precious stones & gold, turn'd poisons on the sultry wastes.
The Gnomes in all that day spar'd not; they curs'd Satan bitterly. 31
To do unkind things in kindness, with power arm'd to say
The most irritating things in the midst of tears and love,
These are the stings of the Serpent: thus did we by them, till thus
They in return retaliated, and the Living Creatures madden'd.
The Gnomes labour'd: I, weeping, hid in Satan's inmost brain. 36
But when the Gnomes refus'd to labour more, with blandishments
I came forth from the head of Satan: back the Gnomes recoil'd
And call'd me Sin, and for a sign portentous held me. Soon
Day sunk, and Palamabron return'd; trembling I hid myself
In Satan's inmost Palace of his nervous fine wrought Brain.
For Elynittria met Satan with all her singing women, 42
Terrific in their joy & pouring wine of wildest power.
They gave Satan their wine: indignant at the burning wrath,
Wild with prophetic fury, his former life became like a dream.

24–28 'Jehovah' is used in the symbol's higher signification: cp. M. 6. 27 *note*. Satan has reference to a false concept of Deity such as Milton presents in *Paradise Lost*. The symbolic details are obscure, but the general drift of this passage seems to repeat the charge of inconsistency against the attribution of 'pity' to a God of Moral Law, the murderer of Albion and Jerusalem.

29–30 See Index, *Serpent*.

41 Cp. J. 89. 14–15, where Blake writes of the Covering Cherub, a symbol not distinguishable from Satan:

> His Head, dark, deadly, in its Brain incloses a reflexion
> Of Eden all perverted.

Cloth'd in the Serpent's folds, in selfish holiness demanding purity,
Being most impure, self-condemn'd to eternal tears, he drove
Me from his inmost Brain, & the doors clos'd with thunder's sound.
O Divine Vision, who didst create the Female to repose
The Sleepers of Beulah, pity the repentant Leutha! My
[11] Sick Couch bears the dark shades of Eternal Death, infolding
The Spectre of Satan: he furious refuses to repose in sleep.
I humbly bow in all my Sin before the Throne Divine.
Not so the Sick-one. Alas, what shall be done him to restore
Who calls the Individual Law Holy, and despises the Saviour,
Glorying to involve Albion's Body in fires of eternal War?"

'Now Leutha ceas'd: tears flow'd; but the Divine Pity supported her.

"All is my fault. We are the Spectre of Luvah, the murderer
Of Albion. O Vala! O Luvah! O Albion! O lovely Jerusalem!
The Sin was begun in Eternity, and will not rest to Eternity,
Till two Eternitys meet together. Ah! lost! lost! lost for ever!"

'So Leutha spoke. But when she saw that Enitharmon had
Created a New Space to protect Satan from punishment,
She fled to Enitharmon's Tent & hid herself. Loud raging
Thunder'd the Assembly, dark & clouded; and they ratify'd
The kind decision of Enitharmon, & gave a Time to the Space,
Even Six Thousand years, and sent Lucifer for its Guard.
But Lucifer refus'd to die, & in pride he forsook his charge.
And they elected Molech; and when Molech was impatient,
The Divine hand found the Two Limits, first of Opacity, then of Contraction.
Opacity was namèd Satan, Contraction was namèd Adam.
Triple Elohim came: Elohim, wearied, fainted: they elected Shaddai.

49 Cp. M. 30. 1–31, and see Index, *Female*.
Page 11. 4–6 Cp. B. U. ii. 9 *note*.
8–9 See Index, *Luvah*.
12–17 See Index, *Space*. 'Enitharmon's Tent' and the 'Space' of six thousand years are equivalent symbols.
17–29 Cp. F. Z. viii. 388–396 and *note*.
20–21 See Index, *Expansion*. The reason for associating the creation of the Limits with Molech is not apparent, unless Blake means that the conception of the Jehovah-God belongs to a period in the history of the Universe later than the limitation of Being to the human. Hence the Limits are not associated with Molech, but are anterior to the emergence of the concept of Jehovah Elohim.

Shaddai angry, Pahad descended: Pahad terrified, they sent Jehovah.
And Jehovah was leprous: loud he call'd, stretching his hand to Eternity;
For then the Body of Death was perfected in hypocritic holiness
Around the Lamb, a Female Tabernacle woven in Cathedron's Looms.
He died as a Reprobate; he was Punish'd as a Transgressor.
Glory! Glory! Glory to the Holy Lamb of God!
I touch the heavens as an instrument to glorify the Lord!

'The Elect shall meet the Redeem'd; on Albion's rocks they shall meet,
Astonish'd at the Transgressor, in him beholding the Saviour.
And the Elect shall say to the Redeem'd: "We behold it is of Divine
Mercy alone, of Free Gift and Election, that we live.
Our Virtues & Cruel Goodnesses have deserv'd Eternal Death."
Thus they weep upon the fatal Brook of Albion's River.

'But Elynittria met Leutha in the place where she was hidden,
And threw aside her arrows and laid down her sounding Bow;
She sooth'd her with soft words, & brought her to Palamabron's bed.
In moments new created for delusion interwoven round about,
In dreams she bore the shadowy Spectre of Sleep, & nam'd him Death:
In dreams she bore Rahab, the mother of Tirzah & her sisters
In Lambeth's vales, in Cambridge & in Oxford, places of Thought,
Intricate labyrinths of Times and Spaces unknown that Leutha livèd
In Palamabron's Tent: and Oothoon was her charming guard.'

25–27 See Index, *Incarnation*.

30–34 Cp. M. 3. 26 *note*. 32–34 Cp. J. 45. 10–16.

35 'The Brook of Albion's River' is another name for 'Tyburn's brook' constantly associated with the idea of the Crucifixion: cp. F. Z. ii. 249 *note*. 42 Cp. M. 4. 14 *note*.

44 For the earlier significance of the symbol 'Oothoon', cp. V. D. A., Introductory Note. Later she is described as the daughter of Los and Enitharmon. In *Europe*, ll. 182–183, she is referred to as purposing to 'give up woman's secrecy', i.e. the power of the moral law. In the later books she is associated with the other children of Los in the work of regeneration (see Index, *Los*, *Note II, a*). Her 'palace' is in Lambeth, remote from 'Ulro', or Error, and opening into 'Beulah' (J. 41. 17–22).

The Bard ceas'd. All consider'd, and a loud resounding murmur
Continu'd round the Halls; and much they question'd the immortal
Loud voic'd Bard: and many condemn'd the high toned Song,
Saying: 'Pity and Love are too venerable for the imputation
Of Guilt.' Others said: 'If it is true, if the acts have been perform'd,
Let the Bard himself witness. Where hadst thou this terrible Song?'

The Bard replied: 'I am Inspired! I know it is Truth! for I Sing
[12] According to the inspiration of the Poetic Genius,
Who is the eternal, all-protecting Divine Humanity,
To whom be Glory & Power & Dominion Evermore. Amen.'

Then there was great murmuring in the Heavens of Albion
Concerning Generation & the Vegetative power & concerning
The Lamb, the Saviour. Albion trembled to Italy, Greece, & Egypt,
To Tartary & Hindostan & China & to Great America,
Shaking the roots & fast foundations of the Earth in doubtfulness.
The loud voic'd Bard, terrify'd, took refuge in Milton's bosom.

Then Milton rose up from the heavens of Albion ardorous.
The whole Assembly wept prophetic, seeing in Milton's face
And in his lineaments divine the shades of Death & Ulro;
He took off the robe of the promise & ungirded himself from the oath of God.

And Milton said: 'I go to Eternal Death! The Nations still
Follow after the detestable Gods of Priam in pomp
Of warlike selfhood, contradicting and blasphеming.
When will the Resurrection come, to deliver the sleeping body
From corruptibility? O when, Lord Jesus, wilt thou come?
Tarry no longer, for my soul lies at the gates of death.
I will arise and look forth for the morning of the grave;
I will go down to the sepulcher to see if morning breaks;

51. See General Introduction, pp. 43–45.

Page 12. 13 These expressions, apparently equivalent, cannot be interpreted with certainty. They may possibly be identical with 'the clothing of the Forgiveness of Sins' (G. A. 46–48), the perfect existence that Milton forgoes in order to accomplish the final annihilation of error,

15 Cp. D. C. iii, p. 21, quoted F. Z. ix. 361 *note*.

20–21 Cp. J. 97. 3–4:

> For lo! the Night of Death is past and the Eternal Day
> Appears upon our Hills.

I will go down to self annihilation and eternal death,
Lest the Last Judgment come & find me unannihilate,
And I be siez'd & giv'n into the hands of my own Selfhood.
The Lamb of God is seen thro' mists & shadows, hov'ring
Over the sepulchers in clouds of Jehovah & winds of Elohim,
A disk of blood, distant: & heav'ns & earths roll dark between.
What do I here before the Judgment, without my Emanation,
With the daughters of memory, & not with the daughters of
inspiration?
I in my Selfhood am that Satan. I am that Evil One.
He is my Spectre: in my obedience to loose him from my Hells,
To claim the Hells, my Furnaces, I go to Eternal Death.'

And Milton said: 'I go to Eternal Death.' Eternity shudder'd;
For he took the outside course among the graves of the dead,
A mournful shade. Eternity shudder'd at the image of eternal
death.

Then on the verge of Beulah he beheld his own Shadow,
A mournful form, double, hermaphroditic, male & female
In one wonderful body; and he enter'd into it
In direful pain; for the dread shadow, twenty-seven fold,
Reach'd to the depths of direst Hell, & thence to Albion's land,
Which is this earth of vegetation on which now I write.

The Seven Angels of the Presence wept over Milton's Shadow.

22 See Index, *Self-annihilation*.
23 Cp. Cat. 1810, quoted F. Z. ix. 32 *note*. 25–27 Cp. J. 66. 40. 43.
28–29 For Blake's criticism of John Milton see the Introduction to *Milton*. The present passage clearly states that part, at all events, of what Milton wrote did not proceed from inspiration and was therefore false. Cp. Cat. 1810: The [? Ancients produce fable] when they Assert that Jupiter usurped the Throne of his Father Saturn, & brought on an Iron Age, & begat on Mnemosyne or Memory The Greek Muses, which are not Inspiration, as the Bible is. Reality was Forgot, & the Vanities of Time & Space only Remember'd, & call'd Reality. Such is the Mighty difference between Allegoric Fable & Spiritual Mystery. Let it here be Noted that the Greek Fables originated in Spiritual Mystery and Real Vision, which are lost & clouded in Fable & Allegory, while the Hebrew Bible & the Greek Gospel are Genuine, Preserv'd by the Saviour's Mercy. The Nature of my Work is Visionary or Imaginative: it is an Endeavour to Restore what the Ancients call'd the Golden Age.' Cp. General Introduction, pp. 32–34.
31–32 The phrase 'in my obedience' may refer to the fact that Milton obeys the Divine 'Dictate' (M. 19. 51–56). The significance of l. 32 can only be interpreted in general as referring to the rectifying of the evil done by the promulgation of the false theology of *Paradise Lost*. Cp. M. H. H., pp. 5–6.
36–41 See Index, *Shadow*, I. *c* and II.
42 This use of the symbol 'Angels of the Presence' differs from that in *The Four Zoas* and M. 11. 15–27; cp. F. Z. viii. 387 *note*. Here they are the 'Eyes of God', ministers of Divine Mercy comforting and sustain-

[14] As when a man dreams, he reflects not that his body sleeps,
Else he would wake, so seem'd he entering his Shadow; but
With him the Spirits of the Seven Angels of the Presence
Entering, they gave him still perceptions of his Sleeping Body,
Which now arose and walk'd with them in Eden, as an Eighth
Image, Divine tho' darken'd, and tho' walking as one walks
In sleep: and the Seven comforted and supported him.

Like as a Polypus that vegetates beneath the deep,
They saw his Shadow vegetated underneath the Couch
Of death: for when he enter'd into his Shadow, Himself,
His real and immortal Self, was, as appear'd to those
Who dwell in immortality, as One sleeping on a couch
Of gold; and those in immortality gave forth their Emanations
Like Females of sweet beauty, to guard round him & to feed
His lips with food of Eden in his cold and dim repose;
But to himself he seem'd a wanderer lost in dreary night.

Onwards his Shadow kept its course among the Spectres call'd
Satan; but swift as lightning passing them, startled the shades
Of Hell beheld him in a trail of light as of a comet
That travels into Chaos: so Milton went, guarded within.

The nature of infinity is this: That every thing has its
Own Vortex; and when once a traveller thro' Eternity
Has pass'd that Vortex, he percieves it roll backward behind
His path, into a globe itself infolding, like a sun
Or like a moon or like a universe of starry majesty,
While he keeps onwards in his wondrous journey on the earth;
Or like a human form, a friend with ⟨with⟩ whom he liv'd
benevolent.
As the eye of man views both the east & west encompassing
Its vortex, and the north & south with all their starry host,
Also the rising sun & setting moon he views, surrounding
His corn-fields and his valleys of five hundred acres square.

ing mortal man in visions of eternity; cp. M. 14. 1–15: 22. 50–52: 23. 7–8: 28. 58–59: extra p. 32*. 8–9.

Page 13 a full-page picture of the risen Milton.

Page 14. 1–16 Though visualized under different forms, Milton, his Shadow or Spectre, and his 'real and immortal Self' represent different 'portions' of the same individuality. The first and second, relating to mundane existence, symbolize respectively the visionary and the materialistic-moralistic principles, the 'angel' and the 'devil' with which Blake declared each man to be born. The third is, as it were, the Idea or perfect form of Man: cp. M. 18. 10–14.

8 See Index, *Mundane Shell, Note I.* B.

20 The phrase 'guarded within' apparently refers to the spiritual protection and guidance described above, ll. 1–15.

21–35 Cp. F. Z. vi. 184 *note*.

Thus is the earth one infinite plane, and not as apparent
To the weak traveller confin'd beneath the moony shade;
Thus is the heaven a vortex pass'd already, and the earth
A vortex not yet pass'd by the traveller thro' Eternity.

First Milton saw Albion upon the Rock of Ages,
Deadly pale, outstretch'd and snowy cold, storm cover'd,
A Giant form of perfect beauty, outstretch'd on the rock
In solemn death; the Sea of Time & Space thunder'd aloud
Against the rock, which was inwrappèd with the weeds of death.
Hovering over the cold bosom in its vortex Milton bent down
To the bosom of death: what was underneath soon seem'd above,
A cloudy heaven mingled with stormy seas in loudest ruin.
But as a wintry globe descends precipitant, thro' Beulah bursting
With thunders loud and terrible, so Milton's shadow fell
Precipitant, loud thund'ring, into the Sea of Time & Space.

Then first I saw him in the Zenith as a falling star,
Descending perpendicular, swift as the swallow or swift;
And on my left foot falling, on the tarsus, enter'd there:
But from my left foot a black cloud redounding spread over Europe.

Then Milton knew that the Three Heavens of Beulah were beheld
By him on earth in his bright pilgrimage of sixty years

32 Crabb Robinson records how an opportunity was lost of hearing Blake develop his argument in favour of the flatness of the earth . . 'He [Blake] declared his opinion that the earth is flat, and not round; and just as I had objected circumnavigation, dinner was announced' (Crabb Robinson, S., p. 291).

36 Cp. F. Z. ix. 284 *note*.

39 The 'Sea of Time and Space' seems to be but a variant of the commoner symbol 'Atlantic Ocean': see Index, *Atlantic*, and cp. F. Z. viii. 4 *note*.

47–50 This, like certain other passages in *Milton*, reads as if it were a transcript from actual visionary experience.

50 Cp. M. 18. 20–24 and *note*.

51 In several passages in *Milton* Beulah cannot be distinguished from Ulro. The 'Three Heavens' here mentioned are apparently the divisions into which the 'Twenty-seven Heavens of Beulah in Ulro' (M. 24. 45) are divided, after the manner of the Heavens of Rahab in the Mundane Shell (J. 75. 10–17). Further, Los labours continually 'Lest these Three Heavens of Beulah should the Creation destroy' (M. 26. 18–20). This divergence of meaning in the same symbol cannot be explained satisfactorily: see Index, *Beulah*, II. ii.

[16] In those three females whom his Wives, & those three whom his Daughters
Had represented and contain'd, that they might be resum'd
By giving up of Selfhood: & they distant view'd his journey
In their eternal spheres, now Human, tho' their Bodies remain clos'd
In the dark Ulro till the Judgment. Also Milton knew they and
Himself was Human, tho' now wandering thro' Death's Vale
In conflict with those Female forms, which in blood & jealousy
Surrounded him, dividing & uniting without end or number.

He saw the Cruelties of Ulro, and he wrote them down
In iron tablets: and his Wives' & Daughters' names were these:
Rahab and Tirzah & Milcah & Malah & Noah & Hoglah.
They sat rang'd round him as the rocks of Horeb round the land
Of Canaan; and they wrote in thunder, smoke and fire
His dictate; and his body was the Rock Sinai, that body
Which was on earth born to corruption; & the six Females
Are Hor & Peor & Bashan & Abarim & Lebanon & Hermon:
Seven rocky masses terrible in the Desarts of Midian.

But Milton's Human Shadow continu'd journeying above
The rocky masses of The Mundane Shell in the Lands
Of Edom & Aram & Moab & Midian & Amalek.

Page 15 contains a full-page drawing of Milton striving against Urizen (see M. 16. 36–17. 14). Beneath is the line 'To Annihilate the Self-hood of Deceit & False Forgiveness', which does not belong to the text as it is now ordered: see Introductory Note.

Page 16. 1–17 Milton's wives and daughters are combined to form the 'Sixfold Emanation', the body of error which Blake imputed to Milton. Emanation is used here in other than its normal Blakean sense: it is equivalent to the common Female symbols, Vala, Rahab, Tirzah, &c.

11 Cp. F. Z. viii. 301 *note*.

12 In l. 16 Blake identifies the six females with six mountains associated with the wanderings of the Israelites through the wilderness—always a symbol of the state of subjection to the moral law—or situated within the borders of hostile heathen tribes: cp. J. 4. 26 *note*.

17 The 'Seven' are the six mountains named in l. 16 and the Rock Sinai (l. 14).

18 The epithet 'Human' distinguishes Milton's Shadow, i. e. Milton descending to Self-annihilation, from the Shadow or Spectre, 'the body born to corruption' referred to in the preceding lines.

The Mundane Shell is a vast Concave Earth, an immense
Harden'd shadow of all things upon our Vegetated Earth,
Enlarg'd into dimension & deform'd into indefinite space
In Twenty-seven Heavens and all their Hells, with Chaos
And Ancient Night & Purgatory. It is a cavernous Earth
Of labyrinthine intricacy, twenty-seven-folds of opakeness,
And finishes where the lark mounts : here Milton journeyèd
In that Region call'd Midian, among the Rocks of Horeb ;
For travellers from Eternity pass outward to Satan's seat,
But travellers to Eternity pass inward to Golgonooza.

Los, the Vehicular terror, beheld him, & divine Enitharmon
Call'd all her daughters, Saying : 'Surely to unloose my bond
Is this Man come ! Satan shall be unloos'd upon Albion.'

Los heard in terror Enitharmon's words : in fibrous strength
His limbs shot forth like roots of trees against the forward path
Of Milton's journey. Urizen beheld the immortal Man,
[17] And he also darken'd his brows, freezing dark rocks between
The footsteps, and infixing deep the feet in marble beds,
That Milton labour'd with his journey & his feet bled sore
Upon the clay now chang'd to marble : also Urizen rose
And met him on the shores of Arnon & by the streams of
the brooks.

Silent they met, and silent strove among the streams of Arnon,
Even to Mahanaim ; when with cold hand Urizen stoop'd down
And took up water from the river Jordan, pouring on
To Milton's brain the icy fluid from his broad cold palm.

21–30 See Index, *Mundane Shell*. 28 Cp. F. Z. viii. 260 *note*.

29–30 The first line refers to those who forsake Imagination, turning their backs upon the Divine Vision ; the second to the spiritual progress of the visionary towards Imagination. The Seat of Satan is Ulro (M. 24. 45) : see Index, *Ulro*.

31 Los is the 'vehicular form of strong Urthona' (J. 53. 1). Vehicular means 'invested with a vehicle or special form : embodied' (*N. E. D.* 'Every Grove, Grot and Stream has its tutelar and vehicular Deity' (S. Holland's *Zara*, 1719, cited *N. E. D.*)). In passages of Milton, as here and 18. 56 foll. : 22. 53–54 traces of the earlier and equivocal use of the symbol Los persist.

32 For the 'bond' cp. M. 6. 43–44 : 11. 12–14.

Page 17. 5 The Arnon, a river of Moab, always in Blake carries a suggestion of error. The phrase 'the streams of the brooks' is slightly modified from Num. xxi. 13. Cp. F. Z. viii. 206 *note*.

6 The similarity of this episode with Jacob's encounter at Peniel (Gen. xxxii. 24–30) marks again the identity of Blake's Urizen and Jehovah, the God of the Sinaitic Law.

8–9 These lines may be a passing condemnation of the Baptist, presumably because he was an ascetic moralist, and therefore in part responsible for the conventional, and Miltonic, misrepresentation of the Christian gospel.

But Milton took of the red clay of Succoth, moulding it with care
Between his palms and filling up the furrows of many years,
Beginning at the feet of Urizen ; and on the bones
Creating new flesh on the Demon cold, and building him,
As with new clay, a Human form in the Valley of Beth Peor.

Four Universes round the Mundane Egg remain Chaotic,
One to the North namèd Urthona ; One to the South namèd Urizen ;
One to the East namèd Luvah ; One to the West namèd Tharmas :
They are the Four Zoa's that stood around the Throne Divine.
But when Luvah assum'd the World of Urizen to the South,
And Albion was slain upon his mountains & in his tent,
All fell towards the Center in dire ruin, sinking down.
And in the South remains a burning fire, in the East a void,
In the West a world of raging waters, in the North a solid,
Unfathomable, without end. But in the midst of these
Is built eternally the Universe of Los and Enitharmon,
Towards which Milton went ; but Urizen oppos'd his path.

The Man and Demon strove many periods. Rahab beheld
Standing on Carmel ; Rahab and Tirzah trembled to behold
The enormous strife, one giving life, the other giving death
To his adversary ; and they sent forth all their sons & daughters
In all their beauty, to entice Milton across the river.

The Twofold form Hermaphroditic, and the Double-sexèd,
The Female-male & the Male-female, self-dividing stood
Before him in their beauty & in cruelties of holiness,
Shining in darkness, glorious upon the deeps of Entuthon,

Saying : 'Come thou to Ephraim ! behold the Kings of Canaan,
The beautiful Amalekites ! behold the fires of youth

10–14 Though obscure in details, the general sense of this passage is clear enough. Urizen, the Jehovah of *Paradise Lost*, the 'giver of death' (l. 29), opposes Milton, the quickening spirit, whose purpose is to annihilate the errors to which he had given wide currency and to substitute a spiritual or 'Human' conception of the 'Divine'. The Valley of Beth-Peor, where Moses was buried, represents the Universe of Moral Law.

31 The Arnon separated Canaan and Moab ; hence, to tempt Milton across it would be to seduce him from Imagination to Natural Religion.

32 See Index, *Hermaphroditic*.

36 The ancient rivalry between Ephraim and Judah is here symbolic of the opposition between Imagination and Natural Religion. Manasseh is often associated with Ephraim in this sense.

37–38 Cp. B. U., chap. vii, and F. Z. v. 97–142

Bound with the Chain of Jealousy by Los & Enitharmon.
The banks of Cam, cold learning's streams, London's dark frowning towers,
Lament upon the winds of Europe in Rephaim's Vale,
Because Ahania, rent apart into a desolate night,
Laments, & Enion wanders like a weeping inarticulate voice,
And Vala labours for her bread & water among the Furnaces.
Therefore bright Tirzah triumphs, putting on all beauty
And all perfection in her cruel sports among the Victims.
Come! bring with thee Jerusalem with songs on the Grecian Lyre,
In Natural Religion, in experiments on Men!
Let her be Offer'd up to Holiness! Tirzah numbers her:
She numbers with her fingers every fibre ere it grow.
Where is the Lamb of God? where is the promise of his coming?
Her shadowy Sisters form the bones, even the bones of Horeb
Around the marrow, and the orbèd scull around the brain.
His Images are born for War, for Sacrifice to Tirzah,
To Natural Religion, to Tirzah, the Daughter of Rahab the Holy.
She ties the knot of nervous fibres into a white brain:
She ties the knot of bloody veins into a red hot heart.

43 It is noteworthy that here, as in *The Four Zoas*, Vala is merely the Emanation of Luvah, Rahab and Tirzah being the symbols of Natural Religion. It is not till *Jerusalem* that Vala becomes the most prominent of the feminine symbols.

45 The Victims of 'the System of Moral Virtue named Rahab' (J. 39. 10), Rahab and Tirzah being interchangeable.

46 All things 'Grecian' are of error; cp. *Milton*, Preface, *note* 1.

48 Cp. Cat. 1810: 'In Hell all is Self Righteousness . . . . he who does Forgive Sins is Crucified as an Abettor of Criminals, & he who performs Works of Mercy in Any shape whatever, is punish'd, & if possible destroy'd —not thro' envy, or Hatred, or Malice, but thro' Self Righteousness that thinks it does God service, which God is Satan.'

51–60 Cp. J. 80. 67–79, where Gwendolen, a Daughter of Albion, only nominally differentiated from Tirzah, gives her 'Victim'

a shape of Moral Virtue against the Lamb,
The invisible lovely one giving him a form according to
His [i.e. the Moral] Law, a form against the Lamb of God, oppos'd to Mercy.

Cp. also 'To Tirzah' (S. E., Clar. Press, p. 123):

Thou Mother of my Mortal part,
With cruelty didst mould my Heart,
And with false self-deceiving tears
Didst bind my Nostrils, Eyes, & Ears,

Didst close my Tongue in senseless clay
And me to Mortal Life betray.

Within her bosom Albion lies embalm'd, never to awake.
Hand is become a rock: Sinai & Horeb is Hyle & Coban:
Scofield is bound in iron armour before Reuben's Gate.
She ties the knot of milky seed into two lovely Heavens,
[18] Two, yet but one, each in the other sweet reflected; these
Are our Three Heavens beneath the shades of Beulah, land of rest.
Come then to Ephraim & Manasseh, O belovèd-one!
Come to my ivory palaces, O belovèd of thy mother,
And let us bind thee in the bands of War, & be thou King
Of Canaan, and reign in Hazor, where the Twelve Tribes meet.'

So spoke they as in one voice. Silent Milton stood before
The darken'd Urizen, as the sculptor silent stands before
His forming image: he walks round it, patient labouring.
Thus Milton stood, forming bright Urizen, while his Mortal part
Sat frozen in the rock of Horeb; and his Redeemèd portion
Thus form'd the Clay of Urizen; but within that portion
His real Human walk'd above in power and majesty,
Tho' darken'd: and the Seven Angels of the Presence attended him.

O how can I with my gross tongue that cleaveth to the dust
Tell of the Four-fold Man in starry numbers fitly order'd,
Or how can I with my cold hand of clay? But thou, O Lord,
Do with me as thou wilt! for I am nothing, and vanity.
If thou chuse to elect a worm, it shall remove the mountains.
For that portion nam'd the Elect, the Spectrous body of Milton,
Redounding from my left foot into Los's Mundane space,
Brooded over his Body in Horeb against the Resurrection,

57 Cp. J. 80. 27–29:
But I, Vala, Luvah's daughter, keep his [Albion's] body embalm'd in moral laws
With spices of sweet odours of lovely jealous stupefaction
Within my bosom, lest he arise to life.

58–59 See Index, *Spectre, Note II* (*a*). Line 59 and the similar passage in J. 15. 2–3 are equally obscure.

60 Cp. J. 80. 72–79.

Page 18. 6 Cp. Joshua xi. 1–5. 10–14 Cp. M. 14. 1 *note*.

16 The 'Four-fold Man' is the symbol of the supreme state: cp. the description of Albion after the regeneration, J. 96. 40–43.

20–22 Cp. M. 14. 49–50 and 16. 14–15. The distinction here set up between the 'Elect, the Spectrous body of Milton' and 'his Body in Horeb', 'that body which was on earth born to corruption', cannot be explained.

Preparing it for the Great Consummation: red the Cherub on Sinai
Glow'd, but in terrors folded round his clouds of blood.

Now Albion's sleeping Humanity began to turn upon his Couch,
Feeling the electric flame of Milton's awful precipitate descent.
See'st thou the little wingèd fly, smaller than a grain of sand?
It has a heart like thee, a brain open to heaven & hell,
Withinside wondrous & expansive: its gates are not clos'd;
I hope thine are not. Hence it clothes itself in rich array:
Hence thou art cloth'd with human beauty, O thou mortal man.
Seek not thy heavenly father then beyond the skies:
There Chaos dwells & ancient Night & Og & Anak old.
For every human heart has gates of brass & bars of adamant,
Which few dare unbar because dread Og & Anak guard the gates
Terrific; and each mortal brain is wall'd and moated round
Within: and Og & Anak watch here: here is the Seat
Of Satan in its Webs; for in brain and heart and loins
Gates open behind Satan's Seat to the City of Golgonooza,
Which is the spiritual fourfold London in the loins of Albion.

Thus Milton fell thro' Albion's heart, travelling outside of Humanity,
Beyond the Stars in Chaos, in Caverns of the Mundane Shell.

But many of the Eternals rose up from eternal tables
Drunk with the Spirit; burning round the Couch of death they stood,

23 Cp. F. Z. ix. 32 *note*. The association of the Spectre in this way with the Consummation may perhaps be explained by a passage in Cat. 1810: 'When Imagination, Art & science & all Intellectual Gifts, all the Gifts of the Holy Ghost, are look'd upon as of no use, & only Contention remains to Man, then the Last Judgment begins.'

23–24 The 'Cherub on Sinai' is the God of Moral Law. Cp. M. 7. 19–22.

25–26 Milton's descent symbolizes an accession of spiritual vitality to mortal life. Cp. the quickening power of Orc, B. U. vii. 21–24.

29 The 'Gates' appear to be symbolic of the fact that men 'are organized by Divine Providence for spiritual communion, though most 'refuse to do spiritual acts because of natural fears or natural desires'. These obstructions, represented by Og and Anak, are ascribed to Natural Religion: see *infra*, ll. 35–38, and see Index, *Giants* II. Other passages on the symbol Gates are J. 38. 55–39. 3: 44. 2–3: 74. 40. Cp. also *The Gates of Paradise*, 1–2 (Clar. Press, p. 372):

> Mutual Forgiveness of each Vice,
> Such are the Gates of Paradise.

38 See Index, *Head, Heart, and Loins*.

39–40 See Index, *Golgonooza*. 41 Cp. F. Z. i. 250 *note*.

Looking down into Beulah, wrathful, fill'd with rage.
They rend the heavens round the Watchers in a fiery circle,
And round the Shadowy Eighth. The Eight close up the Couch
Into a tabernacle and flee with cries down to the Deeps,
Where Los opens his three wide gates surrounded by raging fires :
They soon find their own place & join the Watchers of the Ulro.

Los saw them, and a cold pale horror cover'd o'er his limbs.
Pondering, he knew that Rintrah & Palamabron might depart
Even as Reuben & as Gad, gave up himself to tears.
He sat down on his anvil-stock, and lean'd upon the trough,
Looking into the black water, mingling it with tears.

At last, when desperation almost tore his heart in twain,
He recollected an old Prophecy, in Eden recorded
And often sung to the loud harp at the immortal feasts,
That Milton of the Land of Albion should up ascend,
Forwards from Ulro, from the Vale of Felpham, and set free
Orc from his Chain of Jealousy ; he started at the thought,
[19] And down descended into Udan-Adan : it was night,
And Satan sat sleeping upon his Couch in Udan Adan :
His Spectre slept, his Shadow woke : when one sleeps th' other wakes.

But Milton entering my Foot, I saw in the nether
Regions of the Imagination, also all men on Earth
And all in Heaven saw in the nether regions of the Imagination,
In Ulro beneath Beulah, the vast breach of Milton's descent.
But I knew not that it was Milton, for man cannot know
What passes in his members till periods of Space & Time
Reveal the secrets of Eternity : for more extensive
Than any other earthly things are Man's earthly lineaments.

46–50 For the 'Watchers' see M. 14. 3–15 : the 'fiery circle' afterwards appears as Ololon ; cp. *Milton*, Introduction. The 'Watchers of the Ulro' are Los and his fellows,

plac'd here by the Universal Brotherhood & Mercy
With powers fitted to circumscribe this dark Satanic death,
And that the Seven Eyes of God may have space for Redemption.

52–53 See Index, *Los, Note II (a)*. A similar act of secession as that ascribed to Reuben and Gad is extended to the other sons of Israel (cp. M. 22. 62–23. 4 and J. 93. 12–15), but cannot be explained.

Page 19. 3 No interpretation yet discovered for 'Spectre' and 'Shadow' can be held to explain this line.

4–6 To see in 'the nether regions of the Imagination' appears to be equivalent to life in the state 'Ulro' or error, spiritual events not being rightly apprehended even by the mystic (ll. 8–10). 8–11 See Index, *Albion*.

And all this Vegetable World appear'd on my left Foot
As a bright sandal form'd immortal of precious stones & gold.
I stoopèd down & bound it on to walk forward thro' Eternity.

There is in Eden a sweet River of milk & liquid pearl
Nam'd Ololon, on whose mild banks dwelt those who Milton drove
Down into Ulro ; and they wept in long resounding song
For seven days of eternity, and the river's living banks,
The mountains, wail'd, & every plant that grew in solemn sighs lamented.

When Luvah's bulls each morning drag the sulphur Sun out of the Deep,
Harness'd with starry harness black & shining, kept by black slaves
That work all night at the starry harness—Strong and vigorous,
They drag the unwilling Orb—at this time all the Family
Of Eden heard the lamentation, and Providence began.
But when the clarions of day sounded, they drown'd the lamentations ;
And when night came all was silent in Ololon, & all refus'd to lament
In the still night, fearing lest they should others molest.

Seven mornings Los heard them, as the poor bird within the shell
Hears its impatient parent bird ; and Enitharmon heard them,
But saw them not, for the blue Mundane Shell inclos'd them in.

And they lamented that they had in wrath & fury & fire
Driven Milton into the Ulro, for now they knew too late
That it was Milton the Awakener. They had not heard the Bard,
Whose song call'd Milton to the attempt : and Los heard these laments.
He heard them call in prayer all the Divine Family,
And he beheld the Cloud of Milton stretching over Europe.

12–14 These lines declare the teleological function of mundane life, that it is the means to regeneration : see Index, *Mundane Shell.*

15–17 See *Milton,* Introduction. For the act of expulsion cp. M. 18. 43–50.

20–23 Cp. F. Z. ii. 330 *note.* The punctuation of this passage is conjectural.

23–24 Cp. J. 38. 17–21.

28–30 For a similar inability on the part of Los to interpret vision fully cp. J. 63. 36–41, and see M. 16. 34 *note.*

31 'They' clearly refers to the Eternals: cp. M. 18. 19. 33–34.

36 Cp. M. 14. 50.

But all the Family Divine collected as Four Suns
In the Four Points of heaven, East, West & North & South,
Enlarging and enlarging till their Disks approach'd each other;
And when they touch'd, closèd together Southward in One Sun
Over Ololon; and as One Man who weeps over his brother
In a dark tomb, so all the Family Divine wept over Ololon,

Saying: 'Milton goes to Eternal Death': so saying, they groan'd in spirit
And were troubled; and again the Divine Family groanèd in spirit.

And Ololon said: 'Let us descend also, and let us give
Ourselves to death in Ulro among the Transgressors.
Is Virtue a Punisher? O no! how is this wondrous thing,
This World beneath, unseen before, this refuge from the wars
Of Great Eternity, unnatural refuge, unknown by us till now?
Or are these the pangs of repentance? let us enter into them.'

Then the Divine Family said: 'Six Thousand Years are now
Accomplish'd in this World of Sorrow. Milton's Angel knew
The Universal Dictate, and you also feel this Dictate;
And now you know this World of Sorrow, and feel Pity. Obey
The Dictate. Watch over this World, and with your brooding wings
Renew it to Eternal Life. Lo! I am with you alway.
But you cannot renew Milton: he goes to Eternal Death.'

So spake the Family Divine as One Man, even Jesus,
Uniting in One with Ololon; & the appearance of One Man,
Jesus the Saviour, appear'd, coming in the Clouds of Ololon.
[20] Tho' driven away with the Seven Starry Ones into the Ulro,
Yet the Divine Vision remains Every-where, For-ever. Amen.
And Ololon lamented for Milton with a great lamentation.

While Los heard indistinct in fear, what time I bound my sandals
On to walk forward thro' Eternity, Los descended to me;
And Los behind me stood, a terrible flaming Sun, just close
Behind my back. I turnèd round in terror, and behold,
Los stood in that fierce glowing fire; & he also stoop'd down
And bound my sandals on in Udan-Adan. Trembling I stood

37–42 See Index, *Jesus*. 48–49 See Index, *Mundane Shell*.

60 The coming of Jesus in the Clouds of Ololon would seem to be a vision of the Incarnation, not as a particular, but as a universal act; the revelation of the 'Gospel of Jesus', the visionary metaphysic and ethic, through mundane existence. It is 'the Divine Revelation in the Litteral expression': cp. M. 44. 10–15, a passage reminiscent of Rev. xix. 11–16.

Page 20. 4–5 Cp. M. 19. 12–14 and *note*. 9 See Index, *Ulro, Note III*.

Exceedingly with fear and terror, standing in the Vale
Of Lambeth ; but he kissèd me and wish'd me health,
And I became One Man with him, arising in my strength.
'Twas too late now to recede : Los had enter'd into my soul :
His terrors now possess'd me whole. I arose in fury & strength.

' I am that Shadowy Prophet, who, Six Thousand Years ago,
Fell from my station in the Eternal bosom. Six Thousand Years
Are finish'd. I return : both Time & Space obey my will.
I in Six Thousand Years walk up and down ; for not one Moment
Of Time is lost, nor one Event of Space unpermanent ;
But all remain ; every fabric of Six Thousand Years
Remains permanent : tho' on the Earth, where Satan
Fell and was cut off, all things vanish & are seen no more,
They vanish not from me & mine ; we guard them, first & last.
The generations of men run on in the tide of Time,
But leave their destin'd lineaments permanent for ever & ever.'

So spoke Los as we went along to his supreme abode.

Rintrah and Palamabron met us at the Gate of Golgonooza,
Clouded with discontent, & brooding in their minds terrible things.

They said : ' O Father most belovèd ! O merciful Parent !
Pitying and permitting evil, tho' strong & mighty to destroy,
Whence is this Shadow terrible ? wherefore dost thou refuse
To throw him into the Furnaces ? knowest thou not that he
Will unchain Orc, & let loose Satan, Og, Sihon, & Anak

11–14 Blake becomes identified with the divine purpose of regeneration as embodied in Los.

18–23 Cp. J. 13. 59–14. 1.

24–25 Cp. D. C., iii, p. 9 : ' As one age falls, another rises, different to mortal sight, but to immortals only the same : for we see the same characters repeated again and again, in animals, vegetables, minerals and in men.'

27–28 Rintrah and Palamabron, sons of Los, are unable to see the purpose of Milton's descent. Whatever the primary significance of this episode, it is almost certain that the hostile attitude of these sons of Los towards Blake (M. 22. 18–20), is purposely contrasted with the gentler spirit of Los, in order to stress the mystical doctrines of Brotherhood and Forgiveness. For the earlier use of these symbols see *Europe*, 43 *note* ; for the later, see Index, *Los, Note II*.

32–34 Cp. M. 16. 32–33.

Upon the Body of Albion? For this he is come; behold it written
Upon his fibrous left Foot black, most dismal to our eyes.
The Shadowy Female shudders thro' heaven in torment inexpressible,
And all the Daughters of Los prophetic wail; yet in deceit
They weave a new Religion from new Jealousy of Theotormon.
Milton's Religion is the cause; there is no end to destruction.
Seeing the Churches at their Period in terror & despair,
Rahab created Voltaire, Tirzah created Rousseau,
Asserting the Self-righteousness against the Universal Saviour,
Mocking the Confessors & Martyrs, claiming Self-righteousness,
With cruel Virtue making War upon the Lamb's Redeemèd,
To perpetuate War & Glory, to perpetuate the Laws of Sin.
They perverted Swedenborg's Visions in Beulah & in Ulro,
To destroy Jerusalem as a Harlot & her Sons as Reprobates,
To raise up Mystery, the Virgin Harlot, Mother of War,
Babylon the Great, the Abomination of Desolation.
O Swedenborg! strongest of men, the Samson shorn by the Churches;
Shewing the Transgressors in Hell, the proud Warriors in Heaven,
Heaven as a Punisher, & Hell as One under Punishment,
With Laws from Plato & his Greeks to renew the Trojan Gods
In Albion & to deny the value of the Saviour's blood!
But then I rais'd up Whitefield; Palamabron rais'd up Westley.

34–35 Cp. M. 19. 12–14. Rintrah and Palamabron see 'this Vegetable World' merely as a state of error, its regenerative purpose being hidden from them.

38–49 Cp. F. Z. viii. 598 *note*. Jealousy of Theotormon is the source of the moral tyranny attacked in *The Visions of the Daughters of Albion*, and from him Jesus received the ascetic Gospel, under which the Human race began to wither (*Africa*, 20–27). The nature of the 'new Religion' is vaguely indicated in M. 22. 38–44.

42–45 Cp. J. 52, 'To the Deists', *passim*.

46–54 As in *The Marriage* Blake censures Swedenborg's acceptance of ordinary moral standards and regards his rationalistic method as a betrayal of his visionary powers; but here he estimates more generously the value of his work. So to Crabb Robinson he 'declared him to be a Divine Teacher; he had done and would do much good; yet he did wrong in endeavouring to explain to the reason what it could not comprehend' (S. p. 289).

53 A symbolical derivation from the tradition of Trojan refugees in early Britain. Blake took it from Milton.

55–59 Cp. M. 22. 1–2 and J. 52 § 4. The 'cries of the Churches' may be explained by reference to ll. 57–58, in which case it would seem that Blake accuses the Churches of persecuting in the name of Jesus, thereby crucifying him afresh: cp. Rev. xi.

'And these are the cries of the Churches before the two Witnesses,
Faith in God the dear Saviour, who took on the likeness of men,
Becoming obedient to death, even the death of the Cross.
The Witnesses lie dead in the Street of the Great City.
No Faith is in all the Earth : the Book of God is trodden under Foot.
He sent his two Servants, Whitefield & Westley : were they Prophets,
Or were they Idiots or Madmen ? Shew us Miracles !
[22] Can you have greater Miracles than these, Men who devote
Their life's whole comfort to intire scorn & injury & death ?
Awake, thou sleeper on the Rock of Eternity ! Albion, awake !
The trumpet of Judgment hath twice sounded : all Nations are awake,
But thou art still heavy and dull. Awake, Albion, awake !
Lo, Orc arises on the Atlantic. Lo, his blood and fire
Glow on America's shore. Albion turns upon his Couch :
He listens to the sounds of War, astonish'd and confounded ;
He weeps into the Atlantic deep, yet still in dismal dreams
Unwaken'd : and the Covering Cherub advances from the East.
How long shall we lay dead in the Street of the great City,
How long beneath the Covering Cherub give our Emanations ?

62 The cry for miracles comes apparently from the 'Elect' of the Churches.

Page 21. The full-page design illustrates M. 20. 6–8. Los in the sun, Blake kneeling on left knee fastening a sandal on his right foot, his head raised in terror at the vision.

Page 22. 4 In Rev. xi, after the death and resurrection of the 'witnesses', the kingdoms of the earth become the kingdoms of Christ: so here apparently the rejection of Wesley and Whitefield is the sign of the imminence of the Last Judgement. It may be that the two occasions when the trumpet sounded are to be identified with the Revolutions in America and France.

6 See *Milton*, Introduction. 9 See Index, *Atlantic*.

10 See Index, *Mundane Shell, Note I* (*a*).

11 Rintrah and Palamabron speak as the Witnesses : cp. M. 7. 8.

12 To 'give Emanations' is best explained by reference to M. 14. 3–15, whereby it appears to indicate the granting of visions of Eternity or truth to mortals for their instruction and sustenance. In the present passage, the speakers, being unable to perceive the divine purpose of regeneration immanent in temporal existence (cp. M. 20. 27 *note*), regard their own labours as vain against the opposing error of mundane life. They are not aware of the significance of Milton's descent, wherein, as in the parallel act of the Incarnation, error is assumed that ultimately it may be annihilated by being made manifest, in the Crucifixion by a demonstration of the unreality of the body and of bodily death in the reincarnation of Milton in Blake by a revelation of the spiritual in Art. See Index, *Incarnation*.

' Milton will utterly consume us & thee, our belovèd Father.
He hath enter'd into the Covering Cherub, becoming one with
Albion's dread Sons. Hand, Hyle & Coban surround him as
A girdle, Gwendolen & Conwenna as a garment woven
Of War & Religion. Let us descend & bring him chainèd
To Bowlahoola, O father most beloved ! O mild Parent !
Cruel in thy mildness, pitying and permitting evil,
Tho' strong and mighty to destroy, O Los, our belovèd Father ! '

Like the black storm coming out of Chaos beyond the stars,
It issues thro' the dark & intricate caves of the Mundane Shell,
Passing the planetary visions & the well adornèd Firmament:
The Sun rolls into Chaos & the Stars into the Desarts,
And then the storms, become visible, audible & terrible,
Covering the light of day & rolling down upon the mountains,
Deluge all the country round. Such is a vision of Los
When Rintrah & Palamabron spoke, and such his stormy face
Appear'd, as does the face of heaven when cover'd with thick storms,
Pitying and loving, tho' in frowns of terrible perturbation.

But Los dispers'd the clouds, even as the strong winds of Jehovah.
And Los thus spoke : ' O noble Sons, be patient yet a little.
I have embrac'd the falling Death : he is become One with me.
O Sons, we live not by wrath ; by mercy alone we live.
I recollect an old Prophecy in Eden, recorded in gold, and oft
Sung to the harp, That Milton, of the land of Albion,
Should up ascend forward from Felpham's Vale & break the Chain
Of Jealousy from all its roots : be patient, therefore, O my Sons !
These lovely Females form sweet night and silence and secret
Obscurities to hide from Satan's Watch-Fiends Human loves
And graces, lest they write them in their Books & in the Scroll
Of mortal life, to condemn the accusèd, who at Satan's Bar
Tremble in Spectrous Bodies continually day and night
While on the Earth they live in sorrowful Vegetations.
O when shall we tread our Wine-presses in heaven, and Reap

15 These are sons of Albion. See Index, *Spectre, Note II* (*a*).
18 See Index, *Bowlahoola*. 23 Cp. F. Z. vi. 184 *note*.
33 Cp. M. 20. 4–14.
39–44 'These lovely Females' are the Daughters of Los: see Index, *Los, Note II* (*a*).
40 Cp. M. 28. 47–50. 45 See Index, *Wine-press*, I.

Our wheat with shoutings of joy, and leave the Earth in peace?
Remember how Calvin and Luther in fury premature
Sow'd War and stern division between Papists & Protestants.
Let it not be so now! O go not forth in Martyrdoms & Wars!
We were plac'd here by the Universal Brotherhood & Mercy,
With powers fitted to circumscribe this dark Satanic death,
And that the Seven Eyes of God may have space for Redemption.
But how this is, as yet we know not, and we cannot know
Till Albion is arisen: then patient wait a little while.
Six Thousand Years are pass'd away: the end approaches fast.
This mighty one is come from Eden: he is of the Elect
Who died from Earth, & he is return'd before the Judgment. This thing
Was never known that one of the holy dead should willing return.
Then patient wait a little while till the Last Vintage is over,
Till we have quench'd the Sun of Salah in the Lake of Udan Adan.
O my dear Sons, leave not your Father as your brethren left me.
Twelve Sons successive fled away in that thousand years of sorrow,
[23] Of Palamabron's Harrow, & of Rintrah's wrath & fury.
Reuben & Manazzoth & Gad & Simeon & Levi
And Ephraim & Judah were Generated, because
They left me, wandering with Tirzah. Enitharmon wept
One thousand years, and all the Earth was in a wat'ry deluge.
We call'd him Menassheh because of the Generations of Tirzah,
Because of Satan; & the Seven Eyes of God continually
Guard round them: but I, the Fourth Zoa, am also set

51 See Index, *Self-Annihilation*.
56–58 See *Milton*, Introduction, on the reincarnation of Milton in Blake.
59 See the account of the Last Vintage, F. Z. ix. 691 *seq*.
60 The Sun of Salah is not mentioned elsewhere, though Salah (cf. Gen. x. 24 and Luke iii. 35) is the name of one of the twenty-seven heavens of the Mundane Shell: cp. J. 75. 13. The symbol clearly has reference to the body of error which Los seeks to annihilate: cp. J. 41:

Each Man is in his Spectre's power,
Untill the arrival of that hour
When his Humanity awake
And cast his Spectre into the Lake.

61–62 Cp. M. 18. 52 *note* and see Index, *Los, Note II*.
Page 23. 4–5 Cp. M. 5. 14.

The Watchman of Eternity; the Three are not; & I am preservèd.
Still my four mighty ones are left to me in Golgonooza,
Still Rintrah fierce, and Palamabron mild & piteous,
Theotormon fill'd with care, Bromion loving Science.
You, O my Sons, still guard round Los. O wander not & leave me!
Rintrah, thou well rememberest when Amalek & Canaan
Fled with their Sister Moab into that abhorrèd Void.
They became Nations in our sight beneath the hands of Tirzah.
And Palamabron, thou rememberest when Joseph, an infant
Stolen from his nurse's cradle wrap'd in needle-work
Of emblematic texture, was sold to the Amalekite,
Who carried him down into Egypt, where Ephraim & Menassheh
Gather'd my Sons together in the Sands of Midian.
And if you also flee away and leave your Father's side,
Following Milton into Ulro, altho' your power is great,
Surely you also shall become poor mortal vegetations
Beneath the Moon of Ulro. Pity then your Father's tears.
When Jesus rais'd Lazarus from the Grave, I stood & saw
Lazarus, who is the Vehicular Body of Albion the Redeem'd,
Arise into the Covering Cherub, who is the Spectre of Albion,
By martyrdoms to suffer, to watch over the Sleeping Body
Upon his Rock beneath his Tomb. I saw the Covering Cherub
Divide Four-fold into Four Churches when Lazarus arose,
Paul, Constantine, Charlemaine, Luther: behold they stand before us,
Stretch'd over Europe & Asia. Come, O Sons, come, come away!

14–16 Cp. F. Z. viii. 260 *note*.

17–22 The selling of Joseph into Egypt is elsewhere used, as here, to symbolize the subjection of man to the power of natural religion: cp. J. 55. 15–16. But Blake's variation of the Biblical narrative is not so clear in its details. Ephraim and Manasseh appear to be variants of the symbol Spectre: cp. M. 17. 36 *note*, though in F. Z. viii. 300–301 they appear to represent mankind tormented by the penalties of the moral law.

27–33 The raising of Lazarus is a mediate or 'Vehicular' revelation of the nature of spiritual regeneration. It should have been received as a parabolic or exemplary revelation of the truth concerning death and resurrection (l. 24), keeping the right faith in remembrance, in spite of opposition, during the period of suspended spiritual vitality which is mortal life (ll. 29–30). Cp. John xii. 10–11. But the rationalist *milieu*, the Covering Cherub, refracts the truth, and therefore the episode becomes the basis of the 'warlike Christianity' symbolized by the names in l. 32. The criticism is aimed primarily at the Pauline doctrine of the resurrection of the 'body'.

30–32 Cp. F. Z. viii. 351 *note*.

Arise, O Sons, give all your strength against Eternal Death,
Lest we are vegetated; for Cathedron's Looms weave only Death,
A Web of Death; & were it not for Bowlahoola & Allamanda,
No Human Form, but only a Fibrous Vegetation,
A Polypus of soft affections without Thought or Vision,
Must tremble in the Heavens & Earths thro' all the Ulro space.
Throw all the Vegetated Mortals into Bowlahoola:
But as to this Elected Form who is return'd again,
He is the Signal that the Last Vintage now approaches,
Nor Vegetation may go on till all the Earth is reap'd.'

So Los spoke. Furious they descended to Bowlahoola & Allamanda,
Indignant, unconvinc'd by Los's arguments & thun[d]ers rolling.
They saw that wrath now sway'd, and now pity absorb'd him.
As it was, so it remain'd, & no hope of an end.

Bowlahoola is nam'd Law by mortals. Tharmas founded it
Because of Satan, before Luban, in the City of Golgonooza:
But Golgonooza is nam'd Art & Manufacture by mortal men.

In Bowlahoola Los's Anvils stand & his Furnaces rage;
Thundering the Hammers beat & the Bellows blow loud,
Living, self moving, mourning, lamenting & howling incessantly.
Bowlahoola thro' all its porches feels, tho' too fast founded
Its pillars & porticoes to tremble at the force
Of mortal or immortal arm; and softly lilling flutes,
Accordant with the horrid labours, make sweet melody.
The Bellows are the Animal Lungs, the Hammers the Animal Heart,
The Furnaces the Stomach for digestion; terrible their fury.
Thousands & thousands labour; thousands play on instruments
Stringèd or fluted to ameliorate the sorrows of slavery.
Loud sport the dancers in the dance of death, rejoicing in carnage.
The hard dentant Hammers are lull'd by the flutes' lula lula,
The bellowing Furnaces' blare by the long sounding clarion,

35 See Index, *Weaving*, IV.
36 See Index, *Science*. 43 Cp. M. 25. 59–62 and *note*.
48–50 This passage is wholly obscure. For Luban cp. F. Z. vii. 429 *note*.
59 See Index, *Head, Heart, and Loins*.

The double drum drowns howls & groans, the shrill fife shrieks & cries,
The crooked horn mellows the hoarse raving serpent, terrible but harmonious.

Bowlahoola is the Stomach in every individual man.

Los is by mortals nam'd Time ; Enitharmon is nam'd Space ;
But they depict him bald & agèd who is in eternal youth,
All powerful, and his locks flourish like the brows of morning :
He is the Spirit of Prophecy, the ever apparent Elias.
Time is the mercy of Eternity ; without Time's swiftness,
Which is the swiftest of all things, all were eternal torment.
All the Gods of the Kingdoms of Earth labour in Los's Halls :
Every one is a fallen Son of the Spirit of Prophecy.
He is the Fourth Zoa, that stood arou[n]d the Throne Divine.

[24] But the Wine-press of Los is eastward of Golgonooza, before the Seat
Of Satan : Luvah laid the foundation & Urizen finish'd it in howling woe.
How red the sons & daughters of Luvah ! here they tread the grapes.
Laughing & shouting, drunk with odours, many fall, o'er-wearied ;
Drown'd in the wine is many a youth & maiden : those around
Lay them on skins of Tygers & of the spotted Leopard & the Wild Ass
Till they revive, or bury them in cool grots, making lamentation.

This Wine-press is call'd War on Earth ; it is the Printing-Press
Of Los ; and here he lays his words in order above the mortal brain,
As cogs are form'd in a wheel to turn the cogs of the adverse wheel.

Timbrels & violins sport round the Wine-presses ; the little Seed,
The sportive Root, the Earth-worm, the gold Beetle, the wise Emmet,

69–70 Cp. Cat. 1810 : 'The Greeks represent Chronos, or Time, as a very Aged Man: this is Fable, but the Real Vision of Time is in Eternal Youth.'

Page 24. 1 See Index, *Wine-press.*

3–41 These lines are repeated, with some changes, from F. Z. ix. 741–769.

Dance round the Wine-presses of Luvah: the Centipede is there;
The ground Spider with many eyes, the Mole clothèd in velvet,
The ambitious Spider in his sullen web, the lucky golden Spinnér,
The Earwig arm'd, the tender Maggot, emblem of immortality,
The Flea, Louse, Bug, the Tape-Worm, all the Armies of Disease,
Visible or invisible to the slothful vegetating Man;
The slow Slug, the Grasshopper that sings & laughs & drinks—
Winter comes: he folds his slender bones without a murmur.
The cruel Scorpion is there, the Gnat, Wasp, Hornet & the Honey Bee;
The Toad & venomous Newt, the Serpent cloth'd in gems & gold:
They throw off their gorgeous raiment; they rejoice with loud jubilee
Around the Wine-presses of Luvah, naked & drunk with wine.

There is the Nettle that stings with soft down, and there
The indignant Thistle, whose bitterness is bred in his milk,
Who feeds on contempt of his neighbour; there all the idle Weeds
That creep around the obscure places shew their various limbs
Naked in all their beauty, dancing round the Wine-presses.

But in the Wine-presses the Human grapes sing not nor dance.
They howl & writhe in shoals of torment, in fierce flames consuming,
In chains of iron & in dungeons circled with ceaseless fires,
In pits & dens & shades of death, in shapes of torment & woe—
The plates & screws, & wracks & saws & cords & fires & cisterns,
The cruel joys of Luvah's Daughters lacerating with knives
And whips their Victims & the deadly sport of Luvah's Sons.

They dance around the dying, & they drink the howl & groan;
They catch the shrieks in cups of gold, they hand them to one another;
These are the sports of love, & these the sweet delights of amorous play,

Tears of the grape, the death sweat of the cluster, the last sigh
Of the mild youth who listens to the lureing songs of Luvah.

But Allamanda, call'd on Earth Commerce, is the Cultivated land
Around the City of Golgonooza in the Forests of Entuthon.
Here the Sons of Los labour against Death Eternal through all
The Twenty-seven Heavens of Beulah in Ulro, Seat of Satan,
Which is the False Tongue beneath Beulah: it is the Sense of Touch.
The Plow goes forth in tempests & lightnings, & the Harrow cruel
In blights of the east: the heavy Roller follows in howlings of woe.

Urizen's sons here labour also, & here are seen the Mills
Of Theotormon on the verge of the Lake of Udan-Adan.
These are the starry voids of night & the depths & caverns of earth;
These Mills are oceans, clouds & waters ungovernable in their fury.
Here are the stars created & the seeds of all things planted,
And here the Sun & Moon recieve their fixèd destinations.

But in Eternity the Four Arts, Poetry, Painting, Music,
And Architecture, which is Science, are the Four Faces of Man.
Not so in Time & Space: there Three are shut out, and only
Science remains thro' mercy; & by means of Science the Three
Become apparent in Time & Space, in the Three Professions,
Poetry in Religion; Music, Law; Painting in Physic & Surgery;
That Man may live upon Earth till the time of his awaking.
And from these Three, Science derives every Occupation of Men.
And Science is divided into Bowlahoola & Allamanda.

[25] Loud shout the Sons of Luvah at the Wine-presses as Los descended
With Rintrah & Palamabron in his fires of resistless fury.

46 Cp. M. 3. 10 *note*. 47–48 See Index, *Plow, Harrow, and Roller*.
49–50 Cp. M. 6. 4 *note*.
55–59 See Index, *Science*, and J. 3 *ad fin.*: cp. *Laocoön*, 20: 'A Poet, a Painter, a Musician, an Architect; the Man or Woman who is not one of these is not a Christian.' Line 60 is deleted in the Windus copy and in the Ellis and Yeats facsimile.

Page 25. 1–7 These lines may contain a mystical interpretation of the Napoleonic conquests of 1805 and after, as part of the cosmic strife out of which Los is to bring ultimate regeneration. Characteristically Blake sees a greater evil in the repressive rigour of the Allied governments in their domestic policies.

The Wine-press on the Rhine groans loud, but all its central beams
Act more terrific in the central Cities of the Nations,
Where Human Thought is crush'd beneath the iron hand of Power.
There Los puts all into the Press, the O[p]pressor & the O[p]pressèd
Together, ripe for the Harvest & Vintage & ready for the Loom.

They sang at the Vintage: 'This is the Last Vintage, & Seed
Shall no more be sown upon Earth till all the Vintage is over
And all gather'd in, till the Plow has pass'd over the Nations,
And the Harrow & heavy thundering Roller upon the mountains.'

And loud the Souls howl round the Porches of Golgonooza,
Crying: 'O God, deliver us to the Heavens or to the Earths,
That we may preach righteousness & punish the sinner with death.'
But Los refusèd, till all the Vintage of Earth was gather'd in.

And Los stood & cried to the Labourers of the Vintage in voice of awe:

'Fellow Labourers! The Great Vintage & Harvest is now upon Earth.
The whole extent of the Globe is explorèd. Every scatter'd Atom
Of Human Intellect now is flocking to the sound of the Trumpet.
All the Wisdom which was hidden in caves & dens from ancient
Time is now sought out from Animal & Vegetable & Mineral.
The Awakener is come, outstretch'd over Europe; the Vision of God is fulfilled.
The Ancient Man upon the Rock of Albion Awakes.
He listens to the sounds of War, astonish'd & ashamèd:
He sees his Children mock at Faith and deny Providence.
Therefore you must bind the Sheaves, not by Nations or Families:
You shall bind them in Three Classes; according to their Classes,
So shall you bind them, Separating what has been Mixèd

8–10 Cp. M. 23. 43 and 25. 59–62 *note*.
12–15 Cp. F. Z. ix. 730–740. 18–21 See General Introduction.
22 The Awakener is Milton (M. 19. 33). 27–41 Cp. M. 3. 26 *note*.

Since Men began to be Wove into Nations by Rahab & Tirzah,
Since Albion's Death & Satan's Cutting-off from our awful Fields,
When under pretence to benevolence the Elect Subdu'd All
From the Foundation of the World. The Elect is one Class. You
Shall bind them separate: they cannot Believe in Eternal Life,
Except by Miracle & a New Birth. The other two Classes,
The Reprobate, who never cease to Believe, and the Redeem'd
Who live in doubts & fears, perpetually tormented by the Elect,
These you shall bind in a twin-bundle for the Consummation.
But the Elect must be savèd [from] fires of Eternal Death,
To be formèd into the Churches of Beulah, that they destroy not the Earth.
For in every Nation & every Family the Three Classes are born,
And in every Species of Earth, Metal, Tree, Fish, Bird & Beast.
We form the Mundane Egg, that Spectres coming by fury or amity . . .
All is the same, & every one remains in his own energy.
Go forth, Reapers, with rejoicing! you sowed in tears,
But the time of your refreshing cometh: only a little moment
Still abstain from pleasure & rest in the labours of eternity,
And you shall Reap the whole Earth from Pole to Pole, from Sea to Sea,
Begin[n]ing at Jerusalem's Inner Court, Lambeth, ruin'd and given
To the detestable Gods of Priam, to Apollo, and at the Asylum

30 Cutting-off] not hyphenated in Blake's autotype.

31–32 The reference is to the Satan-Palamabron myth (M. pp. 5–11), Satan being of the 'Elect'.

37 Cp. F. Z. ix. 32 *note*.

38 For the 'fires of Eternal Death' cp. Cat. 1810, quoted F. Z. ix. 32 *note*.

39 Cp. M. 14. 51 *note*.

42 See Index, *Mundane Shell*. One or more lines appear to be missing here, though there is no gap in Blake's autotype.

43 For the permanence of the Individuality cp. M. 4. 14 *note*.

49 The Gods of Priam are the Gods of the Heathen, who 'swore Vengeance for Sin'. See the passage from the *Descriptive Catalogue*, iii, p. 61, quoted F. Z. ix. 361 *note*.

Lines 48–50 contain an extreme instance of Blake's topographical symbolism. His purpose is to show how error has manifested itself even among those who follow vision, in the inner courts of Lambeth: cp. M. 4. 14 *note*. The Everlasting Gospel of Jesus is infected by the heresy

Given to Hercules ; who labour in Tirzah's Looms for bread,
Who set Pleasure against Duty, who Create Olympic crowns
To make Learning a burden & the Work of the Holy Spirit Strife,
The Thor & cruel Odin, who first rear'd the Polar Caves.
Lambeth mourns, calling Jerusalem; she weeps & looks abroad
For the Lord's coming, that Jerusalem may overspread all Nations.
Crave not for the mortal & perishing delights, but leave them
To the weak; and pity the weak as your infant care. Break not
Forth in your wrath, lest you also are vegetated by Tirzah.
Wait till the Judgement is past, till the Creation is consumèd,
And then rush forward with me into the glorious spiritual
Vegetation, the Supper of the Lamb & his Bride and the
Awaking of Albion, our friend and ancient companion.'

So Los spoke. But lightnings of discontent broke on all sides round,
And murmurs of thunder rolling heavy, long & loud over the mountains,
While Los call'd his Sons around him to the Harvest & the Vintage.

Thou seest the Constellations in the deep & wondrous Night :
They rise in order and continue their immortal courses
Upon the mountains & in vales with harp & heavenly song,
With flute & clarion, with cups & measures fill'd with foaming wine.
Glitt'ring the streams reflect the Vision of beatitude,
And the calm Ocean joys beneath & smooths his awful waves.

of the Moral Law of the Heathen Gods. The outward revelation of the change appears in the presence of Apollo and Hercules in Lambeth, the first in the Apollo Gardens, or the Temple of Apollo, a pleasure-haunt in Westminster Bridge Road, the second Bethlehem Hospital on the site of the Old Dog and Duck Tavern opposite Hercules Buildings. The reference to the Asylum might seem to show that this page of *Milton* was written after 18th April 1812, when the foundation-stone of the Hospital was laid. The watermarks in the British Museum Print-room copy of *Milton* show 1808. This page, however, has no watermark.

56–62 These lines show how far Blake has travelled from the revolutionary and antinomian position of the Lambeth books. Cp. Blake's account of a visionary experience, *Poems from Letters*, iv, ll. 59–68, Clar. Press, p. 368. Cp. J., p. 77 *passim*.

59–61 In every passage but this, 'vegetation' refers to corporeal as opposed to spiritual existence. The full exercise of man's higher or imaginative energies is contingent upon the complete annihilation of the error symbolized by mundane or corporeal vegetative life.

66–Page 26. 12 In this passage (cp. M. 26. 31–36) Blake rejoices in natural beauty, and finds therein, symbolically interpreted, messages leading toward truth. Contrast the vehement rejection of the 'imitation of Nature's Images drawn from Remembrance', M. 43. 24.

[26] These are the Sons of Los & these the Labourers of the Vintage.
Thou seest the gorgeous clothèd Flies that dance & sport in summer
Upon the sunny brooks & meadows : every one the dance
Knows in its intricate mazes of delight, artful to weave ;
Each one to sound his instruments of music in the dance,
To touch each other & recede, to cross & change & return.
These are the Children of Los. Thou seest the Trees on mountains :
The wind blows heavy ; loud they thunder thro' the darksom sky,
Uttering prophecies & speaking instructive words to the sons
Of men. These are the Sons of Los, These the Visions of Eternity.
But we see only as it were the hem of their garments
When with our vegetable eyes we view these wondrous Visions.

There are Two Gates thro' which all Souls descend, One Southward
From Dover Cliff to Lizard Point, the other toward the North,
Caithness & rocky Durness, Pentland & John Groat's House.

The Souls descending to the Body wail on the right hand
Of Los, & those deliver'd from the Body on the left hand.
For Los against the east his force continually bends
Along the Valleys of Middlesex from Hounslow to Blackheath,
Lest those Three Heavens of Beulah should the Creation destroy,
And lest they should descend before the north & south Gates.
Groaning with pity, he among the wailing Souls laments.

And these the Labours of the Sons of Los in Allamanda,
And in the City of Golgonooza & in Luban & around

13–17 These Gates would seem to be the Gates of Birth and Death (J. 27. *stanza* 16) between which lie the Furnaces of Los, the world of time and space ; cp. J. 5. 31 :

> They [the Spectres] revolve into the Furnaces Southward & are driven forth Northward.

The word ' descend ' (l. 13) is used loosely : this is clear from ll. 16–17.

18–19 From Hounslow to Blackheath—that is from west to east ' along the Valleys of Middlesex '—represents the direction of the prophetic spirit in its labours against error : see Index, *Cardinal Points*.

20 See Index, *Beulah*, II, ii. 24 Cp. F. Z. vii. 429 *note*.

The Lake of Udan-Adan in the Forests of Entuthon Benython,
Where Souls incessant wail, being piteous Passions & Desires,
With neither lineament nor form, but like to wat'ry clouds;
The Passions & Desires descend upon the hungry winds;
For such alone Sleepers remain, meer passion & appetite.
The Sons of Los clothe them & feed & provide houses & fields.

And every Generated Body in its inward form
Is a garden of delight & a building of magnificence
Built by the Sons of Los in Bowlahoola & Allamanda,
And the herbs & flowers & furniture & beds & chambers
Continually woven in the Looms of Enitharmon's Daughters,
In bright Cathedron's golden Dome with care & love & tears.
For the various Classes of Men are all mark'd out determinate
In Bowlahoola: & as the Spectres choose their affinities,
So they are born on Earth: and every Class is determinate,
But not by Natural, but by Spiritual power alone, Because
The Natural power continually seeks & tends to Destruction
Ending in Death, which would of itself be Eternal Death.
And all are Class'd by Spiritual & not by Natural power.

And every Natural Effect has a Spiritual Cause, and Not
A Natural: for a Natural Cause only seems; it is a Delusion
Of Ulro, & a ratio of the perishing Vegetable Memory.

[27] Some Sons of Los surround the Passions with porches of iron & silver,
Creating form & beauty around the dark regions of sorrow,
Giving to airy nothing a name and a habitation
Delightful, with bounds to the Infinite putting off the Indefinite
Into most holy forms of Thought (such is the power of inspiration).

31 The 'Generated Body' is not merely the 'worm of seventy inches', but implies also capacity for vision.

31–36 Cp. M. H. H., p. 7.:

> How do you know but ev'ry Bird that cuts the airy way
> Is an immense world of delight, clos'd by your senses five?

Cp. also M. 25. 66–26. 12 *note* and F. Z. ii. 337–341 *note*.

46 A 'ratio of the perishing Vegetable Memory' is Blake's name for a deduction from sense-experience, as the antithesis of inspiration or vision. He calls it elsewhere a 'fortuitous concourse of memories' (J. 33. 8). Cp. also M. 43. 23–24.

Page 27. The activities assigned to the several sons of Los cannot be distinguished from their general function (see Index, *Los, Note II a*), but here there appears the underlying idea that their activities are related to the transitory admission of the spiritual worth of natural beauty rightly interpreted.

They labour incessant, with many tears & afflictions
Creating the beautiful House for the piteous sufferer.

Others Cabinets richly fabricate of gold & ivory
For Doubts & fears : unform'd & wretched & melancholy,
The little weeping Spectre stands on the threshold of Death
Eternal ; and sometimes two Spectres, like lamps quivering.
And often malignant they combat (heart-breaking, sorrowful
& piteous).
Antamon takes them into his beautiful flexible hands
As the Sower takes the seed or as the Artist his clay
Or fine wax to mould artful a model for golden ornaments.
The soft hands of Antamon draw the indelible line,
Form immortal, with golden pen, such as the Spectre, admiring,
Puts on the sweet form : then smiles Antamon bright thro' his windows ;
The Daughters of beauty look up from their Loom & prepare
The integument soft for its clothing with joy & delight.

But Theotormon & Sotha stand in the Gate of Luban anxious :
Their numbers are seven million & seven thousand & seven hundred.
They contend with the weak Spectres ; they fabricate soothing forms.
The Spectre refuses : he seeks cruelty : they create the crested Cock.
Terrified, the Spectre screams & rushes in fear into their Net
Of kindness & compassion, & is born a weeping terror :
Or they create the Lion & Tyger in compassionate thunderings.

13 For Antamon cp. *Europe*, l. 43 *note*, and *Africa*, 11 *note*. Here he is no longer the medium through whom Urizen imposes his Laws and Religions upon man, but an agent of spiritual regeneration. The same is true of the other sons, Theotormon and Sotha (*infra*, l. 21).

16 Cp. F. Z. vii. 462–470. The 'indelible line' is the form created for the 'unformed Passions and Desires' of the Spectres, as in ll. 3–5 above. Cp. D. C. xv : 'The great and golden rule of art as well as of life is this, That the more distinct, sharp, and wirey the bounding line, the more perfect the work of art ; . . . Leave out this line, and you leave out life itself : all is chaos again, and the line of the almighty must be drawn out upon it before man or beast can exist.' This passage contains the best statement of Blake's doctrine of the necessity of definiteness of vision, in conduct and in art. This definiteness is constantly connoted of the higher life of the spirit, while its contrary is associated with the false rules in metaphysic, ethic and aesthetic in mundane life : cp. J. 66. 46–54 : 64. 5 : 80. 51.

21 Cp. F. Z. vii. 429 *note*.

22 The number is apparently that of the sons of Theotormon and Sotha : neither to these nor to the sons of Ozoth (l. 30) can any distinctive meaning be attached.

Howling the Spectres flee: they take refuge in Human lineaments.

The Sons of Ozoth within the Optic Nerve stand fiery glowing;
And the number of his Sons is eight millions & eight.
They give delights to the man unknown: artificial riches
They give to scorn, & their possessors to trouble & sorrow & care,
Shutting the sun & moon & stars & trees & clouds & waters
And hills out from the Optic Nerve, & hardening it into a bone
Opake, and like the black pebble on the enragèd beach;
While the poor indigent is like the diamond which, tho' cloth'd
In rugged covering in the mine, is open all within,
And in his hallow'd center holds the heavens of bright eternity.
Ozoth here builds walls of rocks against the surging sea,
And timbers crampt with iron cramps bar in the joys of life
From fell destruction in the Spectrous cunning or rage. He Creates
The speckled Newt, the Spider & Beetle, the Rat & Mouse,
The Badger & Fox: they worship before his feet in trembling fear.

But others of the Sons of Los build Moments & Minutes & Hours,
And Days & Months & Years, & Ages & Periods, wondrous buildings!
And every Moment has a Couch of gold for soft repose,
(A Moment equals a pulsation of the artery)
And between every two Moments stands a Daughter of Beulah
To feed the Sleepers on their Couches with maternal care.
And every Minute has an azure Tent with silken Veils;
And every Hour has a bright golden Gate carvèd with skill;
And every Day & Night has Walls of brass & Gates of adamant,
Shining like precious stones & ornamented with appropriate signs;
And every Month a silver pavèd Terrace builded high;
And every Year invulnerable Barriers with high Towers;

31 Cp. Ross. MS. cxxx, ll. 7–14 (Clar. Press, p. 238).

32–35 The power of vision, symbolized by the Optic Nerve, becomes atrophied in those who give themselves to the 'artificial riches' of this world. Cp. *Laocoön*, 32–35.

44–p. 28. 3 With this vision of Time mystically conceived as the 'mercy of Eternity' (M. 23. 72) cp. J. 48. 27 foll. and the symbol Erin in Index, *Daughters of Beulah, Note I.*

48–49 Cp. J. 56. 8–10.

And every Age is Moated deep, with Bridges of silver & gold ;
And every Seven Ages is Incirclèd with a Flaming Fire.
Now Seven Ages is amounting to Two Hundred Years.
Each has its Guard, each Moment, Minute, Hour, Day, Month & Year :
All are the work of Fairy hands of the Four Elements :
The Guard are Angels of Providence on duty evermore.
Every Time less than a pulsation of the artery
Is equal in its period & value to Six Thousand Years.
[28] For in this Period the Poet's Work is Done; and all the Great
Events of Time start forth & are conciev'd in such a Period,
Within a Moment, a Pulsation of the Artery.

The Sky is an immortal Tent built by the Sons of Los ;
And every Space that a Man views around his dwelling-place,
Standing on his own roof, or in his garden on a mount
Of twenty-five cubits in height, such space is his Universe.
And on its verge the Sun rises & sets, the Clouds bow
To meet the flat Earth & the Sea in such an order'd Space ;
The Starry heavens reach no further, but here bend and set
On all sides, & the two Poles turn on their valves of gold :
And if he move his dwelling-place, his heavens also move
Where'er he goes & all his neighbourhood bewail his loss.
Such are the Spaces callèd Earth & such its dimension.
As to that false appearance which appears to the reasoner,
As of a Globe rolling thro' Voidness, it is a delusion of Ulro.
The Microscope knows not of this nor the Telescope : they alter
The ratio of the Spectator's Organs but leave Objects untouch'd.
For every Space larger than a red Globule of Man's blood
Is visionary, and is created by the Hammer of Los ;
And every Space smaller than a Globule of Man's blood opens
Into Eternity, of which this vegetable Earth is but a shadow.
The red Globule is the unwearied Sun by Los created
To measure Time and Space to mortal Men every morning.
Bowlahoola & Allamanda are placèd on each side
Of that Pulsation & that Globule ; terrible their power.

Page 28. 5–17 Blake's argument is aimed against all astronomical theories, denying the possibility of truth in any. The 'space a man views' is visionary in its nature, its presentation in sense being a perversion of that nature. To assume an objective truth corresponding with the sense-imposed images in the mind, and to erect thereon an elaborate superstructure, to which also is attributed objective truth, is simply to magnify the initial error (cp. J. 83. 40–42 and see M. 14. 32 *note*).
17 this] i.e. the falsity of appearances.

But Rintrah & Palamabron govern over Day & Night
In Allamanda & Entuthon Benython, where Souls wail,
Where Orc incessant howls, burning in fires of Eternal Youth
Within the vegetated mortal Nerves: for every Man born is joinèd
Within into One mighty Polypus, and this Polypus is Orc.

But in the Optic vegetative Nerves Sleep was transformèd
To Death in old time by Satan, the father of Sin & Death:
And Satan is the Spectre of Orc, & Orc is the generate Luvah.

But in the Nerves of the Nostrils, Accident being formèd
Into Substance & Principle by the cruelties of Demonstration,
It became Opake & Indefinite; but the Divine Saviour
Formèd it into a Solid by Los's Mathematic power.
He namèd the Opake Satan; he namèd the Solid Adam.

And in the Nerves of the Ear (for the Nerves of the Tongue are closèd),
On Albion's Rock Los stands, creating the glorious Sun each morning.
And when unwearied in the evening he creates the Moon,
Death to delude, who all in terror at their splendor leaves
His prey; while Los appoints, & Rintrah & Palamabron guide
The Souls clear from the Rock of Death, that Death himself may wake
In his appointed season when the ends of heaven meet.

Then Los conducts the Spirits to be Vegetated into
Great Golgonooza, free from the four iron pillars of Satan's Throne

28 See Index, *Science*, II, and *Ulro, Note*.

29–34 No passage elsewhere throws light on this conception of Orc, nor is there any similar use of the symbol Polypus (l. 31).

37 'It' refers to 'Accident' (l. 35).

38 Generally whatever is of mathematics shares the reprobation with which Blake regarded the uninspired reason and its works: cp. such phrases as 'The Gods of Greece and Egypt were Mathematical Diagrams' (*Laocoön*, 26), and 'Satans Mathematic Holiness' (M. extra p. 32. 18). But here, as in J. 12. 10–15, the doctrine that what was meant for the destruction of man becomes the means to regeneration is again exemplified; the systems of error are to be fixed permanent

by mathematic power,
Giving a body to Falsehood that it may be cast off for ever;
With Demonstrative Science piercing Apollyon with his own bow.

Blake never develops this view.

39 See Index, *Expansion*, &c. 40 Cp. F. Z. i. 100 *note*.

45 The 'Rock of Death' may have some relation to the Stone of Night in the Lambeth books: cp. *Europe*, 96 *note*.

(Temperance, Prudence, Justice, Fortitude, the four pillars of tyranny),
That Satan's Watch-Fiends touch them not before they Vegetate.

But Enitharmon and her Daughters take the pleasant charge
To give them to their lovely heavens till the Great Judgment Day:
Such is their lovely charge. But Rahab & Tirzah pervert
Their mild influences: therefore the Seven Eyes of God walk round
The Three Heavens of Ulro where Tirzah & her Sisters
Weave the black Woof of Death upon Entuthon Benython,
In the Vale of Surrey, where Horeb terminates in Rephaim.
The stamping feet of Zelophehad's Daughters are cover'd with Human gore
Upon the treddles of the Loom; they sing to the wingèd shuttle.
The River rises above his banks to wash the Woof;
He takes it in his arms, he passes it in strength thro' his current.
The veil of human miseries is woven over the Ocean
From the Atlantic to the Great South Sea, the Erythrean.

Such is the World of Los, the labour of six thousand years.
Thus Nature is a Vision of the Science of the Elohim.

End of the First Book

56 See Index, *Vala, Note I.* C. 58 Cp. F. Z. viii. 301 *note.*
63 The Great South Sea, the Erythrean, merely repeats the substance of the symbol Atlantic Ocean (see Index, *Atlantic*).
64 See Index, *Mundane Shell.* 65 Cp. M. 25. 66–26. 12 *note.*

[30]

MILTON

Book the Second

THERE is a place where Contrarieties are equally True.
This place is callèd Beulah. It is a pleasant lovely Shadow
Where no dispute can come, Because of those who Sleep.
Into this place the Sons & Daughters of Ololon descended
With solemn mourning into Beulah's moony shades & hills,
Weeping for Milton. Mute wonder held the Daughters of Beulah
Enraptur'd with affection sweet and mild benevolence.

Beulah is evermore Created around Eternity, appearing
To the Inhabitants of Eden around them on all sides.
But Beulah to its Inhabitants appears within each district
As the belovèd infant in his mother's bosom, round incircled
With arms of love & pity & sweet compassion. But to
The Sons of Eden the moony habitations of Beulah
Are from Great Eternity a mild & pleasant Rest.

And it is thus Created. Lo, the Eternal Great Humanity,
To whom be Glory & Dominion Evermore, Amen,
Walks among all his awful Family, seen in every face.
As the breath of the Almighty, such are the words of man to man
In the great Wars of Eternity, in fury of Poetic Inspiration,
To build the Universe stupendous, Mental forms Creating.

Page 30. The following lines are written in reverse at the top of the page, about the title 'Milton'; they are engraved in reverse and have no place in the text:

How wide the Gulf & Unpassable between Simplicity & Insipidity.
Contraries are Positives./A Negation is not a Contrary.

1–p. 31. 11 See Index, *Beulah*.

4 This takes up the Ololon myth at the point at which it was left on p. 19.

15–20 Beulah appears here to be the reflection of Divine power, of the Divine Family in its aspect as the Ultimate Unity, in so far as it may be expressed in living forms, i.e. by visionary art. It is thus the impulse to imaginative creation (see Index, *Daughters of Beulah*), and not merely repose from error.

But the Emanations trembled exceedingly, nor could they
Live, because the life of Man was too exceeding unbounded :
His joy became terrible to them ; they trembled & wept,
Crying with one voice : ‘ Give us a habitation & a place
In which we may be hidden under the shadow of wings :
For if we who are but for a time & who pass away in winter,
Behold these wonders of Eternity, we shall consume.
But you, O our Fathers & Brothers, remain in Eternity ;
But grant us a Temporal Habitation ; do you speak
To us ; we will obey your words as you obey Jesus
The Eternal, who is blessèd for ever & ever. Amen.’

So spoke the lovely Emanations, & there appear'd a pleasant
Mild Shadow above, beneath, & on all sides round.
[31] Into this pleasant Shadow all the weak & weary,
Like Women & Children, were taken away as on wings
Of dovelike softness & shadowy habitations preparèd for them.
But every Man return'd & went, still going forward thro'
The Bosom of the Father in Eternity on Eternity ;
Neither did any lack or fall into Error without
A Shadow to repose in all the Days of happy Eternity.

Into this pleasant Shadow, Beulah, all Ololon descended.
And when the Daughters of Beulah heard the lamentation,
All Beulah wept, for they saw the Lord coming in the Clouds.
And the Shadows of Beulah terminate in rocky Albion.

And all Nations wept in affliction, Family by Family :
Germany wept towards France & Italy ; England wept & trembled
Towards America ; India rose up from his golden bed,
As one awaken'd in the night ; they saw the Lord coming
In the Clouds of Ololon with Power & Great Glory.

And all the Living Creatures of the Four Elements wail'd
With bitter wailing ; these in the aggregate are namèd Satan

21–31 Cp. Cat. 1810: ‘Beneath these [“the spirits of the just made perfect”], a Cloud of Women & Children are taken up, fleeing from the rolling Cloud which separates the Wicked from the Seats of Bliss. These represent those who, tho' willing, were too weak to Reject Errors without the Assistance & Countenance of those Already in the Truth : for a Man Can only Reject Error by the Advice of a Friend, or by the Immediate Inspiration of God.’

Page 31. 10 The Clouds are the Clouds of Ololon : cp. M. 19. 60 *note*.

17–26 In J. 36. 31–37, ‘ the Living Creatures of the Four Elements ’ are identified with the fallen Zoas : see Index, *Zoas*. They all labour in Los's Halls (M. 23. 74–75). The character here ascribed to them, of knowing

And Rahab they know not of Regeneration, but only of Generation.
The Fairies, Nymphs, Gnomes & Genii of the Four Elements,
Unforgiving & unalterable, these cannot be Regenerated,
But must be Created, for they know only of Generation.
These are the Gods of the Kingdoms of the Earth, in contrarious
And cruel opposition, Element against Element opposèd in War,
Not Mental, as the Wars of Eternity, but a Corporeal Strife,
In Los's Halls continual labouring in the Furnaces of Golgonooza.
Orc howls on the Atlantic : Enitharmon trembles. All Beulah weeps.

Thou hearest the Nightingale begin the Song of Spring.
The Lark, sitting upon his earthy bed, just as the morn
Appears, listens silent ; then, springing from the waving Corn-field, loud
He leads the Choir of Day, trill ! trill ! trill ! trill !
Mounting upon the wings of light into the Great Expanse,
Re-ecchoing against the lovely blue & shining heavenly Shell.
His little throat labours with inspiration ; every feather
On throat & breast & wings vibrates with the effluence Divine.
All Nature listens silent to him, & the awful Sun
Stands still upon the Mountain, looking on this little Bird
With eyes of soft humility & wonder, love & awe.
Then loud from their green covert all the Birds begin their Song :
The Thrush, the Linnet & the Goldfinch, Robin & the Wren
Awake the Sun from his sweet reverie upon the Mountain.
The Nightingale again assays his song, & thro' the day
And thro' the night warbles luxuriant, every Bird of Song
Attending his loud harmony with admiration & love.
This is a Vision of the lamentation of Beulah over Ololon.

Thou percievest the Flowers put forth their precious Odours ;
And none can tell how from so small a center comes such sweet,
Forgetting that within that Center Eternity expands
Its ever during doors that Og & Anak fiercely guard.
First, eer the morning breaks, joy opens in the flowery bosoms,

only of Generation, and not of Regeneration, may be taken as emphasizing the doctrine that of itself mundane life is evil, a state of death ; the powers associated with it err through defect of vision, as in M. 10. 36–39.

25 Cp. M., Preface, *note* 2.

28–63 Cp. M 25. 66–26. 12 and *note*.

Joy even to tears, which the Sun rising dries : first the Wild Thyme
And Meadow-sweet, downy & soft, waving among the reeds,
Light springing on the air, lead the sweet Dance ; they wake
The Honeysuckle sleeping on the Oak ; the flaunting beauty
Revels along upon the wind ; the White-thorn, lovely May,
Opens her many lovely eyes. Listening, the Rose still sleeps ;
None dare to wake her : soon she bursts her crimson curtain'd bed
And comes forth in the majesty of beauty. Every Flower,
The Pink, the Jessamine, the Wall-flower, the Carnation,
The Jonquil, the mild Lilly, opes her heavens ; every Tree
And Flower & Herb soon fill the air with an innumerable Dance,
Yet all in order sweet & lovely. Men are sick with Love.
Such is a Vision of the lamentation of Beulah over Ololon.

[32] And the Divine Voice was heard in the Songs of Beulah, Saying :

' When I first Married you, I gave you all my whole Soul ;
I thought that you would love my loves & joy in my delights,
Seeking for pleasures in my pleasures, O Daughter of Babylon !
Then thou wast lovely, mild, & gentle ; now thou art terrible
In jealousy & unlovely in my sight, because thou hast cruelly
Cut off my loves in fury, till I have no love left for thee.
Thy love depends on him thou lovest, & on his dear loves
Depend thy pleasures, which thou hast cut off by jealousy.
Therefore I shew my Jealousy, & set before you Death.
Behold Milton, descended to Redeem the Female Shade
From Death Eternal ! such your lot, to be continually Redeem'd
By death & misery of those you love & by Annihilation.
When the Sixfold Female percieves that Milton annihilates
Himself, that seeing all his loves by her cut off, he leaves

Page 32. 1–23 Vala or the Shadowy Female is Nature, and in the opening lines of this passage is described as if emblematic of a state of mediate vision. The preceding pages (30–31) are not concerned with the objective reality of Nature, but emphasize its beauty, and the Divine purpose that it shall be as a repose for the spirit of man. The assumption of the permanent reality of the beautiful dream has been in itself the foundation on which is built the superstructure of the ' philosophy of five senses ' with its corollary, the cruelty of restrictive morality. Milton had been among the false teachers ; his doctrine, the ' Sixfold emanation ' (ll. 11 foll.) cannot be corrected, it must be destroyed in order that truth may be revealed. This is the task of Milton incarnate in Blake.

15–17 ' Error or Creation ' symbolized by the Female, and particularly by Vala, ' will be Burned up . . . the Moment Men cease to behold it'

Her also, intirely abstracting himself from Female loves,
She shall relent in fear of death : She shall begin to give
Her maidens to her husband, delighting in his delight.
And then, & then alone begins the happy Female joy,
As it is done in Beulah ; & thou, O Virgin Babylon, Mother of Whoredoms,
Shalt bring Jerusalem in thine arms in the night watches ; and
No longer turning her a wandering Harlot in the streets,
Shalt give her into the arms of God, your Lord & Husband.'

Such are the Songs of Beulah in the Lamentations of Ololon.

[34] And all the Songs of Beulah sounded comfortable notes
To comfort Ololon's lamentation ; for they said :
'Are you the Fiery Circle that late drove in fury & fire
The Eight Immortal Starry-Ones down into Ulro dark,
Rending the Heavens of Beulah with your thunders & lightnings ?
And can you thus lament, & can you pity & forgive ?
Is terror chang'd to pity, O wonder of Eternity ?'

And the Four States of Humanity in its Repose
Were shewèd them. First of Beulah, a most pleasant Sleep
On Couches soft with mild music, tended by Flowers of Beulah,
Sweet Female forms, wingèd or floating in the air spontaneous.
The Second State is Alla, & the third State Al-Ulro ;
But the Fourth State is dreadful ; it is namèd Or-Ulro.
The First State is in the Head, the Second is in the Heart,
The Third in the Loins & Seminal Vessels, & the Fourth
In the Stomach & Intestines, terrible, deadly, unutterable.
And he whose Gates are open'd in those Regions of his Body
Can from those Gates view all these wondrous Imaginations.

But Ololon sought the Or-Ulro & its fiery Gates
And the Couches of the Martyrs ; & many Daughters of Beulah
Accompany them down to the Ulro with soft melodious tears,
A long journey & dark thro' Chaos in the track of Milton's course,

(Cat. 1810) ; that is, when Man, finding no satisfaction for his spiritual life in the objects of mundane experience, wills to 'abstract' himself from them as illusions, these illusions cease to exist : cp. J. 67. 46 : 68. 42.

Page 34. 1 Cp. F. Z. vii *a*. 294–295 :
And all the Songs of Beulah sounded comfortable notes,
Not suffering doubt to rise up from the Clouds of the Shadowy Female.
3–5 Cp. M. 18. 43–50. 8–16 See Index, *Ulro, Note I.*
17–18 Cp. F. Z. i. 250 *note*.

To where the Contraries of Beulah War beneath Negation's Banner.

Then, view'd from Milton's Track, they see the Ulro, a vast Polypus
Of living fibres down into the Sea of Time & Space growing,
A self-devouring, monstrous Human Death Twenty seven fold.
Within it sit Five Females & the nameless Shadowy Mother,
Spinning it from their bowels with songs of amorous delight
And melting cadences that lure the Sleepers of Beulah down
The River Storge (which is Arnon) into the Dead Sea.
Around this Polypus Los continual builds the Mundane Shell.

Four Universes round the Universe of Los remain Chaotic,
Four intersecting Globes, & the Egg form'd World of Los
In midst, stretching from Zenith to Nadir in midst of Chaos.
One of these Ruin'd Universes is to the North, namèd Urthona :
One in the South ; this was the glorious World of Urizen :
One to the East, of Luvah ; One to the West, of Tharmas.
But when Luvah assumèd the World of Urizen in the South,
All fell towards the Center, sinking downward in dire Ruin.

Here in these Chaoses the Sons of Ololon took their abode
In Chasms of the Mundane Shell, which open on all sides round.
Southwards & by the East, within the Breach of Milton's descent,
To watch the time, pitying & gentle, to awaken Urizen,
They stood, in a dark land of death, of fiery corroding waters,
Where lie in evil death the Four Immortals pale and cold,
And the Eternal Man, even Albion, upon the Rock of Ages.

23 The 'Contraries' that are harmonized in Beulah (see Index, *Beulah*) are in opposition in the mortal state of error. The exact nature of these Contraries does not appear. The Negation is the Spectre, the denial of or antithesis of Imagination.

24–31 See Index, *Mundane Shell, Note I*, B and *Note II*.

27 This is the 'Sixfold Emanation' : cp. M. 16. 1 *note*.

30 The name 'Storge' is apparently derived from στοργή ; its significance is indicated in the line 'parental affection, storgous appetite' : cp. F. Z. v. 113 *note*.

32–37 A diagram on p. 32 shows the four worlds as four circles surrounded by flames and intersecting at the central point of the 'Egg-form'd World of Los'. The track of Milton's descent is shown, running up from the bottom right-hand corner through the point of intersection of the circles Urizen and Luvah, the 'breach of Milton's descent' (M. 34. 42), through 'Satan', the lower section of Los's world, and finishing in 'Adam', its upper portion. 38–39 Cp. J. 59. 15–17, and see Index, *Luvah*.

45 See Index, *Zoas*. 46 Cp. F. Z. ix. 284 *note*.

Seeing Milton's Shadow, some Daughters of Beulah trembling
Return'd ; but Ololon remain'd before the Gates of the Dead.

And Ololon lookèd down into the Heavens of Ulro in fear.
They said : ' How are the Wars of Man, which in Great Eternity
Appear around in the External Spheres of Visionary Life,
Here render'd Deadly within the Life & Interior Vision !
How are the Beasts & Birds & Fishes & Plants & Minerals
Here fix'd into a frozen bulk, subject to decay & death !
Those Visions of Human Life & Shadows of Wisdom & Knowledge
[35] Are here frozen to unexpansive deadly destroying terrors ;
And War & Hunting, the Two Fountains of the River of Life,
Are become Fountains of bitter Death & of corroding Hell,
Till Brotherhood is chang'd into a Curse & a Flattery
By Differences between Ideas, that Ideas themselves (which are
The Divine Members) may be slain in offerings for sin.
O dreadful Loom of Death ! O piteous Female forms, compell'd
To weave the Woof of Death ! On Camberwell Tirzah's Courts,
Malah's on Blackheath ; Rahab & Noah dwell on Windsor's heights,
Where once the Cherubs of Jerusalem spread to Lambeth's Vale.

50–55 Cp. J. 92. 13–27, where it is stated that the errors of mortal life remain after the Regeneration in the ' Outward Spheres of Visionary Space and Time/In the shadows of Possibility ' that Man may thenceforward ' Foresee and Avoid ' them and their consequences. Here Man has not yet freed himself from them, but transforms ' Accident ' into ' Substance ' (M. 28. 35–36), neglecting the real and eternal forms for ' an outside shadowy surface superadded to the real Surface' (J. 83. 47) through his reliance upon sense-perception. So the illusion of discrete physical entities displaces the true vision of the union of all forms in the One, the Divine Humanity, the One Man, Jesus.

Page 35. 2–3 Cp. J. 43. 31–32 and M., Preface, *note* 2.

5–6 This is the error of ' Abstract Philosophy warring against Imagination ' :

> rejecting Ideas as nothing & holding all Wisdom
> To consist in the agreements & disagreements of Ideas. (J. 70. 7–8.)

' To reason and compare ' can be no part of the visionary's business, whose perception of all Ideas is immediate and complete.

7–8 See Index, *Weaving*, I.

8–13 The heights here named surround London on all sides ; they represent the stations of the feminine powers of morality and materialism that encompass the visionary activity in mortal life, centred in ' Golgonooza, the Spiritual Fourfold London '.

Milcah's Pillars shine from Harrow to Hampstead, where Hoglah
On Highgate's heights magnificent Weaves over trembling Thames
To Shooter's Hill and thence to Blackheath, the dark Woof. Loud,
Loud roll the Weights & Spindles over the whole Earth, let down
On all sides round to the Four Quarters of the World, eastward on
Europe to Euphrates & Hindu, to Nile & back in Clouds
Of Death across the Atlantic to America North & South.'

So spoke Ololon in reminiscence, astonish'd ; but they
Could not behold Golgonooza without passing the Polypus,
A wondrous journey not passable by Immortal feet ; & none
But the Divine Saviour can pass it without annihilation.
For Golgonooza cannot be seen till, having pass'd the Polypus,
It is viewed on all sides round by a Four-fold Vision,
Or till you become Mortal & Vegetable in Sexuality :
Then you behold its mighty Spires & Domes of ivory & gold.

And Ololon examinèd all the Couches of the Dead,
Even of Los & Enitharmon & all the Sons of Albion,
And his Four Zoas terrified & on the verge of Death.
In midst of these was Milton's Couch, & when they saw Eight
Immortal Starry-Ones guarding the Couch in flaming fires,
They thunderous utter'd all a universal groan, falling down
Prostrate before the Starry Eight, asking with tears forgiveness,
Confessing their crime with humiliation and sorrow.

O how the Starry Eight rejoic'd to see Ololon descended,
And now that a wide road was open to Eternity

15–17 These places, being in the East, share the sinister significance of that quarter.

18–21 This differentiation of the Saviour and Ololon seems quite outside Blake's usual concept of the Eternals as united into One Man in Jesus : see Index, *Jesus*. The whole significance of this ascription of inferior spiritual powers to Ololon, with its outcome in the female form assumed later (M. 36. 13–20), is obscure.

22–25 See Index, *Los, Note III (a)*.

27 Los is classed with the Dead, perhaps as having fallen from his Eternal Station, i.e. having become a power in mortal life : cp. M. 20.15–16.

35 The 'wide road' 'open to Eternity' made by 'Milton the Awakener' appears to be deliberately antithetical to the 'broad and beaten way / Over the dark Abyss' made by Sin and Death in the track of Satan from Hell to this world, according to what Blake thought the perverted account in *Paradise Lost*.

By Ololon's descent thro' Beulah to Los & Enitharmon!

For mighty were the multitudes of Ololon, vast the extent
Of their great sway, reaching from Ulro to Eternity,
Surrounding the Mundane Shell outside in its Caverns
And through Beulah: and all silent forbore to contend
With Ololon, for they saw the Lord in the Clouds of Ololon.

There is a Moment in each Day that Satan cannot find,
Nor can his Watch Fiends find it; but the Industrious find
This Moment, & it multiply: & when it once is found,
It renovates every Moment of the Day, if rightly placèd.
In this Moment Ololon descended to Los & Enitharmon,
Unseen beyond the Mundane Shell, Southward in Milton's track.

Just in this Moment, when the morning odours rise abroad
And first from the Wild Thyme, stands a Fountain in a rock
Of crystal, flowing into two Streams: one flows thro' Golgonooza,
And thro' Beulah to Eden beneath Los's western Wall;
The other flows thro' the Aerial Void & all the Churches,
Meeting again in Golgonooza beyond Satan's Seat.

The Wild Thyme is Los's Messenger to Eden, a mighty Demon;
Terrible, deadly & poisonous his presence in Ulro dark:
Therefore he appears only a small Root creeping in grass,
Covering over the Rock of Odours his bright purple mantle
Beside the Fount above the Lark's Nest in Golgonooza.

41 Cp. M. 19. 60 *note*.

42–45 Cp. J. 41. 15–22. From the tenor of these lines it would appear that Blake refers to the moment of complete communion with Eternity. Cp. F. Z. i. 133–137, where, in creating a 'Space' for the regeneration of the youthful Los and Enitharmon, Eno, a Daughter of Beulah, provided at certain intervals 'windows into Eden', that is, gave 'visions of sweet heaven'.

50–53 The courses of these two streams would appear to symbolize the two paths to regeneration: one, taken by the visionary, leads into Eden through Beulah, the highest spiritual state possible to mortal man; the other, trodden by those who ignore vision, leads through the different states of error, the Void with its Churches, finally coming beneath Los's regenerative power in Golgonooza. The same concept is expressed in obscurer symbols in J. 83. 54–58:

> The land [Albion] is mark'd for desolation, & unless we plant
> The seeds of Cities & of Villages in the Human bosom,
> Albion must be a rock of blood: mark ye the points
> Where Cities shall remain & where Villages: for the rest,
> It must lie in confusion till Albion's time of awaking.

57 The Rock of Odours is not mentioned elsewhere: cp. the description of the 'Stone of Night', *Europe*, ll. 96–107 and *note ad loc.*

Luvah slept here in death, & here is Luvah's empty Tomb.
Ololon sat beside this Fountain on the Rock of Odours.

Just at the place to where the Lark mounts is a Crystal Gate:
It is the enterance of the First Heaven, namèd Luther; for
The Lark is Los's Messenger thro' the Twenty-seven Churches,
That the Seven Eyes of God, who walk even to Satan's Seat
Thro' all the Twenty-seven Heavens, may not slumber nor sleep.
But the Lark's Nest is at the Gate of Los, at the eastern
Gate of wide Golgonooza; & the Lark is Los's Messenger.

[36] When on the highest lift of his light pinions he arrives
At that bright Gate, another Lark meets him, & back to back
They touch their pinions tip [to] tip, and each descend
To their respective Earths, & there all night consult with Angels
Of Providence & with the Eyes of God all night in slumber
Inspirèd; & at the dawn of day send out another Lark
Into another Heaven to carry news upon his wings.
Thus are the Messengers dispatch'd till they reach the Earth again
In the East Gate of Golgonooza: & the Twenty-eighth bright
Lark met the Female Ololon descending into my Garden.
Thus it appears to Mortal eyes & those of the Ulro Heavens:
But not thus to Immortals; the Lark is a mighty Angel.

For Ololon step'd into the Polypus within the Mundane Shell.
They could not step into Vegetable Worlds without becoming
The enemies of Humanity, except in a Female Form.
And as One Female Ololon and all its mighty Hosts
Appear'd, a Virgin of twelve years: nor time nor space was

62–65 For the 'heavens' and 'churches' see Index, *Mundane Shell*.

63–67 The Catalogue of the Grolier Club Exhibition reprints Blake's notes to a number of water-colour drawings for *L'Allegro* and *Il Penseroso*. To the second of the series, illustrating the passage commencing 'To hear the lark begin his flight', Blake notes 'The Lark is an Angel on the Wing. Dull Night starts from her Watch Tower in a Cloud. The Dawn with her Dappled Horses arises above the Earth. The Earth beneath awakes at the Lark's voice.'

Page 36. 10 This incident, like much else in the last pages of Milton, may be a direct transcript from Blake's visionary experiences at Felpham. The design on the page shows Blake walking in the garden before his cottage and Ololon descending to him. Birds soar above the roof.

15 Cp. M., extra p. 17. 34–35, where Orc, addressing the Shadowy Female, says: When wilt thou put on the Female Form as in times of old,
With a Garment of Pity & Compassion like the Garment of God.

16–20 See *Milton*, Introduction.

To the perception of the Virgin Ololon ; but as the
Flash of lightning, but more quick, the Virgin in my Garden
Before my Cottage stood : for the Satanic Space is delusion.

For when Los join'd with me he took me in his fi[e]ry whirlwind.
My Vegetated portion was hurried from Lambeth's shades.
He set me down in Felpham's Vale & prepar'd a beautiful
Cottage for me, that in three years I might write all these Visions
To display Nature's cruel holiness, the deceits of Natural Religion.
Walking in my Cottage Garden, sudden I beheld
The Virgin Ololon, & address'd her as a Daughter of Beulah :

'Virgin of Providence, fear not to enter into my Cottage.
What is thy message to thy friend ? what am I now to do ?
Is it again to plunge into deeper affliction ? behold me
Ready to obey : but pity thou my Shadow of Delight.
Enter my Cottage : comfort her, for she is sick with fatigue.'

[37] The Virgin answer'd : 'Knowest thou of Milton, who descended,
Driven from Eternity ? Him I seek : terrified at my Act
In Great Eternity, which thou knowest, I come him to seek.'

So Ololon utter'd in words distinct the anxious thought.
Mild was the voice, but more distinct than any earthly
That Milton's Shadow heard ; & condensing all his Fibres
Into a strength impregnable of majesty & beauty infinite,
I saw he was the Covering Cherub, & within him Satan
And Rahab, in an outside which is fallacious, within
Beyond the outline of Identity, in the Selfhood deadly.

20 The 'Satanic Space' is the phenomenal universe. 'Nature is the work of the Devil' (Crabb Robinson, S., p. 265).

31–32 The 'Shadow of Delight' is apparently Mrs. Blake, who during her stay at Felpham suffered almost constantly from ague and rheumatism, caused chiefly by the unhealthiness of the place. Cp. Letter to Butts, 10th January 1802 (R. p. 96).

Page 37. 1–2 Cp. M. 19. 15–19 : 31–34.

5–10 The construction of these lines is irregular, but the general purpose is evident enough. The passage and its continuation up to p. 40, l. 2, describe the full vision of the Miltonic error which came to Blake at the same time as the vision of Ololon. The 'outline of Identity', a phrase repeated J. 18. 3, is 'the Outline, the Circumference and Form', the 'lineaments of Man', 'the real and eternal Self'. What lies beyond is the body of error, the Selfhood or Spectre that must be annihilated.

And he appear'd the Wicker Man of Scandinavia, in whom
Jerusalem's children consume in flames among the Stars.

Descending down into my Garden, a Human Wonder of God,
Reaching from heaven to earth, a Cloud & Human Form,
I beheld Milton with astonishment, & in him beheld
The Monstrous Churches of Beulah, the Gods of Ulro dark,
Twelve monstrous dishumaniz'd terrors, Synagogues of Satan,
A Double Twelve & Thrice Nine: such their divisions.

And these their Names & their Places within the Mundane Shell.

In Tyre & Sidon I saw Baal & Ashtaroth. In Moab, Chemosh:
In Ammon, Molech; loud his Furnaces rage among the Wheels
Of Og, & pealing loud the cries of the Victims of Fire;
And pale his Priestesses infolded in Veils of Pestilence border'd
With War, Woven in Looms of Tyre & Sidon by beautiful Ashtaroth:
In Palestine, Dagon, Sea Monster, worship'd o'er the Sea:
Thammuz in Lebanon & Rimmon in Damascus curtain'd:
Osiris, Isis, Orus, in Egypt; dark their Tabernacles on Nile
Floating with solemn songs, & on the Lakes of Egypt nightly
With pomp, even till morning break & Osiris appear in the sky:
But Belial of Sodom & Gomorrha, obscure Demon of Bribes
And secret Assassinations, not worship'd nor ador'd but
With the finger on the lips & the back turn'd to the light:
And Saturn, Jove, & Rhea of the Isles of the Sea remote:
These Twelve Gods are the Twelve Spectre Sons of the Druid Albion.

And these the Names of the Twenty-seven Heavens & their Churches:
Adam, Seth, Enos, Cainan, Mahalaleel, Jared, Enoch,

11–12 The relation of this symbol to the 'Sacrifice', the repressive operation of Morality, is obvious: cp. M. 4. 16 *note* and see Index, *Luvah*, I. iii.

17 The significance of the 'Double Twelve' is obscure unless Blake means that each of the twelve gods is implicitly 'Sexual Twofold' (J. 97. 11). Blake's list gives fourteen names inexplicably. The 'Thrice Nine' may refer to the Twenty-seven Heavens of the Mundane Shell.

19–34 These deities are taken from *Paradise Lost*, i. 381–521. They are 'the Gods of the Heathen', whose religion teaches punishment for sin. Cp. D. C. iii, p. 21, quoted F. Z. ix. 36 *note*.

23–24 Cp. M. extra p. 17. 6–25.

35–43 This passage is repeated J. 75. 10–20: see Index, *Mundane Shell, Note II*.

Methuselah, Lamech ; these are Giants mighty, Hermaphroditic :
Noah, Shem, Arphaxad, Cainan the second, Salah, Heber,
Peleg, Reu, Serug, Nahor, Terah ; these are the Female-Males,
A Male within a Female hid as in an Ark & Curtains :
Abraham, Moses, Solomon, Paul, Constantine, Charlemaine,
Luther ; these seven are the Male-Females, the Dragon Forms,
Religion hid in War, a Dragon red & hidden Harlot.

All these are seen in Milton's Shadow, who is the Covering Cherub,
The Spectre of Albion in which the Spectre of Luvah inhabits,
In the Newtonian Voids between the Substances of Creation.

For the Chaotic Voids outside of the Stars are measured by
The Stars, which are the boundaries of Kingdoms, Provinces,
And Empires of Chaos invisible to the Vegetable Man.
The Kingdom of Og is in Orion : Sihon is in Ophiucus.
Og has Twenty-seven Districts ; Sihon's Districts Twenty-one,
From Star to Star. Mountains & Valleys, terrible dimension
Stretch'd out, compose the Mundane Shell, a mighty Incrustation
Of Forty-eight deformèd Human Wonders of the Almighty,
With Caverns whose remotest bottoms meet again beyond
The Mundane Shell in Golgonooza. But the Fires of Los rage
In the remotest bottoms of the Caves, that none can pass
Into Eternity that way, but all descend to Los,
To Bowlahoola & Allamanda & to Entuthon Benython.

The Heavens are the Cherub : the Twelve Gods are Satan ;

44–45 The Covering Cherub is the total of errors in thought (the Spectre of Albion) and errors in feeling (the Spectre of Luvah): cp. J. 58. 13–20.

46 The antithesis between the 'Newtonian Voids' and the 'Substances of Creation' seems to be parallel to the two forms of perception in mundane life, that of the natural organs of sense, and that of vision. 'The tree which moves some to tears of joy is in the eyes of others only a green thing which stands in the way. Some see Nature all ridicule and deformity . . . and some scarce see Nature at all. But to the eyes of the man of imagination, Nature is Imagination itself' (Letter to Dr. Trusler, 23 August 1799, R., p. 62). Cp. J. 91. 36:

> Los reads the Stars of Albion ; the Spectre reads the Voids
> Between the Stars.

47 In the last quotation of the preceding note, the Stars represent the spiritual light permitted to mortal man, but in the present passage they have the contrary significance, being associated with the spectrous symbols, Og, Sihon and the Mundane Shell.

54 These are identified with the forty-eight cities of the Levites (M. 39. 1, and cp. Num. xxxv. 1–8 and Joshua, xxi. 41), here apparently regarded as centres of Natural Religion.

60 See Index, *Mundane Shell, Note I.*

[39] And the Forty-eight Starry Regions are Cities of the Levites,
The Heads of the Great Polypus, Four-fold twelve enormity,
In mighty & mysterious comingling, enemy with enemy,
Woven by Urizen into Sexes from his mantle of years.
And Milton, collecting all his fibres into impregnable strength,
Descended down a Pavèd work of all kinds of precious stones
Out from the eastern sky, descending down into my Cottage
Garden, clothèd in black: severe & silent he descended.

The Spectre of Satan stood upon the roaring sea, & beheld
Milton within his sleeping Humanity; trembling & shudd'ring,
He stood upon the waves, a Twenty-seven-fold mighty Demon,
Gorgeous & beautiful. Loud roll his thunders against Milton.
Loud Satan thunder'd, loud & dark upon mild Felpham shore:
Not daring to touch one fibre, he howl'd round upon the Sea.

I also stood in Satan's bosom & beheld its desolations,
A ruin'd Man, a ruin'd building of God not made with hands;
Its plains of burning sand, its mountains of marble terrible,
Its pits & declivities flowing with molten ore & fountains
Of pitch & nitre; its ruin'd palaces & cities & mighty works;
Its furnaces of affliction in which his Angels & Emanations
Labour with blacken'd visages among its stupendous ruins;
Arches & pyramids & porches, colonades & domes,
In which dwells Mystery, Babylon: here is her secret place:
From hence she comes forth on the Churches in delight:
Here is her Cup fill'd with its poisons in these horrid vales,
And here her scarlet Veil woven in pestilence & war.
Here is Jerusalem bound in chains in the Dens of Babylon.

In the Eastern porch of Satan's Universe Milton stood & said:

'Satan, my Spectre! I know my power thee to annihilate,
And be a greater in thy place, & be thy Tabernacle,
A covering for thee to do thy will, till one greater comes,
And smites me as I smote thee, & becomes my covering.
Such are the Laws of thy false Heav'ns; but Laws of Eternity

Page 38. Full-page illustration.

Page 39. 9 At this point, Milton's purpose of Self-annihilation manifests itself in a definite separation from the Spectre or Selfhood, called Satan. Hitherto, since Milton's voluntary entry into it (M. 12. 38), these two had been united in the Polypus or Covering Cherub (M. 37, *passim*).

29–33 The interpretation of this passage is uncertain. Apparently it is intended to show that, unless they are inspired, all attempts to subvert any particular manifestation of error (Satan) can only result in the reappearance of the same fundamental fallacy in that which sought to overthrow it. Blake conceived something of this kind to have happened in the case of Deism: cp. M. 42. 9–13 and G. A. 9–15.

Are not such. Know thou, I come to Self Annihilation.
Such are the Laws of Eternity, that each shall mutually
Annihilate himself for others' good, as I for thee.
Thy purpose & the purpose of thy Priests & of thy Churches
Is to impress on men the fear of death, to teach
Trembling & fear, terror, constriction, abject selfishness.
Mine is to teach Men to despise death & to go on
In fearless majesty, annihilating Self, laughing to scorn
Thy Laws & terrors, shaking down thy Synagogues as webs.
I come to discover before Heav'n & Hell the Self righteousness
In all its Hypocritic turpitude, opening to every eye
These wonders of Satan's holiness, shewing to the Earth
The Idol Virtues of the Natural Heart ; & Satan's Seat
Explore in all its Selfish Natural Virtue, & put off
In Self annihilation all that is not of God alone,
To put off Self & all I have, ever & ever. Amen.'

Satan heard, coming in a cloud with trumpets & flaming fire,
Saying : ' I am God, the judge of all, the living & the dead.
Fall therefore down & worship me ; submit thy supreme
Dictate to my eternal Will, & to my dictate bow.
I hold the Balances of Right & Just, & mine the Sword.
Seven Angels bear my Name, & in those Seven I appear :
But I alone am God, & I alone in Heav'n & Earth,
Of all that live, dare utter this ; others tremble & bow,
[40] Till All Things become One Great Satan, in Holiness
Oppos'd to Mercy, and the Divine Delusion, Jesus, be no more.'

Suddenly around Milton on my Path, the Starry Seven
Burn'd terrible : my Path became a solid fire, as bright
As the clear Sun ; & Milton, silent, came down on my Path.
And there went forth from the Starry limbs of the Seven, Forms
Human, with Trumpets innumerable sounding articulate
As the Seven spake ; and they stood in a mighty Column of Fire,

34 See Index, *Self-annihilation*.
40–49 These lines, perfectly applicable to Blake himself, emphasize anew his identification with the descended Milton.
50 coming] Coming, *alternative rdg*.
50–57 Satan is the 'God of this world' 'worshipped as God by the Mighty ones of the Earth' (J. 33. 18). For the Seven Angels see F. Z. i. 242 *note*.
Page 40. 3 Cp. M. 14. 3–7.
6–15 Cp. Rev. viii. 2 and 6. This is the signal of the commencement of the Last Judgement, the final destruction of error. Such forms as those described here appear in all Blake's pictures of the Judgement.

Surrounding Felpham's Vale, reaching to the Mundane Shell, Saying :

'Awake, Albion, awake! reclaim thy Reasoning Spectre! Subdue
Him to the Divine Mercy! Cast him down into the Lake
Of Los that ever burneth with fire, ever & ever, Amen!
Let the Four Zoa's awake from Slumbers of Six Thousand Years.'

Then loud the Furnaces of Los were heard & seen as Seven Heavens,
Stretching from south to north over the mountains of Albion.

Satan heard : trembling round his Body, he incircled it.
He trembled with exceeding great trembling & astonishment,
Howling in his Spectre round his Body, hung'ring to devour,
But fearing for the pain ; for if he touches a Vital,
His torment is unendurable : therefore he cannot devour,
But howls round it as a lion round his prey continually.
Loud Satan thunder'd, loud & dark upon mild Felpham's Shore,
Coming in a Cloud with Trumpets & with Fiery Flame,
An awful Form eastward from midst of a bright Pavèd-work
Of precious stones, by Cherubim surrounded ; so permitted
(Lest he should fall apart in his Eternal Death) to imitate
The Eternal Great Humanity Divine surrounded by
His Cherubim & Seraphim in ever happy Eternity.
Beneath sat Chaos, Sin on his right hand, Death on his left ;
And Ancient Night spread over all the heav'n his Mantle of Laws.
He trembled with exceeding great trembling & astonishment.

Then Albion rose up in the Night of Beulah on his Couch
Of dread repose, seen by the visionary eye : his face is toward
The east, toward Jerusalem's Gates. Groaning he sat above
His rocks. London & Bath & Legions & Edinburgh
Are the four pillars of his Throne : his left foot, near London,
Covers the shades of Tyburn ; his instep from Windsor
To Primrose Hill stretching to Highgate & Holloway.

10–12 Cp. J. 41, quoted M. 22. 60 *note*.
14–15 See Index, *Furnaces*.
34 The association of the East with Jerusalem's Gates is inexplicable.
35 In J. 41. 1 Legions is identified with Bath. Blake may have had a confused recollection of Caerleon the City of Legions, on the Usk in Glamorgan : Geoffrey of Monmouth names it, with London and York, as one of the three noblest cities in the land (Bk. iv, chap. xix).

London is between his knees, its basements fourfold:
His right foot stretches to the sea on Dover cliffs, his heel
On Canterbury's ruins: his right hand covers lofty Wales,
His left Scotland: his bosom girt with gold involves
York, Edinburgh, Durham, & Carlisle; & on the front
Bath, Oxford, Cambridge, Norwich: his right elbow
Leans on the Rocks of Erin's Land, Ireland, ancient nation:
His head bends over London: he sees his embodied Spectre
Trembling before him with exceeding great trembling & fear.
He views Jerusalem & Babylon: his tears flow down.
He mov'd his right foot to Cornwall, his left to the Rocks of Bognor.
He strove to rise to walk into the Deep, but strength failing
Forbad, & down with dreadful groans he sunk upon his Couch
In moony Beulah. Los, his strong Guard, walks round beneath the Moon.

Urizen faints in terror, striving among the Brooks of Arnon
With Milton's Spirit: as the Plowman or Artificer or Shepherd,
While in the labours of his calling, sends his Thought abroad
To labour in the ocean or in the starry heaven, So Milton
Labour'd in Chasms of the Mundane Shell, tho' here before
My Cottage midst the Starry Seven, where the Virgin Ololon
Stood trembling in the Porch. Loud Satan thunder'd on the stormy Sea
Circling Albion's Cliffs in which the Four-fold World resides,
Tho' seen in fallacy outside, a fallacy of Satan's Churches.

[42] Before Ololon Milton stood & perciev'd the Eternal Form
Of that mild Vision: wondrous were their acts by me unknown
Except remotely; and I heard Ololon say to Milton:

'I see thee strive upon the Brooks of Arnon; there a dread
And awful Man I see, o'ercover'd with the mantle of years.
I behold Los & Urizen, I behold Orc & Tharmas,
The Four Zoa's of Albion, and thy Spirit with them striving,
In Self annihilation giving thy life to thy enemies.
Are those who contemn Religion & seek to annihilate it

46 The 'embodied Spectre' is Satan.
53–54 These lines revert to the subject of M. 16. 36–17. 14 and 18. 7–14.
55 calling] Calling, *alternative rdg.*
60–61 Cp. J. 71. 17–19.
Page 42. 4–5 The 'dread and awful Man' would seem to be Urizen: cp. M. 40. 53–54 and F. Z. ix. 187–190.
9–13 Cp. F. Z. viii. 599 *note.*

Become in their Fe[m]inine portions the causes & promoters
Of these Religions ? how is this thing, this Newtonian Phantasm,
This Voltaire & Rousseau, this Hume & Gibbon & Bolingbroke,
This Natural Religion, this impossible absurdity ?
Is Ololon the cause of this ? O where shall I hide my face ?
These tears fall for the little-ones, the Children of Jerusalem,
Lest they be annihilated in thy annihilation.'

No sooner she had spoke but Rahab Babylon appear'd
Eastward upon the Pavèd work across Europe & Asia,
Glorious as the midday Sun, in Satan's bosom glowing,
A Female hidden in a Male, Religion hidden in War,
Nam'd Moral Virtue, cruel two-fold Monster, shining bright,
A Dragon red & hidden Harlot which John in Patmos saw.

And all beneath the Nations innumerable of Ulro
Appear'd the Seven Kingdoms of Canaan & Five Baalim
Of Philistea, into Twelve divided, call'd after the Names
Of Israel as they are in Eden, Mountain, River, & Plain,
City & sandy Desart intermingled beyond mortal ken.

But turning toward Ololon in terrible majesty, Milton
Replied : 'Obey thou the Words of the Inspirèd Man.
All that can be ⟨can be⟩ annihilated must be annihilated,
That the Children of Jerusalem may be savèd from slavery.
There is a Negation & there is a Contrary :
The Negation must be destroy'd to redeem the Contraries.
The Negation is the Spectre, the Reasoning Power in Man :
This is a false Body, an Incrustation over my Immortal
Spirit, a Selfhood which must be put off & annihilated alway.
To cleanse the Face of my Spirit by Self-examination,
[43] To bathe in the waters of Life, to wash off the Not Human,

11 Phantasm] so in the four known copies. The Ellis and Yeats facsimile reads 'Phantasy'.
15 See Index, *Minute Particulars*. 22 Cp. Rev. xvii.
30 Cp. M. extra p. 32*. 36 :

Whatever can be Created, can be Annihilated. Forms [i. e. eternal realities] cannot.

32 Cp. M. 34. 23 *note*.
35 The nature of the 'false Body' is fully set forth on the following page (43).
Page 43. Here, in this challenge, as vigorous as any Blake ever flung to the thought, art, and morality of his time, the identity of Blake and Milton is again clearly evident. This passage is also notable for the light it sheds upon the nature of the mystical Self-annihilation.

I come in Self-annihilation & the grandeur of Inspiration,
To cast off Rational Demonstration by Faith in the Saviour,
To cast off the rotten rags of Memory by Inspiration,
To cast off Bacon, Locke, & Newton from Albion's covering,
To take off his filthy garments & clothe him with Imagination ;
To cast aside from Poetry all that is not Inspiration,
That it no longer shall dare to mock with the aspersion of Madness
Cast on the Inspirèd by the tame high finisher of paltry Blots,
Indefinite or paltry Rhymes or paltry Harmonies,
Who creeps into State Government like a catterpiller to destroy ;
To cast off the idiot Questioner who is always questioning
But never capable of answering, who sits with a sly grin
Silent plotting when to question, like a thief in a cave,
Who publishes doubt & calls it knowledge, whose Science is Despair,
Whose pretence to knowledge is Envy, whose whole Science is
To destroy the Wisdom of ages to gratify ravenous Envy
That rages round him like a Wolf day & night without rest.
He smiles with condescension ; he talks of Benevolence & Virtue,
And those who act with Benevolence & Virtue they murder time on time.
These are the destroyers of Jerusalem : these are the murderers
Of Jesus, who deny the Faith & mock at Eternal Life,
Who pretend to Poetry that they may destroy Imagination
By imitation of Nature's Images drawn from Remembrance.
These are the Sexual Garments, the Abomination of Desolation,
Hiding the Human Lineaments as with an Ark & Curtains,
Which Jesus rent & now shall wholly purge away with Fire,
Till Generation is swallow'd up in Regeneration.'

Then trembled the Virgin Ololon, & reply'd in clouds of despair :

' Is this our Feminine Portion, the Six-fold Miltonic Female ?
Terribly this Portion trembles before thee, O awful Man !

19–24 Cp. J. 91. 24–25, where Blake exclaims, through Los, against the enemies of Imagination :

you talk of benevolence & virtue.
I act with benevolence & virtue & get murder'd time after time.

With the interpretation of Murder in ll. 21–24, cp. J. 91. 11–12.

30 The Feminine Portion is the body of error just described.

Altho' our Human Power can sustain the severe contentions
Of Friendship, our Sexual cannot, but flies into the Ulro.
Hence arose all our terrors in Eternity, & now remembrance
Returns upon us. Are we Contraries, O Milton, Thou & I?
O Immortal! how were we led to War the Wars of Death?
Is this the Void Outside of Existence, which if enter'd into
[44] Becomes a Womb, & is this the Death Couch of Albion?
Thou goest to Eternal Death, & all must go with thee.'

So saying, the Virgin divided Six-fold, & with a shriek
Dolorous that ran thro' all Creation, a Double Six-fold Wonder,
Away from Ololon she divided & fled into the depths
Of Milton's Shadow, as a Dove upon the stormy Sea.

Then as a Moony Ark Ololon descended to Felpham's Vale
In clouds of blood, in streams of gore, with dreadful thunderings,
Into the Fires of Intellect that rejoic'd in Felpham's Vale
Around the Starry Eight. With one accord the Starry Eight became
One Man, Jesus, the Saviour wonderful; round his limbs
The Clouds of Ololon folded as a Garment dippèd in blood,
Written within & without in woven letters: & the Writing
Is the Divine Revelation in the Litteral expression,
A Garment of War. I heard it nam'd the Woof of Six Thousand Years.

And I beheld the Twenty-four Cities of Albion
Arise upon their Thrones to Judge the Nations of the Earth,
And the Immortal Four, in whom the Twenty-four appear Four-fold,
Arose around Albion's body. Jesus wept, & walkèd forth

32–34 Cp. M. 30. 21–31 and *note*. 33 See Index, *Sex*.

35–p. 44. 1 Insistence on differences, the setting of the 'contraries' in opposition is spiritually destructive; it is the 'Wars of Death', the 'Void outside of existence'. It is the error of which the emblem in mortal life is 'Sex' (see Index). Hence it is called also the 'Womb', wherein are vitalized the errors that differentiate the finite from the infinite, Albion's 'Death Couch', or 'Eternal Death' from Eternity.

Page 44. 9 These are the 'Mental flames' 'the fire of thought' (J. 91. 17) in which error is destroyed: cp. M. 43. 25–29 and F. Z. ix. *passim*.

12 Cp. M. 19. 60 *note*. 13–15 Cp. J. 98. 28 *note*.

16 Cp. J. pp. 40–46, where the twenty-four Friends of Albion are identified with an equal number of cathedral cities. They are Eternals who give themselves for Man, and finally relegate their power to Los (J. 44. 28–31). This and the following lines are clearly reminiscent of the Elders and four beasts in Rev. iv. See Index, *Los, Note II, b*.

16–19 Cp. Rev. iv. and F. Z. ix. 277–283. 28 Cp. M. 36. 31 *note*.

From Felpham's Vale, clothèd in Clouds of blood, to enter into
Albion's Bosom, the bosom of death: & the Four surrounded him
In the Column of Fire in Felpham's Vale; then to their mouths the Four
Applied their Four Trumpets, & then sounded to the Four winds.

Terror struck in the Vale I stood at that immortal sound.
My bones trembled, I fell outstretch'd upon the path
A moment, & my Soul return'd into its mortal state
To Resurrection & Judgment in the Vegetable Body;
And my sweet Shadow of Delight stood trembling by my side.

Immediately the Lark mounted with a loud trill from Felpham's Vale,
And the Wild Thyme from Wimbleton's green & impurpled Hills.
And Los & Enitharmon rose over the Hills of Surrey;
Their clouds roll over London with a south wind: soft Oothoon
Pants in the Vales of Lambeth, weeping o'er her Human Harvest;
Los listens to the Cry of the Poor Man; his Cloud
Over London in volume terrific low bended in anger.

Rintrah & Palamabron view the Human Harvest beneath:
Their Wine-presses & Barns stand open; the Ovens are prepar'd,
The Waggons ready; terrific Lions & Tygers sport & play;
All Animals upon the Earth are prepar'd in all their strength
[45] To go forth to the Great Harvest & Vintage of the Nations.

Finis

29–30 Cp. M. 35. 54–67.
29–p. 45. 1 The lines declare the imminence of the Last Judgement.
32 Cp. M. 11. 44 *note*. 34 Cp. M. 27. 36–38.
36–p. 45. 1 Cp. F. Z. ix. 577–853.

Milton

APPENDIX

Of these supernumerary plates, those numbered 2, 3, 8*, 17, and 32* are found in the New York Public Library copy, and, differently numbered, in the Windus copy, which alone possesses the extra plate 5.

Extra p. 2.

By Enitharmon's Looms, when Albion was slain upon his Mountains
And in his Tent thro' envy of Living Form, even of the Divine Vision
And of the sports of Wisdom in the Human Imagination,
Which is the Divine Body of the Lord Jesus blessèd for ever.
Mark well my words; they are of your eternal salvation.

Urizen lay in darkness & solitude, in chains of the mind lock'd up.
Los siez'd his Hammer & Tongs: he labour'd at his resolute Anvil
Among indefinite Druid rocks & snows of doubt & reasoning.

Refusing all Definite Form, the Abstract Horror roof'd stony hard:
And a first Age passèd over & a State of dismal woe.

Down sunk with fright a red round Globe, hot, burning, deep
Deep down into the Abyss, panting, conglobing, trembling:
And a second Age passèd over & a State of dismal woe.

Rolling round into two little Orbs & closèd in two little Caves,
The Eyes beheld the Abyss, lest bones of solidness freeze over all:
And a third Age passèd over & a State of dismal woe.

From beneath his Orbs of Vision Two Ears in close volutions
Shot spiring out in the deep darkness & petrified as they grew:
And a fourth Age passèd over & a State of dismal woe.

Hanging upon the wind Two Nostrils bent down into the Deep:
And a fifth Age passèd over & a State of dismal woe.

Extra p. 2. 6–36 Cp. B. U. iv: B. L. iv: F. Z. iv. 198 seq.
9 Cp. *Europe*, 96–107.

In ghastly torment sick a Tongue of hunger & thirst flamèd out
And a sixth Age passèd over & a State of dismal woe.

Enragèd & stifled without & within, in terror & woe he threw his
Right Arm to the north, his left Arm to the south; & his Feet
Stamp'd the nether Abyss in trembling & howling & dismay:
And a seventh Age passèd over & a State of dismal woe.

Terrified Los stood in the Abyss & his immortal limbs
Grew deadly pale; he became what he beheld; for a red
Round Globe sunk down from his Bosom into the Deep: in pangs
He hover'd over it, trembling & weeping: suspended it shook
The nether Abyss: in tremblings he wept over it: he cherish'd it
In deadly sickening pain, till [it] separated into a Female, pale
As the cloud that brings the snow: all the while from his Back
A blue fluid exuded in Sinews, hardening in the Abyss
Till it separated into a Male Form howling in Jealousy.

Within labouring, beholding Without, from Particulars to Generals,
Subduing his Spectre, they Builded the Looms of Generation.
They Builded Great Golgonooza Times on Times, Ages on Ages.
First Orc was Born; then the Shadowy Female; then All Los's Family.
At last Enitharmon brought forth Satan, Refusing Form in vain,
The Miller of Eternity made subservient to the Great Harvest,
That he may go to his own Place, Prince of the Starry Wheels.

Extra p. 3.

'Beneath the Plow of Rintrah & the Harrow of the Almighty
In the hands of Palamabron, Where the Starry Mills of Satan
Are built beneath the Earth & Waters of the Mundane Shell:
Here the Three Classes of Men take their Sexual texture Woven:
The Sexual is Threefold; the Human is Fourfold.

38 'they' refers to Los and his assistants in the labours of regeneration.
42 The Miller of Eternity is Satan or Urizen as Satan: cp. M., extra p. 8.
1–2. In F. Z. ix. 804–806 Urthona controls the Mills. The contradiction is inexplicable and immaterial.

Extra p. 3. 5 Cp. General Introduction, p. 30. 'Threefold' here is used in a somewhat unusual sense to denote all degrees of defection from the supreme perfection of being and vision expressed by 'Fourfold'. That

" If you account it Wisdom when you are angry to be silent and
Not to shew it, I do not account that Wisdom but Folly.
Every Man's Wisdom is peculiar to his own Individuality.
O Satan, my youngest born, art thou not Prince of the Starry Hosts
And of the Wheels of Heaven, to turn the Mills day & night ?
Art thou not Newton's Pantocrator, weaving the Woof of Locke ?
To Mortals thy Mills seem every thing & the Harrow of Shaddai
A scheme of Human conduct invisible & incomprehensible.
Get to thy Labours at the Mills & leave me to my wrath ! "

' Satan was going to reply, but Los roll'd his loud thunders :

" Anger me not ! thou canst not drive the Harrow in pity's paths.
Thy Work is Eternal Death, with Mills & Ovens & Cauldrons.
Trouble me no more ! thou canst not have Eternal Life."

' So Los spoke. Satan trembling obey'd, weeping along the way.
Mark well my words ; they are of your eternal Salvation.

' Between South Molton Street & Stratford Place, Calvary's foot,
Where the Victims were preparing for Sacrifice, their Cherubim
Around their loins pour'd forth their arrows, & their bosoms beam
With all colours of precious stones, & their inmost palaces
Resounded with preparation of animals wild & tame,
(Mark well my words ; Corporeal Friends are Spiritual Enemies.)

defection is revealed in the declension from the unity of the Fourfold in the Divine Humanity, to the 'divided' or 'sexual' state, wherein is included all mortal conditions, from the merely sense-perceptive to the vision of the mystic.

9 This derivation of Satan is not found elsewhere outside these extra pages : cp. extra p. 5. 41.

11 Pantocrator seems to be a reminiscence of Blake's readings in the Greek New Testament with Hayley at Felpham. Compare his letter to his brother James (30 January 1803, G. L. K., p. 451) : 'I go on Merrily with my Greek & Latin . . . I read Greek as fluently as an Oxford scholar & the Testament is my chief master.' Παντοκράτωρ (Vulgate, *omnipotens*) is found in Rev. i. 8 : iv. 8 : xi. 17 : xv. 3, &c. Its association with Newton seems to have reference to the Blakean significance of the philosopher's name, and not to any passage in his writings.

21 Stratford Place and South Molton Street were some half-mile east of Tyburn Tree : cp. F. Z. 249 *note*.

Mocking Druidical Mathematical Proportion of Length, Bredth, Highth,
Displaying Naked Beauty with Flute & Harp & Song.'

Extra p. 5.

Palamabron with the fiery Harrow in morning returning
From breathing fields. Satan fainted beneath the artillery.
Christ took on Sin in the Virgin's Womb & put it off on the Cross.
All pitied the piteous & was wrath with the wrathful: & Los heard it.
And this is the manner of the Daughters of Albion in their beauty:
Every one is threefold in Head & Heart & Reins; & every one
Has three Gates into the three Heavens of Beulah, which shine
Translucent in their Foreheads & their Bosoms & their Loins,
Surrounded with fires unapproachable: but whom they please
They take up into their Heavens in intoxicating delight.
For the Elect cannot be Redeem'd, but Created continually
By Offering & Atonement in the crue(l)ties of Moral Law.
Hence the three Classes of Men take their fix'd destinations:
They are the Two Contraries & the Reasoning Negative.

While the Females prepare the Victims, the Males at Furnaces
And Anvils dance the dance of tears & pain: loud lightnings
Lash on their limbs as they turn the whirlwinds loose upon
The Furnaces, lamenting around the Anvils: & this their Song:

'Ah weak & wide astray! Ah shut in narrow doleful form,
Creeping in reptile form upon the bosom of the ground!
The Eye of Man a little narrow orb, clos'd up & dark,
Scarcely beholding the great light, conversing with the Void.
The Ear a little shell, in small volutions shutting out
All melodies & comprehending only Discord and Harmony.
The Tongue a little moisture Fills, a little food it cloys,
A little sound it utters & its cries are faintly heard;
Then brings forth Moral Virtue, the cruel Virgin, Babylon.

'Can such an Eye judge of the stars, & looking thro' its tubes
Measure the sunny rays that point their spears on Udanadan?
Can such an Ear, fill'd with the vapours of the yawning pit,
Judge of the pure melodious harp struck by a hand divine?

27 See Index, *Druidism*, and cp. M., extra p. 32*. 16–21, and *Laocoön*, 26.
28 Cp. *Laocoön*, 24: 'Art and Science can never exist without Naked Beauty displayed.' Cp. also M. 43. 2–7.
Extra p. 5. 13 Cp. M. 4. 32 and M. 3*. 4. 19–26 Cp. J. 49. 32–41.

Can such closèd Nostrils feel a joy, or tell of autumn fruits
When grapes & figs burst their covering to the joyful air?
Can such a Tongue boast of the living waters, or take in
Ought but the Vegetable Ratio & loathe the faint delight?
Can such gross Lips percieve? alas, folded within themselves
They touch not ought, but pallid turn & tremble at every wind!'

Thus they sing, Creating the Three Classes among Druid Rocks.
Charles calls on Milton for Atonement; Cromwell is ready;
James calls for fires in Golgonooza, for heaps of smoking ruins
In the night of prosperity and wantonness which he himself Created
Among the Daughters of Albion, among the Rocks of the Druids,
When Satan fainted beneath the arrows of Elynittria,
And Mathematic Proportion was subdued by Living Proportion.

Extra p. 8*.

Then Los & Enitharmon knew that Satan is Urizen
Drawn down by Orc & the Shadowy Female into Generation.
Oft Enitharmon enter'd weeping into the Space, there appearing
An agèd Woman raving along the Streets (the Space is namèd
Canaan): then she return'd to Los, weary, frighted as from dreams.

The nature of a Female Space is this: it shrinks the Organs
Of Life till they become Finite & Itself seems Infinite.

And Satan vibrated in the immensity of the Space, Limited
To those without, but Infinite to those within: it fell down and
Became Canaan, closing Los from Eternity in Albion's Cliffs,
A mighty Fiend against the Divine Humanity must'ring to War.

'Satan, Ah me! is gone to his own place,' said Los: 'their God
I will not worship in their Churches, nor King in their Theatres.
Elynittria, whence is this Jealousy running along the mountains?

Extra p. 8. 6–7 Cp. M. H. H., pp. 17–20. After l. 7 a line *del.*
11 The 'mighty Fiend' is Satan, not Los.

British Women were not Jealous when Greek & Roman were Jealous.
Every thing in Eternity shines by its own Internal light ; but thou
Darkenest every Internal light with the arrows of thy quiver,
Bound up in the horns of Jealousy to a deadly fading Moon :
And Ocalythron binds the Sun into a Jealous Globe,
That every thing is fix'd Opake without Internal light.

So Los lamented over Satan who, triumphant, divided the Nations.

Extra p. 17.

And Tharmas, Demon of the Waters, & Orc who is Luvah.

The Shadowy Female, seeing Milton, howl'd in her lamentation
Over the Deeps, outstretching her Twenty seven Heavens over Albion.

And thus the Shadowy Female howls in articulate howlings :

' I will lament over Milton in the lamentations of the afflicted ;
My Garments shall be woven of sighs & heart broken lamentations ;
The misery of unhappy Families shall be drawn out into its border,
Wrought with the needle with dire sufferings, poverty, pain & woe
Along the rocky Island & thence throughout the whole Earth.
There shall be the sick Father & his starving Family ; there
The Prisoner in the stone Dungeon & the Slave at the Mill.
I will have Writings written all over it in Human Words,
That every Infant that is born upon the Earth shall read
And get by rote as a hard task of a life of sixty years.

Extra p. 17. 5–25 A comparison of this speech with the corresponding passage in M. 17. 36 seq. shows that while this is in the manner of F. Z. viii (cp. ll. 136–174 : 265–319 : 577–597), the other is much more abstruse in symbolic elaboration, being comparable with the style of *Jerusalem*. The inference is that this is earlier than the present p. 17, belonging to the same stage in Blake's development as the later recensions of *The Four Zoas*, a consideration that helps to date the earlier version of *Milton*. Substantially these lines set forth the nature and incidence of the ' Feminine ' fallacies, the ' crucifying cruelties ' of a moral law masking itself in ' Pity and Humanity ' ; they recall passages in *The Four Zoas* like vii *a*. 168–184, ix. 667–679, and vii. 110–129. In this they differ from the contrasted exposition on M., p. 43. The one is still concerned, almost as in the Lambeth books, with the social outcome of tyrannical codes, and looks towards ultimate emancipation through the catastrophic overthrow of civil and religious oppressions, as in F. Z. ix : the other looks forward to the latest phase of Blake's evolution, his faith in the obligation to individual regeneration through the practice of the arts of Imagination.

I will have Kings inwoven upon it & Councellors & Mighty Men;
The Famine shall clasp it together with buckles & Clasps,
And the Pestilence shall be its fringe & the War its girdle,
To divide into Rahab & Tirzah that Milton may come to our tents.
For I will put on the Human Form & take the Image of God,
Even Pity & Humanity; but my Clothing shall be Cruelty.
And I will put on Holiness as a breastplate & as a helmet,
And all my ornaments shall be of the gold of broken hearts,
And the precious stones of anxiety & care & desperation & death
And repentance for sin & sorrow & punishment & fear,
To defend me from thy terrors, O Orc, my only belovèd.'

Orc answer'd: 'Take not the Human Form, O loveliest! Take not
Terror upon thee! Behold how I am, & tremble lest thou also
Consume in my Consummation: but thou maist take a Form
Female & lovely, that cannot consume in Man's consummation.
Wherefore dost thou Create & Weave this Satan for a Covering?
When thou attemptest to put on the Human Form, my wrath
Burns to the top of heaven against thee in Jealousy & fear.
Then I rend thee asunder; then I howl over thy clay & ashes.
When wilt thou put on the Female Form as in times of old,
With a Garment of Pity & Compassion like the Garment of God?
His garments are long sufferings for the Children of Men:
Jerusalem is his Garment, & not thy Covering Cherub, O lovely
Shadow of my delight, who wanderest seeking for the prey!'

So spoke Orc, when Oothoon & Leutha hover'd over his Couch
Of fire in interchange of Beauty & Perfection in the darkness,

Opening interiorly into Jerusalem & Babylon, shining glorious
In the Shadowy Female's bosom. Jealous her darkness grew:
Howlings fill'd all the desolate places in accusations of Sin,
In Female beauty shining in the unform'd void: & Orc in vain
Stretch'd out his hands of fire & wooed: they triumph in his pain.

26 Orc here seems to represent the symbol in an intermediate stage in its development, where it represents neither the insurgent will to freedom, as in *America*, nor, as in the body of *Milton*, enthusiasm or energy enslaved to subserve oppression. Again the present concept seems to be paralleled in the later-written parts of *The Four Zoas*: cp. F. Z. vii, Introductory Note.

Thus darken'd the Shadowy Female tenfold, & Orc tenfold
Glow'd on his rocky Couch against the darkness: loud thunders
Told of the enormous conflict. Earthquake beneath, around,
Rent the Immortal Females limb from limb & joint from joint,
And movèd the fast foundations of the Earth to wake the Dead.

Urizen emergèd from his Rocky Form & from his Snows

Extra p. 32*.

And Milton oft sat up on the Couch of Death & oft conversèd
In vision & dream beatific with the Seven Angels of the Presence:

'I have turnèd my back upon these Heavens builded on cruelty.
My Spectre, still wandering thro' them, follows my Emanation:
He hunts her footsteps thro' the snow & the wintry hail & rain.
The idiot Reasoner laughs at the Man of Imagination,
And from laughter proceeds to murder by undervaluing calumny.'

Then Hillel, who is Lucifer, replied over the Couch of Death,
And thus the Seven Angels instructed him & thus they converse:

'We are not Individuals but States, Combinations of Individuals;
We were Angels of the Divine Presence, & were Druids in Annandale,
Compell'd to combine into Form by Satan, the Spectre of Albion,

51 This line does not link up with p. 18 of *Milton* in its extant form. In the New York Public Library copy and in the Windus copy it is followed by the page which is numbered 17 in the British Museum and the Huntington Library copies.

Extra p. 32*. 2 Cp. F. Z. viii. 387 *note*. 'Hillel who is Lucifer' (l. 8) is one of the Seven.

5 Cp. Ross. MS. (Clar. Press, p. 186):

> He scents thy footsteps in the snow,
> Wheresoever thou dost go,
> Thro' the wintry hail and rain.
> When wilt thou return again?

12–15 In the left margin, over against these lines, is written: כרבים | as multitudes | Vox Populi. The reference of the note is not clear.

Who made himself a God & destroyèd the Human Form Divine.
But the Divine Humanity & Mercy gave us a Human Form,
Because we were combin'd in Freedom & holy Brotherhood;
While those combin'd by Satan's Tyranny first in the blood of War
And Sacrifice, & next in Chains of imprisonment, are Shapeless Rocks
Retaining only Satan's Mathematic Holiness, Length, Bredth & Highth,
Calling the Human Imagination, which is the Divine Vision & Fruition
In which Man liveth eternally, madness & blasphemy against
Its own Qualities which are Servants of Humanity, not Gods or Lords.
Distinguish therefore States from Individuals in those States:
States change, but Individual Identities never change nor cease.
You cannot go to Eternal Death in that which can never Die.
Satan & Adam are States Created into Twenty-seven Churches,
And thou, O Milton, art a State about to be Created,
Callèd Eternal Annihilation, that none but the Living shall
Dare to enter; & they shall enter triumphant over Death
And Hell & the Grave, States that are not, but ah! Seem to be.

Judge then of thy Own Self: thy Eternal Lineaments explore,
What is Eternal & what Changeable & what Annihilable.

The Imagination is not a State: it is the Human Existence itself.
Affection or Love becomes a State when divided from Imagination.
The Memory is a State always; & the Reason is a State
Created to be Annihilated, & a new Ratio Created.
Whatever can be Created can be Annihilated; Forms cannot.
The Oak is cut down by the Ax, the Lamb falls by the Knife;

21 Cp. F. Z. ix. 361 *note*. 22 See Index, *States*.
24 So Milton 'puts off' his 'real and immortal self' before entering his Shadow (M. 12. 10–41).
25 See Index, *Limits*. 29 Cp. M. 39. 37–41.
34 Cp. M. 12. 28 *note*.
36–38 Cp. Cat. 1810: 'The Nature of Visionary Fancy, or Imagination, is very little known, & the Eternal nature & permanence of its ever-Existent Images is consider'd as less permanent than the things of Vegetative & generative Nature; yet the Oak dies as well as the Lettuce: but its Eternal Image & Individuality never dies, but renews by its seed: just so the Imaginative Image returns by the seed of Contemplative Thought.'

But their Forms Eternal Exist For-ever. Amen. Halle[l]ujah.

Thus they converse with the Dead, watching round the Couch of Death.
For God himself enters Death's Door always with those that enter,
And lays down in the Grave with them in Visions of Eternity,
Till they awake & see Jesus & the Linen Clothes lying
That the Females had Woven for them & the Gates of their Father's House.

42 The ' linen clothes ' are the ' woven garments of sleep ', the ' weak visions of time and space ' : cp. M. 44. 7–15 : J. 92. 13–20. The ' Sexual Garments ', an equivalent symbol, are described at length in M. 42. 35–43. 27.

JERUSALEM

Collation : frontispiece 1 plate, title-page 1 plate, *To the Public* 1 plate, chap. 1, 22 plates (pp. 4–25) ; full-page design 1 plate, *To the Jews* 1 plate, chap. 2, 23 plates (pp. 28–50) ; full-page design 1 plate, *To the Deists* 1 plate, chap. 3, 23 plates (pp. 52–75) ; full-page design 1 plate, *To the Christians* 1 plate, chap. 4, 22 plates (pp. 78–99), full-page design 1 plate ; in all 100 plates relief engraving about 9 × 6½ inches.

Keynes in his *Bibliography* (p. 169) gives the following description of a copy of *Jerusalem* in which the page-order of Chapter 2 differs from that in all other known examples : ' 100 plates on 100 leaves. Watermark *J. Whatman*, 1818, 1819, or 1820. Printed in black. Several plates touched up with sepia and chinese white, and on pl. 16 there is some green tinting ; otherwise uncoloured. Foliated by Blake 1–100. Arrangement : 1–28, 33–41, 43–46, 42, 29–32, 47–100. Bound in vellum. Size 32 × 25 cm.

' John Linnell's copy, sold with his collection at Christie's, March 15, 1918 . . .'

The arrangement of plates noted in this description is not noticeably better than that observed in the other copies.

In a letter to George Cumberland, dated the 12th April 1827, Blake says, ' The last work I produced is a poem entitled *Jerusalem, the Emanation of the Giant Albion*, but find that to print it will cost my time the amount of twenty guineas. One I have finished, but it is not likely I shall find a customer for it.' As Mr. Russell points out in a note to this passage, the work described as ' finished ', that is, printed and illuminated, was that which afterwards passed into the hands of Frederick Tatham, and later into the possession of Captain Archibald Sterling. The copy, with which is bound up Tatham's manuscript *Life of William Blake*, two likenesses of Blake at the ages of twenty-eight and sixty-nine years, and George Richmond's portrait of Mrs. Blake, is described by Mr. Russell as ' a magnificent one, illuminated with extreme beauty. . . . It is printed in orange, and measures 13⅜ × 10¾ inches.'

Jerusalem is divided into four chapters, each containing twenty-five pages, including frontispiece and preface. But this semblance of systematic arrangement is not visible in the text, which, though in a different way, is as chaotic as that of *The Four Zoas*. There can be little doubt that some of the plates are later in date than the body of the work, but whether they displaced earlier plates, or were interpolated to complete the tale of leaves in the different chapters, is uncertain. It is, however, noteworthy that these later pages generally elaborate specific points of Blake's mystical doctrine. Attempts were sometimes made by Blake to relate them to their contexts, in other cases no effort of the kind is discernible. To increase the confusion, it is almost certain that several leaves are out of place; and while in a few instances a possible rearrangement can be suggested, it has more often been found impossible to establish a satisfactory alternative. Attempts at readjustment of the pages have invariably resulted in confusion no less bewildering than that which they were to remedy, so that the present edition follows the page sequence which holds in all known copies except that noted above.

It is difficult to trace the history of the text of *Jerusalem.* The date on the title-page, 1804, is also that of *Milton,* yet the difference in symbolism makes it impossible to believe that these two works belong to the same year. In *Milton,* Los plays a much slighter part than in *Jerusalem*; his inspiration is weaker, and nowhere is he identified, as in the longer work, with the supreme manifestation of Being, Jesus. Moreover, in *Milton,* Vala is barely mentioned: in *Jerusalem* she is perhaps even more prominent than Jerusalem herself. *Milton* does little more than mention the Spectre Sons of Albion; and their emanations, the Daughters of Albion, who occupy so large a part of *Jerusalem* do not appear at all except on pp. 4, 25, and 40, whereof 4 and 25 at least are comparatively late additions. *Milton* shows very little use of the geographical symbolism that is so striking a feature of *Jerusalem.* It has been suggested that both of these poems in their original forms were parts of a much more extended work, the 'long poem' of Blake's letters of 1803–1805 and of the *Advertizement.* Against this view must be set the differences of symbolic treatment, expression, and emphasis between *Milton* and *Jerusalem,* differences so great, that, even when full allowance has been made for the effect of Blake's frequent revisions, it is impossible to believe that the two could have been parts of any single work. Again, to whatever poem Blake refers as being descriptive of the spiritual acts of his stay at Felpham, whether it be *Milton,* as is probable, or a lost work, it is unlikely that he intends *Jerusalem,* since the terms of reference, which are substantially identical in all the passages, cannot be applied to it. But in 1809, in the *Descriptive Catalogue* (v, p. 41) there is a specific allusion, the first extant, to *Jerusalem*: 'They [i.e. the Strong Man, the Beautiful Man, and the Ugly Man] were originally one man who was fourfold; he was self-divided, and his real humanity slain on the stems of generation, and the form of the fourth was like the Son of God. How he became divided is a subject of great sublimity and pathos. The artist has written it under inspiration, and will, if God please, publish it; it is voluminous, and contains the ancient history of Britain and the world of Satan and of Adam.' This is a fairly exact statement of the central myth of *Jerusalem* and it also contains an unmistakable reference to the point of symbolism already noticed as peculiar to that poem, namely the identification of Los, the Fourth Zoa or Living Creature in the Fourfold Man, with Jesus. The reference in this passage is to a work completed, but the evidence as to the extent of Blake's revisions furnished by the manuscript of *The Four Zoas* and the extra pages of *Milton* warrants the suspicion that the work as it existed in 1809 may have been widely different from that now extant.

The engraving of *Jerusalem* seems to have been completed about 1820. The date of the title-page, 1804, presumably refers to the year in which the theme was definitely taken up, for the allusion in the *Descriptive Catalogue* is to a work not published, i.e. engraved, in 1809. In Crabb Robinson's diary under date 24th July 1811 there is the statement that Blake had lately shown Southey 'a perfectly mad poem, called *Jerusalem*'. But there is nothing to show whether Southey saw the work in manuscript or partly or wholly engraved. The book is not in the list of engraved books supplied to Dawson Turner on 9th June 1818, and hence it may be presumed that the engraving was not completed at that date. But in *The London Magazine* for September 1820, T. G. Wainwright, 'Janus Weathercock,' writes: 'Talking of articles, my learned friend Dr. Tobias Ruddicombe, M.D., is, at my earnest entreaty, casting a tremendous piece of ordnance, an *eighty-eight pounder*! which he proposeth to fire off in your next. It is an account of an ancient, newly discovered, illuminated MS., which has to name "Jerusalem, the Emanation of the Giant Albion"!!! It contains a good deal anent one "Los", who, it appears, is now, and hath been since the creation, the *sole* and fourfold dominator of the celebrated city of Golgonooza! The doctor assures me that the redemption of mankind hangs on the universal diffusion of the doctrines broached in this MS.' From the mention of an illuminated MS., it is certain that Wainwright had seen the only copy ever completed by the illuminating of the plates. Further, from Wainwright's allusion to the size of the MS. it is reasonable to suppose that he saw the whole of it.

Moreover, 1820 is the watermark of certain pages (58, 69, 71, 74, 82, 84) in the uncoloured copy in the British Museum Printroom, and of the plate (J., p. 51) described under No. 101 in Russell's *Catalogue of Loan Exhibition of Works of William Blake*, 1913. Hence 1820 may reasonably be taken as the earliest possible year of 'publication'.

Whatever unity the poem may have possessed in 1809 was entirely dissipated by 1820. It is now to be read not as an ordered whole, nor even as a series of visions, but as a congeries of episodes bearing upon the conflict between the Everlasting Gospel and Natural Religion, between Forgiveness and Punishment. As in *The Four Zoas*, revision appears never to have been systematic: the work was probably altered by additions and possibly also by eliminations, made without regard to the balance of the poem. What mattered to Blake was obviously the vision that possessed him at the moment: and his unwillingness to do more than merely transcribe it produces frequently the effect of inconsistency. Verbal inconsistencies undoubtedly exist, but generally these can easily be explained, as the notes aim at showing, by keeping in view the point of doctrine or criticism that Blake wishes to emphasize in a particular relation. All the evidence that the present editors have accumulated goes to establish a claim for consistency in fundamentals. Much of the book yet remains to be interpreted, and much can be interpreted, if at all, only by surmise, and has therefore been passed over in the notes to our text. But in the many passages that are interpretable by the light of citations from other writings or from other parts of this book, apparent inconsistencies generally are seen to be the outcome of varying emphasis in the statement of congruent doctrines. One instance, not the most striking, relates to the symbol Enitharmon, at first the most puzzling figure in the book. Passages dealing with the symbol appear violently to conflict, until it is remembered that Enitharmon represents ' Space ', a conception which had for Blake different implications as it was used in a mystical and in a perceptualist connotation. In the former case ' Space ' is valid as, and only as, the expression of the Divine plan of regeneration through mortal life, whereas in the latter it is regarded as valid in itself. The context does not always indicate in which of the two uses the symbol is employed, and hence there remain many passages that are still dark. But the intelligible instances in respect to this and other symbols are held to justify the claim that the essential matter of Blake's vision was so constantly with him and was so entirely the element in which his life was lived, that though limitations of temperament and education obscure it, there is a real, if not always a clearly expressed unity of doctrine in *Jerusalem*.

The General Introduction (section xvii) deals with the central theme of *Jerusalem*, the ethic of Blake's re-interpreted Christianity. Against it is set Natural Religion, the ' Polypus of Death ', ' growing from Albion over the whole Earth ',

Withering the Human Form by Laws of Sacrifice for Sin,
Striving to Create a Heaven in which all shall be pure & holy
In their Own Selfhoods, in Natural Selfish Chastity to banish Pity
And dear Mutual Forgiveness & to become One Great Satan
Inslav'd to the most powerful Selfhood, to murder the Divine Humanity.
(49. 25–30)

Here again Blake intends all illusion proceeding from denial of Vision or Imagination, every fallacy of sense-perception, ' Rational Demonstration ', moral or intellectual or artistic limitation or inhibition. Now for the last time Blake attempts to elaborate a system of fourfold correspondences : it breaks down and resolves into a dualism, and the poem is clogged and broken by the heedless accumulation of unnecessary symbols devised to express it. Opposed to Vision is Reason, with the Spectre and the ' False Female ' as its agents. The Spectre is elaborated into the Twelve Sons of Albion, but its basic meaning is not discernibly altered thereby. The concept of the nature and influence of the Female is one of the most impressive parts of Blake's later symbolism, and here too a twelve-fold division of its function among the Daughters of Albion can be ignored as immaterial : nothing is expressed thereby that is not already present in the wider symbols Vala or Rahab or Tirzah.

Druid symbolism is rare in the latest additions to *The Four Zoas* and in *Milton* : it is in *Jerusalem* that Blake develops the symbolical possibilities of its rites of human sacrifice in order to express the complete negation of Forgiveness. The particularity with which he deploys its resources of suggestive imagery shows how apt he thought it. The central notion is that ' Natural ' or ' Druid ' religion rejects and bans its contrary : its ' Moral and Self-Righteous Law ' sacrifices the freedom of the Individuality to its absolute canons of right and wrong. It is ' swayed by a Providence oppos'd to the Divine Lord Jesus, A Murderous Providence, A Creation that groans, living on Death ' (50. 4–5), for ' Every Religion that Preaches Vengeance for Sin is the Religion of the Enemy & Avenger . . . &

their God is Satan, the Prince of This World' (p. 52). Its precepts of Repentance and Atonement are alike repugnant to the Everlasting Gospel (cp. 61. 17–21 : 29. 12 : 43. 75 : 46. 27) : the former is found very rarely in a higher sense (e. g. 63. 28), Blake in the main consistently regarding both notions as equally false with the concept of positive sin from whence they spring (39. 26–27) : forgiveness dispenses with these coercive disciplines :

> Why should Punishment Weave the Veil with Iron Wheels of War
> When Forgiveness might it weave with Wings of Cherubim ?
> (22. 34–35)

Jerusalem and her 'little ones'—forgiveness and liberty and their implications—are contemned, and she is denounced by the 'Natural religionists' as 'the Shadow of delusions, The harlot Daughter, Mother of pity and dishonourable forgiveness' (18. 11–12). The mystical one-ness of God and Man is denied : Man is but a 'Worm seventy inches long'. The curse of mortality is upon him, 'Born of the Woman to obey the Woman', the arbiter of material existence (33. 51).

Jerusalem shows the fullest and most suggestive development of the mystical significance of Woman's place and power in mortality. The influence that controls our 'vegetative' powers, she besets the life of man with the multitudinous illusions of corporeity and their resultant fallacies. The 'Monstrous Regiment of Women' takes on a new and more devastating meaning as the most perilous antagonism to visionary aspiration. Its symbols betray Blake's dread of the power of sex in life : woman is its embodiment, a spiritually malign influence, perverse and subversive, fascinating but deadly, terrible yet lovely. Such criticism shows how inadequately the phrase 'gentle visionary Blake' describes him and how the dubious gain of a mystical gospeller is paid for with the loss of a notable ironist. Passages like the following sprang from something intenser than the lucky choice of a symbol :

> What may Man be ? Who can tell ! but what may Woman be
> To have power over Man from Cradle to corruptible Grave ?
> There is a Throne in every Man : it is the Throne of God.
> This Woman has claim'd as her own, & Man is no more.
> (34. 28–31)

'This is Woman's World !' cries a Daughter of Albion, describing the material existence of which she is one of the daemonic controllers ; and he who accepts her limitations upon his masculine energies pays the penalty in distraction of thought and purpose, and in consequent ineffectiveness. The rare symbols Arthur and Merlin seem types of too submissive acceptance of the illusory 'Feminine' claim to an idolatrous reverence that ultimately betrays and mocks them, the 'Woman-born and Woman-nourish'd and Woman-educated and Woman-scorn'd' : they represent a notable allegorization of the Arthurian story, one shrewder than Tennyson's. In the same connexion he writes : 'The Man who respects Woman shall be despised by Woman ; And deadly cunning & mean abjectness only shall enjoy them' (88. 37–38). The symbolical intention is plain : Woman is whatever would seduce man's powers from their true allegiance. But no less plainly Blake discovers herein his criticism of Woman's influence in normal life. He was no feminist : he persuaded himself that he had highest spiritual sanction for asserting the supremacy of the masculine genius. Yet his very emphasis betrays his dread of the subtle potency of ' Woman's dominion '. The mystic tries to reassure himself by affirming that ' there is no such thing in Eternity as a Female Will ', but he cannot mask his fears. For him she embodies the power that conceives and gives birth to the illusions of material reality and its associated fallacies. She is the spirit of jealousy that seeks to maintain undivided sway by fettering the will-to-freedom. Her natural timidity, her shrinking from the disconcerting vehemences of passion, her literal and conservative spirit seem wiles to disarm and toils to ensnare Man's creative energies. Her retrogressive bias, determined by limited perceptions and congenital shrinking from the untried, beguile under specious appeals to pity, reverence, love, and chivalrous obligation. Another of her snares is her ' Chastity, not physical merely, but intellectual and aesthetic. Under cover of a tame conformity this ' domineering lust ' shelters itself from the brave venturesomeness of the liberal spirit, from a fear of the unlicensed. To this text Blake speaks with strange bitterness :

> Have you known the Judgment that is arisen among the
> Sons of Albion, where a Man dare hardly to embrace
> His own Wife for the terrors of Chastity that they call
> By the name of Morality : their Daughters govern all
> In hidden deceit.
>
> (36. 43–47)

As poet and as man Blake felt the ' intoxicating beauty and perfection ' of the natural universe, whereof Woman was at once the supreme manifestation and the symbol. He felt and feared its power over himself : it mocked and tormented the mystic in him the more because the ' natural man ' was so susceptible to its spell. *Jerusalem* cannot match the *Milton* passages that turn the beauties of Nature to spiritual significations, but the sense of its power is always there. It is seen obliquely in his denial that this beauty is Nature's own : it is ' stolen ' (74. 32–33) ; it is ' witchcraft ' (90. 68).

This symbolism's ethical content, less distinctly definable than the epistemological and the aesthetic, seems to express the appeal of the ideals of religion and virtue that are founded upon the differentiation of matter and spirit, the theistic concept of Man's relation to God, the false beauty of a fallacious holiness, and the illusion of the resurrection of the body into a life everlasting (49. 25–64).

As this maturer symbolism is found side by side with what is co-temporary with F. Z. vii and viii, so there are passages where Blake lays aside mythopoeic impediments and speaks with the resolved directness of the *Laocoön* sentences and *The Ghost of Abel*, as on pp. 91 and 77. Here is the clarity of *The Marriage of Heaven and Hell*, with a more settled sense of responsibility : if the savour of lively paradox is absent, a high seriousness takes its place, not unimpressively.

Catchwords occur on the following leaves:

Page 5. His	Page 37. His	Page 48. The
,, 8. Con-	,, 38. By	,, 49. The
,, 9. To	,, 40. Bath	,, 70. His
,, 12. And	,, 43. With	,, 79. En-
,, 30. His	,, 47. These	

With the exception of the catchwords on pp. 9 and 70, each of these corresponds with the first word on the succeeding page. Page 9 was originally followed by p. 11, p. 10 being interpolated. Page 70 presents some difficulty. It is likely that it should be read before p. 19.

Jerusalem

The

Emanation of

The Giant

Albion

1804

Printed by W. Blake, S^{th} Molton S^{t}

[3]

SHEEP *GOATS*

To the Public

After my three years' slumber on the banks of the Ocean,[1] I again display my Giant forms to the Public. My former Giants & Fairies having reciev'd the highest reward possible, the . . . and . . . of those with whom to be connected is to be . . . , I cannot doubt that this more consolidated & extended Work will be as kindly recieved . . . The Enthusiasm of the following Poem, the Author hopes . . . I also hope the Reader will be with me wholly One in Jesus our Lord, who is the God . . . and Lord . . . to whom the Ancients [2] look'd, and saw his day afar off with trembling & amazement.

The Spirit of Jesus is continual forgiveness of Sin : he who waits to be righteous before he enters into the Saviour's kingdom, the Divine Body, will never enter there. I am perhaps the most sinful of men : I pretend not to holiness ; yet I pretend to love, to see, to converse with daily, as man with man, & the more to have an interest in the Friend of Sinners. Therefore . . . Reader, . . . what you do not approve, & . . . me for this energetic exertion of my talent.

Reader ! . . . of books ! . . . of heaven,
And of that God from whom . . .[3]
Who in mysterious Sinai's awful cave,
To Man the wond'rous art of writing gave ;
Again he speaks in thunder and in fire,
Thunder of Thought, & flames of fierce desire.
Even from the depths of Hell his voice I hear

The first plate contains a full-page design, without text. A pilgrim, bearing his 'globe of fire' passes through a low door-way, to explore the state of error, the sleep of the spirit. The second plate is the title-page.

Page 3. The gaps in Blake's stereotype seem to be the result of deletions, some of the spaces so left being filled in with broken lines suggesting cloud-forms.

[1] Cp. Letter to Butts, 25 April 1803, quoted *Milton*, Introduction.

[2] For the 'Ancients', the visionaries of a golden age, cp. J. p. 52 and D. C. ii, pp. 3–4, quoted *Laocoön*, 1 *note*. See also Index, *Atlantic*, &c.

[3] Swinburne (Essay, p. 284) gives the following reading of this passage—on what authority is not stated :

Reader ! lover of books ! lover of heaven
And of that God from whom all things are given.

S. Foster Damon (*William Blake, his Philosophy and Symbols*, p. 434), from a collation of unspecified copies gives this second line as

And of that God from whom all hymns are given.

Swinburne's is the more convincing version.

Within the unfathom'd caverns of my Ear.
Therefore I print; nor vain my types shall be:
Heaven, Earth, & Hell henceforth shall live in harmony.

Of the Measure, in which the following Poem is written [1]

We who dwell on Earth can do nothing of ourselves; every thing is conducted by Spirits, no less than Digestion or Sleep. . . .

. . . .

When this Verse was first dictated to me, I consider'd a Monotonous Cadence like that used by Milton & Shakspeare & all writers of English Blank Verse, derived from the modern bondage of Rhyming, to be a necessary and indispensible part of Verse. But I soon found that in the mouth of a true Orator such monotony was not only awkward, but as much a bondage as rhyme itself. I therefore have produced a variety in every line, both of cadences & number of syllables. Every word and every letter is studied and put into its fit place; the terrific numbers are reserved for the terrific parts, the mild & gentle for the mild & gentle parts, and the prosaic for inferior parts; all are necessary to each other.[2] Poetry Fetter'd Fetters the Human Race. Nations are Destroy'd or Flourish in proportion as Their Poetry, Painting and Music are Destroy'd, or Flourish.[3] The Primeval State of Man was Wisdom, Art and Science.[4]

[1] This is obviously in imitation of Milton's note on 'The Verse', prefixed to *Paradise Lost*.
[2] See Index, *Minute Particulars*.
[3] Cp. R. N., p. cxxv, 'The Foundation of Empire is Art & Science. Remove them or Degrade them, & the Empire is No More. Empire follows Art, & not Vice Versa, as Englishmen suppose.'
[4] See Index, *Science*.

[4]

Μονος ο Ιεσους

JERUSALEM

Chap. 1.

Of the Sleep of Ulro and of the passage through Eternal Death and of the awaking to Eternal Life.

THIS theme calls me in sleep night after night & ev'ry morn
Awakes me at sun-rise; then I see the Saviour over me
Spreading his beams of love & dictating the words of this mild song:

Awake! awake! O sleeper of the land of shadows, wake! expand!
I am in you and you in me, mutual in love divine,
Fibres of love from man to man thro' Albion's pleasant land!
In all the dark Atlantic vale down from the hills of Surrey
A black water accumulates: return, Albion! return!
Thy brethren call thee; and thy fathers and thy sons,
Thy nurses and thy mothers, thy sisters and thy daughters
Weep at thy soul's disease, and the Divine Vision is darken'd.
Thy Emanation that was wont to play before thy face,
Beaming forth with her daughters into the Divine bosom,—
Where hast thou hidden thy Emanation, lovely Jerusalem,
From the vision and fruition of the Holy-one?
I am not a God afar off: I am a brother and friend;
Within your bosoms I reside, and you reside in me.
Lo! we are One, forgiving all Evil, Not seeking recompense;
Ye are my members, O ye sleepers of Beulah, land of shades!

But the perturbèd Man away turns down the valleys dark:

Page 4. The Greek phrase is taken, incorrectly, from *John*, viii. 9: εὑρέθη μόνος ὁ Ἰησοῦς. Blake omits breathings and accents. 1 Cp. J. 3, *note* 1.

6 For the image cp. M. 28. 29–34. 7 See Index, *Atlantic*.

9 See Index, *Albion*, III, and *Jesus*, I *a*.

13 bosom] bosom Where *1st rdg.*

19 See Index, *Beulah*, II. ii. After l. 20 a line *del.*: Saying . . .

' Phantom of the over heated brain ! shadow of immortality !
Seeking to keep my soul a victim to thy Love, which binds
Man the enemy of man into deceitful friendships,
Jerusalem is not ; her daughters are indefinite.
By demonstration man alone can live, and not by faith.
My mountains are my own, and I will keep them to myself :
The Malvern and the Cheviot, the Wolds, Plinlimmon & Snowdon
Are mine ; here will I build my Laws of Moral Virtue.
Humanity shall be no more, but war & princedom & victory ! '

So spoke Albion in jealous fears, hiding his Emanation
Upon the Thames and Medway, rivers of Beulah, dissembling
His jealousy before the throne divine, darkening, cold.

[5] The banks of the Thames are clouded ! the ancient porches of Albion are
Darken'd ! they are drawn thro' unbounded space, scatter'd upon
The Void in incoher⟨er⟩ent despair : Cambridge & Oxford & London
Are driven among the starry Wheels, rent away and dissipated
In Chasms & Abysses of sorrow, enlarg'd without dimension, terrible.
Albion's mountains run with blood ; the cries of war & of tumult
Resound into the unbounded night ; every Human perfection

21–29 Fallen man, infected with the errors of empiricism and morality, regards whatever is of vision as a delusion to be rejected for the forms of sense-perception and reason, the basis of 'Natural Religion', 'Rational Truth, Root of Evil and Good'.

26–29 Cp. J. 31. 19. 'Mountains of Moral Virtue' : and J. 28. 9–12, where Albion says :

> These hills & valleys are accursèd witnesses of Sin.
> I therefore condense them into solid rocks, stedfast . . .
> That Man be separate from Man : & here I plant my seat.

30–31 The Emanation is the vision or the capacity for vision : see Index, *Emanation*.

31 In Blake's topographical symbolism the Thames, and here the Medway also, has, in its association with London, the symbol of man's spiritual cosmos, an ancillary sense, the current of man's life.

Page 5. 1–5 The darkening of the porches represents the alteration in Man's relation to the perfect existence of Eternity that follows his fall. It may either have a general reference to this change, or indicate more particularly the narrowing of perception, from the comprehensive vision of the mystic to the restricted outlook of the materialist and moralist. Cp. M. 27. 1–5.

3–12 See Index, *Los, Note II*. B.

7–8 Cp. J. 49. 21–22 :

The Visions of Eternity, by reason of narrowed perception
Are become weak Visions of Time & Space fix'd into furrows of death.

Of mountain & river & city are small & wither'd & darken'd.
Cam is a little stream ! Ely is almost swallow'd up !
Lincoln & Norwich stand trembling on the brink of Udan-Adan !
Wales and Scotland shrink themselves to the west and to the North,
Mourning for fear of the warriors in the Vale of Entuthon-Benython.
Jerusalem is scatter'd abroad like a cloud of smoke thro' non-entity :
Moab & Ammon & Amalek & Canaan & Egypt & Aram
Recieve her little-ones for sacrifices and the delights of cruelty.

Trembling I sit day and night ; my friends are astonish'd at me ;
Yet they forgive my wanderings. I rest not from my great task,
To open the Eternal Worlds, to open the immortal Eyes
Of Man inwards into the Worlds of Thought, into Eternity
Ever expanding in the Bosom of God, the Human Imagination.
O Saviour ! pour upon me thy Spirit of meekness & love.
Annihilate the Selfhood in me ! be thou all my life !
Guide thou my hand which trembles exceedingly upon the rock of ages,
While I write of the building of Golgonooza & of the terrors of Entuthon,
Of Hand & Hyle & Coban, of Kwantok, Peachey, Brereton, Slayd & Hutton ;
Of the terrible sons & daughters of Albion and their Generations !

Scofield, Kox, Kotope and Bowen revolve most mightily upon
The Furnace of Los: before the eastern gate bending their fury,
They war to destroy the Furnaces, to desolate Golgonooza,
And to devour the Sleeping Humanity of Albion in rage & hunger.
They revolve into the Furnaces Southward & are driven forth Northward,

11 Cp. J. 16. 22 :

> Scotland pours out his Sons to labour at the Furnaces,
> Wales gives his Daughters to the Looms.

14 See Index, *Vala, Note II*. B.
16–26 Blake speaks *in propria persona*.
23 Cp. F. Z. ix. 284 *note*. 25–33 See Index, *Spectre, Note II*. A.
28 See Index, *Cardinal Points*.

Divided into Male and Female forms time after time.
From these Twelve all the Families of England spread abroad.

The Male is a Furnace of beryll ; the Female is a golden Loom ;
I behold them and their rushing fires overwhelm my Soul
In London's darkness, and my tears fall day and night
Upon the Emanations of Albion's Sons, the Daughters of Albion,
Names anciently remember'd, but now contemn'd as fictions,
Although in every bosom they controll our Vegetative powers.

These are united into Tirzah and her Sisters on Mount Gilead,
Cambel & Gwendolen & Conwenna & Cordella & Ignoge ;
And these united into Rahab in the Covering Cherub on Euphrates,
Gwiniverra & Gwinefred & Gonorill & Sabrina beautiful,
Estrild, Mehetabel & Ragan, lovely Daughters of Albion ;
They are the beautiful Emanations of the Twelve Sons of Albion.

The Starry Wheels revolv'd heavily over the Furnaces,
Drawing Jerusalem in anguish of maternal love
Eastward, a pillar of a cloud, with Vala upon the mountains
Howling in pain, redounding from the arms of Beulah's Daughters
Out from the Furnaces of Los above the head of Los,
A pillar of smoke writhing afar into Non-Entity, redounding
Till the cloud reaches afar outstretch'd among the Starry Wheels
Which revolve heavily in the mighty Void above the Furnaces.

O what avail the loves & tears of Beulah's lovely Daughters ?
They hold the Immortal Form in gentle bands & tender tears :

34 It has not been found possible to explain these terms. The line recurs J. 90. 27.

39 Cp. J. 3., *To the Public* : 'We who dwell on Earth can do nothing of ourselves ; every thing is conducted by Spirits, no less than Digestion or Sleep.'

40 Cp. F. Z. viii. 2 *note*.

40–44 This partition of Albion's Daughters between Rahab and Tirzah has no apparent significance, beyond emphasizing their identity with the two last named : see Index, *Vala, Note I*. C.

46 Cp. F. Z. i. 260 *note*.

47 The 'maternal' is constantly opposed to the 'Human'. It is identified with the 'mortal and perishing nature', the perverted vision in metaphysic and ethic which Blake symbolizes in the Female : see Index, *Sex*. Here apparently the reference is to the degradation of the spiritual life beneath the distracting influence of mundane environment.

54–59 'The Sanctuary of Eden is in the Camp, in the Outline, in the Circumference' (J. 69. 41–42). Again 'the Outline, the Circumference and

But all within is open'd into the deeps of Entuthon Benython,
A dark and unknown night, indefinite, unmeasurable, without end,
Abstract Philosophy warring in enmity against Imagination,
(Which is the Divine Body of the Lord Jesus, blessèd for ever.)
And there Jerusalem wanders with Vala upon the mountains.
Attracted by the revolutions of those Wheels, the Cloud of smoke
Immense, and Jerusalem & Vala weeping in the Cloud
Wander away into the Chaotic Void, lamenting with her Shadow
Among the Daughters of Albion, among the Starry Wheels,
Lamenting for her children, for the sons & daughters of Albion.

Los heard her lamentations in the deeps afar: his tears fall
Incessant before the Furnaces, and his Emanation divided in pain
Eastward toward the Starry Wheels. But Westward a black Horror,
[6] His Spectre driv'n by the Starry Wheels of Albion's sons, black and
Opake, divided from his back: he labours and he mourns.

For as his Emanation divided, his Spectre also divided
In terror of those starry wheels: and the Spectre stood over Los
Howling in pain, a black'ning Shadow, black'ning dark & opake,
Cursing the terrible Los, bitterly cursing him for his friendship
To Albion, suggesting murderous thoughts against Albion.

Los rag'd and stamp'd the earth in his might & terrible wrath.
He stood and stamp'd the earth: then he threw down his hammer in rage &

Form' are identified with 'Forgiveness of Sins, which is Self-Annihilation' (J. 98. 22–23). These symbols of the supreme state of existence relate to the Human Form, apparent as Jesus: see Index, *Jesus*. The knowledge of this state is preserved in Beulah, whose Daughters are the Daughters of Inspiration.

60–65 The punctuation of this passage is conjectural. 'Her' in l. 63 evidently refers to Jerusalem. The relation between the Cloud, Jerusalem, Jerusalem's Shadow, and Vala, is obscure. See Index, *Shadow*.

66–p. 6. 2 See Index, *Sex*. The whole episode of Los's struggles with his Spectre may be compared with Blake's account of his own spiritual experiences: cp. Letter to Hayley, 23 October 1804 (R., p. 168), and to Butts, 22 November 1802 (R., p. 102).

In fury: then he sat down and wept, terrified: Then arose
And chaunted his song, labouring with the tongs and hammer.
But still the Spectre divided, and still his pain increas'd.

In pain the Spectre divided, in pain of hunger and thirst,
To devour Los's Human Perfection; but when he saw that Los
[7] Was living, panting like a frighted wolf and howling
He stood over the Immortal in the solitude and darkness
Upon the dark'ning Thames across the whole Island westward,
A horrible Shadow of Death among the Furnaces beneath
The pillar of folding smoke; and he sought by other means
To lure Los, by tears, by arguments of science & by terrors,
Terrors in every Nerve, by spasms & extended pains;
While Los answer'd unterrified to the opake blackening Fiend.

And thus the Spectre spoke: 'Wilt thou still go on to destruction
Till thy life is all taken away by this deceitful Friendship?
He drinks thee up like water; like wine he pours thee
Into his tuns; thy Daughters are trodden in his vintage,
He makes thy Sons the trampling of his bulls; they are plow'd
And harrow'd for his profit: lo! thy stolen Emanation
Is his garden of pleasure: all the Spectres of his Sons mock thee.
Look how they scorn thy once admirèd palaces, now in ruins
Because of Albion, because of deceit and friendship! For Lo!
Hand has peopled Babel & Nineveh; Hyle, Ashur & Aram:

Page 7. 3 The spectrous influence acts against the west, the quarter of vision and spiritual liberty.

9–17 The spectre urges the apparent futility of all regenerative labours on man's behalf, seeing that they are perverted at their entry into mundane life. A similar idea is expressed in other symbols and from the point of view of the visionary, in Ross. MS. lxxv. 5–14 (Clar. Press, p. 213). The Greeks and Romans stand for the 'spectrous' illusions, particularly in art.

And if Bezaleel and Aholiab drew
What the finger of God pointed to their View,
Shall we suffer the Roman and Grecian rods
To compell us to worship them as Gods?
They [the Greeks and Romans] stole them from the Temple of the Lord
And worshipp'd them that they might make Inspired Art abhorr'd;
The Wood and Stone were call'd the Holy Things
And their Sublime Intent given to their kings.
All the Atonements of Jehovah spurn'd
And Criminals to Sacrifices turn'd.

15–25 See Index, *Spectre, Note II. a.*

Coban's son is Nimrod : his son Cush is adjoin'd to Aram
By the Daughter of Babel in a woven mantle of pestilence & war.
They put forth their spectrous cloudy sails which drive their immense
Constellations over the deadly deeps of indefinite Udan-Adan.
Kox is the Father of Shem & Ham & Japheth ; he is the Noah
Of the Flood of Udan-Adan. Hut'n is the Father of the Seven
From Enoch to Adam. Schofield is Adam who was New-
Created in Edom. I saw it indignant, & thou art not movèd.
This has divided thee in sunder, and wilt thou still forgive ?
O ! thou seest not what I see, what is done in the Furnaces.
Listen, I will tell thee what is done in moments to thee unknown :
Luvah was cast into the Furnaces of affliction and sealèd ;
And Vala fed in cruel delight the Furnaces with fire.
Stern Urizen beheld, urg'd by necessity to keep
The evil day afar, and if perchance with iron power
He might avert his own despair : in woe & fear he saw
Vala incircle round the Furnaces where Luvah was clos'd.
With joy she heard his howlings & forgot he was her Luvah,
With whom she liv'd in bliss in times of innocence & youth.
Vala comes from the Furnace in a cloud, but wretched Luvah
Is howling in the Furnaces in flames among Albion's Spectres,
To prepare the Spectre of Albion to reign over thee, O Los,
Forming the Spectres of Albion according to his rage,
To prepare the Spectre sons of Adam, who is Scofield, the Ninth
Of Albion's sons & the father of all his brethren in the Shadowy
Generation. Cambel & Gwendolen wove webs of war & of
Religion to involve all Albion's sons, and when they had
Involv'd Eight, their webs roll'd outwards into darkness,
And Scofield the Ninth remain'd on the outside of the Eight,
And Kox, Kotope, & Bowen, One in him, a Fourfold Wonder,

24 The Flood of Udan-Adan is equivalent to the symbol Atlantic Ocean : see Index, *Atlantic*.

30–37 These lines occur F. Z. ii. 282–289.

42–49 It has not been found possible to discriminate between the different Sons of Albion, so that the significance of these intricate combinations remains obscure. It may be noted that 'Fourfold' is very uncommon in its present association with a non-visionary agency. Its normal use is to emphasize the unity of the spiritual elements in the Eternal or Four-fold Man.

44–46 See Index, *Weaving*, I.

Involv'd the Eight. Such are the Generations of the Giant Albion,
To separate a Law of Sin, to punish thee in thy members.'
Los answer'd: 'Altho' I know not this, I know far worse than this:
I know that Albion hath divided me, and that thou, O my Spectre,
Hast just cause to be irritated: but look stedfastly upon me;
Comfort thyself in my strength; the time will arrive
When all Albion's injuries shall cease, and when we shall
Embrace him tenfold bright, rising from his tomb in immortality.
They have divided themselves by Wrath, they must be united by
Pity: let us therefore take example & warning, O my Spectre.
O that I could abstain from wrath! O that the Lamb
Of God would look upon me and pity me in my fury
In anguish of regeneration, in terrors of self annihilation.
Pity must join together those whom wrath has torn in sunder;
And the Religion of Generation which was meant for the destruction
Of Jerusalem become her covering till the time of the End.
O holy Generation, Image of regeneration,
O point of mutual forgiveness between Enemies,
Birthplace of the Lamb of God incomprehensible!
The Dead despise & scorn thee & cast thee out as accursèd,
Seeing the Lamb of God in thy gardens & thy palaces,
Where they desire to place the Abomination of Desolation.
Hand sits before his furnace: scorn of others & furious pride

52–53 Cp. the protest of Los's sons against their father's forbearance: M. 20. 27–23. 43. Both passages emphasize the obligation to continual forgiveness. They deprecate all resentment, such as even the frailer self in the mystic, his Spectre, feels naturally against the hostility of the unregenerate: it is another form of the error of 'self-righteousness'; cp. below, ll. 71–73 and J. 8. 7–17. 58–59 Cp. M. 22. 47–60 and J. 31. 29–38.

61 See Index, *Self-Annihilation*.

63–70 See Index, *Sex*. 'Holy Generation', the union of sexes, figures the unifying of contraries; and its fruitfulness is justified in the Incarnation, the revelation of the supreme truth that the Human and the Divine are one. Against this is set the ascetic reprobation of sex which symbolizes the rationalistic tendency to insist on difference, analytically to divide and not to unite; and this, to Blake, is an activity spiritually sterile, 'the Abomination of Desolation' (see M. p. 43, *passim*). Divine intervention has broken athwart the course of ascetic-rationalist schemes, 'the Religion of Generation'; as, for example, when the Incarnation occurred among the people of the Law of Sinai, so that in its own despite a just interpretation of it is found to express something of truth, i. e. to become the 'covering' of Jerusalem, and serves to give half-veiled expression to an ideal until the coming of the full light of truth (ll. 64–65).

Freeze round him to bars of steel & to iron rocks beneath
His feet: indignant self-righteousness like whirlwinds of the north
[8] Rose up against me thundering from the Brook of Albion's River,
From Ranelagh & Strumbolo, from Cromwell's gardens & Chelsea
The place of wounded Soldiers; but when he saw my Mace
Whirl'd round from heaven to earth, trembling he sat; his cold
Poisons rose up, & his sweet deceits cover'd them all over
With a tender cloud. As thou art now such was he, O Spectre.
I know thy deceit & thy revenges, and unless thou desist
I will certainly create an eternal Hell for thee. Listen!
Be attentive! be obedient! Lo! the Furnaces are ready to recieve thee.
I will break thee into shivers & melt thee in the furnaces of death;
I will cast thee into forms of abhorrence & torment if thou
Desist not from thine own will & obey not my stern command.
I am clos'd up from my children: my Emanation is dividing,
And thou, my Spectre, art divided against me. But mark,
I will compell thee to assist me in my terrible labours, To beat
These hypocritic Selfhoods on the Anvils of bitter Death.
I am inspirèd: I act not for myself: for Albion's sake
I now am what I am, a horror and an astonishment

Page 8. 1 Cp. M. 11. 35 *note*.

2 These places are to the west of London. Ranelagh House and Gardens stood to the east of Chelsea Hospital. Strombolo House in Pimlico was a minor place of entertainment with tea-gardens attached. Cromwell's Gardens, adjoining Hale House, Brompton, traditionally associated with the Protector, was a similar place of popular resort. These places of amusement, situated in the western or visionary quarter, are symbols of the corporeal or 'spectrous' influences that impede and perhaps infect the spiritual labours of the mystic. Cp. J. 77.: 'Every pleasure that intermingles with the duty of our station is a folly unredeemable and is planted like the seed of a wild flower among our wheat.'

4–6 The Spectre's incitements against the Enemies of Vision mask themselves under pretences of loyalty to vision, yet they are but 'deceits' and 'revenges'. 'Uncircumcised pretences to Chastity.' These perverse inclinations within himself the visionary must subdue, at all costs: cp. ll. 16–35 and J. 5. 16–22.

15 See Index, *Spectre*, III. An instance of this subjection of the Spectre is given in the description of Blake's 'Canterbury Pilgrims' (D. C. iii). 'There are always these two classes of learned sages, the poetical and the philosophical. The painter has put them side by side as if the youthful clerk had put himself under the tuition of the mature poet. Let the Philosopher always be the servant and scholar of inspiration, and all will be happy.' So in ll. 23–26 Reason is enlightened by Inspiration, so that it sees from without, the error of which it has been the cause. Similarly, at the final Regeneration, Error appears as a thing remote: cp. J. 92. 13–22.

Shudd'ring the heavens to look upon me. Behold what cruelties
Are practised in Babel & Shinar, & have approach'd to Zion's Hill.'

While Los spoke, the terrible Spectre fell shudd'ring before him,
Watching his time with glowing eyes to leap upon his prey.
Los open'd the Furnaces: in fear the Spectre saw to Babel & Shinar
Across all Europe & Asia; he saw the tortures of the Victims;
He saw now from the outside what he before saw & felt from within.
He saw that Los was the sole uncontroll'd Lord of the Furnaces.
Groaning he kneel'd before Los's iron-shod feet on London Stone,
Hung'ring & thirsting for Los's life, yet pretending obedience,
While Los pursu'd his speech in threat'nings loud & fierce:

'Thou art my Pride & Self-righteousness. I have found thee out.
Thou art reveal'd before me in all thy magnitude & power.
Thy Uncircumcisèd pretences to Chastity must be cut in sunder.
Thy holy wrath & deep deceit cannot avail against me,
Nor shalt thou ever assume the triple-form of Albion's Spectre;
For I am one of the living: dare not to mock my inspirèd fury.
If thou wast cast forth from my life, if I was dead upon the mountains,
Thou mightest be pitied & lov'd; but now I am living: unless
Thou abstain ravening I will create an eternal Hell for thee.
Take thou this Hammer & in patience heave the thundering Bellows;

24 Europe and Asia symbolize states of error: see Introductions to *Europe* and *The Song of Los*.

27 London Stone is consistently regarded by Blake as symbolically equivalent to the Temples of Stonehenge and other Druidical monuments, Druidism being used as synonymous with the error of Natural Religion. The Stone is generally associated with expressions of repressive Morality, as 'Sacrifice' and 'the Sleep of Death'.

32 See Index, *Self-Annihilation, Circumcision.*

34 'The triple form of Albion's Spectre' is in nowise different from the Spectre. It is called the 'Triple Headed Gog-Magog Giant of Albion' (J. 98. 52) and is described at length as Hand, one of Albion's Sons (J. 70, 1–16).

Take thou these Tongs; strike thou alternate with me; labour obedient.
Hand & Hyle & Koban, Skofeld, Kox & Kotope labour mightily
In the Wars of Babel & Shinar; all their Emanations were
Condens'd. Hand has absorb'd all his Brethren in his might;
All the infant Loves & Graces were lost, for the mighty Hand
[9] Condens'd his Emanations into hard opake substances,
And his infant thoughts & desires into cold dark cliffs of death.
His hammer of gold he siez'd and his anvil of adamant.
He siez'd the bars of condens'd thoughts, to forge them
Into the sword of war, into the bow and arrow,
Into the thundering cannon and into the murdering gun.
I saw the limbs form'd for exercise contemn'd, & the beauty of
Eternity look'd upon as deformity, & loveliness as a dry tree.
I saw disease forming a Body of Death around the Lamb
Of God, to destroy Jerusalem & to devour the body of Albion,
By war and stratagem to win the labour of the husbandman;
Awkwardness arm'd in steel, Folly in a helmet of gold,
Weakness with horns & talons, ignorance with a rav'ning beak;
Every Emanative joy forbidden as a Crime,
And the Emanations buried alive in the earth with pomp of religion:
Inspiration deny'd; Genius forbidden by laws of punishment.
I saw terrified: I took the sighs & tears & bitter groans;
I lifted them into my Furnaces, to form the spiritual sword
That lays open the hidden heart: I drew forth the pang
Of sorrow red hot: I work'd it on my resolute anvil:
I heated it in the flames of Hand & Hyle & Coban
Nine times. Gwendolen & Cambel & Gwineverra
Are melted into the gold, the silver, the liquid ruby,
The crysolite, the topaz, the jacinth & every precious stone.
Loud roar my Furnaces and loud my hammer is heard:
I labour day and night. I behold the soft affections

44 See Index, *Minute Particulars*.

Page 9. 9–10 The spectrous power seeks 'to Vegetate the Divine Vision'; to establish the doctrines of physical reality and moral responsibility against Imagination. See *Advertizement* and *Cat.* 1810, *passim*, for Blake's experience of this antagonism in the spheres of poetry and art, and his sense of the significance of his own struggles against it.

26 Cp. Blake's letter to Hayley, 23 October 1804 (R., p. 171): 'Oh! the distress I have undergone, and my poor wife with me; incessantly labouring and incessantly spoiling what I had done well. Every one of my friends was astonished at my faults, and could not assign a reason: they knew my industry and abstinence from every pleasure for the sake of study, and yet—and yet—and yet there wanted the proofs of industry

Condense beneath my hammer into forms of cruelty;
But still I labour in hope, tho' still my tears flow down,
That he who will not defend Truth may be compell'd to defend
A Lie, that he may be snared and caught and snared and taken,
That Enthusiasm and Life may not cease: arise, Spectre, arise!'

Thus they contended among the Furnaces with groans & tears.
Groaning the Spectre heav'd the bellows, obeying Los's frowns,
Till the Spaces of Erin were perfected in the furnaces
Of affliction: and Los drew them forth, compelling the harsh Spectre
[10] Into the Furnaces & into the valleys of the Anvils of Death,
And into the mountains of the Anvils & of the heavy Hammers,
Till he should bring the Sons & Daughters of Jerusalem to be
The Sons & Daughters of Los, that he might protect them from
Albion's dread Spectres: storming, loud, thunderous & mighty
The Bellows & the Hammers move compell'd by Los's hand.

And this is the manner of the Sons of Albion in their strength:
They take the Two Contraries which are call'd Qualities, with which
Every Substance is clothèd; they name them Good & Evil.
From them they make an Abstract, which is a Negation
Not only of the Substance from which it is derived,
A murderer of its own Body, but also a murderer
Of every Divine Member: it is the Reasoning Power,
An Abstract objecting power that Negatives every thing.
This is the Spectre of Man, the Holy Reasoning Power,
And in its Holiness is closèd the Abomination of Desolation.

Therefore Los stands in London building Golgonooza,

in my works.' This obstruction he ascribes earlier in the same letter to his 'spectrous fiend'.

29 Cp. note to Lavater, *Aphorism* 399: 'Active Evil is better than Passive Good': and cp. F. Z. ix. 151–154. 34 See Index, *Erin*.

Page 10 appears to be an interpolation. The catchword 'To' on p. 9 agrees with the first word on p. 11 but not with that on the present page.

1 Here the Anvil is identical in meaning with the 'Mundane Shell' in its regenerative aspect.

10–16 See Index, *Spectre*.

17 It is not easy to formulate a comprehensive definition of the symbol London. Sometimes it is used normally as a place-name (M. 40. ll. 36, 39, and 40: J. 15. 20), while its various districts and environs have the same general significance as the points of compass towards which they lie, with relation to Lambeth. But of the more definitely symbolic uses, the

Compelling his Spectre to labours mighty ; trembling in fear
The Spectre weeps, but Los unmov'd by tears or threats remains.

' I must Create a System, or be enslav'd by another Man's :
I will not Reason & Compare : my business is to Create.'

So Los, in fury & strength, in indignation & burning wrath.
Shudd'ring the Spectre howls : his howlings terrify the night.
He stamps around the Anvil, beating blows of stern despair.
He curses Heaven & Earth, Day & Night & Sun & Moon ;
He curses Forest, Spring & River, Desart & sandy Waste,
Cities & Nations, Families & Peoples, Tongues & Laws,
Driven to desperation by Los's terrors & threat'ning fears.

Los cries : ' Obey my voice & never deviate from my will,
And I will be merciful to thee : be thou invisible to all
To whom I make thee invisible, but chief to my own Children,
O Spectre of Urthona. Reason not against their dear approach
Nor them obstruct with thy temptations of doubt & despair.
O Shame, O strong & mighty Shame ! I break thy brazen fetters.

commonest makes it one of a quaternion, Verulam, London, York, and Edinburgh, that correspond with the four Zoas (J. 46. 24 : 59. 13–14 : 74. 3–4). This use is apparently related to J. 38. 29–39, where London appears as one of the Eternals who enter mortal life to regenerate Man.

> I [Blake] behold London, a Human awful wonder of God.
> He says : ' Return, Albion, return ! I give myself for thee.
> My Streets are my Ideas of Imagination.
> Awake, Albion, awake, and let us awake up together !
> My Houses are Thoughts ; my Inhabitants, Affections,
> The children of my thoughts, walking within my blood-vessels, . . .
> For Albion's sake and for Jerusalem thy Emanation,
> I give myself, and these my brethren give themselves for Albion.

Elsewhere, as a centre of visionary influence in mortal life, it is associated with Golgonooza, the ' Spiritual Fourfold London ' : see Index, *Golgonooza*. In this sense it seems to embody Blake's own experience of London, as a place favourable to seeing visions, dreaming dreams, prophesying, and speaking parables (cp. Letter to Butts, 25 April 1803). In other passages it is taken as the type of existence under various conditions : cp. ' London ' (S. E., Clar. Press, p. 131) ; J. 29. 19 : 79. 24–32

31 The Children of Los in this passage may be either mortal men, Los being the Time-spirit (J. 86. 48), or else the works of the Spirit of Prophecy, its ' births of Intellect ' (*Cat.* 1810). The latter interpretation is the more probable in view of ll. 37–39 below. For the commoner use of the symbol see Index, *Los, Note II. a.*

32 See Index, *Los, Note I.*

34 Shame, Jealousy, Secrecy used in the earlier books to denote the temper of the prudential moralist, here extend to that repugnance to all forms of visionary activity which restrains the powers of man in bondage to the doctrines of Natural Religion.

If thou refuse, thy present torments will seem southern breezes
To what thou shalt endure if thou obey not my great will.'

The Spectre answer'd: 'Art thou not asham'd of those thy Sins
That thou callest thy Children? lo, the Law of God commands
That they be offerèd upon his Altar. O cruelty & torment,
For thine are also mine! I have kept silent hitherto
Concerning my chief delight; but thou hast broken silence.
Now I will speak my mind. Where is my lovely Enitharmon,
O thou my enemy, where is my Great Sin? She is also thine.
I said: "Now is my grief at worst, incapable of being
Surpassed": but every moment it accumulates more & more.
It continues accumulating to eternity: the joys of God advance
For he is Righteous; he is not a Being of Pity & Compassion,
He cannot feel Distress; he feeds on Sacrifice & Offering,
Delighting in cries & tears, & clothèd in holiness & solitude.
But my griefs advance also, for ever & ever without end.
O that I could cease to be! Despair! I am Despair,
Created to be the great example of horror & agony: also my
Prayer is vain. I callèd for compassion; compassion mock'd;
Mercy & pity threw the grave stone over me & with lead
And iron bound it over me for ever. Life lives on my
Consuming, & the Almighty hath made me his Contrary,
To be all evil, all reversèd & for ever dead, knowing
And seeing life, yet living not: how can I then behold
And not tremble? how can I be beheld & not abhorr'd?'

So spoke the Spectre shudd'ring, & dark tears ran down his shadowy face
Which Los wipèd off, but comfort none could give or beam of hope.
Yet ceas'd he not from labouring at the roarings of his Forge,

46–59 This concept of Deity as 'a God afar off' is comparable with the pointed criticism in the vision of Godhead in F. Z. iii. 45 seq.: a 'Shadow' from 'Man's wearied intellect':

> pure, perfect, holy; in white linen pure he hover'd
> A sweet entrancing self delusion, a wat'ry vision of Man,
> Soft exulting in existence, all the Man absorbing.

Cp. J. 23. 29:

> God in the dreary Void
> Dwells from Eternity, wide separated from the Human Soul.

Identifying this God with Satan, 'the Idol Virtues of the Natural Heart, . . . its Selfish Natural Virtue,' Blake writes (M. 39. 37):

> Thy purpose & the purpose of thy Priests & of thy Churches
> Is to impress on men the fear of death, to teach
> Trembling & fear, terror, constriction, abject selfishness.

With iron & brass Building Golgonooza in great contendings,
Till his Sons & Daughters came forth from the Furnaces
At the sublime Labours ; for Los compell'd the invisible Spectre
[11] To labours mighty with vast strength, with his mighty chains :
In pulsations of time & extensions of space, like Urns of Beulah,
With great labour upon his anvils : & in his ladles the Ore
He lifted, pouring it into the clay ground prepar'd with art,
Striving with Systems to deliver Individuals from those Systems,
That whenever any Spectre began to devour the Dead,
He might feel the pain as if a man gnaw'd his own tender nerves.

Then Erin came forth from the Furnaces, & all the Daughters of Beulah
Came from the Furnaces by Los's mighty power for Jerusalem's
Sake, walking up and down among the Spaces of Erin :
And the Sons and Daughters of Los came forth in perfection lovely.
And the Spaces of Erin reach'd from the starry heighth to the starry depth.

Los wept with exceeding joy & all wept with joy together.
They fear'd they never more should see their Father, who
Was built in from Eternity in the Cliffs of Albion.

But when the joy of meeting was exhausted in loving embrace,
Again they lament : ' O what shall we do for lovely Jerusalem,
To protect the Emanations of Albion's mighty ones from cruelty ?
Sabrina & Ignoge begin to sharpen their beamy spears
Of light and love ; their little children stand with arrows of gold.
Ragan is wholly cruel : Scofield is bound in iron armour ;
He is like a mandrake in the earth before Reuben's gate :
He shoots beneath Jerusalem's walls to undermine her foundations.

Page 11. 1–3 The Urns of Beulah cannot be explained.
3–4 Cp. M. H. H., p. 15 and *note*. 5 Cp. M. 7. 13 *note*.
6 Cp. M. 39. 14 and 40. 18–21.
15 This line recurs with slight change in J. 19. 33. Cp. B. U. v. 14–15 ; J. 74. 24–30. 21 Cp. M. 17. 59.
22 Cp. J. 93. 8 and Gen. xxx. 14. The line seems to have the same meaning as l. 23, that is, it relates to the subversion of the visionary by the repressive influence of ' corporeal war ' : see *Milton*, Preface, *note* 2.

Vala is but thy Shadow, O thou loveliest among women :
A shadow animated by thy tears, O mournful Jerusalem !
[12] Why wilt thou give to her a Body whose life is but a Shade,
Her joy and love a shade, a shade of sweet repose ?
But animated and vegetated, she is a devouring worm.
What shall we do for thee, O lovely mild Jerusalem ?'

And Los said : 'I behold the finger of God in terrors.
Albion is dead ; his Emanation is divided from him.
But I am living ; yet I feel my Emanation also dividing.
Such thing was never known. O pity me, thou all-piteous-one!
What shall I do, or how exist, divided from Enitharmon ?
Yet why despair ? I saw the finger of God go forth
Upon my Furnaces from within the Wheels of Albion's Sons,
Fixing their Systems permanent, by mathematic power
Giving a body to Falshood that it may be cast off for ever,
With Demonstrative Science piercing Apollyon with his own bow.
God is within & without : he is even in the depths of Hell !'

Such were the lamentations of the Labourers in the Furnaces.

And they appear'd within & without, incircling on both sides
The Starry Wheels of Albion's Sons, with Spaces for Jerusalem
And for Vala the shadow of Jerusalem, the ever mourning Shade,
On both sides, within & without, beaming gloriously.

Terrified at the sublime Wonder, Los stood before his Furnaces ;
And they stood around, terrified with admiration at Erin's Spaces ;
For the Spaces reach'd from the starry heighth to the starry depth.
And they builded Golgonooza, terrible eternal labour.

24 Jerusalem is the glory or radiance emanating from the perfect state ; its perversion into the body of error, that arises from 'doubts and fears', is Vala.

25 Tears here symbolize the conditions that lead to the distorting or obscuring of spiritual perceptions : cp. J. 66. 30, where the Daughters of Albion

> pour cold water over his [Man's] brain in front to cause
> Lids to grow over his eyes in veils of tears.

Page 12. 1–3 These lines are addressed to Man.

10–15 Cp. M. 28. 39 *note*. In other terms 'Mercy' changes 'Death into 'Sleep', and that which was meant for the destruction of Man becomes his covering till the time of the end ; the Crucifixion becomes the means to the overthrow of the Law that commanded it, and Calvary and Golgotha become Golgonooza, 'a building of pity and compassion'.

What are those golden builders doing? Where was the burying-place
Of soft Ethinthus? Near Tyburn's fatal Tree? Is that
Mild Zion's hill's most ancient promontory, near mournful
Ever weeping Paddington? Is that Calvary and Golgotha
Becoming a building of pity and compassion? Lo!
The stones are pity, and the bricks well wrought affections
Enamel'd with love & kindness; & the tiles engraven gold,
Labour of merciful hands; the beams & rafters are forgiveness,
The mortar & cement of the work tears of honesty, the nails
And the screws & iron braces are well wrought blandishments
And well contrivèd words, firm fixing, never forgotten,
Always comforting the remembrance; the floors humility;
The cielings devotion, the hearths thanksgiving.
Prepare the furniture, O Lambeth, in thy pitying looms!
The curtains woven tears & sighs, wrought into lovely forms
For comfort; there the secret furniture of Jerusalem's chamber
Is wrought. Lambeth! the Bride, the Lamb's Wife, loveth thee.
Thou art one with her & knowest not of self in thy supreme joy.
Go on, builders, in hope! tho' Jerusalem wanders far away
Without the gate of Los, among the dark Satanic wheels.

Fourfold the Sons of Los in their divisions, and fourfold
The great City of Golgonooza: fourfold toward the north,

26 Cp. *Europe*, 158 *note*, and F. Z. viii. 353. For Tyburn's tree cp. F. Z. ii. 249 *note*.

38–42 Cp. M. 4. 14 *note*. It is possible that the 'furniture' here mentioned may allude to Blake's work as a 'prophet', for 'the Building up of Jerusalem'. During the period of his residence in Lambeth he produced the greater part of his earlier symbolic writings.

44 Cp. J. 39. 7–10 and 5. 60–65.

45–60 The 'Four Faces' are the Four Eternal Senses of Man, 'the Human Nerves of Sensation, the Four Rivers of the Water of Life' (J. 98. 12–23). In his scheme of correspondences, consistent so far as it goes, Blake identifies them with the Zoas (see Index, *Zoas*): Tharmas with the Tongue (J. 63. 5), and Los with the Ear (F. Z. i. 14–15: M. 28. 40). Luvah in the East is associated with the 'Nerves of the expansive Nostrils' flowing 'East in Rivers of bliss' exhaling odours and receptive of joy (J. 49. 38), while the Eye can only be connected with Urizen through their possession of a common station in the south. Further they are associated with the Elements and their respective 'Creatures' (J. 36. 31–36): Luvah with Fire and the Genii; Urthona with Earth and its Gnomes; Tharmas with Water and the Nymphs; Urizen with the Air and Fairies. The 'English names' of the Zoas, 'Verulam, London, York and Edinburgh' (J. 59. 14), cannot be allocated. But though Blake returns from time to time to this system of correspondences, it appears to be of no account in the exposition of his doctrine, and is often entirely lost sight of.

And toward the south fourfold, & fourfold toward the east & west,
Each within other toward the four points : that toward
Eden, and that toward the World of Generation,
And that toward Beulah and that toward Ulro.
Ulro is the space of the terrible starry wheels of Albion's sons.
But that toward Eden is wallèd up till time of renovation,
Yet it is perfect in its building, ornaments & perfection.

And the Four Points are thus beheld in Great Eternity :
West the Circumference : South the Zenith : North
The Nadir : East the Center, unapproachable for ever.
These are the four Faces towards the Four Worlds of Humanity
In every Man : Ezekiel saw them by Chebar's flood.
And the Eyes are the South, and the Nostrils are the East,
And the Tongue is the West, and the Ear is the North.

And the North Gate of Golgonooza toward Generation
Has four sculptur'd Bulls terrible before the Gate of iron,
And iron the Bulls : and that which looks toward Ulro,
Clay bak'd & enamel'd, eternal glowing as four furnaces
Turning upon the Wheels of Albion's sons with enormous power.
And that toward Beulah four, gold, silver, brass & iron ;
[13] And that toward Eden, four, form'd of gold, silver, brass & iron.

The South a golden Gate, has four Lions terrible, living ;
That toward Generation four, of iron carv'd wondrous ;
That toward Ulro four, clay bak'd, laborious workmanship ;
That toward Eden four, immortal, gold, silver, brass & iron.

The Western Gate, fourfold, is clos'd, having four Cherubim
Its guards, living, the work of elemental hands, laborious task ;
Like Men hermaphroditic, each wingèd with eight wings.
That towards Generation, iron ; that toward Beulah, stone ;

58 Cp. Ezek. i. 1–28. 63 See Index, *Ulro*.
65 Cp. F. Z. i. 260 *note*.
Page 13. 6–11 The closing of the Western Gate, the Gate of the Tongue, may be said to emphasize the divergence between man's mortal state and his spiritual life in Eternity, Eden, the World of Imagination. It may further signify that from the nature of mundane existence truth cannot be uttered ; or since the tongue is identified with the sense of touch (M. 24. 46), the buttress of the illusion of physical reality, it may represent the obstacle that bars the way of man's return to spiritual modes of perception. Cp. *Paradise Lost*, viii. 579 seq.

That toward Ulro, clay ; that toward Eden, metals ;
But all clos'd up till the last day, when the graves shall yield their dead.

The Eastern Gate, fourfold ; terrible & deadly its ornaments,
Taking their forms from the Wheels of Albion's sons, as cogs
Are form'd in a wheel to fit the cogs of the adverse wheel.

That toward Eden, eternal ice, frozen in seven folds
Of forms of death : and that toward Beulah, stone ;
The seven diseases of the earth are carvèd terrible :
And that toward Ulro, forms of war, seven enormities :
And that toward Generation, seven generative forms.

And every part of the City is fourfold & every inhabitant fourfold,
And every pot & vessel & garment & utensil of the houses,
And every house, fourfold ; but the third Gate in every one
Is clos'd as with a threefold curtain of ivory & fine linen & ermine.
And Luban stands in middle of the City : a moat of fire
Surrounds Luban, Los's Palace & the golden Looms of Cathedron.

And sixty-four thousand Genii guard the Eastern Gate ;
And sixty-four thousand Gnomes guard the Northern Gate ;
And sixty-four thousand Nymphs guard the Western Gate ;
And sixty-four thousand Fairies guard the Southern Gate.

Around Golgonooza lies the land of death eternal, a Land
Of pain and misery and despair and ever brooding melancholy,
In all the Twenty-seven Heavens number'd from Adam to Luther,
From the blue Mundane Shell reaching to the Vegetative Earth.

The Vegetative Universe opens like a flower from the Earth's center,
In which is Eternity. It expands in Stars to the Mundane Shell
And there it meets Eternity again, both within and without :
And the abstract Voids between the Stars are the Satanic Wheels.

There is the Cave, the Rock, the Tree, the Lake of Udan Adan,
The Forest and the Marsh and the Pits of bitumen deadly ;

24 Cp. F. Z. vii. 429 *note*. 32 See Index, *Mundane Shell*, III.
35 Cp. M. 37. 47–54.

The Rocks of solid fire, the Ice valleys, the Plains
Of burning sand, the rivers, cataract & Lakes of Fire,
The Islands of the fiery Lakes, the Trees of Malice, Revenge,
And black Anxiety, and the Cities of the Salamandrine men.
(But whatever is visible to the Generated Man
Is a Creation of mercy & love from the Satanic Void).
The land of darkness flamèd, but no light & no repose :
The land of snows of trembling, & of iron hail incessant ;
The land of earthquakes and the land of woven labyrinths,
The land of snares & traps & wheels & pit-falls & dire mills,
The Voids, the Solids & the land of clouds & regions of waters,
With their inhabitants in the Twenty-seven Heavens beneath Beulah,
Self-righteousnesses conglomerating against the Divine Vision ;
A Concave Earth wondrous, Chasmal, Abyssal, Incoherent,
Forming the Mundane Shell, above, beneath, on all sides surrounding
Golgonooza. Los walks round the walls night and day.

He views the City of Golgonooza & its smaller Cities ;
The Looms & Mills & Prisons & Work-houses of Og & Anak ;
The Amalekite, the Canaanite, the Moabite, the Egyptian,
And all that has existed in the space of six thousand years,
Permanent & not lost, not lost nor vanish'd ; & every little act,
Word, work & wish that has existed, all remaining still
In those Churches ever consuming & ever building by the Spectres
Of all the inhabitants of Earth wailing to be Created ;
Shadowy to those who dwell not in them, meer possibilities,
But to those who enter into them they seem the only substances :
For every thing exists ; & not one sigh nor smile nor tear,
[14] One hair nor particle of dust, not one can pass away.

He views the Cherub at the Tree of Life, also the Serpent
Orc, the first born, coil'd in the south ; the Dragon Urizen ;

43 'Cities of the Salamandrine men' remains unexplained.
44–45 See Index, *Mundane Shell*, IV.
51 See Index, *Mundane Shell, Note II*.
57–58 These are the Nations of the Earth, the enemies of Jerusalem.
59–63 Cp. J. 16. 61–69.
64–p. 14. 1 Blake here defines error as illusion. But the illusions are not to be escaped. They persist to afflict all generation of men : cp. D. C. iii, quoted J. 16. 61–67 *note*.
Page 14. 2 See Index, *Mundane Shell, Note I*, and *Orc*.

Tharmas the Vegetated Tongue, even the Devouring Tongue,
A threefold region, a false brain, a false heart,
And false bowels, altogether composing the False Tongue
Beneath Beulah as a wat'ry flame revolving every way
And as dark roots and stems, a Forest of affliction, growing
In seas of sorrow. Los also views the Four Females,
Ahania and Enion and Vala and Enitharmon lovely,
And from them all the lovely beaming Daughters of Albion.
Ahania & Enion & Vala are three evanescent shades :
Enitharmon is a vegetated mortal Wife of Los,
His Emanation, yet his Wife till the sleep of death is past.

Such are the Buildings of Los, & such are the Woofs of Enitharmon.

And Los beheld his Sons and he beheld his Daughters,
Every one a translucent Wonder, a Universe within,
Increasing inwards into length, and breadth, and heighth,
Starry & glorious : and they, every one in their bright loins,
Have a beautiful golden gate which opens into the vegetative world ;
And every one a gate of rubies & all sorts of precious stones
In their translucent hearts, which opens into the vegetative world ;
And every one a gate of iron dreadful and wonderful
In their translucent heads, which opens into the vegetative world.
And every one has the three regions Childhood, Manhood, & Age.
But the gate of the tongue, the western gate, in them is clos'd,
Having a wall builded against it : and thereby the gates
Eastward & Southward & Northward are incircled with flaming fires.
And the North is Breadth, the South is Heighth & Depth,
The East is Inwards, & the West is Outwards every way.

And Los beheld the mild Emanation Jerusalem eastward bending
Her revolutions toward the Starry Wheels in maternal anguish,

4–9 Cp. M. 3. 10 *note* and Index, *Head, Heart, and Loins.* Threefold is ordinarily connoted of error.

10 See Index, *Ahania, Enion, Vala.* For the symbolic difference between 'Emanation' and 'Wife' see Index, *Sex.*

16–28 The children of Los are spiritual agents in mundane life. They enjoy visionary communion of the completest kind possible to vegetative or mortal existences ; their limitations are indicated by the reference to the closed western gates, that here signifies the absence of fullest vision.

32 Cp. J. 5. 47 *note.*

Like a pale cloud arising from the arms of Beulah's Daughters,
In Entuthon Benython's deep Vales beneath Golgonooza.

[15] And Hand & Hyle rooted into Jerusalem by a fibre
Of strong revenge, & Skofeld Vegetated by Reuben's Gate
In every Nation of the Earth, till the Twelve Sons of Albion
Enrooted into every Nation, a mighty Polypus growing
From Albion over the whole Earth : such is my awful Vision.

I see the Four-fold Man : The Humanity in deadly sleep,
And its fallen Emanation, The Spectre & its cruel Shadow.
I see the Past, Present & Future existing all at once
Before me. O Divine Spirit ! sustain me on thy wings,
That I may awake Albion from his long & cold repose !
For Bacon & Newton, sheath'd in dismal steel, their terrors hang
Like iron scourges over Albion. Reasonings like vast Serpents
Infold around my limbs, bruising my minute articulations.

I turn my eyes to the Schools & Universities of Europe,
And there behold the Loom of Locke, whose Woof rages dire,
Wash'd by the Water-wheels of Newton : black the cloth
In heavy wreathes folds over every Nation : cruel Works
Of many Wheels I view, wheel without wheel, with cogs tyrannic
Moving by compulsion each other ; not as those in Eden, which
Wheel within Wheel in freedom revolve in harmony & peace.

I see in deadly fear in London Los raging round his Anvil
Of death, forming an Ax of gold ; the Four Sons of Los

In the Fitzwilliam Museum copy, End of Chap. 1, *del.* after l. 34. This indication of an earlier arrangement is collateral evidence in support of what is said on pp. 438–439 above.

Page 15. 6–34 Blake speaks.

11 Bacon, Newton, and Locke represent, both individually and collectively, the errors of 'Rational Philosophy and Mathematical Demonstration', and are at all points identical with the generic symbol, 'the Reasoning Spectre'. They are 'the three great teachers of Atheism, or Satan's doctrine' (Crabb Robinson, S., p. 264). Cp. J. 52, '*To the Deists*'.

12–13 Cp. *The Gates of Paradise*, 'The Keys of the Gates', ll. 7–8 (Clar. Press, p. 374) :

> Serpent Reasonings us entice
> Of Good and Evil, Virtue & Vice.

16–20 The antithesis between 'Abstract Philosophy' and 'Imagination' is stated under the same symbols, but with a more definitely moral implication in J. 22. 34–35 :

> Why should Punishment Weave the Veil with Iron Wheels of War,
> When Forgiveness might it Weave with Wings of Cherubim ?

21 Cp. J. 38. 40–43. 22–23 See Index, *Los, Note II.*

Stand round him, cutting the Fibres from Albion's hills,
That Albion's Sons may roll apart over the Nations;
While Reuben enroots his brethren in the narrow Canaanite
From the Limit Noah to the Limit Abram, in whose Loins
Reuben in his Twelve-fold majesty & beauty shall take refuge,
As Abraham flees from Chaldea shaking his goary locks.
But first Albion must sleep, divided from the Nations.

I see Albion sitting upon his Rock in the first Winter,
And thence I see the Chaos of Satan & the World of Adam.
When the Divine Hand went forth on Albion in the mid Winter
And at the place of Death, when Albion sat in Eternal Death
Among the Furnaces of Los in the Valley of the Son of Hinnom. . . .

[16] Hampstead, Highgate, Finchley, Hendon, Muswell hill rage loud
Before Bromion's iron Tongs & glowing Poker reddening fierce.
Hertfordshire glows with fierce Vegetation; in the Forests
The Oak frowns terrible; the Beech & Ash & Elm enroot
Among the Spiritual fires; loud the Corn-fields thunder along;
The Soldier's Fife, the Harlot's shriek, the Virgin's dismal groan,
The Parent's fear, the Brother's jealousy, the Sister's curse
Beneath the Storms of Theotormon; & the thund'ring Bellows
Heaves in the hand of Palamabron, who in London's darkness
Before the Anvil watches the bellowing flames: thundering
The Hammer loud rages in Rintrah's strong grasp, swinging loud
Round from heaven to earth, down falling with heavy blow
Dead on the Anvil, where the red hot wedge groans in pain.
He quenches it in the black trough of his Forge: London's River
Feeds the dread Forge, trembling & shuddering along the Valleys.

Humber & Trent roll dreadful before the Seventh Furnace,
And Tweed & Tyne anxious give up their Souls for Albion's sake.

34 Apparently the conclusion of this passage is to be found on some page uppressed or not yet identified.

Page 16 is clearly out of place, though no alternative position for it can be suggested. 1–15 See Index, *Los*.

5–6 Something appears to be omitted at this point.

16–20 Cp. J. 38. 46–48: Cities
Are Men, fathers of multitudes and Rivers & Mountains
Are also Men; every thing is Human, mighty, sublime.

Lincolnshire, Derbyshire, Nottinghamshire, Leicestershire,
From Oxfordshire to Norfolk on the Lake of Udan Adan,
Labour within the Furnaces, walking among the Fires
With Ladles huge & iron Pokers over the Island white.

Scotland pours out his Sons to labour at the Furnaces;
Wales gives his Daughters to the Looms; England nursing Mothers
Gives to the Children of Albion & to the Children of Jerusalem,
From the blue Mundane Shell even to the Earth of Vegetation,
Throughout the whole Creation which groans to be deliver'd.
Albion groans in the deep slumbers of Death upon his Rock.

Here Los fix'd down the Fifty-two Counties of England & Wales,
The Thirty-six of Scotland & the Thirty-four of Ireland
With mighty power, when they fled out at Jerusalem's Gates
Away from the Conflict of Luvah & Urizen, fixing the Gates
In the Twelve Counties of Wales: & thence Gates looking every way
To the Four Points, conduct to England & Scotland & Ireland,
And thence to all the Kingdoms & Nations & Families of the Earth.
The Gate of Reuben in Carmarthenshire; the Gate of Simeon in
Cardiganshire & the Gate of Levi in Montgomeryshire;
The Gate of Judah, Merionethshire; the Gate of Dan, Flintshire;
The Gate of Napthali, Radnorshire; the Gate of Gad, Pembrokeshire;
The Gate of Asher, Carnarvonshire; the Gate of Issachar, Brecknokshire;
The Gate of Zebulun in Angelsea & Sodor; so is Wales divided:
The Gate of Joseph, Denbighshire; the Gate of Benjamin, Glamorganshire,
For the protection of the Twelve Emanations of Albion's Sons.

And the Forty Counties of England are thus divided: in the Gates

27 Albion's Rock: cp. F. Z. ix. 284 *note*.

28–31 The sons of Israel are elsewhere referred to as those of the Sons of Los who were 'Generated': see Index, *Los*, *Note II. a.* The significance of the partition of the counties among them is not apparent.

31 Cp. F. Z. i. 179 seq.

Of Reuben, Norfolk, Suffolk, Essex ; Simeon, Lincoln, York, Lancashire ;
Levi, Middlesex, Kent, Surrey ; Judah, Somerset, Glouster, Wiltshire ;
Dan, Cornwal, Devon, Dorset ; Napthali, Warwick, Leicester, Worcester ;
Gad, Oxford, Bucks, Harford ; Asher, Sussex, Hampshire, Berkshire ;
Issachar, Northampton, Rutland, Nottgham ; Zebulun, Bedford, Huntgn, Camb ;
Joseph, Stafford, Shrops, Heref ; Benjamin, Derby, Cheshire, Monmouth ;
And Cumberland, Northumberland, Westmoreland & Durham are
Divided in the ⟨the⟩ Gates of Reuben, Judah, Dan & Joseph.

And the Thirty-six Counties of Scotland divided in the Gates
Of Reuben, Kincard, Haddntn, Forfar ; Simeon, Ayr, Argyll, Banff ;
Levi, Edinburgh, Roxbro, Ross ; Judah, Abrdeen, Berwik, Dumfries ;
Dan, Bute, Caitnes, Clakmanan ; Napthali, Nairn, Invernes, Linlithgo ;
Gad, Peebles, Perth, Renfru ; Asher, Sutherlan, Sterling, Wigtoun ;
Issachar, Selkirk, Dumbartn, Glasgo ; Zebulun, Orkney, Shetland, Skye ;
Joseph, Elgin, Lanerk, Kinros ; Benjamin, Kromarty, Murra, Kirkubriht :
Governing all by the sweet delights of secret amorous glances
In Enitharmon's Halls builded by Los & his mighty Children.

All things acted on Earth are seen in the bright Sculptures of
Los's Halls, & every Age renews its powers from these Works,
With every pathetic story possible to happen from Hate or
Wayward Love ; & every sorrow & distress is carvèd here ;
Every Affinity of Parents, Marriages & Friendships are here
In all their various combinations, wrought with wondrous Art,
All that can happen to Man in his pilgrimage of seventy years.
Such is the Divine Written Law of Horeb & Sinai,
And such the Holy Gospel of Mount Olivet & Calvary.

61–67 Cp. D. C. iii, p. 9. : 'As one age falls, another rises, different to mortal sight but to immortals only the same ; for we see the same character repeated again and again in animals, vegetables, minerals and in men ; nothing new occurs in identical existence ; Accident ever varies, Substance can never suffer change nor decay.'

68–69 The labours of Los (ll. 1–60) related to the Holy Gospel are in

[17] His Spectre divides ; & Los in fury compells it to divide,
To labour in the fire, in the water, in the earth, in the air,
To follow the Daughters of Albion as the hound follows the scent
Of the wild inhabitant of the forest, to drive them from his own,
To make a way for the Children of Los to come from the Furnaces.
But Los himself against Albion's Sons his fury bends, for he
Dare not approach the Daughters openly lest he be consumèd
In the fires of their beauty & perfection & be Vegetated beneath
Their Looms, in a Generation of death & resurrection to forgetfulness.
They wooe Los continually to subdue his strength : he continually
Shews them his Spectre, sending him abroad over the four points of heaven
In the fierce desires of beauty & in the tortures of repulse. He is
The Spectre of the Living pursuing the Emanations of the Dead.
Shudd'ring they flee ; they hide in the Druid Temples in cold chastity,
Subdued by the Spectre of the Living & terrified by undisguis'd desire.

For Los said : 'Tho' my Spectre is divided, as I am a Living Man
I must compell him to obey me wholly, that Enitharmon may not

contrast with the labours of the Sons of Albion, the 'Divine Written Law', but the impossibility of rightly placing the page makes the nature of the contrast indefinable.

Page 17. Here an abrupt return is made to the subject of p. 10. Much of this page has an obvious similarity to Blake's own experiences, as described in letters to Butts and Hayley (cp. R., pp. 117–120, 168–172), but cannot safely be restricted thereto. It may be that Blake here recognizes the strength of the appeal of the senses, his position apparently being that the Visionary has no fear of mere intellectual opposition, but much of the 'Emanations of the Dead', united into Vala, the Goddess Nature. And crossing this, there is also a moral purpose.

12 'He' is not Los, but his Spectre.

15 Cp. Ross. MS. xxxv. 2 (Clar. Press, p. 177):

The look of love alarms,
Because it's fill'd with fire ;
But the look of soft deceit
Shall win the lover's hire.

Be lost, & lest he should devour Enitharmon. Ah me!
Piteous image of my soft desires & loves! O Enitharmon!
I will compell my Spectre to obey. I will restore to thee thy Children.
No one bruises or starves himself to make himself fit for labour!

'Tormented with sweet desire for these beauties of Albion,
They would never love my power if they did not seek to destroy
Enitharmon. Vala would never have sought & lovèd Albion
If she had not sought to destroy Jerusalem: such is that false
And Generating Love, a pretence of love to destroy love,
Cruel hipocrisy unlike the lovely delusions of Beulah,
And cruel forms unlike the merciful forms of Beulah's Night.

'They know not why they love nor wherefore they sicken & die,
Calling that Holy Love which is Envy, Revenge & Cruelty,
Which separated the stars from the mountains, the mountains from Man,
And left Man a little grovelling Root outside of Himself.
Negations are not Contraries. Contraries mutually Exist,
But Negations Exist Not. Exceptions & Objections & Unbeliefs
Exist not, nor shall they ever be Organizèd for ever & ever.
If thou separate from me, thou art a Negation, a meer
Reasoning & Derogation from me, an Objecting & cruel Spite

23 'They' relates to the 'Daughters of Albion' who again are equivalent to Vala: see Index, *Vala*. Their purpose to destroy Enitharmon and Jerusalem represents Blake's sense of antagonism in his *milieu* to his aspirations, his 'soft desires and loves', the emanations of the visionary spirit, either in their supreme revelation, as Jerusalem, or their highest potential manifestation in temporal existence as Enitharmon. The two modes approach so nearly that their symbols cannot be differentiated: see Index, *Emanation*.

25–32 This 'false and Generating Love' is 'Natural Religion' in both its ethical and metaphysical aspects, though here, as commonly in the later books, Blake lays emphasis upon the former significance.

32 'Himself, His real and immortal Self' (M. 14–10). The expression 'outside of Himself' means that man is separated from Imagination.

33 Cp. M. 34. 23 *note* and M. 42. 32–36:

> There is a Negation & there is a Contrary.
> The Negation must be destroy'd to redeem the Contraries.
> The Negation is the Spectre, the Reasoning Power in Man:
> This is a false Body, an Incrustation over my Immortal
> Spirit.

35 To be 'organized' is to have the perfection of form, the determinate outline, which comes only of Imagination: all else is indefinite, cloudy, 'with neither lineament nor form.' Cp. M. 26. 25–29, and see Index, *Minute Particulars*: see also General Introduction, p. 36.

37–38 These lines may contain a personal reference. In the *Advertizement*

And Malice & Envy : but my Emanation, Alas ! will become
My Contrary. O thou Negation, I will continually compell
Thee to be invisible to any but whom I please & when
And where & how I please, and never never shalt thou be Organizèd,
But as a distorted & reversèd Reflexion in the Darkness
And in the Non Entity ; nor shall that which is above
Ever descend into thee, but thou shalt be a Non Entity for ever.
And if any enter into thee, thou shalt be an Unquenchable Fire,
And he shall be a never dying Worm, mutually tormented by
Those that thou tormentest, a Hell & Despair for ever & ever.'

So Los in secret with himself communèd, & Enitharmon heard
In her darkness & was comforted : yet still she divided away
In gnawing pain from Los's bosom in the deadly Night,
First as a red Globe of blood trembling beneath his bosom.
Suspended over her he hung : he infolded her in his garments
Of wool : he hid her from the Spectre in shame & confusion of
Face. In terrors & pains of Hell & Eternal Death the
Trembling Globe shot forth Self-living ; & Los howl'd over it,
Feeding it with his groans & tears day & night without ceasing.
And the Spectrous Darkness from his back divided in temptations
And in grinding agonies, in threats, stiflings & direful strugglings.

' Go thou to Skofield : ask him if he is Bath or if he is Canterbury.
Tell him to be no more dubious : demand explicit words.
Tell him I will dash him into shivers where & at what time
I please : tell Hand & Skofield they are my ministers of evil
To those I hate : for I can hate also as well as they ! '

Blake speaks of ' the manner in which my character has been blasted these thirty years both as an Artist and as a Man ' (Ross. MS., p. 51).

42 Cp. J. 89. 14–15. 46 Cp. *Europe*, 158 *note*.

51 Cp. B. U. v. 39 *note*.

62–63 Cp. D. C. iii, p. 18 : ' The uses to society are perhaps equal of the Devil and of the Angel' ; and *ibid.*, p. 22 : 'The Plowman of Chaucer is Hercules in his supreme eternal state, divested of his spectrous shadow, which is the Miller, a terrible fellow, such as exists in all times and places for the trial of men, to astonish every neighbourhood with brutal strength and courage, to get rich and powerful, to curb the pride of Man.'

[18] From every-one of the Four Regions of Human Majesty.
There is an Outside spread Without & an Outside spread Within,
Beyond the Outline of Identity both ways, which meet in One,
An orbèd Void of doubt, despair, hunger & thirst & sorrow.
Here the Twelve Sons of Albion, join'd in dark Assembly,
Jealous of Jerusalem's children, asham'd of her little-ones,
(For Vala produc'd the Bodies, Jerusalem gave the Souls)
Became as Three Immense Wheels, turning upon one-another
Into Non-Entity, and their thunders hoarse appall the Dead
To murder their own Souls, to build a Kingdom among the Dead.

'Cast! Cast ye Jerusalem forth, The Shadow of delusions,
The Harlot daughter, Mother of pity and dishonourable forgiveness,
Our Father Albion's sin and shame! But father now no more,
Nor sons, nor hateful peace & love, nor soft complacencies,
With transgressors meeting in brotherhood around the table
Or in the porch or garden! No more the sinful delights
Of age and youth, and boy and girl, and animal and herb,
And river and mountain, and city & village, and house & family
Beneath the Oak & Palm, beneath the Vine and Fig-tree
In self-denial! But War and deadly contention Between
Father and Son, and light and love! All bold asperities
Of Haters met in deadly strife, rending the house & garden,
The unforgiving porches, the tables of enmity, and beds
And chambers of trembling & suspition, hatreds of age & youth,
And boy & girl, & animal & herb, & river & mountain,

Page 18. This does not follow from the preceding page. Line 1 seems to be left in isolation.

1–4 Whatever is referred to as 'Without' is of error. Cp. J. 71. 7: 'Without is form'd the Selfish [i.e. Spectrous] Center'; and see F. Z. i. 250 *note*. Here it relates to the body of Error, which stands in opposition to the Outline of Identity, the Human Form or Imagination: see Index, *Human Form*, and cp. M. 37. 4–12.

7 Vala is the 'natural', Jerusalem the 'spiritual'. In respect of vision Vala is apparently the symbol, the vehicle exalted by the operations of reason to the prime place, whereas Jerusalem is the vision itself.

8 The 'spectrous' and female symbols are often described as threefold: cp. J. 8. 34 *note*.

11–35 Cp. M. 17. 48 *note*. These lines develop the non-visionary attitude towards Imagination, the Human Existence itself. Contemned as a delusion, its precepts of unity, love, and forgiveness are rejected for the disruptive principles of 'Natural Religion', 'sacrifice', the denial and repression of spiritual impulses.

And city & village, and house & family, That the Perfect
May live in glory, redeem'd by Sacrifice of the Lamb
And of his children before sinful Jerusalem, To build
Babylon the City of Vala, the Goddess Virgin-Mother.
She is our Mother, Nature ! Jerusalem is our Harlot-Sister
Return'd with Children of pollution, to defile our House
With Sin and Shame. Cast, Cast her into the Potter's field !
Her little-ones She must slay upon our Altars, and her agèd
Parents must be carried into captivity to redeem her Soul,
To be for a Shame & a Curse, and to be our Slaves for ever.'

So cry Hand & Hyle, the eldest of the fathers of Albion's
Little-ones, to destroy the Divine Saviour, the Friend of Sinners.
Building Castles in desolated places and strong Fortifications,
Soon Hand mightily devour'd & absorb'd Albion's Twelve Sons ;
Out from his bosom a mighty Polypus vegetating in darkness.
And Hyle & Coban were his two chosen ones, for Emissaries
In War : forth from his bosom they went and return'd,
Like Wheels from a great Wheel reflected in the Deep.
Hoarse turn'd the Starry Wheels, rending a way in Albion's Loins
Beyond the Night of Beulah. In a dark & unknown Night,
Outstretch'd his Giant beauty on the ground in pain & tears :
[19] His Children, exil'd from his breast, pass to and fro before him ;
His birds are silent on his hills, flocks die beneath his branches ;
His tents are fall'n ; his trumpet and the sweet sound of his harp
Are silent on his clouded hills that belch forth storms & fire.
His milk of Cows & honey of Bees & fruit of golden harvest
Is gather'd in the scorching heat & in the driving rain ;
Where once he sat he weary walks in misery and pain,
His Giant beauty and perfection fallen into dust ;

26 The Perfect, the 'Elect' of *Milton*, like the 'Angels' (M. H. H. *passim*) appear to be those who accept the 'moral and self-righteous Law', 'living on Sacrifice', as opposed to 'Self-sacrifice' ; the error is twofold, first it denounces what is of vision as the capital heresy ; then it punishes it.

44 See Index, *Head, Heart, and Loins* : cp. J. 27, stanza 10 :

Albion's Spectre from his Loins
Tore forth in all the pomp of War :
Satan his name : in flames of fire
He stretch'd his Druid Pillars far.

46 See Index, *Giants*.

Page 19. 1–16 See Index, *Albion*, and cp. F. Z. ix. 94–119.

Till from within his wither'd breast grown narrow with his woes,
The corn is turn'd to thistles & the apples into poison,
The birds of song to murderous crows, his joys to bitter groans;
The voices of children in his tents to cries of helpless infants;
And self-exilèd from the face of light & shine of morning,
In the dark world, a narrow house, he wanders up and down,
Seeking for rest and finding none: and hidden far within,
His Eon weeping in the cold and desolated Earth.

All his Affections now appear withoutside: all his Sons,
Hand, Hyle & Coban, Guantok, Peachey, Brereton, Slayd & Hutton,
Scofeld, Kox, Kotope & Bowen, his Twelve Sons, Satanic Mill,
Who are the Spectres of the Twenty-four, each Double-form'd,
Revolve upon his mountains groaning in pain, beneath
The dark incessant sky seeking for rest and finding none,
Raging against their Human natures, rav'ning to gormandize
The Human majesty and beauty of the Twentyfour,
Condensing them into solid rocks with cruelty and abhorrence,
Suspition & revenge: & the seven diseases of the Soul
Settled around Albion and around Luvah in his secret cloud.
Willing the Friends endur'd for Albion's sake and for
Jerusalem his Emanation shut within his bosom,
Which harden'd against them more and more as he builded onwards
On the Gulph of Death in self-righteousness, that roll'd
Before his awful feet in pride of virtue for victory.
And Los was roof'd in from Eternity in Albion's Cliffs
Which stand upon the ends of Beulah; and withoutside all
Appear'd a rocky form against the Divine Humanity.

16 The 'Eon' is the Emanation, here Jerusalem: cp. M. 9. 1.

17 Cp. F. Z. i. 250 *note*.

19 Cp. J. 39. 3–5:

Withoutside is the Mill, intricate, dreadful,
And fill'd with cruel tortures; but no mortal man can find the Mill
Of Satan in his mortal pilgrimage of seventy years.

20 It is difficult to discover whether the 'Twenty-four' here mentioned are the 'Friends of Albion', who seem to be alluded to in l. 24. The 'Spectre Sons of Albion' are not elsewhere related to them. See Index, *Los, Note II*.

25 Cp. J. 4. 26 *note*. 26 Cp. J. 9. 9 *note*.

27 See Index, *Luvah*, I. i.

33 Cp. B. U. v. 1–21: M. 19. 28–30: and J. 74. 28–29. The confinement of Los within the limits of mundane life is the condition of the spiritualizing of the world.

34 Cp. J. 18. 1 *note*.

Albion's Circumference was clos'd : his Center began dark'ning
Into the Night of Beulah, and the Moon of Beulah rose
Clouded with storms. Los, his strong Guard, walk'd round
    beneath the Moon,
And Albion fled inward among the currents of his rivers.

He found Jerusalem upon the River of his City soft repos'd
In the arms of Vala, assimilating in one with Vala,
The Lilly of Havilah : and they sang soft thro' Lambeth's vales,
In a sweet moony night & silence that they had created
With a blue sky spread over with wings and a mild moon,
Dividing & uniting into many female forms, Jerusalem
Trembling ; then in one comingling in eternal tears,
Sighing to melt his Giant beauty on the moony river.

[20] But when they saw Albion fall'n upon mild Lambeth's vale,
Astonish'd, Terrified, they hover'd over his Giant limbs.
Then thus Jerusalem spoke while Vala wove the veil of tears,
Weeping in pleadings of Love in the web of despair :

'Wherefore hast thou shut me into the winter of human life,
And clos'd up the sweet regions of youth and virgin innocence,
Where we live, forgetting error, not pondering on evil,
Among my lambs & brooks of water, among my warbling
    birds ;
Where we delight in innocence before the face of the Lamb,
Going in and out before him in his love and sweet affection ?'

36 Cp. J. 71. 6–9:

What is Above is Within, for everything in Eternity is translucent.
The Circumference is Within ; Without is formed the Selfish Center :
And the Circumference still expands, going forward to Eternity,
And the Center has Eternal States ; these States we now explore.

38 Cp. M. 40. 52.

40 'He' is Los : the 'River of his City' is the Thames: cp. J. 4. 31 *note*.

41 Cp. J. 5. 60–65.

42 The only passage that seems to throw any light on this title for Vala is F. Z. vii. 237 seq. For what may be Havilah in another sense cp. J. 49. 15–16.

44 The Moon, associated with the Night of Error, the 'dim region of death' (J. 34. 11), is regarded from two points of view that arise from the dual concept of mundane life. In the first place, it is part of the illusion created by perverted vision (J. 45. 20 : 66. 34), and is joined with the feminine symbols, Vala or Nature, the Daughters of Albion, and the Fairies, spirits of vegetative life. But it is also a means to regeneration through the power of Los and his fellows (M. 28. 40–44 : J. 56. 18) in which sense it is often connected with Beulah. In the present passage the first meaning is intended.

Page 20. 3 The 'veil of tears' is used here in the contrary sense to J. 12. 39–40. In association with Vala and kindred symbols it is the 'veil of human miseries' (M. 28. 62), the 'veil of tears & sorrows' (J. 60. 34), and not distinguishable from the Veil of Vala. See Index, *Weaving*, I.

Vala replied, weeping & trembling, hiding in her veil :

' When winter rends the hungry family and the snow falls
Upon the ways of men, hiding the paths of man and beast,
Then mourns the wanderer ; then he repents his wanderings & eyes
The distant forest ; then the slave groans in the dungeon of stone,
The captive in the mill of the stranger, sold for scanty hire.
They view their former life : they number moments over and over,
Stringing them on their remembrance as on a thread of sorrow.
Thou art my sister and my daughter : thy shame is mine also :
Ask me not of my griefs : thou knowest all my griefs.'

Jerusalem answer'd with soft tears over the valleys :

' O Vala, what is Sin, that thou shudderest and weepest
At sight of thy once lov'd Jerusalem ! What is Sin but a little
Error & fault that is soon forgiven ! But mercy is not a Sin,
Nor pity nor love nor kind forgiveness. O, if I have Sinnèd
Forgive & pity me ! O, unfold thy Veil in mercy and love !
Slay not my little ones, belovèd Virgin daughter of Babylon,
Slay not my infant loves & graces, beautiful daughter of Moab.
I cannot put off the human form. I strive but strive in vain.
When Albion rent thy beautiful net of gold and silver twine—
Thou hadst woven it with art : thou hadst caught me in the bands
Of love : thou refusedst to let me go—Albion beheld thy beauty,
Beautiful thro' our Love's comeliness, beautiful thro' pity.
The Veil shone with thy brightness in the eyes of Albion,
Because it inclos'd pity & love, because we lov'd one-another.
Albion lov'd thee : he rent thy Veil : he embrac'd thee : he lov'd thee.

11–20 This representation of Vala is unique, being dramatic rather than symbolic. Vala speaks as if she were as much the victim of man's changed state as Jerusalem.

15–16 Cp. M., extra p. 17. 11. 22–25 See General Introduction, p. 73.

27–28 See Index, *Minute Particulars*.

30–41 The mythical incident alluded to here and in p. 23. 5–6 cannot be related to anything else in Blake. To rend the net or veil of the Female generally symbolizes the achievement of emancipation from the delusions of morality and empiricism : cp. J. 68. 42–43 and F. Z. viii. 290 *note*. But from the latter part of this passage such interpretation scarcely seems possible. It may, however, be surmised that, since the reference is clearly to the ' golden age ' before the fall (cp. l. 41), the veil relates to the ' allegoric and mental signification ' which when man fell, was perverted into 'corporeal command' (D. C. v, p. 41). If this be so, Blake may intend an

Astonish'd at his beauty & perfection, thou forgavest his furious love.
I redounded from Albion's bosom in my virgin loveliness ;
The Lamb of God reciev'd me in his arms, he smil'd upon us :
He made me his Bride & Wife ; he gave thee to Albion.
Then was a time of love. O why is it passèd away ?'

Then Albion broke silence and with groans reply'd :

[21] ' O Vala ! O Jerusalem ! do you delight in my groans !
You O lovely forms, you have preparèd my death-cup.
The disease of Shame covers me from head to feet : I have no hope.
Every boil upon my body is a separate & deadly Sin.
Doubt first assail'd me ; then Shame took possession of me.
Shame divides Families ; Shame hath divided Albion in sunder.
First fled my Sons, & then my Daughters, then my Wild Animations ;
My Cattle next; last ev'n the Dog of my Gate; the Forests fled,
The Corn-fields & the breathing Gardens outside separated,
The Sea, the Stars, the Sun, the Moon, driv'n forth by my disease.
All is Eternal Death unless you can weave a chaste
Body over an unchaste Mind ! Vala ! O that thou wert pure,
That the deep wound of Sin might be clos'd up with the Needle
And with the Loom, to cover Gwendolen & Ragan with costly Robes
Of Natural Virtue ; for their Spiritual forms without a Veil
Wither in Luvah's Sepulcher. I thrust him from my presence
And all my Children follow'd his loud howlings into the Deep.
Jerusalem ! dissembler Jerusalem ! I look into thy bosom :

intermediate state between the 'golden' and the fallen ages wherein communion with the truth of eternity is mediate, and accompanied by consciousness of the symbol : see note on twofold vision, General Introduction, p. 25. Ethically the veil represents a state of untrammelled pity and love : cp. ll. 34–35.

Page 21. 3 Cp. J. 10. 34 *note*.

7–10 See Index, *Albion*.

11–15 Albion speaks in terms of 'Natural Morality', so that the 'chaste body' is the pretence to prudence that inhibits native impulse. Repression, failing to eradicate, is content to hide with its 'costly robe', its sacraments and religious sanctions, the reprobated impulsive acts.

15–17 See Index, *Luvah*. The reference in ll. 16–17 is obscure, unless it is to F. Z. iii. 44–96 and J. 29. 33–80.

18–27 Albion again speaks as one obsessed by illusions of morality, so that Jerusalem seems to him an evil : cp. J. 4. 21 *note*.

I discover thy secret places. Cordella ! I behold
Thee whom I thought pure as the heavens in innocence & fear,
Thy Tabernacle taken down, thy secret Cherubim disclosèd.
Art thou broken ? Ah me, Sabrina, running by my side !
In childhood what wert thou ? unutterable anguish ! Conwenna !
Thy cradled infancy is most piteous. O hide, O hide !
Their secret gardens were made paths to the traveller.
I knew not of their secret loves with those I hated most,
Nor that their every thought was Sin & secret appetite.
Hyle sees in fear ; he howls in fury over them. Hand sees
In jealous fear ; in stern accusation, with cruel stripes,
He drives them thro' the Streets of Babylon before my face
Because they taught Luvah to rise into my clouded heavens.
Battersea and Chelsea mourn for Cambel & Gwendolen ;
Hackney and Holloway sicken for Estrild & Ignoge,
Because the Peak, Malvern & Cheviot Reason in Cruelty ;
Penmaenmawr & Dhinas-bran Demonstrate in Unbelief ;
Manchester & Liverpool are in tortures of Doubt and Despair ;
Malden & Colchester Demonstrate. I hear my Children's voices ;
I see their piteous faces gleam out upon the cruel winds
From Lincoln & Norwich, from Edinburgh & Monmouth.
I see them distant from my bosom scourg'd along the roads ;
Then lost in clouds I hear their tender voices : clouds divide ;
I see them die beneath the whips of the Captains ; they are taken
In solemn pomp into Chaldea across the bredths of Europe.
Six months they lie embalm'd in silent death, worshippèd,
Carried in Arks of Oak before the armies : in the spring

32–35 Cp. J. 33. 12. Battersea and Chelsea, being to the west of London, apparently represent the state of visionary activity in mortal life, the west being always the quarter of Imagination. The north and east are associated with the contrary state of subjection to error, so that Hackney and Holloway would seem to be significant of that condition. This interpretation would give a definite value to the contrasted verbs 'mourn' and 'sicken'. The mountains are 'barren Mountains of Moral Virtue' (J. 31. 19, and cp. J. 4. 28–31)

36–37 These places have the same general meaning as Hackney and Holloway, noted above. The symbolism of the cities in ll. 36–39 cannot be interpreted with certainty.

42–47 This passage emphasizes the connexion between the 'False Female' and 'Corporeal War' (see M., Preface, *note* 2). The symbols Chaldea, Europe, and the Ark have all a sinister connotation. The periods of alternate suspension and revival in the activities of the 'Female' seem to stand in contrast to the parallel phenomenon described in connexion with Ahania : cp. F. Z. ix. 209 *note*.

Bursting their Arks they rise again to life; they play before
The Armies. I hear their loud cymbals & their deadly cries.
Are the Dead cruel? are those who are infolded in moral Law
Revengeful? O that Death & Annihilation were the same!'

Then Vala answer'd, spreading her scarlet Veil over Albion:

[22] 'Albion thy fear has made me tremble; thy terrors have surrounded me.
Thy Sons have nail'd me on the Gates, piercing my hands & feet;
Till Skofield's Nimrod, the mighty Huntsman Jehovah came,
With Cush his Son & took me down. He in a golden Ark
Bears me before his Armies, tho' my Shadow hovers here.
The flesh of multitudes fed & nouris'd me in my childhood;
My morn & evening food were prepar'd in Battles of Men.
Great is the cry of the Hounds of Nimrod along the Valley
Of Vision: they scent the odor of War in the Valley of Vision.
All Love is lost: terror succeeds & Hatred instead of Love,
And stern demands of Right & Duty instead of Liberty.
Once thou wast to me the loveliest Son of heaven, but now
Where shall I hide from thy dread countenance & searching eyes?
I have lookèd into the secret Soul of him I lovèd
And in the dark recesses found Sin & can never return.'

Albion again utter'd his voice beneath the silent Moon:

'I brought Love into light of day to pride in chaste beauty,
I brought Love into light & fancied Innocence is no more.'

Then spoke Jerusalem: 'O Albion! my Father Albion!
Why wilt thou number every little fibre of my Soul,
Spreading them out before the Sun like stalks of flax to dry?
The Infant Joy is beautiful, but its anatomy

49 Annihilation here is utter extinction, and not the mystical putting off of the Selfhood, for which see Index, *Self-Annihilation*.

50 See Index, *Weaving*, I, and cp. J. 22. 30.

Page 22. 1 Cp. F. Z. i. 29.

3 Messrs. Russell and Maclagan read 'before Jehovah': some such words may be necessary. But in any case the association of Nimrod with Jehovah, the God of Sinai and Horeb, is significant: see below, ll. 8–11.

8 For the 'valley of vision' cp. Isa. xxii. 1–5.

10–12 Lines repeated from F. Z. i. 30–32.

14–15 Repeated with slight verbal changes from F. Z. i. 38–39.

20–24 These lines are taken, with slight verbal changes, from F. Z. i. 41–45. Their theme appears frequently in the poems of the Rossetti and Pickering MSS.

Horrible, ghast & deadly : nought shalt thou find in it
But dark despair & everlasting brooding melancholy ! '

Then Albion turn'd his face toward Jerusalem & spoke :

' Hide thou, Jerusalem, in impalpable voidness, not to be
Touch'd by the hand nor seen with the eye. O Jerusalem,
Would thou wert not, & that thy place might never be found.
But come, O Vala, with knife & cup : drain my blood
To the last drop, then hide me in thy Scarlet Tabernacle !
For I see Luvah whom I slew. I behold him in my Spectre,
As I behold Jerusalem in thee, O Vala dark and cold ! '

Jerusalem then stretch'd her hand toward the Moon & spoke :

' Why should Punishment Weave the Veil with Iron Wheels of War,
When Forgiveness might it Weave with Wings of Cherubim ? '

Loud groan'd Albion from mountain to mountain & replied :

[23] ' Jerusalem ! Jerusalem ! deluding shadow of Albion !
Daughter of my phantasy ! unlawful pleasure ! Albion's curse !
I came here with intention to annihilate thee. But
My soul is melted away, inwoven within the Veil.
Hast thou again knitted the Veil of Vala which I for thee
Pitying rent in ancient times ? I see it whole and more
Perfect and shining with beauty ! But thou, O wretched Father ! '

Jerusalem reply'd, like a voice heard from a sepulcher
' Father ! once piteous ! Is Pity a Sin ? Embalm'd in Vala's bosom
In an Eternal Death for Albion's sake, our best belovèd !
Thou art my Father & my Brother ! Why hast thou hidden me
Remote from the divine Vision, my Lord & Saviour ? '

29 Cp. J. 63. 39 : ' The Druid Knife of Revenge & the Poison Cup of Jealousy.' See Index, *Druid*.

Page 23. 4 Cp. J. 68. 48–68 for a fuller description of the spiritual enervation induced by the manifold illusion which is the Veil of Vala.

6 Cp. J. 20. 36.

7 It may be that a line has been deleted after l. 7. The indications in the originals suggest it, but not clearly.

11–12 Cp. J. 4. 15–16.

Trembling stood Albion at her words, in jealous dark despair.

He felt that Love and Pity are the same, a soft repose,
Inward complacency of Soul, a Self-annihilation.

'I have errèd. I am ashamèd, and will never return more.
I have taught my children sacrifices of cruelty: what shall I answer?
I will hide it from Eternals. I will give myself for my Children.
Which way soever I turn, I behold Humanity and Pity!'

He recoil'd: he rush'd outwards: he bore the Veil whole away.
His fires redound from his Dragon Altars in Errors returning.
He drew the Veil of Moral Virtue, woven for Cruel Laws,
And cast it into the Atlantic Deep to catch the Souls of the Dead.
He stood between the Palm tree & the Oak of weeping
Which stand upon the edge of Beulah, and there Albion sunk
Down in sick pallid languor. These were his last words, relapsing
Hoarse from his rocks, from caverns of Derbyshire & Wales
And Scotland, utter'd from the Circumference into Eternity:

'Blasphemous Sons of Feminine delusion! God in the dreary Void
Dwells from Eternity, wide separated from the Human Soul.
But thou, deluding Image, by whom imbu'd the Veil I rent,
Lo! here is Vala's Veil whole, for a Law, a Terror & a Curse!
And therefore God takes vengeance on me: from my clay-cold bosom
My children wander, trembling victims of his Moral Justice.
His snows fall on me and cover me, while in the Veil I fold

19 Cp. J. 12. 15: 'God is within and without: he is even in the depths of Hell', God here being the 'Divine Pity and Humanity', not the God of ll. 29–34 below.

23 See Index, *Atlantic Continent*. 24 Cp. F. Z. ii. 206 *note*.

25 For the 'edge' or the 'Ends' of Beulah, cp. F. Z. viii. 231–232:

> We now behold the Ends of Beulah; & we now behold
> Where Death Eternal is put off Eternally.

27–28 These caves Blake associates with 'the Druidical age, which began to turn allegoric and mental signification into corporeal command, whereby human sacrifice would have depopulated the earth' (D. C. v, p. 41). Among the monuments of this period he mentions 'the caves in Cornwall, Wales, Derbyshire and Scotland' (*ibid.*, p. 40).

29 The identity of the 'Blasphemous Sons of Feminine delusion' is not clearly apparent, though the tone of hostility to Imagination in the rest of the speech would suggest that it is a reference to the Eternals; cp. l. 28. God here is 'the God of this world, Satan', who 'made himself a God & destroyed the Human Form Divine' (M., extra p. 32*. 13): see below, l. 38, and J. 10. 46–49. 31 Cp. J. 20. 36.

My dying limbs. Therefore, O Manhood, if thou art aught
But a meer Phantasy, hear dying Albion's Curse!
May God, who dwells in this dark Ulro & voidness, vengeance take,
And draw thee down into this Abyss of sorrow and torture,
Like me thy Victim. O that Death & Annihilation were the same!

[24] 'What have I said? What have I done? O all-powerful Human Words!
You recoil back upon me in the blood of the Lamb slain in his Children.
Two bleeding Contraries, equally true, are his Witnesses against me.
We rearèd mighty Stones: we dancèd naked around them,
Thinking to bring Love into light of day to Jerusalem's shame,
Displaying our Giant limbs to all the winds of heaven. Sudden
Shame siez'd us; we could not look on one-another for abhorrence: the Blue
Of our immortal Veins & all their Hosts fled from our Limbs,
And wander'd distant in a dismal Night clouded & dark.
The Sun fled from the Briton's forehead, the Moon from his mighty loins:
Scandinavia fled with all his mountains fill'd with groans.

'O what is Life & what is Man? O what is Death? Wherefore
Are you, my Children, natives in the Grave to where I go!
Or are you born to feed the hungry ravenings of Destruction,
To be the sport of Accident, to waste in Wrath & Love a weary
Life, in brooding cares & anxious labours that prove but chaff?
O Jerusalem! Jerusalem! I have forsaken thy Courts,
Thy Pillars of ivory & gold, thy Curtains of silk & fine
Linen, thy Pavements of precious stones, thy Walls of pearl
And gold, thy Gates of Thanksgiving, thy Windows of Praise,
Thy Clouds of Blessing, thy Cherubims of Tender-mercy

36 The Manhood is Jesus, the Divine Humanity: see Index, *Jesus*.

40 Cp. J. 21. 49 *note*.

Page 24. 2 Apparently 'Albion's Curse', that the 'Manhood be drawn into the Abyss of sorrow and torture' is fulfilled in the Incarnation. See Index, *Incarnation*, and cp. J. 27, *poem*, ll. 57–64.

3 The 'Two bleeding Contraries' may refer to the Incarnation and Crucifixion. For the 'Two Witnesses' cp. M. 22. 4 *note*.

4–11 See Index, *Albion*, and cp. J. 21. 5–10.

5 Cp. J. 22. 17–18.

18–22 Compare the similar description of Golgonooza, J. 12. 30–41.

Stretching their Wings sublime over the Little-ones of Albion.
O Human Imagination! O Divine Body! I have Crucified,
I have turnèd my back upon thee into the Wastes of Moral Law:
There Babylon is builded in the Waste, founded in Human desolation.
O Babylon! thy Watchman stands over thee in the night;
Thy severe Judge all the day long proves thee, O Babylon,
With provings of destruction, with giving thee thy heart's desire.
But Albion is cast forth to the Potter, his Children to the Builders,
To build Babylon, because they have forsaken Jerusalem.
The Walls of Babylon are Souls of Men; her Gates the Groans
Of Nations; her Towers are the Miseries of once happy Families;
Her Streets are pavèd with Destruction, her Houses built with Death,
Her Palaces with Hell & the Grave, her Synagogues with Torments
Of ever-hardening Despair, squar'd & polish'd with cruel skill.
Yet thou wast lovely as the summer cloud upon my hills
When Jerusalem was thy heart's desire in times of youth & love.
Thy Sons came to Jerusalem with gifts: she sent them away
With blessings on their hands & on their feet, blessings of gold,
And pearl, & diamond; thy Daughters sang in her Courts;
They came up to Jerusalem; they walkèd before Albion.
In the Exchanges of London every Nation walk'd,
And London walk'd in every Nation, mutual in love & harmony.
Albion cover'd the whole Earth, England encompass'd the Nations,
Mutual each within other's bosom in Visions of Regeneration.
Jerusalem cover'd the Atlantic Mountains & the Erythrean

26 Los, 'the Watchman of Eternity' (M. 23. 9) may be intended here: his purpose is to annihilate the error of Vala or Babylon at the end of time.

31–35 Contrast with this the parallel description of Jerusalem and Golgonooza, J., pp. 12–13. And cp. F. Z. viii. 211–220.

34–49 The general reference of the whole passage is, in diverse symbols, to the ideal Unity anterior to the Fall.

36–50 For the significance of Vala before the Fall, see J. 20. 30 *note*.

40 Cp. J. 10. 17 *note*.

45 Cp. J. 88. 3–5:

When in Eternity Man converses with Man, they enter
Into each other's Bosom (which are Universes of delight)
In mutual interchange.

From bright Japan & China to Hesperia, France & England.
Mount Zion lifted his head in every Nation under heaven,
And the Mount of Olives was beheld over the whole Earth.
The footsteps of the Lamb of God were there; but now no more,
No more shall I behold him; he is clos'd in Luvah's Sepulcher.
Yet why these smitings of Luvah, the gentlest mildest Zoa?
If God was Merciful this could not be. O Lamb of God,
Thou art a delusion and Jerusalem is my Sin! O my Children,
I have educated you in the crucifying cruelties of Demonstration
Till you have assum'd the Providence of God & slain your Father.
Dost thou appear before me, who liest dead in Luvah's Sepulcher?
Dost thou forgive me, thou who wast Dead & art Alive?
Look not so merciful upon me, O thou Slain Lamb of God!
I die! I die in thy arms, tho' Hope is banish'd from me.'

Thund'ring the Veil rushes from his hand, Vegetating Knot by
Knot, Day by Day, Night by Night: loud roll the indignant Atlantic
Waves & the Erythrean, turning up the bottoms of the Deeps.

[25] And there was heard a great lamenting in Beulah: all the Regions
Of Beulah were movèd as the tender bowels are movèd, & they said:

'Why did you take Vengeance, O ye Sons of the mighty Albion,
Planting these Oaken Groves, Erecting these Dragon Temples?
Injury the Lord heals but Vengeance cannot be healèd.
As the Sons of Albion have done to Luvah, so they have in him

47 That is, from East to West: see Index, *Cardinal Points*.

49 The association of the Mount of Olives with Jesus' life and its proximity to Jerusalem suggest its significance here.

50–51 See Index, *Luvah, Note I*. 52 Cp. J. 29. 61–64.

55 Cp. J. 65. 22–28.

57 Albion addresses Jesus. To read, 'thou who liest', etc. would make the sense plainer. 61 Cp. J. 23. 20–23.

Page 25. 4 Symbols relating to Natural Religion, drawn from Druidical tradition, often occur in the later writings. The term 'Dragon' or 'Serpent Temples' (J. 42. 76) may be derived from Jacob Bryant or contemporary antiquarians who explained the monuments at Abury in Wiltshire and elsewhere to be dragon temples, Arkite symbols of the Deluge.

5–11 See General Introduction, p. 73.

6 Luvah in this passage, as in J. 65. 56–79, appears to be the 'Victim' of the Spectre Sons of Albion: cp. J. 58. 13–15, and Index, *Luvah*.

Done to the Divine Lord & Saviour, who suffers with those that suffer.
For not one sparrow can suffer, & the whole Universe not suffer also
In all its Regions, & its Father & Saviour not pity and weep.
But Vengeance is the destroyer of Grace & Repentance in the bosom
Of the Injurer, in which the Divine Lamb is cruelly slain.
Descend, O Lamb of God & take away the imputation of Sin
By the Creation of States & the deliverance of Individuals Evermore. Amen.'

Thus wept they in Beulah over the Four Regions of Albion :
But many doubted & despair'd & imputed Sin & Righteousness
To Individuals & not to States : and these Slept in Ulro.

12–13 See Index, *States.*
Page 26. A full-page design, the figures of ' Hand ' and ' Jerusalem ', while in the space about them is the rude quatrain :

SUCH VISIONS HAVE APPEAR'D TO ME
AS I MY ORDER'D RACE HAVE RUN.
JERUSALEM IS NAMED LIBERTY
AMONG THE SONS OF ALBION.

For the ' Sons of Albion ' in the last line of the quatrain cp. M. 3. 23 *note* and J. 54. 5.

[27]

To the Jews

Jerusalem the Emanation of the Giant Albion! Can it be! Is it a Truth that the Learned have explored? Was Britain the Primitive Seat of the Patriarchal Religion.[1] If it is true, my title-page is also True, that Jerusalem was & is the Emanation of the Giant Albion. It is True, and cannot be controverted. Ye are united, O ye Inhabitants of Earth, in One Religion, The Religion of Jesus, the most Ancient, the Eternal & the Everlasting Gospel.[2] The Wicked will turn it to Wickedness, the Righteous to Righteousness. Amen! Huzza! Selah!

'All things Begin & End in Albion's Ancient Druid Rocky Shore.' [3]

Your Ancestors derived their origin from Abraham,[4] Heber, Shem, and Noah, who were Druids, as the Druid Temples (which are the Patriarchal Pillars & Oak Groves) over the whole Earth witness to this day.

You have a tradition, that Man anciently contain'd in his mighty limbs all things in Heaven & Earth:[5] this you recieved from the Druids.

Page 27. The significance of the title 'To the Jews' is not clear. They are called the 'Inhabitants of Earth' and may comprehend both the 'Wicked' and the 'Righteous', who are addressed in the prologues to the succeeding chapters as 'Deists' and 'Christians' respectively.

[1] Cp. Milton's *Areopagitica* (ed. Arber, p. 68): 'Therefore the studies of learning in her deepest Sciences have bin so ancient, and so eminent among us, that Writers of good antiquity, and ablest judgement have been perswaded that ev'n the school of *Pythagoras*, and the *Persian* wisdom took beginning from the old Philosophy of this Iland.'

[2] Cp. D. C., pp. 43–44: 'The antiquities of every Nation under Heaven is no less sacred than that of the Jews. They are the same thing, as Jacob Bryant, and all antiquaries have proved. . . . All had originally one language and one religion, the Everlasting Gospel. Antiquity preaches the Gospel of Jesus.' The reference is to Jacob Bryant's *New System or An Analysis of Ancient Mythology* (1774–1776), or to William Stukeley's *Stonehenge* (1740), or *Abury* (1743).

[3] This line occurs J. 32. 15. The quotation marks are Blake's. The line below, 'But now the Starry Heavens are fled from the mighty limbs of Albion', is similarly marked. It repeats J. 75. 27. It is possible for these points to be taken as evidence proving that this page was composed later than pages 32 and 75, from which the quotations were made.

[4] Cp. D. C., p. 41: 'Adam was a Druid, and Noah; also Abraham was called to succeed the Druidical age, which began to turn allegoric and mental signification into corporeal command, whereby human sacrifice would have depopulated the earth.'

[5] Possibly Blake had some knowledge of the Cabbalah, with its doctrine

'But now the Starry Heavens are fled from the mighty limbs of Albion.'

Albion was the Parent of the Druids,[6] & in his Chaotic State of Sleep Satan & Adam & the whole World was Created by the Elohim.[7]

The fields from Islington to Marybone,
To Primrose Hill and Saint John's Wood,
Were builded over with pillars of gold;
And there Jerusalem's pillars stood.

Her Little-ones ran on the fields,
The Lamb of God among them seen,
And fair Jerusalem, his Bride,
Among the little meadows green.

Pancrass & Kentish-town repose
Among her golden pillars high,
Among her golden arches which
Shine upon the starry sky.

The Jew's-harp-house & the Green Man,
The Ponds where Boys to bathe delight,
The fields of Cows by Wil[la]ns farm,
Shine in Jerusalem's pleasant sight.

She walks upon our meadows green;
The Lamb of God walks by her side;
And every English Child is seen,
Children of Jesus & his Bride,

of the union of the Sephiroth with the Archetypal and heavenly Man, and its theory of the revealed universe, wherein Man unites in himself all forms, see Index, *Albion*.

[6] Cp. *Cat.* 1810: 'an Aged patriarch is awaked by his aged wife: he is Albion, our Ancestor, patriarch of the Atlantic Continent, whose History Preceded that of the Hebrews, in whose Sleep, or Chaos, Creation began.'

[7] Cp. Crabb Robinson (S., p. 274): 'Atheism consists in worshipping the natural world, which same natural world, properly speaking, is nothing real, but a mere illusion produced by Satan.'

Poem: 1–24 Cp. J. 29. 1–26. The districts named, lying to the west or north-west of London, indicate the state of visionary activity symbolically associated with the western quarter.

13 The Jew's Harp House stood in Marylebone Park: it was pulled down in 1812 to give place to Regent's Park. The Green Man was a coaching inn at Waltham.

14 These may be the ponds afterwards traced to their source by Mr. Pickwick.

15 The name of the farm is illegible in Blake's autograph. The following readings have been suggested: Willan's (Shepherd); Welling's (W. B. Yeats); William's (E. J. Ellis and Clar. Press). Willan's farm stood where Regent's Park is now.

Forgiving trespasses and sins 21
Lest Babylon, with cruel Og,
With Moral & Self-righteous Law,
Should Crucify in Satan's Synagogue.

What are those golden Builders doing 25
Near mournful ever-weeping Paddington,
Standing above that mighty Ruin
Where Satan the first victory won;

Where Albion slept beneath the fatal Tree, 29
And the Druids' golden Knife
Rioted in human gore,
In Offerings of Human Life?

They groan'd aloud on London Stone, 33
They groan'd aloud on Tyburn's Brook;
Albion gave his deadly groan,
And all the Atlantic Mountains shook.

Albion's Spectre from his Loins, 37
Tore forth in all the pomp of War;
Satan his name; in flames of fire
He stretch'd his Druid Pillars far.

Jerusalem fell from Lambeth's Vale, 41
Down thro' Poplar & Old Bow,
Thro' Malden & acros[s] the Sea
In War & howling, death & woe.

The Rhine was red with human blood; 45
The Danube roll'd a purple tide;
On the Euphrates Satan stood,
And over Asia stretch'd his pride.

He wither'd up sweet Zion's Hill 49
From every Nation of the Earth;
He wither'd up Jerusalem's Gates,
And in a dark Land gave her birth.

He wither'd up the Human Form 53
By laws of sacrifice for sin,
Till it became a Mortal Worm,
But O! translucent all within.

25–26 Cp. J. 12. 25–28. 36 See Index, *Atlantic.*

41–44 Jerusalem falls from Lambeth, the spiritual centre (cp. M. 4. 14 *note*) eastward, i.e. into Ulro, or error.

48 For Asia see *The Song of Los*, Introduction.

53–57 The same idea is expressed in different symbols, B. U., chap. ix.

The Divine Vision still was seen, 57
Still was the Human Form Divine;
Weeping in weak & mortal clay,
O Jesus, still the Form was thine!

And thine the Human Face, & thine 61
The Human Hands & Feet & Breath,
Entering thro' the Gates of Birth,
And passing thro' the Gates of Death.

And O thou Lamb of God, whom I 65
Slew in my dark self-righteous pride,
Art thou return'd to Albion's Land,
And is Jerusalem thy Bride?

Come to my arms, & never more 69
Depart, but dwell for ever here;
Create my Spirit to thy Love;
Subdue my Spectre to thy Fear.

Spectre of Albion! warlike Fiend! 73
In clouds of blood & ruin roll'd,
I here reclaim thee as my own,
My Selfhood! Satan arm'd in gold!

Is this thy soft Family-Love, 77
Thy cruel Patriarchal pride,
Planting thy Family alone,
Destroying all the World beside?

A man's worst enemies are those 81
Of his own house & family;
And he who makes his law a curse
By his own law shall surely die.

In my Exchanges every Land 85
Shall walk; & mine in every Land
Mutual shall build Jerusalem
Both heart in heart & hand in hand. 88

75–76 Cp. M. 40. 10–12:
Awake, Albion, awake! reclaim thy Reasoning Spectre. Subdue
Him to the Divine Mercy: cast him down into the Lake
Of Los that ever burneth with fire, ever & ever, Amen.

77 Cp. J. 38. 12 *note*.

81 Cp. J. 46. 25–28:
Alas! The time will come when a man's worst enemies
Shall be those of his own house and family in a Religion
Of Generation to destroy by Sin and Atonement happy Jerusalem,
The Bride and Wife of the Lamb.

85–88 Cp. J. 24. 42–43.

If Humility is Christianity, you, O Jews, are the true Christians. If your tradition that Man contained in his Limbs all Animals is True, & they were separated from him by cruel Sacrifices, and when compulsory cruel Sacrifices had brought Humanity into a Feminine Tabernacle in the loins of Abraham & David, the Lamb of God, the Saviour, became apparent on Earth as the Prophets had foretold.[1] The Return of Israel is a Return to Mental Sacrifice & War. Take up the Cross, O Israel, & follow Jesus!

[1] The apodosis of this conditional clause seems to be missing. Abraham would be defined as a 'State' wherein the process of regeneration begins, either for the individual or the race, that process being foreshadowed in the promise of the Incarnation. All the references to David, with the doubtful exception of J. 90. 30, have regenerative connotation: cp. J. 73. 28 : 73. 40 : 85. 5. Mention of 'compulsory cruel Sacrifices' recalls the passage from D. C. p. 41, quoted under *note* 4 above, which, with other references to Druidism on this page bear a strong likeness to the fantastic archaeological theories of William Stukeley: see General Introduction, p. 79, *note*.

[28]

Jerusalem

Chap: 2.

Every ornament of perfection and every labour of love
In all the Garden of Eden & in all the golden mountains,
Was become an envied horror and a remembrance of jealousy,
And every Act a Crime, and Albion the punisher & judge.

And Albion spoke from his secret seat and said :

'All these ornaments are crimes ; they are made by the labours
Of loves, of unnatural consanguinities and friendships,
Horrid to think of when enquired deeply into ; and all
These hills & valleys are accursèd witnesses of Sin.
I therefore condense them into solid rocks, stedfast,
A foundation and certainty and demonstrative truth,
That Man be separate from Man : & here I plant my seat.'

Cold snows drifted around him : ice cover'd his loins around.
He sat by Tyburn's brook, and underneath his heel shot up
A deadly Tree : he nam'd it Moral Virtue and the Law
Of God who dwells in Chaos hidden from the human sight.

The Tree spread over him its cold shadows ; (Albion groan'd).
They bent down ; they felt the earth ; and again enrooting
Shot into many a Tree, an endless labyrinth of woe.

From willing sacrifice of Self, to sacrifice of (miscall'd) Enemies
For Atonement, Albion began to erect twelve Altars
Of rough unhewn rocks before the Potter's Furnace.

2 See Index, *Eden* and *Atlantic*.

4 The 'Indefinite Spectre who is the Rational power' (J. 64. 5) opposes 'temptations of doubt and despair' to the definite expression of inspiration in act. This is developed on the artistic side in the *Descriptive Catalogue*, §§ ix and xv.

6 Judged according to the Moral Law, the visionary ethic is immoral : compare the frequent references to Jerusalem as the 'harlot', e. g. J. 18. 11–12 : 23. 1–2.

10–12 Cp. J. 4. 26 *note*, and see Index, *Minute Particulars*.

14 Cp. F. Z. ii. 249 *note*.

15 See Index, *Mundane Shell, Note I*. ii.

18 Cp. B. A. ii i. 5–21.

20 *Read* Turning from willing sacrifice *&c*.

He nam'd them Justice and Truth. And Albion's Sons
Must have become the first Victims, being the first transgressors :
But they fled to the mountains to seek ransom, building A Strong
Fortification against the Divine Humanity and Mercy,
In Shame & Jealousy to annihilate Jerusalem.

[29] Then the Divine Vision like a silent Sun appear'd above
Albion's dark rocks, setting behind the Gardens of Kensington
On Tyburn's River in clouds of blood, where was mild Zion Hill's
Most ancient promontory : and in the Sun a Human Form appear'd.
And thus the Voice Divine went forth upon the rocks of Albion :

' I elected Albion for my glory. I gave to him the Nations
Of the whole Earth. He was the Angel of my Presence, and all
The Sons of God were Albion's Sons, and Jerusalem was my joy.
The Reactor hath hid himself thro' envy. I behold him,
But you cannot behold him till he be reveal'd in his System.
Albion's Reactor must have a Place prepar'd. Albion must Sleep
The Sleep of Death, till the Man of Sin & Repentance be reveal'd.
Hidden in Albion's Forests he lurks ; he admits of no Reply
From Albion, but hath founded his Reaction into a Law

23–27 The altars of Justice and Truth, operating even from the moment of man's entry into the world, the Potter's Furnace, represent the false ideals, the ' hypocritic holiness of the moral law '. Cp. M. 28. The conduct of the Sons of Albion is difficult to interpret, unless it repeat a fairly familiar Blakean criticism that the perverted Justice of Natural Religion fails to touch the true offenders.

Page 29. 4 Cp. Poems from Letters, ii, ll. 45–78 (Clar. Press, p. 303).

7 See Index, *Albion*, III.

9–18 The symbol Reactor is found only here. The context shows that it is equivalent to ' Spectre '. It is suggested, with diffidence, that the passage ll. 33–82 below, repeated from F. Z. iii, is the revelation of the Reactor ' in his System ' (l. 10), as the Man-created Deity, in this case Luvah who appears in the cloud of the ' sorrows of Man '. The ' System ' of moral justice reveals the immorality of this conception of deity.

12 ' The Man of Sin and Repentance ' is the Reactor. Sin and Repentance are ' Ideas of Moral Virtue ', the negation of Forgiveness, the basis of the great body of error which man must prove and reject before he can attain to liberty : cp. M. 12. 23 *note*, and see Index, *Incarnation* and *Crucifixion*. For a similar reprobation of Repentance cp. J. 43. 75–76.

14–15 ' The Reasoning Power, An Abstract objecting power that Negatives every thing ' (J. 10. 13–14) ' frames Laws & Moralities to destroy Imagination.'

Of Action, for Obedience to destroy the Contraries of Man.
He hath compell'd Albion to become a Punisher & hath possess'd
Himself of Albion's Forests & Wilds : and Jerusalem is taken,
The City of the Woods in the Forest of Ephratah is taken.
London is a stone of her ruins : Oxford is the dust of her walls :
Sussex & Kent are her scatter'd garments, Ireland her holy place,
And the murder'd bodies of her little ones are Scotland and Wales.
The Cities of the Nations are the smoke of her consummation :
The Nations are her dust, ground by the chariot wheels
Of her lordly conquerors : her palaces levell'd with the dust.
I come that I may find a way for my banishèd ones to return.
Fear not, O little Flock, I come : Albion shall rise again.'

So saying, the mild Sun inclos'd the Human Family.

Forthwith from Albion's dark'ning locks came two Immortal forms,
Saying : 'We alone are escapèd, O merciful Lord and Saviour.
We flee from the interiors of Albion's hills and mountains,
From his Valleys Eastward, from Amalek, Canaan & Moab,
Beneath his vast ranges of hills surrounding Jerusalem.

'Albion walk'd on the steps of fire before his Halls,
And Vala walk'd with him in dreams of soft deluding slumber.
He lookèd up & saw the Prince of Light with splendor faded.
Then Albion ascended mourning into the porches of his Palace.
Above him rose a Shadow from his wearied intellect
Of living gold, pure, perfect, holy ; in white linen pure he hover'd,
A sweet entrancing self-delusion, a wat'ry vision of Albion,
Soft exulting in existence, all the Man absorbing.

'Albion fell upon his face prostrate before the wat'ry Shadow,
Saying : "O Lord whence is this change ? thou knowest I am nothing ! "
And Vala trembled & cover'd her face, & her locks were spread on the pavement.

22 Cp. F. Z. ix. 32 *note*.

28 The 'two Immortal forms' are 'the Emanation of Los and his Spectre' : cp. J. 30. 1–2.

33–82 This episode is repeated, with slight verbal changes, from F. Z. iii. 41–98. It is a notable piece of irony.

35 The title of 'Prince of Light' is frequently given to Urizen in *The Four Zoas*, but is not found elsewhere than here in *Jerusalem*.

43 Vala would appear to be the source of the false vision that deludes Albion : see Index, *Vala*.

'We heard astonish'd at the Vision & our hearts trembled within us;
We heard the voice of slumberous Albion, and thus he spake,
Idolatrous to his own Shadow, words of eternity uttering:

'"O I am nothing when I enter into judgment with thee!
If thou withdraw thy breath, I die & vanish into Hades.
If thou dost lay thine hand upon me, behold! I am silent:
If thou withhold thine hand, I perish like a fallen leaf.
O I am nothing, and to nothing must return again:
If thou withdraw thy breath, Behold, I am oblivion."

'He ceas'd; the shadowy voice was silent: but the cloud hover'd over their heads
In golden wreathes, the sorrow of Man; & the balmy drops fell down.
And lo! that son of Man, that Shadowy Spirit of mild Albion,
Luvah, descended from the cloud: in terror Albion rose;
Indignant rose the awful Man, & turn'd his back on Vala.

We heard the voice of Albion starting from his sleep:

'"Whence is this voice crying 'Enion!' that soundeth in my ears?
O cruel pity! O dark deceit! can love seek for dominion?"

'And Luvah strove to gain dominion over Albion:
They strove together above the Body where Vala was inclos'd,
And the dark Body of Albion left prostrate upon the crystal pavement,
Cover'd with boils from head to foot, the terrible smitings of Luvah.

'Then frown'd the fallen Man, and put forth Luvah from his presence,
Saying: "Go and Die the Death of Man for Vala the sweet wanderer.
I will turn the volutions of your ears outward, and bend your nostrils

59 The meaning of this line is obscure. For all that can be said concerning Enion see Index, *Enion*.

62 Cp. J. 23. 9 *note*. The Body inclosing Vala is the symbol of the fallen state of man, wherein vision is displaced by sense-perception and the obsessions of morality. Cp. J. 34. 27–28:

> There is a Throne in every Man; it is the Throne of God:
> This Woman has claim'd as her own, & Man is no more.

64 Cp. J. 21. 4.

Downward; and your fluxile eyes, englob'd, roll round in fear;
Your with'ring lips and tongue shrink up into a narrow circle,
Till into narrow forms you creep. Go take your fiery way;
And learn what 'tis to absorb the Man, you Spirits of Pity & Love!"

'They heard the voice and fled swift as the winter's setting sun.
And now the human blood foam'd high: the Spirits Luvah & Vala
Went down the Human Heart, where Paradise & its joys abounded,
In jealous fears & fury & rage: & flames roll round their fervid feet,
And the vast form of Nature like a serpent play'd before them.
And as they fled in folding fires & thunders of the deep,
Vala shrunk in like the dark sea that leaves its slimy banks,
And from her bosom Luvah fell, far as the east and west;
And the vast form of Nature like a serpent roll'd between,
Whether of Jerusalem's or Vala's ruins congenerated we know not.
All is confusion: all is tumult: & we alone are escapèd.'
So spoke the fugitives; they join'd the Divine Family, trembling.

[30] And the Two that escaped were the Emanation of Los & his
Spectre; for where ever the Emanation goes, the Spectre
Attends her as her Guard: & Los's Emanation is namèd
Enitharmon, & his Spectre is namèd Urthona: they knew
Not where to flee: they had been on a visit to Albion's Children,
And they strove to weave a Shadow of the Emanation

Page 30. 1–15 The best commentary on this passage is perhaps to be found in certain letters to Butts (R., pp. 114–116, 119–124), for there would seem to be some ground for regarding it as a veiled account of the visit of Blake and his wife to Felpham. Their purpose to escape the worldly counsel of Fuseli and Johnson the publisher (cp. R., p. 99) and their desire to carry on their visionary labours in peace are possibly indicated in ll. 6–7, while their difficulties with Hayley (see *Milton*, Introduction) may be alluded to in the passage on corporeal friendship. Finally, there would seem to be a reference (l. 11) to the clearer vision that came to Blake during his stay in Felpham (cp. R., pp. 98, 106, 170–171), and to the hopes raised by the prospect of his return to London (ll. 12–13: cp. R., p. 114).

4 The 'Spectre named Urthona', 'Urthona's Spectre' (l. 14), and the Spectre of Los (ll. 1–2) are here synonymous symbols not distinguishable, except dramatically, from the normal signification of Los; elsewhere Blake apparently intends that they should be distinguished: see Index, *Los, Note I.*

To hide themselves, weeping & lamenting for the Vegetation
Of Albion's Children, fleeing thro' Albion's vales in streams of gore.

Being not irritated by insult, bearing insulting benevolences,
They percieved that corporeal friends are spiritual enemies :
They saw the Sexual Religion in its embryon Uncircumcision.
And the Divine hand was upon them, bearing them thro' darkness
Back safe to their Humanity as doves to their windows :
Therefore the Sons of Eden praise Urthona's Spectre in Songs
Because he kept the Divine Vision in time of trouble.

They wept & trembled : & Los put forth his hand, & took them in,
Into his Bosom, from which Albion shrunk in dismal pain,
Bending the fibres of Brotherhood, & in Feminine Allegories
Inclosing Los ; but the Divine Vision appear'd with Los,
Following Albion into his Central Void among his Oaks.

And Los prayed and said : ' O Divine Saviour, arise
Upon the Mountains of Albion as in ancient time. Behold !
The Cities of Albion seek thy face. London groans in pain
From Hill to Hill & the Thames laments along the Valleys.
The little Villages of Middlesex & Surrey hunger & thirst :
The Twenty-eight Cities of Albion stretch their hands to thee,
Because of the Op[p]ressors of Albion in every City & Village.
They mock at the Labourer's limbs ; they mock at his starv'd Children.
They buy his Daughters that they may have power to sell his Sons ;
They compell the Poor to live upon a crust of bread by soft mild arts ;

18 Allegory, according to Blake (*Cat.* 1810), proceeding from the Daughters of Memory, is entirely distinct from and inferior to Vision or Imagination. Blake's valuation of allegory is not constant. Here, and in J. 50. 2, and J. 89, ll. 5 and 45, the unreality of the ' things of memory ' is emphasized, making allegory equivalent to the illusions of empiricism and morality usually associated with the feminine symbols, e. g. Vala : ' Allegories are things that Relate to Moral Virtues. Moral Virtues do not Exist ; they are Allegories and dissimulations ' (*Cat.* 1810). But elsewhere allegory has a functional value, as a means to regeneration, and may be compared with the dual significance of the Mundane Shell (see Index, *Mundane Shell*).

19–20 Cp. J. 38. 10–13.

26 The ' Twenty-eight Cities ' are the Twenty-four that are identified with the Friends of Albion (see Index, *Los, Note II. β*), together with the four that correspond to the Zoas : cp. J. 12. 45 *note*.

28–32 Cp. F. Z. vii. 109–129.

They reduce the Man to want; then give with pomp & ceremony.
The praise of Jehovah is chaunted from lips of hunger & thirst.
Humanity knows not of Sex: wherefore are Sexes in Beulah?
In Beulah the Female lets down her beautiful Tabernacle,
Which the Male enters, magnificent, between her Cherubim,
And becomes One with her, mingling, condensing in Self-love,
The Rocky Law of Condemnation & double Generation & Death.
Albion hath enter'd the Loins, the place of the Last Judgment,
And Luvah hath drawn the Curtains around Albion in Vala's bosom.
The Dead awake to Generation! Arise O Lord, & rend the Veil!'

So Los in lamentations follow'd Albion. Albion cover'd
[31] His western heaven with rocky clouds of death & despair.

Fearing that Albion should turn his back against the Divine Vision,
Los took his globe of fire to search the interiors of Albion's
Bosom in all the terrors of friendship, entering the caves

34–37 See Index, *Beulah*, 11.

37 'Generation' is used as equivalent to mundane existence in both its aspects, that is, as a state wherein the ideas of Sin and Atonement militate against Imagination (J. 46. 26) and also as a means to regeneration through mercy (J. 58. 18, and see Index, *Generation*). The epithet 'double', always used with sinister significance, and possibly referring to the symbolic fact of Sex, indicates that the second sense holds here. The other meaning appears in l. 40.

Page 31. 3–4 Cp. J. 71. 17–19:

> in your own Bosom you bear your Heaven
> And Earth & all you behold: tho' it appears Without it is Within
> In your Imagination.

Compare Los's Journey with that of Urizen, B. U. vii. 25 seq.: and F. Z. vi. *passim*. His course skirts London on the north, east, and south, the west being omitted, no doubt intentionally, since the western quarter is 'closed' in Man's fallen state: cp. J. 13. 6 *note*.

4 Friendship, 'the willing sacrifice of self', is not mere passivity but the supreme exercise of spiritual energy, possible only in the highest state of being: cp. M. 43. 32–33:

> Altho' our Human Power can sustain the severe contentions
> Of Friendship, our Sexual cannot, but flies into the Ulro.

4–5 Cp. J. 64. 20–22:

> All Quarrels arise from Reasoning, the secret Murder and
> The violent Manslaughter: these are the Spectre's double Cave,
> The Sexual Death, living on accusation of Sin & Judgment.

'Murder' is defined as envy and calumny (J. 91. 11), the denial of the visionary faith (M. 43. 21–22), and the destructive operation of analytic Reason (J. 91. 26–27).

Of despair & death to search the tempters out, walking among
Albion's rocks & precipices, caves of solitude & dark despair;
And saw every Minute Particular of Albion degraded & murder'd,
But saw not by whom; they were hidden within in the minute particulars
Of which they had possess'd themselves: and there they take up
The articulations of a man's soul, and laughing throw it down
Into the frame, then knock it out upon the plank; & souls are bak'd
In bricks to build the pyramids of Heber & Terah. But Los
Search'd in vain; clos'd from the minutia he walk'd difficult;
He came down from Highgate thro' Hackney & Holloway towards London,
Till he came to old Stratford, & thence to Stepney & the Isle
Of Leutha's Dogs; thence thro' the narrows of the River's side
And saw every minute particular, the jewels of Albion, running down
The kennels of the streets & lanes as if they were abhorr'd.
Every Universal Form was become barren mountains of Moral
Virtue, and every Minute Particular harden'd into grains of sand,
And all the tendernesses of the soul cast forth as filth & mire
Among the winding places of deep contemplation intricate,
To where the Tower of London frown'd dreadful over Jerusalem,
A building of Luvah builded in Jerusalem's eastern gate to be
His secluded Court: thence to Bethlehem where was builded
Dens of despair in the house of bread; enquiring in vain
Of stones and rocks he took his way, for human form was none:
And thus he spoke, looking on Albion's City with many tears:

'What shall I do? what could I do, if I could find these Criminals?

6–12 The tradition of idolatry associated with the ancestors of Abraham explains their use as symbols equivalent to the Spectre. This passage is a good instance of the impressiveness that could invest Blake's symbolism: the imaginative intensity of this vision of human helplessness beneath the stress of perverting error almost masters the intractable symbols. Cp. J. 24. 31, The Walls of Babylon are Souls of Men.

19–22 See Index, *Minute Particulars*.

25–26 Bethlehem, 'the house of Bread', with its 'dens of despair' is Bethlehem Hospital, Bedlam, in Lambeth: cp. M. 25. 49 *note*. The ironical antithesis is intentional.

29–38 See General Introduction, p. 73.

I could not dare to take vengeance; for all things are so constructed
And builded by the Divine hand that the sinner shall always escape;
And he who takes vengeance alone is the criminal of Providence.
If I should dare to lay my finger on a grain of sand
In way of vengeance, I punish the already punish'd. O whom
Should I pity if I pity not the sinner who is gone astray?
O Albion, if thou takest vengeance, if thou revengest thy wrongs,
Thou art for ever lost! What can I do to hinder the Sons
Of Albion from taking vengeance or how shall I them perswade?'

So spoke Los, travelling thro' darkness & horrid solitude.
And he beheld Jerusalem in Westminster & Marybone,
Among the ruins of the Temple; and Vala, who is her Shadow,
Jerusalem's Shadow, bent northward over the Island white.
At length he sat on London Stone, & heard Jerusalem's voice:

'Albion, I cannot be thy Wife: thine own Minute Particulars
Belong to God alone, and all thy little ones are holy;
They are of Faith & not of Demonstration. Wherefore is Vala
Cloth'd in black mourning upon my river's currents? Vala awake!
I hear thy shuttles sing in the sky, and round my limbs
I feel the iron threads of love & jealousy & despair.'

Vala reply'd: 'Albion is mine! Luvah gave me to Albion,
And now recieves reproach & hate. Was it not said of old,
Set your Son before a man & he shall take you & your sons
For slaves; but set your Daughter before a man and She
Shall make him & his sons & daughters your slaves for ever?
And is this Faith? Behold the strife of Albion & Luvah
Is great in the east; their spears of blood rage in the eastern heaven.
Urizen is the champion of Albion; they will slay my Luvah:
And thou, O harlot daughter, daughter of despair, art all

41 Cp. J. 11. 24–25. 42 Cp. M. 4. 20 *note.* 43 Cp. J. 8. 27 *note.*

44 The symbol Wife relates to the state of 'Conjugal Love', the 'false and Generating Love' (J. 17. 25–28) that seeks to destroy the spiritual life of man.

48–49 See Index, *Weaving*, I.

57 Vala's accusation that Urizen is the champion of Albion against Luvah and herself is a reversion to the complicated Luvah-Urizen myth of the earlier parts of *The Four Zoas.*

This cause of these shakings of my towers on Euphrates.
Here is the House of Albion, & here is thy secluded place,
And here we have found thy sins ; & hence we turn thee forth
For all to avoid thee, to be astonish'd at thee for thy sins,
Because thou art the impurity & the harlot, & thy children
Children of whoredoms, born for Sacrifice, for the meat & drink
Offering, to sustain the glorious combat & the battle & war,
That Man may be purified by the death of thy delusions.'

So saying she her dark threads cast over the trembling River
And over the valleys, from the hills of Hertfordshire to the hills
Of Surrey across Middlesex & across Albion's House
Of Eternity : pale stood Albion at his eastern gate,
[32] Leaning against the pillars, & his disease rose from his skirts.
Upon the Precipice he stood, ready to fall into Non-Entity.

Los was all astonishment & terror ; he trembled sitting on the Stone
Of London ; but the interiors of Albion's fibres & nerves were hidden
From Los ; astonish'd he beheld only the petrified surfaces,
And saw his Furnaces in ruins ; for Los is the Demon of the Furnaces.
He saw also the Four Points of Albion revers'd inwards.
He siez'd his Hammer & Tongs, his iron Poker & his Bellows
Upon the valleys of Middlesex, Shouting loud for aid Divine.

In stern defiance came from Albion's bosom Hand, Hyle, Koban,
Gwantok, Peachy, Brertun, Slaid, Huttn, Skofeld, Kock, Kotope,
Bowen, Albion's Sons : they bore him a golden couch into the porch,

66 Purification here is purification according to the moral law, and not the mystical annihilation of error. Cp. J. 28. 6 *note*.

67–70 As the course of Los's journey, so Vala's Veil passes from the north to the east and south. Albion's 'House of Eternity' is the 'Spiritual Fourfold London'.

Page 32. 5 The 'petrified surfaces' are the illusions of corporeity and morality, the 'excrementitious husk and covering' (J. 98. 18–19) obscuring the spiritual form of truth.

7 Cp. J. 59. 10–20. 8 See Index, *Furnaces*.

9 Middlesex appears to have the same symbolic reference to regenerative activity as London (cp. J. 10. 17 *note*). Cp. J. 90. 39 : 'So cried Los in the Valley of Middlesex in the Spirit of Prophecy.'

12 Compare the description of Ahania's Couch, F. Z. ii. 383 seq. The porch is 'the Eastern porch of Satan's Universe' (M. 39. 28), the East being the quarter of Ulro or error.

And on the Couch repos'd his limbs trembling from the bloody field,
Rearing their Druid Patriarchal rocky Temples around his limbs.
(All things begin & end in Albion's Ancient Druid Rocky Shore.)

[33] Turning his back to the Divine Vision, his Spectrous
Chaos before his face appear'd, an Unformèd Memory.

Then spoke the Spectrous Chaos to Albion, dark'ning cold
From the back & loins where dwell the Spectrous Dead :

' I am your Rational Power, O Albion, & that Human Form
You call Divine is but a Worm seventy inches long
That creeps forth in a night & is dried in the morning sun,
In fortuitous concourse of memorys accumulated & lost.
It plows the Earth in its own conceit ; it overwhelms the Hills
Beneath its winding labyrinths, till a stone of the brook
Stops it in midst of its pride among its hills & rivers.
Battersea & Chelsea mourn ; London & Canterbury tremble ;
Their place shall not be found as the wind passes over.
The ancient Cities of the Earth remove as a traveller ;
And shall Albion's Cities remain when I pass over them
With my deluge of forgotten remembrances over the tablet ?'

So spoke the Spectre to Albion : he is the Great Selfhood
Satan, Worship'd as God by the Mighty Ones of the Earth ;
Having a white Dot call'd a Center from which branches out
A Circle in continual gyrations : this became a Heart
From which sprang numerous branches varying their motions,
Producing many Heads, three or seven or ten, & hands & feet
Innumerable at will of the unfortunate contemplator
Who becomes his food : such is the way of the Devouring Power.

Page 33. 1–4 The Spectrous Chaos is synonymous with the Spectre.

6 Cp. B. U. vi. 10 *note* and J. 27, *poem* ll. 53–56.

12 Cp. J. 21. 32 *note*.

14–15 ' The ancient Cities of the Earth ' may be intended literally ; cp. M. 25. 4–5 : ' The central Cities of the Nations | Where Human Thought is crushed beneath the iron hand of Power.' Albion's Cities seem to be contrasted with these, and to have reference to the higher mode of existence : cp. J. 38. 46–47 : ' Cities are Men, fathers of Multitudes ' and J. 71. 15 : ' For all are Men in Eternity : Rivers, Mountains, Cities, Villages, | All are Human.'

17 Cp. F. Z. vii *a*. 17–37.

23 The ' unfortunate contemplator ' would seem to be he who, having forsaken Imagination, becomes subject to ' temptations of doubt and despair ', ' serpent reasonings ' of ' good and evil, virtue, vice '. Cp. J. 68. 65–70.

And this is the cause of the appearance in the frowning Chaos.
Albion's Emanation which he had hidden in Jealousy
Appear'd now in the frowning Chaos, prolific upon the Chaos,
Reflecting back to Albion in Sexual Reasoning Hermaphroditic.

Albion spoke: 'Who art thou that appearest in gloomy pomp,
Involving the Divine Vision in colours of autumn ripeness?
I never saw thee till this time, nor beheld life abstracted,
Nor darkness immingled with light on my furrow'd field.
Whence camest thou? who art thou, O loveliest? the Divine Vision
Is as nothing before thee; faded is all life and joy.'

Vala replied in clouds of tears, Albion's garment embracing:

'I was a City & a Temple built by Albion's Children.
I was a Garden planted with beauty. I allured on hill & valley
The River of Life to flow against my walls & among my trees.
Vala was Albion's Bride & Wife in great Eternity,
The loveliest of the daughters of Eternity, when in day-break
I emanated from Luvah over the Towers of Jerusalem
And in her Courts among her little Children, offering up
The Sacrifice of fanatic love: why lovèd I Jerusalem?
Why was I one with her, embracing in the Vision of Jesus?
Wherefore did I loving create love, which never yet
Immingled God & Man, when thou & I hid the Divine Vision
In cloud of secret gloom which, behold, involve me round about?
Know me now, Albion! look upon me! I alone am Beauty!
The Imaginative Human Form is but a breathing of Vala.
I breathe him forth into the Heaven from my secret Cave,
Born of the Woman to obey the Woman, O Albion the mighty!
For the Divine appearance is Brotherhood, but I am Love
[34] Elevate into the Region of Brotherhood with my red fires.'

31 Blake consistently applies the term 'abstract' to analytic reason and its works. Here it describes the false idea of existence divorced from vision.

36–44 It is difficult to discover the exact significance of Vala in this 'golden age' before the Fall. It may be suggested quite tentatively that she represents Nature regarded as symbol, and not, as in the fallen state, as ultimate reality. The description in the present passage suggests a parallel between the state Vala and Eden in Genesis.

43 'Fanatic love' is the criticism which Natural Religion directs against the visionary ethic: cp. J. 28. 6 *note*.

50–51 This is the symbolic interpretation of Sex, the subjection of man to the illusions of physical reality and moral virtue. See Index, *Sex*, and cp. J. 34. 39–40.

' Art thou Vala ? ' replied Albion ' image of my repose ?
O how I tremble ! how my members pour down milky fear !
A dewy garment covers me all over ; all manhood is gone.
At thy word & at thy look death enrobes me about
From head to feet, a garment of death & eternal fear.
Is not that Sun thy husband & that Moon thy glimmering Veil ?
Are not the Stars of heaven thy Children ? Art thou not Babylon ?
Art thou Nature, Mother of all ? Is Jerusalem thy Daughter ?
Why have thou elevate inward, O dweller of outward chambers,
From grot & cave beneath the Moon, dim region of death,
Where I laid my Plow in the hot noon, where my hot team fed,
Where implements of War are forgèd, the Plow to go over the Nations,
In pain girding me round like a rib of iron in heaven. O Vala !
In Eternity they neither marry nor are given in marriage.
Albion, the high Cliff of the Atlantic, is become a barren Land.'

Los stood at his Anvil : he heard the contentions of Vala.
He heav'd his thund'ring Bellows upon the valleys of Middlesex ;
He open'd his Furnaces before Vala : then Albion frown'd in anger
On his Rock, ere yet the Starry Heavens were fled away
From his awful Members ; and thus Los cried aloud
To the Sons of Albion & to Hand the eldest Son of Albion.

' I hear the screech of Childbirth loud pealing, & the groans
Of Death in Albion's clouds dreadful utter'd over all the Earth.
What may Man be ? who can tell ! but what may Woman be,
To have power over Man from Cradle to corruptible Grave ?
There is a Throne in every Man : it is the Throne of God.

Page 34. 2–16 These lines describe the condition of man in the state called Vala, the image of his ' repose ', or ' sleep of death ' : cp. J. 68. 65–70

10 This would seem to be a restatement of the fact that Natural Religion has taken the place of Vision in the life of man. For Blake's use of the expressions ' inner ' and ' outer ', cp. F. Z. i. 250 *note* and M. 37. 8–9.

11 Cp. J. 19. 44 *note*. 12 See Index, *Plow*, &c.

16 Cp. M. 4. 20 *note*. 18 Cp. J. 32. 9 *note*.

23 The ' screech of Childbirth ' images the difficulty and pain attending the processes of ' sexual reasoning ' as compared with the spontaneity of visionary knowledge, the ' births of intellect '.

25–35 An explicit statement of the symbolic significance of Sex, its power over man within the limits of mortality, and its negation of vision.

27 Cp. E. G. 31–32 (Clar. Press, p. 250) :

Thou art a Man, God is no more.
Thy own Humanity learn to adore.

This Woman has claim'd as her own & Man is no more :
Albion is the Tabernacle of Vala & her Temple,
And not the Tabernacle & Temple of the Most High.
O Albion ! why wilt thou Create a Female Will
To hide the most evident God in a hidden covert, even
In the shadows of a Woman & a secluded Holy Place,
That we may pry after him as after a stolen treasure,
Hidden among the Dead & murèd up from the paths of life ?
Hand ! art thou not Reuben enrooting thyself into Bashan,
Till thou remainest a vaporous Shadow in a Void ? O Merlin,
Unknown among the Dead, where never before Existence came !
Is this the Female Will, O ye lovely Daughters of Albion, To
Converse concerning Weight & Distance in the Wilds of Newton & Locke ? '

So Los spoke standing on Mam-Tor, looking over Europe & Asia :
The Graves thunder beneath his feet from Ireland to Japan.

Reuben slept in Bashan like one dead in the valley,
Cut off from Albion's mountains & from all the Earth's summits
Between Succoth & Zaretan beside the Stone of Bohan,
While the Daughters of Albion divided Luvah into three Bodies.
Los bended his Nostrils down to the Earth, then sent him over
Jordan to the Land of the Hittite ; every-one that saw him
Fled ; they fled at his horrible Form ; they hid in caves
And dens ; they lookèd on one-another & became what they beheld.

Reuben return'd to Bashan : in despair he slept on the Stone.
Then Gwendolen divided into Rahab & Tirza[h] in Twelve Portions.
Los rollèd his Eyes into two narrow circles, then sent him
Over Jordan ; all terrified fled ; they became what they beheld.

36 Cp. J. 8. 34 *note*, and see Index, *Reuben*.

37 Merlin is one of the 'Giants of Albion' (J. 93. 13) : see Index, *Giants*, and J. Introduction, p. 441.

41 Cp. J. 23. 27 *note*. 42 Cp. F. Z. ii. 269 *note*.

45 For Zaretan or Zarthon see Joshua iii. 16 and 1 Kings vii. 46. For the 'Stone of Bohan' see Joshua xv. 6, and cp. *Europe*, l. 96 and *note*.

47 For the changes of Reuben here and in J. 36. 1–12 cp. *Europe*, ll. 80–85 ; 'his' relates to Reuben, cp. l. 53.

' If Perceptive Organs vary, Objects of Perception seem to vary :
If the Perceptive Organs close, their Objects seem to close also.
Consider this, O mortal Man, O worm of sixty winters,' said Los,
' Consider Sexual Organization & hide thee in the dust.'

[35] Then the Divine hand found the Two Limits, Satan and Adam,
In Albion's bosom ; for in every Human bosom those Limits stand.
And the Divine voice came from the Furnaces; as multitudes without
Number the voices of the innumerable multitudes of Eternity.
And the appearance of a Man was seen in the Furnaces,
Saving those who have sinnèd from the punishment of the Law,
(In pity of the punisher whose state is eternal death)
And keeping them from Sin by the mild counsels of his love.

' Albion goes to Eternal Death. In Me all Eternity
Must pass thro' condemnation, and awake beyond the Grave.
No individual can keep these Laws, for they are death
To every energy of man, and forbid the springs of life.
Albion hath enter'd the State Satan. Be permanent, O State,
And be thou for ever accursèd, that Albion may arise again !
And be thou created into a State ! I go forth to Create
States to deliver Individuals evermore. Amen.'

So spoke the voice from the Furnaces, descending into Non Entity.

[36] Reuben return'd to his place ; in vain he sought beautiful Tirzah,
For his Eyelids were narrow'd, & his Nostrils scented the ground.
And Sixty Winters Los ragèd in the Divisions of Reuben,
Building the Moon of Ulro, plank by plank & rib by rib.
Reuben slept in the Cave of Adam, and Los folded his Tongue
Between Lips of mire & clay ; then sent him forth over Jordan

Page 35 interrupts the sequence of pp. 34 and 36. It is either interpolated or misplaced : no better place can be suggested. Its reiteration of the ethic of Forgiveness and its corollary, Regeneration, is notable.
1 See Index, *Expansion*.
13 See Index, *States*.
17 See Index, *Incarnation*. After l. 17 a line *del. illeg.*
Page 36. 4 Cp. J. 19. 44 *note* and J. 56. 18–21.

In the love of Tirzah : he said : ' Doubt is my food day & night.'
All that beheld him fled howling, and gnawed their tongues
For pain : they became what they beheld. In reasonings Reuben returnèd
To Heshbon : disconsolate he walk'd thro' Moab & he stood
Before the Furnaces of Los in a horrible dreamful slumber
On Mount Gilead looking toward Gilgal : and Los bended
His Ear in a spiral circle outward ; then sent him over Jordan.

The Seven Nations fled before him ; they became what they beheld :
Hand, Hyle & Coban fled ; they became what they beheld ;
Gwantock & Peachy hid in Damascus beneath Mount Lebanon,
Brereton & Slade in Egypt, Hutton & Skofeld & Kox
Fled over Chaldea in terror, in pains in every nerve ;
Kotope & Bowen became what they beheld, fleeing over the Earth :
And the Twelve Female Emanations fled with them agonizing.

Jerusalem trembled, seeing her Children driv'n by Los's Hammer
In the visions of the dreams of Beulah on the edge of Non-Entity.
Hand stood between Reuben & Merlin, as the Reasoning Spectre
Stands between the Vegetative Man & his Immortal Imagination.

And the Four Zoas clouded rage East & West & North & South :
They change their situations in the Universal Man.
Albion groans ; he sees the Elements divide before his face :
And England, who is Brittannia, divided into Jerusalem & Vala.

7 Cp. J. 33. 23 *note*. The speaker is Reuben.
9 Cp. J. 47. 13–15 : F. Z. iv. 203 : vii. 465 : M. 27. 10–18.
20 These Emanations are the Daughters of Albion.
25–26 In Eternity the positions of the Zoas are, Urthona, north ; Luvah, east ; Urizen, south ; Tharmas, north (F. Z. vi. 272–273, and M. 32, *diagram*). In F. Z. vi. 264 seq. Urizen falls into the west, Orc or Luvah into the south, Urthona keeps the north, while the east is void, Tharmas wandering through the other three quarters. In the present passage Urizen and Luvah only are affected. Interpretation has not been found possible, since the nature of the Zoas in Eternity is quite uncertain. For the general significance of the four quarters see Index, *Cardinal Points*. For the correspondences see J. 12. 45–60 *note*.
28 Brittannia, or Brittannica, is the wife of Los and mother of Jerusalem (*Cat.* 1810), or according to J. 77, stanza 1, her sister. There is not sufficient material to establish any interpretation. In J. 94. 20–27 she is not distinguishable from Vala. Her division into Jerusalem and Vala may refer

And Urizen assumes the East ; Luvah assumes the South,
In his dark Spectre ravening from his open Sepulcher.

And the Four Zoas, who are the Four Eternal Senses of Man,
Became Four Elements separating from the Limbs of Albion.
These are their names in the Vegetative Generation

. . . .

And Accident & Chance were found hidden in Length, Bredth & Highth :
And they divided into Four ravening deathlike Forms,
Fairies & Genii & Nymphs & Gnomes of the Elements :
These are States Permanently Fixèd by the Divine Power.
The Atlantic Continent sunk round Albion's cliffy shore,
And the Sea pourèd in amain upon the Giants of Albion
As Los bended the Senses of Reuben. Reuben is Merlin
Exploring the Three States of Ulro—Creation, Redemption, & Judgment.

And many of the Eternal Ones laughèd after their manner :

'Have you known the Judgment that is arisen among the
[Zoas] of Albion, where a Man dare hardly to embrace
His own Wife for the terrors of Chastity that they call
By the name of Morality ? their Daughters govern all
In hidden deceit : they are Vegetable, only fit for burning.
Art & Science cannot exist but by Naked Beauty display'd.'

Then those in Great Eternity who contemplate on Death
Said thus : 'What seems to Be, Is, To those to whom
It seems to Be ; & is productive of the most dreadful
Consequences to those to whom it seems to Be, even of
Torments, Despair, Eternal Death : but the Divine Mercy
Steps beyond and Redeems Man in the Body of Jesus. Amen.

to the presence in mortal life of the contrary modes, the visionary and the materialistic or moral. England (J. 54. 27) is apparently a variant of the same symbol. After l. 33 a line has been erased.

38–39 See Index, *Atlantic*. 40 Cp. J. 34. 37 *note*.

42 Cp. *Paradise Lost*, xii. 59. 61:

> Great laughter was in Heaven,
> And looking down to see the hubbub strange
> And hear the din.

44 The word we read as 'Zoas' is indistinct in Blake's autotype: it may be 'Sons'.

54 Cp. E. G. β. ll. 50–54 (Clar. Press, p. 248) :

> [Jesus] in his Body tight doth bend
> Satan & all his Hellish Crew ;
> And thus with wrath he did subdue
> The Serpent Bulk of Nature's Dross
> Till he had nail'd it on the Cross.

See Index, *Incarnation* and *Crucifixion*.

And Length, Bredth, Highth again Obey the Divine Vision.
Hallelujah.'

[37] And One stood forth from the Divine Family & said:

'I feel my Spectre rising upon me. Albion! arouze thyself!
Why dost thou thunder with frozen Spectrous wrath against us?
The Spectre is in Giant Man insane and most deform'd.
Thou wilt certainly provoke my Spectre against thine in fury.
He has a Sepulcher hewn out of a Rock ready for thee,
And a Death of Eight thousand years forg'd by thyself, upon
The point of his Spear, if thou persistest to forbid with Laws
Our Emanations and to attack our secret supreme delights.'

So Los spoke. But when he saw pale death in Albion's feet,
Again he join'd the Divine Body, following merciful;
While Albion fled more indignant, revengeful, covering
[38] His face and bosom with petrific hardness, and his hands
And feet, lest any should enter his bosom & embrace
His hidden heart: his Emanation wept & trembled within him.
Uttering not his jealousy, but hiding it as with
Iron and steel, dark and opake, with clouds & tempests brooding,
His strong limbs shudder'd upon his mountains high and dark.

Turning from Universal Love, petrific as he went,
His cold against the warmth of Eden rag'd with loud
Thunders of deadly war (the fever of the human soul),
Fires and clouds of rolling smoke: but mild the Saviour follow'd him,
Displaying the Eternal Vision, the Divine Similitude,
In loves and tears of brothers, sisters, sons, fathers and friends,
Which if Man ceases to behold, he ceases to exist;

Saying: 'Albion! Our wars are wars of life & wounds of love,
With intellectual spears & long wingèd arrows of thought.
Mutual in one another's love and wrath all renewing,
We live as One Man: for, contracting our infinite senses,
We behold multitude; or, expanding, we behold as one,

Page 37. 1 The 'One' is Los: cp. l. 10. 4 See Index, *Giant*.

6 The absence of definite sequence in the mythical events described in *Jerusalem* makes the interpretation of this passage difficult. If the statement of J. 34. 20 holds, that the separation between Albion and his eternal state is not yet fully accomplished, then the present passage may be taken to foretell mortality, the place of Man's 'sleep of death', his Sepulchre. But Blake usually puts the duration of mundane existence at six thousand years (cp. M. 19. 51–52).

As One Man all the Universal Family ; and that One Man
We call Jesus the Christ : and he in us and we in him
Live in perfect harmony in Eden, the land of life,
Giving, recieving, and forgiving each other's trespasses.
He is the Good shepherd, he is the Lord and master ;
He is the Shepherd of Albion, he is all in all
In Eden, in the garden of God and in heavenly Jerusalem.
If we have offended, forgive us ! take not vengeance against us ! '

Thus speaking, the Divine Family follow Albion.
I see them in the Vision of God upon my pleasant valleys.

I behold London, a Human awful wonder of God.
He says : ' Return, Albion, return ! I give myself for thee.
My Streets are my Ideas of Imagination.
Awake, Albion, awake ! and let us awake up together.
My Houses are Thoughts ; my Inhabitants Affections,
The children of my thoughts, walking within my blood-vessels,
Shut from my nervous form which sleeps upon the verge of Beulah
In dreams of darkness, while my vegetating blood in veiny pipes
Rolls dreadful thro' the Furnaces of Los and the Mills of Satan.
For Albion's sake and for Jerusalem thy Emanation
I give myself, and these my brethren give themselves for Albion.'

So spoke London, immortal Guardian. I heard in Lambeth's shades :
In Felpham I heard and saw the Visions of Albion :
I write in South Molton Street what I both see and hear
In regions of Humanity, in London's opening streets.

Page 38. 28 Blake speaks in his own person.

29 London here appears as one of the Twenty-eight Cities, the spiritual Friends of Albion : cp. J. 30. 26 *note* and Index, *Los, Note II*. B. Cp. also the description of Golgonooza and Jerusalem, J. pp. 12–13.

35 Cp. J. 23. 25 *note*. The ' nervous form ' stands here for the fallen state of man. The ' nerves ' as symbol may have the sinister sense deduced from the evil results of the sense of touch (cp. J. 13. 6 *note*). They are frequently, though not consistently used to symbolize the ramifications of error throughout mundane existence (J. 68. 26 : 80. 64 : 87. 5–6). In M. 28. 29–31 the ' nervous form ' appears to be identified with the Polypus ; see Index, *Mundane Shell, Note I*. B.

37 See Index, *Furnaces*, and J. 35. 5 *note*. 40 Cp. M. 4. 14 *note*.

42 Blake lived at 17 South Molton St. from 1803 to 1820. Here he engraved *Milton* and part, if not the whole, of *Jerusalem*.

I see thee, awful Parent Land, in light : behold ! I see
Verulam, Canterbury, venerable parent of men,
Generous immortal Guardian golden clad—for Cities
Are Men, fathers of multitudes ; and Rivers & Mountains
Are also Men ; every thing is Human, mighty, sublime.
In every bosom a Universe expands, as wings
Let down at will around, and call'd the Universal Tent—
York, crown'd with loving kindness ; Edinburgh, cloth'd
With fortitude as with a garment of immortal texture
Woven in looms of Eden, in spiritual deaths of mighty men
Who give themselves in Golgotha, Victims to Justice, where
There is in Albion a Gate of precious stones and gold
Seen only by Emanations, by vegetations viewless,
Bending across the road of Oxford Street ; it from Hyde Park
To Tyburn's deathful shades admits the wandering souls
Of multitudes who die from Earth : this Gate cannot be found
[39] By Satan's Watch-fiends : tho' they search, numbering every grain
Of sand on Earth every night, they never find this Gate.
It is the Gate of Los. Withoutside is the Mill, intricate, dreadful
And fill'd with cruel tortures : but no mortal man can find the Mill
Of Satan in his mortal pilgrimage of seventy years ;
For Human beauty knows it not, nor can Mercy find it. But
In the Fourth region of Humanity, Urthona nam'd,
Mortality begins to roll the billows of Eternal Death
Before the Gate of Los. Urthona here is namèd Los,

44–50 Cp. J. 71. 12–19, and see Index, *Human Form*.
50 For a possible meaning of the obscure expression ' Universal Tent ' cp. M. 28. 4–14.
53 Cp. J. 96. 27–28 :

every kindness to another is a little Death
In the Divine Image, nor can Man exist but by Brotherhood.

54 Justice here is ' Moral Justice ' : cp. J. 23. 32–36.
59 For the ' Gates of Los ' cp. M. 35. 66 and Blake's Dedication of his Illustrations to Blair's ' The Grave ' to Queen Charlotte :

The Door of Death is made of Gold
That Mortal Eyes cannot behold ;
But when the Mortal Eyes are clos'd,
And cold and pale the Limbs repos'd,
The Soul awakes ; and, wond'ring, sees
In her mild Hand the golden Keys :
The Grave is Heaven's golden Gate
And rich and poor around it wait ;
O Shepherdess of England's Fold
Behold this Gate of Pearl and Gold !

And here begins the System of Moral Vìrtue, namèd Rahab.
Albion fled thro' the Gate of Los, and he stood in the Gate.

Los was the friend of Albion who most lov'd him. In Cambridgeshire
His eternal station ; he is the twenty-eighth, & is four-fold.
Seeing Albion had turn'd his back against the Divine Vision,
Los said to Albion : ' Whither fleest thou ? ' Albion reply'd :

' I die ! I go to Eternal Death ! the shades of death
Hover within me & beneath, and spreading themselves outside
Like rocky clouds, build me a gloomy monument of woe.
Will none accompany me in my death, or be a Ransom for me
In that dark Valley ? I have girded round my cloke, and on my feet
Bound these black shoes of death, & on my hands death's iron gloves.
God hath forsaken me, & my friends are become a burden,
A weariness to me, & the human footstep is a terror to me.'

Los answer'd, troubled, and his soul was rent in twain :
' Must the Wise die for an Atonement ? does Mercy endure Atonement ?
No ! It is Moral Severity, & destroys Mercy in its Victim.'
So speaking, not yet infected with thè Error & Illusion,
[40] Los shudder'd at beholding Albion, for his disease
Arose upon him pale and ghastly : and he call'd around
The Friends of Albion : trembling at the sight of Eternal Death
The four appear'd with their Emanations in fiery
Chariots : black their fires roll, beholding Albion's House of Eternity.

13 The four Cities, corresponding to the four Zoas (cp. J. 12. 45 *note*), of whom Los is the fourth (J. 42. 24), are added to the twenty-four that are the spiritual friends of Albion (see Index, *Los*). Hence the reference to Los as the twenty-eighth may be a restatement of his regenerative function, with a possible allusion to the fact that the other twenty-seven relegate their powers to him (J. 44. 28). ' Fourfold ' always connotes spiritual perfection.

19 The doctrine of atonement or ransom is contrary to the visionary ethic ; it implies a punitive code that must be satisfied. Vicarious sacrifice has no place in Blake's interpretation of the Crucifixion : see Index, *Crucifixion*, and cp. J. 61. 17–21 :

> Doth Jehovah Forgive a Debt only on condition that it shall
> Be Payed ? Doth he Forgive Pollution only on condition of Purity ?
> That Debt is not Forgiven, That Pollution is not Forgiven.
> Such is the Forgiveness of the Gods, the Moral Virtues of the
> Heathen, whose tender Mercies are Cruelty.

Cp. *infra*, ll. 25–26.

Damp couch the flames beneath, and silent, sick, stand shuddering
Before the Porch of sixteen pillars: weeping, every one
Descended and fell down upon their knees round Albion's knees,
Swearing the Oath of God with awful voice of thunders round
Upon the hills & valleys; and the cloudy Oath roll'd far and wide.

'Albion is sick!' said every Valley, every mournful Hill
And every River: 'our brother Albion is sick to death.
He hath leaguèd himself with robbers: he hath studied the arts
Of unbelief. Envy hovers over him: his Friends are his abhorrence:
Those who give their lives for him are despisèd.
Those who devour his soul are taken into his bosom.
To destroy his Emanation is their intention.
Arise! awake, O Friends of the Giant Albion!
They have perswaded him of horrible falshoods:
They have sown errors over all his fruitful fields!'

The Twenty-four heard; they came trembling on wat'ry chariots,
Borne by the Living Creatures of the third procession
Of Human Majesty: the Living Creatures wept aloud as they
Went along Albion's roads, till they arriv'd at Albion's House.

O! how the torments of Eternal Death waited on Man;
And the loud-rending bars of the Creation ready to burst,

7 Cp. J. 48. 6–11 and *note*. 9 Cp. M. 12. 13 and *note*.
11–12 Cp. J. 71. 15–16:

For all are Men in Eternity, Rivers, Mountains, Cities, Villages.
All are Human.

22–23 These 'Living Creatures of the third procession of Human Majesty' are not mentioned elsewhere. A drawing on p. 46 shows two of them as beasts with heavy bodies supported on hoofed feet, and having the heads of bearded men. From each forehead springs a spiral horn, terminating in a human hand; upon their backs sit winged cherubim. The shafts of the chariot are serpents, whose tails, convolved, form the wheels; in the chariot sit a venerable man and a woman, the Friend and his Emanation. The twenty-four Friends appear as so many British cathedral cities: see Index, *Los, Note II*. B.

26–44 The 'loud-rending bars of the Creation' (l. 26) appears to repeat something of the meaning of the 'torments of Eternal Death' (l. 25). Therefore Creation connotes here, as in ll. 31–44, the divinely ordered defence for man against Eternal Death. It is an evil, but a less evil than would have followed the infraction of the Eternal Unity, had Divine Mercy not intervened (see Index, *Mundane Shell*).

That the wide world might fly from its hinges, & the immortal mansion
Of Man for ever be possess'd by monsters of the deeps;
And Man himself become a Fiend, wrap'd in an endless curse,
Consuming and consum'd for-ever in flames of Moral Justice.

For had the Body of Albion fall'n down, and from its dreadful ruins
Let loose the enormous Spectre on the darkness of the deep,
At enmity with the Merciful & fill'd with devouring fire,
A nether-world must have reciev'd the foul enormous spirit,
Under pretence of Moral Virtue fill'd with Revenge and Law;
There to eternity chain'd down and issuing in red flames
And curses, with his mighty arms brandish'd against the heavens,
Breathing cruelty, blood & vengeance, gnashing his teeth with pain,
Torn with black storms & ceaseless torrents of his own consuming fire;
Within his breast his mighty Sons chain'd down & fill'd with cursings;
And his dark Eon, that once fair crystal form divinely clear,
Within his ribs producing serpents whose souls are flames of fire.
But, glory to the Merciful-One, for he is of tender mercies!
And the Divine Family wept over him as One Man.

And these the Twenty-four in whom the Divine Family
Appear'd; and they were One in Him, A Human Vision,
Human Divine, Jesus the Saviour, blessèd for ever and ever.

Selsey, true friend, who afterwards submitted to be devour'd
By the waves of Despair, whose Emanation rose above
The flood, and was nam'd Chichester, lovely mild & gentle. Lo!
Her lambs bleat to the sea-fowls' cry, lamenting still for Albion.

Submitting to be call'd the son of Los the terrible vision,
Winchester stood devoting himself for Albion, his tents
Outspread with abundant riches, and his Emanations
Submitting to be call'd Enitharmon's daughters and be born
In vegetable mould, created by the Hammer and Loom
In Bowlahoola & Allamanda where the Dead wail night & day.

48–51 At Felpham Blake learned that coast-erosion had caused the seat of the bishopric to be transferred in 1075 from Selsey to Chichester. The mystical rendering of this fact is made memorable by the striking l. 51.

(I call them by their English names, English, the rough basement.
Los built the stubborn structure of the Language, acting against
Albion's melancholy, who must else have been a Dumb despair.)

Gloucester and Exeter and Salisbury and Bristol, and benevolent
[41] Bath who is Legions ; he is the Seventh, the physician and
The poisoner, the best and worst in Heaven and Hell,
Whose Spectre first assimilated with Luvah in Albion's mountains.
A triple octave he took to reduce Jerusalem to twelve,
To cast Jerusalem forth upon the wilds to Poplar & Bow,
To Malden & Canterbury in the delights of cruelty.
The Shuttles of death sing in the sky to Islington & Pancrass,
Round Marybone to Tyburn's River, weaving black melancholy as a net,
And despair as meshes closely wove over the west of London
Where mild Jerusalem sought to repose in death & be no more.
She fled to Lambeth's mild Vale and hid herself beneath
The Surrey Hills where Rephaim terminates; her Sons are siez'd
For victims of sacrifice, but Jerusalem cannot be found, Hid
By the Daughters of Beulah, gently snatch'd away and hid in Beulah.

There is a Grain of Sand in Lambeth that Satan cannot find,
Nor can his Watch Fiends find it ; 'tis translucent & has many Angles :
But he who finds it will find Oothoon's palace ; for within,
Opening into Beulah, every angle is a lovely heaven.
But should the Watch Fiends find it, they would call it Sin,
And lay its Heavens & their inhabitants in blood of punishment.
Here Jerusalem & Vala were hid in soft slumberous repose,
Hid from the terrible East, shut up in the South & West.

Page 41. 1 The equivocal nature of Bath is reflected in such conflicting passages as J. 46. 1–2 and J. 75. 1–3. Its significance is undetermined ; and though frequently mentioned it remains as obscure as the 'triple octave' of l. 4, which occurs nowhere else.

5–6 These places to the east of London symbolize the state of error or Ulro, the eastern quarter : see below, ll. 21–22. In ll. 8–9 the west is the quarter of visionary activity, which the spectrous powers strive to destroy through melancholy, doubt and despair.

15–20 Cp. M. 35. 42–43 and J. 38. 55–39. 3. There probably is in this a reference to Blake's own work either as mystic or artist. Cp. M. 4. 14 *note*.

17 Cp. V. D. A., Introductory Note.

21 This association of Jerusalem with Vala in Lambeth, the visionary

The Twenty-eight trembled in Death's dark caves; in cold despair
They kneel'd around the Couch of Death in deep humiliation
And tortures of self condemnation, while their Spectres rag'd within.
The Four Zoas in terrible combustion clouded rage,
Drinking the shuddering fears & loves of Albion's Families,
Destroying by selfish affections the things that they most admire,
Drinking & eating & pitying & weeping; as at a trajic scene
The soul drinks murder & revenge, & applauds its own holiness.

They saw Albion endeavouring to destroy their Emanations.

42] Thus Albion sat, studious of others in his pale disease,
Brooding on evil; but when Los open'd the Furnaces before him,
He saw that the accursèd things were his own affections
And his own belovèds: then he turn'd sick: his soul died within him.
Also Los, sick & terrified, beheld the Furnaces of Death,
And must have died, but the Divine Saviour descended
Among the infant loves & affections, and the Divine Vision wept
Like evening dew on every herb upon the breathing ground.

centre in London, or mortal existence, may be compared with the state described (J. 20. 6–10) as the

sweet regions of youth and virgin innocence
Where we live, forgetting error, not pondering on evil,
Among my [Jerusalem's] lambs & brooks of water, among my warbling birds;
Where we delight in innocence before the face of the Lamb,
Going in and out before him in his love and sweet affection.

26 Los is clearly not included here among the Zoas, though later (J. 42. 24) he calls himself the 'Fourth Zoa'. Possibly the fourth in this instance is the spectre of Los.

Beneath l. 31 the following quatrain is engraved in reverse upon a scroll:

Each Man is in his Spectre's power,
Untill the arrival of that hour
When his Humanity awake
And cast his Spectre into the Lake.

Here, as elsewhere, the use of reversed characters may indicate that the lines so written are not to be taken as part of the text.

Page 42. The transition from the preceding page is abrupt. The evidence of the engraved script seems to show that originally p. 41 was followed by p. 44, and that pp. 42–43, written in a finer and more compact hand, were interpolated to introduce a more direct exposition of Blake's visionary doctrine and his antagonism to punitive morality. If this hypothesis be just, page 43 was adapted to the opening lines of p. 44 and the catchword 'With' added.

Albion spoke in his dismal dreams: 'O thou deceitful friend,
Worshipping mercy & beholding thy friend in such affliction!
Los! thou now discoverest thy turpitude to the heavens.
I demand righteousness & justice. O thou ingratitude!
Give me my Emanations back, food for my dying soul!
My daughters are harlots: my sons are accursèd before me.
Enitharmon is my daughter, accursèd with a father's curse.
O! I have utterly been wasted. I have given my daughters to devils.'

So spoke Albion in gloomy majesty; and deepest night
Of Ulro roll'd round his skirts from Dover to Cornwall.

Los answer'd: 'Righteousness & justice I give thee in return
For thy righteousness; but I add mercy also, and bind
Thee from destroying these little ones. Am I to be only
Merciful to thee and cruel to all that thou hatest?
Thou wast the Image of God surrounded by the Four Zoas.
Three thou hast slain. I am the Fourth: thou canst not destroy me.
Thou art in Error; trouble me not with thy righteousness.
I have innocence to defend and ignorance to instruct:
I have no time for seeming, and little arts of compliment
In morality and virtue, in self-glorying and pride.
There is a limit of Opakeness, and a limit of Contraction
In every Individual Man; and the limit of Opakeness,
Is namèd Satan, and the limit of Contraction is namèd Adam.
But when Man sleeps in Beulah, the Saviour in mercy takes
Contraction's Limit, and of the Limit he forms Woman, That
Himself may in process of time be born Man to redeem.
But there is no Limit of Expansion, there is no Limit of Translucence
In the bosom of Man for ever from eternity to eternity.
Therefore I break thy bonds of righteousness; I crush thy messengers,
That they may not crush me and mine: do thou be righteous,

12 'Righteousness and justice', cp. ll. 19–21 below.
13–16 Cp. J. 21. 18–49.
18 This appears to indicate the spread of error into the sphere of visionary activity in mortal life: compare the similar movement from east to west, J. 41. 7–10. 21 See below, ll. 37–45. 23 Cp. J. 96. 41–43.
24 Cp. M. 23. 8. 29–36 See Index, *Expansion*.
37–45 Blake maintains that 'the Will must not be bended' [J. 44. 18]. External interference, implying an act of judgement, violates that rule. Therefore Los, in ordering the divine purpose of regeneration in mortality, lets error run its course, while he protects visionary integrity from its influence. An illustration of this from Blake's own life is given in his letter to Butts, 6 July 1803 (R., pp. 122–123).

And I will return it ; otherwise I defy thy worst revenge.
Consider me as thine enemy : on me turn all thy fury ;
But destroy not these little ones, nor mock the Lord's anointed.
Destroy not by Moral Virtue the little ones whom he hath chosen,
The little ones whom he hath chosen in preference to thee.
He hath cast thee off for ever ; the little ones he hath anointed.
Thy Selfhood is for ever accursèd from the Divine presence.'

So Los spoke : then turn'd his face & wept for Albion.

Albion replied : ' Go, Hand & Hyle ! sieze the abhorrèd friend,
As you have siez'd the Twenty-four rebellious ingratitudes,
To atone for you, for spiritual death. Man lives by deaths of Men.
Bring him to justice before heaven here upon London stone,
Between Blackheath & Hounslow, between Norwood & Finchley.
All that they have is mine : from my free gen'rous gift
They now hold all they have : ingratitude to me,
To me their benefactor, calls aloud for vengeance deep.'

Los stood before his Furnaces awaiting the fury of the Dead ;
And the Divine hand was upon him, strengthening him mightily.

The Spectres of the Dead cry out from the deeps beneath
Upon the hills of Albion. Oxford groans in his iron furnace,
Winchester in his den & cavern : they lament against
Albion ; they curse their human kindness & affection ;
They rage like wild beasts in the forests of affliction ;
In the dreams of Ulro they repent of their human kindness :

' Come up ! build Babylon ! Rahab is ours & all her multitudes
With her, in pomp and glory of victory. Depart,
Ye twenty-four, into the deeps ! let us depart to glory ! '

Their Human majestic forms sit up upon their Couches
Of death : they curb their Spectres as with iron curbs.
They enquire after Jerusalem in the regions of the dead,
With the voices of dead men, low, scarcely articulate,
And with tears cold on their cheeks they weary repose.

49 Cp. J. 39. 19 *note*. 50 Cp. J. 8. 27 *note* and M. 4. 4 *note*.

57–74 The conflict between the 'Human Majestic Forms' (l. 66) of Albion's Friends and their Spectres, with the protest of the latter against the altruism of the former, may be compared with the long debate between Los and his Spectre, J. pp. 6–7.

'O when shall the morning of the grave appear, and when
Shall our salvation come? we sleep upon our watch:
We cannot awake; and our Spectres rage in the forests.
O God of Albion, where art thou! pity the watchers!'

Thus mourn they. Loud the Furnaces of Los thunder upon
The clouds of Europe & Asia among the Serpent Temples.

And Los drew his Seven Furnaces around Albion's Altars:
And as Albion built his frozen Altars, Los built the Mundane Shell
In the Four Regions of Humanity, East & West & North & South,
Till Norwood & Finchley & Blackheath & Hounslow cover'd the whole Earth:
This is the Net & Veil of Vala among the Souls of the Dead.

[43] They saw their Wheels rising up poisonous against Albion:
Urizen, cold & scientific; Luvah, pitying & weeping;
Tharmas, indolent & sullen; Urthona, doubting & despairing;
Victims to one another & dreadfully plotting against each other
To prevent Albion walking about in the Four Complexions.

They saw America clos'd out by the Oaks of the western shore,
And Tharmas dash'd on the Rocks of the Altars of Victims in Mexico:
'If we are wrathful Albion will destroy Jerusalem with rooty Groves;

73 Cp. M. 4. 3 *note*.

76 Cp. J. 25. 4 *note*. For Europe and Asia as symbols cp. Introduction to *Europe* and *The Song of Los*.

77–81 Los strives to subdue Albion's Spectre, opposing the regenerative purpose in the Mundane Shell to the destructive principle of sacrifice implied in the reference to Albion's Altars. Line 81 would seem to refer to the latter, not to the former.

Page 43. 'They' refers to the Friends of Albion. For the Wheels cp. F. Z. i. 260 *note*.

2–3 The identity of the Twenty-four Friends of Albion with the Zoas is again mentioned in l. 14, and more definitely in J. 46. 23–24:

And then the Four in whom the twenty-four appear'd fourfold,
Verulam, London, York, Edinburgh,

the 'English names' of the Zoas. But elsewhere (J. 57. 1) they combine into Bath, Canterbury, York, and Edinburgh. The significance of these correspondences and their variations does not appear.

5 The 'Four Complexions', only mentioned here, seem to relate to the Four Regions of the World of Eternity, identified with the Four Arts, 'Poetry, Painting, Music, and Architecture' (cp. M. 24. 35 *note*). The expression may have been derived from Böhme, though the meaning is not.

6 This is another reference to the closing of the Western Gate: cp. J. 13. 6. The Oaks are the Druid Oaks, symbols of Natural Religion: cp. l. 8, 'rooty grove', and see Index, *Druid*.

If we are merciful, ourselves must suffer destruction on his Oaks.
Why should we enter into our Spectres, to behold our own corruptions?
O God of Albion, descend! deliver Jerusalem from the Oaken Groves!'

Then Los grew furious, raging: 'Why stand we here trembling around,
Calling on God for help, and not ourselves in whom God dwells,
Stretching a hand to save the falling Man? Are we not Four,
Beholding Albion upon the Precipice ready to fall into Non-Entity,
Seeing these Heavens & Hells conglobing in the Void, Heavens over Hells
Brooding in holy hypocritic lust, drinking the cries of pain
From howling victims of Law, building Heavens Twenty-seven-fold,
Swell'd & bloated General Forms repugnant to the Divine-
Humanity, who is the Only General and Universal Form,
To which all Lineaments tend & seek with love & sympathy?
All broad & general principles belong to benevolence,
Who protects minute particulars, every one in their own identity.
But here the affectionate touch of the tongue is clos'd in by deadly teeth;
And the soft smile of friendship & the open dawn of benevolence
Become a net & a trap, & every energy render'd cruel,
Till the existence of friendship & benevolence is denied.
The wine of the Spirit & the vineyards of the Holy-One
Here turn into poisonous stupor & deadly intoxication,
That they may be condemn'd by Law & the Lamb of God be slain.
And the two Sources of Life in Eternity, Hunting and War,

10 Cp. Milton's descent into his Spectre for the same purpose of self-annihilation (M. 12. 33–41).

13 Cp. J. 34. 28 *note*.

16 This line would seem to refer to the formation of particular ethical systems within the general body of error: cp. J. 49. 60–64. And see Index, *Mundane Shell*, II–III.

19–21 See Index, *Human Form*.

28–30 The enslavement of energy in Orc, and the change in Luvah from Love to Hate may illustrate these lines: see Index, *Orc*, § II (*a*), and *Luvah*, § II.

31 Cp. M. 35. 2–3.

Are become the Sources of dark & bitter Death & of corroding Hell.
The open heart is shut up in integuments of frozen silence,
That the spear that lights it forth may shatter the ribs & bosom,
A pretence of Art to destroy Art, a pretence of Liberty
To destroy Liberty, a pretence of Religion to destroy Religion.
Oshea and Caleb fight: they contend in the valleys of ⟨of⟩ Peor,
In the terrible Family Contentions of those who love each other.
The Armies of Balaam weep: no women come to the field.
Dead corses lay before them, & not as in Wars of old:
For the Soldier who fights for Truth calls his enemy his brother:
They fight & contend for life, & not for eternal death.
But here the Soldier strikes, & a dead corse falls at his feet;
Nor Daughter nor Sister nor Mother come forth to embosom the Slain.
But Death, Eternal Death, remains in the Valleys of Peor.
The English are scatter'd over the face of the Nations: are these
Jerusalem's children? Hark! hear the Giants of Albion cry at night:
"We smell the blood of the English! we delight in their blood on our Altars.

33–34 The meaning of these lines is not quite certain. It may be intended to describe the difficulty and pain that attends the attempt to pierce with 'intellectual spears' (J. 38. 15) the 'petrific body' of moral and empirical and artistic error enclosing fallen man.

35–36 Cp. R. N.: 'Concession to Truth for the sake of Oversetting Truth' and *Auguries of Innocence*, ll. 53–54 (Clar. Press, p. 290):

> Truth that's told with bad intent
> Beats all the Lies you can invent.

Cp. also D. C. iii, p. 27: 'As there is a class of men whose sole delight is the destruction of men, so there is a class of artist whose sole art and science is fabricated for the purpose of destroying art.'

37 This reference to the story of Numbers xiii–xiv, with the similar passage in J. 49. 56–59, cannot be interpreted on the material available.

40 The 'Wars of old' 'that ancient happy period which history has recorded' (D. C. v, p. 50) are 'the severe contentions of friendship' (J. 91. 17). 43–45 Cp. M., Preface, *note* 2.

46 Cp. J. 92. 1–2, where at Albion's 'resurrection into Unity' the British, Saxon, Roman, and Norman 'amalgamate' into 'One Nation, the English'.

47 This adaptation of a familiar rhyme to the purposes of mystical symbolism does not appear to modify or extend the sinister significance of the term 'Giant': see Index, *Giant*.

The living & the dead shall be ground in our rumbling Mills
For bread of the Sons of Albion, of the Giants Hand & Scofield."
Scofeld & Kox are let loose upon my Saxons : they accumulate
A World in which Man is by his Nature the Enemy of Man,
In pride of Selfhood unwieldy stretching out into Non Entity,
Generalizing Art & Science till Art & Science is lost.
Bristol & Bath, listen to my words ! & ye Seventeen, give ear !
It is easy to acknowledge a man to be great & good while we
Derogate from him in the trifles & small articles of that goodness.
Those alone are his friends, who admire his minutest powers.
Instead of Albion's lovely mountains & the curtains of Jerusalem,
I see a Cave, a Rock, a Tree deadly and poisonous, unimaginative :
Instead of the Mutual Forgivenesses, the Minute Particulars, I see
Pits of bitumen ever burning, artificial Riches of the Canaanite
Like Lakes of liquid lead ; instead of heavenly Chapels, built
By our dear Lord, I see Worlds crusted with snows & ice.
I see a Wicker Idol woven round Jerusalem's children. I see
The Canaanite, the Amalekite, the Moabite, the Egyptian,
By Demonstrations the cruel Sons of Quality & Negation,
Driven on the Void in incoherent despair into Non Entity.
I see America clos'd apart, & Jerusalem driven in terror
Away from Albion's mountains, far away from London's spires.
I will not endure this thing : I alone withstand to death
This outrage. Ah me ! how sick & pale you all stand round me !

52 'Man [that is, mortal man] is born a Spectre or Satan' (J. 52) and is thereby opposed to Eternal Man, the Divine Humanity.

54 Elsewhere Blake develops this criticism on the artistic side, applying it to Titian and Correggio : 'They cause that every thing in art shall become a Machine. They cause that the execution shall all be blocked up with brown shadows. They put the original Artist in fear and doubt of his own original conception . . . for when the Artist took up his pencil to execute his ideas, his power of imagination weakened so much and darkened, that memory of nature and of Pictures of the various Schools possessed his mind, instead of appropriate execution resulting from the inventions, like walking in another man's style, or speaking or looking in another man's style and manner' (D. C. ix, p. 55).

55 The Seventeen are of the Friends of Albion : cp. J. 45. 37–46. 19.

60–65 See Index, *Druid*.

71 Cp. *Advertizement*, pp. 18–19. 'If all the princes in Europe, like Louis XIV and Charles I, were to patronize such blockheads, I, William Blake, a Mental Prince, would decollate and hang their souls as guilty of mental high treason.'

Ah me! pitiable ones! do you also go to death's vale?
All you my Friends & Brothers, all you my belovèd Companions,
Have you also caught the infection of Sin & stern Repentance?
I see Disease arise upon you: yet speak to me and give
Me some comfort! Why do you all stand silent? I alone
Remain in permanent strength. Or is all this goodness & pity only
That you may take the greater vengeance in your Sepulcher?'

So Los spoke. Pale they stood around the House of Death
In the midst of temptations & despair, among the rooted Oaks,
Among rearèd Rocks of Albion's Sons: at length they rose
[44] With one accord in love sublime, & as on Cherubs' wings
They Albion surround with kindest violence to bear him back
Against his will thro' Los's Gate to Eden, Four-fold, loud,
Their Wings waving over the bottomless Immense, to bear
Their awful charge back to his native home: but Albion, dark,
Repugnant, roll'd his Wheels backward into Non-Entity.
Loud roll the Starry Wheels of Albion into the World of Death;
And all the Gate of Los clouded with clouds redounding from
Albion's dread Wheels, stretching out spaces immense between,
That every little particle of light & air became Opake,
Black & immense, a Rock of difficulty & a Cliff
Of black despair, that the immortal Wings labour'd against
Cliff after Cliff & over Valleys of despair & death.
The narrow Sea between Albion & the Atlantic Continent,
Its waves of pearl became a boundless Ocean, bottomless,
Of grey obscurity, fill'd with clouds & rocks & whirling waters,
And Albion's Sons ascending & des[c]ending in the horrid Void.

But as the Will must not be bended but in the day of Divine
Power, silent, calm & motionless, in the mid-air sublime,
The Family Divine hover around the darken'd Albion.

79 Cp. J. 37. 6 *note*. Here the Sepulchre, the state of spiritual death, darkness and corruption, has a more particular reference to the tyranny of the Moral Virtues. Once more the reference is to the fallacy of an abstract standard of right and wrong, perplexing the spirit by calls to repentance and inhibiting individual freedom. Cp. M., extra p. 17. 19–24.

Page 44. 1 Cp. J. 22. 34–35:

> Why should Punishment Weave the Veil with Iron Wheels of War,
> When Forgiveness might it Weave with Wings of Cherubim?

8 Cp. J. 38. 55–39. 3, and cp. M. 35. 66–67 and *note*.

10 Cp. F. Z. iv. 274 *note*, and J. 77, *poem*, 8–11, where the 'Wheel of Religion' is described in its effects upon man's perceptions.

14–16 See Index, *Atlantic*.

18–19 Cp. F. Z. vi. 280–281, and General Introduction, p. 90.

Such is the nature of the Ulro, that whatever enters
Becomes Sexual, & is Created and Vegetated and Born.
From Hyde Park spread their vegetating roots beneath Albion
In dreadful pain, the Spectrous Uncircumcisèd Vegetation
Forming a Sexual Machine, an Agèd Virgin Form
In Erin's Land toward the north, joint after joint, & burning
In love & jealousy immingled & calling it Religion.
And feeling the damps of death they with one accord delegated
Los,
Conjuring him by the Highest that he should Watch over them
Till Jesus shall appear : & they gave their power to Los,
Naming him the Spirit of Prophecy, calling him Elijah.

Strucken with Albion's disease they become what they behold.
They assimilate with Albion in pity & compassion :
Their Emanations return not : their Spectres rage in the Deep :
The Slumbers of Death came over them around the Couch of
Death,
Before the Gate of Los & in the depths of Non Entity,
Among the Furnaces of Los, among the Oaks of Albion.

Man is adjoin'd to Man by his Emanative portion,
Who is Jerusalem in every individual Man ; and her
Shadow is Vala, builded by the Reasoning power in Man.
O search & see ; turn your eyes inward : open, O thou World
Of Love & Harmony in Man ! expand thy ever lovely Gates !

They wept into the deeps a little space : at length was heard
The voice of Bath, faint as the voice of the Dead in the House
of Death,
45] Bath, healing City ! whose wisdom, in midst of Poetic
Fervor, mild spoke thro' the Western Porch in soft gentle tears.

23–27 The punctuation of this passage presents considerable difficulty, partly because its meaning is uncertain. The 'vegetating roots', the 'Spectrous Uncircumcised Vegetation', the 'Sexual Machine', and 'Aged Virgin Form' seem to repeat the commoner symbols of the Tree of Moral Virtue and the Veil of the Female 'woven for Moral Laws'. Hence their identification with 'Religion'. The passage relates to the Spectres of Albion's Friends : see below, ll. 32–37.

28 'They' are the Friends of Albion. 32 Cp. J. 36. 9 *note*.

38–39 Cp. J. 88. 3–15, and see Index, *Emanation*.

40 See Index, *Vala*.

Page 45. Like pp. 42–43, this appears to be an interpolation, Blake's desire being apparently to emphasize at this point the power of the Divine Humanity. The engraved script differs from that of pages 44 and 46.

1–2 Its association with the west, with Wisdom, and Poetic Fervour, indicate the visionary nature of Bath at this point : cp J. 41. 1 *note*, 45. 33, and 46. 1–2.

‘ O Albion, mildest Son of Eden ! clos’d is thy Western Gate !
Brothers of Eternity, this Man whose great example
We all admir’d & lov’d, whose all benevolent countenance, seen
In Eden, in lovely Jerusalem, drew even from envy
The tear, and the confession of honesty, open & undisguis’d,
From mistrust and suspition, The Man is himself become
A piteous example of oblivion, To teach the Sons
Of Eden, that however great and glorious, however loving
And merciful the Individuality, however high
Our palaces and cities, and however fruitful are our fields,
In Selfhood we are nothing, but fade away in morning’s breath.
Our mildness is nothing : the greatest mildness we can use
Is incapable and nothing : none but the Lamb of God can heal
This dread disease : none but Jesus. O Lord, descend and save !
Albion’s Western Gate is clos’d : his death is coming apace :
Jesus alone can save him : for alas, we none can know
How soon his lot may be our own. When Africa in sleep
Rose in the night of Beulah, and bound down the Sun & Moon,
His friends cut his strong chains, & overwhelm’d his dark
Machines in fury & destruction ; and the Man reviving repented.
He wept before his wrathful brethren, thankful & considerate
For their well timèd wrath. But Albion’s sleep is not
Like Africa’s ; and his machines are woven with his life.
Nothing but mercy can save him, nothing but mercy, interposing
Lest he should slay Jerusalem in his fearful jealousy.
O God, descend ! gather our brethren ! deliver Jerusalem !
But that we may omit no office of the friendly spirit,
Oxford, take thou these leaves of the Tree of Life : with eloquence,
That thy immortal tongue inspires, present them to Albion :
Perhaps he may recieve them, offer’d from thy lovèd hands.’

So spoke, unheard by Albion, the merciful Son of Heaven
To those whose Western Gates were open, as they stood weeping

9 Cp. Swedenborg, *The Apocalypse Revealed*, § 758 : ‘ The selfhood of man is nothing but evil ; wherefore he who attaches what is Divine to himself as his own, not only defiles but profanes it.’

19–25 This myth of Africa is not developed elsewhere : cp. *The Song of Los*, Introduction.

30 Cp. Rev. xxii. 2 : ‘ and the leaves of the tree [of life] were for the healing of the nations.’ Cp. J. 46. 7 *note*.

Around Albion: but Albion heard him not: obdurate, hard,
He frown'd on all his Friends, counting them enemies in his sorrow.

And the Seventeen conjoining with Bath, the Seventh
In whom the other Ten shone manifest, a Divine Vision,
Assimilated and embrac'd Eternal Death for Albion's sake.

And these the names of the Eighteen combining with those Ten.
[46] Bath, mild Physician of Eternity, mysterious power,
Whose springs are unsearchable & knowledg[e] infinite ;
Hereford, ancient Guardian of Wales, whose hands
Builded the mountain palaces of Eden, stupendous works ;
Lincoln, Durham & Carlisle, Councellors of Los ;
And Ely, Scribe of Los, whose pen no other hand
Dare touch ; Oxford, immortal Bard ; with eloquence
Divine he wept over Albion, speaking the words of God
In mild perswasion, bringing leaves of the Tree of Life :

'Thou art in Error, Albion, the Land of Ulro.
One Error not remov'd will destroy a human Soul.
Repose in Beulah's night, till the Error is remov'd.
Reason not on both sides. Repose upon our bosoms
Till the Plow of Jehovah and the Harrow of Shaddai
Have passèd over the Dead to awake the Dead to Judgment.'
But Albion turn'd away refusing comfort.

37–39 This passage repeats the thesis of *Milton*, Self-annihilation, willing sacrifice of Self. For the significance of the Seventeen, cp. J. 43. 55 *note*.

Page 46. 7–9 Cp. J. 45. 30–32. In a letter to Hayley, 27th January 1804, Blake speaks of a 'much admired and respected Edward, the bard of Oxford, whose verses still sound upon my ear like the distant approach of things mighty and magnificent, like the sound of harps which I hear before the sun's rising' (R., pp. 141–142). Gilchrist (1880), vol. i, p. 203, identifies him with 'a certain young Mr. Edward Marsh, of Oriel College, who when visiting Hayley while Blake was also his frequent guest and fellow labourer, had been wont to read aloud to them the Hermit's own compositions in a singularly melodious voice'. Blake's name, with those of Hayley, Edward Marsh, Fellow of Oriel College, and others of the Felpham circle, appears among the subscribers to the three-volume edition of *Poems by the Rev. James Hurdis, D.D., Late Fellow of Magdalen College, and Professor of Poetry in the University of Oxford* (Oxford, 1808). Hurdis was a friend of Cowper and Hayley, and Blake may have met him at Hayley's house. He died in December 1801, that is, during Blake's stay at Felpham, and it is just possible that it is to his works that Blake refers in the present passage.

13 With the phrase 'Reason not on both sides' cp. Blake's letter to George Cumberland, 12th April 1827 : 'God keep you and me from the divinity of yes and no too—the yea, nay, creeping Jesus—from supposing up and down to be the same thing as all experimentalists must suppose ?' (R., p. 222). It is no part of man's business to 'reason and compare' ; this is the error of the philosophers. 14–15 See Index, *Plow*.

Oxford trembled while he spoke, then fainted in the arms
Of Norwich, Peterboro, Rochester, Chester awful, Worcester,
Litchfield, Saint David's, Landaff, Asaph, Bangor, Sodor,
Bowing their heads devoted : and the Furnaces of Los
Began to rage ; thundering loud the storms began to roar
Upon the Furnaces, and loud the Furnaces rebellow beneath.

And these the Four in whom the twenty-four appear'd four-fold :
Verulam, London, York, Edinburgh, mourning one towards another:
'Alas ! The time will come, when a man's worst enemies
Shall be those of his own house and family, in a Religion
Of Generation to destroy by Sin and Atonement happy Jerusalem,
The Bride and Wife of the Lamb. O God, thou art Not an Avenger !'

. . . .

[47] From Camberwell to Highgate where the mighty Thames shudders along,
Where Los's Furnaces stand, where Jerusalem & Vala howl,
Luvah tore forth from Albion's Loins in fibrous veins, in rivers
Of blood over Europe, a Vegetating Root in grinding pain,
Animating the Dragon Temples, soon to become that Holy Fiend
The Wicker Man of Scandinavia, in which cruelly consumèd
The Captives, rear'd to heaven, howl in flames among the stars.
Loud the cries of War on the Rhine & Danube with Albion's Sons.
Away from Beulah's hills & vales break forth the Souls of the Dead,
With cymbal, trumpet, clarion & the scythèd chariots of Britain.

25–26 J. 27. 77–84.

Page 47. The sequence here is uncertain : the first two lines read like the conclusion of a passage that cannot be found. At the top of the page are traces of a deleted line, the last portion of which is faintly discernible, 'Hope is banished from me', as if l. 17 of this page had been written out of its right order.

1–2 From Camberwell to Highgate, from south to north, is the direction in which Los's Furnaces are ranged (J. 53. 14). The 'Spectres of the Dead' with whom Luvah is sometimes identified 'revolve into the Furnace Southward & are driven forth Northward' (J. 5. 31).

6 Cp. M. 37. 11 *note*.

8 This may be a reference to the Napoleonic campaigns of 1805–1806 (cp. M. 25. 1 *note*). For Blake's symbolic interpretation of 'War' cp. M., Preface, *note* 1.

10 These are symbols of 'Corporeal War', 'contradicting & blaspheming'. Vision or Imagination (M. 12. 16).

Bath, mild Physician of Eternity, mysterious power
Whose springs are unsearchable & knowledg infinite:
Hereford, ancient Guardian of Wales, whose hands
Builded the mountain palaces of Eden, stupendous works!
Lincoln, Durham & Carlisle, Councellors of Los.
And Ely, Scribe of Los, whose pen no other hand
Dare touch: Oxford, immortal Bard! with eloquence
Divine, he wept over Albion: speaking the words of God
In mild perswasion: bringing leaves of the Tree of Life.

Thou art in Error Albion, the Land of Ulro:
One Error not removd, will destroy a human Soul
Repose in Beulahs night, till the Error is removd
Reason not on both sides. Repose upon our bosoms
Till the Plow of Jehovah, and the Harrow of Shaddai
Have passed over the Dead, to awake the Dead to Judgment.
But Albion turnd away refusing comfort.

Oxford trembled while he spoke, then fainted in the arms
Of Norwich, Peterboro, Rochester, Chester awful, Worcester,
Litchfield, Saint Davids, Landaff, Asaph, Bangor, Sodor,
Bowing their heads devoted: and the Furnaces of Los
Began to rage, thundering loud the storms began to roar
Upon the Furnaces, and loud the Furnaces rebellow beneath

And these the Four in whom the twenty-four appeard four-fold:
Verulam, London, York, Edinburgh, mourning one towards another
Alas!—The time will come, when a mans worst enemies
Shall be those of his own house and family: in a Religion
Of Generation, to destroy by Sin and Atonement, happy Jerusalem,
The Bride and Wife of the Lamb. O God thou art Not an Avenger!

Jerusalem: page 46

And the Veil of Vala is composèd of the Spectres of the Dead.

Hark! the mingling cries of Luvah with the Sons of Albion!
Hark! & Record the terrible wonder, that the Punisher
Mingles with his Victim's Spectre, enslavèd & tormented
To him whom he has murder'd, bound in vengeance & enmity.
Shudder not, but Write, & the hand of God will assist you!
Therefore I write Albion's last words: 'Hope is banish'd from me.'

[48] These were his last words; and the merciful Saviour in his arms
Reciev'd him, in the arms of tender mercy, and repos'd
The pale limbs of his Eternal Individuality
Upon the Rock of Ages. Then, surrounded with a Cloud,
In silence the Divine Lord builded with immortal labour,
Of gold & jewels, a sublime Ornament, a Couch of repose,
With Sixteen pillars canopied with emblems & written verse,
Spiritual Verse, order'd & measur'd, from whence time shall reveal
The Five books of the Decalogue, the books of Joshua & Judges,
Samuel a double book, & Kings a double book, the Psalms & Prophets,
The Four-fold Gospel, and the Revelations everlasting.
Eternity groan'd & was troubled at the image of Eternal Death!

Beneath the bottoms of the Graves, which is Earth's central joint,
There is a place where Contrarieties are equally true:
(To protect from the Giant blows in the sports of intellect,
Thunder in the midst of kindness, & love that kills its belovèd;
Because Death is for a period, and they renew tenfold).
From this sweet Place Maternal Love awoke Jerusalem.

11 Cp. J. 24. 31–35, and see Index, *Vala, Note II.*

13–15 Cp. J. 36. 9 *note*. *The Ghost of Abel* develops this theme.

16 The doubtful order of the pages at this point make it impossible to discover the speaker of these lines, which are apparently addressed to Blake, or to discover the point at which the speech begins.

Page 48. 3–4 Cp. M. 14. 10–16. For the Rock of Ages, cp. F. Z. ix. 284 *note*.

7–11 Cp. *Cat.* 1810: 'The Hebrew Bible & the Greek Gospel are Genuine, preservèd by the Saviour's Mercy.' The omission of the Pauline writings is noteworthy and in harmony with the estimate of Paul implied in the symbolic use of the apostle's name: cp. F. Z. viii. 351 *note* and J. 98. 28 *note*.

13–20 See Index, *Beulah*. 18 Cp. J. 5. 47 *note*.

With pangs she forsook Beulah's pleasant lovely shadowy Universe
Where no dispute can come, created for those who Sleep.

Weeping was in all Beulah, and all the Daughters of Beulah
Wept for their Sister the Daughter of Albion, Jerusalem,
When out of Beulah the Emanation of the Sleeper descended
With solemn mourning out of Beulah's moony shades and hills
Within the Human Heart, whose Gates closèd with solemn sound.

And this the manner of the terrible Separation.
The Emanations of the grievously afflicted Friends of Albion
Concenter in one Female form, an Agèd pensive Woman.
Astonish'd, lovely, embracing the sublime shade, the Daughters of Beulah
Beheld her with wonder. With awful hands she took
A Moment of Time, drawing it out with many tears & afflictions
And many sorrows oblique across the Atlantic Vale,
Which is the Vale of Rephaim dreadful, from East to West
Where the Human Harvest waves abundant in the beams of Eden,
Into a Rainbow of jewels and gold, a mild Reflection from
Albion's dread Tomb, Eight thousand and five hundred years
In its extension. Every two hundred years has a door to Eden.
She also took an Atom of Space, with dire pain opening it a Center
Into Beulah: trembling the Daughters of Beulah dried
Her tears; she ardent embrac'd her sorrows, occupied in labours
Of sublime mercy in Rephaim's Vale. Perusing Albion's Tomb
She sat: she walk'd among the ornaments solemn mourning:
The Daughters attended her shudderings, wiping the death sweat.

21–25 Cp. J. 5. 46–53 and 14. 31–34. The closing of the Gate of the Human Heart has apparently something of the meaning of the closing of the Western Gate: cp. J. 13. 6 *note*. 32–37 See Index, *Atlantic*.

35–39 The Rainbow is mentioned in J. 83. 67 and 86. 21. It is the symbol of the promise of regeneration in the 8,500 years of mortality (cp. J. 37. 7). As the reflection of Albion's dread tomb (M. 9. 9 *note*) it represents the specious illusion of an objectively real Universe of Man: it is beautiful by reason of the promise defined by the 'doors' or 'windows into Eden' that give 'visions to sweet heaven': cp. F. Z. i. 135 and *note*. Cp. Enitharmon's space created for Satan, M. 11. 12–17.

Los also saw her in his seventh Furnace ; he also terrified
Saw the finger of God go forth upon his seventh Furnace,
Away from the Starry Wheels to prepare Jerusalem a place;
When with a dreadful groan the Emanation mild of Albion
Burst from his bosom in the Tomb like a pale snowy cloud,
Female and lovely, struggling to put off the Human form,
Writhing in pain. The Daughters of Beulah in kind arms reciev'd
Jerusalem, weeping over her among the Spaces of Erin
In the Ends of Beulah, where the Dead wail night & day.

And thus Erin spoke to the Daughters of Beulah, in soft tears :

' Albion the Vortex of the Dead, Albion the Generous,
Albion the mildest son of Heaven, The Place of Holy Sacrifice
Where Friends Die for each other, will become the Place
Of Murder, & Unforgiving Never-awaking Sacrifice of Enemies.
The Children must be sacrific'd (a horror never known
Till now in Beulah,) unless a Refuge can be found
To hide them from the wrath of Albion's Law, that freezes sore
Upon his Sons & Daughters self-exilèd from his bosom.
Draw ye Jerusalem away from Albion's Mountains
To give a Place for Redemption : let Sihon and Og
Remove Eastward to Bashan and Gilead, and leave
[49] The secret coverts of Albion & the hidden places of America.
Jerusalem ! Jerusalem ! why wilt thou turn away ?
Come ye, O Daughters of Beulah, lament for Og & Sihon
Upon the Lakes of Ireland from Rathlin to Baltimore.
Stand ye upon the Dargle from Wicklow to Drogheda,

44 Cp. J. 16. 16 and Index, *Furnaces*. 49 Cp. J. 20. 29.
54 Cp. F. Z. vi. 184 *note*. 58 Cp. J. 20. 27–28 : 31. 44–46 : 42. 42–44 : and Index, *Minute Particulars*.
63–64 The expulsion of the heathen races from Canaan is made the symbol of that putting off of error which is the condition of regeneration. ' Eastward ' has its usual Blakean significance, being the quarter proper to error. For the Mountains cp. J. 4. 26 *note*.
Page 49. This page appears to have been inserted later. It contains such definite statements of Blake's doctrines as have already been noticed on the similar pages 42, 43, and 45. The final lines of this page repeat the substance of the concluding lines of p. 48, so that p. 50 reads continuously with it.
4–5 Ireland is ' Erin's Continent ' (J. 78. 26–27), the western land, and like America, the place of liberty and Imagination. Here the Giants dwelt before the floods of abstraction overwhelmed them (J. 89. 50) and here are laid the foundations of Jerusalem (J. 29. 20 : 71. 52 : 72. 14).

Come & mourn over Albion the White Cliff of the Atlantic,
The Mountain of Giants. All the Giants of Albion are become
Weak, wither'd, darken'd ; & Jerusalem is cast forth from Albion.
They deny that they ever knew Jerusalem or ever dwelt in Shiloh.
The Gigantic roots & twigs of the vegetating Sons of Albion,
Fill'd with the little-ones, are consumèd in the Fires of their Altars.
The vegetating Cities are burnèd & consumèd from the Earth,
And the Bodies in which all Animals & Vegetations, the Earth & Heaven,
Were contain'd in the All Glorious Imagination are wither'd & darken'd.
The golden Gate of Havilah and all the Garden of God
Was caught up with the Sun in one day of fury and war.
The Lungs, the Heart, the Liver shrunk away far distant from Man
And left a little slimy substance floating upon the tides.
In one night the Atlantic Continent was caught up with the Moon
And became an Opake Globe far distant, clad with moony beams.
The Visions of Eternity, by reason of narrowèd perceptions,
Are become weak Visions of Time & Space fix'd into furrows of death,
Till deep dissimulation is the only defence an honest man has left.
O Polypus of Death ! O Spectre over Europe and Asia,
Withering the Human Form by Laws of Sacrifice for Sin !

6 Cp. M. 4. 20 *note*. 7 See Index, *Giants*.

9 Shiloh is constantly associated with Jerusalem ; cp. F. Z. i. 238 : J. 49. 46 : 55. 28–29 : 79. 10 : 85. 22 : 86. 44. As the abiding place of the Ark, where God revealed himself to the Israelites, before the Temple was built, it apparently has something of the symbolic significance of Jerusalem. No explanation can be offered of J. 49. 48 and J. 55. 29 where Shiloh is the Emanation of France, nor of J. 49. 47.

10 See Index, *Mundane Shell, Note I* i.

12 Cp. J. 33. 14 *note*.

15–16 The loss of Eden is treated symbolically : cp. Gen. ii. 11–12. Havilah is mentioned in the same manner in J. 55. 22. For another use of the symbol cp. J. 19. 42 *note*.

17–18 Cp. B. L., chaps. ii–iii. No satisfactory explanation has been found possible.

20 Cp. M. 28. 15–16 :

As to that false appearance which appears to the reasoner
As of a Globe rolling thro' Voidness, it is a delusion of Ulro.

24 See Index, *Mundane Shell, Note I*. B.

By Laws of Chastity & Abhorrence I am wither'd up,
Striving to Create a Heaven in which all shall be pure & holy
In their Own Selfhoods, in Natural Selfish Chastity to banish Pity
And dear Mutual Forgiveness & to become One Great Satan
Inslav'd to the most powerful Selfhood, to murder the Divine Humanity,
In whose sight all are as the dust & who chargeth his Angels with folly!
Ah! weak & wide astray! Ah! shut in narrow doleful form,
Creeping in reptile flesh upon the bosom of the ground!
The Eye of Man, a little narrow orb clos'd up & dark,
Scarcely beholding the Great Light, conversing with the ground;
The Ear, a little shell, in small volutions shutting out
True Harmonies, & comprehending great as very small;
The Nostrils, bent down to the earth & clos'd with senseless flesh,
That odours cannot them expand nor joy on them exult;
The Tongue, a little moisture fills, a little food it cloys,
A little sound it utters, & its cries are faintly heard.
Therefore they are removèd: therefore they have taken root
In Egypt & Philistea, in Moab & Edom & Aram.
In the Erythrean Sea their Uncircumcision in Heart & Loins
Be lost for ever & ever: then they shall arise from Self
By Self Annihilation into Jerusalem's Courts & into Shiloh,
Shiloh, the Masculine Emanation among the Flowers of Beulah.
Lo, Shiloh dwells over France, as Jerusalem dwells over Albion!
Build & prepare a Wall & Curtain for America's shore!
Rush on! Rush on! Rush on, ye vegetating Sons of Albion!
The Sun shall go before you in Day: the Moon shall go

27–28 Cp. J. 52, '*To the Deists*', *passim*.

32–35 These lines apostrophize mortal man, the 'worm of sixty winters' (J. 34. 57).

42 'They' refers to the Giants of Albion: see above, ll. 7–8.

44 The Erythrean is apparently equivalent to the Atlantic Ocean, for which see Index. Some word such as 'till' would seem to be needed after 'Sea'. Cp. J. 41:

> Each Man is in his Spectre's power,
> Untill the arrival of that hour,
> When his Humanity awake
> And cast his Spectre into the Lake.

49 This refers to spiritual labours such as those of Los, to defend the innocent and instruct the ignorant.

50–59 Again that which was meant for the destruction of Man becomes subservient to the divine purpose of regeneration in mortality: see below, ll. 54–55.

Before you in Night. Come on ! Come on ! Come on ! The Lord
Jehovah is before, behind, above, beneath, around !
He has builded the arches of Albion's Tomb, binding the Stars
In merciful Order, bending the Laws of Cruelty to Peace.
He hath placèd Og & Anak, the Giants of Albion, for their Guards,
Building the Body of Moses in the Valley of Peor, the Body
Of Divine Analogy : and Og & Sihon in the tears of Balaam,
The Son of Beor, have given their power to Joshua & Caleb.
Remove from Albion, far remove these terrible surfaces.
They are beginning to form Heavens & Hells in immense
Circles, the Hells for food to the Heavens, food of torment,
Food of despair : they drink the condemn'd Soul & rejoice
In cruel holiness in their Heavens of Chastity & Uncircumcision.
Yet they are blameless ; & Iniquity must be imputed only
To the State they are enter'd into that they may be deliver'd :
Satan is the State of Death & not a Human existence ;
But Luvah is namèd Satan, because he has enter'd that State,
A World where Man is by Nature the enemy of Man ;
Because the Evil is Created into a State that Men
May be deliver'd time after time, evermore. Amen.
Learn therefore, O Sisters, to distinguish the Eternal Human
That walks about among the stones of fire in bliss & woe
Alternate, from those States or Worlds in which the Spirit travels.
This is the only means to Forgiveness of Enemies.
Therefore remove from Albion these terrible Surfaces ;
And let wild seas & rocks close up Jerusalem away from
[50] The Atlantic Mountains where Giants dwelt in Intellect ;
Now given to stony Druids and Allegoric Generation,

54 Cp. J. 50. 20–21.

56–59 The present lines seem to restate J. 48. 4–12, in which case the Body of Moses, the Body of Divine Analogy, might be the Mosaic books interpreted as a divine allegory, and not as literal statements of mundane history. Elsewhere Og, Anak, and Sihon are purely spectrous symbols (cp. M. 18. 29 *note*). Joshua and Caleb, the spies who brought the just report of Canaan, appear to symbolize visionary agencies : cp. J. 43. 37 and J. 98. 28 *note*.

60 The ' surfaces ' appear to be the errors that gather about the fallen man, the ' excrementitious husk and covering ' of delusion that enshrouds him. Cp. J. 83. 46–48, and see Index, *Vala, Note II*.

62–64 Moral Virtue exists by the repression of those activities that it arbitrarily declares to be evil, ' The Sexual Death living on accusation of Sin & Judgment ' (J. 64. 22).

64 Uncircumcision is the state in which Error has not yet been annihilated.

66–74 See Index, *States*.

Page 50. 2 See Index, *Generation*, and cp. J. 30. 18 *note*.

To the Twelve Gods of Asia, the Spectres of those who Sleep,
Sway'd by a Providence oppos'd to the Divine Lord Jesus,
A murderous Providence, A Creation that groans, living on Death,
Where Fish & Bird & Beast & Man & Tree & Metal & Stone
Live by Devouring, going into Eternal Death continually.
Albion is now possess'd by the War of Blood : the Sacrifice
Of envy Albion is become, and his Emanation cast out.
Come, Lord Jesus, Lamb of God, descend ! for if, O Lord,
If thou hadst been here, our brother Albion had not died.
Arise, sisters ! Go ye & meet the Lord, while I remain.
Behold the foggy mornings of the Dead on Albion's cliffs !
Ye know that if the Emanation remains in them
She will become an Eternal Death, an Avenger of Sin,
A Self-righteousness, the proud Virgin-Harlot, Mother of War,
And we also, & all Beulah, consume beneath Albion's curse.'

So Erin spoke to the Daughters of Beulah. Shuddering
With their wings they sat in the Furnace in a night
Of stars ; for all the Sons of Albion appear'd distant stars,
Ascending and descending into Albion's sea of death :
And Erin's lovely Bow enclos'd the Wheels of Albion's Sons.

Expanding on wing, the Daughters of Beulah replied in sweet response :

'Come, O thou Lamb of God, and take away the remembrance of Sin.
To Sin & to hide the Sin in sweet deceit is lovely :

3 The Twelve Gods of Asia, identified with the Sons and Daughters of Albion (J. 74. 22), are not distinguishable from the 'Spectre'. They are the 'Gods of the Heathen' (J. 60. 52) :

who labour in Tirzah's Looms for bread ;
Who set Pleasure against Duty, who Create Olympic crowns
To make Learning a burden & the Work of the Holy Spirit Strife.
(M. 25. 50–52.)

Cp. D. C. iii, p. 21 : 'The Grecian gods were the ancient Cherubim of Phoenicia, but the Greeks and since them the Moderns have neglected to subdue the gods of Priam. These gods are visions of the eternal attributes or divine names, which, when erected into gods, become destructive to humanity. They ought to be the servants and not the masters of man or of society.'

5–7 Cp. B. U. viii. 5 : 'For he [Urizen] saw that life liv'd upon death', i.e. mundane life, with its illusions of corporeity and morality, persists by the destruction or atrophy of the spiritual powers.

10 Cp. F. Z. vii *a*. 288–295.

14–16 See Index, *Emanation*. 20 Cp. M. 37. 47 *note*.

22 Cp. J. 48. 35 *note*. The regenerative purpose expressed in Erin's Rainbow manifests itself on all sides in mundane existence : cp. J. 12. 15 : 'God is within and without : he is even in the depths of Hell.' And cp. J. 49. 53.

To Sin in the open face of day is cruel & pitiless. But
To record the Sin for a reproach, to let the Sun go down
In a remembrance of the Sin, is a Woe & a Horror,
A brooder of an Evil Day and a Sun rising in blood !
Come then, O Lamb of God, and take away the remembrance
of Sin.'

End of Chap. 2^d^

26 This is a difficult saying, chiefly because it is impossible to be certain as to how much of its strangeness proceeds from the imperfectly understood significance of the Daughters of Beulah, who utter it. But this much emerges, that however great the sin, the obligation to forgiveness is greater.

30 Cp. J. 25. 12–13 :

Descend, O Lamb of God, & take away the imputation of Sin
By the Creation of States & the deliverance of Individuals Evermore, Amen.

Page 51 contains a full-page design showing two figures crouching with heads bowed ; that to the left bears crown and sceptre, and in some copies her name ' Vala ' is written beneath. Her companion is identified in the same way as ' Hyle '. Another figure to the right stands manacled : he is ' Scofield '. The background is flame : at the bottom left corner ' W. B [word *illeg.*] '.

[52]

Rahab is an Eternal State.

To the Deists

The Spiritual States of the Soul are all Eternal. Distinguish between the Man & his present State.

He never can be a Friend to the Human Race who is the Preacher of Natural Morality or Natural Religion; he is a flatterer who means to betray,[1] to perpetuate Tyrant Pride & the Laws of that Babylon which, he foresees, shall shortly be destroyed with the Spiritual and not the Natural Sword. He is in the State named Rahab; which State must be put off before he can be the Friend of Man.

You, O Deists, profess yourselves the Enemies of Christianity; and you are so: you are also the Enemies of the Human Race & of Universal Nature. Man is born a Spectre or Satan, & is altogether an Evil, & requires a New Selfhood continually, & must continually be changed into his direct Contrary. But your Greek Philosophy (which is a remnant of Druidism) teaches that Man is Righteous in his Vegetated Spectre, an Opinion of fatal & accursed consequence to Man, as the Ancients saw plainly by Revelation, to the intire abrogation of Experimental Theory:[2] and many believed what they saw, and Prophecied of Jesus.

Man must & will have Some Religion: if he has not the Religion of Jesus, he will have the Religion of Satan,[3] & will erect the Synagogue of Satan, calling the Prince of this World, God, and destroying all who do not worship Satan under the Name of God. Will any one say: 'Where are those who worship Satan under the Name of God?' Where are they? Listen! Every Religion that Preaches Vengeance for Sin is the Religion of the Enemy & Avenger, and not of the Forgiver

[1] Cp. J. 90. 63–66:

Plotting to devour Albion & Los the friend of Albion;
Denying in private, mocking God & Eternal Life; & in Public
Collusion calling themselves Deists, worshipping the Maternal
Humanity, calling it Nature and Natural Religion.

[2] Cp. Ross. MS. (Clar. Press, p. 200):

Reason says 'Miracle': Newton says 'Doubt'.
Aye! that 's the way to make all Nature out.
'Doubt, Doubt, & don't believe without experiment;'
That is the very thing that Jesus meant
When he said 'Only Believe! Believe & try!
Try, Try, & never mind the Reason why!'

'Reason' in the first line of this quotation is clearly equivalent to visionary perception, an unusual sense in Blake.

[3] Cp. M. 7. 19–29.

of Sin ; and their God is Satan, Named by the Divine Name. Your Religion, O Deists, Deism, is the Worship of the God of this World by the means of what you call Natural Religion and Natural Philosophy, and of Natural Morality or Self-Righteousness, the Selfish Virtues of the Natural Heart. This was the Religion of the Pharisees who murder'd Jesus. Deism is the same, & ends in the same.

Voltaire, Rousseau, Gibbon, Hume charge the Spiritually Religious with Hypocrisy ; but how a Monk, or a Methodist either, can be a Hypocrite, I cannot concieve. We are Men of like passions with others, & pretend not to be holier than others ; therefore, when a Religious Man falls into Sin, he ought not to be call'd a Hypocrite ; this title is more properly to be given to a Player who falls into Sin, whose profession is Virtue & Morality, & the making Men Self-Righteous.[4] Foote, in calling Whitefield Hypocrite, was himself one ;[5] for Whitefield pretended not to be holier than others, but confessed his Sins before all the World. Voltaire ! Rousseau ! You cannot escape my charge that you are Pharisees & Hypocrites ; for you are constantly talking of the Virtues of the Human Heart and particularly of your own, that you may accuse others, & especially the Religious, whose errors you, by this display of pretended Virtue, chiefly design to expose. Rousseau thought Men Good by Nature : he found them Evil & found no friend. Friendship cannot exist without Forgiveness of Sins continually. The Book written by Rousseau, call'd his Confessions, is an apology & cloke for his sin, & not a confession.

But you also charge the poor Monks & Religious with being the causes of War, while you acquit & flatter the Alexanders & Caesars, the Lewis's & Fredericks, who alone are its causes & its actors. But the Religion of Jesus, Forgiveness of Sin, can never be the cause of a War, nor of a single Martyrdom.

Those who Martyr others, or who cause War, are Deists, but never can be Forgivers of Sin. The Glory of Christianity is To Conquer by Forgiveness. All the Destruction, therefore, in Christian Europe has arisen from Deism, which is Natural Religion.

[4] Cp. J. 41. 29–30.

[5] In *The Minor*, one of the most successful of his farces, Samuel Foote represents Methodism as a cloak for vice, and Whitefield, in the character of Mr. Squintum of the Tabernacle, as an unscrupulous hypocrite. The following quotation sufficiently indicates the general line of Foote's criticism of Methodism : 'No wonder these preachers have plenty of proselytes, whilst they have the address so comfortably to blend the hitherto jarring interests of the two worlds.'

To the Deists

I saw a Monk of Charlemaine
Arise before my sight:
I talk'd with the Grey Monk as we stood
In beams of infe[r]nal light.

Gibbon arose with a lash of steel,
And Voltaire with a wracking wheel;
The Schools, in clouds of learning roll'd,
Arose with War in iron & gold.

'Thou lazy Monk!' they sound afar,
'In vain condemning glorious War;
And in your Cell you shall ever dwell:
Rise, War, & bind him in his Cell!'

The blood red ran from the Grey Monk's side,
His hands & feet were wounded wide,
His body bent, his arms & knees
Like to the roots of ancient trees.

When Satan first the black bow bent
And the Moral Law from the Gospel rent,
He forg'd the Law into a Sword,
And spill'd the blood of mercy's Lord.

Titus! Constantine! Charlemaine!
O Voltaire! Rousseau! Gibbon! Vain
Your Grecian Mocks & Roman Sword
Against this image of his Lord!

For a Tear is an Intellectual thing;
And a Sigh is the Sword of an Angel King;
And the bitter groan of a Martyr's woe
Is an Arrow from the Almightie's Bow.

Stanzas. Cp. Clar. Press, p. 360: 'The original version [of this poem] forms part of a larger poem found in first draft on p. 12 of the MS. Book. This Blake afterwards separated into two distinct poems, engraving seven stanzas here as part of *Jerusalem*, and transcribing others, under the title "The Grey Monk", into the Pickering MS. . . . The first four stanzas are practically the same as those of the version in the MS. Book; stanza 5, "When Satan first the black bow bent", is a revised version of the original stanza 12; stanza 7 is also the final version of the original draft; and stanza 6 is a marginal addition, probably added by Blake when about to engrave this poem. Stanzas 4 and 6 occur also as stanzas 2 and 8 of the version in the Pickering MS.' See also Ross. MS. xlii, prefatory and textual notes (Clar. Press, p. 194), and 'The Grey Monk' (Clar. Press, p. 283).

5–7 Cp. J. 15. 14–20.

13–16 Cp. Watson Marginalia, p. 427: 'Was not Christ martered because he taught that God loved all Men & was their father, & forbad all contention for worldly prosperity; in opposition to the Jewish Scriptures? . . . Christ died as an Unbeliever, & if the Bishops had their way, so would Paine.' And *ibid.*, p. 436: 'The Gospel is Forgiveness of Sins & has no moral precepts; these belong to Plato & Seneca & Nero.'

17 Cp. B. A., chap. ii.

23 Cp. *Milton*, Preface; *On Homer's Poetry* and *On Virgil*.

[53]

Jerusalem

Chap. 3

BUT Los, who is the Vehicular Form of strong Urthona,
Wept vehemently over Albion where Thames' currents spring
From the rivers of Beulah, pleasant river, soft, mild, parent stream.
And the roots of Albion's Tree enter'd the Soul of Los
As he sat before his Furnaces clothèd in sackcloth of hair,
In gnawing pain dividing him from his Emanation,
Inclosing all the Children of Los time after time,
Their Giant forms condensing into Nations & Peoples & Tongues.
Translucent the Furnaces, of Beryll & Emerald immortal,
And Seven-fold each within other, incomprehensible
To the Vegetated Mortal Eye's perverted & single vision.
The Bellows are the Animal Lungs, the Hammers, the Animal Heart,
The Furnaces, the Stomach for Digestion ; terrible their fury
Like seven burning heavens rang'd from South to North.

Here, on the banks of the Thames, Los builded Golgonooza,
Outside of the Gates of the Human Heart beneath Beulah
In the midst of the rocks of the Altars of Albion. In fears
He builded it, in rage & in fury. It is the Spiritual Fourfold
London, continually building & continually decaying desolate.
In eternal labours loud the Furna[c]es & loud the Anvils
Of Death thunder incessant around the flaming Couches of
The Twenty-four Friends of Albion, and round the awful Four,
For the protection of the Twelve Emanations of Albion's Sons,

Page 53. 1 Cp. M. 16. 31 *note*.
4–8 See Index, *Mundane Shell, Note I*. ii. β. Los here becomes infected by the errors and delusions of his environment.
12–13 These lines occur in *Milton*, 23. 58–59. No explanation can be suggested.
15 See Index, *Golgonooza*. 16 Cp. J. 48. 21 *note*.
17 Cp. J. 42. 77–78, and J. 13. 30 :

> Around Golgonooza lies the land of death eternal, a Land
> Of pain and misery and despair and ever brooding melancholy.

22 Cp. J. 43. 2 *note*.
23–25 Cp. J. 49. 75–50. 22 for another symbolic statement of the

The Mystic Union of the Emanation in the Lord; Because
Man divided from his Emanation is a dark Spectre,
His Emanation is an ever-weeping melancholy Shadow;
But she is made receptive of Generation thro' mercy
In the Potter's Furnace, among the Funeral Urns of Beulah,
From Surrey hills thro' Italy and Greece to Hinnom's vale.

[54] In Great Eternity every particular Form gives forth or Emanates
Its own peculiar Light; & the Form is the Divine Vision,
And the Light is his Garment. This is Jerusalem in every Man,
A Tent & Tabernacle of Mutual Forgiveness, Male & Female Clothings.
And Jerusalem is callèd Liberty among the Children of Albion.

But Albion fell down, a Rocky fragment, from Eternity hurl'd
By his own Spectre, who is the Reasoning Power in every Man,
Into his own Chaos, which is the Memory between Man & Man.

The silent broodings of deadly revenge, springing from the
All powerful parental affection, fills Albion from head to foot,
Seeing his Sons assimilate with Luvah, bound in the bonds
Of spiritual Hate from which springs Sexual Love as iron chains.
He tosses like a cloud outstretch'd among Jerusalem's Ruins
Which overspread all the Earth: he groans among his ruin'd porches.

obligation to defend the Emanation, here the mystical ethic of Forgiveness, against the fallacies of Natural Religion, 'the Religion of the Enemy & Avenger'. The 'Mystic Union' is the highest form of existence.

26–28 See Index, *Incarnation*, and cp. J. 42. 32–34:

> But when Man sleeps in Beulah, the Saviour in mercy takes
> Contraction's Limit, and of the Limit he forms Woman, That
> Himself may in process of time be born Man to redeem.

29 Cp. J. 15. 34 *note*. It is uncertain whether this line belongs to what has gone before, or whether it is part of another sentence left incomplete owing to some irregularity in the arrangement of the pages at this point. Cp. J. 15. 34 *note*.

Page 54. 4 This equivalence of Tent, Tabernacle and Garment, as symbolizing the ethical content of the Emanation, holds throughout the later books. In relation to Vala, the symbols refer to Natural Religion; with Jerusalem, they signify the doctrines of Mutual Forgiveness and Liberty.

5 Cp. J. 26 *note*. 8 Cp. M. 12. 29 *note*.

9–14 The punctuation of this passage is based on the identification of Luvah and the 'spiritual Hate' (l. 12).

10 Cp. F. Z. v. 113 *note*. 12 Cp. J. 17. 25 *note*.

After l. 14 is drawn a rough circle inscribed 'This World', and to the N. 'Reason', S. 'Desire', E. 'Wrath', W. 'Pity'. Cp. J. 12. 45–60 *note*.

But the Spectre like a hoar frost & a Mildew rose over Albion,
Saying: 'I am God, O Sons of Men! I am your Rational Power!
Am I not Bacon & Newton & Locke, who teach Humility to Man,
Who teach Doubt & Experiment, & my two Wings Voltaire, Rousseau?
Where is that Friend of Sinners, that Rebel against my Laws,
Who teaches Belief to the Nations & an unknown Eternal Life?
Come hither into the Desart & turn these stones to bread.
Vain foolish Man, wilt thou believe without Experiment,
And build a World of Phantasy upon my Great Abyss,
A World of Shapes in craving lust & devouring appetite?'

So spoke the hard cold constrictive Spectre: he is namèd Arthur,
Constricting into Druid Rocks round Canaan, Agag & Aram & Pharoh.

Then Albion drew England into his bosom in groans & tears;
But she stretch'd out her starry Night in Spaces against him like
A long Serpent in the Abyss of the Spectre which augmented
The Night with Dragon wings cover'd with stars; & in the Wings
Jerusalem & Vala appear'd; & above, between the Wings, magnificent,
The Divine Vision dimly appear'd in clouds of blood weeping.

17–24 Cp. E. G. γ^2, ll. 43–48 (Clar. Press, p. 252):

> For thus the Gospel St. Isaac [Newton] confutes;
> 'God can only be known by His Attributes;
> And as for the Indwelling of the Holy Ghost,
> Or of Christ & His Father, it 's all a boast
> And pride & vanity of the imagination,
> That disdains to follow this world's fashion.

Cp. J. 15. 11 *note* and J. 52 *passim*.

19 Cp. M. H. H., p. 23, and E. G. ϵ. *passim* (Clar. Press, pp. 256–257).

25 Cp. D. C. v, pp. 42–43: 'The stories of Arthur are the acts of Albion, applied to a Prince of the fifth century who conquered Europe and held the Empire of the world in the dark age.' Cp. also J. 64. 15–17:

> Go assume Papal dignity, thou Spectre, thou Male Harlot! Arthur,
> Divide into the Kings of Europe in times remote, O Woman-born
> And Woman-nourish'd & Woman-educated & Woman-scorn'd.

The evidence is slight, but Arthur seems to be a spectrous symbol analogous to Reuben.

26 Canaan is here the Land of Promise, and so the symbol of the visionary state. Agag and the others are 'states' of error besetting it.

27 Cp. J. 36. 28 *note*.

[55] When those who disregard all Mortal Things saw a Mighty-One
Among the Flowers of Beulah still retain his awful strength,
They wonder'd, checking their wild flames: & Many gathering
Together into an Assembly, they said: 'let us go down
And see these changes'. Others said: 'If you do so, prepare
For being driven from our fields: what have we to do with the Dead?
To be their inferiors or superiors we equally abhor.
Superior none we know; inferior, none: all equal share
Divine Benevolence & Joy: for the Eternal Man
Walketh among us, calling us his Brothers & his Friends,
Forbidding us that Veil which Satan puts between Eve & Adam,
By which the Princes of the Dead enslave their Votaries,
Teaching them to form the Serpent of precious stones & gold
To sieze the Sons of Jerusalem & plant them in One Man's Loins,
To make One Family of Contraries, that Joseph may be sold
Into Egypt for Negation, a Veil the Saviour born & dying rends.'

But others said: 'Let us to him who only Is & who
Walketh among us, give decision: bring forth all your fires!'

So saying, an eternal deed was done: in fiery flames
The Universal Concave ragèd, such thunderous sounds as never
Were sounded from a mortal cloud, nor on Mount Sinai old,
Nor in Havilah where the Cherub roll'd his redounding flame.

Page 55. This and the following page appear to be later additions, though perhaps added at different times. The present page is complete in itself and constitutes a digression from the main course of the story at this point. Like the additions already noticed in chapter ii, it states with more than usual explicitness important points of doctrine.

1 'Those' are the Eternals: cp. J. 36. 42–55, and see below, l. 44 *note*. The 'Mighty One' is Albion.

2 Cp. F. Z. vii. 237 *note*.

3 Cp. J. 86. 23–25 and 91. 17: 'the burning fires of thought'.

5 Cp. the Ololon episode in *Milton*, especially M. 18. 43–50 and Introduction to *Milton*.

11 The 'Veil' is apparently the 'Veil of Moral Virtue'. See Index, *Vala, Note I*. E, and cp. J. 36. 44–46. There appears also to be a reference to the creation of the mortal and of sex: see Index, *Sex*.

13 See Index, *Serpent*.

14 Cp. J. 33. 4: 'The back & loins where dwell the Spectrous Dead.'

15 The meaning of this line remains obscure: the only passage remotely like it is M. H. H., pp. 16–17. For Joseph cp. M. 23. 17 *note*.

17–18 'He who only Is' is the Unity of the Eternals, not the supreme Deity in the conventional sense: see Index, *Jesus*.

Loud, loud the Mountains lifted up their voices ; loud the Forests ;
Rivers thunder'd against their banks ; loud Winds furious fought ;
Cities & Nations contended in fires & clouds & tempests ;
The Seas rais'd up their voices & lifted their hands on high ;
The Stars in their courses fought, the Sun, Moon, Heaven, Earth,
Contending for Albion & for Jerusalem his Emanation,
And for Shiloh the Emanation of France, & for lovely Vala.

Then far the greatest number were about to make a Separation.
And they Elected Seven, call'd the Seven Eyes of God,
Lucifer, Molech, Elohim, Shaddai, Pahad, Jehovah, Jesus.
They nam'd the Eighth : he came not, he hid in Albion's Forests.
But first they said (& their Words stood in Chariots in array,
Curbing their Tygers with golden bits & bridles of silver & ivory) :

'Let the Human Organs be kept in their perfect Integrity,
At will Contracting into Worms or Expanding into Gods,
And then, behold ! what are these Ulro Visions of Chastity ?
Then as the moss upon the tree, or dust upon the plow,
Or as the sweat upon the labouring shoulder, or as the chaff
Of the wheat-floor or as the dregs of the sweet wine-press.
Such are these Ulro Visions : for tho' we sit down within
The plowed furrow, list'ning to the weeping clods till we
Contract or Expand Space at will ; or if we raise ourselves
Upon the chariots of the morning, Contracting or Expanding Time,
Every one knows, we are One Family, One Man blessèd for ever.'

Silence remain'd & every one resum'd his Human Majesty.
And many conversèd on these things as they labour'd at the furrow,

29 Cp. J. 49. 9 *note*. 31 Cp. F. Z. viii. 388 *note*.

33 The Eighth cannot be identified. 36–37. See Index, *Expansion*.

42–46 The Seven Eyes of God, ministers of Providence, keep themselves free from the delusions and error of their mundane environment. Cp. *Cat.* 1810 : 'If the Spectator could Enter into these Images in his Imagination, approaching them on the Fiery Chariot of his Contemplative Thought ; if he could Enter into Noah's Rainbow, or into his bosom or could make a Friend & Companion of one of these Images of wonder, which always intreats him to leave mortal things . . . then would he arise from his Grave, then would he meet the Lord in the Air, & then he would be happy.'

48 See Index, *Plow*.

Saying : ' It is better to prevent misery than to release from misery ;
It is better to prevent error than to forgive the criminal.
Labour well the Minute Particulars : attend to the Little-ones :
And those who are in misery cannot remain so long,
If we do but our duty : labour well the teeming Earth.'

They Plow'd in tears : the trumpets sounded before the golden Plow :
And the voices of the Living Creatures were heard in the clouds of heaven,
Crying : ' Compell the Reasoner to Demonstrate with unhewn Demonstrations.
Let the Indefinite be explorèd, and let every Man be Judgèd
By his own Works ! Let all Indefinites be thrown into Demonstrations
To be pounded to dust & melted in the Furnaces of Affliction !
He who would do good to another, must do it in Minute Particulars.
General Good is the plea of the Scoundrel hypocrite & flatterer;
For Art & Science cannot exist but in minutely organizèd Particulars,
And not in generalizing Demonstrations of the Rational Power.
The Infinite alone resides in Definite & Determinate Identity.
Establishment of Truth depends on destruction of Falshood continually,
On Circumcision, not on Virginity, O Reasoners of Albion ! '

So cried they at the Plow. Albion's Rock frownèd above,
And the Great Voice of Eternity rollèd above terrible in clouds,
Saying : ' Who will go forth for us & Who shall we send before our face ? '

56–59 See below, ll. 65–66, and M. 27. 16 *note*. Cp. *Cat.* 1810 : ' No man can Embrace True Art till he has Explor'd & cast out False Art (such is the Nature of Mortal Things) ; or he will be himself Cast out by those who have Already Embraced True Art.'

61–64 Cp. *Cat.* 1810 : ' General Knowledge is Remote Knowledge : it is in Particulars that Wisdom consists, & Happiness too. Both in Art & in Life General Masses are as Much Art as a Pasteboard Man is Human. Every Man has Eyes, Nose, & Mouth ; this Every Idiot knows ; but he who enters into & discriminates most minutely the Manners & Intentions, the Characters in all their branches, is the alone Wise or Sensible Man : and on this discrimination All Art is founded.'

66 See Index, *Self-Annihilation*, &c. Virginity is the refusal to employ ' the liberty both of body & mind to exercise the Divine Arts of Imagination '. See also *Reynolds's Notes*, p. 15.

[56] Then Los heavèd his thund'ring Bellows on the Valley of Middlesex
And thus he chaunted his Song: the Daughters of Albion reply:

'What may Man be? who can tell! But what may Woman be,
To have power over Man from Cradle to corruptible Grave?
He who is an Infant, and whose Cradle is a Manger,
Knoweth the Infant sorrow, whence it came, and where it goeth,
And who weave it a Cradle of the grass that withereth away.
This World is all a Cradle for the errèd wandering Phantom,
Rock'd by Year, Month, Day & Hour; and every two Moments
Between dwells a Daughter of Beulah, to feed the Human Vegetable.
Entune, Daughters of Albion, your hymning Chorus mildly,
Cord of affection thrilling extatic on the iron Reel
To the golden Loom of Love, to the moth-labour'd Woof,
A Garment and Cradle weaving for the infantine Terror;
For fear, at entering the gate into our World of cruel
Lamentation, it flee back & hide in Non-Entity's dark wild,
Where dwells the Spectre of Albion, destroyer of Definite Form.
The Sun shall be a Scythèd Chariot of Britain; the Moon, a Ship
In the British Ocean, Created by Los's Hammer, measured out
Into Days & Nights & Years & Months, to travel with my feet
Over these desolate rocks of Albion. O daughters of despair!
Rock the Cradle, and in mild melodies tell me where found
What you have enwoven with so much tears & care, so much
Tender artifice, to laugh, to weep, to learn, to know!
Remember! recollect! what dark befel in wintry days.'

Page 56. The singular character of the engraved script would seem to indicate that this is an added page. The number '56' is engraved on the plate, whereas Blake usually paginated the printed sheets. The fact that ll. 1 and 3–4 repeat J. 34. 18 and 34. 25–26 is remarkable.

1 Cp. J. 34. 18 and J. 32. 9 *note*.

8–10 This is a clear statement of the teleological function of mundane life. Cp. M. 27. 44–61.

11–17 This is an aspect of the Daughters of Albion not generally stressed. It is perhaps most explicitly stated in J. 83. 33–48. They appear to have almost identical functions with the Daughters of Los: see Index, *Los, Note II. a.* For a corresponding passage relating to the Sons of Albion, cp. J. 49. 50–59.

22 A word may be missing here. Messrs. Russell and Maclagan read 'where you found'.

'O it was lost for ever, and we found it not: it came
And wept at our wintry Door. Look! look! behold! Gwendolen
Is become a Clod of Clay! Merlin is a Worm of the Valley!'

Then Los utterèd with Hammer & Anvil: 'Chaunt! revoice!
I mind not your laugh, and your frown I not fear; and
You must my dictate obey from your gold-beam'd Looms. Trill
Gentle to Albion's Watchman on Albion's mountains. Reeccho,
And rock the Cradle while—Ah me!—Of that Eternal Man,
And of the cradle'd Infancy in his bowels of compassion,
Who fell beneath his instruments of husbandry & became
Subservient to the clods of the furrow: the cattle and even
The emmet and earth-worm are his superiors & his lords.'

Then the response came warbling from trilling Looms in Albion:
'We Women tremble at the light, therefore hiding fearful
The Divine Vision with Curtain & Veil & fleshly Tabernacle.'
Los utter'd, swift as the rattling thunder upon the mountains:
'Look back into the Church Paul! Look! Three Women around
The Cross! O Albion why didst thou a Female Will Create?'

[57] And the voices of Bath & Canterbury & York & Edinburgh Cry
Over the Plow of Nations, in the strong hand of Albion thundering along

26 The allusion here may be to the 'cradled Infancy' of l. 34 below, where there may be an obscure reference to the Incarnation: see Index, *Incarnation*.

28 Cp. M. 34. 37 *note*. 32 Albion's Watchman is Los: cp. M. 23. 8–9.

33 This line is more than usually incoherent. For 'while' read 'awhile'.

35–36 'Who' may refer either to 'that Eternal Man' (l. 33) or to the 'cradled Infancy' who becomes subservient to the conditions of mortal life for man's salvation. The former view seems to derive support from J. 56. 11–16.

36–37 Blake may here intend to suggest superiority of instinct over the 'abstract reasoning power', the Spectre in fallen man.

39–40 Cp. M. 30. 21–30. See Index, *Emanation*. From the context it is to be deduced that the 'Three Women' with 'Curtain & Veil' hide the true significance of the Crucifixion, and are associated with the Pauline fallacy in its misinterpretation of that event in dogmatic Christianity. Cp. F. Z. viii. 351 *note*. For 'Church' see Index, *Mundane Shell, Note II*, and J. 75. 16.

Page 57 appears to follow directly upon p. 54. The text is engraved across a circle apparently representing the earth. In the upper part of it are the names 'York' and 'London' to left and right of a rough sketch of St. Paul's. In the lower portion a drawing of a Gothic building with spires is marked 'Jerusalem'.

1 These are the Friends of Albion: cp. J. 30. 26 *note*.

Among the Fires of the Druid & the deep black rethundering Waters
Of the Atlantic which pourèd in, impetuous, loud, loud, louder & louder.
And the Great Voice of the Atlantic howlèd over the Druid Altars,
Weeping over his Children in Stone-henge, in Malden & Colchester,
Round the Rocky Peak of Derbyshire, London Stone & Rosamond's Bower:

'What is a Wife & what is a Harlot? What is a Church & What
Is a Theatre? are they Two & not One? can they Exist Separate?
Are not Religion & Politics the Same Thing? Brotherhood is Religion,
O Demonstrations of Reason Dividing Families in Cruelty & Pride!'

But Albion fled from the Divine Vision with the Plow of Nations enflaming.
The Living Creatures madden'd and Albion fell into the Furrow, and
The Plow went over him & the Living was Plowèd in among the Dead:
But his Spectre rose over the starry Plow. Albion fled beneath the Plow
Till he came to the Rock of Ages, & he took his Seat upon the Rock.

Wonder siez'd all in Eternity to behold the Divine Vision open
The Center into an Expanse; & the Center rolled out into an Expanse.

[58] In beauty the Daughters of Albion divide & unite at will.

5 The 'Great Voice of the Atlantic' is not mentioned elsewhere. It appears to be identical with Albion, as represented in J. 21, *passim.*

8–11 The distinctions set up by the Moral Law are entirely factitious, and in direct opposition to the unifying spirit of Imagination.

12 See Index, *Plow.* 13 See Index, *Zoas.*

16 Cp. F. Z. ix. 284 *note.*

17–18 Behind the obscure symbolism of 'Center' and 'Expanse' the general reference to providential interference is clear enough.

Page 58. 1 The conception of the Daughters of Albion in the present passage is quite different from that on the added page 56. There they were in some manner subject to the power of Los. Here no such suggestion is visible: they are the powers that govern vegetable or mortal life to the destruction of everything that belongs to Imagination.

Naked & drunk with blood, Gwendolen, dancing to the timbrel
Of War ; reeling up the Street of London, she divides in twain
Among the Inhabitants of Albion : the People fall around.
The Daughters of Albion divide & unite in jealousy & cruelty.
The Inhabitants of Albion at the Harvest & the Vintage
Feel their Brain cut round beneath the temples, shrieking,
Bonifying into a Scull, the Marrow exuding in dismal pain.
They flee over the rocks bonifying. Horses, Oxen, feel the knife ;
And while the Sons of Albion by severe War & Judgment bonify,
The Hermaphroditic Condensations are divided by the Knife,
The obdurate Forms are cut asunder by Jealousy & Pity.

Rational Philosophy and Mathematic Demonstration
Is divided in the intoxications of pleasure & affection ;
Two Contraries War against each other in fury & blood,
And Los fixes them on his Anvil : incessant his blows.
He fixes them with strong blows, placing the stones & timbers
To Create a World of Generation from the World of Death,
Dividing the Masculine & Feminine : for the comingling
Of Albion's & Luvah's Spectres was Hermaphroditic.

Urizen wrathful strode above directing the awful Building
As a Mighty Temple delivering Form out of confusion.

2 Gwendolen is a Daughter of Albion.

5 This would seem to be a symbolic statement of the instability of mundane perceptions, the Female being both the vision and the power inducing and controlling the vision.

6–9 Cp. J. 66. 81–84 :

> The Stars flee remote : the heaven is iron, the earth is sulphur,
> And all the mountains & hills shrink up like a withering gourd,
> As the Senses of Men shrink together under the Knife of flint
> In the hands of Albion's Daughters among the Druid Temples.

For the 'bonifying' of the skull cp. *Europe*, ll. 94–99.

11 See Index, *Hermaphroditic*.

15 The 'Two Contraries' are 'Rational Philosophy and Mathematic Demonstration' on one hand, and 'the intoxications of pleasure & affection' on the other : see Index, *Luvah*, II.

18–19 Cp. J. 73. 24–26 :

> Los, who is of the Elohim,
> Opens the Furnaces of affliction in the Emanation,
> Fixing the Sexual into an ever-prolific Generation.

21–51 In F. Z. ii. 229–494 Urizen builds a 'Golden World' in the Abyss : it is identified with the Mundane Shell in its regenerative aspect by the insertion of the later lines 235 and 494. Urizen's association with such a labour both here and in *The Four Zoas* can hardly be reconciled with the general tendency of the symbol. It may be, though the suggestion is offered with hesitation, that though Urizen's world is evil, it is a less evil

Jordan sprang beneath its threshold, bubbling from beneath
Its pillars : Euphrates ran under its arches : white sails
And silver oars reflect on its pillars, & sound on its ecchoing
Pavements, where walk the Sons of Jerusalem who remain Ungenerate.
But the revolving Sun and Moon pass thro' its porticoes
Day & night : in sublime majesty & silence they revolve,
And shine glorious within. Hand & Koban arch'd over the Sun
In the hot noon, as he travel'd thro' his journey : Hyle & Skofield
Arch'd over the Moon at midnight, & Los fix'd them there
With his thunderous Hammer : terrified the Spectres rage & flee.
Canaan is his portico : Jordan is a fountain in his porch,
A fountain of milk & wine to relieve the traveller.
Egypt is the eight steps within ; Ethiopia supports his pillars :
Lybia & the Lands unknown are the ascent without :
Within is Asia & Greece, ornamented with exquisite art :
Persia & Media are his halls : his inmost hall is Great Tartary.
China & India & Siberia are his temples for entertainment :
Poland & Russia & Sweden his soft retirèd chambers :
France & Spain & Italy & Denmark & Holland & Germany
Are the temples among his pillars : Britain is Los's Forge :
America North & South are his baths of living waters.

Such is the Ancient World of Urizen in the Satanic Void,
Created from the Valley of Middlesex by London's River,
From Stone-henge & from London Stone, from Cornwall to Cathnes.
The Four Zoas rush around on all sides in dire ruin.
Furious in pride of Selfhood the terrible Spectres of Albion
Rear their dark Rocks among the Stars of God, stupendous
Works ! A World of Generation continually Creating out of
The Hermaphroditic Satanic World of rocky destiny,

[59] And formèd into Four precious stones, for enterance from Beulah.

than the 'Hermaphrodite Satanic World of rocky destiny' (l. 51) which would have resulted from the infraction of Ideal Unity had not Divine Mary intervened to justify the 'place apart' by making it the place of human regeneration, the sphere of Los's labours. Cp. J. 13. 44–45.

26 These are Bromion, Theotormon, Rintrah, and Palamabron. See Index, *Los, Note II.*

45 Cp. J. 32. 9 *note.* 46 'Cathnes' is Caithness : cp. J. 83. 70.

51 See Index, *Ulro*, II.

Page 59 does not follow from the preceding page. A better place for it might be between pp. 72 and 73, though no known copies have this arrange-

For the Veil of Vala, which Albion cast into the Atlantic Deep
To catch the Souls of the Dead, began to Vegetate & Petrify
Around the Earth of Albion among the Roots of his Tree.
This Los formèd into the Gates & mighty Wall between the Oak
Of Weeping & the Palm of Suffering beneath Albion's Tomb.
Thus in process of time it became the beautiful Mundane Shell,
The Habitation of the Spectres of the Dead & the Place
Of Redemption & of awaking again into Eternity.

For Four Universes round the Mundane Egg remain Chaotic:
One to the North, Urthona; One to the South, Urizen;
One to the East, Luvah; One to the West, Tharmas.
They are the Four Zoas that stood around the Throne Divine;
Verulam, London, York & Edinburgh, their English names.
But when Luvah assumèd the World of Urizen Southward,
And Albion was slain upon his Mountains & in his Tent,
All fell towards the Center, sinking downwards in dire ruin.
In the South remains a burning Fire; in the East, a Void;
In the West, a World of raging Waters; in the North, solid Darkness,
Unfathomable, without end: but in the midst of these
Is Built eternally the sublime Universe of Los & Enitharmon.

And in the North Gate, in the West of the North, toward Beulah,
Cathedron's Looms are builded; and Los's Furnaces in the South.
A wondrous golden Building immense with ornaments sublime
Is bright Cathedron's golden Hall, its Courts, Towers & Pinnacles.

And one Daughter of Los sat at the fiery Reel, & another
Sat at the shining Loom, with her Sisters attending round:
Terrible their distress, & their sorrow cannot be utter'd.
And another Daughter of Los sat at the Spinning Wheel:
Endless their labour, with bitter food, void of sleep:

ment. It may have been placed here because Blake wishes once more to emphasize his conviction that Divine Mercy uses the 'Ancient World of Urizen' as the place of man's redemption and return to Unity, i.e. it becomes the 'sublime Universe of Los & Enitharmon' (l. 21).

2–9 See Index, *Mundane Shell*, § IV. 5–6 Cp. F. Z. ii. 206 *note*.

10–21 This passage, except l. 14, occurs in M. 17. 15–25. The matter is restated in M. 34. 32–39 and is illustrated in the diagram, M., p. 32.

14 Cp. J. 36. 25 *note*.

22–25 See Index, *Los*. The Daughters of Los here appear to be equivalent to the Daughters of Beulah: see below, l. 44, and cp. J. 11. 8–12.

Tho' hungry, they labour: they rouze themselves, anxious,
Hour after hour labouring at the whirling Wheel;
Many Wheels, & as many lovely Daughters sit weeping.
Yet the intoxicating delight that they take in their work
Obliterates every other evil: none pities their tears,
Yet they regard not pity & they expect no one to pity;
For they labour for life & love, regardless of any one
But the poor Spectres that they work for always, incessantly.
They are mock'd by every one that passes by: they regard not:
They labour; & when their Wheels are broken by scorn & malice
They mend them sorrowing with many tears & afflictions.

Other Daughters Weave on the Cushion & Pillow Network fine,
That Rahab & Tirzah may exist & live & breathe & love.
Ah, that it could be as the Daughters of Beulah wish!

Other Daughters of Los, labouring at Looms less fine,
Create the Silk-worm & the Spider & the Catterpiller
To assist in their most grievous work of pity & compassion.
And others Create the wooly Lamb & the downy Fowl
To assist in the work: the Lamb bleats: the Sea-fowl cries.
Men understand not the distress & the labour & sorrow
That in the Interior Worlds is carried on in fear & trembling,
Weaving the shudd'ring fears & loves of Albion's Families.
Thunderous rage the Spindles of iron, & the iron Distaff
Maddens in the fury of their hands, weaving in bitter tears
The Veil of Goats'-hair & Purple & Scarlet & fine twined Linen.

[60] The clouds of Albion's Druid Temples rage in the eastern heaven,
While Los sat terrified beholding Albion's Spectre, who is Luvah,
Spreading in bloody veins in torments over Europe & Asia,

42–43 Beyond a vague reference to the 'Sleep of Death' no interpretation can be discovered for the Cushion & Pillow, with their Network. See Index, *Weaving*, II. For the general doctrine cp. J. 62. 20–22, where Jesus says:

> Luvah must be Created,
> And Vala; for I cannot leave them in the gnawing Grave,
> But will prepare a way for my banished-ones to return.

49 Apparently, like the Lark in M. 35. 63, these are 'Mighty Angels', 'Los's Messengers'.

50–55 Cp. J. 3: 'We who dwell on Earth can do nothing of ourselves: every thing is conducted by Spirits, no less than Digestion or Sleep.'

Page 60. 2 See Index, *Luvah*, I.

3 Albion's Spectre or Luvah is identified with the Polypus: see Index, *Mundane Shell, Note I*, ii. a.

Not yet formèd, but a wretched torment unformèd & abyssal.
In flaming fire within the Furnaces the Divine Vision appear'd
On Albion's hills, [and] often walking from the Furnaces in clouds
And flames among the Druid Temples & the Starry Wheels,
Gather'd Jerusalem's Children in his arms & bore them like
A Shepherd in the night of Albion which overspread all the Earth.

'I gave thee liberty and life, O lovely Jerusalem,
And thou hast bound me down upon the Stems of Vegetation.
I gave thee Sheep-walks upon the Spanish Mountains, Jerusalem!
I gave thee Priam's City and the Isles of Grecia lovely;
I gave thee Hand & Scofield & the Counties of Albion.
They spread forth like a lovely root into the Garden of God;
They were as Adam before me: united into One Man,
They stood in innocence, & their skiey tent reach'd over Asia
To Nimrod's Tower, to Ham & Canaan walking with Mizraim
Upon the Egyptian Nile with solemn songs, to Grecia
And sweet Hesperia, even to Great Chaldea & Tesshina,
Following thee as a Shepherd by the Four Rivers of Eden.
Why wilt thou rend thyself apart, Jerusalem,
And build this Babylon & Sacrifice in secret Groves
Among the Gods of Asia, among the fountains of pitch & nitre?
Therefore thy Mountains are become barren, Jerusalem!
Thy Valleys, Plains of burning sand; thy Rivers, waters of death.
Thy Villages die of the Famine, and thy Cities
Beg bread from house to house, lovely Jerusalem!
Why wilt thou deface thy beauty & the beauty of thy little-ones
To please thy Idols in the pretended chastities of Uncircumcision?
Thy Sons are lovelier than Egypt or Assyria: wherefore
Dost thou blacken their beauty by a Secluded place of rest,

6 Messrs. Russell and Maclagan supply 'and' after 'Albion's hills'; and so give coherence to the passage.

10–37 See Index, *Jerusalem, Note I*. The binding down of Christ upon the 'Stems of Vegetation' refers to the misinterpretation of Christ's gospel into formal Christianity. For 'Stems of Vegetation' (= Albion's Tree or the Tree of Mystery) see Index, *Mundane Shell, Note I*. ii.

18 Mizraim was the son of Ham (Gen. x. 6): the name was also used to designate Egypt.

22–23 Cp. J. 11. 24–12. 3. 23 Cp. J. 24. 31–35.

32–33 The Secluded place of rest, the peculiar Tabernacle, is the contrary

And a peculiar Tabernacle, to cut the integuments of beauty
Into veils of tears and sorrows, O lovely Jerusalem?
They have perswaded thee to this; therefore their end shall come:
And I will lead thee thro' the Wilderness in shadow of my cloud,
And in my love I will lead thee, lovely Shadow of Sleeping Albion.'

This is the Song of the Lamb, sung by Slaves in evening time.

But Jerusalem faintly saw him: clos'd in the Dungeons of Babylon,
Her Form was held by Beulah's Daughters; but all within unseen
She sat at the Mills, her hair unbound, her feet naked,
Cut with the flints; her tears run down; her reason grows like
The Wheel of Hand, incessant turning day & night without rest.
Insane she raves upon the winds, hoarse, inarticulate.
All night Vala hears; she triumphs in pride of holiness
To see Jerusalem deface her lineaments with bitter blows
Of despair, while the Satanic Holiness triumph'd in Vala,
In a Religion of Chastity & Uncircumcisèd Selfishness

to Jerusalem, 'in every Man/A Tent & Tabernacle of Mutual Forgiveness'. Cp. below, ll. 45–49.

34 Cp. M. 28. 62 where the Veil of Vala is 'the Veil of Human miseries', the reference being to the spiritual desolation following upon the denial of Imagination and the consequent subjection to error.

38 The Slaves or Captives are the victims of Natural Religion or Corporeal War: see J. 65. 22–28, and F. Z. ix. 10–31 and 234–276.

39 Cp. J. 20. 5–7 where Jerusalem pleads with Vala:

> Wherefore hast thou shut me into the winter of human life
> And clos'd up the sweet regions of youth and virgin innocence
> Where we live, forgetting error, not pondering on evil.

40 The Form is the 'real and immortal Self' (M. 14. 11) as it were the Idea of perfect existence. Cp. J. 5. 55 *note*. For the use of 'within' here, cp. Ross. MS. xxxvii, ll. 1–4 (Clar. Press, p. 186):

> My Spectre around me night & day
> Like a Wild beast guards my way;
> My Emanation, far within,
> Weeps incessantly for my sin.

41 Cp. M. 6. 4 *note*.

42 The mention of reason in this connexion is remarkable; it is nowhere else associated with Jerusalem. Apparently it is used in the sense of the highest order of reason, never defined by Blake.

46–47 'Temptations of doubt & despair' (J. 10. 33) obstruct and destroy vision: cp. D. C. ix, p. 55, quoted J. 43. 54 *note*.

48 The Chastity of Natural Religion is the insistence on 'purity', the negation of passion and imagination: cp. J. 91. 54 *note*. Its 'Uncircumcised Selfishness' is its belief in the validity of Reason or Selfhood, an error the visionary must cut away, or annihilate, continually.

Both of the Head & Heart & Loins, clos'd up in Moral Pride.

But the Divine Lamb stood beside Jerusalem ; oft she saw
The lineaments Divine & oft the Voice heard, & oft she said :
' O Lord & Saviour, have the Gods of the Heathen piercèd thee ;
Or hast thou been piercèd in the House of thy Friends ?
Art thou alive, & livest thou for evermore ? or art thou
Not but a delusive shadow, a thought that liveth not ?
Babel mocks, saying there is no God nor Son of God ;
That thou, O Human Imagination, O Divine Body, art all
A delusion : but I know thee, O Lord, when thou arisest upon
My weary eyes, even in this dungeon & this iron mill.
The Stars of Albion cruel rise ; thou bindest to sweet influences :
For thou also sufferest with me altho' I behold thee not ;
And altho' I sin & blaspheme thy holy name, thou pitiest me,
Because thou knowest I am deluded by the turning mills,
And by these visions of pity & love because of Albion's death.'

Thus spake Jerusalem, & thus the Divine Voice replied :

' Mild Shade of Man, pitiest thou these Visions of terror & woe?
Give forth thy pity & love. Fear not ! Lo ! I am with thee always.
Only believe in me that I have power to raise from death
Thy Brother who Sleepeth in Albion : fear not, trembling Shade.

[61] Behold in the Visions of Elohim Jehovah, behold Joseph & Mary;
And be comforted, O Jerusalem, in the Visions of Jehovah Elohim.'

She lookèd & saw Joseph the Carpenter in Nazareth, & Mary

49 See Index, *Head, Heart and Loins.* 52 Cp. J. 50. 3 *note.*
60 Cp. M. 37. 47 *note* and J. 67. 31–34.
61 Cp. M., extra p. 32*. 39–43.
64 Cp. J. 29. 28–71 for an account of the deluding of Albion by the 'Spirits of Pity and Love', Luvah and Vala.

Page 61 appears to have been inserted between pp. 60 and 62. It is engraved in a different hand and is complete in itself as a mystical revelation of the doctrine of unconditional forgiveness. The original conclusion of the speech, p. 60, ll. 60–69, is now p. 62, l. 1.

1 See Index, *Jesus,* III. Here Jehovah Elohim is one of the 'Seven Eyes of God' who instruct man : cp. M., extra p. 32*. 9, and J. 61. 24 *note.*

3–p. 62. 1 With this passage may be compared *The Ghost of Abel,* another instance of a scriptural episode being treated not as a record of an historical event, but as a parabolic revelation of truth ; in both instances the necessity of continual and complete forgiveness, of 'Perpetual Mutual Sacrifice', is exemplified.

His espousèd Wife. And Mary said: 'If thou put me away from thee
Dost thou not murder me?' Joseph spoke in anger & fury: 'Should I
Marry a Harlot & an Adulteress?' Mary answer'd: 'Art thou more pure
Than thy Maker, who forgiveth Sins & calls again Her that is Lost?
Tho' She hates, he calls her again in love. I love my dear Joseph,
But he driveth me away from his presence; yet I hear the voice of God
In the voice of my Husband: tho' he is angry for a moment, he will not
Utterly cast me away: if I were pure, never could I taste the sweets
Of the Forgive[n]ess of Sins; if I were holy, I never could behold the tears
Of love, of him who loves me in the midst of his anger in furnace of fire.'

'Ah my Mary!' said Joseph, weeping over & embracing her closely in
His arms, 'Doth he forgive Jerusalem & not exact Purity from her who is
Polluted? I heard his voice in my sleep & his Angel in my dream
Saying: "Doth Jehovah Forgive a Debt only on condition that it shall
Be Payed? Doth he Forgive Pollution only on conditions of Purity?
That Debt is not Forgiven! That Pollution is not Forgiven!
Such is the Forgiveness of the Gods, the Moral Virtues of the
Heathen, whose tender Mercies are Cruelty. But Jehovah's Salvation
Is without Money & without Price, in the Continual Forgiveness of Sins,
In the Perpetual Mutual Sacrifice in Great Eternity: for behold,
There is none that liveth & Sinneth not! And this is the Covenant

17–26 See General Introduction, pp. 66–75.
24–25 Cp. G. A. 46–48: Thou stood'st
Forth, O Elohim Jehovah, in the midst of the darkness of the Oath, All Clothed
In thy Covenant of the Forgiveness of Sins.

Of Jehovah: 'If you Forgive one-another, so shall Jehovah Forgive You;
That He Himself may Dwell among You.' Fear not then to take
To thee Mary thy Wife, for she is with Child by the Holy Ghost."'

Then Mary burst forth into a Song: she flowed like a River of
Many Streams in the arms of Joseph, & gave forth her tears of joy
Like many waters, and Emanating into gardens & palaces upon
Euphrates & to forests & floods & animals, wild & tame, from
Gihon to Hiddekel, & to corn fields & villages & inhabitants
Upon Pison & Arnon & Jordan. And I heard the voice among
The Reapers, Saying: 'Am I Jerusalem, the lost Adulteress, or am I
Babylon come up to Jerusalem?' And another voice answer'd, Saying:
'Does the voice of my Lord call me again? am I pure thro' his Mercy
And Pity? Am I become lovely as a Virgin in his sight, Who am
Indeed a Harlot drunken with the Sacrifice of Idols? does he
Call her pure as he did in the days of her Infancy, when She
Was cast out to the loathing of her person? The Chaldean took
Me from my Cradle. The Amalekite stole me away upon his Camels,
Before I had ever beheld with love the Face of Jehovah, or known
That there was a God of Mercy. O Mercy! O Divine Humanity!
O Forgiveness & Pity & Compassion! If I were Pure I should never
Have known Thee. If I were Unpolluted I should never have
Glorified thy Holiness, or rejoicèd in thy great Salvation.'

31–33 Cp. Gen. ii. 11–14. The significance of Arnon and Jordan in this passage does not appear.

33 Blake speaks in his own person. The voice is apparently that of Jerusalem, answered (l. 35) by Mary, who seems in this passage to be the type of 'the lapsed soul' whose return from the errors of the Moral Law to the light and liberty of the Covenant of Jehovah is marked by the birth of Jesus into this world, the manifestation of mystical truth in mundane life. There is also apparently a collateral reference to the historic birth of Christ.

Mary leanèd her side against Jerusalem. Jerusalem receivèd
The Infant into her hands in the Visions of Jehovah. Times passèd on.
Jerusalem fainted over the Cross & Sepulcher. She heard the voice:
'Wilt thou make Rome thy Patriarch Druid, & the Kings of Europe his
Horsemen? Man in the Resurrection changes his Sexual Garments at Will:
Every Harlot was once a Virgin, every Criminal an Infant Love.
[62] Repose on me till the morning of the Grave. I am thy life.'
Jerusalem replied. 'I am an outcast: Albion is dead;
I am left to the trampling foot & the spurning heel;
A Harlot I am call'd; I am sold from street to street;
I am defaced with blows & with the dirt of the Prison:
And wilt thou become my Husband, O my Lord & Saviour?
Shall Vala bring thee forth? shall the Chaste be ashamèd also?
I see the Maternal Line; I behold the Seed of the Woman:
Cainah & Ada & Zillah & Naamah, Wife of Noah.
Shuah's daughter & Tamar & Rahab the Canaanites,
Ruth the Moabite & Bathsheba of the daughters of Heth,
Naamah the Ammonite, Zibeah the Philistine, & Mary.
These are the Daughters of Vala, Mother of the Body of death.

49 'the voice' is the Divine voice, cp. J. 60. 66–69.

50 Rome is the symbol of the false ethic and metaphysic which the visionary rejects as being the body which Jesus put off on the Cross: see J. 62. 13 and Index, *Incarnation*.

51 This appears to mean that by an act of will, man may cast off the Sexual Garments, the forms of error enumerated in M. 42. 35–43.

Page 62. 2–5 This describes man's neglect and contempt of the visionary life in his state of spiritual death. See Index, *Jerusalem, Note I.*

7 Cp. J. 53. 26–27:

[Vala, fallen Man's] Emanation is an ever-weeping melancholy Shadow
But she is made receptive of Generation thro' mercy.

8–12 Cp. J. 61. 33 *note*. Blake adapts the divine promise concerning the seed of the woman to his own doctrine of regeneration through mundane existence. He sets out to trace the ancestry of Jesus on the maternal side in such a manner as to stress the element of 'feminine delusion' noticed elsewhere in his use of the term 'maternal': cp. J. 5. 47 *note*. Of the list that he draws up from women associated with the male line of Jesus' ancestry every name belongs either to the idolatrous age before Noah, or to members of heathen tribes of Canaan, the enemies of Israel. Cainah appears to be a feminine form derived from Cain: Ada and Zillah were wives of Lamech; Shuah (Gen. xxxviii. 2) and Tamar, wives of Judah, were Canaanitish women, as was also Rahab the harlot of Jericho; Naamah was Rehoboam's mother, and Zillah the mother of Joash. Ruth and Bathsheba were both outlandish women.

But I, thy Magdalen, behold thy Spiritual Risen Body.
Shall Albion arise? I know he shall arise at the Last Day.
I know that in my flesh I shall see God: but Emanations
Are weak; they know not whence they are, nor whither tend.'

Jesus replied: 'I am the Resurrection & the Life.
I Die & pass the limits of possibility as it appears
To individual perception. Luvah must be Created,
And Vala; for I cannot leave them in the gnawing Grave,
But will prepare a way for my banished-ones to return.
Come now with me into the villages; walk thro' all the cities.
Tho' thou art taken to prison & judgment, starvèd in the streets,
I will command the cloud to give thee food & the hard rock
To flow with milk & wine: tho' thou seest me not a season,
Even a long season, & a hard journey & a howling wilderness,
Tho' Vala's cloud hide thee & Luvah's fires follow thee,
Only believe & trust in me. Lo, I am always with thee!'

So spoke the Lamb of God, while Luvah's Cloud reddening above
Burst forth in streams of blood upon the heavens, & dark night
Involv'd Jerusalem, & the Wheels of Albion's Sons turn'd hoarse
Over the Mountains, & the fires blaz'd on Druid Altars,
And the Sun set in Tyburn's Brook where Victims howl & cry.

But Los beheld the Divine Vision among the flames of the Furnaces:
Therefore he livèd & breathèd in hope; but his tears fell incessant
Because his Children were clos'd from him apart & Enitharmon
Dividing in fierce pain: also the Vision of God was clos'd in clouds
Of Albion's Spectres, that Los in despair oft sat, & often pondered
On Death Eternal, in fierce shudders upon the mountains of Albion
Walking, & in the vales in howlings fierce: then to his Anvils
Turning anew, began his labours, tho' in terrible pains.

16 This appears to mean that the vision of Eternity, the Divine Humanity, is made perceptible to mortals in and through mundane life.

30 Cp. J. 29. 36–57 for an example of the spiritually perversive influence of Luvah and Vala.

39–42 Los's despair may be a reflection of moods Blake knew as a spiritual artist: cp. Letter to Hayley, 23 October 1804 (R., pp. 169–172).

[63] Jehovah stood among the Druids in the Valley of Annandale,
When the Four Zoas of Albion, the Four Living Creatures, the Cherubim
Of Albion, tremble before the Spectre in the starry Harness of the Plow
Of Nations. And their Names are Urizen & Luvah &Tharmas & Urthona.

Luvah slew Tharmas the Angel of the Tongue, & Albion brought him
To Justice in his own City of Paris, denying the Resurrection.
Then Vala the Wife of Albion, who is the Daughter of Luvah,
Took vengeance Twelve-fold among the Chaotic Rocks of the Druids,
Where the Human Victims howl to the Moon, & Thor & Friga
Dance the dance of death, contending with Jehovah among the Cherubim.
The Chariot Wheels fillèd with Eyes rage along the howling Valley
In the Dividing of Reuben & Benjamin, bleeding from Chester's River.

The Giants & the Witches & the Ghosts of Albion dance with
Thor & Friga ; & the Fairies lead the Moon along the Valley of Cherubim,
Bleeding in torrents from Mountain to Mountain, a lovely Victim.
And Jehovah stood in the Gates of the Victim, & he appeared
A weeping Infant in the Gates of Birth in the midst of Heaven.

Page 63. 1 Jehovah here may be Jehovah Elohim, one of the Seven Eyes of God. Cp. M., extra p. 32. 9–15. It is, however, possible that Jehovah may be 'The Divine Humanity, Jesus, that God who is the intellectual fountain of Humanity' : cp. J. 98. 40. The difference seems to be chiefly formal.

5–8 For Tharmas, Angel of the Tongue, cp. M. 3. 10 *note*. The passage reads like a symbolic interpretation of the French Revolution, Luvah or Orc representing revolt against the tyranny of civil and religious authority, while Albion's interference and Vala's vengeance symbolize the reactionary policy of Britain and the allies and the triumph of the young republic. Cp. J. 66. 15 :

For Luvah is France, the Victim of the Spectres of Albion,

and R. N., p. ciii :

When France got Free, Europe, 'twixt Fools & Knaves,
Were Savage first to France, & after Slaves.

The course of the Revolution no longer had Blake's sympathy.

9 Thor and Friga are ' Gods of the Heathen ' : cp. J. 50. 3 *note*.

13 See Index, *Giants*. Witches and Ghosts are spectrous symbols. The Valley of Cherubim is not mentioned elsewhere.

16–22 The illusion of multitudinous discrete forms in mundane life

The Cities & Villages of Albion became Rock & Sand Unhumanizèd,
The Druid Sons of Albion; & the Heavens a Void around unfathomable:
No Human Form but Sexual, & a little weeping Infant pale reflected
Multitudinous in the Looking Glass of Enitharmon on all sides
Around in the clouds of the Female, on Albion's Cliffs of the Dead.

Such the appearance in Cheviot in the Divisions of Reuben,
When the Cherubim hid their heads under their wings in deep slumbers,
When the Druids demanded Chastity from Woman & all was lost.

'How can the Female be Chaste, O thou stupid Druid,' Cried Los,
'Without the Forgiveness of Sins in the merciful clouds of Jehovah,
And without the Baptism of Repentance to wash away Calumnies and
The Accusations of Sin, that each may be Pure in their Neighbours' sight?
O, when shall Jehovah give us Victims from his Flocks & Herds
Instead of Human Victims by the Daughters of Albion & Canaan?'

Then laugh'd Gwendolen, & her laughter shook the Nations & Familys of

marks the triumph of Reason; but throughout all there is the pale reflection of the child, which, according to ll. 16–17, means that there is, if men would but see it, the perpetual promise of regeneration through the Incarnation.

21 The 'Looking Glass of Enitharmon' is a rare symbol the meaning of which can only be conjectured. It may be derived from Böhme (see *Treatise of the Incarnation*, Part I, chap. vi, § 4), but if so, its significance is altered. Cp. *Cat.* 1810: 'There exist in that eternal world the eternal realities of every thing which we see reflected in this vegetable glass of nature.'

24 The Cherubim are the spirits of Forgiveness: cp. J. 22. 34–35.

30–31 Cp. G. A.:

Abel. Are these the Sacrifices of Eternity, O Jehovah, a Broken Spirit
And a Contrite Heart? O I cannot Forgive! the Accuser hath
Enter'd into Me as into his House & I loathe thy Tabernacles.
As thou hast said, so is it come to pass. My desire is unto Cain
And he doth rule over Me: therefore My Soul in Fumes of Blood
Cries for Vengeance, Sacrifice on Sacrifice, Blood on Blood.
Jehovah. Lo I have given you a Lamb for an Atonement, instead
Of the Transgressor, or no Flesh or Spirit could ever Live.

The Dead beneath Beulah from Tyburn to Golgotha and from
Ireland to Japan : furious her Lions & Tygers & Wolves sport before
Los on the Thames & Medway : London & Canterbury groan in pain.

Los knew not yet what was done : he thought it was all in Vision,
In Visions of the Dreams of Beulah among the Daughters of Albion.
Therefore the Murder was put apart in the Looking-Glass of Enitharmon.

He saw in Vala's hand the Druid Knife of Revenge & the Poison Cup
Of Jealousy, and thought it a Poetic Vision of the Atmospheres ;
Till Canaan roll'd apart from Albion across the Rhine, along the Danube.

And all the Land of Canaan suspended over the Valley of Cheviot
From Bashan to Tyre & from Troy to Gaza of the Amalekite :
And Reuben fled with his head downwards among the Caverns
[64] Of the Mundane Shell, which froze on all sides round Canaan on
The vast Expanse, where the Daughters of Albion Weave the Web
Of Ages & Generations, folding & unfolding it like a Veil of Cherubim :
And sometimes it touches the Earth's summits, & sometimes spreads
Abroad into the Indefinite Spectre, who is the Rational Power.

41–43 Blake appears to describe under this curious geographical symbolism Man's separation from Eternity. Albion or Albion's Land is apparently the supreme state, the Humanity ; and Canaan, passing thence over Europe (see *Europe*, Introduction) to Palestine, images Man's decline in spirituality. The direction in which Canaan travels, towards the East, is also significant, that quarter being constantly associated with Error, the state Ulro. It may also be that this passage restates the origin of all religions in Albion the Parent of the Druids : cp. J. 27. *note* 6.

44 See Index, *Reuben*.

Page 64. 1–5 See Index, *Mundane Shell*, III. The 'Web of Ages and Generations' is 'the Woof of Six Thousand Years' (M. 44. 15), the sum of man's endeavours after religious and moral expression, here attributed to the powers that govern mortal life, the 'Daughters of Albion' (J. 5. 37–39). The two extremes in mundane perception, the highest and the lowest, are indicated, the mortal visionary and the merely physical.

Then All the Daughters of Albion became One before Los, even Vala.
And she put forth her hand upon the Looms in dreadful howlings,
Till she vegetated into a hungry Stomach & a devouring Tongue.
Her Hand is a Court of Justice, her Feet two Armies in Battle;
Storms & Pestilence in her Locks, & in her Loins Earthquake
And Fire & the Ruin of Cities & Nations & Families & Tongues.

She cries: 'The Human is but a Worm, & thou, O Male, Thou art
Thyself Female, a Male, a breeder of Seed, a Son & Husband: & Lo!
The Human Divine is Woman's Shadow, a Vapor in the summer's heat.
Go assume Papal dignity, thou Spectre, thou Male Harlot! Arthur,
Divide into the Kings of Europe in times remote, O Woman-born
And Woman-nourish'd & Woman-educated & Woman-scorn'd!'

'Wherefore art thou living' said Los, '& Man cannot live in thy presence?
Art thou Vala the Wife of Albion, O thou lovely Daughter of Luvah?
All Quarrels arise from Reasoning, the secret Murder and
The violent Man-slaughter; these are the Spectre's double Cave,
The Sexual Death living on accusation of Sin & Judgment,
To freeze Love & Innocence into the gold & silver of the Merchant.
Without Forgiveness of Sin Love is Itself Eternal Death.'

Then the Spectre drew Vala into his bosom, magnificent, terrific,

8 See Index, *Head, Heart and Loins* and M. 3. 10 *note*.

12–17 Cp. J. 33. 48–51. Vala claims that what is of the Female, the forms of sense-perception and moral ideas, is alone real, the visionary metaphysic and ethic being but perverted forms, and therefore delusions derived therefrom. Her claim is therefore a restatement of the attitude of the materialists. The masculine creative energies, no longer responding solely to imaginative impulses, are controlled entirely by the sense-perceptive, the feminine, powers. The outcome is 'papal' and 'regal' tyranny. Arthur is practically synonymous with Albion: cp. D. C., pp. 40 and 42, and cp. J. 54. 25 *note*. 20–21 Cp. J. 31. 4 *note*.

Glittering with precious stones & gold, with Garments of blood & fire.
He wept in deadly wrath of the Spectre, in self-contradicting agony,
Crimson with Wrath & green with Jealousy, daz[z]ling with Love
And Jealousy immingled; & the purple of the violet darken'd deep
Over the Plow of Nations thund'ring in the hand of Albion's Spectre.

A dark Hermaphrodite they stood, frowni⟨ni⟩ng upon London's River:
And the Distaff & Spindle in the hands of Vala, with the Flax of
Human Miseries, turn'd fierce with the Lives of Men along the Valley,
As Reuben fled before the Daughters of Albion Taxing the Nations.

Derby Peak yawn'd a horrid Chasm at the Cries of Gwendolen & at
The stamping feet of Ragan upon the flaming Treddles of her Loom,
That drop with crimson gore with the Loves of Albion & Canaan,
Opening along the Valley of Rephaim, weaving over the Caves of Machpelah.

[65] To decide Two Worlds with a great decision, a World of Mercy, and
A World of Justice; the World of Mercy for Salvation,
To cast Luvah into the Wrath and Albion into the Pity,
In the Two Contraries of Humanity & in the Four Regions.

For in the depths of Albion's bosom, in the eastern heaven,
They sound the clarions strong: they chain the howling Captives:

30 See Index, *Plow*. 31 See Index, *Hermaphrodite*.

32–33 See Index, *Weaving*, and J. 60. 34 *note*.

34 Whether 'Taxing the Nations' relates to the Daughters of Albion or to Reuben or to both is uncertain. Taxation here, as in J. 98. 52–53, suggests the spiritually oppressive and repressive operation of the anti-visionary fallacies.

38 The Valley of Rephaim or of the Giants is identical with the Atlantic Vale, see Index, *Atlantic*. The Caves of Machpelah are not mentioned elsewhere: for the general significance of Caves, cp. J. 31, 4 *note*.

Page 65. This and the following page, both engraved in the same style, appear to be interpolations: they have no clear connexion with their contexts, so that it is impossible to say who 'they' (l. 6) are.

6–55 This passage is repeated from F. Z. vii *a*. 162–207, with the addition of the geographical symbols and certain minor changes.

They cast the lots into the helmet : they give the oath of blood in Lambeth :
They vote the death of Luvah & they nail'd him to Albion's Tree in Bath.
They stain'd him with poisonous blue : they inwove him in cruel roots,
To die a death of Six thousand years bound round with vegetation.
The sun was black & the moon roll'd a useless globe thro' Britain.

Then left the Sons of Urizen the plow & harrow, the loom,
The hammer & the chisel, & the rule & compasses ; from London fleeing,
They forg'd the sword on Cheviot, the chariot of war & the battle-ax,
The trumpet fitted to mortal battle & the flute of summer in Annandale.
And all the Arts of Life they chang'd into the Arts of Death in Albion.
The hour-glass contemn'd because its simple workmanship
Was like the workmanship of the plowman, & the water wheel
That raises water into cisterns broken & burn'd with fire,
Because its workmanship was like the workmanship of the shepherd ;
And in their stead intricate wheels invented, wheel without wheel,
To perplex youth in their outgoings, & to bind to labours in Albion
Of day & night the myriads of eternity that they may grind
And polish brass & iron hour after hour, laborious task,
Kept ignorant of its use that they might spend the days of wisdom
In sorrowful drudgery to obtain a scanty pittance of bread,
In ignorance to view a small portion & think that All,
And call it Demonstration, blind to all the simple rules of life.

'Now, now the battle rages round thy tender limbs, O Vala !
Now smile among thy bitter tears ; now put on all thy beauty.
Is not the wound of the sword sweet, & the broken bone delightful ?
Wilt thou now smile among the scythes when the wounded groan in the field ?

8–9 Cp. F. Z. vii *a.* 164 *note.*

We were carried away in thousands from London, & in tens
Of thousands from Westminster & Marybone, in ships clos'd up,
Chain'd hand & foot, compell'd to fight under the iron whips
Of our captains, fearing our officers more than the enemy.
Lift up thy blue eyes, Vala, & put on thy sapphire shoes :
O melancholy Magdalen, behold the morning over Malden break !
Gird on thy flaming zone : descend into the sepulcher of Canterbury.
Scatter the blood from thy golden brow, the tears from thy silver locks :
Shake off the waters from thy wings, & the dust from thy white garments.
Remember all thy feignèd terrors on the secret couch of Lambeth's Vale,
When the sun rose in glowing morn with arms of mighty hosts
Marching to battle, who was wont to rise with Urizen's harps
Girt as a sower with his seed to scatter life abroad over Albion.
Arise, O Vala ! bring the bow of Urizen : bring the swift arrows of light.
How rag'd the golden horses of Urizen, compell'd to the chariot of love,
Compell'd to leave the plow to the ox, to snuff up the winds of desolation,
To trample the corn fields in boastful neighings ! This is no gentle harp,
This is no warbling brook nor shadow of a mirtle tree ;
But blood and wounds and dismal cries and shadows of the oak,
And hearts laid open to the light by the broad grizly sword :
And bowels hid in hammer'd steel rip'd quivering on the ground.
Call forth thy smiles of soft deceit ! call forth thy cloudy tears !
We hear thy sighs in trumpets shrill when morn shall blood renew.'

So sang the Spectre Sons of Albion round Luvah's Stone of Trial,
Mocking and deriding at the writhings of their Victim on Salisbury,

33–36 These lines, that glance at the work of the press-gangs, are not found in *The Four Zoas*.

38 Magdalen here is Vala. In J. 62. 14 the name is applied to Jerusalem. Malden is constantly associated with error : cp. J. 41. 5 *note*.

39 Why into the sepulchre of Canterbury is not apparent.

Drinking his Emanation in intoxicating bliss, rejoicing in Giant dance.
For a Spectre has no Emanation but what he imbibes from decieving
A Victim. Then he becomes her Priest & she his Tabernacle
And his Oak Grove, till the Victim rend the woven Veil
In the end of his sleep when Jesus calls him from his grave.

Howling the Victims on the Druid Altars yield their souls
To the stern Warriors ; lovely sport the Daughters round their Victims,
Drinking their lives in sweet intoxication : hence arose from Bath
Soft deluding odours, in spiral volutions intricately winding
Over Albion's mountains, a feminine indefinite cruel delusion.
Astonish'd, terrified & in pain & torment, Sudden they behold
Their own Parent, the Emanation of their murder'd Enemy,
Become their Emanation and their Temple and Tabernacle.
They knew not this Vala was their belovèd Mother, Vala, Albion's Wife.

Terrified at the sight of the Victim, at his distorted sinews,
The tremblings of Vala vibrate thro' the limbs of Albion's Sons.
While they rejoice over Luvah in mockery & bitter scorn,
Sudden they become like what they behold, in howlings & deadly pain.
Spasms smite their features, sinews & limbs ; pale they look on one another ;
They turn, contorted ; their iron necks bend unwilling towards
Luvah ; their lips tremble ; their muscular fibres are cramp'd & smitten ;

59–62 Perhaps this abstruse piece of mystical dogmatism can best be explained by reference to *The Ghost of Abel*, ll. 10–13 and 29–33, if it be remembered that Tent, Tabernacle, Oak-Grove and House are equivalent in meaning to certain aspects of the symbol Emanation : cp. J. 54. 4 *note*. Satan, who is also the Gods of the Heathen, the Elohim of the Heathen who live on sacrifice, opposed to Jehovah who is Forgiveness of Sins, enters into the deluded spirit, the 'Ghost' of Abel, and dominates him so that through him is made manifest by emanation the false ethic of sin and atonement, which in earlier works would have been represented as Rahab or Vala. Satan is the Spectre, the Priest, the executive force behind the error ; Abel is its Victim.

65 Bath is an equivocal symbol ; all that can be said of it is that here it is associated with the springs of error.

72–79 Cp. J. 36. 9 *note*. 74 Cp. J. 63. 5 *note*.

They become like what they behold. Yet immense in strength & power,
[66] In awful pomp & gold, in all the precious unhewn stones of Eden,
They build a stupendous Building on the Plain of Salisbury: with chains
Of rocks, round London Stone, of Reasonings, of unhewn Demonstrations,
In labyrinthine arches, (Mighty Urizen the Architect,) thro' which
The Heavens might revolve & Eternity be bound in their chain,
Labour unparallell'd, a wondrous rocky World of cruel destiny,
Rocks pilèd on rocks reaching the stars, stretching from pole to pole.
The Building is Natural Religion, & its Altars Natural Morality;
A building of eternal death, whose proportions are eternal despair.
Here Vala stood turning the iron Spindle of destruction
From heaven to earth, howling, invisible: but not invisible
Her Two Covering Cherubs, afterwards namèd Voltaire & Rousseau,
Two frowning Rocks on each side of the Cove & Stone of Torture,
Frozen Sons of the feminine Tabernacle of Bacon, Newton & Locke.
For Luvah is France, the Victim of the Spectres of Albion.

Los beheld in terror: he pour'd his loud storms on the Furnaces.
The Daughters of Albion, clothèd in garments of needle work,
Strip them off from their shoulders and bosoms: they lay aside

Page 66. 1–15 Cp. J. 68. 21–51, where, however, there are references to an ulterior regenerative purpose not explicit here. The 'precious unhewn stones of Eden' is a phrase that scarcely seems in accord with the general tenor of these lines: no explanation can, however, be offered.

12–14 See Index, *Mundane Shell, Note II*.

15–34 It is possible that this passage may refer to the decline of the French Revolution from what Blake had hoped of it. The 'spiritual cause' of this failure is represented as the perverting influence of the Daughters of Albion, the sources of rationalism and morality, or in Blake's own term, of Deism. But whether or not this be the true interpretation of the passage in its particular application, its general purpose clearly is to describe the 'Crucifying Cruelties of Demonstration' (J. 24. 55) in their operation, 'the Moral Virtues of the Heathen whose tender Mercies are Cruelty' (J. 61. 20). Particularly in ll. 23–24 Blake urges once more against official Christianity the accusation of hostility to the spirit of Christ's teaching, while zealous in the observation of the letter, the 'linen garments' and 'vesture'.

Their garments : they sit naked upon the Stone of trial.
The Knife of flint passes over the howling Victim : his blood
Gushes & stains the fair side of the fair Daug[h]ters of Albion.
They put aside his curls : they divide his seven locks upon
His forehead : they bind his forehead with thorns of iron :
They put into his hand a reed ; they mock, Saying : ' Behold
The King of Canaan, whose are seven hundred chariots of iron ! '
They take off his vesture whole with their Knives of flint :
But they cut asunder his inner garments, searching with
Their cruel fingers for his heart ; & there they enter in pomp,
In many tears ; & there they erect a temple & an altar.
They pour cold water on his brain in front, to cause
Lids to grow over his eyes in veils of tears and caverns
To freeze over his nostrils, while they feed his tongue from cups
And dishes of painted clay. Glowing with beauty & cruelty,
They obscure the sun & the moon : no eye can look upon them.

Ah ! alas ! at the sight of the Victim & at sight of those who are smitten,
All who see become what they behold : their eyes are cover'd
With veils of tears, and their nostrils & tongues shrunk up,
Their ear bent outwards : as their Victim, so are they in the pangs
Of unconquerable fear, amidst delights of revenge Earth-shaking.
And as their eye & ear shrunk, the heavens shrunk away.
The Divine Vision became first a burning flame, then a column
Of fire, then an awful fiery wheel surrounding earth & heaven,
And then a globe of blood wandering distant in an unknown night.
Afar into the unknown night the mountains fled away :
Six months of mortality, a summer ; & six months of mortality, a winter.
The Human form began to be alter'd by the Daughters of Albion
And the perceptions to be dissipated into the Indefinite, Becoming
A mighty Polypus nam'd Albion's Tree. They tie the Veins

22–23 Cp. Judges xvi. 13. 35 Cp. J. 36. 9 *note*.
40–52 Cp. J. 49. 21–22 :

The Visions of Eternity, by reason of narrowed perceptions,
Are become weak Visions of Time & Space, fix'd into furrows of death.

The changes in man's perception of the Divine Vision cannot be interpreted.
46–55 See Index, *Mundane Shell, Note I.* B.

And Nerves into two knots, & the Seed into a double knot.
They look forth : the Sun is shrunk : the Heavens are shrunk
Away into the far remote, and the Trees & Mountains wither'd
Into indefinite cloudy shadows in darkness & separation.
By Invisible Hatreds adjoin'd, they seem remote and separate
From each other ; and yet are a Mighty Polypus in the Deep.
As the Misletoe grows on the Oak, so Albion's Tree on Eternity. Lo !
He who will not comingle in Love must be adjoin'd by Hate.

They look forth from Stone-henge : from the Cove round London Stone
They look on one another : the mountain calls out to the mountain :
Plinlimmon shrunk away : Snowdon trembled : the mountains
Of Wales & Scotland beheld the descending War, the routed flying.
Red run the streams of Albion : Thames is drunk with blood,
As Gwendolen cast the shuttle of war, as Cambel return'd the beam.
The Humber & the Severn are drunk with the blood of the slain :
London feels his brain cut round : Edinburgh's heart is circumscribèd :
York & Lincoln hide among the flocks, because of the griding Knife.
Worcester & Hereford, Oxford & Cambridge reel & stagger,
Overwearied with howling : Wales & Scotland alone sustain the fight.
The inhabitants are sick to death : they labour to divide into Days
And Nights the uncertain Periods, and into Weeks & Months. In vain
They send the Dove & Raven, & in vain the Serpent over the mountains,

53–54 The diverse and conflicting modes of error are united in their common hostility to the mystical ethic and metaphysic.

56 Cp. J. 9. 26–31.

57 The Cove round London Stone is not mentioned elsewhere : for London's Stone, cp. J. 8. 27 *note*, and see Index, *Druid*.

61–66 The streams of Albion 'give up their souls for Albion's sake' (J. 16. 16–17). The cities mentioned are among the Twenty-four Friends of Albion : see Index, *Los*, *Note II*. B. The purpose of this passage would seem to be to describe the temporary checks of visionary activity in mundane life.

67 Cp. J. 5. 11 *note*. The significance of the endurance of Wales and Scotland in the struggle is hidden.

70–73 These lines seem to suggest unsuccessful attempts on the part

And in vain the Eagle & Lion over the four-fold wilderness.
They return not, but generate in rocky places desolate :
They return not, but build a habitation separate from Man.
The Sun forgets his course like a drunken man : he hesitates
Upon the Cheselden hills, thinking to sleep on the Severn.
In vain : he is hurried afar into an unknown Night ;
He bleeds in torrents of blood as he rolls thro' heaven above.
He chokes up the paths of the sky : the Moon is leprous as snow,
Trembling & descending down, seeking to rest on high Mona,
Scattering her leprous snows in flakes of disease over Albion.
The Stars flee remote : the heaven is iron, the earth is sulphur,
And all the mountains & hills shrink up like a withering gourd,
As the Senses of Men shrink together under the Knife of flint
In the hands of Albion's Daughters among the Druid Temples.

[67] By those who drink their blood & the blood of their Covenant.

And the Twelve Daughters of Albion united in Rahab & Tirzah,
A Double Female : and they drew out from the Rocky Stones
Fibres of Life to Weave ; for every Female is a Golden Loom,
The Rocks are opake hardnesses covering all Vegetated things.
And as they Wove & Cut from the Looms in various divisions,
Stretching over Europe & Asia from Ireland to Japan,
They divided into many lovely Daughters to be counterparts
To those they Wove : for when they Wove a Male, they divided
Into a Female to the Woven Male : in opake hardness
They cut the Fibres from the Rocks ; groaning in pain they Weave,
Calling the Rocks Atomic Origins of Existence, denying Eternity
By the Atheistical Epicurean Philosophy of Albion's Tree.

of man to find a resting-place amid the flood of rationalistic and ethical abstractions and in the deserts of the Moral Law.

83–84 Cp. M. 4. 16 *note*.

Page 67. The sequence here is disordered. The first line does not clearly follow from the preceding page, nor yet from p. 64.

3–4 See Index, *Weaving*, I.

8 The Counterpart is evidently not to be distinguished from the Female : see Index, *Sex*.

13 Cp. Crabb Robinson's letter to Dorothy Wordsworth (S., p. 274) : 'Now according to Blake, Atheism consists in worshipping the natural world, which same natural world, properly speaking, is nothing real but a mere illusion produced by Satan.' Cp. also R. N., p. 197 : 'The Artifice of the Epicurean Philosophers is to Call all other Opinions Unsolid & Unsubstantial than those which are derived from Earth', and *ibid.*, p. 204 :

Such are the Feminine & Masculine when separated from Man.
They call the Rocks Parents of Men, & adore the frowning Chaos,
Dancing around in howling pain clothèd in the bloody Veil,
Hiding Albion's Sons within the Veil, closing Jerusalem's
Sons without, to feed with their Souls the Spectres of Albion,
Ashamèd to give Love openly to the piteous & merciful Man,
Counting him an imbecile mockery : but the Warrior
They adore, & his revenge cherish with the blood of the Innocent.
They drink up Dan & Gad to feed with milk Skofeld & Kotope :
They strip off Joseph's Coat & dip it in the blood of battle.

Tirzah sits weeping to hear the shrieks of the dying : her Knife
Of flint is in her hand : she passes it over the howling Victim.
The Daughters Weave their Work in loud cries over the Rock
Of Horeb, still eyeing Albion's Cliffs eagerly, siezing & twisting
The threads of Vala & Jerusalem running from mountain to mountain
Over the whole Earth : loud the Warriors rage in Beth Peor
Beneath the iron whips of their Captains & consecrated banners :
Loud the Sun & Moon rage in the conflict : loud the Stars
Shout in the night of battle & their spears grow to their hands
With blood, weaving the deaths of the Mighty into a Tabernacle
For Rahab & Tirzah, till the Great Polypus of Generation coverèd the Earth.

' Here is a plain confession that he [Reynolds] Thinks Mind & Imagination not to be above the Mortal & Perishing Nature. Such is the Epicurean or Newtonian Philosophy : it is Atheism.'

19–21 Cp. J. 81. 1–5. The ' piteous & merciful Man ' is Jesus, in whom the mystical ethic of the forgiveness of sins is revealed. The Warrior is the representative of the ' Religion that Preaches Vengeance for Sin ' (J. 52). Cp. M. 28. 51–54 and *Auguries of Innocence*, ll. 59-60 (Clar. Press, p. 290) :

Joy & Woe are woven fine
A Clothing for the soul divine.

29 Beth Peor, where Moses rehearsed the Law of Sinai to the Israelites, represents the fullest power of the ' Religion of the Enemy & Avenger ' whose ' God is Satan '.

33 Cp. D. C. viii, p. 53 : ' Unworthy Men who gain fame among Men continue to govern mankind after death, and in their spiritual bodies oppose the spirits of those who worthily are famous ; and, as Swedenborg observes, by entering into disease and excrement, drunkenness, and concupiscence, they possess themselves of the bodies of mortal men, and shut the doors of mind and of thought by placing Learning above Inspiration.'

34–40 See Index, *Mundane Shell, Note II*. ii.

In Verulam the Polypus's Head, winding around his bulk
Thro' Rochester and Chichester & Exeter & Salisbury,
To Bristol; & his Heart beat strong on Salisbury Plain,
Shooting out Fibres round the Earth, thro' Gaul & Italy
And Greece, & along the Sea of Rephaim into Judea
To Sodom & Gomorrha; thence to India, China & Japan.

The Twelve Daughters in Rahab & Tirzah have circumscrib'd the Brain
Beneath & piercèd it thro' the midst with a golden pin.
Blood hath stain'd her fair side beneath her bosom.

'O thou poor Human Form!' said she. 'O thou poor child of woe!
Why wilt thou wander away from Tirzah? why me compel to bind thee?
If thou dost go away from me, I shall consume upon these Rocks.
These fibres of thine eyes, that usèd to beam in distant heavens
Away from me I have bound down with a hot iron.
These nostrils, that expanded with delight in morning skies,
I have bent downward with lead melted in my roaring furnaces
Of affliction, of love, of sweet despair, of torment unendurable.
My soul is seven furnaces; incessant roars the bellows
Upon my terribly flaming heart; the molten metal runs
In channels thro' my fiery limbs. O love! O pity! O fear!
O pain! O the pangs, the bitter pangs of love forsaken!
Ephraim was a wilderness of joy where all my wild beasts ran.
The River Kanah wander'd by my sweet Manasseh's side,
To see the boy spring into heavens sounding from my sight.
Go Noah, fetch the girdle of strong brass; heat it red-hot;
Press it around the loins of this ever expanding cruelty.
Shriek not so, my only love: I refuse thy joys: I drink
Thy shrieks because Hand & Hyle are cruel & obdurate to me.
[68] O Skofield why art thou cruel? Lo Joseph is thine, to make
You One, to weave you both in the same mantle of skin.

35–37 Like the 'Wheel of Religion' (J. 77. 1–13), the Polypus winds out of the East, the quarter of error against the West, the quarter of vision. Salisbury Plain, from its Druidical associations, is represented as the heart of the false 'Natural Religion'.

39 Cp. J. 64. 38 *note*.

41–42 The reference is to the limitation of mental or spiritual activity in life by the Daughters of Albion who 'control our vegetative powers'.

44 From this point to p. 68. 9 Blake repeats, with slight verbal changes, F. Z. viii. 288–310.

54–55 This is the 'false Female Love'.

Bind him down, Sisters, bind him down on Ebal, Mount of cursing !
Malah, come forth from Lebanon ! & Hoglah, from Mount Sinai !
Come ! circumscribe this tongue of sweets, & with a screw of iron
Fasten this ear into the rock. Milcah, the task is thine.
Weep not so, Sisters, weep not so ! our life depends on this ;
Or mercy & truth are fled away from Shechem & Mount Gilead,
Unless my belovèd is bound upon the Stems of Vegetation.'

And thus the Warriors cry in the hot day of Victory in Songs :

' Look ! the beautiful Daughter of Albion sits naked upon the Stone,
Her panting Victim beside her ; her heart is drunk with blood,
Tho' her brain is not drunk with wine ; she goes forth from Albion
In pride of beauty, in cruelty of holiness, in the brightness
Of her tabernacle & her ark & secret place : the beautiful Daughter
Of Albion delights the eyes of the Kings ; their hearts & the
Hearts of their Warriors glow hot before Thor & Friga. O Molech !
O Chemosh ! O Bacchus ! O Venus ! O Double God of Generation !
The Heavens are cut like a mantle around from the Cliffs of Albion,
Across Europe, across Africa, in howlings & deadly War.
A sheet & veil & curtain of blood is let down from Heaven
Across the hills of Ephraim, & down Mount Olivet to

Page 68. 3 ' him ' may refer to the ' Human Form ' (J. 67. 44), to its equivalent, ' the boy ' (J. 67. 58), possibly to a second equivalent, ' Joseph ' (J. 68. 1), or much less probably to ' Skofield ' (J. 68. 1).

8 Shechem, Rehoboam's capital set up against Jerusalem, represents the hostility of Natural Religion against Imagination. For Gilead cp. F. Z. viii. 2 *note*.

10 The ' warriors ' are they who delight in ' Corporeal War ', the fundamental principle of Natural Religion.

11 The ' Stone ' is the Stone of Sacrifice : cp. Index, *Druid*, and M. 4. 16 *note*.

17–18 Cp. J. 50. 3 *note*. The Double God of Generation may be related to the ' Hermaphroditic Blasphemy ' of a ' Vegetated Christ and a Virgin Eve ' (J. 90. 34), that is, to the sterile body of moral and metaphysical ideas which is a perversion of ' the Everlasting Gospel ' of liberty and forgiveness into a travesty of Christianity.

22–23 Mount Ephraim in which Shechem stood (see above, l. 8 *note*), Mount Olivet, where Solomon built high places to strange gods, and the Valley of the Jebusites, are all associated with the veil of Natural Religion by reason of their connexion with ancient idolatries.

The Valley of the Jebusite. Molech rejoices in heaven :
He sees the Twelve Daughters naked upon the Twelve Stones,
Themselves condensing to rocks & into the Ribs of a Man.
Lo, they shoot forth in tender Nerves across Europe & Asia !
Lo, they rest upon the Tribes, where their panting Victims lie!
Molech rushes into the Kings in love to the beautiful Daughters,
But they frown & delight in cruelty, refusing all other joy.
Bring your Offerings, your first begotten pamper'd with milk & blood,
Your first born of seven years old, be they Males or Females,
To the beautiful Daughters of Albion ! They sport before the Kings
Clothèd in the skin of the Victim! blood, human blood, is the life
And delightful food of the Warrior : the well fed Warrior's flesh
Of him who is slain in War fills the Valleys of Ephraim with
Breeding Women walking in pride & bringing forth under green trees
With pleasure, without pain ; for their food is blood of the Captive.
Molech rejoices thro' the Land from Havilah to Shur : he rejoices
In moral law & its severe penalties. Loud Shaddai & Jehovah
Thunder above, when they see the Twelve panting Victims
On the Twelve Stones of Power, & the beautiful Daughters of Albion :
" If you dare rend their Veil with your spear, you are healèd of Love."
From the Hills of Camberwell & Wimbledon, from the Valleys
Of Walton & Esher, from Stone-henge & from Malden's Cove,
Jerusalem's Pillars fall in the rendings of fierce War

24–25 The cognate illusions of physical reality and morality are here attributed to the Female : in J. 90. 19–20 they are traced to the Spectre. This confusion of masculine and feminine activities is not uncommon in Blake's application of his symbols.

26 Cp. J. 38. 35 *note*.

39 Shaddai and Jehovah are 'Angels of the Presence' : see F. Z. viii. 387 *note*.

41 The 'Twelve Stones' are apparently identical with the Druid Temples, or the Altars of Sacrifice called Justice and Truth (J. 28. 21–23) : cp. J. 25. 4 *note*. The name is probably taken from Ossian, *Sul-malla of Lumon* : 'Near were two circles of Loda with the stone of power, where spirits descended by night in dark-red streams of fire.'

42 Cp. F. Z. viii. 290 *note*. Love is here the 'False Generative Love', the contrary of 'Universal Brotherhood and Love'. The 'spear' is the 'intellectual spear' that 'puts off' or 'annihilates' error.

45–46 Cp. J. 47. 8 *note*.

Over France & Germany, upon the Rhine & Danube.
Reuben & Benjamin flee : they hide in the Valley of Rephaim.
Why trembles the Warrior's limbs when he beholds thy beauty
Spotted with Victims' blood, by the fires of thy secret tabernacle
And thy ark & holy place : at thy frowns, at thy dire revenge,
Smitten as Uzzah of old, his armour is soften'd : his spear
And sword faint in his hand from Albion across Great Tartary.
O beautiful Daughter of Albion, cruelty is thy delight !
O Virgin of terrible eyes, who dwellest by Valleys of springs
Beneath the Mountains of Lebanon in the City of Rehob in Hamath,
Taught to touch the harp, to dance in the Circle of Warriors
Before the Kings of Canaan, to cut the flesh from the Victim,
To roast the flesh in fire, to examine the Infant's limbs
In cruelties of holiness, to refuse the joys of love, to bring
The Spies from Egypt to raise jealousy in the bosoms of the Twelve
Kings of Canaan, then to let the Spies depart to Meribah Kadesh
To the place of the Amalekite ! I am drunk with unsatiated love.
I must rush again to War ; for the Virgin has frown'd & refus'd.
Sometimes I curse & sometimes bless thy fascinating beauty.
Once Man was occupied in intellectual pleasures & energies :
But now my Soul is harrow'd with grief & fear & love & desire,
And now I hate, & now I love, & Intellect is no more.
There is no time for any thing but the torments of love & desire :
The Feminine & Masculine Shadows soft, mild & ever varying
In beauty, are Shadows now no more, but Rocks in Horeb.'

[69] Then all the Males conjoinèd into One Male, & every one
Became a ravening eating Cancer growing in the Female,

48–52 The lines image the atrophy of man's spiritual powers so long as he persists in the attitude of mind symbolized by the Daughters of Albion, i.e. so long as he accepts the witness of his senses.

58–59 Cp. F. Z. i. 43–47.

69–70 The constrictive arbitrariness of the forms, intellectual, moral, and aesthetic, of the 'Satanic world' is set over against the unconstrained freedom of the world of Imagination, where forms are 'mental' and the spirit is liberty : cp. J. 69. 6–25 for a parallel passage.

Page 69. 1–11 See Index, *Mundane Shell, Note I.* ii. The Male here is symbolic of 'sexual' schisms and discords, and the union of all such activities into One is parallel with and opposed to the union of the Eternals, the Divine Family, into 'One Man, Jesus'. The 'One Male', the 'enormous Form' of l. 6, Hand as described on p. 70, is ultimately Satan, 'God of this World'.

2 The illusions of false reason and morality originate in the perversion

A Polypus of Roots of Reasoning, Doubt, Despair & Death,
Going forth & returning from Albion's Rocks to Canaan,
Devouring Jerusalem from every Nation of the Earth.

Envying stood the enormous Form at variance with Itself
In all its Members, in eternal torment of love & jealousy,
Driv'n forth by Los time after time from Albion's cliffy shore,
Drawing the free loves of Jerusalem into infernal bondage,
That they might be born in contentions of Chastity & in
Deadly Hate between Leah & Rachel, Daughters of Deceit & Fraud,
Bearing the Images of various Species of Contention
And Jealousy & Abhorrence & Revenge & deadly Murder,
Till they refuse liberty to the Male ; & not like Beulah
Where every Female delights to give her maiden to her husband.
The Female searches sea & land for gratifications to the
Male Genius, who in return clothes her in gems & gold,
And feeds her with the food of Eden ; hence all her beauty beams.
She Creates at her will a little moony night & silence
With Spaces of sweet gardens & a tent of elegant beauty,
Closèd in by a sandy desart & a night of stars shining,
And a little tender moon & hovering angels on the wing.
And the Male gives a Time & Revolution to her Space
Till the time of love is passèd in ever varying delights.
For All Things Exist in the Human Imagination,
And thence in Beulah they are stolen by secret amorous theft,
Till they have had Punishment enough to make them commit Crimes.

of man's perceptions, of which the Female is the mythical cause and the symbol. Cp. E. G. γ^2. 89–94 :

> that which was of woman born,
> When the soul fell into sleep . . .
> Shooting out against the Light
> Fibres of a deadly night,
> Reasoning upon its own dark Fiction,
> In doubt which is Self Contradiction.

For the Cancer or Polypus see Index, *Mundane Shell, Note I.* ii.

9–10 Cp. J. 64. 22–23 :

> The Sexual Death, living on accusations of Sin & Judgment,
> To freeze Love & Innocence into the gold & silver of the Merchant.

11–12 The references to the double-dealing of Laban, to the jealousy of his daughters, the wives of Jacob, and to Rachel's theft of the images are not interpretable in detail, though the justification of interpreting the particular fact in terms of a general spiritual experience is made in D. C. iii, pp. 9 and 21.

25–31 Here Beulah is a phase in individual and in universal Experience wherein the symbol and its spiritual meaning appear to be seen and known

Hence rose the Tabernacle in the Wilderness & all its Offerings,
From Male & Female Loves in Beulah & their Jealousies.
But no one can consummate Female bliss in Los's World without
Becoming a Generated Mortal, a Vegetating Death.

And now the Spectres of the Dead awake in Beulah : all
The Jealousies become Murderous, uniting together in Rahab,
A Religion of Chastity, forming a Commerce to sell Loves,
With Moral Law, an Equal Balance, not going down with decision.
Therefore the Male, severe & cruel, fill'd with stern Revenge,
Mutual Hate returns & mutual Deceit & mutual Fear.

Hence the Infernal Veil grows in the disobedient Female,
Which Jesus rends & the whole Druid Law removes away
From the Inner Sanctuary, a False Holiness hid within the Center.
For the Sanctuary of Eden is in the Camp, in the Outline,
In the Circumference : & every Minute Particular is Holy.
Embraces are Cominglings from the Head even to the Feet,
And not a pompous High Priest entering by a Secret Place.

Jerusalem pinèd in her inmost soul over Wandering Reuben
As she slept in Beulah's Night hid by the Daughters of Beulah.

[70] And this the form of mighty Hand sitting on Albion's cliffs
Before the face of Albion, a mighty threat'ning Form.

His bosom wide & shoulders huge, overspreading, wondrous,
Bear Three strong sinewy Necks & Three awful & terrible Heads,
Three Brains in contradictory council brooding incessantly,

together, as 'Contraries' equally true : hence 'no dispute can come'. Later 'allegoric and mental signification' is perverted 'into corporeal command' (D. C., p. 41). It is as if Blake declares (ll. 30–31) that no truth revealed in mortality can escape perversion after the manner described in ll. 32–37.

36–37 Cp. J. 68. 62–70.

40–42 Cp. J. 71. 6–9.

43–44 The 'Cominglings' signify that man's perceptions of the real and eternal world of Imagination is immediate by virtue of his identity with it. On the other hand, in his state of error he loses sight of this 'one-ness' and becomes subject to the arbitrary and external authority of moral law, and to the partial revelations of a reason limited to the data of sense.

Page 70 may be misplaced, since its catchword 'His' does not correspond to the first word of p. 71.

5 Cp. E. G. γ^2. 95–96 (Clar. Press, p. 254) :

Reasoning upon its own dark Fiction
In doubt which is Self Contradiction.

Neither daring to put in act its councils, fearing each-other,
Therefore rejecting Ideas as nothing & holding all Wisdom
To consist in the agreements & disagree[me]nts of Ideas,
Plotting to devour Albion's Body of Humanity & Love.

Such Form the aggregate of the Twelve Sons of Albion took, & such
Their appearance when combin'd : but often by birth-pangs & loud groans
They divide to Twelve : the key-bones & the chest dividing in pain
Disclose a hideous orifice ; thence issuing the Giant-brood
Arise as the smoke of the furnace, shaking the rocks from sea to sea ;
And there they combine into Three Forms, namèd Bacon & Newton & Locke
In the Oak Groves of Albion which overspread all the Earth.

Imputing Sin & Righteousness to Individuals, Rahab
Sat deep within him hid, his Feminine Power, u[n]reveal'd,
Brooding Abstract Philosophy to destroy Imagination, the Divine-
Humanity ; A Three-fold Wonder, feminine, most beautiful, Three-fold
Each within other. On her white marble & even Neck her Heart
Inorb'd and bonified, with locks of shadowing modesty shining.
Over her beautiful Female features, soft, flourishing in beauty,
Beams mild all love and all perfection, that when the lips
Recieve a kiss from Gods or Men, a threefold kiss returns
From the press'd loveliness ; so her whole immortal form, three-fold,
Three-fold embrace returns, consuming lives of Gods & Men,
In fires of beauty melting them as gold & silver in the furnace.
Her Brain enlabyrinths the whole heaven of her bosom & loins

7–9 Cp. M. 35. 5 *note*. 'Albion's Body of Humanity & Love' is the 'real and Immortal self' of Man, his spiritual life, the Divine Humanity.

16 See Index, *Druid*.

17 Cp. J. 49. 65–66 :

Yet they [the Spectres] are blameless, & Iniquity must be imputed only
To the States that they are enter'd into that they may be deliver'd.

See Index, *States*.

17–31 With this description of Rahab or Vala, cp. 'The Crystal Cabinet' (Clar. Press, pp. 282–283).

21–24 This passage is more than usually incoherent, and punctuation is uncertain.

To put in act what her Heart wills. O who can withstand her power!
Her name is Vala in Eternity: in Time her name is Rahab.

The Starry Heavens all were fled from the mighty limbs of Albion,
[71] And above Albion's Land was seen the Heavenly Canaan,
As the Substance is to the Shadow; and above Albion's Twelve Sons
Were seen Jerusalem's Sons and all the Twelve Tribes spreading
Over Albion. As the Soul is to the Body, so Jerusalem's Sons
Are to the Sons of Albion: and Jerusalem is Albion's Emanation.

What is Above is Within, for every-thing in Eternity is translucent.
The Circumference is Within: Without, is formèd the Selfish Center.
And the Circumference still expands, going forward to Eternity:
And the Center has Eternal States: these States we now explore.

And these the Names of Albion's Twelve Sons & of his Twelve Daughters,
With their Districts. Hand dwelt in Selsey, & had Sussex & Surrey
And Kent & Middlesex, all their Rivers & their Hills of flocks & herds,
Their Villages, Towns, Cities, Sea-Ports, Temples, sublime Cathedrals:
All were his Friends & their Sons & Daughters intermarry in Beulah;
For all are Men in Eternity, Rivers, Mountains, Cities, Villages.

Page 71. See note on J., p. 70. Nothing can be said in explanation of the distribution of the districts among the Sons of Albion and their Emanations.

1–2 Albion's Land in the present passage is mundane life, the state of fallen man. The Heavenly Canaan is the World of Eternity or Imagination.

6–9 Cp. F. Z. i. 250 *note*.

9 Cp. *Cat.* 1810: 'Man passes on but States remain for ever: he passes thro' them like a traveller'; and J. 4:

> Of the Sleep of Ulro and of the passage through
> Eternal Death, and of the awaking to Eternal Life.

10–53 This account of the Sons of Albion with their Emanation relates to the time before the Fall; cp. l. 54:

> But now Albion is darkened & Jerusalem lies in ruins.

15 Cp. Poems from Letters, ii. 25–32 (Clar. Press, p. 303).

All are Human, & when you enter into their Bosoms you walk
In Heavens & Earths, as in your own Bosom you bear your Heaven
And Earth; & all you behold, tho' it appears Without, it is Within
In your Imagination, of which this World of Mortality is but a Shadow.

Hyle dwelt in Winchester, comprehending Hants, Dorset, Devon, Cornwall,
Their Villages, Cities, Sea Ports, their Corn fields & Gardens, spacious
Palaces, Rivers & Mountains: and between Hand & Hyle arose
Gwendolen & Cambel who is Boadicea: they go abroad & return
Like lovely beams of light from the mingled affections of the Brothers.
The Inhabitants of the whole Earth rejoice in their beautiful light.

Coban dwelt in Bath: Somerset, Wiltshire, Gloucestershire,
Obey'd his awful voice: Ignoge is his lovely Emanation.
She adjoin'd with Gwantoke's Children: soon lovely Cordella arose.
Gwantoke forgave & joy'd over South Wales & all its Mountains.

Peachey had North Wales, Shropshire, Cheshire & the Isle of Man.
His Emanation is Mehetabel, terrible & lovely upon the Mountains.

Brertun had Yorkshire, Durham, Westmoreland; & his Emanation
Is Ragan: she adjoin'd to Slade, & produced Gonorill far beaming.

Slade had Lincoln, Stafford, Derby, Nottingham; & his lovely
Emanation Gonorill rejoices over hills & rocks & woods & rivers.

Huttn had Warwick, Northampton, Bedford, Buckingham,
Leicester & Berkshire; & his Emanation is Gwinefred beautiful.

Skofeld had Ely, Rutland, Cambridge, Huntingdon, Norfolk,
Suffolk, Hartford & Essex; & his Emanation is Gwinevera:

23 See Index, *Vala*, *Note I*. i.

Beautiful she beams towards the east all kinds of precious stones
And pearl, with instruments of music in holy Jerusalem.

Kox had Oxford, Warwick, Wilts ; his Emanation is Estrild :
Join'd with Cordella she shines southward over the Atlantic.

Kotope had Hereford, Stafford, Worcester, & his Emanation
Is Sabrina : join'd with Mehetabel she shines west over America.

Bowen had all Scotland, the Isles, Northumberland & Cumberland :
His Emanation is Conwenna ; she shines a triple form
Over the north with pearly beams gorgeous & terrible.
Jerusalem & Vala rejoice in Bowen & Conwenna.

But the Four Sons of Jerusalem that never were Generated
Are Rintrah and Palamabron and Theotormon and Bromion. They
Dwell over the Four Provinces of Ireland in heavenly light,
The Four Universities of Scotland, & in Oxford & Cambridge & Winchester.

But now Albion is darkenèd & Jerusalem lies in ruins
Above the Mountains of Albion, above the head of Los.

And Los shouted with ceaseless shoutings, & his tears pourèd down
His immortal cheeks, rearing his hands to heaven for aid Divine.
But he spoke not to Albion, fearing lest Albion should turn his Back
Against the Divine Vision & fall over the Precipice of Eternal Death.
But he receded before Albion & before Vala weaving the Veil
With the iron shuttle of War among the rooted Oaks of Albion,
Weeping & shouting to the Lord day & night : and his Children
Wept round him as a flock silent Seven Days of Eternity.

50–53 See Index, *Los, Note II*. In J. 15. 14–20 Blake speaks in condemnation of the 'Schools and Universities of Europe' : it is to be remembered that Europe is always the symbol of intellectual and moral error ; see *Europe*, Introduction. Here the Universities of Albion are 'places of thought' standing 'in heavenly light', as their association with the Sons of Los who were never 'Generated' indicates.

63 The significance of the 'Seven Days of Eternity' is not clear. It would seem to be connected in some way with the duration of mundane life,

[72] And the Thirty-two Counties of the Four Provinces of Ireland
Are thus divided : The Four Counties are in the Four Camps ;
Munster South in Reuben's Gate, Connaut West in Joseph's Gate,
Ulster North in Dan's Gate, Leinster East in Judah's Gate.

For Albion in Eternity has Sixteen Gates among his Pillars,
But the Four towards the West were Wallèd up, & the Twelve
That front the Four other Points were turnèd Four Square
By Los for Jerusalem's sake & callèd the Gates of Jerusalem ;
Because Twelve Sons of Jerusalem fled successive thro' the Gates.
But the Four Sons of Jerusalem who fled not but remain'd
Are Rintrah & Palamabron & Theotormon & Bromion,
The Four that remain with Los to guard the Western Wall.
And these Four remain to guard the Four Walls of Jerusalem,
Whose foundations remain in the Thirty-two Counties of Ireland,
And in Twelve Counties of Wales, & in the Forty Counties
Of England, & in the Thirty-six Counties of Scotland.

And the names of the Thirty-two Counties of Ireland are these :
Under Judah & Issachar & Zebulun are Lowth, Longford,
Eastmeath, Westmeath, Dublin, Kildare, King's County,
Queen's County, Wicklow, Catherloh, Wexford, Kilkenny.
And those under Reuben & Simeon & Levi are these,
Waterford, Tipperary, Cork, Limerick, Kerry, Clare.
And those under Ephraim, Manasseh & Benjamin are these,
Galway, Roscommon, Mayo, Sligo, Leitrim.
And those under Dan, Asher & Napthali are these,
Donnegal, Antrim, Tyrone, Fermanagh, Armagh, Londonderry,
Down, Monaghan, Cavan. These are the Land of Erin.

All these Center in London & in Golgonooza, from whence
They are Created continually, East & West & North & South :

the time of man's regeneration. Blake may here have adopted the eschatology of the Millennarians based on Psalm xc. 4.

Page 72. 5 Cp. the description of Golgonooza (J., pp. 12–13), with its four Gates, each fourfold. 6 Cp. J. 13. 6 *note*.

7 The mention of ' the Four other Points ' would seem to be a slip of the pen. Ellis, however, maintains that the phrase has a definite significance ; cp. Blake's *Poetical Works* (Chatto & Windus), vol. ii, pp. 490–492.

9 Cp. F. Z. viii. 362–366.

17 Cp. J. 49. 4 *note*.

And from them are Created all the Nations of the Earth,
Europe & Asia & Africa & America, in fury Fourfold.

And Thirty-two the Nations to dwell in Jerusalem's Gates.
O Come, ye Nations ! Come, ye People ! Come up to Jerusalem !
Return, Jerusalem, & dwell together as of old ! Return !
Return, O Albion, let Jerusalem overspread all Nations
As in the times of old ! O Albion, awake ! Reuben wanders :
The Nations wait for Jerusalem : they look up for the Bride.

France, Spain, Italy, Germany, Poland, Russia, Sweden, Turkey,
Arabia, Palestine, Persia, Hindostan, China, Tartary, Siberia,
Egypt, Lybia, Ethiopia, Guinea, Caffraria, Negroland, Morocco,
Congo, Zaara, Canada, Greenland, Carolina, Mexico,
Peru, Patagonia, Amazonia, Brazil—Thirty-two Nations :
And under these Thirty-two Classes of Islands in the Ocean,
All the Nations, Peoples & Tongues throughout all the Earth.

And the Four Gates of Los surround the Universe Within and
Without ; & whatever is visible in the Vegetable Earth, the same
Is visible in the Mundane Shell, revers'd in mountain & vale.
And a Son of Eden was set over each Daughter of Beulah, to guard
In Albion's Tomb the wondrous Creation : & the Four-fold Gate
Towards Beulah is to the South : Fenelon, Guion, Teresa,
Whitefield & Hervey guard that Gate, with all the gentle Souls
Who guide the great Wine-press of Love. Four precious Stones that Gate.

31 Below this line is a drawing of the terrestrial globe, showing the continents mentioned in the text. Within the circle of the earth this line is engraved spirally : 'Continually Building, Continually Destroying, because of Love & Jealousy '. Generally when Blake intends a line not to be included in the body of the poem he engraves it in reversed characters, not as here, in the normal way. The present verse might well follow l. 31, but the line engraved within the design on p. 93, though written in the ordinary way, cannot conceivably be made part of the text. Since, therefore, there is a doubt as to Blake's intention in the present instance, the line has not been printed in the body of the text.

47 See Index, *Mundane Shell.* 49–52 See Index, *Wine-press*, III.

51 Samuel Palmer writes of Blake : 'He was fond of the works of St. Theresa, and often quoted them, with other writers on the interior life.'

52 Written in reverse at the foot of the page is the line :

Women, the comforters of Men, become the Tormenters & Punishers

Cp. F. Z. ii. 29.

[73] Such are Cathedron's golden Halls in the City of Golgonooza.

And Los's Furnaces howl loud, living, self-moving, lamenting
With fury & despair; & they stretch from South to North
Thro' all the Four Points. Lo! the Labourers at the Furnaces,
Rintrah & Palamabron, Theotormon & Bromion, loud lab'ring
With the innumerable multitudes of Golgonooza round the Anvils
Of Death! But how they came forth from the Furnaces & how long,
Vast & severe the anguish eer they knew their Father, were
Long to tell; & of the iron rollers, golden axle-trees & yokes
Of brass, iron chains & braces & the gold, silver & brass,
Mingled or separate, for swords, arrows, cannons, mortars,
The terrible ball, the wedge, the loud sounding hammer of destruction,
The sounding flail to thresh, the winnow to winnow kingdoms,
The water wheel & mill of many innumerable wheels resistless
Over the Four fold Monarchy from Earth to the Mundane Shell.

Perusing Albion's Tomb in the starry characters of Og & Anak,
To Create the lion & wolf, the bear, the tyger & ounce:
To Create the wooly lamb & downy fowl & scaly serpent,
The summer & winter, day & night, the sun & moon & stars,
The tree, the plant, the flower, the rock, the stone, the metal
Of Vegetative Nature by their hard restricting condensations.

Where Luvah's World of Opakeness grew to a period, It
Became a Limit, a Rocky hardness without form & void,
Accumulating without end. Here Los, who is of the Elohim,
Opens the Furnaces of affliction in the Emanation,

Page 73. This page follows awkwardly upon p. 72. It may be that p. 59 should come between them.

9–14 The instruments of war and husbandry symbolize the spiritual labours of the Sons of Los for man's regeneration. For the use of the same terms in the contrary sense, cp. F. Z. vii *a*. 168–184.

15 Fourfold seems to be used in an unusual association. It is generally connoted of the supreme state of Imagination. Cp. below, l. 33.

16–21 Difficulty arises from the uncertainty as to the subject of this passage. It may relate to the Spectrous activities, or to those regenerative powers just mentioned who create the forms of mundane life as part of their labours to redeem man; cp. J. 13. 44–45:

whatever is visible to the Generated Man
Is a Creation of mercy & love from the Satanic Void.

22 Luvah's World of Opakeness, not mentioned elsewhere, is apparently equivalent to the Satanic World of Ulro. Here Luvah is Albion's Spectre (J. 60. 2) or Satan (J. 49. 68).

Fixing the Sexual into an ever-prolific Generation,
Naming the Limit of Opakeness Satan, & the Limit of Contraction
Adam, who is Peleg & Joktan & Esau & Jacob & Saul & David.

Voltaire insinuates that these Limits are the cruel work of God,
Mocking the Remover of Limits & the Resurrection of the Dead,
Setting up Kings in wrath, in holiness of Natural Religion,
Which Los with his mighty Hammer demolishes time on time
In miracles & wonders in the Four-fold Desart of Albion,
Permanently Creating, to be in Time Reveal'd & Demolish'd,
Satan, Cain, Tubal, Nimrod, Pharoh, Priam, Bladud, Belin,
Arthur, Alfred, the Norman Conqueror, Richard, John,
. . . .
And all the Kings & Nobles of the Earth & all their Glories,
These are Created by Rahab & Tirzah in Ulro: but around
These, to preserve them from Eternal Death, Los Creates
Adam, Noah, Abraham, Moses, Samuel, David, Ezekiel,
. . . .
Dissipating the rocky forms of Death by his thunderous Hammer.
As the Pilgrim passes, while the Country permanent remains,
So Men pass on, but States remain permanent for ever.

The Spectres of the Dead howl round the porches of Los
In the terrible Family feuds of Albion's cities & villages,
To devour the Body of Albion, hung'ring & thirsting & rav'ning.
The Sons of Los clothe them & feed, & provide houses & gardens;
And every Human Vegetated Form in its inward recesses
Is a house of ple[as]antness & a garden of delight Built by the
Sons & Daughters of Los in Bowlahoola & in Cathedron.

27 See Index, *Expansion*.

28 Nothing can be found to explain this line. For Peleg and Joktan see Gen. x. 25.

33 'Fourfold' here, as in l. 15 above, does not appear to have its usual significance of 'eternal' or 'imaginative'; the phrase 'fourfold Desart' expresses the fallen state of the Fourfold Man.

35 Bladud and Belin, the names of legendary British kings, are probably taken from Milton's *History of England*, to which Blake refers in his *Descriptive Catalogue*.

36 After l. 36 a line has been erased in Blake's stereotype. Another is deleted after l. 40.

42–43 See Index, *States*, and cp. J. 71. 9 *note*.

47–50 Cp. M. 26. 23–36.

From London to York & Edinburgh the Furnaces rage terrible:
Primrose Hill is the mouth of the Furnace & the Iron Door.

[74] The Four Zoa's clouded rage. Urizen stood by Albion,
With Rintrah and Palamabron and Theotormon and Bromion :
These Four are Verulam & London & York & Edinburgh.
And the Four Zoa's are Urizen & Luvah & Tharmas & Urthona
In opposition deadly, and their Wheels in poisonous
And deadly stupor turn'd against each other loud & fierce.
Entering into the Reasoning Power, forsaking Imagination,
They became Spectres : & their Human Bodies were reposèd
In Beulah by the Daughters of Beulah with tears & lamentations.

The Spectre is the Reasoning Power in Man ; & when separated
From Imagination and closing itself as in steel in a Ratio
Of the Things of Memory, It thence frames Laws & Moralities
To destroy Imagination, the Divine Body, by Martyrdoms & Wars.

Teach me, O Holy Spirit, the Testimony of Jesus ! let me
Comprehend wonderous things out of the Divine Law.
I behold Babylon in the opening Streets of London ; I behold
Jerusalem in ruins wandering about from house to house.
This I behold : the shudderings of death attend my steps.
I walk up and down in Six Thousand Years : their Events are present before me,
To tell how Los in grief & anger, whirling round his Hammer on high,
Drave the Sons & Daughters of Albion from their ancient mountains :
They became the Twelve Gods of Asia Opposing the Divine Vision.

The Sons of Albion are Twelve : the Sons of Jerusalem Sixteen.
I tell how Albion's Sons by Harmonies of Concords & Discords

51–52 Cp. M. 4. 7 *note*.

Page 74. The sequence is again broken at this point. It is possible, though by no means certain, that p. 16 should follow p. 73.

1 Cp. J. 31. 57. 'Urizen is the champion of Albion', an unusual and so far an unexplained use of the symbol Urizen.

3 These are the 'English names' of the four Zoas : cp. J. 59. 13–14.

5 Cp. F. Z. i. 260 *note*. 8–9 Cp. M. 31. 1–7.

12 Cp. M. 12. 28 *note*.

14–22 Blake invokes the Holy Ghost, the 'Intellectual Fountain', whose gifts are 'Every thing to Man' (J. 77, 'To the Christians').

19 Six thousand years is the duration of mundane existence, according to the Millennarian estimate adopted by Blake.

22 Cp. J. 50. 3 *note*.

Opposèd to Melody, and by Lights & Shades opposèd to Outline,
And by Abstraction opposèd to the Visions of Imagination,
By cruel Laws divided Sixteen into Twelve Divisions :
How Hyle roof'd Los in Albion's Cliffs, by the Affections rent
Asunder & opposèd to Thought, to draw Jerusalem's Sons
Into the Vortex of his Wheels : therefore Hyle is callèd Gog,
Age after age drawing them away towards Babylon,
Babylon, the Rational Morality, deluding to death the little ones
In strong temptations of stolen beauty. I tell how Reuben slept
On London Stone & the Daughters of Albion ran around admiring
His awful beauty ; with Moral Virtue the fair deciever, offspring
Of Good & Evil, they divided him in love upon the Thames & sent
Him over Europe in streams of gore out of Cathedron's Looms :
How Los drave them from Albion & they became Daughters of Canaan :
Hence Albion was call'd the Canaanite & all his Giant Sons.
Hence is my Theme. O Lord my Saviour, open thou the Gates,
And I will lead forth thy Words, telling how the Daughters
Cut the Fibres of Reuben, how he roll'd apart & took Root
In Bashan. Terror-struck Albion's Sons look toward Bashan.
They have divided Simeon : he also roll'd apart in blood
Over the Nations, till he took Root beneath the shining Looms
Of Albion's Daughters in Philistea by the side of Amalek.

25 Cp. D. C. xv, pp. 63 and 64 : 'The great and golden rule of art as well as of life is this, That the more distinct, sharp and wirey the bounding line, the more perfect the work of art ; and the less keen and sharp, the greater is the evidence of weak imagination, plagiarism and bungling. . . . What is it that distinguishes honesty from knavery, but the hard and wirey line of rectitude and certainty in the actions and intentions? Leave out this line and you leave out life itself ; all is chaos again.' Cp. also D. C., pp. 55–56.

27 Cp. J. 41. 4–5 :

A triple octave he [the Spectre of Bath, with Luvah] took to reduce Jerusalem to twelve,
To cast Jerusalem forth upon the wilds.

Jerusalem's Gates are sixteen (J. 72. 5), and the reduction to twelve may be connected with the closing of the fourfold Western Gate.

29 It would seem as if Blake in this passage identifies Thought with Imagination. If this be so, the association of terms is unusual.

30–33 Cp. the poem quoted J. 7. 9 *note*. 33 See Index, *Reuben*.

42–51 The establishment of the twelve tribes in the midst of the heathen

They have divided Levi ; he hath shot out into Forty eight Roots
Over the land of Canaan : they have divided Judah ;
He hath took Root in Hebron, in the Land of Hand & Hyle.
Dan, Napthali, Gad, Asher, Issachar, Zebulun roll apart
From all the Nations of the Earth to dissipate into Non Entity.

I see a Feminine Form arise from the Four terrible Zoas,
Beautiful but terrible, struggling to take a form of beauty,
Rooted in Shechem : this is Dinah, the youthful form of Erin.
The Wound I see in South Molton Street & Stratford place,
Whence Joseph & Benjamin roll'd apart away from the Nations.
In vain they roll'd apart : they are fix'd into the Land of Cabul.

[75] And Rahab, Babylon the Great, hath destroyèd Jerusalem.
Bath stood upon the Severn with Merlin & Bladud & Arthur,
The Cup of Rahab in his hand, her Poisons Twenty-seven-fold.

And all her Twenty-seven Heavens, now hid & now reveal'd,
Appear in strong delusive light of Time & Space, drawn out
In shadowy pomp, by the Eternal Prophet created evermore.

For Los in Six Thousand Years walks up & down continually,
That not one Moment of Time be lost ; & every revolution
Of Space he makes permanent in Bowlahoola & Cathedron.

And these the names of the Twenty-seven Heavens & their Churches :
Adam, Seth, Enos, Cainan, Mahalaleel, Jared, Enoch,

races of Canaan becomes the symbol of Man's fall and division. Blake makes frequent symbolic use of the proximity of certain tribes, e.g. Reuben and Simeon, to heathen nations.

47–48 Cp. M. 39. 1–2 :

And the Forty-eight Starry Regions [of the Mundane Shell] are Cities of the Levites,
The Heads of the Great Polypus, Four-fold twelve enormity.

For the forty-eight cities of the Levites, cp. Joshua xxi. 41.

52–54 See Index, *Daughters of Beulah, Note I.*

55 The 'Wound' is not mentioned elsewhere. Stratford Place ran into Oxford Street opposite to South Molton Street, where Blake lived from 1803 to 1821. Cp. M., extra p. 3. 21.

57 For the 'Land of Cabul' cp. 1 Kings ix. 13 ; it appears to be symbolically equivalent to Ulro, the state of error.

Page 75. 2 Bath here is the Spectre of Bath (J. 41. 3–6). For Merlin, see J. 34. 37 *note* ; Arthur, J. 54. 25 *note* ; Bladud, J. 73. 35 *note*.

3 The number 'three' is frequently associated with the forms of reason and morality : hence powers of three express error, as powers of four, the perfect number, express truth.

7–9 Cp. J. 16. 61–67. 10–27 See Index, *Mundane Shell, Note II.*

Methuselah, Lamech: these are the Giants mighty, Hermaphroditic.
Noah, Shem, Arphaxad, Cainan the Second, Salah, Heber,
Peleg, Reu, Serug, Nahor, Terah: these are the Female Males,
A Male within a Female hid as in an Ark & Curtains.
Abraham, Moses, Solomon, Paul, Constantine, Charlemaine,
Luther, these Seven are the Male Females, the Dragon Forms,
The Female hid within a Male: thus Rahab is reveal'd,
Mystery, Babylon the Great, the Abomination of Desolation,
Religion hid in War, a Dragon red & hidden Harlot.
But Jesus breaking thro' the Central Zones of Death & Hell
Opens Eternity in Time & Space, triumphant in Mercy.

Thus are the Heavens form'd by Los within the Mundane Shell:
And where Luther ends Adam begins again in Eternal Circle,
To awake the Prisoners of Death, to bring Albion again
With Luvah into light eternal in his eternal day.

But now the Starry Heavens are fled from the mighty limbs of Albion.

For Salah see Genesis x. 24. 18–20 Cp. F. Z. viii. 238–249.

Page 76. A full-page design: a figure, with outstretched arms, looks up to the crucified Jesus upon the Tree of Mystery: faintly at the foot of the Cross is written 'Jesus', and between the feet of the second figure 'Albion'.

[77]

To the Christians

I give you the end of a golden string:
  Only wind it into a ball,
It will lead you in at Heaven's gate,
  Built in Jerusalem's wall.

Devils are | False Religions.
"Saul, Saul, | Why persecutest thou me?"

We are told to abstain from fleshly desires that we may lose no time from the Work of the Lord. Every moment lost is a moment that cannot be redeemed; every pleasure that intermingles with the duty of our station is a folly unredeemable, & is planted like the seed of a wild flower among our wheat. All the tortures of repentance are tortures of self-reproach on account of our leaving the Divine Harvest to the Enemy,[1] the struggles of intanglement with incoherent roots.[2] I know of no other Christianity and of no other Gospel than the liberty both of body & mind to exercise the Divine Arts of Imagination—Imagination, the real & eternal World of which this Vegetable Universe is but a faint shadow, & in which we shall live in our Eternal or Imaginative Bodies, when these Vegetable Mortal Bodies are no more. The Apostles knew of no other Gospel. What were all their spiritual gifts? What is the Divine Spirit? is the Holy Ghost any other than an Intellectual Fountain? What is the Harvest of the Gospel & its Labours? What is that Talent which it is a curse to hide? What are the Treasures of Heaven which we are to lay up for ourselves? are they any other than Mental Studies & Performances? What are all the Gifts of the Gospel? are they

[1] Cp. Letter to Butts, 10 January 1802 (R., p. 100): 'But if we fear to do the dictates of our angels, and tremble at the tasks set before us; if we refuse to do spiritual acts because of natural fears or natural desires, who can describe the dismal torments of such a state! I too well remember the threats I heard!—"If you who are organised by Divine Providence for spiritual communion, refuse, and bury your talent in the earth, even though you should want natural bread, sorrow and desperation pursue you through life, and after death, shame and confusion of face to eternity. Every one in eternity will leave you, aghast at the man who was crowned with glory and honour by his brethren, and betrayed their cause to their enemies. You will be called the base Judas who betrayed his friend!"'

[2] This phrase throws light on Blake's use of the symbol 'forest': cp. *Europe*, 88 *note*.

not all Mental Gifts? Is God a Spirit who must be worshipped in Spirit & in Truth, and are not the Gifts of the Spirit Everything to Man? O ye Religious, discountenance every one among you who shall pretend to despise Art & Science! I call upon you in the Name of Jesus! What is the Life of Man but Art & Science? is it Meat & Drink? is not the Body more than Raiment? What is Mortality but the things relating to the Body which Dies? What is Immortality but the things relating to the Spirit which Lives Eternally? What is the Joy of Heaven but Improvement in the things of the Spirit? What are the Pains of Hell but Ignorance, Bodily Lust, Idleness & devastation of the things of the Spirit? Answer this to yourselves, & expel from among you those who pretend to despise the labours of Art & Science, which alone are the labours of the Gospel. Is not this plain & manifest to the thought? Can you think at all, & not pronounce heartily: That to Labour in Knowledge is to Build up Jerusalem, and to Despise Knowledge is to Despise Jerusalem & her Builders? And remember, He who despises & mocks a Mental Gift in another, calling it pride & selfishness & sin, mocks Jesus, the giver of every Mental Gift, which always appear to the ignorance-loving Hypocrite as Sins: but that which is a Sin in the sight of cruel Man is not so in the sight of our kind God. Let every Christian, as much as in him lies, engage himself openly & publicly before all the World in some Mental pursuit for the Building up of Jerusalem.

I stood among my valleys of the south,
And saw a flame of fire, even as a Wheel
Of fire surrounding all the heavens: it went
From west to east against the current of
Creation, and devour'd all things in its loud
Fury & thundering course round heaven & earth.

The blank verse is written in two columns, the second commencing with l. 19.

1 The mention of the 'valleys of the south' may indicate that these lines, like the two poems from Blake's letters (Poems from Letters, ii and iv, Clar. Press, pp. 302 and 305), record a vision seen in or about 'Felpham's Vale'.

3–5 Cp. F. Z. ii. 269 *note*. The 'current of Creation' cannot be reconciled with Blake's ordinary attitude towards Creation, which usually stands for the illusory phenomenal universe. Here apparently it relates to some form of visionary activity. A similar difficulty arises in ll. 20–23, where Nature is Created by Jesus either as a refuge from the 'fiery Law' of Natural Religion, when it may be regarded as repeating the regenerative significance of the Mundane Shell (see Index, *Mundane Shell*, IV), or as an act of re-creation or redemption from error.

By it the Sun was roll'd into an orb ;
By it the Moon faded into a globe,
Travelling thro' the night ; for from its dire
And restless fury Man himself shrunk up
Into a little root a fathom long.
And I askèd a Watcher & a Holy-One
Its Name : he answer'd : ' It is the Wheel of Religion.'
I wept & said : ' Is this the law of Jesus,
This terrible devouring sword turning every way ? '
He answer'd : ' Jesus died because he strove
Against the current of this Wheel : its Name
Is Caiaphas, the dark Preacher of Death,
Of sin, of sorrow & of punishment,
Opposing Nature. It is Natural Religion.
But Jesus is the bright Preacher of Life,
Creating Nature from this fiery Law
By self-denial & forgiveness of Sin.
Go, therefore, cast out devils in Christ's name !
Heal thou the sick of spiritual disease !
Pity the evil ; for thou art not sent
To smite with terror & with punishments
Those that are sick, like to the Pharisees,
Crucifying, & encompasing sea & land
For proselytes to tyranny & wrath.
But to the Publicans & Harlots go !
Teach them True Happiness, but let no curse
Go forth out of thy mouth to blight their peace.
For Hell is open'd to Heaven ; thine eyes beheld
The dungeons burst, & the Prisoners set free.'

7–11 Cp. J. 49. 2–45.

18 Throughout *The Everlasting Gospel* Caiaphas, the typical priest, is joined with Caesar, the civil tyrant, as a minister of Satan's ' Moral and Self-righteous Law '. In Blake's interpretation of the second temptation in the wilderness, Satan urges :

> If Caiaphas You will obey,
> If Herod You with bloody Prey
> Feed with the Sacrifice & be
> Obedient ; fall down, worship me.
> (E. G. β. 21–24, Clar. Press, p. 248.)

24 Cp. above : ' Devils are False Religions ' ; cp. E. G. ζ. 43–52 (Clar. Press, p. 259), where Jesus addresses the woman taken in adultery :

> Mary, Fear Not. Let me see
> The Seven Devils that torment thee . . .
> . . . . Come ye forth,
> Fallen fiends of Heavenly birth,
> That have forgot your ancient love,
> And driven away my trembling Dove.

England ! awake ! awake ! awake !
  Jerusalem thy Sister calls !
Why wilt thou sleep the sleep of death,
  And close her from thy ancient walls ?

Thy hills & valleys felt her feet,
  Gently upon their bosoms move :
Thy gates beheld sweet Zion's ways ;
  Then was a time of joy and love.

And now the time returns again :
  Our souls exult, & London's towers
Recieve the Lamb of God to dwell
  In England's green & pleasant bowers.

[78]

Jerusalem. C. 4.

THE Spectres of Albion's Twelve Sons revolve mightily
Over the Tomb & over the Body, rav'ning to devour
The Sleeping Humanity. Los with his mace of iron
Walks round: loud his threats; loud his blows fall
On the rocky Spectres, as the Potter breaks the potsherds,
Dashing in pieces Self-righteousnesses, driving them from Albion's
Cliffs, dividing them into Male & Female forms in his Furnaces
And on his Anvils: lest they destroy the Feminine Affections
They are broken. Loud howl the Spectres in his iron Furnace.

While Los laments at his dire labours, viewing Jerusalem
Sitting before his Furnaces clothèd in sackcloth of hair,
Albion's Twelve Sons surround the Forty-two Gates of Erin
In terrible armour, raging against the Lamb & against Jerusalem,
Surrounding them with armies to destroy the Lamb of God.
They took their Mother Vala, and they crown'd her with gold:
They nam'd her Rahab, & gave her power over the Earth,
The Concave Earth round Golgonooza in Entuthon Benython,
Even to the stars exalting her Throne, to build beyond the Throne
Of God and the Lamb, to destroy the Lamb & usurp the Throne of God,
Drawing their Ulro Voidness round the Four-fold Humanity.

Naked Jerusalem lay before the Gates upon Mount Zion,
The Hill of Giants, all her foundations levell'd with the dust,

Page 78. 1–3 Cp. J. 73. 44–46. 3–9 Cp. J. 73. 32–41.

12 The 'Forty-two Gates of Erin' cannot be explained, unless the number is an error of transcription, and is to be read as 'thirty-two'. This would identify the Gates with the Divisions of Erin described in J. 72. 1–37.

15–16 Cp. J. 70. 31:

Her name is Vala in Eternity: in Time her name is Rahab.

17 Cp. J. 13. 30–32:

Around Golgonooza lies the land of death eternal, a Land
Of pain and misery and despair and ever brooding melancholy
In all the Twenty-seven Heavens.

18–19 Cp. J. 34. 27–28.

Her Twelve Gates thrown down; her children carried into captivity,
Herself in chains; this from within was seen in a dismal night
Outside, unknown before in Beulah: & the twelve gates were fill'd
With blood, from Japan eastward to the Giants causway west
In Erin's Continent: and Jerusalem wept upon Euphrates' banks;
Disorganiz'd, an evanescent shade, scarce seen or heard among
Her children's Druid Temples dropping with blood, wander'd weeping;
And thus her voice went forth in the darkness of Philisthea:

'My brother & my father are no more! God hath forsaken me!
The arrows of the Almighty pour upon me & my children!
I have sinnèd and am an outcast from the Divine Presence!
[79] My tents are fall'n: my pillars are in ruins: my children dash'd
Upon Egypt's iron floors & the marble pavements of Assyria.
I melt my soul in reasonings among the towers of Heshbon:
Mount Zion is become a cruel rock, & no more dew
Nor rain, no more the spring of the rock appears: but cold,
Hard & obdurate are the furrows of the mountain of wine & oil;
The mountain of blessing is itself a curse & an astonishment.
The hills of Judea are fallen with me into the deepest hell,
Away from the Nations of the Earth & from the Cities of the Nations.
I walk to Ephraim; I seek for Shiloh; I walk like a lost sheep
Among precipices of despair: in Goshen I seek for light
In vain, and in Gilead for a physician and a comforter.
Goshen hath follow'd Philistea: Gilead hath join'd with Og:
They are become narrow places in a little and dark land,
How distant far from Albion! his hills & his valleys no more
Recieve the feet of Jerusalem: they have cast me quite away,
And Albion is himself shrunk to a narrow rock in the midst of the sea.
The plains of Sussex & Surrey, their hills of flocks & herds,

23 Cp. J. 72. 5–9. 26 Cp. F. Z. ii. 269 *note*.
27 Cp. J. 49. 4 *note*.
Page 79. 3 Heshbon is associated with Natural Religion, as being the city of Sihon (Joshua iii. 10 and cp. J. 48. 63 *note*), and one of the Levitical cities (J. 74. 47–48).
4–5 Cp. 1 Kings xvii. 1. 10 Cp. J. 49. 9 *note*.
17 Cp. F. Z. viii. 4 *note*.

No more seek to Jerusalem nor to the sound of my Holy-ones.
The Fifty-two Counties of England are harden'd against me
As if I was not their Mother; they despise me & cast me out.
London cover'd the whole Earth, England encompass'd the Nations,
And all the Nations of the Earth were seen in the Cities of Albion.
My pillars reach'd from sea to sea; London beheld me come
From my east & from my west: he blessèd me and gave
His children to my breasts, his sons & daughters to my knees.
His agèd parents sought me out in every city & village:
They discern'd my countenance with joy; they shew'd me to their sons,
Saying: "Lo, Jerusalem is here! she sitteth in our secret chambers.
Levi and Judah & Issachar, Ephram, Manasseh, Gad and Dan
Are seen in our hills & valleys: they keep our flocks & herds:
They watch them in the night, and the Lamb of God appears among us."
The river Severn stay'd his course at my command:
Thames pourèd his waters into my basons and baths.
Medway mingled with Kishon: Thames reciev'd the heavenly Jordan.
Albion gave me to the whole Earth to walk up & down, to pour
Joy upon every mountain, to teach songs to the shepherd & plowman.
I taught the ships of the sea to sing the songs of Zion.
Italy saw me in sublime astonishment: France was wholly mine,
As my garden & as my secret bath: Spain was my heavenly couch;
I slept in his golden hills. The Lamb of God met me there;
There we walkèd as in our secret chamber among our little ones.
They lookèd upon our loves with joy: they beheld our secret joys,
With holy raptures of adoration rap'd sublime in the Visions of God.
Germany, Poland & the North wooed my footsteps; they found
My gates in all their mountains & my curtains in all their vales:
The furniture of their houses was the furniture of my chamber.
Turkey & Grecia saw my instr[u]ments of music; they arose,
They siez'd the harp, the flute, the mellow horn of Jerusalem's joy;

22–54 This relates to a 'golden age' before the Fall.

They sounded thanksgivings in my courts. Egypt & Lybia heard ;
The swarthy sons of Ethiopia stood round the Lamb of God
Enquiring for Jerusalem : he led them up my steps to my altar.
And thou, America ! I once beheld thee, but now behold no more
Thy golden mountains where my Cherubim & Seraphim rejoic'd
Together among my little-ones. But now, my Altars run with blood.
My fires are corrupt : my incense is a cloudy pestilence
Of seven diseases ! Once a continual cloud of salvation rose
From all my myriads : once the Four-fold World rejoic'd among
The pillars of Jerusalem, between my wingèd Cherubim.
But now I am clos'd out from them in the narrow passages
Of the valleys of destruction, into a dark land of pitch & bitumen,
From Albion's Tomb afar and from the four-fold wonders of God,
Shrunk to a narrow doleful form in the dark land of Cabul.
There is Reuben & Gad & Joseph & Judah & Levi, clos'd up
In narrow vales. I walk & count the bones of my belovèds
Along the Valley of Destruction, among these Druid Temples
Which overspread all the Earth in patriarchal pomp & cruel pride.
Tell me, O Vala, thy purposes ! tell me wherefore thy shuttles
Drop with the gore of the slain, why Euphrates is red with blood,
Wherefore in dreadful majesty & beauty outside appears
Thy Masculine from thy Feminine hardening against the heavens
To devour the Human ! Why dost thou weep upon the wind among
These cruel Druid Temples ? O Vala ! Humanity is far above
Sexual organization, & the Visions of the Night of Beulah,

53–55 This may be another reference to the 'closing of the Western Gate' : cp. J. 13. 6 *note*.

57 Blake here alludes to the seven cardinal virtues, which are to him forms of spiritual disease. Cp. the 'seven devils' in the passage from *The Everlasting Gospel*, quoted J. 77. 24 *note*. In F. Z. vii. 116–118 they are 'seven diseases of Man' ; in J. 19. 26 'seven diseases of the Soul'.

58 The Fourfold World is apparently identical with the Fourfold Man : see Index, *Albion*. 62 Cp. M. 9. 9 *note*. 63 Cp. J. 74. 57 *note*.

71–74 See Index, *Sexes*. The meaning is that the 'Visions of the Night of Beulah', like 'Humanity', are 'far above Sexual organization'. The point is noteworthy. 74–77 See Index, *Beulah*, II. ii.

Where Sexes wander in dreams of bliss among the Emanations,
Where the Masculine & Feminine are nurs'd into Youth and Maiden
By the tears and smiles of Beulah's Daughters till the time of Sleep is past.
Wherefore then do you realize these nets of beauty & delusion
In open day to draw the souls of the Dead into the light,
Till Albion is shut out from every Nation under Heaven,
[80] Encompass'd by the frozen Net and by the rooted Tree!
I walk weeping in pangs of a Mother's torment for her Children.
I walk in affliction: I am a worm, and no living soul,
A worm going to eternal torment, rais'd up in a night
To an eternal night of pain, lost! lost! lost! for ever!'

Beside her Vala howl'd upon the winds in pride of beauty,
Lamenting among the timbrels of the Warriors, among the Captives
In cruel holiness: and her lamenting songs were from Arnon
And Jordan to Euphrates. Jerusalem follow'd, trembling,
Her children in captivity, listening to Vala's lamentation
In the thick cloud & darkness: & the voice went forth from
The cloud: 'O rent in sunder from Jerusalem the Harlot daughter
In an eternal condemnation, in fierce burning flames
Of torment unendurable! And if once a Delusion be found
Woman must perish & the Heavens of Heavens remain no more.

My Father gave to me command to murder Albion
In unreviving Death: my Love, my Luvah, order'd me in night
To murder Albion, the King of Men: he fought in battles fierce:
He conquer'd Luvah my belovèd: he took me and my Father:
He slew them: I revivèd them to life in my warm bosom.
He saw them issue from my bosom: dark in Jealousy

78–80 Cp. J. 22. 17–18 and J. 12. 1–3:

Why wilt thou give to her [Vala] a Body, whose life is but a Shade,
Her joy and love a shade, a shade of sweet repose;
But animated and vegetated she is a devouring worm.

Page 80. 1 See Index, *Mundane Shell, Note I*, and *Vala, Note II*.
2 Cp. J. 5. 47 *note*.
8 Cp. M. 17. 5 *note*. 12 Cp. J. 18. 11 *note*.
14–15 Cp. F. Z. viii. 290 *note*.
16–24 Not least among the difficulties of this obscure passage is the impossibility of relating the pronouns to their antecedents, and of accounting for the abrupt change to the plural form in l. 20.

He burn'd before me : Luvah fram'd the Knife & Luvah gave
The Knife into his daughter's hand : such thing was never known
Before in Albion's land, that one should die a death never to be reviv'd.
For in our battles we the Slain men view with pity and love.
We soon revive them in the secret of our tabernacles.
But I, Vala, Luvah's daughter, keep his body embalm'd in moral laws
With spices of sweet odours of lovely jealous stupefaction
Within my bosom, lest he arise to life & slay my Luvah.
Pity me then, O Lamb of God ! O Jesus, pity me !
Come into Luvah's Tents and seek not to revive the Dead ! '

So sang she : and the Spindle turn'd furious as she sang.
The Children of Jerusalem, the Souls of those who sleep,
Were caught into the flax of her Distaff & in her Cloud,
To weave Jerusalem a body according to her will,
A Dragon form on Zion Hill's most ancient promontory.

The Spindle turn'd in blood & fire : loud sound the trumpets
Of war : the cymbals play loud before the Captains
With Cambel & Gwendolen in dance and solemn song,
The Cloud of Rahab vibrating with the Daughters of Albion.
Los saw terrified, melted with pity & divided in wrath :
He sent them over the narrow seas in pity and love
Among the Four Forests of Albion which overspread all the Earth.
They go forth & return swift as a flash of lightning,
Among the tribes of warriors, among the Stones of power :
Against Jerusalem they rage thro' all the Nations of Europe,
Thro' Italy & Grecia to Lebanon & Persia & India.

The Serpent Temples thro' the Earth from the wide Plain of Salisbury,

25–26 Cp. J. 43. 39–45, where a similar comparison between 'Corporeal' and 'Spiritual' warfare is put, appropriately enough, into the mouth of Los. Why Vala should utter what seems to be good Blakean doctrine in the midst of so much that is characteristically froward, cannot be explained.

27 'His' apparently relates to Albion.

27–31 Cp. F. Z. viii. 321 *note*.

32–36 See Index, *Weaving*, I. Vala is 'the Mother of the Body of Death' (J. 62. 13), 'a shape of Moral Virtue against the Lamb' and 'opposed to Mercy' (J. 80. 77).

43 Cp. M. 4. 3. *note*. Los's purpose in this passage is inscrutable.

45 Cp. J. 68. 41 *note*.

47 The direction is that of the 'Wheel of Religion', 'from west to east against the current of Creation' (J. 78. 2–5).

48 Cp. J. 67. 35 *note*.

Resound with cries of Victims, shouts & songs & dying groans
And flames of dusky fire, to Amalek, Canaan and Moab.
And Rahab like a dismal and indefinite hovering Cloud
Refus'd to take a definite form: she hover'd over all the Earth
Calling the definite, sin, defacing every definite form
Invisible or Visible, stretch'd out in length or spread in breadth
Over the Temples, drinking groans of victims, weeping in pity
And joying in the pity, howling over Jerusalem's walls.

Hand slept on Skiddaw's top, drawn by the love of beautiful
Cambel, his bright beaming Counterpart, divided from him.
And her delusive light beam'd fierce above the Mountain,
Soft, invisible, drinking his sighs in sweet intoxication,
Drawing out fibre by fibre, returning to Albion's Tree
At night and in the morning to Skiddaw: she sent him over
Mountainous Wales into the Loom of Cathedron fibre by fibre.
He ran in tender nerves across Europe to Jerusalem's Shade,
To weave Jerusalem a Body repugnant to the Lamb.

Hyle on East Moor in rocky Derbyshire rav'd to the Moon
For Gwendolen: she took up in bitter tears his anguish'd heart
That apparent to all in Eternity glows like the Sun in the breast.
She hid it in his ribs & back: she hid his tongue with teeth
In terrible convulsions, pitying & gratified, drunk with pity,
Glowing with loveliness before him, becoming apparent
According to his changes: she roll'd his kidneys round
Into two irregular forms; and looking on Albion's dread Tree,
She wove two vessels of seed, beautiful as Skiddaw's snow,
Giving them bends of self interest & selfish natural virtue.
She hid them in his loins: raving he ran among the rocks,
Compell'd into a shape of Moral Virtue against the Lamb,
The invisible lovely one giving him a form according to
His Law, a form against the Lamb of God, oppos'd to Mercy,
And playing in the thunderous Loom in sweet intoxication,

52–53 Cp. M. 27. 16 *note* and J. 74. 25 *note*.

57–82 With this example of the power of the Female to pervert the masculine activities, cp. J. 68. 53–70.

64 Cp. J. 78. 27–28: Jerusalem wept upon Euphrates' banks,
Disorganiz'd, an evanescent shade, scarce seen or heard among
Her children's Druid Temples.

66 Cp. J. 23. 27 *note*.

67–76 The Daughters of Albion 'control our Vegetative powers' (J. 5. 39). In the present passage the disposition of the physical organs is ascribed to one of these females and is made the symbol of the perversion of Man's spiritual powers: cp. J. 43. 24–36: 49. 13–31.

Filling cups of silver & crystal with shrieks & cries, with groans
And dolorous sobs, the wine of lovers in the Wine-press of Luvah.

'O sister Cambel,' said Gwendolen, as their long beaming light
Mingled above the Mountain, 'what shall we do to keep
These awful forms in our soft bands: distracted with trembling
[81] I have mock'd those who refusèd cruelty, & I have admired
The cruel Warrior. I have refusèd to give love to Merlin the piteous.
He brings to me the Images of his Love & I reject in chastity
And turn them out into the streets for Harlots, to be food
To the stern Warrior. I am become perfect in beauty over my Warrior:
For Men are caught by Love, Woman is caught by Pride,
That Love may only be obtain'd in the passages of Death.
Let us look! let us examine! is the Cruel become an Infant
Or is he still a cruel Warrior? look Sisters, look! O piteous!
I have destroy'd Wand'ring Reuben who strove to bind my Will.
I have strip'd off Joseph's beautiful integument for my Belovèd,
The Cruel-one of Albion, to clothe him in gems of my Zone.
I have namèd him Jehovah of Hosts. Humanity is become
A weeping Infant in ruin'd lovely Jerusalem's folding Cloud!

82 See Index, *Wine-press*.

84–85 Cp. J. 82. 1–4 and F. Z. viii. 290 *note*.

Page 81. A line appears to have been deleted at the top of this plate.

2 Cp. J. 34. 37 *note*.

7 'Love' here is the false Love that is the negation of the visionary Brotherhood and Forgiveness.

8 Blake's use of the symbol 'Infant' in this passage, as in 'The Mental Traveller' (Clar. Press, p. 274) and 'The Crystal Cabinet', still remains obscure.

10 See Index, *Reuben* and *Sex*.

11–12 Cp. M. 23. 17–22 *note*. Cp. also M. 28. 51–59 and J. 34. 27–28. Comparison with J. 68. 1 seq. shows that the 'Beloved' is Hand, the aggregate of the Spectres.

11 See Index, *Weaving*, III.

13 'Jehovah of Hosts' is Satan, the God of this World.

13–14 Humanity reduced to a weeping Infant, apparently the triumph of the Satanic Holiness (cp. J. 60. 45–48), is in reality the sign of its imminent annihilation through the Incarnation. Gwendolen's words in J. 82. 1–4 shows her dramatically aware of this, at least in part.

14 The lower part of this page, beneath l. 14, is occupied by a vigorous drawing of Gwendolen and her sisters: about it Blake has engraved the following lines which, written in reversed characters, do not seem to have any place in the body of the text:

In Heaven the only Art of Living
Is Forgetting & Forgiving:
But if you on Earth Forgive,
You shall not find where to Live.
Especially to the Female.

The fifth line seems to be the title of the preceding quatrain, the final

In Heaven Love begets Love: but Fear is the Parent of Earthly Love;
And he who will not bend to Love must be subdu'd by Fear.

[82] 'I have heard Jerusalem's groans; from Vala's cries & lamentations
I gather our eternal fate. Outcasts from life and love,
Unless we find a way to bind these awful Forms to our
Embrace we shall perish annihilate, discover'd our Delusions.
Look! I have wrought without delusion. Look! I have wept,
And given soft milk mingled together with the spirits of flocks
Of lambs and doves, mingled together in cups and dishes
Of painted clay; the mighty Hyle is become a weeping infant.
Soon shall the Spectres of the Dead follow my weaving threads.'

The Twelve Daughters of Albion attentive listen in secret shades,
On Cambridge and Oxford beaming soft, uniting with Rahab's cloud,
While Gwendolen spoke to Cambel, turning soft the spinning reel,
Or throwing the wing'd shuttle, or drawing the cords with softest songs.
The golden cords of the Looms animate beneath their touches soft
Along the Island white among the Druid Temples, while Gwendolen
Spoke to the Daughters of Albion standing on Skiddaw's top.

So saying she took a Falshood & hid it in her left hand:
To entice her Sisters away to Babylon on Euphrates.
And thus she closèd her left hand and utter'd her Falshood.
Forgetting that Falshood is prophetic, she hid her hand behind her
Upon her back behind her loins, & thus utter'd her Deceit:

couplet of which expresses the antithesis of the two Gospels, of Jesus and of Satan.

15–16 This candid statement by Gwendolen interrupts her story but is valuable as a comparison of the contrasted ethics.

Page 82. 10–16 These lines read as if they were an interpolation: l. 17 follows naturally after l. 9 but awkwardly after l. 16.

20 The first part of the line appears to mean that Gwendolen's statement (ll. 22–29), though believed by her to be false, is actually fulfilled. The manner of its fulfilment is not, however, made clear.

'I heard Enitharmon say to Los: "Let the Daughters of Albion
Be scatter'd abroad and let the name of Albion be forgotten:
Divide them into three; name them Amalek, Canaan & Moab.
Let Albion remain a desolation without an inhabitant,
And let the Looms of Enitharmon & the Furnaces of Los
Create Jerusalem & Babylon & Egypt & Moab & Amalek
And Helle & Hesperia & Hindostan & China & Japan;
But hide America, for a Curse, an Altar of Victims & a Holy Place."
See Sisters, Canaan is pleasant, Egypt is as the Garden of Eden:
Babylon is our chief desire, Moab our bath in summer.
Let us lead the stems of this Tree; let us plant it before Jerusalem,
To judge the Friend of Sinners to death without the Veil,
To cut her off from America, to close up her secret Ark,
And the fury of Man exhaust in War, Woman permanent remain.
See how the fires of our loins point eastward to Babylon!
Look, Hyle is become an infant Love! look! behold! see him lie
Upon my bosom! look! here is the lovely wayward form
That gave me sweet delight by his torments beneath my Veil!
By the fruit of Albion's Tree I have fed him with sweet milk,
By contentions of the mighty for Sacrifice of Captives.
Humanity, the Great Delusion, is chang'd to War & Sacrifice.
I have nail'd his hands on Beth Rabbim & his hands on Heshbon's Wall.
O that I could live in his sight! O that I could bind him to my arm!'

So saying, She drew aside her Veil from Mam-Tor to Dovedale,
Discovering her own perfect beauty to the Daughters of Albion
And Hyle a winding Worm beneath . . . .
. . . . and not a weeping Infant.
Trembling & pitying she scream'd & fled upon the wind.
Hyle was a winding Worm and herself perfect in beauty:
The desarts tremble at his wrath; they shrink themselves in fear.

32 The Tree is Albion's 'Tree of Good and Evil' (J. 92. 25): see Index, *Mundane Shell, Note I.* B.

33 See Index, *Crucifixion*. 35 Cp. J. 68. 48–70.

45–82 The inspissated darkness of this myth admits no ray of light unless it come from J. 9. 26–31, where Los restates the Blakean concept, exemplified here, that in the divine plan of regeneration through mundane life, even error has its place, unwitting but effective.

Cambel trembled with jealousy : she trembled : she envied.
The envy ran thro' Cathedron's Looms into the Heart
Of mild Jerusalem, to destroy the Lamb of God. Jerusalem
Languish'd upon Mount Olivet, East of mild Zion's Hill.

Los saw the envious blight above his Seventh Furnace
On London's Tower on the Thames : he drew Cambel in wrath
Into his thundering Bellows, heaving it for a loud blast :
And with the blast of his Furnace upon fishy Billingsgate
Beneath Albion's fatal Tree, before the Gate of Los,
Shew'd her the fibres of her belovèd to ameliorate
The envy : loud she labour'd in the Furnace of fire
To form the mighty form of Hand according to her will
In the Furnaces of Los, & in the Wine-press treading day & night,
Naked among the human clusters, bringing wine of anguish
To feed the afflicted in the Furnaces : she minded not
The raging flames, tho' she return'd . . . . .
. . . . instead of beauty
Deformity : she gave her beauty to another, bearing abroad
Her struggling torment in her iron arms, and like a chain
Binding his wrists & ankles with the iron arms of love.

Gwendolen saw the Infant in her siste[r]'s arms : she howl'd
Over the forests with bitter tears, and over the winding Worm
Repentant : and she also in the eddying wind of Los's Bellows
Began her dolorous task of love in the Wine-press of Luvah
To form the Worm into a form of love by tears & pain.
The Sisters saw : trembling ran thro' their Looms, soften[in]g mild
Towards London : then they saw the Furna[c]es open'd, & in tears
Began to give their souls away in the Furna[c]es of affliction.

Los saw & was comforted at his Furnaces, uttering thus his voice :

'I know I am Urthona, keeper of the Gates of Heaven,
And that I can at will expatiate in the Gardens of bliss.
But pangs of love draw me down to my loins, which are

54 Cp. J. 68. 22 *note*. East here has its usual meaning : see Index, *Cardinal Points*.

66–67 The latter part of l. 66 and the first part of l. 67 have been deleted.

79–80 See Index, *Los, Note I*.

81–82 According to Swedenborg, 'Those who are in the loins are in conjugal love'. The 'fountain of veiny pipes' is identified with Enitharmon (J. 86. 50–64), at this point the symbol of perversive 'feminine'

Become a fountain of veiny pipes. O Albion ! my brother !
[83] Corruptibility appears upon thy limbs, and never more
Can I arise and leave thy side, but labour here incessant
Till thy awaking : yet alas, I shall forget Eternity !
Against the Patriarchal pomp and cruelty labouring incessant
I shall become an Infant horror. Enion ! Tharmas ! friends !
Absorb me not in such dire grief. O Albion, my brother !
Jerusalem hungers in the desart ; affection to her children.
The scorn'd and contemn'd youthful girl, where shall she fly ?
Sussex shuts up her Villages ; Hants, Devon & Wilts,
Surrounded with masses of stone in order'd forms, determine then
A form for Vala and a form for Luvah here on the Thames,
Where the Victim nightly howls beneath the Druid's knife,
A Form of Vegetation. Nail them down on the stems of Mystery.
O when shall the Saxon return with the English his redeemèd brother ?
O when shall the Lamb of God descend among the Reprobate ?
I woo to Amalek to protect my fugitives : Amalek trembles.
I call to Canaan & Moab in my night watches : they mourn ;
They listen not to my cry ; they rejoice among their warriors.
Woden and Thor and Friga wholly consume my Saxons
On their enormous Altars built in the terrible north
From Ireland's rocks to Scandinavia, Persia and Tartary,
From the Atlantic Sea to the universal Erythrean.
Found ye London, enormous City ! Weeps thy River ?
Upon his parent bosom lay thy little ones, O Land

influence, the temporary triumph of which over the visionary Los is attributed to the power of the Spectre (J. 88. 34–36).

Page 83. 7 Something is clearly lacking in this line. Blake has a colon or semicolon after 'desart', where 'in' or 'from' might otherwise be taken as a possible reading.

10 The 'masses of stone' are the 'Druid Temples' of Abury and Stonehenge : see Index, *Druid*.

10–13 Cp. J. 12. 13 :

Giving a body to Falshood that it may be cast off for ever.

The 'stems of Mystery' are equivalent to 'the Tree of Mystery' (see Index, *Mundane Shell, Note I*. B.) : to nail the forms of Luvah and Vala thereon is to demonstrate the falsity of the systems of metaphysic and morality that they represent : see Index, *Crucifixion*.

14 When Albion is regenerated into Unity, the 'British, Saxon, Roman and Norman' amalgamate 'into One Nation, the English' (J. 92. 1–2).

16–17 Cp. M. 23. 74–75 :

All the Gods of the Kingdoms of Earth labour in Los's Halls.
Every one is a fallen son of the Spirit of Prophecy.

21–22 It is uncertain whether these lines relate to what precedes or to what follows them, so that the punctuation must be entirely conjectural.

Forsaken. Surrey and Sussex are Enitharmon's Chamber,
Where I will build her a Couch of repose & my pillars
Shall surround her in beautiful labyrinths. Oothoon,
Where hides my child ? in Oxford hidest thou with Antamon ?
In graceful hidings of error, in merciful deceit,
Lest Hand the terrible destroy his Affection, thou hidest her,
In chaste appearances for sweet deceits of love & modesty,
Immingled, interwoven, glistening to the sickening sight.
Let Cambel and her Sisters sit within the Mundane Shell,
Forming the fluctuating Globe according to their will.
According as they weave the little embryon nerves & veins,
The Eye, the little Nostrils & the delicate Tongue & Ears
Of labyrinthine intricacy, so shall they fold the World ;
That whatever is seen upon the Mundane Shell, the same
Be seen upon the Fluctuating Earth woven by the Sisters.
And sometimes the Earth shall roll in the Abyss & sometimes
Stand in the Center & sometimes stretch flat in the Expanse,
According to the will of the lovely Daughters of Albion.
Sometimes it shall assimilate with mighty Golgonooza,
Touching its summits ; & sometimes divided roll apart.
As a beautiful Veil : so these Females shall fold & unfold
According to their will the outside surface of the Earth,
An outside shadowy Surface superadded to the real Surface,
Which is unchangeable for ever & ever. Amen : so be it !
Separate Albion's Sons gently from their Emanations,
Weaving bowers of delight on the current of infant Thames
Where the old Parent still retains his youth, as I, alas,
Retain my youth eight thousand and five hundred years,
The labourer of ages in the Valleys of Despair.
The land is mark'd for desolation ; & unless we plant
The seeds of Cities & of Villages in the Human bosom
Albion must be a rock of blood. Mark ye the points
Where Cities shall remain, & where Villages : for the rest,
It must lie in confusion till Albion's time of awaking.

27–28 For Oothoon cp. V. D. A., Introductory Note, and M. 11. 44 *note* ; for Antamon cp. M. 27. 13 *note* : both are children of Los.

33–48 See Index, *Mundane Shell*, II. 3 and III, and cp. M. 28. 5–17 and *note*.

51 'The old Parent' cannot be identified with certainty : the term may refer to Albion.

52 The significance of this period of time is not apparent.

54–58 Cp. J. 85. 27–29 : plant ye
The Seeds, O Sisters, in the bosom of Time & Space's womb
To spring up for Jerusalem.

The implication in the present passage is that regeneration during the course of mundane life can only be partial : the complete annihilation of error can only be achieved when time shall end.

Place the Tribes of Llewellyn in America for a hiding place,
Till sweet Jerusalem emanates again into Eternity.
The night falls thick. I go upon my watch : be attentive.
The Sons of Albion go forth ; I follow from my Furnaces
That they return no more, that a place be prepar'd on Euphrates.
Listen to your Watchman's voice : sleep not before the Furnaces.
Eternal Death stands at the door. O God, pity our labours.'

So Los spoke to the Daughters of Beulah, while his Emanation
Like a faint rainbow wavèd before him in the awful gloom
Of London City on the Thames from Surrey Hills to Highgate.
Swift turn the silver spindles, & the golden weights play soft
And lulling harmonies beneath the Looms from Caithness in the north
To Lizard-point & Dover in the south : his Emanation
Joy'd in the many weaving threads in bright Cathedron's Dome,
Weaving the Web of life for Jerusalem : the Web of life
Down flowing into Entuthon's Vales glistens with soft affections.

While Los arose upon his Watch, and down from Golgonooza,
Putting on his golden sandals to walk from mountain to mountain,
He takes his way, girding himself with gold & in his hand
Holding his iron mace, The Spectre remains attentive.
Alternate they watch in night, alternate labour in day,
Before the Furnaces labouring ; while Los all night watches
The stars rising & setting, & the meteors & terrors of night.
With him went down the Dogs of Leutha ; at his feet
They lap the water of the trembling Thames, then follow swift.
And thus he heard the voice of Albion's daughters on Euphrates:

'Our Father Albion's land, O, it was a lovely land ! & the Daughters of Beulah

62–63 Cp. J. 17. 6 :

But Los himself against Albion's Sons his fury bends.

Cp. also J. 9. 35–10. 6.

64 Cp. J. 24. 26 *note*.

68 From Surrey's Hills to Highgate, that is, from south to north, is the direction of Los's Furnaces : cp. M. 4. 7 *note*. Enitharmon's Looms are similarly disposed : see below, ll. 70–71.

73–74 See Index, *Weaving*, II.

76–78 Los is here imaged as the Sun, a common association in Blake's concept of the Eternal Prophet.

82 Cp. J. 31. 15, where the Isle of Dogs, on the north side of the Thames, is called 'the Isle of Leutha's Dogs'.

Walkèd up and down in its green mountains : but Hand is fled
Away, & mighty Hyle ; & after them Jerusalem is gone.
Awake !

[84] Highgate's heights & Hampstead's, to Poplar, Hackney & Bow,
To Islington & Paddington & the Brook of Albion's River.
We builded Jerusalem as a City & a Temple ; from Lambeth
We began our Foundations, lovely Lambeth ! O lovely Hills
Of Camberwell, we shall behold you no more in glory & pride,
For Jerusalem lies in ruins, & the Furnaces of Los are builded there. 6
You are now shrunk up to a narrow Rock in the midst of the Sea.
But here we build Babylon on Euphrates, compell'd to build
And to inhabit, our Little-ones to clothe in armour of the gold
Of Jerusalem's Cherubims & to forge them swords of her Altars. 10
I see London blind & age bent begging thro' the Streets
Of Babylon, led by a child ; his tears run down his beard.
The voice of Wandering Reuben ecchoes from street to street
In all the Cities of the Nations, Paris, Madrid, Amsterdam.
The Corner of Broad Street weeps ; Poland Street languishes
To Great Queen Street & Lincoln's Inn : all is distress & woe.

The night falls thick. Hand comes from Albion in his strength:
He combines into a Mighty-one, the Double Molech & Chemosh,
Marching thro' Egypt in his fury : the East is pale at his course. 19
The Nations of India, the Wild Tartar that never knew Man,
Starts from his lofty places & casts down his tents & flees away.

Page 84. Something appears to have broken the sequence at this point, though the present page is connected with the preceding in that it concludes the Song of the Daughters, begun on p. 83. 85. It may be noticed here that this lamentation of the Daughters seems at times to clash with the normal concept of these females as the source and symbol of mundane error. It almost appears as if they become assistant to Los's regenerative labours. Yet in ll. 26 seq. they 'unite into One with Rahab'.

11 'I' relates to Rahab, in whom the Daughters unite : see below, ll. 26–27.

13 See Index, *Reuben*.

15–16 The desolation of these places in the west of London symbolizes the neglected state of visionary pursuits in mundane life. Blake lived at 27 Broad Street (1784–1787) and at 28 Poland Street (1787–1793).

After l. 16, three lines deleted in Blake's autotype.

18 Molech and Chemosh, Gods of the Heathen (J. 50. 3 *note*) are the 'Generalizing Gods' holding Israel in bondage (J. 89. 30). Molech 'rejoices in moral law and its severe penalties' (J. 68. 38–39).

But we woo him all the night in songs. O Los, come forth! O Los!
Divide us from these terrors & give us power them to subdue.
Arise upon thy Watches; let us see thy Globe of fire
On Albion's Rocks & let thy voice be heard upon Euphrates.'

Thus sang the Daughters in lamentation, uniting into One
With Rahab as she turn'd the iron Spindle of destruction.

Terrified at the Sons of Albion they took the Falshood which
Gwendolen hid in her left hand: it grew & grew till it
[85] Became a Space & an Allegory around the Winding Worm.
They nam'd it Canaan & built for it a tender Moon.
Los smil'd with joy, thinking on Enitharmon; & he brought
Reuben from his twelvefold wand'rings & led him into it,
Planting the Seeds of the Twelve Tribes & Moses & David:
And gave a Time & Revolution to the Space, Six Thousand Years.
He call'd it Divine Analogy; for in Beulah the Feminine
Emanations Create Space, the Masculine Create Time, & plant
The Seeds of beauty in the Space. List'ning to their lamentation
Los walks upon his ancient Mountains in the deadly darkness
Among his Furnaces, directing his laborious Myriads, watchful
Looking to the East: & his voice is heard over the whole Earth
As he watches the Furnaces by night & directs the labourers.

And thus Los replies upon his Watch: the Valleys listen silent,
The Stars stand still to hear: Jerusalem & Vala cease to mourn.
His voice is heard from Albion: the Alps & Appenines
Listen: Hermon & Lebanon bow their crownèd heads:
Babel & Shinar look toward the Western Gate: they sit down
Silent at his voice; they view the red Globe of fire in Los's hand,

28 Though Gwendolen's Falsehood remains unexplained, the general meaning of this passage is clear enough. It repeats the doctrine of a providential purpose in mortal life. Mercy changes Death into Sleep, that which was meant for Jerusalem's destruction into a covering, the Veil of Vala into the Mundane Shell, Gwendolen's Falsehood into a 'Divine Analogy'.

Page 85. 1 Cp. J. 30. 18 *note*. 2 Cp. J. 19. 44 *note*.

12 Los continually labours against error, quartered in the east.

18 Cp. J. 13. 6 *note*.

19 Cp. J. 31. 2–4:

> Fearing that Albion should turn his back against the Divine Vision,
> Los took his globe of fire to search out the interiors of Albion's
> Bosom in all the terrors of friendship.

As he walks from Furnace to Furnace directing the Labourers.
And this is the Song of Los, the Song that he sings on his Watch:

‘ O lovely mild Jerusalem ! O Shiloh of Mount Ephraim !
I see thy Gates of precious stones ; thy Walls of gold & silver.
Thou art the soft reflected Image of the Sleeping Man,
Who, stretch’d on Albion’s rocks, reposes amidst his Twenty-eight
Cities where Beulah lovely terminates in the hills & valleys of Albion,
Cities not yet embodied in Time and Space. Plant ye
The Seeds, O Sisters, in the bosom of Time & Space’s womb
To spring up for Jerusalem, lovely Shadow of Sleeping Albion.
Why wilt thou rend thyself apart & build an Earthly Kingdom,
To reign in pride & to op[p]ress & to mix the Cup of Delusion,
O thou that dwellest with Babylon? Come forth, O lovely-one !

[86] ‘ I see thy Form, O lovely mild Jerusalem, Wing’d with Six Wings
In the opacous Bosom of the Sleeper, lovely, Three fold
In Head & Heart & Reins, three Universes of love & beauty !
Thy forehead bright, Holiness to the Lord, with Gates of pearl
Reflects Eternity beneath thy azure wings of feathery down,
Ribb’d delicate & cloth’d with feather’d gold & azure & purple,
From thy white shoulders shadowing purity in holiness ;
Thence, feather’d with soft crimson of the ruby, bright as fire,
Spreading into the azure Wings which, like a canopy,
Bends over thy immortal Head in which Eternity dwells.
Albion, belovèd Land ! I see thy mountains & thy hills
And valleys & thy pleasant Cities, Holiness to the Lord !
I see the Spectres of thy Dead, O Emanation of Albion !

22 Cp. J. 49. 9 *note*. 24 See Index, *Jerusalem*, II.
25 Cp. J. 30. 26 *note*. 26 Cp. J. 23. 25 *note*.
27–29 Cp. J. 83. 54–56 and *note*. The Sisters are the Daughters of Beulah : cp. J. 83. 66.
30–31 Cp. J. 11. 24–12. 3.
32 See Index, *Jerusalem, Note I*.
Page 86. The description of Jerusalem on this page is to be compared with that of the Covering Cherub, J. 89. 9–62.
2 The use of the symbolic expression ‘ Three-fold ’ accords with the description of Jerusalem as the ‘ Lovely Shadow of Sleeping Albion ’ (J. 85. 29). It indicates a state lower than the supreme life of Eternity.

'Thy Bosom white, translucent, cover'd with immortal gems,
A sublime ornament not obscuring the outlines of beauty,
Terrible to behold for thy extreme beauty & perfection :
Twelve-fold here all the Tribes of Israel I behold
Upon the Holy Land. I see the River of Life & Tree of Life.
I see the New Jerusalem descending out of Heaven
Between thy Wings of gold & silver feather'd immortal,
Clear as the rainbow, as the cloud of the Sun's tabernacle.

'Thy Reins, cover'd with Wings translucent, sometimes covering
And sometimes spread abroad, reveal the flames of holiness,
Which like a robe covers, & like a Veil of Seraphim
In flaming fire unceasing burns from Eternity to Eternity.
Twelvefold I there behold Israel in her Tents.
A Pillar of a Cloud by day, a Pillar of fire by night
Guides them ; there I behold Moab & Ammon & Amalek ;
There Bells of silver round thy knees, living, articulate
Comforting sounds of love & harmony, & on thy feet
Sandals of gold & pearl ; & Egypt & Assyria before me,
The Isles of Javan, Philistea, Tyre and Lebanon.'

Thus Los sings upon his Watch, walking from Furnace to Furnace.
He siezes his Hammer every hour : flames surround him as
He beats ; seas roll beneath his feet ; tempests muster
Around his head ; the thick hail stones stand ready to obey
His voice in the black cloud : his Sons labour in thunders
At his Furnaces ; his Daughters at their Looms sing woes.
His Emanation separates in milky fibres agonizing
Among the golden Looms of Cathedron, sending fibres of love
From Golgonooza with sweet visions for Jerusalem, wanderer.

Nor can any consummate bliss without being Generated
On Earth of those whose Emanations weave the loves
Of Beulah for Jerusalem & Shiloh in immortal Golgonooza,
Concentering in the majestic form of Erin in eternal tears,
Viewing the Winding Worm on the Desarts of Great Tartary,
Viewing Los in his shudderings, pouring balm on his sorrows.
So dread is Los's fury, that none dare him to approach
Without becoming his Children in the Furnaces of affliction.

18 Cp. Rev. xxii. 1–2. 38 Cp. J. 59. 26–41.

43–45 Those whose Emanations concentre in Erin are the Friends of Albion : cp. J. 48. 27–52 and see Index, *Erin*. The whole of this passage (ll. 42–49) stresses the regenerative purpose of mundane existence by representing it as the only means to the annihilation of error through the ministration of Los and Enitharmon and the Daughters of Los and of Beulah who 'give sweet visions' to mortal men.

And Enitharmon like a faint rainbow wavèd before him,
Filling with Fibres from his loins which redden'd with desire
Into a Globe of blood beneath his bosom, trembling in darkness
Of Albion's clouds. He fed it with his tears & bitter groans,
Hiding his Spectre in invisibility from the timorous Shade
Till it became a separated cloud of beauty, grace & love
Among the darkness of his Furnaces, dividing asunder till
She separated stood before him, a lovely Female weeping,
Even Enitharmon, separated outside; & his Loins closèd
And heal'd after the separation: his pains he soon forgot,
Lured by her beauty outside of himself in shadowy grief.
Two Wills they had, Two Intellects, & not as in times of old.

Silent they wander'd hand in hand like two Infants wand'ring
From Enion in the desarts, terrified at each other's beauty,
Envying each other, yet desiring in all devouring Love,
[87] Repelling weeping Enion, blind & age-bent, into the fourfold
Desarts. Los first broke silence & began to utter his love:

'O lovely Enitharmon! I behold thy graceful forms
Moving beside me till, intoxicated with the woven labyrinth
Of beauty & perfection, my wild fibres shoot in veins
Of blood thro' all my nervous limbs: soon overgrown in roots
I shall be closèd from thy sight. Sieze therefore in thy hand
The small fibres as they shoot around me: draw out in pity
And let them run on the winds of thy bosom. I will fix them
With pulsations: we will divide them into Sons & Daughters
To live in thy Bosom's translucence as in an eternal morning.'

Enitharmon answer'd: 'No. I will sieze thy Fibres & weave
Them not as thou wilt but as I will; for I will Create

50–62 The relevancy of this myth of Enitharmon is not apparent. It is found in B. U., chap. v, and in F. Z. ii, and relates to the origin and significance of Sex (see Index, *Sex*). Cp. J. 82. 81 *note* and B. U. v. 39 *note*. Blake's purpose in these passages of retrogressive myth and symbol is obscure.

60 This may refer to the distracting influence of the beauty of mundane things upon the spirit of the artist: to Blake the 'outward creation' was a 'hindrance'.

62–p. 87. 2 Cp. F. Z. i. 127–134.

Page 87. 1–2 Cp. J. 73. 33 *note*.

6–11 The roots and fibres are of the Tree of Mystery: see Index, *Mundane Shell, Note II*. Los's proposal to 'divide them into Sons and Daughters' would seem to be equivalent to the regenerative purpose that creates 'sweet forms' to redeem the Spectres.

12–15 Cp. J. 88. 51–53. Enitharmon, here the type of the 'disobedient Female', seeks, in jealousy of Jerusalem, to create 'a Form repugnant to the Lamb', that is, an ethical system opposed to the mystical ideas of Brotherhood and Forgiveness: see Index, *Incarnation*, II. *b*. ii.

A round Womb beneath my bosom, lest I also be overwoven
With Love. Be thou assurèd I never will be thy slave.
Let Man's delight be Love, but Woman's delight be Pride.
In Eden our Loves were the same; here they are opposite.
I have Loves of my own; I will weave them in Albion's Spectre.
Cast thou in Jerusalem's shadows thy Loves, silk of liquid
Rubies, Jacinths, Crysolites, issuing from thy Furnaces. While
Jerusalem divides thy care, while thou carest for Jerusalem,
Know that I never will be thine. Also thou hidest Vala:
From her these fibres shoot to shut me in a Grave.
You are Albion's Victim: he has set his Daughter in your path.'

[88] Los answer'd, sighing like the Bellows of his Furnaces:

'I care not! the swing of my Hammer shall measure the starry round.
When in Eternity Man converses with Man they enter
Into each other's Bosom (which are Universes of delight)
In mutual interchange. And first their Emanations meet
Surrounded by their Children: if they embrace & comingle
The Human Four-fold Forms mingle also in thunders of Intellect.
But if the Emanations mingle not, with storms & agitations
Of earthquakes & consuming fires they roll apart in fear;
For Man cannot unite with Man but by their Emanations,
Which stand both Male & Female at the Gates of each Humanity.
How then can I ever again be united as Man with Man
While thou, my Emanation, refusest my Fibres of dominion?
When Souls mingle & join thro' all the Fibres of Brotherhood
Can there be any secret joy on Earth greater than this?'

16–17 See Index, *Incarnation, Note*. For the conflict of the 'sexes' contrasted with the harmony of the supreme spiritual state, Eden, cp. J. 68. 65–70.

22–23 In these lines jealous Enitharmon is not to be distinguished from Vala.

24 Cp. J. 31. 51–54. Albion's 'Daughter' is Jerusalem or her 'shadow' Vala.

Page 88. 2 The swing of Los's hammer is Mercy: see below, l. 49.

4 Cp. J. 38. 49–50.

5–13 The significance of Emanation in this passage, which is without parallel, remains obscure. The commingling of the Emanations vaguely suggests community of vision.

15 Secrecy is for Blake the seminal fallacy in the 'feminine' illusions, especially in religion and morals, as well as in the preference for mediate sense-perception before the immediacy of vision. For the term's earlier ethical connotation see B. A. ii. 26 *note*.

Enitharmon answer'd: 'This is Woman's World, nor need she any
Spectre to defend her from Man. I will Create secret places,
And the masculine names of the places Merlin & Arthur.
A triple Female Tabernacle for Moral Law I weave
That he who loves Jesus may loathe terrified Female love,
Till God himself become a Male subservient to the Female.'

She spoke in scorn & jealousy, alternate torments; and
So speaking she sat down on Sussex shore, singing lulling
Cadences & playing in sweet intoxication among the glistening
Fibres of Los, sending them over the Ocean eastward into
The realms of dark death. O perverse to thyself, contrarious
To thy own purposes! for when she began to weave,
Shooting out in sweet pleasure, her bosom in milky Love
Flow'd into the aching fibres of Los, yet contending against him
In pride, send⟨ind⟩ing his Fibres over to her objects of jealousy
In the little lovely Allegoric Night of Albion's Daughters
Which stretch'd abroad, expanding east & west & north & south
Thro' all the World of Erin & of Los & all their Children.

A sullen smile broke from the Spectre in mockery & scorn,
Knowing himself the author of their divisions & shrinkings: gratified
At their contentions, he wipèd his tears; he wash'd his visage:

'The Man who respects Woman shall be despisèd by Woman,
And deadly cunning & mean abjectness only shall enjoy them.
For I will make their places of joy & love excrementitious,

16 Cp. J. 78. 15–20 and *Europe*, ll. 33–41. See also Index, *Incarnation, Note.*

18 For Merlin cp. J. 34. 37 *note*: for Arthur cp. J. 54. 25 *note*.

31 Cp. J. 30. 18 *note*. 'The lovely Allegoric Night of Albion's Daughters' is the world of sense-perception created by these females: cp. J. 83. 33–48.

33 See Index, *Erin*.

37–38 The 'feminine delusions' of morality foster hypocrisy and cunning to the scorning of honest purpose. The theme is common in the earlier poems of the Rossetti MS.:

> I told my love, I told my love,
> I told her all my heart;
> Trembling, cold, in ghastly fears,
> Ah! she doth depart.
>
> Soon as she was gone from me,
> A traveller came by,
> Silently, invisibly—
> O! was no deny. (Clar. Press, p. 156.)

Continually building, continually destroying in Family feuds.
While you are under the dominion of a jealous Female,
Unpermanent for ever because of love & jealousy,
You shall want all the Minute Particulars of Life.'

Thus joy'd the Spectre in the dusky fires of Los's Forge, eyeing
Enitharmon who at her shining Looms sings lulling cadences;
While Los stood at his Anvil in wrath, the victim of their love
And hate, dividing the Space of Love with brazen Compasses
In Golgonooza & in Udan-Adan & in Entuthon of Urizen.

The blow of his Hammer is Justice, the swing of his Hammer
    Mercy:
The force of Los's Hammer is eternal Forgiveness: but
His rage or his mildness were vain; she scatter'd his love on
    the wind
Eastward into her own Center, creating the Female Womb
In mild Jerusalem around the Lamb of God. Loud howl
The Furnaces of Los: loud roll the Wheels of Enitharmon.
The Four Zoa's in all their faded majesty burst out in fury
And fire. Jerusalem took the Cup which foam'd in Vala's hand,
Like the red Sun upon the mountains in the bloody day,
Upon the Hermaphroditic Wine-presses of Love & Wrath.

[89] Tho' divided by the Cross & Nails & Thorns & Spear,
In cruelties of Rahab & Tirzah permanent endure

40 Cp. J. 27, stanza 20:

Is this thy soft Family-Love,
Thy cruel Patriarchal pride,
Planting thy Family alone,
Destroying all the World beside.

41–43 Cp. J. 68. 63–70. 43 See Index, *Minute Particulars*.

47 The Space of Love, not mentioned elsewhere, may possibly be identical with the Space of Six Thousand Years providentially prepared for the Spectre: cp. M. 11. 12–17.

52 The 'Selfish Center', the seat of error, is opposed to the Circumference, the Sanctuary of Eden: cp. J. 69. 40–42.

52–53 Cp. J. 87. 12–15 and *note*. 56 Cp. J. 85. 30–31.

Page 89. The sequence is again doubtful. It is possible that the opening lines depend for their explanation upon some antecedent passage now lost. The description of the Covering Cherub is to be set against that of Jerusalem (J., p. 86).

1–3 The reference is apparently to the 'Covering Cherub,

majestic image
Of Selfhood, Body put off, the Antichrist accursed,

which Man in the Regeneration 'puts off', a spiritual act symbolized in the Crucifixion and Resurrection. The doctrine of the persistence of this body of error after its rejection is elaborated below, J. 92. 13–27. It is equally possible that the allusion may be to the historical event, the Crucifixion, which demonstrated the unreality of all that Rahab and Tirzah stand for, though they still remain. Cp. also Colossians ii. 13–14.

A terrible indefinite Hermaphroditic form,
A Wine-press of Love & Wrath, double, Hermaphroditic,
Twelvefold in Allegoric pomp, in selfish holiness;
The Pharisaion, the Grammateis, the Presbuterion,
The Archiereus, the Iereus, the Saddusaion, double
Each withoutside of the other, covering eastern heaven.

Thus was the Covering Cherub reveal'd, majestic image
Of Selfhood, Body put off, the Antichrist accursèd,
Cover'd with precious stones, a Human Dragon terrible
And bright, stretch'd over Europe & Asia gorgeous.
In three nights he devour'd the rejected corse of death.

His Head, dark, deadly, in its Brain incloses a reflexion
Of Eden all perverted; Egypt on the Gihon, many tongued
And many mouth'd, Ethiopia, Lybia, the Sea of Rephaim.
Minute Particulars in slavery I behold among the brick-kilns
Disorganiz'd, & there is Pharoh in his iron Court
And the Dragon of the River & the Furnaces of iron.
Outwoven from Thames & Tweed & Severn, awful streams,
Twelve ridges of Stone frown over all the Earth in tyrant pride,
Frown over each River, stupendous Works of Albion's Druid Sons.
And Albion's Forests of Oaks cover'd the Earth from Pole to Pole.

3 See Index, *Hermaphroditic*.

11–12 See Index, *Serpent*. The eastern position of Europe and Asia in relation to Albion gives them the symbolic significance of error attaching to that quarter.

13 The evils symbolized by the Serpent are sustained by the delusions rejected by the spiritually regenerate man as 'the body of death', the 'excrementitious husk and covering' the 'Dust and Clay' 'which never was made for Man to Eat'. Cp. E. G. ζ, ll. 81–94 (Clar. Press, pp. 260–261):

> Then Roll'd the shadowy Man [the Spectre or Covering Cherub] away
> From the limbs of Jesus, to make them his prey,
> An ever devouring appetite,
> Glittering with festering Venoms bright;
> Crying: 'Crucify this cause of distress,
> Who don't keep the secrets of holiness!
> The Mental Powers by Diseases we bind;
> But he heals the deaf, the dumb, & the Blind.
> Whom God has afflicted for secret ends,
> He comforts and Heals and calls them Friends.'
> But when Jesus was crucified,
> Then was perfected his galling pride.
> In three Nights he devour'd his prey,
> And still he devours the Body of Clay.

17 Cp. J. 31. 3–21.

19 Cp. Ezek. xxix. 3: 'Pharaoh, king of Egypt, the great dragon that lieth in the midst of his rivers, which hath said, My river is my own, and I have made it for myself.'

His Bosom wide reflects Moab & Ammon on the River
Pison, since call'd Arnon : there is Heshbon beautiful,
The flocks of Rabbath on the Arnon & the Fish-pools of Heshbon
Whose currents flow into the Dead Sea by Sodom & Gomorra.
Above his Head high arching Wings, black, fill'd with Eyes,
Spring upon iron sinews from the Scapulæ & Os Humeri ;
There Israel in bondage to his Generalizing Gods,
Molech & Chemosh : & in his left breast is Philistea
In Druid Temples over the whole Earth with Victims' Sacrifice,
From Gaza to Damascus, Tyre & Sidon & the Gods
Of Javan, thro' the Isles of Grecia & all Europe's Kings,
Where Hiddekel pursues his course among the rocks.
Two Wings spring from his ribs of brass, starry, black as night,
But translucent their blackness as the daz[z]ling of gems.

His Loins inclose Babylon on Euphrates beautiful,
And Rome in sweet Hesperia : there Israel scatter'd abroad
In martyrdoms & slavery I behold, ah, vision of sorrow !
Inclosèd by eyeless Wings, glowing with fire as the iron
Heated in the Smith's forge : but cold the wind of their dread Fury.

But in the midst of a devouring Stomach, Jerusalem
Hidden within the Covering Cherub as in a Tabernacle
Of threefold workmanship, in allegoric delusion & woe.
There the Seven Kings of Canaan & Five Baalim of Philistea,
Sihon & Og, the Anakim & Emim, Nephilim & Gibborim,
From Babylon to Rome : & the Wings spread from Japan,
Where the Red Sea terminates the World of Generation & Death
To Ireland's farthest rocks where Giants builded their Causeway
Into the Sea of Rephaim : but the Sea o'erwhelm'd them all.

A Double Female now appear'd within the Tabernacle,
Religion hid in War, a Dragon red & hidden Harlot,
Each within other ; but without, a Warlike Mighty-one

25 Cp. J. 79. 3 *note*.

26 Rabbath or Rabbah was the chief city of the Ammonites (Deut. iii. 11). For the Fishpools of Heshbon cp. Song of Solomon vii. 4.

28–35 Satisfactory pointing in this passage appears to be impossible. Blake's autotype gives no assistance.

31 Cp. J. 84. 18 *note*. 35 Cp. Gen. ii. 14.

43 See Index, *Head, Heart, Loins, and Stomach*, and *Jerusalem, Note I*.

45 The 'Threefold is Sexual', that is, it is of the error of morality and sense-perception. 48–51 Cp. F. Z. ii. 269 *note*.

52 The Female is Rahab or Vala : cp. J. 75. 18–20.

Of dreadful power sitting upon Horeb, pondering dire
And mighty preparations, mustering multitudes innumerable
Of warlike sons among the sands of Midian & Aram.
For multitudes of those who sleep in Alla descend,
Lurèd by his warlike symphonies of tabret, pipe & harp,
Burst the bottoms of the Graves & Funeral Arks of Beulah.
Wandering in that unknown Night beyond the silent Grave
They become One with the Antichrist & are absorb'd in him.

[90] The Feminine separates from the Masculine & both from Man,
Ceasing to be His Emanations, Life to Themselves assuming:
And while they circumscribe his Brain, & while they circumscribe
His Heart, & while they circumscribe his Loins, a Veil & Net
Of Veins of red Blood grows around them like a scarlet robe,
Covering them from the sight of Man like the woven Veil of Sleep,
Such as the Flowers of Beulah weave to be their Funeral Mantles,
But dark, opake, tender to touch, & painful & agonizing
To the embrace of love & to the mingling of soft fibres
Of tender affection, that no more the Masculine mingles
With the Feminine, but the Sublime is shut out from the Pathos
In howling torment, to build stone walls of separation, compelling
The Pathos to weave curtains of hiding secresy from the torment.

Bowen & Conwenna stood on Skiddaw cutting the Fibres
Of Benjamin from Chester's River: loud the River, loud the Mersey

58 Alla, one of 'the four states of Humanity in its repose' is only mentioned once elsewhere: cp. M. 34. 8–16, and see Index, *Ulro*, I. *Note*.

Page 90. 1–13 An instance of this separation is to be found in the division of Spectre and Emanation from Los: cp. J. 5. 67–6. 7. Cp. below, ll. 52–56, and see Index, *Sex*.

5–6 This limitation of Man's perceptions is described more fully, J. 49. 7–41 and J. 66. 17–54. In l. 6 Man is again the Divine Humanity. The 'woven Veil of Sleep' hardly seems to differ from Beulah itself, as a state created by Divine mercy that the 'weak and weary', those incapable of sustaining immediate communion with the Infinite and Eternal of the Divine Humanity, may receive a mediate vision adapted to their feebler powers: cp. M. 30. 21–31. 7.

11 The 'Sublime' and the 'Pathos' are apparently equivalent to Male and Female respectively. The 'stone walls of separation' seem identical in meaning with the veil of Moral Virtue 'that Satan puts between Eve and Adam': cp. J. 55. 11–16.

14 Bowen and Conwenna, son and daughter of Albion, represent the Spectre and Emanation, as do Hyle and Gwendolen (J. 82. 49) and Hand and Cambel (*ibid*. l. 62).

And the Ribble thunder into the Irish sea, as the Twelve Sons
Of Albion drank & imbibèd the Life & eternal Form of Luvah.
Cheshire & Lancashire & Westmoreland groan in anguish.
As they cut the fibres from the Rivers he sears them with hot
Iron of his Forge, & fixes them into Bones of chalk & Rock.
Conwenna sat above: with solemn cadences she drew
Fibres of life out from the Bones into her golden Loom.
Hand had his Furnace on Highgate's heights & it reach'd
To Brockley Hills across the Thames; he with double Boadicea
In cruel pride cut Reuben apart from the Hills of Surrey,
Comingling with Luvah & with the Sepulcher of Luvah.
For the Male is a Furnace of beryll: the Female is a golden Loom.

Los cries: 'No Individual ought to appropriate to Himself
Or to his Emanation any of the Universal Characteristics
Of David or of Eve, of the Woman or of the Lord,
Of Reuben or of Benjamin, of Joseph or Judah or Levi.
Those who dare appropriate to themselves Universal Attributes
Are the Blasphemous Selfhoods & must be broken asunder.
A Vegetated Christ & a Virgin Eve are the Hermaphroditic
Blasphemy: by his Maternal Birth he is that Evil-One,
And his Maternal Humanity must be put off Eternally,
Lest the Sexual Generation swallow up Regeneration.
Come Lord Jesus, take on thee the Satanic Body of Holiness!'

19 The Rivers here, as elsewhere, appear to have something of a visionary character, almost as if they were rivers of the wells of life. Separation from them leads to subjection to error.

20 The petrifaction or condensation of spiritual forms into the delusions of mundane existence is frequently alluded to: cp. J. 19. 17–25; 73. 16–21; 90. 49; and see below, ll. 49–50.

21–22 Cp. J. 67. 2–18.

23–24 The high places, hills and mountains, are associated with the power of Natural Religion in this world.

26 Luvah's Sepulchre denotes some undefined form of moral fallacy.

27 This line occurs in J. 5. 34.

28–33 Cp. J. 90. 1–13, and below, ll. 40–43, 52–56. The appropriation of universality by the Individual implies the negation of universal brotherhood and the unity of all in the Divine Family. This passage also stresses the fallacy of assuming that any single form of law or belief can claim universal validity.

34–35 See Index, *Hermaphroditic*.

35–38 See Index, *Incarnation*, and cp. E. G. β. 55–57 (Clar. Press, p. 249):

He took on Sin in the Virgin's Womb
And put it off on the Cross & Tomb
To be Worship'd by the Church of Rome.

The 'Maternal Humanity', the 'Satanic Body of Holiness', is the sum of mundane error: cp. J. 89. 1 *note* and J. 62. 8 *note*. So too 'Sexual Generation' symbolizes temporal existence apart from any regenerative purpose: for its content in art and morals cp. M. 42. 32–43. 28.

So Los cried in the Valleys of Middlesex in the Spirit of Prophecy,
While in Selfhood Hand & Hyle & Bowen & Skofeld appropriate
The Divine Names: seeking to Vegetate the Divine Vision
In a corporeal & ever dying Vegetation & Corruption.
Mingling with Luvah in One, they become One Great Satan.

Loud scream the Daughters of Albion beneath the Tongs & Hammer:
Dolorous are their lamentations in the burning Forge.
They drink Reuben & Benjamin as the iron drinks the fire:
They are red hot with cruelty, raving along the Banks of Thames
And on Tyburn's Brook, among the howling Victims in loveliness;
While Hand & Hyle condense the Little-ones & erect them into
A mighty Temple even to the stars: but they Vegetate
Beneath Los's Hammer, that Life may not be blotted out.

For Los said: 'When the Individual appropriates Universality
He divides into Male & Female: & when the Male & Female
Appropriate Individuality, they become an Eternal Death,
Hermaphroditic worshippers of a God of cruelty & law.
Your Slaves & Captives you compell to worship a God of Mercy.
These are the Demonstrations of Los & the blows of my mighty Hammer.'

So Los spoke. And the Giants of Albion, terrified & ashamèd
With Los's thunderous Words, began to build trembling rocking Stones—
For his Words roll in thunders & lightnings among the Temples,
Terrified, rocking to & fro upon the earth, & sometimes

39 Cp. J. 32. 9 *note*.

43 Cp. J. 47. 12 and J. 49. 68–69:

Luvah is named Satan because he has enter'd that State,
A World where Man is by Nature the enemy of Man.

48 Cp. F. Z. ii. 249 *note*.

49–50 Cp. J. 91. 26–27:

You [the Spectres] accumulate Particulars, & murder by analyzing, that you
May take the aggregate; & you call the aggregate Moral Law.

Cp. J. 31. 3–12.

59–62 Blake here remembers speculations among archaeologists concerning the 'rocking stones'. He relates them to his symbolic use of Druid Temples: see Index, *Druid*. In the design on M., p. 4, that shows a trilithon, there is also a perched rock or rocking stone. Lines 60–62 are in parenthesis: ll. 63–66 relate back to the Giants (l. 58).

60 Cp. J. 55. 4 *note*.

Resting in a Circle in Malden or in Strathness or Dura—
Plotting to devour Albion & Los the friend of Albion,
Denying in private, mocking God & Eternal Life ; & in Public
Collusion calling themselves Deists, Worshipping the Maternal
Humanity, calling it Nature and Natural Religion.

But still the thunder of Los peals loud & thus the thunders cry :
'These beautiful Witchcrafts of Albion are gratifyd by Cruelty.

[91] It is easier to forgive an Enemy than to forgive a Friend !
The man who permits you to injure him deserves your vengeance ;
He also will recieve it. Go, Spectre ! obey my most secret desire,
Which thou knowest without my speaking. Go to these Fiends of Righteousness !
Tell them to obey their Humanities, & not pretend Holiness,
When they are murderers : as far as my Hammer & Anvil permit.
Go ! tell them that the Worship of God is honouring his gifts
In other men, & loving the greatest men best, each according
To his Genius, which is the Holy Ghost in Man : there is no other
God than that God who is the intellectual fountain of Humanity.
He who envies or calumniates, which is murder & cruelty,
Murders the Holy-one. Go ! tell them this & overthrow their cup,
Their bread, their altar-table, their incense & their oath,
Their marriage & their baptism, their burial & consecration.

64–66 Cp. F. Z. viii. 598 *note*.

68 These 'beautiful Witchcrafts' are the 'feminine' delusions of Natural Religion, and may refer more particularly either to what Blake regarded as the specious doctrines and ceremonies of current religions, or to the loveliness of the natural world. But these only exist in the negation of imagination, that is, in cruel repression of man's true Humanity.

Page 91. 1 Cp. Ross. MS. (Clar. Press, p. 204) :

At a Friend's Errors anger shew,
Mirth at the Errors of a Foe.

6 See below, ll. 11–12. The latter portion of l. 6 cannot be related with any certainty to the context. Blake's punctuation has therefore been retained.

7–12 Cp. M. H. H., p. 22 : 'The worship of God is, Honouring his gifts in other men, each according to his genius ; and loving the greatest men best : those who envy or calumniate great men hate God, for there is no other God.' Cp. also J., p. 77 : 'What is the Divine Spirit ? Is the Holy Ghost any other than an Intellectual Fountain ?'

I have tried to make friends by corporeal gifts but have only
Made enemies. I never made friends but by spiritual gifts,
By severe contentions of friendship & the burning fire of thought.
He who would see the Divinity must see him in his Children,
One first in friendship & love, then a Divine Family, & in the midst
Jesus will appear: so he who wishes to see a Vision, a perfect Whole,
Must see it in its Minute Particulars, Organizèd, & not as thou,
O Fiend of Righteousness, pretendest: thine is a Disorganizèd
And snowy cloud, brooder of tempests & destructive War.
You smile with pomp & rigor, you talk of benevolence & virtue;
I act with benevolence & Virtue, & get murder'd time after time.
You accumulate Particulars & murder by analyzing, that you
May take the aggregate; & you call the aggregate Moral Law,
And you call that swell'd & bloated Form a Minute Particular.
But General Forms have their vitality in Particulars; & every
Particular is a Man, a Divine Member of the Divine Jesus.

So Los cried at his Anvil in the horrible darkness weeping.

The Spectre builded stupendous Works, taking the Starry Heavens
Like to a curtain & folding them according to his will,
Repeating the Smaragdine Table of Hermes to draw Los down
Into the Indefinite, refusing to believe without demonstration.
Los reads the Stars of Albion: the Spectre reads the Voids

15–17 Cp. J. 30. 10: 'Corporeal friends are spiritual enemies'; and cp. Letter to Butts, 25 April 1803 (R., p. 114): 'If a man is the enemy of my spiritual life while he pretends to be the friend of my corporeal, he is a real enemy; but the man may be the friend of my spiritual life while he seems the enemy of my corporeal, though not *vice versa*.'

18–30 See Index, *Minute Particulars*, and General Introduction, p. 39.

24–25 Cp. M. 43. 19–20.

34 The source of Blake's knowledge of the Emerald Table of Hermes is still to seek.

35 The demonstrations of reason blur and confuse the definite and simple outlines of truth: they are the antithesis of imagination or vision: cp. J. 4. 25 and J. 52 *note* 2. For Blake's use of 'Indefinite', cp. M. 27. 16 *note*. It is here identical with the 'Indefinite Udan-Adan' the state of error: see Index, *Ulro*, II.

36 Cp. E. G., Prologue, ll. 1–2 and 13–14, where Blake addresses his adversary:

> The Vision of Christ that thou dost see
> Is my Vision's Greatest Enemy . . .
> Both read the Bible day & night,
> But thou read'st black where I read white.

Between the Stars, among the arches of Albion's Tomb sublime
Rolling the Sea in rocky paths, forming Leviathan
And Behemoth, the War by Sea enormous & the War
By Land astounding, erecting pillars in the deepest Hell
To reach the heavenly arches. Los beheld, undaunted; furious
His heav'd Hammer; he swung it round & at one blow
In unpitying ruin driving down the pyramids of pride,
Smiting the Spectre on his Anvil & the integuments of his Eye
And Ear unbinding in dire pain, with many blows
Of strict severity self-subduing, & with many tears labouring.

Then he sent forth the Spectre: all his pyramids were grains
Of sand & his pillars dust on the fly's wing, & his starry
Heavens a moth of gold & silver mocking his anxious grasp.
Thus Los alter'd his Spectre, & every Ratio of his Reason
He alter'd time after time with dire pain & many tears,
Till he had completely divided him into a separate space.

Terrified Los sat to behold, trembling & weeping & howling.
'I care not whether a Man is Good or Evil; all that I care
Is whether he is a Wise Man or a Fool. Go! put off Holiness,
And put on Intellect; or my thund'rous Hammer shall drive thee
To wrath which thou condemnest, till thou obey my voice.'

So Los terrified cries, trembling & weeping & howling. Beholding . . .

[92] 'What do I see! The Briton, Saxon, Roman, Norman amalgamating

38–39 Compare the titles of the companion pictures numbered I and II in the *Descriptive Catalogue*. The first reads 'The spiritual form of Nelson guiding Behemoth, in whose wreathings are infolded the Nations of the Earth'; the second reads 'The spiritual form of Pitt, guiding Behemoth; He is that Angel who, pleased to perform the Almighty's orders, rides on the whirlwind, directing the storms of war. He is ordering the Reaper to reap the Vine of the Earth, and the Plowman to plow up the Cities and Towers.'

43 Cp. J. 31. 8–12.

44–45 The reference here is to the destruction of the delusions arising from sense-perception.

46 For 'self-subduing' see Index, *Self-Annihilation*.

47–49 The pyramids and starry heavens are the delusions of the Spectre, the 'unreal forms' of error: cp. J. 31. 12 *note*.

54–55 Cp. *Cat.* 1810: 'Men are admitted into Heaven not because they have curbed & govern'd their Passions, or have No Passions, but because they have Cultivated their Understandings. The Treasures of Heaven are not Negations of Passion, but Realities of Intellect, from which all the Passions Emanate, Uncurbed in their Eternal Glory.'

Page 92. The sequence is again interrupted at this point.

1 This amalgamation marks the beginning of the Resurrection into Unity.

In my Furnaces into One Nation, the English, & taking refuge
In the Loins of Albion! The Canaanite united with the fugitive
Hebrew, whom she divided into Twelve & sold into Egypt,
Then scatter'd the Egyptian & Hebrew to the four Winds.
This sinful Nation Created in our Furnaces & Looms is Albion.'

So Los spoke. Enitharmon answer'd in great terror in Lambeth's Vale:

'The Poet's Song draws to its period & Enitharmon is no more.
For if he be that Albion I can never weave him in my Looms;
But when he touches the first fibrous thread, like filmy dew
My Looms will be no more & I annihilate vanish for ever.
Then thou wilt Create another Female according to thy Will.'

Los answer'd, swift as the shuttle of gold: 'Sexes must vanish & cease
To be when Albion arises from his dread repose, O lovely Enitharmon!
When all their Crimes, their Punishments, their Accusations of Sin,
All their Jealousies, Revenges, Murders, hidings of Cruelty in Deceit,
Appear only in the Outward Spheres of Visionary Space and Time,
In the shadows of Possibility by Mutual Forgiveness for evermore,
And in the Vision & in the Prophecy, that we may Foresee & Avoid
The terrors of Creation & Redemption & Judgment, Beholding them
Display'd in the Emanative Visions of Canaan, in Jerusalem & in Shiloh

3–4 The Loins are 'the place of the Last Judgment' (J. 30. 38). Neither the Canaanite nor 'the fugitive Hebrew' can be identified or explained.

9 The allusion to the ultimate disappearance of Enitharmon or Space apparently refers to the final destruction of mundane existence: cp. M. 25. 38 *note*. The same idea is expressed as the cessation of Sex; see below, ll. 13–20.

10–11 Cp. F. Z. viii. 290 *note*. Between these lines is engraved the desolate figure of a woman, crouching among the dead: her name is written 'Jerusalem'. In the distance are Druid temples.

13–27 See Index, *Sexes*, and cp. M. 34. 50 *note*. Cp. also J. 98. 28 *note*.

20 These are the three States of Ulro: cp. J. 36. 41.

And in the Shadows of Remembrance & in the Chaos of the Spectre,
Amalek, Edom, Egypt, Moab, Ammon, Ashur, Philistea around Jerusalem,
Where the Druids rear'd their Rocky Circles to make permanent Remembrance
Of Sin, & the Tree of Good & Evil sprang from the Rocky Circle & Snake
Of the Druid along the Valley of Rephaim from Camberwell to Golgotha,
And framèd the Mundane Shell Cavernous in Length, Bredth & Highth.'

[93] Enitharmon heard. She rais'd her head like the mild Moon:

'O Rintrah! O Palamabron! What are your dire & awful purposes?
Enitharmon's name is nothing before you: you forget all my Love.
The Mother's love of obedience is forgotten, & you seek a Love
Of the pride of dominion, that will Divorce Ocalythron & Elynittria
Upon East Moor in Derbyshire & along the Valleys of Cheviot.
Could you Love me, Rintrah, if you Pride not in my Love,
As Reuben found Mandrakes in the field & gave them to his Mother?
Pride meets with Pride upon the Mountains in the stormy day,
In that terrible Day of Rintrah's Plow & of Satan's driving the Team.
Ah! then I heard my little ones weeping along the Valley.
Ah! then I saw my belovèd ones fleeing from my Tent.

22–27 These lines include almost all the more important symbols of the state of mundane error.

Page 93. At the head of this page the following sentence is engraved across the forms of three kneeling figures: 'Anytus, Melitus, & Lycon thought Socrates a very Pernicious Man. So Caiaphas thought Jesus.' With this cp. *Cat.* 1810 (Ross. MS., p. 86): 'The painter [Blake] hopes that his Friends Anytus, Melitus & Lycon will perceive that they are not now in Ancient Greece; & tho' they can use the Poison of Calumny, the English Public will be convinc'd that such a Picture as this [Blake's *Canterbury Pilgrims*] Could never be Painted by a Madman, or by one in a State of Outrageous manners.'

2–16 Little can be made of this speech, which reads like a final attempt to divert the spiritual activities denoted by the Sons of Los away from their regenerative labours in order to establish Woman's dominion, the reign of Moral Law.

5 Cp. *Europe*, ll. 46–49 and *notes ad loc.*

6 Cp. J. 23. 27 *note*. 8 Cp. J. 11. 22 *note*.

10 Cp. F. Z. viii. 358–396 and M., pp. 5–7.

Merlin was like thee, Rintrah, among the Giants of Albion.
Judah was like Palamabron. O Simeon ! O Levi ! ye fled away !
How can I hear my little ones weeping along the Valley,
Or how upon the distant Hills see my belovèds' Tents ! '

Then Los again took up his speech as Enitharmon ceast :

' Fear not, my Sons, this Waking Death : he is become One with me.
Behold him here ! We shall not Die : we shall be united in Jesus.
Will you suffer this Satan, this Body of Doubt that Seems but Is Not,
To occupy the very threshold of Eternal Life ? If Bacon, Newton, Locke,
Deny a Conscience in Man & the Communion of Saints & Angels,
Contemning the Divine Vision & Fruition, Worship[p]ing the Deus
Of the Heathen, The God of This World, & the Goddess Nature,
Mystery, Babylon the Great, The Druid Dragon & hidden Harlot,
Is it not that Signal of the Morning which was told us in the Beginning ? '

Thus they converse upon Mam-Tor : the Graves thunder under their feet.

[94] Albion cold lays on his Rock ; storms & snows beat round him,
Beneath the Furnaces & the starry Wheels & the Immortal Tomb ;
Howling winds cover him ; roaring seas dash furious against him ;
In the deep darkness broad lightnings glare, long thunders roll.

18 ' This Waking Death ' is, of course, Albion awaking from his sleep of Death.

21–26 Following the Biblical prophecy concerning the signs of the second coming and the end of the world (Matt. xxiv. 3–15), Blake makes the declaration of the Deistical heresy the signal of the complete revelation of the Divine Humanity and the destruction of error in the Last Judgement.

22 Conscience is elsewhere called ' Con—or Innate Science ' (R. N. iv, p. 47). Cp. also R. N., p. 58 : ' Innate Ideas are in Every Man, Born with him ; they are truly Himself.' Cp. with this passage F. Z. viii. 598 *note*.

27 Mam-Tor, one of the ' barren mountains of Moral Virtue ' (J. 31. 19).

Page 94. 17 Cp. M. 14. 36–40.

2 Cp. F. Z. iv. 274 *note* and M. 7. 2 *note*.

The weeds of Death inwrap his hands & feet, blown incessant
And wash'd incessant by the for-ever restless sea-waves foaming abroad
Upon the white Rock. England, a Female Shadow, as deadly damps
Of the Mines of Cornwall & Derbyshire, lays upon his bosom heavy,
Movèd by the wind in volumes of thick cloud, returning, folding round
His loins & bosom, unremovable by swelling storms & loud rending
Of enragèd thunders. Around them the Starry Wheels of their Giant Sons
Revolve, & over them the Furnaces of Los & the Immortal Tomb, around
Erin sitting in the Tomb, to Watch them unceasing night and day.
And the Body of Albion was closèd apart from all Nations.

Over them the famish'd Eagle screams on boney Wings, and around
Them howls the Wolf of famine : deep heaves the Ocean black, thundering
Around the wormy Garments of Albion, then pausing in deathlike silence.

Time was Finishèd ! The Breath Divine Breathèd over Albion
Beneath the Furnaces & starry Wheels and in the Immortal Tomb;
And England who is Brittannia awoke from Death on Albion's bosom.
She awoke pale & cold : she fainted seven times on the Body of Albion.

' O pitious Sleep ! O pitious Dream ! O God, O God, awake ! I have slain
In Dreams of Chasti⟨ti⟩ty & Moral Law, I have Murderèd Albion ! Ah !
In Stone-henge & on London Stone & in the Oak Groves of Malden
I have Slain him in my Sleep with the Knife of the Druid. O England,
O all ye Nations of the Earth, behold ye the Jealous Wife !

7 Cp. J. 36. 28 *note*. 8 Cp. J. 23. 27 *note*. 13 See Index, *Erin*. 16 The Atlantic Ocean. See Index, *Atlantic*. 24–25 Cp. J. 8. 27 *note* and M. 4. 16 *note*. 26 See Index, *Sex*, &c.

The Eagle & the Wolf & Monkey & Owl & the King & Priest were there!'

[95] Her voice pierc'd Albion's clay cold ear: he movèd upon the Rock.
The Breath Divine went forth upon the morning hills. Albion mov'd
Upon the Rock: he open'd his eyelids in pain; in pain he mov'd
His stony members: he saw England. Ah! shall the Dead live again?

The Breath Divine went forth over the morning hills. Albion rose
In anger, the wrath of God, breaking bright, flaming on all sides around
His awful limbs: into the Heavens he walkèd, clothèd in flames
Loud thund'ring, with broad flashes of flaming lightning & pillars
Of fire, speaking the Words of Eternity in Human Forms, in direful
Revolutions of Action & Passion, thro' the Four Elements on all sides
Surrounding his awful Members. Thou seest the Sun in heavy clouds
Struggling to rise above the Mountains; in his burning hand
He takes his Bow, then chooses out his arrows of flaming gold.
Murmuring the Bowstring breathes with ardor; clouds roll round the
Horns of the wide Bow; loud sounding winds sport on the mountain brows.
Compelling Urizen to his Furrow & Tharmas to his Sheepfold
And Luvah to his Loom, Urthona he beheld, mighty, labouring at

Page 95. 9 Cp. J. 98. 28–32 and Swedenborg, *Arcana Caelestia*, § 1641: 'Of the converse of spirits in the Intermediate State: Spirits converse with each other in the other life just as men do on earth; they that are in good, with all familiarity of friendship and love—of which I have frequently been a witness: and this they do in their own language by which they express more in a minute than man can do in an hour. For their speech is the universal of all languages, by means of ideas, the primitives of words.'

10 The Elements are the Zoas: see Index, *Zoas*, and J. 12. 45 *note*.

11–18 Los is frequently associated with the Sun (cp. B. L. iv. 21 *note*) and with the Divine Vision, Jesus, or the Divine Family appearing as One Man. This fact may explain the present passage.

16–17 See Index, *Zoas*.

17–18 See Index, *Los, Note I*.

His Anvil in the Great Spectre Los, unwearied labouring & weeping.
Therefore the Sons of Eden praise Urthona's Spectre in songs,
Because he kept the Divine Vision in time of trouble.

As the Sun & Moon lead forward the Visions of Heaven & Earth,
England, who is Brittannia, enter'd Albion's bosom rejoicing,
Rejoicing in his indignation, adoring his wrathful rebuke.
She who adores not your frowns will only loathe your smiles.

[96] As the Sun & Moon lead forward the Visions of Heaven & Earth
England, who is Brittannia, enterèd Albion's bosom rejoicing.

Then Jesus appearèd standing by Albion, as the Good Shepherd
By the lost Sheep that he hath found : & Albion knew that it
Was the Lord, the Universal Humanity ; & Albion saw his Form
A Man, & they conversèd as Man with Man, in Ages of Eternity.
And the Divine Appearance was the likeness & similitude of Los.

Albion said : ' O Lord, what can I do ! my Selfhood cruel
Marches against thee, deceitful, from Sinai & from Edom
Into the Wilderness of Judah to meet thee in his pride.
I behold the Visions of my deadly Sleep of Six Thousand Years
Daz[z]ling around thy skirts like a Serpent of precious stones & gold.
I know it is my Self, O my Divine Creator & Redeemer ! '

Jesus replied : ' Fear not, Albion ! unless I die thou canst not live :
But if I die I shall arise again & thou with me.
This is Friendship & Brotherhood : without it Man Is Not.'

So Jesus spoke : the Covering Cherub coming on in darkness
Overshadow'd them ; & Jesus said : ' Thus do Men in Eternity,
One for another to put off by forgiveness every sin.'

19–20 These lines are repeated from J. 30. 14–15. Cp. J. 44. 28–31.
Page 96. 7 See Index, *Los*, III.
9–10 These places derive their significance from their association with the wanderings in the desert, the ' wilderness of moral law '.
11–12 Cp. M. 44. 7–15. 12 See Index, *Serpent*.
13 The Self here is the Spectre. See below, l. 31 *note*.
16 Cp. J. 45. 4–15.

Albion reply'd : ' Cannot Man exist without Mysterious
Offering of Self for Another ? is this Friendship & Brotherhood ?
I see thee in the likeness and similitude of Los my Friend.'

Jesus said : ' Wouldest thou love one who never died
For thee, or ever die for one who had not died for thee ?
And if God dieth not for Man, & giveth not himself
Eternally for Man, Man could not exist ; for Man is Love,
As God is Love : every kindness to another is a little Death
In the Divine Image, nor can Man exist but by Brotherhood.'

So saying the Cloud overshadowing divided them asunder.
Albion stood in terror, not for himself but for his Friend
Divine ; & Self was lost in the contemplation of faith
And wonder at the Divine Mercy & at Los's sublime honour.

' Do I sleep amidst danger to Friends ! O my Cities & Counties,
Do you sleep ! rouze up, rouze up ! Eternal Death is abroad ! '

So Albion spoke, & threw himself into the Furnaces of affliction.
All was a Vision, all a Dream : the Furnaces became
Fountains of Living Waters flowing from the Humanity Divine.
And all the Cities of Albion rose from their Slumbers, and All
The Sons & Daughters of Albion on soft clouds Waking from Sleep.
Soon all around remote the Heavens burnt with flaming fires,
And Urizen & Luvah & Tharmas & Urthona arose into
Albion's Bosom. Then Albion stood before Jesus in the Clouds
Of Heaven, Fourfold among the Visions of God in Eternity.

[97] ' Awake, Awake, Jerusalem ! O lovely Emanation of Albion,
Awake, and overspread all Nations as in Ancient Time !
For lo ! the Night of Death is past and the Eternal Day
Appears upon our Hills. Awake, Jerusalem, and come away ! '

So spake the Vision of Albion, & in him so spake in my hearing

23–28 See General Introduction, pp. 96–97.

29 The irregular structure of this sentence is confusing. ' So saying ' clearly relates to Jesus : the ' Cloud ' is the Covering Cherub (cp. above, ll. 17–18), the source of division, the ' Eternal Death ' of l. 34.

30–43 Albion's recognition of the doctrine of ' Friendship ' is immediately followed by Regeneration. The narrow visions of Time and Space become Visions of Eternity and Man reassumes his ancient Unity. Cp. F. Z. ix. 823–841.

31 The ' Self ' is the Selfhood or Spectre, the Reasoning Power and the Punisher, whose belief in ' Experimental theory ' (cp. J. 52 *note*) and Moral Law is the negation of the visionary doctrine here enunciated.

The Universal Father. Then Albion stretch'd his hand into Infinitude,
And took his Bow. Fourfold the Vision : for bright beaming Urizen
Lay'd his hand on the South & took a breathing Bow of carvèd Gold ;
Luvah his hand stretch'd to the East & bore a Silver Bow bright shining ;
Tharmas Westward a Bow of Brass pure flaming, richly wrought ;
Urthona Northward in thick storms a Bow of Iron, terrible thundering.

And the Bow is Male & Female, & the Quiver of the Arrows of Love
Are the Children of his Bow ; a Bow of Mercy & Loving-kindness, laying
Open the hidden Heart in Wars of mutual Benevolence, Wars of Love.
And the Hand of Man grasps firm between the Male & Female Loves :
And he Clothèd himself in Bow & Arrows in awful state, Fourfold,
In the midst of his Twenty-eight Cities, each with his Bow breathing.

[98] Then each an Arrow flaming from his Quiver fitted carefully.
They drew fourfold the unreprovable String, bending thro' the wide Heavens
The hornèd Bow Fourfold : loud sounding flew the flaming Arrow fourfold.

Murmuring the Bowstring breathes with ardor. Clouds roll round the horns
Of the wide Bow ; loud sounding Winds sport on the Mountains' brows.
The Druid Spectre was Annihilate, loud thund'ring, rejoicing terrific, vanishing,

Page 97. 7 Nothing can be discovered outside of the present passage, to throw light on this use of the Bow.
13–14 Cp. J. 9. 17–19 :

I [Los] took the sighs & tears & bitter groans.
I lifted them into my Furnaces to form the spiritual sword
That lays open the hidden heart.

For the 'hidden heart' cp. J. 37. 11–38. 3.
17 Cp. J. 30. 26 *note*.

Fourfold Annihilation: & at the clangor of the Arrows of Intellect
The innumerable Chariots of the Almighty appear'd in Heaven,
And Bacon & Newton & Locke, & Milton & Shakspear & Chaucer,
A Sun of blood red wrath surrounding heaven on all sides around,
Glorious, incompreh[en]sible by Mortal Man: & each Chariot was Sexual Twofold.

And every Man stood Fourfold; each Four Faces had, One to the West,
One toward the East, One to the South, One to the North: the Horses Fourfold.
And the dim Chaos brighten'd beneath, above, around, Eyed as the Peacock,
According to the Human Nerves of Sensation, the Four Rivers of the Water of Life.

South stood the Nerves of the Eye; East in Rivers of bliss the Nerves of the
Expansive Nostrils; West flow'd the Parent Sense, the Tongue; North stood
The labyrinthine Ear: Circumscribing & Circumcising the excrementitious
Husk & Covering into Vacuum evaporating, revealing the lineaments of Man,
Driving outward the Body of Death in an Eternal Death & Resurrection,
Awaking it to Life among the Flowers of Beulah, rejoicing in Unity
In the Four Senses, in the Outline, the Circumference & Form for ever
In Forgiveness of Sins which is Self Annihilation: it is the Covenant of Jehovah.

Page 98. 9–11 Bacon, Newton, and Locke, in Man's unregenerate state 'the teachers of Atheism, Satan's doctrine' (Crabb Robinson), become in the Resurrection Chariots of the Almighty, that is, apparently, vehicles of the Holy Spirit. The statement that 'each Chariot was Sexual Twofold' is inexplicable in its present connexion. For a like vision of the sun, as: 'an innumerable company of the heavenly host crying: "Holy! Holy! Holy is the Lord God Almighty!"' cp. *Cat.* 1810 *ad fin.*

15–27 See Index, *Zoas.*

21 Cp. F. Z. vii. 237 *note.*

23 Cp *The Ghost of Abel,* 46–48.

The Four Living Creatures, Chariots of Humanity, Divine, Incomprehensible,
In beautiful Paradises expand. These are the Four Rivers of Paradise
And the Four Faces of Humanity fronting the Four Cardinal Points
Of Heaven, going forward, forward irresistible from Eternity to Eternity.

And they conversèd together in Visionary forms dramatic, which bright
Redounded from their Tongues in thunderous majesty, in Visions,
In new Expanses, creating exemplars of Memory and of Intellect,
Creating Space, Creating Time, according to the wonders Divine
Of Human Imagination throughout all the Three Regions immense
Of Childhood, Manhood & Old Age : & the all tremendous unfathomable Non Ens
Of Death was seen in regeneration terrific or complacent, varying
According to the subject of discourse : & every Word & every Character
Was Human according to the Expansion or Contraction, the Translucence or

28 Cp. J. 95. 9 *note* : see also J. 88. 3–5 :

> When in Eternity Man converses with Man they enter
> Into each other's Bosom (which are Universes of delight)
> In mutual interchange.

Instances of these 'Emanative Visions' are the visions of mortal life, which when time is past, persist in the 'Outward Spheres of Visionary Space and Time' as 'exemplars of Memory and of Intellect', that their errors may be 'seen and avoided'. Apparently identical in nature and purpose are the episodes of the Bible. 'The Bible is fill'd with Imagination and Visions from End to End' (*Siris*) ; and again : 'I cannot conceive the Divinity of the Bible to consist in who they were written by or at what time, or in the historical evidence which may all be false in the eyes of one & true in the eyes of another, but in the Sentiments & Examples which, whether true or Parabolic, are equally useful as Examples given to us of the perverseness of some & of its subsequent evil, & the honesty of others & its consequent good. This sense of the Bible is equally true to all & equally plain to all. None can doubt of the impression he receives from a book of Examples' (Watson's *Apology*). Another instance is the parabolic vision given in 'Visionary form dramatic' in the 'Visions of Jehovah Elohim' in J., p. 61.

33 The Non Ens is the Chaos or Ulro : see Index, *Ulro*.

36 See Index, *Expansion*, &c.

Opakeness of Nervous fibres. Such was the variation of Time & Space
Which vary according as the Organs of Perception vary: & they walkèd
To & fro in Eternity as One Man, reflecting each in each & clearly seen
And seeing, according to fitness & order. And I heard Jehovah speak
Terrific from his Holy Place, & saw the Words of the Mutual Covenant Divine
On Chariots of gold & jewels with Living Creatures, starry & flaming
With every Colour. Lion, Tyger, Horse, Elephant, Eagle, Dove, Fly, Worm,
And the all wondrous Serpent clothèd in gems & rich array, Humanize
In the Forgiveness of Sins according to thy Covenant, Jehovah! They Cry:

'Where is the Covenant of Priam, the Moral Virtues of the Heathen?
Where is the Tree of Good & Evil that rooted beneath the cruel heel
Of Albion's Spectre, the Patriarch Druid? Where are all his Human Sacrifices
For Sin in War & in the Druid Temples of the Accuser of Sin beneath
The Oak Groves of Albion that cover'd the whole Earth beneath his Spectre?
Where are the Kingdoms of the World & all their glory that grew on Desolation,
The Fruit of Albion's Poverty Tree, when the Triple Headed Gog-Magog Giant

38 Cp. *Gates of Paradise* [from the Legends to the Plates], i. (Clar. Press, p. 378):

> The Sun's Light, when he unfolds it,
> Depends on the Organ that beholds it.

Cp. J. 34. 55–56:

> If Perceptive Organs vary, Objects of Perception seem to vary:
> If the Perceptive Organs close, their Objects seem to close also.

46 Cp. J. 50. 3 *note*.

47–52 Cp. J. 28. 13–19, and see Index, *Mundane Shell, Note I*. ii. For the explanation of the name 'Albion's Poverty Tree' (l. 52), cp. F. Z. vii. 111–129.

52 Compare the descriptions of the Triple Form of Hand, the combined Spectre of Albion's Sons, J. 70. 1–16. In J. 74. 30 Blake writes: 'Hyle is called Gog.' It may be again noticed that the Sons of Albion have no apparent meaning beyond that of the generic symbol Spectre. Hence they can be taken as equivalents.

Of Albion Taxèd the Nations into Desolation & then gave the Spectrous Oath ?'
Such is the Cry from all the Earth from the Living Creatures of the Earth
And from the great City of Golgonooza in the Shadowy Generation,
And from the Thirty-two Nations of the Earth among the Living Creatures.

[99] All Human Forms identified, even Tree, Metal, Earth, & Stone ; all
Human Forms identified, living, going forth & returning wearied
Into the Planetary lives of Years, Months, Days & Hours ; reposing,
And then Awaking into his Bosom in the Life of Immortality.
And I heard the Name of their Emanations : they are namèd Jerusalem.

The End of The Song of Jerusalem.

53 For the Spectrous Oath cp. *The Ghost of Abel*, ll. 46–50.
56 Cp. J. 72. 32–44.
Page 99. 1–4 Nothing has been found to throw light on this doctrine of an eternal cycle in existence. The ' Forms identified ' are the ' Eternal Forms ' of what appear to mortal sense-perception as discrete physical entities : cp. J. 71. 15–19.

APPENDIX

THE copy of *Jerusalem* in the Fitzwilliam Museum, printed from the original plates in 1832, after Blake's death, shows on its frontispiece three fragments of partially deleted text that are not visible in the copies printed by Blake himself. They are as follows :

(a) *above the arch :*

[T]here is a Void outside of Existence which if enter'd into
Englobes itself & becomes a Womb : such was Albion's Couch,
A pleasant Shadow of Repose call'd Albion's lovely Land.

His Sublime & Pathos become Two Rocks fix'd in the Earth.
His Reason, his Spectrous Power, covers them above,
Jerusalem his Emanation is a . . . ing beneath.
O . . .
. . . Vision of Albion

(b) *written downwards on the right side of the doorway :*

. . . said Los
. . . Death for Albion's sake [?Ins]pired
The . . . gs of . . . are not for ever : there is a Judgment

(c) *written in reverse along the right side of the arch :*

Every thing
has its
. . . O Spectres of the . . . g Dead

1–2 Cp. M. 43. 37–44. 1. 4 Cp. J. 90. 11

ON HOMER'S POETRY
ON VIRGIL

These notes are engraved on one side of a single plate ($4\frac{1}{2} \times 3\frac{7}{8}$), without date, but apparently belonging to the latest period, *c.* 1820.

On Homer's Poetry

EVERY Poem must necessarily be a perfect Unity, but why Homer's is peculiarly so I cannot tell: he has told the story of Bellerophon, & omitted the Judgment of Paris, which is not only a part but a principal part of Homer's subject.

But when a Work has Unity, it is as much in a Part as in the Whole: the Torso is as much a Unity as the Laocoön.

As Unity is the cloke of folly, so Goodness is the cloke of knavery. Those who will have Unity exclusively in Homer come out with a Moral like a sting in the tail. Aristotle says Characters are either Good or Bad; now Goodness or Badness has nothing to do with Character: an Apple tree, a Pear tree, a Horse, a Lion, are Characters; but a Good Apple tree or a Bad is an Apple tree still: a Horse is not more a Lion for being a Bad Horse; that is its Character: its Goodness or Badness is another consideration.

It is the same with the Moral of a whole Poem as with the Moral Goodness of its parts. Unity & Morality are secondary considerations & belong to Philosophy & not to Poetry, to Exception & not to Rule, to Accident & not to Substance: the Ancients call'd it eating of the tree of good & evil.

The Classics! it is the Classics, & not Goths nor Monks, that Desolate Europe with Wars.

On Virgil

SACRED Truth has pronounced that Greece & Rome, as Babylon & Egypt, so far from being parents of Arts & Sciences, as they pretend, were destroyers of all Art. Homer, Virgil & Ovid confirm this opinion, & make us reverence The Word of God, the only light of antiquity that remains unperverted by War. Virgil in the Eneid, Book VI., line 848,[1] says: 'Let others study Art. Rome has somewhat better to do, namely War & Dominion.'

Rome & Greece swept Art into their maw & destroy'd it: a Warlike State never can produce Art. It will Rob & Plunder & accumulate into one place, & Translate & Copy & Buy & Sell & Criticise, but not Make. Grecian is Mathematic Form: Gothic is Living Form.[2]

Mathematic Form is Eternal in the Reasoning Memory;[3] Living Form is Eternal Existence.

[1] Virgil . . . says] cp. *Aeneid*, vi. 847–853:

Excudent alii spirantia mollius aera,
Credo equidem, vivos ducent de marmore vultus,
Orabunt causas melius, caelique meatus
Describent radio, et surgentia sidera dicent;
Tu regere imperio populos, Romane, memento;
Hae tibi erunt artes, pacisque imponere morem,
Parcere subjectis, et debellare superbos.

[2] Gothic . . . Form] Cp. *Cat.* 1810: 'Multitudes are seen ascending from the Green fields of the blessed in which a Gothic Church is representative of true Art, Call'd Gothic in All Ages by those who Follow'd the Fashion, as that is call'd which is without Shape or Fashion.' Cp. also the note engraved beneath the design known as 'Joseph of Arimathea among The Rocks of Albion': 'This is One of the Gothic Artists who Built the Cathedrals in what we call the Dark Ages / Wandering about in sheep skins & goat skins, of whom the World was not worthy.'

[3] Mathematic . . . Memory] The content of Mathematic Form is set forth in M. 42. 35–43. 26. The statement that it is 'Eternal in the Reasoning Memory' may refer either to its continuance even after the final Regeneration, as described in J. 92. 15–27, or to the illusion of absolute truth with which the 'Reasoning Power in Man' invests it.

THE LAOCOÖN

Collation : single print, line engraving, 10 13/16 × 9 1/16 inches. *Imprint:* Drawn and Engraved by William Blake. *Without date, but belonging to Blake's latest period.*

In the space surrounding the group Blake has written a number of disconnected aphorisms. These have been re-arranged as far as possible according to their subject-matter. The first section, nos. 1–10, interprets the sculptured figures in terms of Blake's conception of the Creation and the Natural Man, as opposed to the Imagination, the Divine Body. Nos. 11–25 deal with art in its relation to Christianity, while nos. 26–31 show the opposition between art and Natural religion, identified with the influence of the ancients. 'To his half-trained apprehension Rome seemed mere violence and Greece mere philosophy' (Swinburne, *Essay*, p. 144). Of the two remaining groups, the first (32–35) treats of 'artificial riches' in the same manner as M. 27. 31–38, while the second repeats characteristic criticisms of current morality.

1. *Blake's interpretation of the group, engraved below the pedestal* : יה & his two Sons, Satan & Adam, as they were copied from the Cherubim of Solomon's Temple by three Rhodians, & applied to Natural Fact, or History of Ilium.

2. *Above the father's head* : The Angel of the Divine Presence. מלאך יהוה

3. *To the left of the same* : ϲφιȣχος.

4. He repented that he had made Adam (of the Female, the Adamah), & it grieved him at his heart.

5. *About the serpent to the right* : Good, לילית, Satan's Wife, The Goddess Nature, is War & Misery ; & Heroism a Miser.

6. *About the serpent to the left* : Evil.

1 יה : cp. the next aphorism and F. Z. viii. 394 *note*. Cp. also D. C. ii, p. 3 : 'The two Pictures of Nelson and Pitt are compositions of a mythological cast, similar to those Apotheoses of Persian, Hindoo, and Egyptian Antiquity which are still preserved on rude monuments, being copies of some stupendous originals now lost or perhaps buried till some happier age. The Artist, having been taken in vision into the ancient republics, monarchies and patriarchates of Asia, has seen those wonderful originals called in the Sacred Scriptures the Cherubim, which were sculptured and painted on walls of Temples, Towers, Cities, Palaces, and erected in the highly cultivated states of Egypt, Moab, Edom, Aram, among the Rivers of Paradise, being the originals from which the Greeks and Hetrurians copied Hercules Farnese, Venus de Medicis, Apollo Belvedere and all the grand works of ancient art.'

2 King Jehovah. Cp. M. 6. 27 *note*.

3 Cp. M. 37. 50 : 'Sihon is in Ophiucus', and cp. M. 37. 47 *note*.

5 Lilith is here equivalent to the symbol 'Vala' : see Index, *Vala*.

7. Good & Evil are Riches & Poverty, a Tree of Misery, propagating Generation & Death.

8. What can be Created Can be Destroyed. Adam is only The Natural Man, & not the Soul or Imagination.

9. The Eternal Body of Man is The Imagination, that is, God Himself, The Divine Body, ישוע, Jesus; we are his Members. It manifests itself in his Works of Art. (In Eternity All is Vision.)

10. All that we See is Vision; from Generated Organs gone as soon as come; Permanent in The Imagination, Consider'd as Nothing by the Natural Man.

11. The whole Business of Man Is The Arts & All Things Common.

12. Jesus & his Apostles & Disciples were all Artists. Their Works were destroy'd by the Seven Angels of the Seven Churches in Asia, Antichrist, Science.

13. Art is the Tree of Life. God is Jesus.

14. Science is the Tree of Death.

15. The Old & New Testaments are the Great Code of Art.

16. What we call Antique Gems are the Gems of Aaron's Breast Plate.

17. Hebrew Art is called Sin by the Deist Science.

18. Prayer is the Study of Art, Praise is the Practise of Art. Fasting &c all relate to Art. The outward Ceremony is Antichrist.

19. Without Unceasing Practise nothing can be done. Practise is Art. If you leave off you are Lost.

20. A Poet, a Painter, a Musician, an Architect—the Man Or Woman who is not one of these is not a Christian.

21. The unproductive Man is not a Christian; much less the Destroyer.

22. You must leave Fathers & Mothers & Houses & Lands if they stand in the way of Art.

23. Spiritual War: Israel deliver'd from Egypt is Art deliver'd from Nature & Imitation.

24. Art can never exist without Naked Beauty displayed.

25. No Secresy in Art.

26. The Gods of Greece & Egypt were Mathematical Diagrams. See Plato's Works.

9 ישוע . . . members] added, in parenthesis, to the right of the phrase 'God . . . Body'. Blake writes ישע.

12 Science here denotes the whole body of error, metaphysical, moral, and aesthetic.

20 Cp. M. 24. 55 *note*.

26–28 Cp. D. C. iii, quoted F. Z. ix. 361 *note* and M. 28. 38 *note*.

27. The Gods of Priam are the Cherubim of Moses & Solomon. The Hosts of Heaven.

28. Divine Union Deriding, And Denying Immediate Communion with God. The Spoilers say: 'Where are his Works That he did in the Wilderness? Lo! what are these? Whence came they? These are not the Works Of Egypt nor Babylon, Whose Gods are the Powers Of this World, Goddess Nature; Who first spoil & then destroy Imaginative Art; For their Glory is War and Dominion.'

29. Empire against Art. See Virgil's Eneid Lib. VI. v. 848.

30. Art Degraded, Imagination Denied, War Governed the Nations.

31. There are States in which all Visionary Men are accounted Mad Men: such are Greece & Rome, Such is Empire or Tax. See Luke Ch. 2. v. 1.

32. Christianity is Art & not Money. Money is its Curse.

33. The True Christian Charity not dependent on Money (the life blood of Poor Families); that is, on Cæsar or Empire or Natural Religion: Money, which is The Great Satan or Reason, the Root of Good & Evil, In The Accusation of Sin.

34. Where any view of Money exists, Art cannot be carried on, but War only, by pretences to the Two Impossibilities, Chastity & Abstinence, Gods of the Heathen. Read Matthew C. x, 9 & 10 v.

35. For every Pleasure Money Is Useless.

36. Is not every Vice possible to Man described in the Bible openly?

37. All is not Sin that Satan calls so, All the Loves & Graces of Eternity.

38. If Morality was Christianity, Socrates was the Saviour.

29 Cp. *On Virgil, note* 1. 30 Cp. M. Preface, *note* 1.
35 Cp. M. 27. 31–38 and *note*.
38 See General Introduction, section xvii *ad fin*.

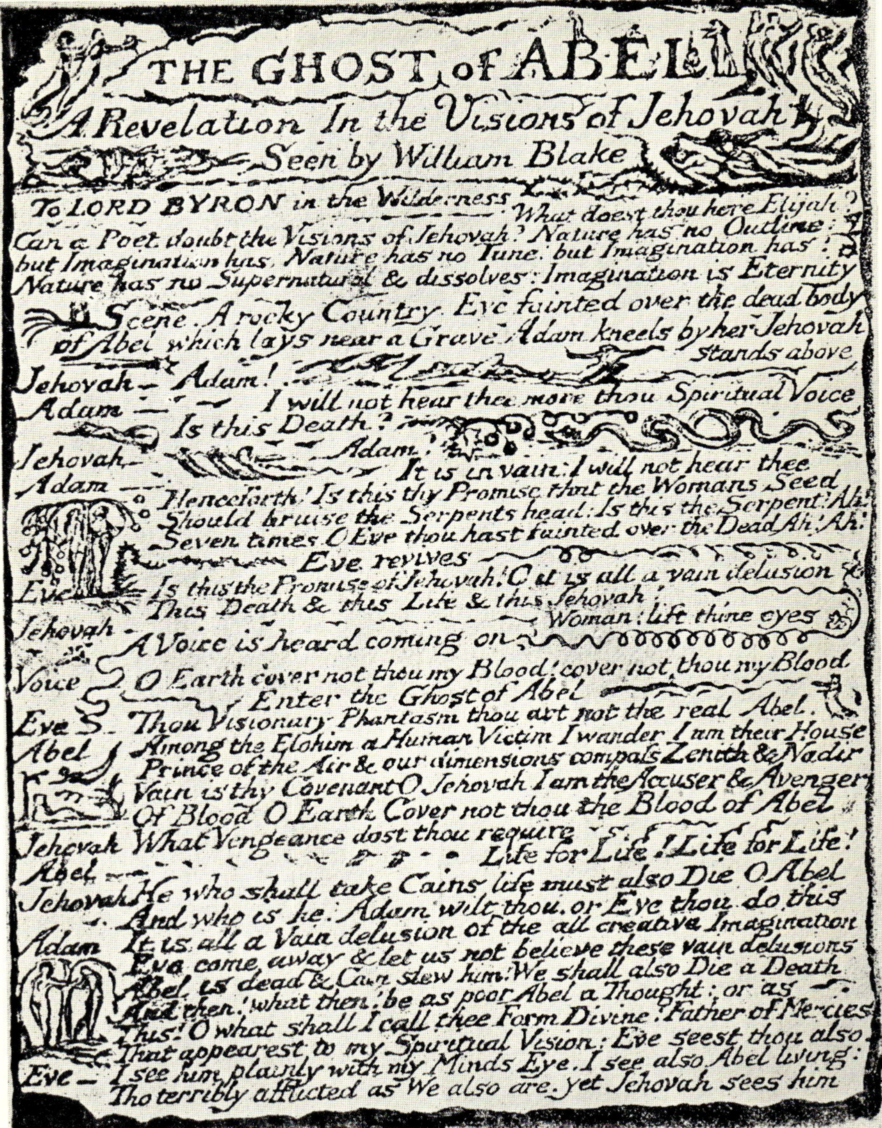

THE GHOST of ABEL

A Revelation In the Visions of Jehovah

Seen by William Blake

To LORD BYRON in the Wilderness
What doest thou here Elijah?

Can a Poet doubt the Visions of Jehovah? Nature has no Outline:
but Imagination has. Nature has no Tune: but Imagination has!
Nature has no Supernatural & dissolves: Imagination is Eternity

Scene. A rocky Country. Eve fainted over the dead body
of Abel which lays near a Grave. Adam kneels by her Jehovah
stands above

Jehovah — Adam!

Adam — I will not hear thee more thou Spiritual Voice
Is this Death?

Jehovah — Adam!

Adam — It is in vain: I will not hear thee
Henceforth! Is this thy Promise that the Womans Seed
Should bruise the Serpents head: Is this the Serpent? Ah!
Seven times O Eve thou hast fainted over the Dead Ah! Ah!

Eve revives

Eve — Is this the Promise of Jehovah! O it is all a vain delusion
This Death & this Life & this Jehovah!

Jehovah — Woman: lift thine eyes

A Voice is heard coming on

Voice — O Earth cover not thou my Blood! cover not thou my Blood

Enter the Ghost of Abel

Eve — Thou Visionary Phantasm thou art not the real Abel.

Abel — Among the Elohim a Human Victim I wander I am their House
Prince of the Air & our dimensions compass Zenith & Nadir
Vain is thy Covenant O Jehovah I am the Accuser & Avenger
Of Blood O Earth Cover not thou the Blood of Abel

Jehovah — What Vengeance dost thou require

Abel — Life for Life! Life for Life!

Jehovah — He who shall take Cains life must also Die O Abel
And who is he: Adam wilt thou, or Eve thou do this

Adam — It is all a Vain delusion of the all creative Imagination
Eve come away & let us not believe these vain delusions
Abel is dead & Cain slew him! We shall also Die a Death
And then! what then! be as poor Abel a Thought: or as
This! O what shall I call thee Form Divine! Father of Mercies
That appearest to my Spiritual Vision: Eve seest thou also.

Eve — I see him plainly with my Minds Eye. I see also Abel living:
Tho terribly afflicted as We also are. yet Jehovah sees him

The Ghost of Abel: Plate I

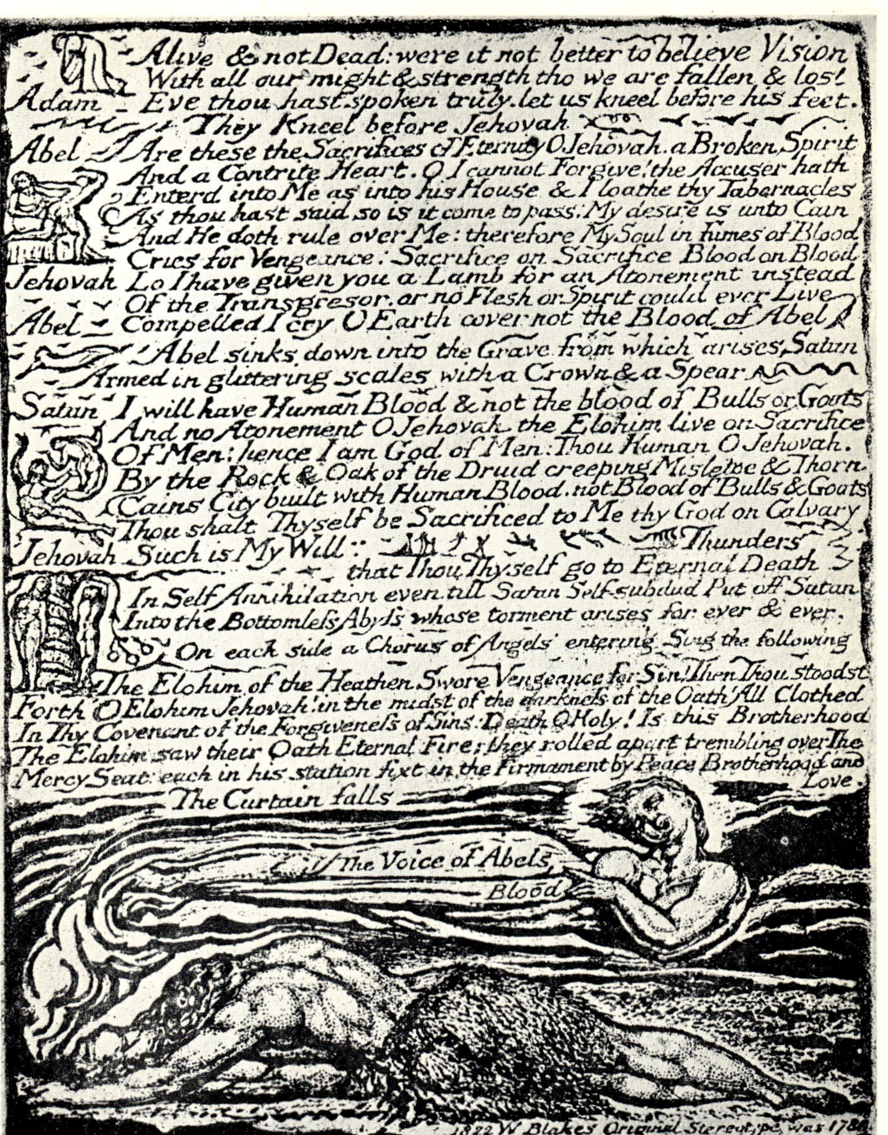

Alive & not Dead: were it not better to believe Vision
With all our might & strength tho we are fallen & lost!
Adam Eve thou hast spoken truly. let us kneel before his feet.
They Kneel before Jehovah
Abel Are these the Sacrifices of Eternity O Jehovah. a Broken Spirit
And a Contrite Heart. O I cannot Forgive! the Accuser hath
Enterd into Me as into his House & I loathe thy Tabernacles
As thou hast said so is it come to pass: My desire is unto Cain
And He doth rule over Me: therefore My Soul in fumes of Blood
Cries for Vengeance: Sacrifice on Sacrifice Blood on Blood
Jehovah Lo I have given you a Lamb for an Atonement instead
Of the Transgresor. or no Flesh or Spirit could ever Live
Abel Compelled I cry O Earth cover not the Blood of Abel
Abel sinks down into the Grave. from which arises Satan
Armed in glittering scales with a Crown & a Spear
Satan I will have Human Blood & not the blood of Bulls or Goats
And no Atonement O Jehovah the Elohim live on Sacrifice
Of Men: hence I am God of Men: Thou Human O Jehovah.
By the Rock & Oak of the Druid creeping Mistletoe & Thorn
Cains City built with Human Blood. not Blood of Bulls & Goats
Thou shalt Thyself be Sacrificed to Me thy God on Calvary
Jehovah Such is My Will: Thunders
that Thou Thyself go to Eternal Death
In Self Annihilation even till Satan Self-subdud Put off Satan
Into the Bottomless Abyss whose torment arises for ever & ever.
On each side a Chorus of Angels entering Sing the following
The Elohim of the Heathen Swore Vengeance for Sin! Then Thou stoodst
Forth O Elohim Jehovah! in the midst of the darkness of the Oath! All Clothed
In Thy Covenant of the Forgiveness of Sins: Death O Holy! Is this Brotherhood
The Elohim saw their Oath Eternal Fire; they rolled apart trembling over The
Mercy Seat: each in his station fixt in the Firmament by Peace Brotherhood and Love.
The Curtain falls

The Voice of Abels Blood

1822 W Blakes Original Stereotype was 1788

The Ghost of Abel: Plate 2

THE GHOST OF ABEL

Collation: 2 plates, relief engraving, about $4\frac{7}{8} \times 6\frac{9}{16}$ inches. *Colophon*: 1822. W. Blake's Original Stereotype was 1788.

It has been supposed that the earlier date mentioned in the Colophon is that of an earlier work on the subject, possibly suggested by Gesner's 'Death of Abel'. But the editor of the Clarendon Press edition of the *Poetical Works* believes that 'the reference to Blake's first stereotype probably refers to his earliest use of this process in the *Songs of Innocence*' (Clar. Press, p. 341).

The Ghost of Abel is Blake's latest and, artistically, one of his most effective statements of the mystical Gospel of Jesus against the moralistic heresies of the 'Churches'. Its immediate occasion was the publication of Byron's 'Mystery', *Cain*, which may have suggested the form, as it certainly suggested the theme of Blake's work. The public outcry against *Cain*, on the grounds of its alleged blasphemy and atheism, would not be likely to influence Blake, who, perhaps chiefly on account of the general condemnation, would seem to have regarded Byron as belonging, spiritually, to his own party. So he hails him as Elijah, that is, as the 'spirit of prophecy' (J. 44. 31) comprehending within himself 'all the prophetic characters' (*Cat.* 1810). But at the same time Blake urges a criticism of his own, that the author of *Cain* has been so far infected with the heresies of the 'Churches' as to identify the supreme being with the author of the curse laid upon the first fratricide. He therefore proceeds to show that the sentence was pronounced, not by Jehovah, but by Satan, the God of this world, a fallen Angel of the Divine Presence. Jehovah is 'Universal Brotherhood and Mercy', the spirit of Love and unconditional forgiveness of sins; Satan, the source of the moral law, exacts punishment for all offences.

The work is simple in style and treatment, and is almost entirely free from the distractions of uncouth symbolism. Like the *Laocoön* aphorisms, it shows how completely Blake, towards the end of his long spiritual pilgrimage, had found a resting-place in a re-interpretation of the fundamental Christian doctrines. The theme of the present work, the exaltation of the law of Forgiveness of Sins, seems always to have been the source of powerful inspiration for Blake; but, although some of the most notable passages in his maturer work deal with it, as, for example, the Vision of Mary and Joseph (J., p. 61) and the Magdalen episode in *The Everlasting Gospel*, none surpasses *The Ghost of Abel* in simple nobility of outlook and expression.

In the original autograph, text, names of speakers, and directions are all engraved in Blake's usual italic script.

The lower part of the second plate shows the body of Abel. From it issues a tormented human form, inscribed 'The Voice of Abel's Blood'.

[1]

THE GHOST OF ABEL

A Revelation In the Visions of Jehovah
Seen by William Blake

To LORD BYRON in the Wilderness

What doest thou here, Elijah ?
Can a Poet doubt the Visions of Jehovah ? Nature has no Outline,
but Imagination has. Nature has no Tune, but Imagination has.
Nature has no Supernatural, & dissolves : Imagination is Eternity.

Scene : *A rocky Country.* Eve *fainted over the dead body of* Abel, *which lays near a Grave.* Adam *kneels by her.* Jehovah *stands above.*

Jehovah. Adam !
Adam. I will not hear thee more, thou Spiritual Voice.
Is this Death ?
Jehovah. Adam !
Adam. It is in vain. I will not hear thee
Henceforth. Is this thy Promise, that the Woman's Seed
Should bruise the Serpent's head ? Is this the Serpent ? Ah !
Seven times, O Eve ! thou hast fainted over the Dead. Ah ! Ah !

Eve *revives.*

Eve. Is this the Promise of Jehovah ! O, it is all a vain delusion,
This Death & this Life & this Jehovah !

Jehovah. Woman, lift thine eyes !

A Voice is heard coming on.

Voice. O Earth, cover not thou my Blood ! cover not thou my Blood !

Enter the Ghost of Abel.

Eve. Thou Visionary Phantasm, thou art not the real Abel.

Abel. Among the Elohim, a Human Victim I wander. I am their House,
Prince of the Air, & our dimensions compass Zenith & Nadir.
Vain is thy Covenant, O Jehovah ! I am the Accuser & Avenger
Of Blood. O Earth, Cover not thou the Blood of Abel.

Jehovah. What Vengeance dost thou require ?

Abel. Life for Life ! Life for Life !

Jehovah. He who shall take Cain's life must also Die, O Abel,
And who is he ? Adam, wilt thou, or Eve, thou do this ?

Adam. It is all a Vain delusion of the all creative Imagination.
Eve, come away, & let us not believe these vain delusions.
Abel is dead, & Cain slew him. We shall also Die a Death,
And then—what then ? be as poor Abel, a Thought ; or as
This ? O what shall I call thee, Form Divine, Father of Mercies,
That appearest to my Spiritual Vision ? Eve, seest thou also ?

Eve. I see him plainly with my Mind's Eye. I see also Abel living,
Tho' terribly afflicted, as We also are ; yet Jehovah sees him

[2] Alive & not Dead: were it not better to believe Vision
With all our might & strength, tho' we are fallen & lost?

Adam. Eve, thou hast spoken truly: let us kneel before his feet.

They Kneel before Jehovah.

Abel. Are these the Sacrifices of Eternity, O Jehovah—a Broken Spirit
And a Contrite Heart? O, I cannot Forgive!. the Accuser hath
Enter'd into Me as into his House, & I loathe thy Tabernacles.
As thou hast said, so is it come to pass. My desire is unto Cain,
And He doth rule over Me; therefore My Soul in fumes of Blood
Cries for Vengeance, Sacrifice on Sacrifice, Blood on Blood!

Jehovah. Lo! I have given you a Lamb for an Atonement instead
Of the Transgressor, or no Flesh or Spirit could ever Live.

Abel. Compellèd I cry: 'O Earth, cover not the Blood of Abel!'

Abel *sinks down into the Grave from which arises* Satan *Armed in glittering scales with a Crown & a Spear.*

Satan. I will have Human Blood, & not the blood of Bulls or Goats
And no Atonement. O Jehovah! the Elohim live on Sacrifice
Of Men: hence I am God of Men, Thou Human, O Jehovah!
By the Rock & Oak of the Druid, creeping Misletoe & Thorn,
Cain's City built with Human Blood, not Blood of Bulls & Goats,
Thou shalt Thyself be Sacrificed to Me, Thy God, on Calvary.

Jehovah. Such is My Will, *Thunders*
That Thou Thyself go to Eternal Death
In Self Annihilation, even till Satan, Self-Subdu'd, Put off Satan
Into the Bottomless Abyss, whose torment arises for ever & ever.

On each side a Chorus of Angels, entering, Sing the following:

The Elohim of the Heathen Swore Vengeance for Sin. Then Thou stood'st
Forth, O Elohim Jehovah, in the midst of the darkness of the Oath, All Clothèd
In Thy Covenant of the Forgiveness of Sins. Death, O Holy! Is this Brotherhood?
The Elohim saw their Oath, Eternal Fire: they rollèd apart, trembling, over The
Mercy Seat, each in his station fixt in the Firmament by Peace, Brotherhood and Love.

The Curtain falls.

[Colophon] 1822. W. Blake's Original Stereotype was 1788.